Food for Today

First Canadian Edition

CANADIAN EDITION AUTHORS

SENIOR AUTHOR

Jane Witte

Independent Educational Consultant

Innerkip, Ontario

AUTHORS

Helen Miller

Pickering High School

Ajax, Ontario

Lisa O'Leary-Reesor

St. Thomas Aquinas Catholic Secondary School

London, Ontario

CONTRIBUTING AUTHOR

Zita Bersenas-Cers, B.A.A., B.Ed., R.D.

Delta Secondary School

Hamilton, Ontario

U.S. EDITION AUTHORS

Helen Kowtaluk

Alice Orphanos Kopan, M.Ed., M.A., CFCS

McGraw-Hill Ryerson

Toronto   Montréal   Boston   Burr Ridge, IL   Dubuque, IA   Madison, WI   New York
San Francisco   St. Louis   Bangkok   Bogotá   Caracas   Kuala Lumpur   Lisbon   London
Madrid   Mexico City   Milan   New Delhi   Santiago   Seoul   Singapore   Sydney   Taipei

COPIES OF THIS BOOK
MAY BE OBTAINED
BY CONTACTING:
McGraw-Hill Ryerson Ltd.

WEB SITE:
http://www.mcgrawhill.ca

E-MAIL:
orders@mcgrawhill.ca

TOLL-FREE FAX:
1-800-463-5885

TOLL-FREE CALL:
1-800-565-5758

OR BY MAILING YOUR
ORDER TO:
McGraw-Hill Ryerson
Order Department
300 Water Street
Whitby, ON L1N 9B6

Please quote the ISBN and
title when placing your order.

Student text ISBN:
0-07-087761-0

McGraw-Hill Ryerson

Food For Today, First Canadian Edition

Brand Name Disclaimer:
Publisher does not necessarily recommend or endorse any particular company or brand name product that may be discussed or pictured in this text. Brand name products are used because they are readily available, likely to be known to the reader, and their use may aid in the understanding of the text. Publisher recognizes other brand name or generic products may be substituted and work as well or better than those featured in the text.

ISBN 0-07-087761-0
http://www.mcgrawhill.ca

3 4 5 6 7 8 9 10 TCP 0 9 8 7 6

Printed and bound in Canada

Care has been taken to trace ownership of copyright material contained in this text. The publishers will gladly accept any information that will enable them to rectify any reference or credit in subsequent printings.

National Library of Canada Cataloging in Publication Data

Witte, Jane
   Food for today/senior author: Jane Witte; authors: Helen Miller, Lisa O'Leary-Reesor; author/consultants: Zita Bersenas-Cers. — 1st Canadian ed.

For use in grade 9.

ISBN 0-07-087761-0

   1. Food—Textbooks. 2. Nutrition—Textbooks. 3. Cookery—Textbooks. I. Miller, Helen II. O'Leary-Reesor, Lisa III. Bersenas-Cers, Zita IV. Title.

TX663.W58 2003   641   C2003-904329-0

PUBLISHER: Patty Pappas
DEVELOPMENTAL EDITORS: Jocelyn Wilson, Ellen Munro, Sheila Wawanash
SUPERVISING EDITOR: Cathy Deak
COPY EDITOR: Karen Rolfe
PERMISSIONS EDITOR: Paula Joiner, Krista Alexander
EDITORIAL ASSISTANT: Erin Parton Hartley
PRODUCTION SUPERVISOR: Yolanda Pigden
COVER DESIGN: ArtPlus Ltd.
INTERIOR DESIGN: MKR Design, Inc.
PAGE MAKE-UP: Heather Brunton, Alicia Countryman, Ruth Nicholson/ArtPlus Ltd.
ILLUSTRATIONS: ArtPlus Ltd.
COVER IMAGE: FPG International/Denis Scott

Acknowledgements

Reviewers of *Food For Today, First Canadian Edition*

The authors and editors of *Food For Today, First Canadian Edition* wish to thank the reviewers listed below for their thoughtful comments and suggestions. Their input has been invaluable in ensuring that this text meets the needs of the students and teachers taking this course.

Reviewers

Janet Dryden
Adam Scott Collegiate and Vocational Institute
Kawartha Pine Ridge District School Board

Nancy Fitzpatrick
R.S. McLaughlin Collegiate and Vocational Institute
Durham District School Board

Laura Gini-Newman
Instructional Co-ordinator, Curriculum
  Implementation
Canadian Studies, Social Sciences and the
  Humanities
Peel District School Board

Heather Lush
Program Advisor
School of Nutrition
Ryerson University

Suzanne Robertson
Holy Name of Mary Secondary School
Dufferin Peel Catholic District School Board

Family Studies Advisory Group

Patricia Andres
Eden High School
Niagara District School Board

Penny Ballagh
Ontario Institute for Studies in Education
University of Toronto

Janet Dryden
Adam Scott Collegiate and Vocational Institute
Kawartha Pine Ridge District School Board

Ann Harrison
Social Sciences and Humanities
Toronto District School Board

Maureen Holloway
David and Mary Thompson Collegiate Institute
Toronto District School Board

Maria McLellan
Iroquois Ridge High School
Halton District School Board

Michelyn Putignano
Delta Secondary School
Hamilton District School Board

Karen Wilson
Westdale Secondary School
Hamilton District School Board

Justice Marvin A. Zuker
Ontario Family Court Judge and Associate
  Professor at Ontario Institute for Studies
  in Education

CONTENTS

Unit 2 Food Needs of Individuals and Families 66

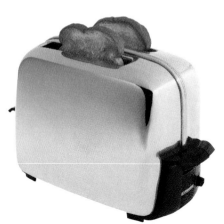

Unit 3 Nutrition, Health, and Well-Being. 220

Unit 4 Achieving Wellness 338

Unit 5 Food From Canadian and Global Perspectives 448

Unit 6 Issues and Trends in Food and Nutrition 578

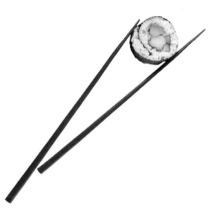

FEATURES LIST

Safety Check

Social Science Skills

A TOUR OF YOUR TEXTBOOK

Welcome to *Food for Today, First Canadian Edition*. This textbook provides a solid background in food and nutrition, as well as an introduction to many other aspects related to these topics. The textbook also provides guidelines for learning basic Social Science skills, recipes from many parts of the world, food-related science experiments, information about careers in the food and nutrition industries, and tips on health and safety.

Unit Opener

- **Unit Expectations** list the topics from the curriculum that are examined in the unit.
- A **photograph** captures the essence of what the unit is about.
- A **Mini Table of Contents** lists the chapters in the unit.
- An **Overview** outlines the content that will be explored in the unit.

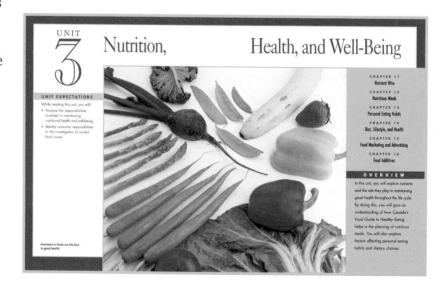

- **Chapter Expectations** list the topics from the curriculum that are studied in the chapter.
- A **photograph** that represents the chapter content is featured.
- **Chapter Introduction** describes what the chapter will be about.
- **Key Terms** found within the chapter are listed.
- **Social Science Skills** outlined in a feature within the chapter are identified.

Chapter Review and Activities

- A **Summary** of the chapter content is provided.
- **Questions and activities** satisfy the four areas of the Achievement Chart—Knowledge and Understanding, Thinking and Inquiry, Communication, and Application.
- Activities are geared toward a variety **of learning styles.**

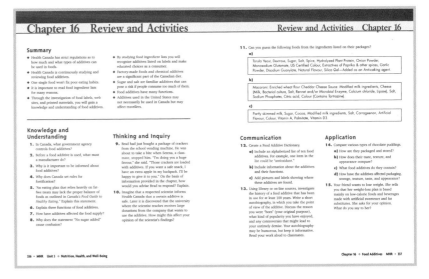

This textbook was designed and written to make Food and Nutrition understandable, interesting, and appealing to today's students

Food for Today, First Canadian Edition, has a number of features that will make food and nutrition relevant to you, will provide practical health and safety tips, and will inform you of a variety of careers available in the food and nutrition industries.

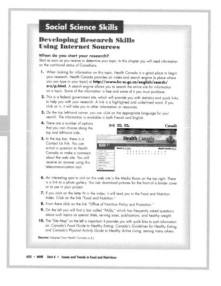

Social Science Skills

• The research skills required of students who study the Food and Nutrition course are featured throughout the text in easy-to-understand language, and include practical applications and formats.

Career Profiles

• Highlight individuals who represent a diverse range of career possibilities in the food and nutrition industries, as well as their recommendations on the education, skills, and experience needed to do the job. Each person also identifies the food and nutrition trend that is of most concern to him or her at the present time.

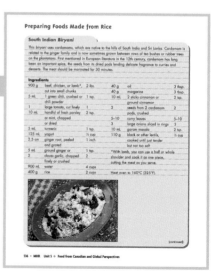

Recipes

• Recipes from many cultures around the world are presented in a variety of ways and include standard and additional information found in cookbooks.

Food Science Labs

- Provide experiments for students to discover facts about foods for themselves.

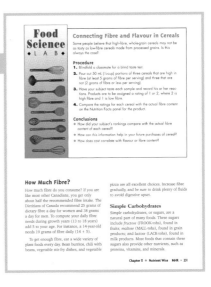

Internet Connects

- Web sites are provided throughout the textbook to assist students in researching topics related to content for both assignments and personal interest.

For Your Health

- Brief items provides a variety of information about aspects of health that relate to the topic under study.

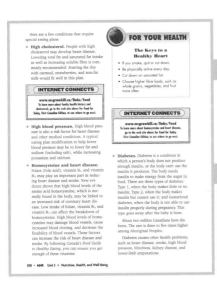

FYI

- This feature provides interesting information that is relevant to the topic under study but is not part of the curriculum expectations.

Safety Checks

- For topics where safety is a concern, this feature supplies helpful tips for preventing accidents from happening.

UNIT
1

Our Food

UNIT EXPECTATION

While reading this unit, you will:

- Identify the variety of reasons behind the choices people make about food.

Your food choices have an impact on your overall health and wellness, now and in the future.

Choices

OVERVIEW

In this unit, you will explore factors affecting people's food choices. As a result, you will gain an understanding of how these factors affect people's overall health and wellness now and in the future. An exploration of career opportunities will begin in this unit and continue throughout the text.

CHAPTER EXPECTATION

While reading this chapter, you will:

- Categorize the reasons people eat the foods they eat.

Our Food Needs

Food plays an important role in all people's lives.

CHAPTER INTRODUCTION

Many different things influence people's food choices. This chapter will focus on how your needs influence your food choices. As a result, you will gain an understanding of the physical requirements and psychological associations relating to food choices.

Food is a basic need for life. Your body signals its need for food with hunger pangs.

Food and Health

Physical Needs

Food does more than stop hunger pangs. It supplies you with **nutrients**, chemicals from food that your body uses to carry out its functions. These chemicals are so important that they have given rise to a branch of science. That science, called **nutrition**, is the study of nutrients and how they are used by the body.

You have probably also seen or heard the word *nutrition* used in a more popular sense to refer to the effects of a person's food choices on his or her health. If your food choices provide all the nutrients you need in the right amounts, you are said to be practising good nutrition.

Good nutrition has many benefits. It helps you feel and look your best as well as grow and become strong. Practising good nutrition is important for your overall physical, emotional, and intellectual health and wellbeing. The principles of good nutrition provide your body with the optimum conditions for a healthy life.

FOR YOUR HEALTH

All's Well That Starts Well

Wellness is affected by many decisions you make. Do your decisions promote wellness? To find out, privately answer the following statements "true" or "false" on a separate sheet of paper. Be honest with yourself.

- I eat at least three regular meals each day, beginning with breakfast.
- I have a varied eating plan that includes plenty of fruits, vegetables, and whole grains.
- I drink at least six to eight cups of water every day.
- I get between seven and eight hours of sleep each night.
- I exercise at least 20 to 30 minutes three to four times a week.
- I take safety precautions, such as wearing a seat belt and using protective sporting gear.
- I avoid harmful substances, such as tobacco, alcohol, and other drugs.
- I ask for help when I need it.
- I know where to turn for current and reliable health and nutrition information.
- I can manage stress.
- I get along well with others.
- If I have a problem, I try to work it out.

If you answered "true" to eight or more statements, your health and wellness levels are high. Seven or fewer "true" answers means you should take a close look at your wellness plan. Learning about nutrition and wellness is a good place to start.

Wellness

Good nutrition is part of a bigger health picture known as wellness. **Wellness** is a philosophy

◆ Getting the most out of life depends on feeling your best.

that encourages people to take responsibility for their own health. It focuses on the overall health of a person. It considers factors beyond physical health, such as social, emotional, and intellectual health. Wellness is reflected in both your attitudes and your behaviours. Decisions that influence your health include:

◆ The food choices you make.

◆ The amount of physical activity you get.

◆ How you manage your feelings and emotions.

◆ How you handle certain social situations.

◆ How much sleep you get.

By developing habits that promote wellness, you have a better chance of staying healthy and happy throughout your life. Benefits of improving your overall health and wellness include:

◆ Improved quality of life.

◆ Increased life span.

◆ Greater energy levels.

◆ Stronger immune system.

◆ Improved self-confidence and self-esteem.

◆ Improved relationships.

◆ Improved ability to manage and control stress.

Practising wellness doesn't guarantee you will never get sick or feel upset. It will, however, help you achieve the highest level of overall health and wellness possible.

Psychological Needs

Although you may not know it, food also helps you meet psychological needs. **Psychological** (sye-kuh-LODGE-ih-kuhl) means having to do with the mind and emotions. The psychological needs that food helps meet include security, a sense of belonging, and enjoyment.

Security and Comfort

Security is feeling free from harm and want. The love of family and friends is an important source of security. Another type of security comes from knowing you have the basic necessities of life. Having an ample supply of food helps you feel secure. In Canada, we are fortunate because most people experience **food security**. But, there are many Canadians who suffer from insecurity about food. Not knowing if there will be enough food to feed their families is a concern for many Canadians. A secure source of food is an important aspect of an individual's and a family's overall health and wellness.

Food also provides people with another form of security. During stressful periods, some people turn to foods that they believe will make them feel better. These foods provide them with a secure and comfortable feeling. They may crave **comfort foods** from childhood that they associate with feelings of being cared for or rewarded. Later, you will learn more about how emotions influence food choices.

A Sense of Belonging in Social Groups

People are social beings. They need to feel that they are accepted by others—that they belong. Food can help create a bond between people, giving them a sense of belonging.

Food is associated with many social events. When planning a party, the host(s) will often take great care to ensure that appropriate food and beverages are served. In fact, some parties are planned around the food to be served— an example would be a Mexican party. Food for major social events, such as a wedding, is given careful consideration by the people planning the event. In many instances, religion, culture, and customs influence the type of food that is served and when the meal is eaten.

Food is not only associated with bigger social events but also linked with regular social events as well. When friends come over to visit, often they are offered something to eat or drink. Many times social occasions, like going to a movie, involve food before, during, or after the occasion.

People often use food to welcome friends and guests or to show their appreciation or concern for someone. Sharing a meal or snack puts people at ease and adds to conversation. Food has a major impact on our social lives.

Food and Family

Food can also help strengthen family relationships. Do you help with the preparation of family meals or the shopping? Tasks like these make a positive contribution to the family's health.

They also can create feelings of self-pride. When families are able to share meals together, they have a chance to talk and laugh together.

◆ **Involving the whole family in food preparation is not only fun but also provides opportunities for passing on family traditions.** Write a short paragraph about one family food tradition practised in your home or in the home of a relative.

Both parents and children have the opportunity to catch up on one another's lives. Spending time with family helps to provide members with an added sense of security and belonging. Family meals can be a special time.

Food and customs help extended families connect with one another. Many extended families share special occasions and religious and cultural celebrations. Often, a major part of the occasion is a meal. Families pass down special recipes from generation to generation, and those recipes are an important part of the family celebration.

Enjoyment

What are your favourite foods? Do you most enjoy sinking your teeth into a slice of pizza oozing with cheese and zesty tomato sauce? Are you tempted by the aroma of fresh-baked cookies? It is easy to see that food satisfies the senses.

Food can add to your sense of enjoyment in many ways. Often the way in which you enjoy food is dependent on the situation in which you consume food. What type of food do you enjoy at a movie? A theme park? While shopping? First thing in the morning? Are they the same or different? A mug of hot chocolate would be enjoyed differently after a walk on a cold winter day than in the heat of the summer.

Preparing food can bring pleasure as well. Many people enjoy the chance to be creative and the challenge of learning new skills. Turning an assortment of ingredients into a delicious dish for yourself and others to enjoy can bring a great sense of satisfaction.

FYI

Food Advertising

Each year, advertisers spend millions of dollars to sell food products. What types of foods are advertised the most? Why?

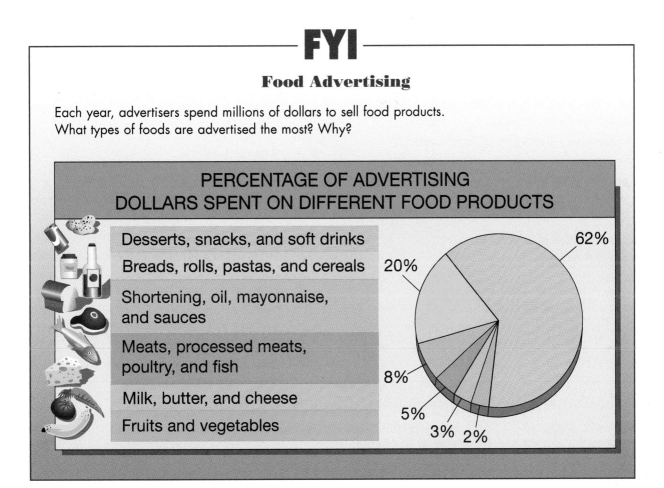

PERCENTAGE OF ADVERTISING
DOLLARS SPENT ON DIFFERENT FOOD PRODUCTS

Desserts, snacks, and soft drinks

Breads, rolls, pastas, and cereals

Shortening, oil, mayonnaise, and sauces

Meats, processed meats, poultry, and fish

Milk, butter, and cheese

Fruits and vegetables

62%

20%

8%

5%

3%   2%

Chapter 1 Review and Activities

Summary

- Food supplies your body with the nutrients it needs to help it grow and become strong.
- Food is also important for your overall physical, emotional, and intellectual health and well-being.
- Wellness is a philosophy that encourages you to take care of your physical, social, emotional, and intellectual health.
- Food fulfills your psychological needs by making you feel secure or free from hunger.
- Meals shared with family, friends, and other social groups provide you with a sense of belonging and enjoyment.
- Shared food shopping, preparation, and eating together strengthen family relations.
- Food satisfies your senses and gives you enjoyment.

Knowledge and Understanding

1. What is nutrition? Describe three health benefits of practising good nutrition.

2. What is wellness? What are four things you can do to improve your overall health and wellness?

3. Define psychological needs. Give an example of two food-related psychological needs that people have.

4. How can food provide a sense of belonging?

Thinking and Inquiry

5. After completing the "All's Well That Starts Well" quiz on page 4, how would you rate your overall wellness? Make a list of goals to improve your wellness. Develop an action plan for a one-week period that will help you meet your goals.

6. Food security is an important issue. Make a list of ways in which a stable source of food can have an impact on the overall health and wellness of teenagers.

7. Make a list of situations that cause you to turn to comfort foods. Make a list of those comfort foods and their source. Compare your list to a classmate's, then write one paragraph describing the similarities and differences between the two of you.

8. Make a list of foods and beverages that you would serve in the following situations:
   - A special dinner for your family.
   - An after-school snack for your friends.
   - A birthday party.
   - A cultural celebration.

   For each one, make a list of the physical and psychological needs met by your selections.

Communication

9. Find pictures from magazines that represent people eating food. Divide them into two categories, physical and psychological. Make them into a collage. Write a one-page reflection on your collage, expressing the physical benefits of eating a variety of foods and the psychological benefits of enjoying foods and sharing meals with others.

Application

10. Keep a food record for three days—two weekdays and one weekend day. Record everything that you eat, as well as the reason you ate it. Write a summary of the reasons, answering the following questions as part of the summary:

- Were the reasons you ate mainly for health and wellness, or were there other reasons?
- Does the situation you are in have an impact on the food you eat? Do your eating patterns change on weekends? If so, how?

CHAPTER

2

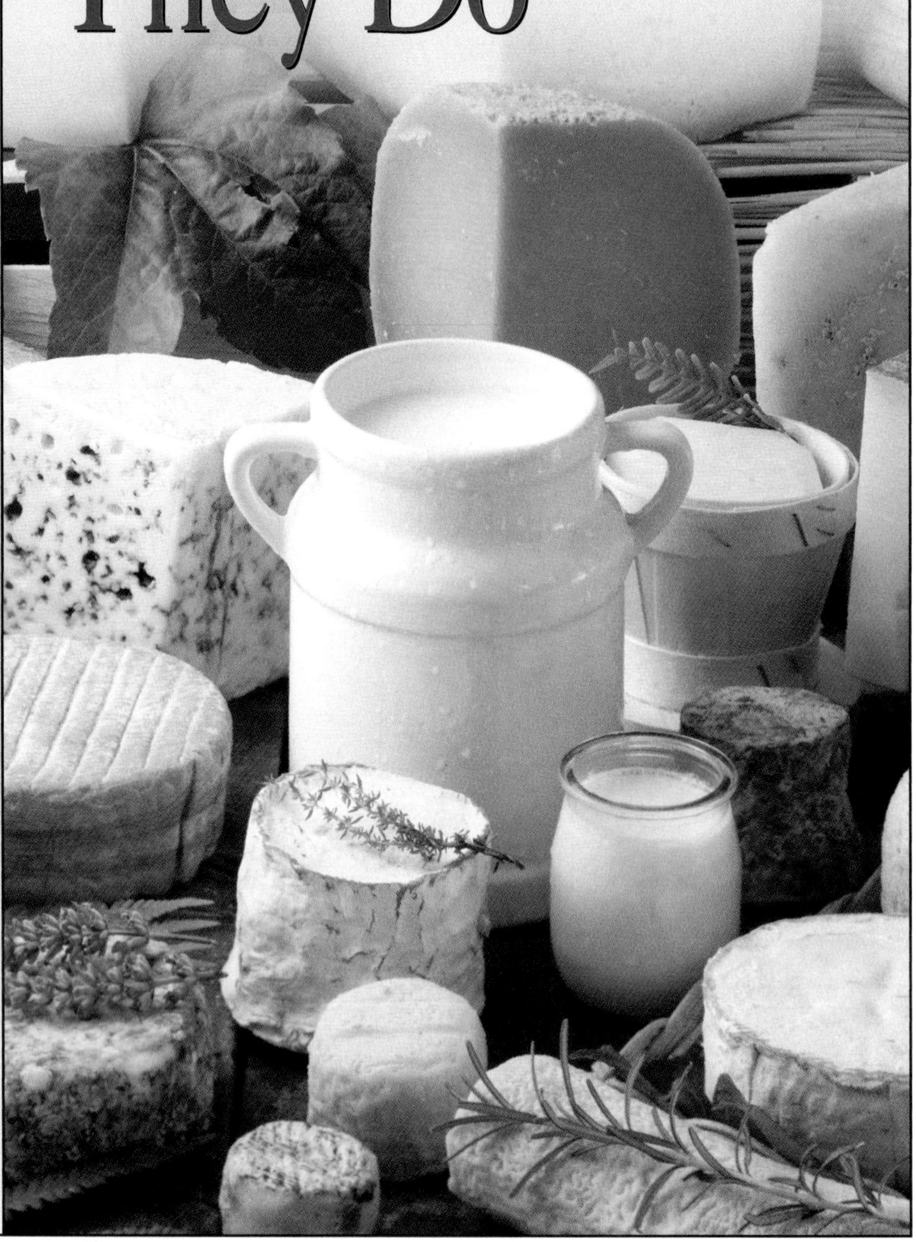

Why People Eat the Foods They Do

CHAPTER EXPECTATION

While reading this chapter, you will:

- Categorize the reasons people eat the foods they eat.

Many foods were once only available in certain areas of the globe, but today they are enjoyed worldwide.

CHAPTER INTRODUCTION

In this chapter, you will examine social influences on your food choices. These will include factors such as family, friends, and the media. You will consider how your lifestyle, values, and emotions may affect what you eat. You will also explore how different cultures have an impact on food and food practices.

Most people enjoy the foods they ate as children with their families.

Influences on Food Choices

Social Influences

Although you are an individual, you are also a member of various social groups. Many of your food preferences begin with the influence of family, friends, the media, and culture.

Family

Your family probably has had the single greatest influence on your food choices. When you were very young, family members made most of your food choices for you. As you grew, you learned food habits by following your family's example. You saw them enjoying certain foods at certain times of the day, for instance.

A family's food customs often reflect cultural background. For instance, an Italian family might always have two main dishes at Thanksgiving—turkey and spaghetti.

Families sometimes develop their own food rituals. In one family, pancakes might be a traditional Saturday night meal. Another family might never think of serving pork chops without applesauce.

Families also have an influence on the way that foods are prepared. Different families have their own recipes and/or ingredients for similar dishes. You become used to a dish being prepared and served the way that your family traditionally does it.

People tend to feel comfortable with foods that are familiar. If certain foods were never served in your home, you may think you would dislike them. Part of the adventure of eating, however, is trying new foods and finding ones that you enjoy.

Friends

As you grow older, friends play an increasingly greater role in your food choices. As discussed in Chapter 1, eating is a social experience, and part of the time you spend with friends involves food. When you are out together, your friends influence where and what you eat, and vice versa. When you go to your friends' homes, you may be served a snack or a meal. Have you ever cooked a dish for your family that you were introduced to first at a friend's?

If your friends are from cultural backgrounds different from your own, you might learn to enjoy the foods they commonly eat. Can you think of foods from different cultures you have learned to enjoy as a result of a friendship?

The Media

We live in an information age. Each day, we are bombarded with messages from many communication sources, including television, radio, movies, newspapers, magazines, advertisements, and the Internet. These sources, known collectively as the **media,** are a major influence in the food choices you make. News reports may shape your decision to eat—or not eat—a certain food. The media reports on news about food and nutrition. As an informed consumer who is concerned about your overall health and wellness, you need to carefully consider the validity of these reports. How to judge the soundness of information is something that will be discussed later in this textbook. There are many programs on television dedicated to cooking. Watching cooking shows can inspire you to be more creative with food selection and preparation. Magazines may make you aware of new food trends.

One medium that has an especially powerful influence on your food choices is advertising. Have you ever bought a particular cereal or snack food because a TV commercial made it sound so good?

In order to make wise food choices, you need to be aware of media influences. You need to analyze the messages you see and hear. It is important that you gain a good understanding of the principles of good nutrition, so that you can evaluate the claims of advertisers.

Available Resources

Your choice of foods depends a great deal on the resources available to you. **Resources** are objects and qualities that can help you reach a goal. For example, this textbook is a resource that helps you learn about food and nutrition.

Many resources are involved in obtaining the food you need. Money is the most important one. Time, knowledge, abilities, equipment, and a place to buy food are also important.

The Social Science Research Process

The Social Sciences study groups of people in order to understand their behaviour. This feature will familiarize you with various aspects of Social Science skills that can be used to increase your understanding of the world in which you live.

Social scientists have a specific process or model that they apply to their research. The model is outlined in the chart below. This is the process that must be followed in order to do valid Social Science research.

Social Science Research Model

STAGE I	*Defining question*
Preparing for research	1. Define the topic of investigation. 2. Find out what others have learned about the topic. 3. Specify the research question.

STAGE II	*Locating information*
Accessing resources	4. Access the requirements for carrying out the research. 5. Consider ethical issues. 6. Devise a research strategy.

STAGE III	*Evaluating information*
Processing information	7. Gather data. 8. Interpret data.

STAGE IV	*Presenting information*
Transferring learning	9. State your conclusions. 10. Share your results.

Source: Ontario Family Studies Leadership Council (n.d.).

People's food choices differ because their resources differ. No one has an endless supply of all resources, but everyone has some. You can often substitute one resource for another that is in short supply. For instance, if you have time and skills, you can save money by cooking at home instead of eating out.

In order to make wise decisions about food choices, individuals and families need to look at all their resources. It is important that families make use of their resources to their own advantage. Sometimes, families forget that personal skills are resources.

Technology and the Food Supply

One of the resources that influences your food choices is the basic food supply. In other words, the choices you make depend on the foods you can choose from. **Technology,** the practical application of scientific knowledge, influences the food supply and, therefore, your choices.

Suppose you could step into a time machine that could whisk you 300 years into the past. What would your food choices be like? In this world of long ago, almost everything you ate would be grown by your family or your neighbours. In warm weather, food would be plentiful, but spoilage would be a problem. In cold weather, the challenge would be to make food last until the next harvest.

◆ **Technology has had an enormous impact on the foods available to us.** Look up the term *agriculture* in an encyclopedia or other resource. Explain how changes in technology have increased the availability of foods to enjoy.

Today, modern technology has greatly increased your options. Planes and trucks bring food from around the world to your local market. You can also take a frozen, already-prepared main dish out of the freezer and pop it in the microwave. In just minutes it's hot and ready to eat.

Advances in technology will continue to add to people's food choices. Can you imagine what foods might be available 300 years from now?

Personal Influences

Have you ever wondered how two people raised in the same family can be so different? Your lifestyle, values, priorities, and emotions influence your choice of foods. They are part of the reason that your food choices are uniquely your own.

Your Lifestyle

Lifestyle refers to a person's typical way of life. Your lifestyle includes how you spend your time and what is most important to you. Lifestyle has a strong influence on what and where you eat, how and where you shop, and how you prepare food.

A teen's lifestyle commonly revolves around school, family, friends, leisure activities, and, possibly, a part-time job. A busy lifestyle can affect your food choices. For instance, you may buy a snack from a fast-food outlet just because the food is available, easy to carry, and easy to eat quickly.

Lifestyle changes as people go through life. Moving away from home to go to post-secondary school will change your lifestyle. Most of your food may no longer be prepared by and consumed with your family.

Many college and university students learn to appreciate home cooking while away at school. Moving through the stages of life will influence food choices as well.

Values and Priorities

Not everyone spends time or money in the same way. People make choices based on their personal values and priorities.

Food choices also depend on personal values and priorities. Some people enjoy the time they spend preparing meals. Others would rather spend the time on another activity, such as a hobby or a sport.

It's not always easy to juggle your priorities. Time, money, health, enjoyment—all are important to most people. As you continue to study food, you will learn ways to meet the challenge of a busy lifestyle.

Your Emotions

Emotions and moods can influence food choices. Some people rely on certain foods to make them feel better when they are sad or depressed. They may choose different foods if they are happy or when they are celebrating an event. Think about the foods that you eat often, such as when you are happy, sad, or celebrating something. How does the food suit your mood?

Food often carries strong associations—both pleasant and unpleasant. For instance, one boy can still remember being forced to eat spinach as a child. He does not like spinach to this day. On the other hand, one girl loves spinach. It reminds her of meals at her grandmother's house and the associated feelings of comfort and security.

◆ **Every culture has its own way of preparing, serving, and eating foods.**

Food and Culture

Understanding Culture

Culture

Culture refers to the shared customs, traditions, and beliefs of a large group of people, such as a nation, race, or religious group. These customs are part of what defines a group's unique identity.

Food customs are one aspect of culture. Every culture has its own traditional ways of preparing, serving, and eating foods. Some of these customs are one of a kind. The Mexican dish *pollo con mole poblano*, for instance, combines chicken with chocolate. Other customs are dictated by geography. The hot climate throughout much of southeastern Asia is ideal for growing rice, which is why rice is a staple starch in most southeast Asian cuisine.

Modern trends that have "shrunk" the world—high-speed transportation and communication, for instance—have made it possible for people to share and experience the foods of many cultures. Most cities in this country have Chinese and Italian restaurants. What foods from other cultures have you tried?

How do we determine a "group of people" as defined by their culture? This question has several possible answers:

◆ **Geography.** People who live in a particular region or part of the world may be said to make up a cultural group.

◆ **Heritage.** A common heritage, or past, is another defining feature of a cultural group. Aboriginal Peoples, descendants of the first people to live in this country, are one such group. Some people now living in Canada were born or have ancestral roots in other cultures. A cultural group based on common heritage is often called an **ethnic group**.

◆ **Religion.** Religion is another basis for defining cultural groups. Members of a particular faith usually have a common set of beliefs and follow specific practices.

If you were to take a survey of students in your school, you would probably find many cultures represented. Some students might trace their cultural roots to Ireland, others to Japan, still others to India. As such a mix reveals, Canada is a society made up of many cultures. This cultural richness is a great strength. People within the society are free to share and explore the customs of all the different cultures.

INTERNET CONNECTS

www.mcgrawhill.ca/links/food
To learn more about cultural profiles, food celebrations, and festivals, go to the web site above for *Food for Today, First Canadian Edition*, to see where to go next.

Understanding Cultural Food Customs

Food is essential in the everyday life of individuals and families. It can also play an important role in celebrations and ceremonies. It is not surprising that food customs are often a focal point in cultural traditions.

Food customs usually involve certain kinds of food, but that's just the beginning. They also include how food is prepared, how it is served, and how it is eaten.

Unique Foods

Wonton soup is a dish that originated in China. Wontons are dumplings filled with minced vegetables and meat. Shish kebab, chunks of meat threaded on a skewer, originated in the Middle East. So did pita bread, a distinctive flat bread that forms a pocket.

Within a nation, there may also be distinct regional food traditions. Different regions of Canada are known for different foods—for example, lobster from the Maritimes, tourtière from Québec, and salmon from British Columbia. Although all of these foods are available across the country, they originate in a particular region.

◆ **Food-related celebrations are common in this country. One town's annual pumpkin festival offers everything from pumpkin ice cream to pumpkin chili. Name a food custom associated with each of the four seasons.**

◆ **Food customs affect not only what is eaten, but also how foods are served.** With what cultures do you associate the eating utensils in these two pictures? In what ways have lines between the customs of these cultures been blurred?

Dietary Laws

Religious beliefs often include dietary laws, or rules about what foods may be eaten. For example, Jews who follow a kosher diet do not eat meat and dairy products in the same meal. Hindus do not eat beef because they consider cattle sacred animals. Muslims eat no pork.

Cultural Etiquette

Social customs for serving and eating food also vary depending on the culture. Not all cultures use forks, knives, and spoons for eating. In China, Japan, and Korea, chopsticks are the traditional eating utensils. In some countries, such as India, Afghanistan, Algeria, and Morocco, it is considered proper to eat many foods using the fingers. In some nations of Africa, food is scooped up with a flat bread called *injera*.

Special Occasions

Some food customs relate to holidays, festivals, and religious observances. To celebrate the Chinese New Year, Judy Chen helps her mother make New Year's dumplings. The small, smooth, round dumplings are made of rice powder and water and are filled with a sweet soybean paste. Their shape symbolizes good fortune. For Easter, Ukrainians colour eggs in complex designs. In Italy, a popular Easter food is a ring-shaped coffee cake with coloured eggs tucked into the top.

Sometimes food itself is the theme for a festival. Harvest festivals have been common since ancient times. In Canada, Thanksgiving is the official harvest festival. Many communities also have their own festivals to celebrate the harvest of locally grown foods, such as pumpkin fest and apple days.

Not all holiday customs involve special foods. On Yom Kippur, the Jewish faith observes the Day of Atonement by fasting. Catholics refrain from eating meat on certain church holy days. During Ramadan, a month-long religious observance, Muslims do not eat or drink during daylight hours.

How Food Customs Evolve

The many cultural groups dispersed throughout the world have many varied ways of preparing, serving, and eating food. None of these food customs can be considered better than any other. Different customs arise naturally as a result of different circumstances.

For instance, you may be used to eating leftovers for lunch or dinner. In Japan, this would be considered unusual, even strange. This cultural difference can be understood if you realize that most Japanese do not have large refrigerators for food storage. Food is purchased fresh to be eaten that day. Dining on leftovers would be viewed as eating "old" food.

Food Customs Throughout History

A journey through history can help you understand food customs. In the distant past, cultural groups were limited in their food choices to items they could raise or gather locally. How these foods were cooked often

◆ The status of regional dishes sometimes changes. Bouillabaisse, an elegant fish stew served in the south of France, began as a "peasant" dish consisting of leftover fish sold at day's end.

depended on the types and amount of fuel available. For example, in many Asian countries, cooking fuel was scarce. To conserve fuel, food was cut into small pieces that would cook quickly.

Economic conditions in some cultures led to food distinctions along social class lines. The rich, who could afford the finest foods, dined on elegant fare prepared by top chefs. The rest of the people ate simple meals—typically, soup made from whatever food was available, accompanied by coarse, dark bread made from ground whole grains.

Many food traditions have been passed down through generations. Changes to these traditions occurred because different groups influenced one another. When the early explorers travelled the world, they brought their own food with them. When the explorers arrived in a new land, the people who lived there often introduced the explorers to new foods and food customs. The explorers would leave their customs in the new land and bring back some of the new foods and food customs to their homelands.

European explorers who reached the Western Hemisphere found an abundance of foods eaten by Aboriginal Peoples. The explorers brought back samples and seeds of foods that were not found in Europe, such as dry beans, corn, tomatoes, potatoes, sweet potatoes, and cassava, a type of root. Over the centuries, some of these foods became popular in the Eastern Hemisphere.

As improvements in transportation made travel easier, people went farther and farther from home. As they travelled, they began to share foods and food customs. Original recipes changed for many reasons. When a recipe was brought to a different country, sometimes ingredients were not available,

so substitutions were made. Other recipes were altered due to personal preferences. Chop suey, considered by some people to be a Chinese food, is not authentic Chinese, but an American recipe based on the Chinese style of cooking.

A World of Food Choices

Today, the world is becoming "smaller." People and foods can be flown thousands of kilometres in a few hours. Satellite links and the Internet allow instant communication between people in remote corners of the globe. As a result, food customs are shared the world over. Foods grown halfway around the world are sold in your local supermarket. While surfing the Internet or watching television, you can learn about life in other countries. You can see how people prepare and serve food, as well as learn how to prepare dishes from other cultures.

It is no surprise that ethnic and international foods are now an everyday part of our lives. Supermarkets often stock a wide variety of ethnic foods, and many restaurants include an assortment on their menus.

◆ Evidence that the world is "shrinking" may be seen in the North American fast-food restaurant chains cropping up in other countries.

You probably enjoy many such foods, from tacos to pasta, without thinking of them as being unusual. They have become as familiar to Canadians as steak and potatoes.

This variety is one of the benefits of living in a society of many cultures. Consider the mingling of international flavours in this meal: chicken vindaloo and rice (India), steamed snow peas and water chestnuts (China), and a dessert of guava shells and cream cheese (Mexico).

Flavours from around the world are being combined in recipes. A person might make pizza with chili-seasoned ground meat and top it with grated sharp cheese and salsa— a spicy Mexican fresh tomato sauce. Fast-food chains featuring fried chicken and hamburgers have sprung up around the globe. Such global diversity enriches everyone's life. No matter where people go, they can find foods they enjoy and can experience the adventure of new flavours.

FOR YOUR HEALTH

"Vegging" at Lunchtime

Many Canadians fail to meet the minimum recommendation in *Canada's Food Guide to Healthy Eating* of five to ten fruit or vegetable servings per day. One way to meet this requirement is to build a sandwich around vegetables. Here are some nutrition-packed vegetarian sandwich ideas:

- For a fresh and crunchy choice, top whole wheat bread with thinly sliced cucumber, diced green onions, fat-free cream cheese, and pepper.

- Instead of the usual grilled cheese, slip some sliced tomatoes in with low-fat cheese. You might also microwave cheese and tomato, open-face, on a bagel half.

- Place a mixed green salad or a grain salad, such as tabbouleh, in a whole wheat pita pocket.

- Go Italian with mozzarella cheese, tomato, and fresh basil on Italian bread with a splash of flavoured vinegar for a burst of flavour.

- Spread vegetarian refried beans, diced tomatoes, salsa, and shredded cheese on a tortilla. Roll it up. Then heat and eat.

- Grill or roast your favourite vegetables. Then layer them on whole-grain bread and enjoy the natural taste of the veggies.

National Food Writer

Judy Creighton

What education is required for your job?

• A degree in journalism.

• If possible, courses in nutrition, education, and cooking.

What skills does a person need to be able to do your job?

• A love and understanding of food.

• An inquiring mind.

What do you like most about your job?

Dreaming up stories, researching them, and getting positive feedback from my readers.

What other jobs/job titles have you had in the past?

I've worked as a lifestyles reporter and editor for the *Victoria-Times Colonist*, *London Free Press*, and the *Toronto Star*; as a reporter covering courts and education for the *Victoria-Times Colonist*; and as a lifestyles editor and columnist on aging issues for *The Canadian Press* in Toronto.

What advice would you give a person who is considering a career as a food columnist?

Enroll in a journalism school to learn the practical side of writing, and surround yourself with as much information as possible about food and nutrition. Spend time in supermarkets, health food stores, and farmers' markets. Read about the sources, economics, and history of food. Scan newspaper and magazine business pages for food-related articles. Search the Internet and watch food shows on television. Use public libraries to find resource books about food. Buy a good food encyclopedia and dictionary. Most of all, get into the kitchen and experiment!

Comment on what you consider to be important issues or trends in food and nutrition.

I am most concerned about the trend toward convenience and fast foods to the detriment of home cooking and its pleasures. Also a concern is the rise in childhood and adolescent obesity, as well as the onset of Type 2 diabetes among young people. There must be more done to discourage the suppliers of junk and unhealthy food. I would like to see a return to the school curriculum of food and nutrition classes beginning in Grade 5 or 6. Also, parents must be encouraged to include their children in the cooking experience from an early age.

Chapter 2 Review and Activities

Summary

- Your family has had the greatest influence on your food choices, customs, and the way foods are prepared.

- Friends are often the first to introduce you to new foods.

- Media reports on food and nutrition, and you adjust your food choices according to new knowledge. Television cooking shows, recipes and food articles in magazines and newspapers, and advertising also influence your food choices and may inspire you to become more creative with the foods you eat.

- Families use different resources to obtain and provide the foods they need and want.

- Modern technology has enabled foods to be preserved, shipped around the world, and packaged as ready-made meals.

- Lifestyle, personal values and priorities, and emotions influence your food choices.

- A person's culture, which includes his or her geography, heritage, and religion, affects the foods he or she eats and how they are prepared, served, and eaten.

- Historically, cultural groups were limited to their food choices because of where they lived and the amount of fuel that was available to cook the food. Later, economics determined what different social classes could afford to eat. With the advent of the European explorers, different foods and customs were exchanged between the Eastern and Western Hemispheres. Improved transportation made the exchange of foods and customs even easier. Today, they are shared worldwide.

Knowledge and Understanding

1. Define the term *culture*. Make a list of the cultural backgrounds of the students in your class. For each one, list a food eaten as part of the culture.

2. What is a resource? Make a list of resources that are involved in obtaining food. Which ones do you use?

3. What are three aspects of culture?

4. What is lifestyle? How can lifestyle influence a person's food choices? Give two examples.

5. How did geography affect food customs in the past? Why does it have less influence today? Give two examples.

6. How does religion affect food choices? Give two examples.

Thinking and Inquiry

7. Choose a dish that you eat on a regular basis. Do some research on the origins of that dish. Write a one-page description on where the food originated.

   a) What happens when food customs are introduced into a new area? Why?

   b) Do you think food customs will continue to exist? Why or why not?

8. Think about ways that your family has influenced your personal food choices. Describe three family food traditions that you value. Does your extended family have similar traditions?

9. Do you think it is important for members of a particular culture to retain some distinct food customs? Why or why not?

Communication

10. Interview a senior about his or her food habits, customs, and practices. Include the following topics:

- Family's favourite foods.
- Foods not eaten by the family but enjoyed now.
- Family's traditional foods.
- Family's celebration foods; for instance, on birthdays.
- Personal comfort foods.
- Cultural foods.
- How often the family ate together.
- Which foods and customs the family still celebrates.
- Did the seniors pass on any to the next generation?

11. Write a report on changing food customs and traditions to share with the class. Follow the procedure outlined in the Social Science Research Process on page 13.

Application

12. a) With a partner, make a list of special occasions. Put the list into into chart form, similar to the one below.

Occasion	Foods Served
Example: Thanksgiving	*Turkey, mashed potatoes, peas, gravy*

b) Ask several people to tell you what they eat on that occasion. Make a summary of the foods that are common and the foods that are different. Put the information in a chart to present to the class.

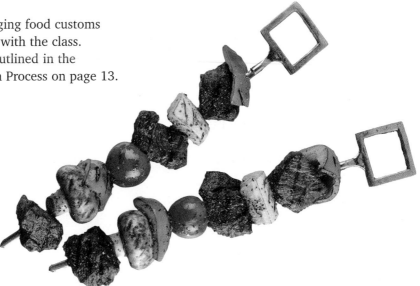

CHAPTER

3

The Effects of Childhood Eating Patterns

CHAPTER EXPECTATION

While reading this chapter, you will:

- Observe the effect of early childhood eating habits on current eating patterns and on nutritional well-being throughout life.

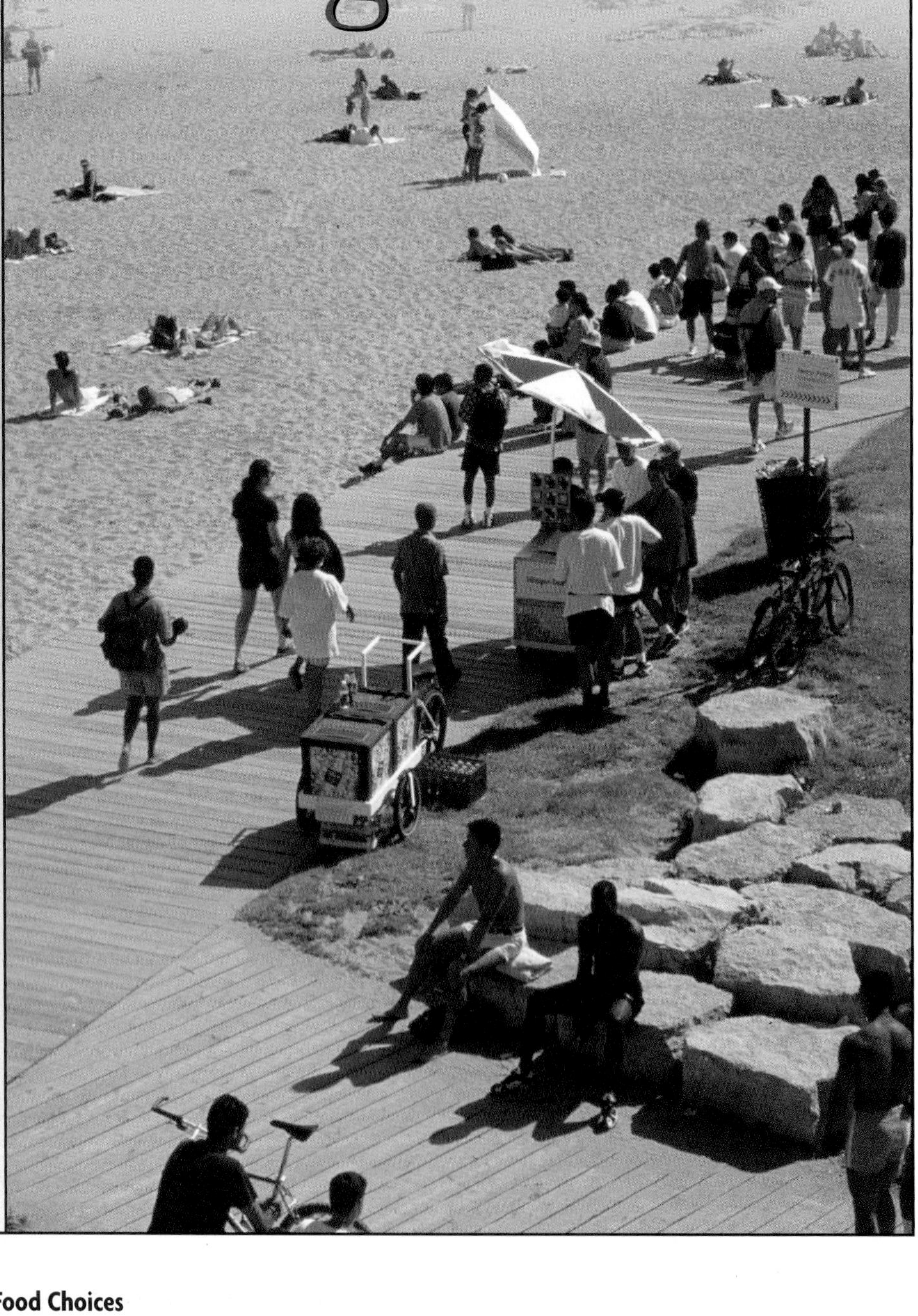

Children who have treats in moderation and are physically active have a good chance at becoming healthy adults.

KEY TERMS
adult modelling
key issues
obesity
supporting issues

SOCIAL SCIENCE SKILLS
• key and supporting
  issues when developing
  questions

CHAPTER INTRODUCTION

In this chapter you will learn how the eating habits developed in childhood stay with people throughout their lives. Eating habits developed and practised during childhood can have a positive or a negative effect on a person's future health. Negative effects of unhealthy eating habits will be discussed, as well as factors that influence a child's eating habits.

This child is enjoying his food. As young children, people develop food habits and eating practices that stay with them throughout their lifetimes.

The Importance of Healthy Eating During Childhood

"Childhood is a critical time to see, to learn, and to practise good eating behaviours" (Krebs, January 2000). The consequences of unhealthy habits will have long-term negative effects, such as obesity, heart disease, and diabetes. Research has shown that poor habits developed in childhood put adults at risk.

In the federal government report *Trends in the Health of Canadian Youth* (2002), the importance of healthy eating is emphasized. It is noted that healthy eating contributes to both the physical and emotional health of a student.

It is never too early to teach a child the importance of good nutrition. It is key to a child's growth and development. Providing a child with a healthy diet gives them the best start possible. It is essential to develop healthy eating habits at a young age in order to achieve optimum health as an adult.

Problems Caused by Unhealthy Eating Habits

Developing unhealthy eating habits and practices while you are young can have life-long consequences. A lifestyle that is less active, has a high-fat diet, and is exposed to cigarette smoke leads to an increased risk of heart problems. Normally, these risk factors are associated with adults; but studies done in Ontario show that 40 percent of children between the ages of five and eight are already at risk for at least one of these factors, and 20 percent have two or more. By the time these children reach their teenage years, their habits will be difficult to change and they may experience the long-term consequences of unhealthy behaviours (Partridge, 1998).

If these children's eating habits do not change, then as adults they will be at higher risk for the following:

- **Psychological problems, including lack of self-esteem and depression.** Poor eating habits can lead to **obesity**. Being obese affects the way you see yourself and the way other people see you. This can lead to depression and low self-esteem.

- **Breathing disorders.** People who are obese put a strain on their respiratory system. This can lead to breathing problems.

- **Bone and joint problems.** Poor eating habits can lead to bone and joint problems later in life for a number of reasons. Lack of calcium in the diet leads to poor bone development and a deficiency in bone density. If a person becomes obese, the extra weight is hard for the bones and joints to carry.

- **Diabetes.** Type 2 Diabetes is more likely to occur in the general population over the age of 45, and more often in people who are overweight.

- **High cholesterol.** Diet is a main factor in the development of high cholesterol. People who have diets high in fat and cholesterol run the risk of developing cholesterol-related problems later in life, such as heart disease and stroke. An inactive lifestyle also increases the chances that cholesterol will be a problem in the future.

- **Gall bladder disease.** The risk factors for gall bladder disease include obesity and diabetes. Both are conditions affected by poor eating habits and practices throughout a person's life.

- **High blood pressure or hypertension.** This disease is linked to poor eating habits. People diagnosed with high blood pressure are told to decrease their salt intake and to increase the amount of fruits, vegetables, whole grains, and fibre in their diets. High blood pressure is one of the main risk factors for stroke, heart disease, and kidney failure.

- **Stroke.** The risk factors for having a stroke include high blood pressure, diabetes, and obesity. Poor eating habits are a contributing factor for all of these conditions.

- **Heart disease.** The risk factors for heart disease are similar to that of a stroke, high blood pressure, high cholesterol, and obesity. Healthy eating habits and an active lifestyle can reduce the risk of heart disease later in life.

Other long-term problems that can be related to a poor diet throughout life are liver disease and some forms of cancer (Ontario Ministry of Health, 2002).

Having read about the above conditions and seeing how eating habits have an impact on all of them, it is easy to see why developing healthy eating habits as a child will have lifelong benefits.

Factors Influencing Children's Eating Habits

Adult Modelling

"To bring up a child in the way he should go, travel that way yourself once in a while."

—Josh Billings

One of the ways in which children learn is by watching others. Parents and other significant adults have a major impact on children. Therefore, it is important that adults model appropriate behaviours for children. Children need to develop the same healthy habits recommended for adults. One way they will do this is by watching their parents practising those habits. When parents tell children that they are not allowed to eat something that the parents eat, they give the child a mixed message. Sometimes children view the forbidden food as more desirable than the foods their parents give them permission to eat. This may cause children to eat more of that food, thus having the opposite effect of what their parents wanted. A more productive solution for parents is to show their children,

through their own actions, how to follow good eating practices. They can show their children how to get a variety of different foods in their diet, and how to balance eating for health and pleasure. Parents can ensure that they pass on a healthy attitude toward eating and enjoying food.

Food habits and eating practices are an important part of children's health now and in the future. Adults need to ensure that when it comes to food, they practise what they preach by eating regular, healthy meals and snacks. Children are unlikely to develop healthy eating patterns if their parents do not practise them. The role of parents in modelling healthy behaviour is critical to children's development of healthy eating practices. It is in their children's best interest that they become role models for healthy living. It is important for the overall health of the entire family that all members practise good eating habits. Making sure that everyone follows Canada's Food Guide to Healthy Eating and selects healthy choices for snacks is an important step in building healthy bodies for all members of the family.

Often parents who are picky eaters raise children who are also picky eaters. Parents need to understand how their behaviours have an impact on their children's ability to have a balanced diet that meets all the nutritional requirements. Parents who are picky eaters should try new foods with their children, teaching them how to introduce new foods into their diets. How often did your parents offer you foods that were unfamiliar? Do you try new foods often or shy away from them?

Children are better at copying behaviours than listening to rules. They will often model parents' unhealthy eating habits. Unfortunately, parents are not always the best role models for their children when it comes to eating habits and practices. Parents need to take a serious look at their own food habits in order to help their children develop healthy ones. Once parents identify problems with their own eating habits, they need to be honest with themselves about the long-term consequences of these habits for both themselves and their children. The future health of both generations of the family depends on healthy eating habits and practices. Beginning with small steps, parents can guide change in the family's eating practices that will benefit everyone.

INTERNET CONNECTS

www.mcgrawhill.ca/links/food
To learn more about eating and nutrition for children, go to the web site above for *Food for Today,*
First Canadian Edition, to see where to go next.

Adult Control of Children's Eating

It is better for parents to teach children healthy eating practices than to try to exercise complete control over what they eat. Parents who monitor their children's food habits too strictly may find that when they are absent, their children will eat foods they have been forbidden to eat. Often these foods become their children's most desired foods. At some point in time, children will have their own money and will buy foods that their parents will not purchase for them.

Parents shouldn't use food to reward or punish children. They should also avoid rules such as "You can't have dessert if you don't eat everything on your plate." Parents are telling their children that healthy food is something to suffer through in order to get the reward of the good food—dessert. When children become older, they will continue to reward and punish themselves with food, and this can lead to all kinds of health problems in later life. These may include eating disorders, such as anorexia, bulimia, and compulsive overeating. Not learning to control your own behaviour concerning food can have negative consequences.

A research study looked at the impact of parents' practice of restricting the foods that they allowed their daughters to eat. The study showed that restricting certain foods the girls liked caused them to want the foods more. It also caused the girls to feel bad about themselves when they ate the restricted foods, creating a negative self-image. Parents who exert high levels of control over their children's eating practices cause their children to be less able to regulate their energy intake. Restricted foods become more attractive and children want them more than the foods they are allowed to eat.

Pediatric Occupational Therapist

Diana Matovich

What education is required for your job?

- Bachelor of Science degree in Occupational Therapy.
- One thousand hours of field-work education.
- National certification exam.

What skills does a person need to be able to do your job?

- Enjoy working with people.
- Strong organizational and communication skills.
- Openness to learn about other cultures and how culture affects feeding practices.

What do you like most about your job?

Certainly, the opportunity to work with children and their families is the most rewarding aspect of this job. In addition, feeding, swallowing, and nutrition problems are often complex, offering the opportunity to take a team approach and work with other health care professionals.

What other jobs/job titles have you had in the past?

Initially, I worked as a school-care occupational therapist, providing consultations in the schools to help children with special needs learn to integrate into their school environment and play at school to the best of their abilities. From there, I came to work at the McMaster Children's Hospital in acute care with children ranging from newborns to teenagers who have suffered congenital problems, illness, or accidents. Occupational therapists provide therapy to enhance development in all areas including cognition, mobility, self-care, and feeding.

What advice would you give a person who is considering a career as an occupational therapist?

This is an excellent career choice in terms of the diversity that is available. Occupational therapists work with people of all ages, in all settings. Our aim is to assist our clients and patients to be as independent as possible in all of the tasks of their daily life.

Comment on what you see as important issues/trends in food and nutrition.

More and more, there is a focus on good health and what is required to maintain it. Increased education and public awareness of food, nutrition, and exercise are truly important trends that I believe will continue to be a focus for Canadian society.

As adults, they will continue to experience cravings for the foods that were forbidden to them as children. Many a "chocoholic" will tell you that chocolate was a restricted food when he or she was young. Forbidden foods are often those that are high in fat or sugar content. It is better to teach children to eat less healthy foods in moderation than to forbid them.

Experts suggest that people should treat children the way they would like to be treated. Remembering a few simple rules will help to develop healthy eating habits in children. Children do not need as much food as adults, so it is better to give them small servings and allow seconds. Toddlers often eat many small meals because they cannot eat one large one. Providing them with healthy snacks in between meals is one way to ensure they get the nutrition they need throughout the day, instead of just at mealtimes.

Parents should avoid having power struggles with their children over food. Eating or not eating should not become an issue of who has the most power in the relationship. If parents force children to finish meals when they are full, then children will not learn when they are full. Recognition of their body signals helps to prevent obesity later in life. Children will learn that eating or not eating gives them a sense of control over their parents. Children can refuse to eat until they are rewarded. This sets up a situation where food is being used for the wrong reasons. Parents can provide a variety of healthy food choices for their children, ensuring that there are enough choices that the child can eat a healthy diet without power struggles occurring.

Childhood Obesity

Childhood obesity is becoming a serious health issue in the industrialized world. The World Health Organization has called childhood obesity an "epidemic." Over the past ten years, the number of children who are obese has risen dramatically (Ontario Ministry of Health, 2002).

◆ **Childhood obesity is a growing concern in North America.** What factors do you think are contributing to this increasing problem?

Childhood obesity is a serious problem. There are many factors that contribute to it, including overeating, lack of exercise, high-fat meals and snacks, and social behaviours and practices children learn at home. Parents need to look at their own eating habits and practices to determine their impact on their children's.

The food preparation habits of adults can also have a negative impact on their children's weight. If children are constantly being served foods high in fat, then they learn to crave them. As well, they are getting more fat in their diet than the recommended daily amount. Parents who are concerned about their child's weight should cook with less fat and serve less fatty foods.

Obese children experience physical, social, and emotional problems because they are overweight. If they continue to be overweight as adults, these problems become life-long ones. Obese children are at higher risk of becoming obese adults. Since the consequences of obesity in children are serious, children should be helped to deal with

it at an early age. Parents need to be involved in the treatment, and to be shown how to make family food habits and eating practices healthier.

Physical Activity

Healthy living involves a wide variety of factors. It is difficult to discuss healthy eating habits and practices without also mentioning healthy activity patterns. No matter how well you eat, your level of physical activity has a major impact on your overall health. There is a growing concern about the reduced activity levels of today's children. Children are seen as spending too much time watching television, playing video games, and using the computer. People are less physically active and obesity rates are rising in both the adult and child populations. In 1991, 24 percent of Canadian children aged four to nine were overweight, while in 1981 the figure was 14 percent. Twenty-six percent of Canadian adults are obese, and 35 percent of Canadians are not even moderately active on a weekly basis (Moscovitch, 1998a).

FOR YOUR HEALTH

Obesity in Children

In the past, many people thought that obesity was simply caused by overeating and under-exercising due to a lack of willpower and self-control. Today, doctors recognize that obesity is a serious medical problem due to multiple factors: genetic, environmental, behavioural, and social. All these factors play a role in determining a person's weight.

Research has shown that television viewing has been associated with obesity in children of all ages (preschool-aged, school-aged, and adolescents). Obesity is even more common if there is a television in the child's bedroom.

The diagnosis of obesity is usually based on a physical examination and patient history (i.e., eating and exercise habits). Children are considered "medically obese" when their weight poses health risks. The degree of obesity is often measured using the body mass index (BMI). BMI is calculated as follows:

$$\text{BMI} = \text{body weight (kg)} \div \text{height}^2 \text{ (m)}$$

Example: If a 4-year-old boy weighs 18 kg and is 0.95 m tall, you divide 18 by 0.95^2 (or 0.95×0.95). The result is 19.9.

The normal ranges for BMI are different for boys and girls of different ages. If you are concerned about your weight, you should consult your doctor or healthcare professional. He or she will compare your BMI result to a standard chart, and will then be able to tell whether you should start weight loss therapy.

Source: Ontario Ministry of Health (2002, p. 1).

◆ Children need to be physically active. Developing an active lifestyle when you are young has lifelong benefits. How can parents encourage their children to lead an active lifestyle?

As with healthy eating habits and practices, active lifestyles begin in childhood. It is important for parents to model an active lifestyle, as well as to actively participate with their children. An active lifestyle affects both the current and the future health of children. Parents need to take the time to ensure that their children develop healthy activity habits as well as healthy eating habits. It is important that parents model for their children. Parents who pursue an active lifestyle with their children will also benefit from the increased activity level. Once again, the entire family's health will benefit from a healthier lifestyle.

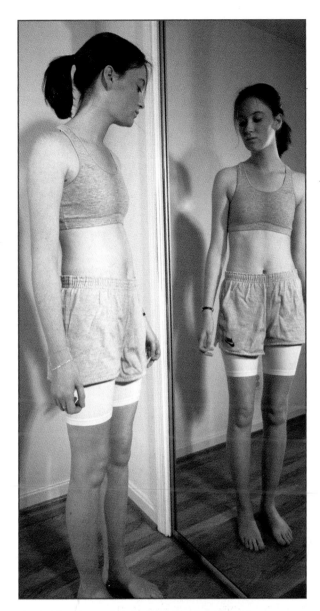

◆ Childhood struggles over food can lead to eating disorders later in life.

Disordered Eating

Early eating problems can lead to eating disorders later in life. Childhood eating conflicts and unpleasant mealtime experiences are seen as risk factors for the development of eating disorders later in life (Sandler, 2002). Eating disorders, such as anorexia, may develop as children grow and learn to reward and punish themselves with food. People diagnosed with anorexia starve themselves in an attempt to be slim. For some people, eating disorders are about control, which may be the result of learning from power struggles over food when they were younger.

Compulsive overeaters and bulimics will gorge on foods they crave. This may result from parents who were too restrictive with their children's food habits and eating practices. Being too restrictive does not allow children to learn how to eat all foods in a healthy way. Compulsive overeaters do not recognize their body signals of fullness and eat much more than they need to be healthy. This may be a result of being forced to ignore those signals as young children. Bulimics overeat and then force their bodies to get rid of the food in an attempt to control their weight. They may make themselves vomit or take laxatives in order to get rid of the food they've eaten. They recognize that the foods that they crave may not give them the body they want, so they satisfy their desire for the food but then go to extreme measures to get rid of the consequences of eating them.

Parents need to promote positive eating experiences and develop healthy eating practices in their children to provide them with a good start in life and the best chance of a healthy future. Developing a positive attitude toward eating and food will have lifelong benefits for children. Making sure that children see food as enjoyable and that they learn to eat all foods in a healthy way is an important step to avoiding eating disorders later in life.

Lifelong Benefits of Healthy Eating Patterns

The benefits of developing healthy eating patterns as a child show themselves in a healthier life as an adult. Taking a proactive approach to disease prevention will benefit the health

◆ **Healthy eating habits developed in childhood will help you become a healthy adult. How does your family influence your eating habits?**

of future generations. The health-care system and health-care workers are beginning to look at health promotion and wellness instead of only trying to heal the sick. The new direction in the medical community is to work to prevent some of the illnesses that develop from known causes. As you have seen in this chapter, the development of good eating habits and practices in children can go a long way to ensuring that future generations have healthier adult lives.

"An ounce of prevention is worth a pound of cure."

—author unknown

Key and Supporting Issues When Developing Questions

One of the key aspects of doing research is developing questions. Questions help to guide your research and give you a focus. The ability to develop questions is an important Social Science research tool.

When you are studying a new topic, you need to decide what the **key issues** are. Key issues are those that are critical to the understanding of a topic. **Supporting issues** are those that reinforce the key issues. Supporting issues help define the key issues.

One way to develop key and supporting issues for a topic is by using a web. Write the key issue in the centre and have the supporting issues branch out from it, as shown in the example below.

Key and Supporting Issues Web

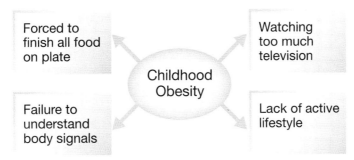

Once you have determined the key and supporting issues, you can begin to develop questions about your topic. Questions are most often developed to guide research. Well-developed questions can help you find the information you are looking for.

When you are developing questions, make sure you relate the supporting issues back to the key issue. Your questions should help you define the key issue.

Example

Key issue: childhood obesity

Main question: What are the causes of childhood obesity?

Supporting questions:
- How does the increased number of hours Canadian children spend watching television relate to childhood obesity?
- How does the less-active lifestyle of Canadian children relate to the increasing number of children who are obese?
- How can failing to recognize the body signal of fullness lead to obesity?
- How does parents' insistence that a child finish his or her meal contribute to child-hood obesity?
- How does the use of food for reward or punishment contribute to childhood obesity?

Chapter 3 Review and Activities

Summary

- Childhood is the most important time to see and learn good eating habits. Developing poor ones can lead to life-long health problems.

- Almost half of today's children between the ages of five and eight are already at risk for one of the diseases that normally occur in adults.

- It is necessary that adults model healthy eating habits so their children will adopt them.

- Parents and caregivers who exert too much control over what their children eat cause them to sneak forbidden foods and make these foods more desirable.

- Food shouldn't be used to reward or punish children. This system may be carried on by the children throughout their lives and may result in eating disorders.

- Power struggles between parents and children over food should be avoided so that children learn to recognize when their bodies signal they are full or hungry.

- Childhood obesity has risen dramatically over the past ten years due to overeating, lack of exercise, high-fat meals and snacks, and social behaviours and practices learned at home.

- Parents need to model an active lifestyle for their children to prevent future health problems among family members.

- Many eating disorders are a result of eating problems experienced in early childhood. Eating disorders include anorexia, when people starve themselves to be thin; compulsive overeating, when people do not recognize their body signal of fullness; and bulimia, when people binge-eat to satisfy a craving, then rid their body of the food unnaturally in an attempt to control their weight.

- Parents and caregivers need to develop a positive attitude toward healthy eating and living in their children to prevent them from having health problems when they are adults.

Knowledge and Understanding

1. What is a key issue?

2. What are supporting issues? How do they differ from key issues? Give an example.

3. Were you ever told by your parents that you were not allowed to eat something that they did? How did that make you feel? Do you enjoy that food now? Is it better because you were denied it as a child? Explain how this is an example of the concept of adult modelling of eating practices.

4. Name two physical activities that families can do together when the children are young and when they are older.

5. What are the risks associated with childhood obesity? Why is obesity being called an epidemic? What can parents and other caregivers do to reduce the risks of childhood obesity?

Thinking and Inquiry

6. You are studying the effects of parental control on the eating habits of young children. You have found that the more control a parent exerts over a child's food habits and choices, the more likely the child is to try to eat forbidden foods and sneak snacks. You also observe that these children are unable to read their body signals of feeling hunger and fullness.

- What is the key issue in this case?
- What are the supporting issues?
- Write four questions to use to survey parents regarding this issue.

7. Think back to your childhood. Make a list of foods that you commonly ate and a list of foods that your parents usually ate. How similar are they? Did your parents follow the same eating guidelines they set for you? Explain.

8. What rules did your parents or caregivers have about food when you were younger? What impact do they have on your current eating patterns and habits? Do you think those rules will result in any long-term positive or negative consequences for you? Explain.

9. What is an eating disorder? How can childhood eating patterns have an impact on the development of an eating disorder? What can parents do? What can you do to change your eating patterns in order to have healthier ones?

10. Make a list of healthy eating practices for families to follow.

Communication

11. Develop a poster aimed at parents of preschool children, explaining to them the importance of developing healthy food habits and eating practices in their children. Include the following points:

- Influences on a young child's food habits.
- Risk factors of unhealthy eating habits.
- A list of things parents can do to encourage healthy eating practices.

12. Create a brochure that deals with the issue of childhood obesity and physical activity. The brochure should be aimed at parents and include the following points:

- The dangers of obesity.
- Some reasons children may become obese.
- The role of physical activity in a healthy lifestyle.
- The ways parents can help children to develop healthy habits.

Application

13. Using the survey questions developed in question 6, survey ten parents. Tally the results of your survey and create a chart to show your results. Write a one-page summary of your survey.

While reading this chapter, you will:

- Observe how families, peers, and media influence an individual's food choices and habits.

- Investigate current food marketing techniques directed at different age groups.

Food Marketing

Often when people socialize with their friends, eating is involved. Have you ever considered how much influence your friends have on your food choices and habits?

KEY TERMS

peers
primary research
primary source
secondary research
secondary source

SOCIAL SCIENCE SKILLS

- primary research
- secondary research

In this chapter you will explore the influences of family, peers, and the media on an individual's food choices. You will also examine food marketing techniques, with a focus on how different age groups are targeted.

Children often respond to food advertising, asking their parents to purchase the desired product.

Family Influence on Food Choices

Family is the major influence on the food choices and habits of its members. It is the first influence on a young child's food choices, since very young children eat the foods that their family provides for them.

As children grow older, they begin to develop likes and dislikes. Young children will refuse to eat a food they do not like the taste of. At an early age, children will show preferences for certain foods.

Once children begin to socialize with people outside the family unit, they will introduce them to new foods. Families can restrict what

◆ **The first and primary influence on your food habits is your family.**

their members eat within the home, but they have little control over what they eat outside it. Did you ever eat foods at a friend's house that you were not allowed to eat at home?

Providing food for its members is one of the main functions of a family. As a result, families continue to have an influence on the food habits of their members for a long time. An individual's favourite foods are often those they ate at home.

Family members use food to celebrate special occasions during their lives. The influence of your family on your food habits and eating practices will last a lifetime.

Influences of Peers

Peers are people who belong to the same societal group. They are based on age, school grade, or status. As you get older, your peers will begin to have a greater influence on both your food choices and your food habits.

The more time you spend with your peers away from your family, the more influence peers will have.

During the preschool years, the food choices and food habits of children who attend day cares, preschools, and play groups, and who socialize with other children, begin to be influenced by their peers. If a best friend likes broccoli, a child may eat it to impress the friend. Likewise, the child may decide he or she no longer likes broccoli because the friend does not. Parents who limit their children's intake of sweet and salty foods may be pressured by them to allow these foods, since they are exposed to others who are allowed to eat them. Children are often served food in playgroups or at preschool, and they experience new foods and new ways of serving familiar foods there. As a result, children may begin to ask for these foods at home.

Many children who attend school take food with them either for snacks or for lunch. Children often share and trade foods at school. This exposure to different foods influences their food habits. Did you ever ask your parents to include something in your lunch that you first ate at school? Did you ever trade your food for someone else's? When children begin to play more with their friends, they sometimes have snacks at friends' houses. When children visit other homes, they encounter different food habits and practices. Sometimes, children will visit a friend's house in order to eat a food that they can't have at home. The more children are exposed to different food habits and practices, the more they are influenced by them.

◆ Often, children's first exposure to foods from other families is at birthday parties for friends.

◆ **Eating lunch at school with friends is part of a young person's social life.** Does your school have more than one lunch period? Have you ever had a different lunch period than your friends? How did you feel about that?

As teenagers become more independent of their parents, their peers begin to exert a greater influence on their lives. This influence is extended to food habits, practices, and beliefs about food. Food is an important part of a teen's social life. In secondary school, most teens eat lunch in the school cafeteria and chose who they will sit with. They are no longer eating with a class group as in most elementary school settings. The social aspect of lunch becomes an important part of the secondary school experience.

Media Influence

The media has a large influence on all our lives because it is all around us, even though we may not always be aware of it. Canadians are exposed to many forms of media, as indicated by the list below.

What Media Canadians Own

◆ 99 percent of Canadian households own a radio and a television set.

◆ **Advertisers use the media in many ways to influence your food choices and habits.** Sometimes there are so many ads in the environment that they become part of the scenery. Do you see any food ads on your way to school or work? About how many are there? What products are being advertised?

- 59 percent of all households have two television sets, and more than a third own at least three TV sets.

- 81 percent of all homes with TV have cable and 84 percent have VCRs.

- More than 70 percent of households rent at least one video a week; 83 percent own at least one video; 40 percent own more than 20.

- One in three households uses a computer for communications or surfing the Internet. Adults with children aged 12–17 are most likely to own a computer.

- Canada is, per capita, the most "wired" country in the world, followed by the United States and Australia (Moscovitch, 1998).

How does your family compare to these statistics? Do families in your classroom match these statistics?

FYI

Marketing to Children

Marketing to children is now a multi-billion-dollar business. The spending power of children has risen dramatically in recent years. In Canada, four million children, aged 2 to 12, spend $1.5 billion of their own money in one year and influence an additional $15 billion in home purchases. Advertisers see children as future lifetime customers. They want to make them loyal to their product at a young age (Moscovitch, 1998).

Advertisers use the media to sell their products. There are many different ways in which they use the media. The following are some examples:

- **Newspapers.** Advertisers use newspapers to reach a broad audience, usually adults. Newspapers are used at the local level. In Canada, there are a few papers that reach a national audience; however, the cost of national advertising is high.

- **Consumer magazines.** Magazines target special audiences. Advertisers will choose the magazine based on their target audience. Advertisers use age-related magazines to target different age groups. Magazines tend to stay in households longer than newspapers, so the target audience sees the ad more than once. Do the food ads in your favourite magazine appeal to you and influence your food choices?

- **Radio.** Like magazines, radio audiences vary. Each station has its own group of listeners. Advertisers will use a station whose main audience is their target. Tie-ins to events sponsored by the radio station can give a product extra exposure. Often food companies will give free samples at events.

- **Television.** Television has mass audience appeal. It is very visible and has a high impact on consumers. It has a broad market, but can be used to reach specific audiences as well. Ads can be placed within shows for specific audiences, or they can be placed during shows that have a broader appeal. These ads reach 98 percent of Canadians on a weekly basis. Television ads are very costly to make and to air. However, they do give advertisers broad exposure, an opportunity to demonstrate their product, to create name identity, and to build an image around their product.

◆ Advertisers sometimes give away free samples of a new product to make people aware of it.

◆ **Outdoor ads.** Outdoor ads are a highly visible means of reaching a large audience. Their audience is very broad, since anyone who passes them sees them. Advertisers can choose the location for the ad in order to reach a specific target market. This type of advertising tends to be done around major markets, larger cities, and on main transportation routes.

◆ **Direct mail.** More and more advertisers are using direct mail to advertise their products. Direct mail targets audiences in a specific location or group. Some consumers see direct mail as junk mail and throw it away; other consumers find direct mailings valuable. Have you ever used a coupon you received in the mail to make a food-related purchase?

◆ **The Yellow Pages.** The Yellow Pages are used to reach the telephone owner. Many consumers look up places to shop in the Yellow Pages. It is a great way to introduce a product or service to someone who is new to an area.

◆ **Internet marketing.** The Internet offers a variety of ways to reach consumers. Advertisers develop web sites, pop-up ads, and banner ads for their products. These are used to promote products, communicate with consumers about products, and reinforce advertising in other mediums. The Internet is a fast-growing medium that is offering a world of opportunities to advertisers.

◆ Canadians of all ages spend many hours watching television. The amount of time they watch television has an influence on them.

Advertisers are also looking for different ways of advertising their products. Products are often used in movies and television shows to get extra exposure. Advertising during sporting events increases consumer awareness of a product, as well as giving the product a positive image by associating it with the event. Advertising is beginning to appear in many unexpected places as well. For instance, have you ever seen an ad while using a public washroom facility?

Advertising Techniques

Are there TV commercials you enjoy watching? Advertising can be informative and entertaining. Advertisers use different techniques to entice consumers to purchase their products. Food advertisers use these same techniques to convince people that they want to eat their products. Following are some of the techniques that advisers use to influence consumers' purchases.

◆ **Limited information.** Advertisements often give only the facts that will encourage you to buy, without telling the whole story. Can you think of an ad that gives limited information? What effect does that have on your consumer decisions? Can you think of one ad that leaves out important information?

◆ **Positive images.** An ad may use images of things that people feel positively about, such as friendship or a good appearance. The advertiser's hope is that the consumer will associate these images and feelings with the product.

◆ **Celebrity endorsement.** Some ads show popular performers or athletes promoting the product. They don't tell you whether the person actually uses the product in real life.

FYI

Average Hours Per Week of Television Viewing

Television is seen as one of the most powerful advertising techniques for marketers (Wright et al, 1984). The time spent watching television can influence the amount of food and other advertising one sees.

Look at the chart below. How does the television viewing of children and adolescents differ from that of men and women? How might advertisers use this information?

Average Hours Per Week of Television Viewing (Fall 1996)

	Total Population	Children 2–11	Adolescents 12–17	Men 18 and Over	Women 18 and Over
Canada	22.8	17.9	17.3	21.9	26.5
Newfoundland	24.0	21.9	18.9	21.8	28.0
Prince Edward Island	21.3	17.1	18.9	20.3	24.4
Nova Scotia	24.5	19.7	18.1	23.5	28.3
New Brunswick	24.5	19.7	18.1	23.5	28.3
Québec					
Total	26.0	20.1	18.3	24.6	30.7
English	22.5	18.2	18.3	21.6	25.4
French	26.6	20.5	18.3	25.2	31.7
Ontario	21.8	17.6	17.2	21.0	25.0
Manitoba	22.3	16.1	18.0	21.7	26.2
Saskatchewan	22.5	17.4	16.4	21.3	27.3
Alberta	20.3	16.5	16.0	19.5	23.7
British Columbia	21.0	15.5	16.0	21.1	23.7

Source: Statistics Canada (1997).

Different people have different tastes. Look at the chart below that shows the types of programs watched on television. How might advertisers use this information?

Television Viewing Time

	Fall 2001 Anglophones Aged 2 and Older		
	Total	Canadian Programs	Foreign Programs
	Percent of Viewing Time		
All programs	**100.0**	**28.6**	**71.4**
News and public affairs	22.3	14.6	7.7
Documentary	3.8	1.2	2.7

FYI

Television Viewing Time (continued)

	Fall 2001 Anglophones Aged 2 and Older		
	Total	Canadian Programs	Foreign Programs
	Percent of Viewing Time		
Instructional:			
Academic	2.6	1.2	1.4
Social/recreational	1.2	0.4	0.8
Religion	0.4	0.2	0.2
Sports	9.9	5.1	4.6
Variety and games	11.6	1.1	10.4
Music and dance	1.4	0.9	0.5
Comedy	11.9	0.5	11.4
Drama	28.0	3.5	24.5
Other/unknown:			
VCR	4.8	0.0	4.8
Other	2.2	0.0	2.2

Source: Statistics Canada (2003).

◆ **Appeal to basic needs.** Advertisers may focus on ways the product meets a need for security or self-esteem. They try to convince you that the product will make you look or feel better. This technique is used in different ways for different age groups. For example, a young child's needs are different than an adult's needs. Selling cereal to children would mean that advertisers would promote cereal that tastes good. However, the children's parents would look at the same cereal and want to know if it provides their children with good nutrition.

◆ **Scare tactics.** Advertisers may play on people's fears of aging or developing a medical condition by claiming that their product can prevent or relieve the symptoms or provide essential nutrients.

◆ **False claims.** Ads may make claims that are not true, such as fast or guaranteed results. Remember, if a claim sounds too good to be true, it usually is. Can you think of an ad that claims something that is too good to be true? At whom is the ad directed? Why do you think the advertiser used this appeal to sell the product?

◆ **Infomercials.** Infomercials are TV ads made to look like regular consumer programs or televised news reports. Unless you look carefully, you may believe you're watching something you are not!

Besides advertising, companies use other techniques to promote their products. A soft drink company may lend its name to a sports event or arrange to have its product shown in a movie. Coupons and eye-catching store displays encourage consumers to buy. Even product packages are a form of advertising.

Remember that the purpose of advertising is to get people to buy a product. The goal is to get good nutrition at a fair price. All consumers, regardless of age, need to be aware of advertising's effect on their food habits and eating practices. Consumers need to be sure that their buying decisions are based on their own priorities and not on the advertisers'.

FYI

Teen Consumerism

The purpose of advertising is to sell, and today's teens are a target market. Think about the kinds of promotions that have inspired you to try a new product. A recent marketing and lifestyle study revealed the following buying habits in response to various promotions.

| | **AGE** | | |
Promotion	12–15	16–17	18–19
Free sample	48%	47%	38%
Coupon	35%	40%	42%
Contest/ sweepstakes	26%	21%	19%
Free gift with purchase	25%	21%	20%
Cash rebate	11%	10%	11%
Frequent-buyer clubs	6%	8%	9%

INTERNET CONNECTS

www.mcgrawhill.ca/links/food
To learn more about teen health and the media, go to the web site above for *Food for Today, First Canadian Edition,* to see where to go next.

◆ Teenagers find cents-off coupons like these are a good way to save money and try new items on the market.

Primary and Secondary Research

Primary and secondary research are terms used to define the *distance* from the research.

Primary research refers to research where the researcher is the first person (primary) to view the research. This means that the person who actually performs the research is the person reporting on the research. You will be a primary researcher when you design and implement a questionnaire or survey.

A **primary source** is an *original* document or account that is not about another document or account but stands on its own. For example, any novel, poem, play, diary, letter, or other creative work is a primary source. The data from a research study also constitutes a primary source because it comes straight from the participants' responses. Interviews of people actually experiencing something "on the scene" are also primary sources. If you were doing a paper on the physical effects of stress, talking to someone who is under stress would be about as close to your topic as you could get. That's what is meant by *distance*.

Primary research involves the collection of *original* data on a specific research topic. There are three methods of primary research:

1. Survey Research

- Gathers brief answers from many people.
- Involves using questionnaires by mail, phone, in person.
- Needs a representative sample.
- Questionnaires must be carefully planned and well written.
- Quality of data is dependent on quality of questionnaire.
- Least expensive form of data collection.
- Low response rate, since fewer people complete and return the data.
- Good way of collecting a lot of information in a short period of time, but it is not an in-depth method of collecting information.

2. In-Depth Personal Interviews

- Costly and time-consuming method of research collection.
- Allows for greater understanding of lifestyles and personal feelings.
- May encourage participants to project their feelings and attitudes and to talk at length on topic; not as structured as a questionnaire.
- Interviewer's personality and skills will affect the outcome of the interview.

3. Personal Observation

- Family interaction can be studied through observation.
- One-way mirrors, or observation in natural settings.
- Participant observation sometimes used by becoming a member of the group.
- Need to be well trained in the skills of observation.
- Must be careful not to let bias show through.

(continued)

Social Science Skills (continued)

Secondary sources are ones that interpret primary sources or are otherwise a step removed. A journal article or book about a poem, novel, or play, or a commentary about what an interview signifies is a secondary source. When you perform secondary research on a subject and write a paper on it, it becomes a secondary source.

Secondary research involves researching information and/or data that someone else has collected. You can find this type of information in printed sources (books, magazines, and newspapers) and in electronic sources (CD-ROM encyclopedias, software packages, Internet). Whenever a primary or secondary source is used, it must be referenced.

Source: Ontario Family Studies Leadership Council and Ontario Family Studies Home Economics Educators Association (2002).

Chapter 4 Review and Activities

Summary

- Family is the major influence on your food choices and eating habits, both during childhood and throughout adulthood.
- Children and adolescents are exposed to different foods and food habits through their peers.
- Advertisers use media, including television, the Internet, newspapers and magazines, radio, outdoor ads, direct mail, and the Yellow Pages, to market food products and food-related businesses, such as restaurants and fast-food outlets.
- Advertisers use different techniques to convince consumers to purchase their products. Some of these include limiting information about the product to encourage you to buy it; associating positive images with the product; including celebrities in their ads to endorse a product; focusing on the way a product will help you look or feel better; playing on your fears about something, such as a medical condition, and telling how their product will help; making false claims about a product that offer guaranteed results; and airing infomercials that seem like regular programs so the audience doesn't realize they are watching or hearing a commercial.
- Companies also use special events, coupons, in-store displays, and eye-catching packaging to encourage consumers to buy and use their products.

Knowledge and Understanding

1. What is the difference between primary and secondary research? Give two examples of each.

2. Define the term *peer*. Explain how your peers have had an influence on your personal eating habits. Include whether or not your peers have influenced your family's eating habits and, if so, how.

3. Think of an ad for a snack food that gives limited information. Do you think the advertisers are leaving out other information that might be important to know? Explain.

Thinking and Inquiry

4. Make a list of your favourite foods in a chart like the one that follows. Record them in two-year intervals since you were two years old. Ask your parents or caregivers to help you recall your favourite foods from when you were very young. Decide who or what influenced your favourite foods as you have grown.

My Favourite Foods

Age	Food	Influence
2	*artny yulmo frnso*	*artny yulmo frnso*
4	*artny yulmo frnso*	*artny yulmo frnso*
6	*artny yulmo frnso*	*artny yulmo frnso*
8	*artny yulmo frnso*	*artny yulmo frnso*
10	*artny yulmo frnso*	*artny yulmo frnso*
12	*artny yulmo frnso*	*artny yulmo frnso*
14	*artny yulmo frnso*	*artny yulmo frnso*

5. Compare your answers to question 4 to those of four classmates, then write a one-page summary on the influence of family and peers on people of different ages.

6. Choose three different ads. Describe each ad in a paragraph, making note of the different techniques being used to appeal to consumers. Is the ad successful? Explain why or why not.

7. Note the different techniques advertisers use on pages 46–49. For each technique, explain how it would be used to appeal to each of the following age groups: young children, teens, young adults, middle-aged adults, older adults.

Communication

8. Looking at the techniques used in your answer to question 7, explain how advertisers might change their appeal for males and females.

9. Choose three different types of magazines, one for adults, one for teens, and one for children. Cut out food advertisements from each of these magazines. Make a collage of each group of ads. Write a one-page analysis explaining the differences and similarities between the ads geared to the different age groups.

Application

10. Choose an hour time slot to watch television. While watching, make a list of the commercials that relate to food and nutrition and note other relevant information in a chart like the following one:

Time	Network	Commercial	Age Group Targeted
artny yulmo frmso	*artny yulmo frmso*	*artny yulmo frmso*	*artny yulmo frmso*
artny yulmo frmso	*artny yulmo frmso*	*artny yulmo frmso*	*artny yulmo frmso*
artny yulmo frmso	*artny yulmo frmso*	*artny yulmo frmso*	*artny yulmo frmso*

Is there one particular age group being targeted? Who? How?

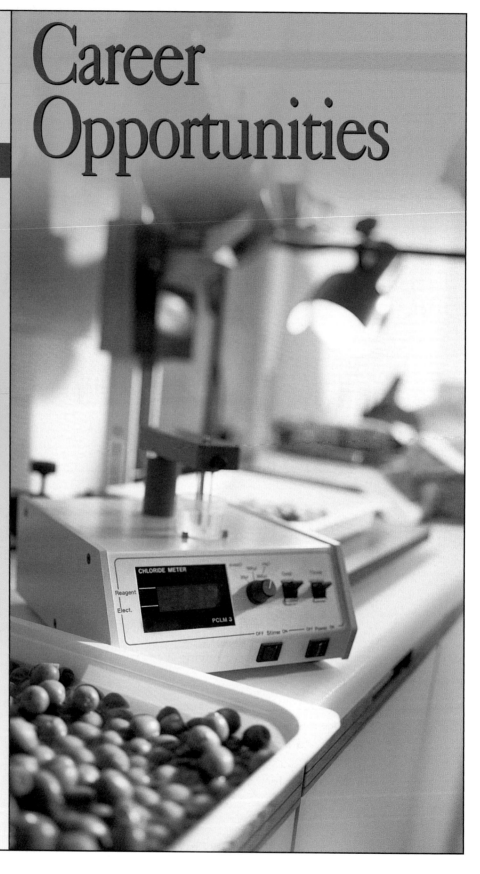

CHAPTER EXPECTATION

While reading this chapter, you will:

- Discover career opportunities related to food and nutrition.

Career Opportunities

People often think of traditional careers relating to food and nutrition. In this chapter you will learn about some of these as well as some careers you may not have considered.

CHAPTER INTRODUCTION

There are many different careers that involve food and nutrition. Many of us think only of the basic career options, such as chef, dietitian, and cookbook author. As you will see in the Career Profiles throughout this text, there are a wide variety of careers that involve foods. This chapter will discuss some of the factors to consider while exploring food and nutrition as a career option. Read over the Career Profiles in this and other chapters to come to a better understanding of the extensive career choices available in the field of food and nutrition.

Now that you are nearing adulthood, it is time to consider what career you would like to pursue.

Career Opportunities

Thinking about Careers

A **career** is a profession or a life's work within a certain field. It usually begins with an **entry-level job**, a job that requires little or no experience. These jobs often lead to better-paying jobs with more responsibility.

Employees will advance in their careers by mastering the skills needed for their jobs and showing they are qualified to take on new responsibilities. Many seek additional education or training throughout their lives to further their careers.

◆ **An interest in food now could turn into a career someday.**

◆ **Many entry-level jobs are available in the food service industry. List characteristics that can help a person move up the ladder to higher-paying jobs.**

Food-Related Careers

A recent study on job growth for the coming years predicted great expansion in service industries, including those pertaining to food and nutrition. The job outlook for this field is bright. Consider these trends:

◆ More people are eating out.

◆ Consumers are more interested in the relationship between food and health.

◆ The growing world population and other global factors make efficient production and use of high-quality food more important than ever.

Food Service

The food service industry includes all aspects of preparing and serving food for the public. It is expected to create more new jobs than any other retail industry in the next decade.

Jobs in food service can vary from serving food to developing recipes to merchandising food products. These jobs are usually available in every part of the country. If you like to travel, you might consider food service jobs with cruise lines or airlines, or jobs in other countries.

Educational Background

Educational requirements in food service vary, depending on the job you want. Part-time, entry-level jobs are often a good start. Foods classes in secondary school can also provide a valuable foundation. To further your education, you may have to consider courses at a community college or university. There are also private schools where you can train for food-related careers. Canada has many award-winning schools that are recognized internationally for their graduates. There are such a wide variety of careers related to foods and the food industry that it is worth spending some time doing an Internet search to see what options are available to you if you are interested in the field. See the Internet Connects opposite to find sites where you can explore career options. It is important to begin to explore career possibilities now, since they affect your course choices during secondary school and your post-secondary options.

Once you have started working for a company, you can upgrade your qualifications. Many companies offer on-the-job training to help employees advance. Taking advantage of these opportunities can lead you to some exciting career choices.

Personal Qualifications

Food service jobs require certain personal traits. Employees must enjoy and be able to work successfully with people. They must be willing to do their share as part of a team. Producing quality food on a schedule can mean hard work and long hours. Good health, enthusiasm, ambition, and a sense of humour are essential. So are good work habits, such as punctuality and the ability to follow directions and accept criticism.

Job Advancement

Brent started working in a restaurant clearing and cleaning tables. Through hard work and study, he moved up the career ladder to the position of assistant manager. His goal now is to become a manager.

As a rule, more education and training allow you to start on a higher rung of the career ladder. Food service offers many different career ladders.

◆ Having a long-range goal, such as becoming an executive chef, can help you plan your career. An entry-level job, such as a kitchen helper, is often the first step. From there, you can work your way up the career ladder. Each promotion takes you a step closer to your long-term goal.

```
INTERNET CONNECTS
```
www.mcgrawhill.ca/links/food
To learn more about jobs related to the food and nutrition industries, go to the web site above for *Food for Today, First Canadian Edition,* to see where to go next.

Family and Consumer Studies

Family and consumer studies—called home economics, human ecology, or family studies at some universities—involves using knowledge and skills to solve problems and make decisions about the home and family. Professionals with degrees in food and nutrition or consumer foods have many career options in addition to food service. These include teaching, communication, and research and development.

The Successful Worker

The qualities Canadian employers look for in a worker are listed below. Which ones do you possess? Which are your strengths? Which are your weaknesses? How can you make yourself more employable?

Academic Skills: Those skills which provide the basic foundation to get, keep, and progress on a job and to achieve the best results.

Communicate

- Understand and speak the languages in which business is conducted.
- Listen to understand and learn.
- Read, comprehend, and use written materials, including graphs, charts, and displays.
- Write effectively in the languages in which business is conducted.

Think

- Think critically and act logically to evaluate situations, solve problems, and make decisions.
- Understand and solve problems involving mathematics and use the results.
- Use technology, instruments, tools, and information systems effectively.
- Access and apply specialized knowledge from various fields.

Learn

- Continue to learn for life.

Personal Management Skills:

The combination of skills, attitudes, and behaviours required to get, keep, and progress on a job, and to achieve the best results.

Source: Conference Board of Canada, 2003.

Positive attitudes and behaviours

- Self-esteem and confidence.
- Honesty, integrity, and personal ethics.
- A positive attitude toward learning, growth, and personal health.
- Initiative, energy, and persistence to get the job done.

Responsibility

- The ability to set goals and priorities in work and personal life.
- The ability to plan and manage time, money, and other resources to achieve goals.
- Accountability for actions taken.
- Adaptability.
- A positive attitude toward change.
- The ability to identify and suggest new ideas to get the job done—creativity.

Teamwork Skills: Those skills needed to work with others on a job and to achieve the best results.

- Work with others.
- Understand and contribute to the organization's goals.
- Understand and work within the culture of the group.
- Plan and make decisions with others and support the outcomes.
- Respect the thoughts and opinions of others in the group.
- Exercise "give and take" to achieve group results.
- Seek a team approach as appropriate.
- Lead where appropriate, mobilizing the group for high performance.

Teaching

Family and consumer sciences specialists may teach in schools, colleges, and universities. They may teach secondary school programs in food and nutrition, as well as other courses related to families. Nutritionists may work for public health units, teaching consumers about food preparation and related topics. They are also hired by other organizations to instruct consumers on how to make wise food choices. Many national marketing boards provide an educational component as well as service for consumers. These instructors write resources and provide workshops for teachers to help them provide their students with good information about nutrition.

Governments at all levels hire educators to provide nutrition information to Canadians. These educators will also write resources and provide workshops for both teachers and students. Governments know the importance of providing valid information to consumers in order to help them make wise food choices.

INTERNET CONNECTS

www.mcgrawhill.ca/links/food
To learn more about what nutrition educators do, go to the web site above for *Food for Today, First Canadian Edition*, to see where to go next.

Communication

This area involves communicating information to the public through television, magazines, books, and newspapers. People with strong communication skills are needed to help write speeches, articles, and advertisements about food products and services. Food stylists create attractive arrangements of foods for photographs. Employers include food producers, manufacturers, government agencies, and trade associations.

Research and Development

Food researchers help develop new products and appliances in test kitchens or research laboratories. They may work for universities, food producers, appliance manufacturers, or the government.

Many jobs in family and consumer studies require at least a bachelor's degree. Some, such as teaching, research, and management, may require higher degrees. Study and experience in related fields also helps. Specialists in communications, for example, might have a background in journalism or public relations.

Food Science

Food science is the study of the physical, chemical, and microbiological make-up of food. Food scientists develop food products and new ways to process and package them. They also test foods and beverages for quality and purity to be sure they meet company standards and federal food regulations.

◆ A university education can lead to a rewarding career as a food scientist.

Food scientists are generally employed by the food-processing industry. They may work in laboratories, in test kitchens, or on the production line. The many careers in food science include basic research, product development, quality control, and sales.

Food scientists need at least a bachelor's degree with a major in food science, food engineering, or food technology. Higher degrees are needed for research and managerial jobs.

Dietetics

A dietitian is a professional trained in the principles of food and nutrition. Dietitians may work for large institutions such as hospitals, health maintenance organizations, company cafeterias, and food service companies. They help develop special diets and counsel groups or individuals in making wise food choices.

Dietitians must have a bachelor's degree in food and nutrition. After graduation from an approved course, those wishing to become a registered dietitian in Canada must successfully complete a practicum experience program. This program is a supervised practical experience that is accredited by the Dietitians of Canada. Dietitians have a code of ethics and follow standards of practice that are approved by the Dietitians of Canada (n.d.).

Your Basic Health and Safety Rights

The *Occupational Health and Safety Act* (OHSA) gives every worker important rights. What are some of these basic rights?

1. **The right to know.** You have the right to know the hazards in your job. Your employer or supervisor must tell you about anything in your job that can hurt you. Your employer must make sure you are provided with the information you need so that you can work safely.

2. **The right to participate.** You have the right to take part in keeping your workplace healthy and safe. Depending on the size of the company, you can be part of the Health and Safety Committee or be a Health and Safety Representative. You also have the right to participate in training and information sessions to help you do your job safely.

3. **The right to refuse unsafe work.** If you believe your job is likely to endanger you, you have an obligation to report the unsafe situation to management. If the situation is not corrected and you feel your health and safety is still in danger, you have the right under the OHSA to refuse to perform the work without reprisal.

INTERNET CONNECTS

www.mcgrawhill.ca/links/food
To learn more about young workers' rights and responsibilities and tips for new workers and volunteers, go to the web site above for *Food for Today, First Canadian Edition*, to see where to go next.

Food Production, Processing, and Marketing

As you will see throughout the text, an extensive network of people is involved in producing food and getting it to the marketplace. Career opportunities vary from hydroponic farming to supermarket management.

Training and education also vary, but a combination of experience and formal education is best. Farmers, for example, need to know how to do the everyday work on the farm itself but can also benefit from studies in related topics, such as soil conservation and plant and animal genetics. With all of the changes in science and technology applied to agriculture, some farmers now attend college or university in order to obtain valuable information about making their farms as productive as possible. Farmers are continually updating their knowledge as the changes in agriculture demand. A bakery owner must have experience in preparing the food as well as knowledge about business management, marketing techniques, human resource management, and tax laws.

INTERNET CONNECTS

www.mcgrawhill.ca/links/food
To learn more about careers in agriculture and food science, go to the web site above for *Food for Today, First Canadian Edition,* to see where to go next.

Entrepreneurship

Many people dream of owning their own businesses. A person who runs his or her own business is called an **entrepreneur** (AHN-truh-pruh-NOOR). Successful entrepreneurs share certain personal qualities. They are willing to work hard and take risks. They can make sound decisions, are well organized, and understand basic business management practices. Opportunities for entrepreneurs in food and nutrition include catering, running a snack shop, providing home delivery from restaurants or supermarkets, providing nutritional consultation, and preparing and selling food, to name a few.

Franchises

Entrepreneurs sometimes invest in a **franchise,** an individually owned and operated branch of a business with an established name and guidelines. Some fast-food restaurants are franchises. Not all franchises are reliable, however, so potential owners should investigate carefully before buying. Also, the fact that the business is a franchise cannot guarantee success. It's up to the individual businessperson to provide the skills and commitment needed to succeed.

◆ Owning a business takes hard work, but the results are worthwhile. Entrepreneurs feel the special satisfaction of building their own success.

FOR YOUR HEALTH

TAP-ping Your Strengths

According to a popular saying, "You get only one chance to make a first impression." While this advice is useful in all social situations, it comes in especially handy in a job interview. To make a positive impression, remember the TAP strategy:

- **(T)horoughness.** Learn all you can about the company, including the job you are applying for. Make up an interview packet. Include your résumé (if needed), a good pen, and a small notebook.

- **(A)ppearance.** Dress neatly. Avoid jeans, excessive makeup, and excessive jewellery. Go to the interview alone. Don't bring family members or friends.

- **(P)unctuality.** Be sure to arrive on time. Write down the time and place of the interview. Be sure you know how to get there and how long the trip will take.

◆ Learning to communicate effectively—for example, by speaking to adults who can help you with career decisions—is an important aspect of preparing for the future.

Family Studies Teacher

Calvin Knight

What education is required for your job?

- Honours Bachelor of Arts (with three courses in Family Studies or the Humanities).

- Bachelor of Education with Family Studies as a teachable subject or additional qualifications in Family Studies.

What skills does a person need to be able to do your job?

- Patience.

- Public speaking.

- Creativity.

- Empathy.

- A sense of humour.

What do you like most about your job?

I like the challenge of taking the curriculum and making it interesting, and the freedom to be "wacky" to help students enjoy what I am teaching more. Getting to know students and helping them grow to be more self-confident is also a very enjoyable and satisfying part of my job.

What other jobs/job titles have you had in the past?

I have worked as an English teacher in Korea, an assistant in the Ministry of Disability and Work, a construction worker, and a cook at McDonald's.

What advice would you give a person who is considering a career as a Family Studies teacher?

Get to know a person before you make a judgment. Don't take yourself too seriously. Don't be afraid to be vulnerable in front of your students.

Comment on what you consider to be important issues or trends in food and nutrition.

Issues I consider important are hunger in Canada and in developing countries; illness caused by foods; and how we make food dangerous to eat without realizing it.

Chapter 5 Review and Activities

Summary

- A career is a profession within a certain field.
- It usually begins with an entry-level job that leads to better paying positions.
- Recent studies have predicted that there will be great expansion in the food and nutrition industries.
- The food service industry includes all aspects of preparing and serving food to the public. Foods classes in secondary school provide a good foundation for these jobs, but you will also need courses at a community college, university, or private food schools to receive training for specific food-related careers.
- Once you are working for a company, you can upgrade your qualifications or receive on-the-job training.
- Family and Consumer Studies involve problem solving and making decisions about the home and family, and include the areas of teaching, communication, and research and development.
- Communication jobs involve conveying information to the public through the media. Employers include food producers, manufacturers, government agencies, and trade associations.
- Research and Development positions require people who develop new products and appli-

ances in test kitchens or research laboratories. Universities, food producers, appliance manufacturers, or the government are places where researchers work.

- Food Sciences is another career area in which scientists develop food products and new ways to process and package them. Food scientists are employed by the food-processing industry and work in test kitchens, laboratories, or on the production line.
- Dietetics is the area of work in which dietitians are trained in the principles of food and nutrition. Dietitians work in hospitals, health maintenance organizations, company cafeterias, and food service companies.
- Food Production, Processing, and Marketing is another area of the food industry. Farmers are part of this group.
- People who own their own business are called entrepreneurs. Catering, running a snack bar, providing home delivery from a restaurant or supermarket, providing nutritional consultation, and preparing and selling food are examples of businesses run by entrepreneurs.
- Sometimes entrepreneurs operate a franchise, an individually owned branch of a larger business, such as a fast-food restaurant that is one of a chain.

Knowledge and Understanding

1. Make a list of six food-related jobs. What type of education or work experience do they require?

2. What is an entry-level job? What type of training does it require? Where do these jobs lead?

Job	Education Needed	Work Experience Needed
1	srtny yulmo frmso	srtny yulmo frmso
2	srtny yulmo frmso	srtny yulmo frmso
3	srtny yulmo frmso	srtny yulmo frmso
4	srtny yulmo frmso	srtny yulmo frmso
5	srtny yulmo frmso	srtny yulmo frmso
6	srtny yulmo frmso	srtny yulmo frmso

3. Describe the education and training required for a dietitian in Canada.

4. Give three reasons why there is expected job growth in the area of food and nutrition.

5. Make a list of ten food entrepreneurs in your community.

6. Make a list of ten food franchises that can be purchased in Canada. How many of them are in your local community? How many are in a neighbouring community?

Thinking and Inquiry

7. Perform a career search using one of the web sites recommended in the Internet Connects within this chapter. Make a list of qualifications that you would need to apply for the job. Include personal attributes as well as educational and career paths.

8. Choose a common processed food, then make a graphic organizer to show all the different people's jobs that are involved in taking the original food from a raw state to the processed food. Put your findings on chart paper and be prepared to share it with the class.

9. Investigate a food franchise that you are interested in. Write a report on the franchise and how to get involved in it.

Communication

10. Choose one of the Career Profiles in this text. Write a classified ad for the job that could appear in a newspaper or on the Internet. Include the following information in the ad:

- Job type.
- Job description.
- Educational background.
- Career experience.
- Personal qualities needed to fulfill the job.

11. Create a brochure to describe a career related to food and nutrition that could be given to secondary school students. Include the following information:

- Job description.
- Educational requirements.
- Schools or training centres for that career.
- Skills required.
- Employment opportunities.
- Starting salary and salary range.

Application

12. Look at the Career Profiles included in this text. Make a career ladder for at least two of them (see page 57 for an example). Compare the people's educational backgrounds and their work experiences. Present your career ladders to the class.

UNIT 2

Food Needs of

UNIT EXPECTATIONS

While reading this unit, you will:

- Summarize the practical factors and demonstrate the skills involved in producing appetizing and healthy foods for yourself and others.

- Complete an assessment of the importance of meeting the food needs of family members.

- Analyse the importance of each member's contribution to the selection, preparation, and serving of food.

- Demonstrate knowledge of the rules of mealtime etiquette.

- Demonstrate effective collaborative group skills.

Time-saving appliances and food products are available to help busy people produce nutritious meals quickly.

Individuals and Families

OVERVIEW

With today's fast-paced lifestyle, producing healthy and delicious foods to eat can be a challenge for individuals and families. Knowing proper food handling and preparation techniques and using resources found in cookbooks and grocery stores will assist you in planning and preparing meals that will meet your food needs and goals.

CHAPTER

6

CHAPTER EXPECTATIONS

While reading this chapter, you will:

- Safely use, maintain, clean, and store tools and equipment used in food preparation.

- Identify and demonstrate safe food-handling practices, including kitchen safety, sanitary methods, and proper food storage.

- Demonstrate collaborative problem-solving, conflict-resolution, and planning skills, and be able to explain the need for these skills by referring to organization theory.

You need to know how to store and handle food and kitchen utensils safely to keep food-related illnesses and accidents to a minimum.

Kitchen Know-How

composting
conservation
CPR
cross-contamination
danger zone
food safety
freezer burn
Heimlich manoeuvre
inventory
major appliance
micro-organisms
polarized plugs
recycling
shelf life
shelf-stable
small appliance
spores
toxins
utensils
work centre

SOCIAL SCIENCE SKILLS
- problem-solving

CHAPTER INTRODUCTION

Meeting your own and your family's food needs is not just about producing a meal. It involves knowing the rules of kitchen safety, including safe food-handling practices and correct methods of food storage. To help run a kitchen effectively, it is essential to plan out your tasks and to use other time-management and organizational skills.

Food preparation involves many tasks. Many tools have been designed for a specific purpose and to save time, like this blender.

Introduction to the Kitchen

Types of Kitchen Equipment

Kitchens contain three basic kinds of equipment: major appliances, small appliances, and utensils.

A **major appliance** is a large device that gets its energy from electricity or gas. Most kitchens have at least two major appliances: a refrigerator-freezer for cold storage and a stove for cooking. Some kitchens have a separate cooktop and oven instead of a single stove unit. Some kitchens also have a microwave oven and a dishwasher.

A **small appliance** is a small electrical household device used to perform simple tasks. A mixer, food processor, blender, and toaster are examples of small kitchen appliances.

Utensils are kitchen tools, such as measuring cups, knives, and peelers. Other kitchen utensils include pots, pans, and other cookware.

Safety Check

As any cook who has ever shorted out a microwave oven or burned a pot can tell you, appliances and utensils require careful use and regular care. Before using or cleaning any appliance, read the owner's manual.

Kitchen Work Centres

You wouldn't store videotapes or CDs in a different location from the VCR or CD player. The same principle applies to kitchen organization. Organizing a kitchen efficiently can save time and energy by reducing the steps you need to take to carry out a task.

Many home kitchens and school food labs are organized around work centres. A **work centre** is an area designed for specific kitchen tasks. A well-designed work centre has the equipment you need for a task, enough storage space, and a safe, convenient work space.

Technological advances are making kitchen designs more user-friendly. One example is an adjustable cooktop that can be raised or lowered to a convenient height.

Basic Work Centres

The refrigerator-freezer, sink, and stove—and the counters and cabinets around them—form the three basic kitchen centres.

◆ **Cold storage centre.** The refrigerator-freezer is the focus of this centre. Items stored nearby might include plastic storage bags, food wraps, and containers for leftover foods.

◆ **Sink centre.** This centre is the main source of water. It is used for a variety of tasks, including washing fresh fruits and vegetables, draining foods, and washing dishes. Dishpans and other clean-up supplies should be kept handy.

◆ The overall design of a kitchen depends on lifestyle and budget. Which of the kitchen work centres can be seen in the kitchen shown here?

- **Cooking centre.** This centre includes the stove and related items, such as cooking tools, pots and pans, and pot-holders. Small cooking appliances might be kept near the range. Some canned and packaged foods might also be stored here.

Sometimes there is more than one logical place for equipment. For instance, a microwave oven may be part of the cooking centre. However, it could also be placed near the refrigerator-freezer for quick heating of leftovers and frozen food. Some families keep the microwave oven on a sturdy rolling cart so that it can be moved to wherever it's needed.

Other Work Centres

Some kitchens contain additional, separate work centres.

- **Mixing centre.** This area is used for preparing and mixing foods. Measuring cups, bowls, mixing spoons, and an electric mixer are commonly stored here, along with foods such as flour and spices. In a small kitchen, this centre might be combined with one of the others.

- **Planning centre.** Some home kitchens include a planning centre with space to store cookbooks, recipes, and coupons. A desk provides a convenient place for writing out meal plans and shopping lists. Other useful features are a calendar, a bulletin board, a telephone, and perhaps a computer.

A well-organized and well-equipped kitchen is a place where good food can be prepared quickly, easily, and safely.

- **An egg dropped accidentally on the floor is very slippery and should be cleaned up immediately to prevent an accident.**

Preventing Kitchen Accidents

An Accident-Free Kitchen

A kitchen should be a place to prepare enjoyable food. Yet, just a few seconds of carelessness can set the stage for an accident. Falls, electrical shocks, cuts, burns, and poisoning are all kitchen hazards. The keys to preventing kitchen accidents are careful kitchen management and proper work habits.

General Safety Guidelines

Your work habits are vital to your safety in the kitchen. Here are some general guidelines:

- Tie back hair, remove jewellery, roll up sleeves, and tightly tie back apron strings. These items could catch on fire or become tangled in appliances if left dangling.

- Keep your mind on what you're doing.

- Prevent clutter. Put items back where they belong as you finish with them or after you've washed them.

- Close drawers and doors completely after you open them. You could be seriously hurt if you bump into an open door or drawer.

- Use the right tool for the job. Don't use a knife to pry off a jar lid, for example. Take the time to find the tool you need.

- Store heavy or bulky items, such as cookware, on low shelves so that you can reach them easily.

Preventing Falls

Spills on the floor can cause accidents. To prevent falls, keep the floor clean and clear of clutter. Wipe up spills, spatters, and peelings so that no one will slip on them. Eliminate other hazards, such as slippery throw rugs, and replace damaged or worn flooring. Don't wear untied shoes, floppy slippers, or long clothing that could cause you to trip.

To reach higher shelves, use a steady step-stool. If you use a chair or a box, you could fall and be injured.

Preventing Cuts

Cuts are an everyday hazard for the cook. Here are some safety guidelines for handling knives, other sharp tools, and broken glass:

- Keep knives sharp and use them properly.

- Use a drawer divider, knife block, or knife rack for storing sharp cutting tools.

- Don't try to catch a falling knife—you might grab the blade instead of the handle. Step aside and let it fall.

- Sweep up broken glass from the floor immediately with a broom and dustpan. If you need to pick up pieces by hand, use a wet paper towel instead of bare fingers. Wrap broken glass in layers of paper and place in a garbage container. Take out the garbage as soon as possible.

◆ Accidents can be prevented in the kitchen if simple safety rules are followed. **How is the person in the picture using proper safety techniques?**

◆ **Storing knives in a block or special rack helps prevent cuts.** Identify two other precautions to take when using knives.

◆ Don't soak knives or other sharp-edged utensils in a sink or dishpan with water in it. When you reach into the water, you could cut yourself. Wash and dry knives immediately after using them and return them to their proper storage place.

Using Electricity Safely

To avoid accidents, carefully read the owner's manual that comes with each kitchen appliance. Follow the directions for using the appliance safely. In addition, remember these basic guidelines:

◆ **Water and electricity don't mix.** Never use an electrical appliance when your hands are wet or when you are standing on a wet floor. Keep small electrical appliances away from water when you use them. Don't run cords around a sink. If an electrical appliance falls into water or becomes wet, unplug it immediately without touching the appliance itself. Don't put small appliances in water for cleaning unless the owner's manual says it's safe to do so.

◆ **Avoid damage to electrical cords.** Even a single exposed wire could start a fire or produce a shock. To keep from damaging cords, don't let them rest on a hot surface or try to staple or nail them in place. Never disconnect an appliance by tugging on the cord. Instead, grasp the plug at the electrical outlet to remove it.

◆ **Use outlets properly.** Plugging too many cords into an electrical outlet can cause a fire. Some appliances are equipped with **polarized plugs**—plugs made with one blade wider than the other and designed to fit in the outlet in only one way. You may not be able to fit a polarized plug into an older outlet. If that's the case, don't try to force the plug in or change the shape of the plug. Instead, have the outlet replaced, or buy an adapter.

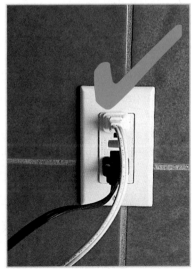

◆ **Exercising electrical safety can help prevent a kitchen disaster.** In what ways is the situation in the left photo an accident waiting to happen?

- **Use care with any plugged-in appliance.** Never put your fingers or a kitchen tool inside an appliance that is plugged in. You might touch parts that could shock you, or you might accidentally turn the appliance on and injure yourself. Don't let the cords dangle off the counter—an appliance could accidentally be pulled over while in use. Turn off small appliances as soon as you are through with them.

- **Watch for problems.** Don't try to use a damaged appliance or one that gives you a shock. Have it repaired before you use it again. If an appliance starts to burn, unplug it immediately.

Hazardous Chemicals

Hazardous chemicals are not limited to use in industries. Many can be found in most households. Hazardous household chemicals include oven cleaners, disinfectants, bleach, and drain cleaners. Some of these chemicals can cause burns, breathing difficulties, and poisoning.

Before you buy any household chemical, read the label carefully to be sure you understand the directions. You'll find important information about adequate ventilation, ways to protect yourself, and proper disposal of any unused product. You will also learn what to do if the product is accidentally swallowed or inhaled. Here are some additional tips:

- Never transfer a hazardous product to another container. Other people may mistake the product for the original contents, especially food or drinks. You'll need the directions that appear on the original container each time you use the product as well.

- Never mix different chemical products. They could combine to give off poisonous fumes.

- Store hazardous chemical products away from food. Be sure children can't reach them. Flammable products, such as kerosene, lighter fluid, and aerosol sprays, must be stored away from any source of heat.

- Avoid using hazardous chemicals unnecessarily. Whenever you can, substitute simple, safe cleaners, such as lemon juice, vinegar, club soda, soap flakes, baking soda, washing soda, or borax.

INTERNET CONNECTS

www.mcgrawhill.ca/links/food
To learn more about hazardous chemicals in the home and safer substitutes, go to the web site above for *Food for Today, First Canadian Edition,* to see where to go next.

Preventing Stove and Microwave Accidents

The stove is the most likely place for fires and burns to occur. The microwave oven also presents some hazards. Here are some rules for using these appliances safely:

- Use potholders or oven mitts when picking up or uncovering hot pots and pans.

- Do not use a kitchen towel to take out hot items in the oven or on the stove. It can touch an element and catch fire.

- When uncovering a pot or pan, lift up the far edge of the cover first so that the steam will flow away from you. Otherwise, it could burn your face and hands.

- Use only pots and pans in good condition. A loose handle or warped bottom could cause an accident.

- Keep pan handles turned toward the back or middle of the stove top. Otherwise, someone might bump into a handle, causing a spill, and possibly be burned by a hot liquid.

- Keep flammable items, such as paper towels, away from the stove. A draft could blow them onto the stove and start a fire. For the same reason, do not put curtains on a window that is close to the stove.

FOR YOUR HEALTH

Safe Cleaning Substitutes

Before reaching for a potentially hazardous cleaning product, consider using a safe substitute. Not only do the following suggestions make a safer cleaner, they are more environmentally friendly and more economical than other household cleaning products.

Cleaning Product	Safe Substitute
Dishwashing liquid	Use a combination of soap flakes and vinegar.
Dishwasher detergent	Use equal parts borax and washing soda (hydrated sodium carbonate).
Oven cleaner	In a cold oven, use a paste of baking soda, salt, and hot water, or sprinkle baking soda on the soiled area and scrub it with a damp cloth after about five minutes. Be sure not to let the baking soda touch the heating elements.
Drain cleaner	Pour 50 mL (¼ cup) baking soda followed by 125 mL (½ cup) white vinegar in the drain. Cover the drain until the fizzing stops. Then flush by running hot water in the drain.
Window cleaner	Use rubbing alcohol to remove the residues. When the glass is dry, spray it with a mixture of equal parts white vinegar and water. You can recycle newspaper by drying the window with a crumpled page.

◆ Do not use plastic items near the stove except for those made of heatproof plastic, such as plastic turners and spoons for non-stick pans. Some plastics are highly flammable and give off poisonous fumes when they burn.

◆ Arrange oven racks properly before you turn the oven on. You risk being burned if you have to change them once the oven is hot.

◆ **Oven mitts provide more protection than potholders. Explain why both should be inspected from time to time.**

- Stand to the side when you open the oven door. The heat rushing from the oven could burn your face.

- Don't reach into a hot oven. Pull out the rack first, using a potholder or an oven mitt.

- Clean up spills and crumbs after the oven has cooled. If allowed to build up in the oven, they could catch fire.

- Be sure stovetop and oven/broiler controls are turned off when not in use.

- Keep a fire extinguisher handy, and be sure everyone knows how to use it.

✚ Safety Check

Be sure to inspect oven mitts and potholders for wear and tear from time to time. Worn or scorched spots will not protect you from getting burned by hot pots and pans.

If a Fire Starts

You've followed all the proper safety procedures, but suddenly there's a fire in your kitchen. What should you do? It depends on where the fire occurs.

- **Stove top or electric skillet.** Turn off the heat. Put the cover on the pan, or pour salt or baking soda on the flames. Never use water—the grease will splatter and spread the fire, and it could burn you. Don't use baking powder—it could make the fire worse.

- **Oven, broiler, microwave, toaster oven.** Turn off or disconnect the appliance. Keep the oven door closed until the fire goes out.

Never attempt to carry a pan with burning contents. You could cause an injury or a bigger fire. If you can't immediately put out a fire, go outdoors and call the fire department.

Accommodations for Accident Prevention

As a rule, anything you could do to prevent accidents will benefit the entire family. Certain family members may need special consideration.

Children

Small children like to be where adults are—especially in the kitchen. They want to watch you and do what you're doing. If your household includes young children, follow these guidelines for accident prevention:

- Never leave young children alone in the kitchen, even for a few seconds.

- Protect toddlers by using safety latches on drawers and cabinet doors.

- If children want to help you work, set up a child-size table or a safe stepstool. Provide small utensils they can use easily for simple tasks such as mixing and mashing. Don't let young children use knives or work near the stove. Supervise them at all times.

- Model safe work habits for children. Use the accident prevention skills you have learned. If you practise safe work habits in the kitchen, they will too.

◆ **No kitchen should be without a fire extinguisher. Do you know how to use one correctly?**

People with Special Needs

Certain accommodations may be required to ensure kitchen safety for a family member who has a physical challenge, such as low vision or arthritis. Changes in the workspace or equipment may be needed so that the person can use the kitchen safely and with a minimum of frustration. Ask the person the following questions so that he or she may make suggestions:

◆ What kitchen tasks are difficult to perform?

◆ How could the kitchen be reorganized to make jobs easier and safer?

◆ Barrier-free kitchen design makes it easier for everyone to use the kitchen. What specific features would make a kitchen convenient for the person shown?

Here are some ideas for creating a barrier-free kitchen:

◆ Keep a magnifying glass in the kitchen to aid with reading small print.

◆ Relabel items in larger letters, if necessary, using stick-on labels and a marking pen.

◆ Add more or better lighting.

◆ Store frequently used equipment and foods in easy-to-reach places.

◆ Add a cart with wheels to the kitchen to make it easier to move food and equipment from place to place.

◆ Use non-breakable dishes and glassware.

◆ Replace hard-to-open cabinet hardware with U-shaped or pull handles.

◆ Provide tongs or grippers to grab items that would otherwise be out of reach.

◆ Put mixing bowls on a damp dishcloth or a rubber disk jar opener to keep them from sliding on a slippery countertop during mixing.

◆ Use rubber disk jar openers for gripping appliance knobs.

◆ Provide a stool or tall chair so that the person can sit while working at the counter.

✚ Safety Check

The kitchen can be a great learning environment for children. But it is not surprising that the kitchen is the room where children are burned most frequently. It is important to take extra precautions when working with children in the kitchen.

INTERNET CONNECTS

www.mcgrawhill.ca/links/food
To learn more about aids to independent living, go to the web site above for *Food for Today, First Canadian Edition,* to see where to go next.

In Case of Accident

In spite of all your precautions, an accident may happen when you are working in the kitchen. If you have practised the management skills discussed in this chapter, you will be prepared for that possibility. You will have a list of emergency numbers next to the phone and a first aid kit in a handy location. If you don't know how to administer first aid, contact your local St. John Ambulance Canada branch to find out about training.

One first aid technique everyone should know is how to administer the **Heimlich manoeuvre**—a technique used to rescue victims of choking. You can even perform the technique on yourself. Another vital technique is **CPR**, or cardiopulmonary resuscitation (KARD-ee-oh-PULL-muh-nare-ee ree-SUSS-uh-TAY-shun), a technique used to revive a person whose breathing and heartbeat have stopped. Knowing these techniques can save a life.

If an accident does occur, stay calm. Panic will keep you from thinking clearly. If necessary, take a few deep breaths to get yourself under control first.

Never hesitate to call for help, whether for yourself or someone else. It is better to summon help, even though you may not need it, than to try to handle the accident yourself.

Keeping Food Safe to Eat

Food Safety

Food safety means following practices that help prevent foodborne illness and keep food safe to eat.

It's estimated that up to 2.2 million Canadians suffer from foodborne illness, also known as food poisoning, every year (Lambton Health, 2002). The illness may be mild, lasting just a day or two, or severe enough to require hospitalization. In some cases it can even result in death. Children, women who are pregnant, aging adults, and people with chronic illness are most at risk.

Most cases of foodborne illness can be traced to harmful **micro-organisms**—tiny living creatures visible only through a microscope. Improper food handling practices allow harmful micro-organisms to grow and spread. It's up to you to handle food properly to prevent illness.

INTERNET CONNECTS

www.mcgrawhill.ca/links/food
To learn more about foodborne illness and food safety, go to the web site above for *Food for Today, First Canadian Edition,* to see where to go next.

◆ Keeping a clean kitchen and keeping your hands clean helps maintain food safety. How might rubber gloves keep food safe?

Harmful Micro-Organisms

Most harmful micro-organisms associated with foodborne illness are bacteria—and they're everywhere. Bacteria are carried by people, animals, insects, and objects. Many bacteria are harmless, but others can cause illness. Sometimes the illness is not caused by the bacteria themselves but by the **toxins**, or poisons, they produce.

Most harmful bacteria can be tolerated by the human body in small amounts. When the amounts multiply to dangerous levels, they create a health hazard. Bacteria reproduce quickly in the presence of food, moisture, and warmth. In just a few hours, one bacterium can multiply into thousands. You can't tell whether food contains harmful bacteria. The food generally looks, smells, and tastes normal.

The chart below describes some bacteria that cause foodborne illness and where those bacteria are found.

Bacteria That Cause Foodborne Illness

Bacteria	Where Bacteria Are Found
E. coli	Contaminated water, raw or rare ground beef, unpasteurized milk, or apple juice.
Listeria monocytogenes	Contaminated soil and water; meat and dairy products; ready-to-eat foods, such as hot dogs, luncheon meats, cold cuts, dry sausages, and deli-style meats and poultry.
Salmonella	Raw or undercooked foods, such as poultry, eggs, and meat; unpasteurized milk.
Clostridium botulinum	Improperly processed canned foods, garlic in oils, vacuum-packed or tightly wrapped food—environments where there is little or no oxygen.
Campylobacter jejuni	Contaminated water, unpasteurized milk, or undercooked meat or poultry.
Staphylococcus aureus	On human skin, in nose, and in throat—spread by improper food handling.
Clostridium perfringens	Environments where there is little or no oxygen; spores can survive cooking; often called the "cafeteria germ" because it most often strikes food served in quantity and left for long periods on a steam table or at room temperature.

Cleanliness in the Kitchen

Cleanliness is one of the keys to food safety. Whenever you work with food, be sure to keep yourself and the kitchen clean.

Personal Hygiene

When you're handling food, you don't have to scrub as surgeons do before operating. Remember that keeping clean is important. Here are suggestions for minimizing the risk of introducing harmful micro-organisms when you are working in the kitchen:

◆ Wear clean clothes and cover them with a clean apron. Spots and stains can harbour bacteria.

◆ Remove dangling jewellery, roll up long sleeves, and tie back long hair. That will help keep them out of food.

◆ Using soap and warm water, scrub your hands for 20 seconds before you begin to handle food. Use a brush to clean under and around your fingernails.

◆ Wear rubber or plastic gloves if you have an open wound on your hands. Because gloves can pick up bacteria, wash gloved hands as often as you wash bare hands.

◆ Scrub your hands immediately after using the washroom or blowing your nose.

◆ Do not sneeze or cough into food.

◆ Do not touch your face, your hair, or any other part of your body while working with food. If you do, stop working and scrub your hands.

Work Methods for Food Safety

In addition to keeping yourself clean, remember to follow these important guidelines:

◆ Be sure that work areas and equipment are clean before you start preparing food.

◆ Avoid **cross-contamination**—letting micro-organisms from one food get into another. For example, the juices from raw meat, poultry, and fish and other seafood contain harmful micro-organisms. A knife used to cut raw meat could contaminate raw vegetables. After you have handled raw meat, poultry, or seafood, wash everything that came in contact with those foods. This includes tools, work surfaces, and your hands.

◆ **Washing cutting boards and other equipment in between uses can prevent cross-contamination of foods.** Explain why juices from raw meat, poultry, fish, or other seafood should not come in contact with other foods.

◆ If possible, avoid using cutting boards made of porous materials, such as soft wood. Such materials provide a breeding ground for harmful bacteria. A safe way to prevent cross-contamination is to use two different cutting boards—one for raw meat, poultry, and seafood, and the other for washed produce and cooked foods.

◆ Wash the top of a can before opening it to keep dirt from getting into the food.

◆ If you use a spoon to taste food during preparation, use two spoons. Remove food that is to be sampled with one spoon and pour the contents into another spoon for tasting.

◆ Keep pets out of the kitchen.

◆ Keep two towels handy in the kitchen—one for wiping hands and a second one for drying dishes.

◆ Dishcloths and sponges can harbour harmful bacteria. Use a clean dishcloth each day. Wash sponges at the end of the day and allow them to air-dry before reuse.

Clean-up Time

After food has been prepared and eaten, it's time to clean up. A clean kitchen has no food particles and spills to encourage bacterial growth or to attract insects or rodents.

Using Clean-up Appliances

Many kitchens are equipped with a food waste disposal and a dishwasher to help speed clean-up. A food waste disposal system grinds food waste and flushes it down the drain. Always run plenty of cold water when grinding food. Don't overfill the disposal. Instead, grind small bunches at a time. To avoid clogging the disposal, don't put fibrous food, such as onion skins and corn husks, in it.

When using an automatic dishwasher, follow the instructions in the owner's manual. Be sure the dishwasher is full before running it. Small loads waste water and energy.

Washing Dishes by Hand

Washing dishes can go faster and more easily if you're well organized. The following suggestions can help you with this task.

Rinse soiled dishes and place them on one side of the sink. Group like items and arrange them in this order: glasses, cutlery, plates, kitchen tools, and cookware. Keep sharp knives separate. If food is stuck to cookware, presoak it. Pour a little dish detergent in, add hot water, and let the pan stand for a while.

Fill a dishpan or sink with soapy water—hot enough to remove grease but not hot enough to burn your hands. Using a sponge or dishcloth, wash the dishes in the order you grouped them. Wash glasses first and greasy cookware last. When necessary, refill the sink or dishpan with clean, hot, soapy water.

FIGHT BAC!
Keep Food Safe From Bacteria

CLEAN
Wash hands and surfaces often.

SEPARATE
Don't cross-contaminate.

CHILL
Refrigerate promptly.

COOK
Cook to proper temperatures.

BAC

TM

◆ Clean, separate, cook and chill, are the four steps to food safety.

Reduce the risk of food-borne illness by following these four simple steps:

Clean
Wash hands, utensils, and surfaces with hot soapy water before, during, and after preparing foods. Sanitize countertops, cutting boards, and utensils with a mild bleach and water solution. Wash all produce thoroughly before eating or cooking.

Separate
Keep raw meats and poultry away from other foods during storage and preparation. Keep separate cutting boards for raw meats and vegetables. Always keep foods covered.

Cook
Cook food thoroughly—cooking times and temperatures vary for different meat and poultry. Prepare foods quickly, and serve immediately so foods don't linger at room temperatures where bacteria can grow.

Chill
Refrigerate or freeze perishables, prepared food, and leftovers within two hours. Make sure the refrigerator is set at a temperature of 4°C (40°F), and keep the freezer at −18°C (0°F).

Rinse dishes thoroughly in hot water. Be sure the insides of containers are well rinsed. A safe and easy way to rinse the outsides is to put the dish rack in the sink and let hot water run over it. Let the dishes air-dry in the rack, or dry them with a clean, dry towel.

Cleaning the Work and Eating Areas

When you are through washing dishes, wipe the table. For added protection, clean the work areas and appliances that were used with a bleach solution. To make your own bleach solution, mix 5 mL (1 tsp) of household bleach to 750 mL (3 cups) of water Don't forget to wash the can-opener blade and the cutting board. Rinse the dishcloth often as you work, using hot, soapy water.

Wipe up any spills on the floor. Wash the sink to remove grease and food particles. If the kitchen is equipped with a disposal, run it a final time.

Finally, put any garbage in a plastic bag, close the bag tightly, and put it in the garbage can outside. Wash garbage cans regularly so that they don't attract insects and rodents.

Controlling Pests

Insects can bring disease into the kitchen. However, chemical insecticides can be hazardous to humans and the environment. Here are some ways to control household insects without using insecticides:

◆ Repair holes in walls and screens. Fill in caulk cracks and crevices.

◆ Keep the kitchen and other areas clean.

◆ Sprinkle chili powder, paprika, or dried peppermint across ant trails.

◆ To control roaches, dust borax lightly around the refrigerator and stove.

Proper Food Temperatures

Temperature is one of the most important factors in food safety. Keeping food at proper temperatures can be critical to preventing foodborne illness.

How Temperatures Affect Micro-Organisms

Bacteria multiply rapidly at temperatures between 16°C and 60°C (60°F to 140°F). Note that this range includes room temperatures. Most foodborne illnesses are caused by bacteria that thrive in these temperatures.

High food temperatures, from 71°C to 100°C (160°F to 212°F), kill most harmful bacteria. These temperatures are normally reached during cooking. However, some bacteria produce **spores**, cells that will develop into bacteria if conditions are right. Spores can survive cooking heat.

Cold refrigerator temperatures, below 4°C (40°F), slow down the growth of some bacteria but do not kill them.

If food is frozen at –18°C (0°F), bacteria stop growing. Bacteria or spores already present in food, however, will not be killed. When the food is thawed, bacteria will start to grow again.

The diagram below shows the proper temperatures for storing and cooking food. Red is the **danger zone**—where bacteria grow rapidly. Bacteria also grow in the orange zone, but more slowly than in the red zone.

As you have learned, foodborne illness can also be caused by toxins. Some types of toxins are destroyed by heat. Others remain unchanged even after food is cooked.

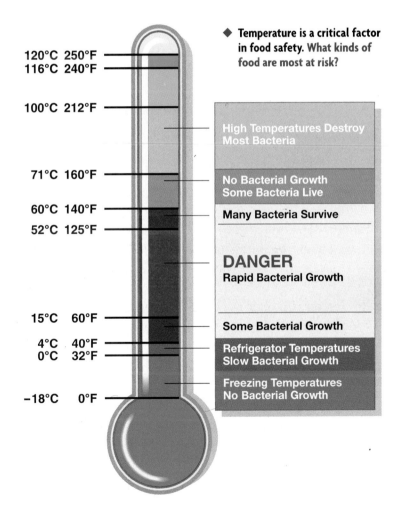

◆ Temperature is a critical factor in food safety. What kinds of food are most at risk?

120°C 250°F	
116°C 240°F	
100°C 212°F	High Temperatures Destroy Most Bacteria
71°C 160°F	No Bacterial Growth Some Bacteria Live
60°C 140°F	Many Bacteria Survive
52°C 125°F	**DANGER** Rapid Bacterial Growth
15°C 60°F	Some Bacterial Growth
4°C 40°F	Refrigerator Temperatures Slow Bacterial Growth
0°C 32°F	
–18°C 0°F	Freezing Temperatures No Bacterial Growth

Food-Handling Guidelines

Many foods require special care to keep them out of the danger zone. Meat, poultry, fish and other seafood, eggs, and dairy products are some of these foods.

When cooking and serving food, follow these guidelines:

◆ Cook food to the proper internal temperature or until thoroughly cooked. Avoid partial cooking—cook the food completely at one time.

◆ Taste foods containing ingredients from animal sources only after they are fully cooked. Do not taste them when they are raw or during cooking (for example, eggs).

◆ When microwaving, take steps to ensure even, thorough cooking.

◆ Do not leave food out more than two hours at room temperature or more than one hour if the temperature is above 32°C (90°F).

◆ Keep extra quantities of food either hot—on the stove or in another cooking appliance— or cold—in the refrigerator.

◆ Do not add more food to a serving dish of food that has been out for a while. Instead, use a clean dish.

◆ Discard foods that have been held at room temperature for more than two hours.

◆ Refrigerate food in shallow containers. Large, deep containers keep the food from cooling rapidly and evenly.

◆ When reheating food that has been refrigerated, bring it to an internal temperature of 74°C (165°F) or higher to kill any bacteria. Keep in mind that if the food has not been properly stored, it can't be made safe just by reheating.

◆ Thawing food at proper temperatures is another important safeguard. How would you thaw a frozen turkey safely?

Social Science Skills

Problem-Solving

Problem-solving is the process of dealing with a challenge. There are five steps that can assist you in dealing with a problem. These five steps will be explained using the following scenario:

> Your food lab group is in charge of preparing the main entrée, chicken wraps, for a luncheon fundraiser at your school. You have pre-sold tickets for the fundraiser. On the morning of the event, you arrive at school to find out that the refrigerator in the foods lab has broken down. What do you and your group do?

1. Identify the problem.

The chicken for the wraps is in the refrigerator. The luncheon is scheduled to begin in three hours and the tickets have been pre-sold.

2. List the alternatives for solving the problem.

i) Use the chicken, because you are uncertain when the refrigerator broke down.
ii) Go to the grocery store to purchase more chicken, even though this purchase will put your fundraising campaign in debt.
iii) Choose another less-expensive menu item and risk complaints from your clients.
iv) Cancel the fundraiser and return the money to the ticket buyers.

3. Choose one of the alternatives and justify why you feel that this is the best solution.

You and your group decide to choose alternative ii because this is the first of four planned fundraising events for the school year. You don't want your customers to be dissatisfied.

4. Carry out the solution.

Your teacher rushes to the grocery store to purchase more chicken. You and your group prepare the wraps for the fundraiser using the fresh chicken.

5. Reflect on and evaluate the results of your decision.

As a result of this expensive fundraiser, your class has to conduct five fundraisers in total to help cover the costs of this first fundraising event.

Thawing Food Safely

Anita was about to leave a package of frozen chicken on the counter to thaw when she remembered what she had learned in foods lab: Never thaw food at room temperature. Quickly, she put the package on a clean plate and placed it in the refrigerator to thaw.

When food is thawed at room temperature, the outside of the item may contain millions of harmful bacteria by the time the inside is thawed. To thaw food safely, use one of these methods:

◆ Place food in the refrigerator where it will thaw slowly. Be sure to place a package of thawing food on a plate so that it does not leak onto other foods.

◆ For faster thawing, put the package in a watertight plastic bag and submerge it in cold water. Change the water every 30 minutes. The cold slows down the growth of bacteria as the food thaws.

◆ Use a microwave for quick, safe defrosting. Follow the manufacturer's directions. Foods thawed this way should be cooked immediately.

◆ Thaw frozen meat safely to prevent the growth of bacteria.

◆ Sealable plastic storage bags help foods keep their nutrients. **How do they help keep foods safe to eat?**

Proper Food Storage

Spoilage and Nutrient Loss

When food is not properly stored, it begins to lose quality and nutrients. Eventually, it will spoil. Spoiled food often develops bad tastes and odours and must be thrown out. Some types of spoilage can cause foodborne illness.

What causes spoilage? Under the right conditions, harmful bacteria, yeasts, and moulds can spoil food. Spoilage can also be caused by natural chemical changes within the cells of the food. Yet another cause is conditions in the environment, which can cause or speed up nutrient loss and spoilage.

◆ **Heat.** Heat speeds up chemical reactions that cause spoilage.

◆ **Air.** Exposure to oxygen can destroy some nutrients, such as vitamins C and E. It can also cause oils to become rancid and develop an unpleasant flavour.

◆ **Moisture.** Moisture is a double-edged sword. Too little moisture can cause fresh foods to dry out, wilt, and lose nutrients. Too much moisture can provide a breeding ground for bacteria and moulds.

- **Light.** Light can destroy nutrients, especially vitamin C and riboflavin.

- **Dirt.** Dirt contains harmful micro-organisms.

- **Damage to food or packaging.** Both these conditions make spoilage by micro-organisms more likely. Be alert for signs of spoilage in packaging, such as bulging cans, liquids that spurt when you open the container, or liquids that are cloudy when they should be clear.

◆ Blue cheese gets its flavour from a special type of mould. However, most foods with mould must be thrown out. Name two ways of retarding the formation of mould in the foods you store.

INTERNET CONNECTS

www.mcgrawhill.ca/links/food
To learn more about food spoilage,
go to the web site above for *Food for Today,*
First Canadian Edition, to see where to go next.

When Food Is Spoiled

How do you know when food is starting to spoil? Some fresh foods, such as apples and celery, may wilt, get wrinkled, or turn brown. Some foods become slimy, a sign that decay has started. Other signs of spoilage are spots of fuzzy mould; damage such as bruises; bad flavours; and bad odours.

Safety Check

Homemade flavoured oils are popular and tasty gifts, but they have a limited shelf life of one week and must be kept refrigerated at all times. Oils made with fresh foods, for instance, garlic and herbs, pose the greatest risk. Before purchasing, ensure these oils have been refrigerated and check the preparation date. Do not purchase them if they are more than one week old.

Spoiled foods should be discarded. Those that have turned mouldy require special handling because mould gives off spores, which can easily spread. Very gently wrap the mouldy food, or place it in a bag, before discarding it. Examine other foods that may have been in contact with the mouldy food. Clean the container that held the mouldy food, and if necessary, wash out the refrigerator.

Basic Storage Principles

No food can be stored indefinitely. Each food has a **shelf life,** the length of time it can be stored and still retain its quality. Shelf life depends on the type of food, packaging, and storage temperature, as well as how the food is handled.

Food Science ◆ L A B ◆

Growing Micro-Organisms

You can't see a single micro-organism, but you can see colonies of micro-organisms, called *cultures*. In this experiment, you'll discover just how widespread micro-organisms really are.

Procedure

1. With a felt-tip pen, divide into quarters a Petri dish coated with nutrient agar. Number the quarters 1 to 4.

2. Touch the end of a 10-cm (4-inch) strip of cellophane tape to a doorknob, and press it into area 1 of the Petri dish. Touch another tape strip to a clean dish and a third strip to your hair, and press these into areas 2 and 3.

3. Touch a fourth piece of tape to the agar without letting it touch any other surface, including your fingers.

4. Leave the Petri dish at room temperature for three days. Observe it each day, and describe any growths that have appeared.

Conclusions

◆ Were any of the surfaces you tested free of micro-organisms? Was the tape itself free of micro-organisms?

◆ Which surfaces produced the most bacterial growth? Why do you think this occurred?

◆ What changes in your food preparation practices might you consider making as a result of this experiment?

To avoid loss of quality in stored food, follow these guidelines:

◆ Buy only what you need.

◆ Follow the principle of "first in, first out." Store new food behind the same kind of older food. Use the older food first.

◆ Look for "best before" or "packaged on" dates on the containers. If there are none, you may want to write the purchase dates on the containers before storing them. Use canned food within a year.

◆ Clean storage areas regularly. Throw out food that has started to spoil or containers that have been damaged. Wash and dry surfaces thoroughly.

INTERNET CONNECTS

www.mcgrawhill.ca/links/food
To learn more about proper storage of food, go to the web site above for *Food for Today, First Canadian Edition,* to see where to go next.

Room Temperature Storage

Many canned, bottled, and packaged foods are **shelf-stable,** which means they are able to last for weeks or even months at room temperatures below 30°C (85°F). Examples are most unopened canned foods, dry beans and peas, oils and shortening, and many grain products (except whole grains). In general, foods that you find on grocery shelves can be stored at room temperature when you bring them home.

Kitchen cabinets are used for most room temperature storage. They should be clean and dry, with doors to keep out light and dirt. Temperatures should be no higher than 30°C (85°F) and no lower than freezing, 0°C (32°F). Do not store food on shelves near or above heat sources, such as a stove, toaster, refrigerator, or radiator. Also avoid areas that may be wet, such as cabinets under the sink.

Once packages or containers have been opened, storage requirements differ. Some shelf-stable foods, including most canned goods, must be refrigerated after opening. Others, such as a bag of dry beans or a box of cereal, can remain at room temperature. Reseal the package if possible. Otherwise, transfer the contents to a storage container with a tight-fitting cover. Do the same with the foods you buy in bulk.

Safety Check

If you have to stack items to store them, put the lightest on top so that you'll be less likely to accidentally knock over heavy items that could cause injury. Boxes of dried soup mix, for example, can be stored on top of canned soups.

◆ **Shelf-stable foods may be stored at normal room temperature. Which of the two foods shown has telltale signs of possible bacterial contamination?**

Cold Storage

Perishable foods spoil quickly at room temperature. They require cold storage in the refrigerator or freezer, depending on the kind of food and how long you want to store it. The package may give instructions for storage. The chart below and on the next page gives you a general timetable for keeping foods in cold storage.

Refrigerator Storage

Foods normally refrigerated include:

- Foods that were refrigerated in the store, such as milk and milk products, eggs, delicatessen foods, and fresh meat, poultry, fish, and other seafood.

- Most fresh fruits and vegetables. Exceptions are onions, potatoes, and sweet potatoes, which should be stored in a cool, dry area.

- Whole-grain products, seeds, and nuts. They contain oils that can spoil and give foods an off-flavour.

- Leftover cooked foods.

- Baked goods with fruit or cream fillings.

- Any foods that according to label directions say "keep refrigerated" or "refrigerate after opening."

Cold Storage Chart

NOTE: The dash (—) means food should not be stored in that area.

Type of Food	Refrigerator Storage 4°C (40°F)	Freezer Storage −18°C (0°F)
Meats, Poultry, Fish		
Beef, lamb, pork, or veal chops, steaks, roast	2–4 days	8–12 months
Chicken or turkey, whole	2–3 days	1 year
Chicken or turkey, pieces	2–3 days	6 months
Ground meats or poultry	1–2 days	2–3 months
Lean fish (cod)	3–4 days	6 months
Fatty fish (salmon)	3–4 days	2 months
Shellfish (shrimp)	12–24 hours	2–4 months
Dairy Products		
Fresh milk, cream	Check "best before" date	6 weeks
Salted butter, margarine	8 weeks	1 year
Unsalted butter, margarine	8 weeks	3 months
Buttermilk	Check "best before" date	6 weeks
Sour cream	Check "best before" date	—
Yogurt, plain or flavoured	Check "best before" date	1–2 months
Cottage cheese	Check "best before" date	—
Hard cheese (cheddar), opened	3–4 weeks	—
Hard cheese, unopened	10 months	1 year
Ice cream, sherbet	—	2–4 months

Cold Storage Chart

NOTE: The dash (——) means food should not be stored in that area.

Type of Food	Refrigerator Storage 4°C (40°F)	Freezer Storage –18°C (0°F)
Miscellaneous Foods		
Bread	check "best before" date	3 months
Cakes, pies (not cream-filled)	7 days	2–3 months
Cream pies	1–2 days	——
Fresh eggs, in shell	3–4 weeks	——
Raw yolks, whites	2–4 days	4 months
Hard-cooked eggs	1 week	——
Egg substitutes	3 days	——
Egg substitutes, unopened	10 days	——
Mayonnaise, opened	2 months	——
Salad dressing, opened	3 months	——
Salsa, opened	3 months	——
Cookies	2 months	8–12 months
Cooked Foods, Leftovers		
Cooked meats, meat dishes	3–4 days	2–3 months
Fried chicken	3–4 days	4 months
Poultry covered in broth	3–4 days	6 months
Fish stews, soups (not creamed)	3–4 days	4–6 months
Cured Meats		
Hot dogs, opened	1 week	1–2 months
Lunch meats, opened	3–4 days	1–2 months
Hot dogs, lunch meats, unopened	2 weeks	1–2 months
Bacon	7 days	1 month
Smoked sausage (beef, pork, turkey)	7 days	1–2 months
Hard sausage (pepperoni)	2–3 weeks	1–2 months
Ham, canned (refrigerated, unopened)	6–9 months	——
Ham, fully cooked, whole	7 days	1–2 months
Ham, fully cooked, half or slices	3–5 days	1–2 months

Source: Canadian Partnership for Consumer Food Safety Education. (n.d.)

◆ **Not all areas of the refrigerator have the same temperature. Which areas offer the coldest storage? Which foods should be stored in the door?**

Refrigeration Guidelines

Avoid overloading the refrigerator when storing foods. If the cold air can't circulate well, some areas may become too warm to store perishables safely. Be sure, also, that foods are tightly covered. This will keep them from drying out and will also prevent odours from being picked up by other foods. Opened canned foods may pick up an off-flavour from the can, so transfer them to another storage container.

Store meat, poultry, fish, and other seafood in the store wrap in a plastic bag to prevent leakage. Leaking foods can contaminate other stored foods.

When storing fruits and vegetables, wash them only if necessary to remove dirt. Wipe hard-skinned fruits and vegetables dry, and drain others well.

Leftovers require special care. To ensure thorough chilling, use shallow containers. Large, deep containers keep food from cooling rapidly and evenly. Cut large pieces of meat into smaller ones so that they cool quickly. Close the containers tightly, and label them with the current date. Be sure to use the food within a few days. (Remember that some foods can be frozen for longer storage.) You may want to keep all leftovers on the same shelf so that none get overlooked.

Every refrigerator has a temperature control or coldness setting. To promote freshness and retard spoilage of stored foods, follow the manufacturer's recommended settings. Do not let the temperature fall to a point where frost or ice forms. Foods with a high water content, such as lettuce, may freeze and be damaged.

Freezer Storage

Freezing allows long-term storage of many foods. At temperatures of –18°C (0°F) or below, foods keep from one month to a year, depending on the type of food and proper packaging.

Foods purchased frozen should be stored promptly in the home freezer. Many other foods can also be frozen to increase shelf life. These include fresh meats, poultry, fish, and other seafood baked goods such as breads and rolls; and many leftovers.

Some foods don't freeze well. Examples are fresh vegetables that are to be eaten raw, cooked or whole raw eggs, products made with mayonnaise, meat and poultry stuffing, cream- or egg-based sauces, custards, baked goods with cream filling, and many cheeses.

To freeze foods at home, you need a two-door refrigerator-freezer or a separate freezer unit. Separate freezer units generally maintain food quality longer than refrigerator-freezers.

Some refrigerators have only one outside door and a small freezer compartment inside. The freezer compartment maintains a temperature of –12°C to –10°C (10°F to 15°F). It can be used for storing already frozen food for several weeks. However, it is not cold enough to freeze fresh or leftover food satisfactorily.

A freezer functions best when fairly full. Some freezers need regular defrosting.

Packaging and Freezing Foods

Foods that are purchased already frozen can be stored in their original packaging. Foods frozen at home must be specially packaged to avoid freezer burn. **Freezer burn** is a condition that results when food is improperly packaged or stored in the freezer too long. The food dries out and loses flavour and texture.

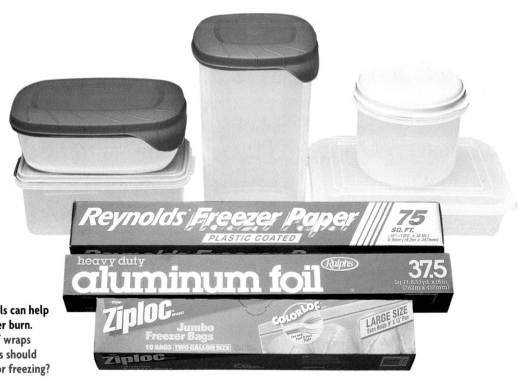

◆ These materials can help prevent freezer burn. What types of wraps and containers should not be used for freezing?

Packaging materials for freezing must be vapour- and moisture-resistant. Plastic containers with tight-fitting covers, heavy-duty plastic freezer bags, and wraps such as heavy-duty foil and freezer wrap are recommended. Don't use regular refrigerator storage bags or plastic tubs from foods such as margarine and yogurt. They do not provide enough protection. Fresh meat, poultry, fish, and other seafood need additional wrap for freezing because the lightweight store wrapping does not provide sufficient protection.

When wrapping solid foods, such as meat, squeeze out as much air as possible to prevent freezer burn. Seal packages with freezer tape. When filling storage containers, leave enough space for food to expand as it freezes—about 2.5 cm (1 inch) in a 1 L (1 quart) container. Then seal the container tightly. Label all packages and containers with the contents, amount (or number of servings), date frozen, and any special instructions.

For best quality, freeze food quickly. Spread the packages out so that they touch the coils or sides of the freezer. Leave enough space between packages for air to circulate. When the food is frozen (at least 24 hours later), you can stack it according to the kind of food.

Keep an **inventory,** or ongoing record, of the food in the freezer. Include the food, date frozen, and quantity. As you remove food, change the quantity on the inventory so that you know how much is left.

Power Outages

When the power goes off or the refrigerator-freezer breaks down, the food inside is in danger of spoiling. In general, avoid opening the door of the freezer or refrigerator. This will help maintain cold temperatures longer.

Keeping Frozen Foods Safe

A full freezer will keep food frozen for about two days after losing power. A half-full freezer will keep food frozen for about one day. If the freezer is not full, stack packages closely together so that they will stay cold. However, separate frozen meat, poultry, fish, and other seafood from other foods. That way, if they begin to thaw, their juices will not get into other foods.

If you know the power will be off longer than two days, you can put dry ice (frozen carbon dioxide) in the freezer. Be careful! Never touch dry ice with bare hands or breathe its vapours in an enclosed area. Carbon dioxide gas in high concentration is poisonous.

When the freezer is working again, follow these guidelines to decide what to do with the food:

◆ If ice crystals are still visible or the food feels as cold as if it were refrigerated, it's safe to refreeze. Some foods may lose quality, but they can still be eaten.

◆ Discard any food that thawed or was held above 4°C (40°F) for more than two hours. Discard any food that has a strange odour.

Once the freezer is working again, wash up any food spills and wipe surfaces dry. If odours remain, wash again with a solution of 30 mL (2 tablespoons) baking soda dissolved in 1 L (1 quart) warm water. Leave an open box of baking soda inside the freezer to absorb odours.

Keeping Refrigerated Foods Safe

During a power outage, food will usually keep in the refrigerator for four to six hours, depending on the temperature of the room. If you know the power will be out for a long time, you can place a block of ice in the refrigerator.

When the refrigerator is working again, follow these guidelines to decide what to do with the food:

◆ Discard fresh meats, poultry, fish, lunch meats, hot dogs, eggs, milk, soft cheeses, and cooked foods if they have been held above 4°C (40°F) for more than two hours.

◆ Keep butter or margarine if it has not melted and does not have a rancid odour.

◆ Other foods, including fresh fruits and vegetables, are safe if they show no signs of mould or sliminess and do not have a bad odour.

Once the refrigerator is working again, clean it as described for the freezer.

◆ **Washing the dishes in a sink full of soapy water instead of under a running tap is one way to save water.**

Conserving Natural Resources

Conserve Energy

Conservation is concern about, and action taken to ensure, the preservation of the environment. The kitchen accounts for a major portion of household garbage. In addition, it is also an energy-guzzler, filled with appliances that liberally use natural gas, electricity, and water. We often take for granted the precious resources that we have readily available, such as water and electricity. This creates much waste. By keeping a few simple suggestions in mind, we can all help to preserve and conserve the environment.

What can you as a consumer do to save energy? For starters, remember to turn off lights and appliances when they are not in use.

Cook as many foods as possible when using the oven, and freeze the extra for future meals. Here are some other tips:

- Use small appliances or a microwave oven when cooking small amounts of food. They use less energy than the stove.

- Match the pan size to the size of the burner or heating unit for stovetop cooking so that less energy will be lost.

- Decide what you want to eat before opening the refrigerator door. The air in the refrigerator warms up if you leave the door open. Then more energy is needed to cool it down.

- Keep the refrigerator and freezer well organized so that you can find food easily.

- Don't run the dishwasher unless it's full.

Safety Check

Never try to save energy by letting hot food cool to room temperature before refrigerating it. Remember, harmful bacteria grow quickly at room temperature.

Conserve Water

Clean and safe water is a precious natural resource that we must help to preserve because our supply of fresh water is dwindling. One of the reasons for this is because the average Canadian family of four uses over 1500 L of water per day (Waste Reduction Week Canada, 2002). The pressure for people to conserve this natural resource is growing. By conserving water in your home, you can help preserve this precious resource for people in the future.

Here are some other suggestions:

- Look for ways to use less water during food preparation. For example, don't let tap water run unnecessarily as you pare vegetables.

- When washing dishes by hand, don't keep the water running. Wash all dishes first; then rinse them at the same time, as quickly as possible.

- If you need to run the tap to get cold or hot water, catch the water in a can to be used for other things, such as watering plants.

- Keep a jug of water in the refrigerator so that it is cold for drinking.

- Be sure to repair dripping taps immediately.

- Install an aerator on the kitchen tap. The finer spray will cut down on water waste.

Reduce Garbage

Household Waste

"Each year Canadians throw away enough garbage to fill nearly one billion garbage cans. If these cans were lined up side by side, they would form a line long enough to encircle the earth twelve and one-half times" (Recycle Plus, 2003). A major portion of this garbage comes from household waste. It is estimated that one-third of our household waste is paper and paper products, another third is kitchen waste and yard materials, and the remainder is divided among glass, metals, plastics, textiles, wood, and other materials (Regional District of Kootenay Boundary, 2003). Most of this garbage ends up in landfill sites, which can pollute soil, water, and the air. Communities are running out of landfill space to bury their "garbage". Yet, much of this is not garbage at all. It is materials that can be used in other ways. For example, plastic containers can be recycled into plant watering cans. That is why it is important to remember these three key words: reduce, reuse, and recycle.

◆ **The mobius loop is the international logo for recycling. Which products have the mobius loop on them?**

Reduce

One way to reduce residential garbage is to reduce the amount of waste production in our households. This is the most effective way to reduce garbage. We can look to the following points as suggestions:

◆ Kitchen waste accounts for a major portion of household waste. For helpful suggestions on ways to reduce kitchen waste, refer to the ways to store food properly that were discussed earlier in this chapter. Reducing food waste will help to save the environment and will save you money.

◆ As a consumer, you can do your part in reducing household waste by choosing to purchase products that can be reused, that have less packaging, or that are in recyclable containers. Some specific suggestions on how to do this in the kitchen include:

  • Using dishcloths instead of paper towels to wipe up spills and to clean.

  • Using cloth napkins instead of paper.

  • Buying reusable plastic bins or making cloth bags to carry groceries.

  • Avoiding the use of paper cups, paper plates, and plastic cutlery.

  • Buying food in bulk quantities so that there is little packaging.

Source: Environment Canada. (n.d.)

Reuse

Reusing gives second life to materials. Find creative ways to reuse items that might otherwise be thrown away. In the kitchen, you might:

◆ Wash plastic tubs from margarine, yogurt, and cottage cheese and use them to refrigerate leftovers. Do not use them for freezing—they aren't heavy enough and food will dry out.

◆ Turn glass jars and bottles with tight-fitting covers into storage containers. Use them for foods such as rice, pasta, and dry beans. Wash the jars and covers carefully; then let them dry for at least 24 hours to remove odours.

◆ Reuse plastic or paper grocery bags as garbage bags.

Recycle

We could not live without water and many other natural resources. Recycling is a chance to give something back to the planet. **Recycling** is the treating of waste so that it can be reused, as well as an awareness of such practices.

All Canadian provinces and territories participate in some kind of recycling program. They may have curb-side pickup, where materials are sorted into different boxes according to what they are made of, for instance, paper in one box, and plastic, glass, and metals in another box. Other households may have to take their recyclables to a recycle depot. Materials that may be included in a recycling program are paper, metals such as aluminum cans, glass bottles, and some plastics. In addition, many supermarkets collect plastic shopping bags for recycling. For further information regarding the recycling program in your area, contact your local municipality.

Another way to recycle is to compost kitchen waste. **Composting** is a process in which organic material is converted into a soil-like product called *compost* or *humus*. Compost can be used in the garden to enrich plants and the soil. Kitchen waste that can be composted includes fruit and vegetable scraps, crushed eggshells, coffee grounds, and tea bags. Leaves, grass, and other yard materials may also be composted. A composter is easy to build in your backyard and can help to recycle as much as one-third of your household waste.

Show Your Concern

Some people believe they can't do much to help solve environmental problems. Yet conservation begins with the individual. As a consumer you can choose to buy items or services that are more "environmentally friendly" than other products. You can participate in your community's local recycling program, encourage others to recycle, and build and use a backyard composter. If each person does his or her share to help conserve natural resources, waste and pollution can be reduced.

◆ **Many materials can be recycled and used again. Find out what steps your community has taken to recycle waste.**

Public Health Inspector

Veronica Kozelj

What education is required for your job?

- A Bachelor of Applied Science (Environmental Health), or a Diploma in Environmental Health.

- A six-month practicum in a health agency.

What skills does a person need to be able to do your job?

- Investigative, observational, and decision-making skills to act independently and to take appropriate action in relation to potential and existing health hazards.

- Oral and written communication skills.

- A valid driver's licence.

- A thorough knowledge of legislation, standards, and judicial process related to environmental and public health.

What do you like most about your job?

The diversity.

What other jobs/job titles have you had in the past?

I have been a public health inspector for 25 years. During this time I have worked in different capacities within the field. As the educator for the City of Hamilton's Health Protection Branch, I am responsible for the development, promotion, presentation, and evaluation of educational material and courses. I have also worked as a manager, supervising public health inspectors.

What advice would you give a person who is considering a career as a public health inspector?

Go for it!

Comment on what you consider to be important issues or trends in food and nutrition.

Public health inspectors are, and will continue to be, challenged by the following issues and trends: genetically modified foods; increases in international importing of food products; new and emerging or mutating bacteria and viruses; more processing and handling of foodstuffs; and less governmental control.

Chapter 6 Review and Activities

Summary

- Kitchens are equipped with major appliances, small appliances, and utensils.
- Kitchens are organized around work centres; the three basic ones are cold storage, sink, and cooking centres.
- Good management and safe work habits are the keys to kitchen safety.
- Common kitchen hazards include falls, cuts, shock, and burns.
- Children and people with special needs require special safety measures.
- Learn first aid, including the Heimlich manoeuvre and CPR.
- If food is handled improperly, micro-organisms can multiply and cause foodborne illness.
- Prevent illness by practicing good personal hygiene, using sanitary work methods, keeping the kitchen clean, and keeping food at proper temperatures.
- Proper food storage prevents spoilage and nutrient loss.
- Shelf-stable foods may be stored at room temperature.
- Store perishable foods in the freezer or in the refrigerator.
- Frozen and refrigerated foods require special handling after a power outage.
- Conservation begins with the individual.
- Consider measures for saving energy and conserving water.
- To reduce trash, identify ways to reduce, reuse, and recycle.

Knowledge and Understanding

1. Why is it important to organize a kitchen around work centres?

2. List three safety precautions to take when having children participate in the kitchen.

3. Define cross-contamination. Identify safety guidelines for handling foods to ensure that you do not cross-contaminate.

4. Make a list of ways to store foods properly to ensure that the foods do not lose quality, nutrients, or become unsafe to eat.

5. Identify ways in which you can reduce, reuse, and recycle in the kitchen.

Thinking and Inquiry

6. Describe the most serious kitchen accident that you ever had. Why did it happen? How could it have been prevented?

7. The Ameslers are designing a new kitchen. The family does a lot of baking. Identify which work centres they should plan their kitchen around. Explain your answer.

8. Some people are in the habit of unplugging toasters and other small kitchen appliances after every use. Discuss how this practice might lead to an accident.

9. Propose guidelines as to whether a food should be stored in the refrigerator or in the freezer.

Communication

10. Draw a rough floor plan of your school foods lab kitchen. Show the location of the sink, major appliances, cabinets, and counters. Circle and label each work centre. Identify the location of at least two small appliances and of at least three kinds of utensils. Discuss the efficiency, safety, and convenience of the work centres in your school foods lab kitchen.

11. Make a mini-poster for the school foods lab to remind class members of one of the accident-prevention pointers discussed in this chapter. Compose a slogan that will help people remember the tip. Display your poster in the classroom.

12. School lunches are often left in the "danger zone" for three hours or more. Present a list of suggestions that ensure optimum safety and nutrition for people eating lunches at school. Your list of suggestions should include tips that include the 3 Rs when packing a lunch.

Application

13. a) Research the Internet to discover toxic ingredients that are used in household cleaners. Then check the content labels of several household cleaners used in the kitchen to discover which ones contain toxic ingredients. What effect could these ingredients have on the environment? Do you feel safe using products that contain these ingredients?

b) Research the Internet to discover other safe cleaning substitutes that may be used in the kitchen. Make a list of at least five ingredients that you should keep on hand to be used as safe substitutes in the kitchen.

CHAPTER

7

CHAPTER EXPECTATIONS

While reading this chapter, you will:

- Identify, select, and effectively use appropriate kitchen tools to plan and prepare interesting and appealing meals in co-operation with others.

- Demonstrate accurate measuring skills and appropriate food-preparation techniques.

- Demonstrate basic cooking and baking skills.

At Home in the Kitchen

The right tools and techniques make cooking interesting and fun.

KEY TERMS

arcing
bakeware
baking
cookware
dry-heat cooking
folding
frying
heating units
hot spot
moist-heat cooking
pare
poaching
preheating
purée
roasting
sautéing
score
serrated
sharpening steel
smoking point
stewing
whisk
wok

CHAPTER INTRODUCTION

There are many kitchen tools and a wide variety of equipment available to use when planning and preparing meals. These include major appliances, small appliances, and an assortment of utensils. Using these tools properly will help turn ingredients into interesting and appealing dishes that will tempt your senses.

How many of these utensils can you recognize?

Equipment for Cooking

Major Cooking Appliances

The major appliances used for cooking are the conventional stove, the convection oven, and the microwave oven. At least one of the first two appliances is found in most kitchens. Some kitchens have all three.

The Stove

A stove usually consists of a cooktop, an oven, and a broiler. The stovetop has either dials or push buttons to control the heat. The heat is generated by **heating units**— energy sources in stoves used to heat foods. Ovens have thermostatic controls so that you can set precise temperatures. Oven temperature settings vary from "warm"—below 93°C (200°F)—to "broil," which is generally about 260°C (500°F). The broiler cooks food by direct heat from a heating unit located in the top of the oven.

Instead of a freestanding stove, some kitchens have separate cooktop and oven units built into cabinets. Some cooktops include features such as a grill for indoor grilling or a centre warmer to keep foods warm.

Stoves use either gas or electricity for heat. The two types of stoves have slightly different features.

Gas Stove

In a gas stove, the oven and broiler are often in separate compartments. The broiler is generally located below the oven. When you're broiling in a gas range, keep the compartment door closed.

The heating units in a gas stove are called burners. The burners in gas cooktops heat with a flame that is easily regulated. The change in heat level is almost immediate. Some gas ranges have sealed burners that show no visible flame.

In most newer stoves, when a burner is turned on, gas flows through and is ignited by an electronic spark. Older ranges contain pilot lights—small gas flames that burn continuously. When the burner is turned on, the pilot light ignites the gas. Sometimes, however, the pilot light goes out and must be relighted. This should be done by lighting a match and *then* turning on the burner. If the burner is turned on first, gas will accumulate and could cause an explosion when you strike the match.

Air flow is needed for burning gas, so take care not to block the vents in a gas range (by, for example, lining the burner bowls with foil). If air flow is blocked, the gas will not burn properly, resulting in the release of carbon monoxide, a deadly gas.

♦ **The two most common types of cooktops for electric ranges are coil elements (below) and induction.** Name two things that might make an induction cooktop preferable to one with coil elements.

Electric Stove

The heating units in electric ranges are called elements. Electricity passes through the element, causing it to heat up.

The oven and broiler in an electric stove are in the same compartment. The compartment has two heating elements, one at the top and one at the bottom. The bottom element heats the compartment for all cooking purposes except broiling. For broiling, only the top element comes on. When you're broiling food in an electric stove, leave the door slightly open.

There are two main cooktops available in electric stoves, each with unique characteristics:

♦ **Coil elements.** Elements heat up and cool down relatively quickly, although more slowly than gas burners. Coils may vary in size to fit smaller and larger cooking containers.

♦ **Induction cooktops.** A glass-ceramic top covers the heating elements, making this cooktop very easy to keep clean. With induction cooktops, heat is produced when a ferrous metal pan—such as stainless steel or cast iron—is placed on the element. The magnetic attraction between the pan and the heating element produces heat. This cooktop stays cool, except for any heat transferred from the pan.

The Convection Oven

A convection oven is similar to a conventional oven except that a fan circulates the heated air. This speeds cooking and keeps temperatures even throughout the oven. As a result, foods brown more evenly than in a conventional oven. A convection oven cooks more quickly than a conventional oven, but not as quickly as a microwave oven.

A convection oven can be combined with either a conventional or a microwave oven. The combination oven has more advantages than any single type.

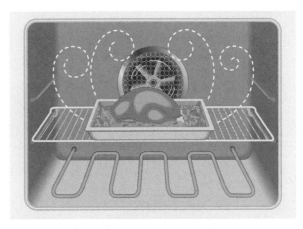

◆ Convection ovens use a built-in fan to circulate hot air in the oven compartment. **Explain the advantages of this method of cooking.**

The Microwave Oven

Microwaves are a form of energy that travel like radio waves. In a microwave oven, a magnetron (MAG-nuh-trahn) tube turns electricity into microwaves. The microwaves are distributed throughout the oven by a stirrer blade, a fan-like device. The microwaves bounce off the oven's walls and floor until they are absorbed by the food. Microwave energy is reflected from metal but passes through glass, paper, and plastic to get to food.

Microwaves make food molecules vibrate against each other, producing friction. This friction produces heat that cooks the food. Microwave ovens cook many foods in one-quarter the time that it takes to cook them conventionally, making this an energy-efficient way to cook.

FYI

The EnerGuide Label

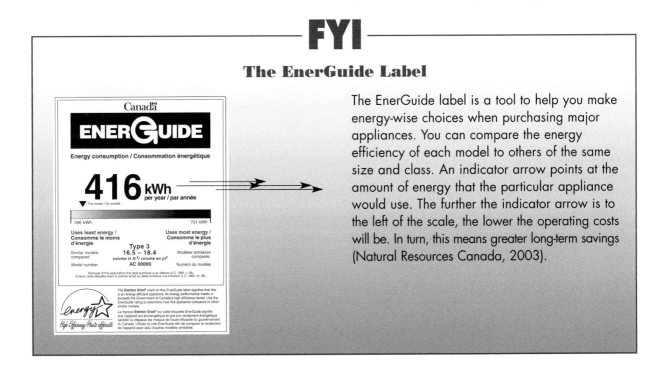

The EnerGuide label is a tool to help you make energy-wise choices when purchasing major appliances. You can compare the energy efficiency of each model to others of the same size and class. An indicator arrow points at the amount of energy that the particular appliance would use. The further the indicator arrow is to the left of the scale, the lower the operating costs will be. In turn, this means greater long-term savings (Natural Resources Canada, 2003).

Rice cooker/steamer

Broiler/grill

Electric skillet

Toaster oven

Slow cooker

Toaster

Small Cooking Appliances

Many small appliances are available to help you perform certain cooking tasks quickly and easily. Here are some basic ones:

◆ **Toaster.** Browns bread products on both sides at the same time. You set the controls for the degree of browning. Two- and four-slice models are available, as well as wide-slice models.

◆ **Toaster oven.** Toasts bread, heats up foods, and bakes small amounts of many foods. Some toaster ovens can broil food.

◆ **Electric skillet.** A thermostat controls the temperature of the skillet. This appliance is useful for frying, roasting, steaming, and baking.

◆ **Portable electric burner.** A small appliance that works like the cooktop on a stove.

◆ **Slow cooker.** A deep pot with a heating element in the base that allows food to cook slowly over many hours. It's a convenient way to cook one-dish meals such as stews.

◆ **Broiler/grill.** A small, portable electric grill used to broil or grill food indoors.

◆ **Rice cooker/steamer.** Used to cook large quantities of rice, vegetables, poultry, fish, or other seafood. The controlled heat cooks all types of rice perfectly.

Cookware and Bakeware

Cookware is equipment for cooking food on top of the stove. **Bakeware** is equipment for cooking food in an oven. Both cookware and bakeware are available in a variety of materials. Microwave ovens have special requirements for cooking containers.

As a general rule, all types of cookware and bakeware should be washed in hot water with dish detergent. To remove baked-on food, soak pans in hot water with a little detergent prior to washing them.

Cookware

If you were packing for an overnight trip, you'd use a lightweight travel bag, not a huge trunk. In much the same way, you can choose cookware, which comes in many shapes and sizes, depending on how you plan to use it. Here is a guide to some common items:

◆ **Saucepans.** Saucepans have one long handle and often come with a cover. Some types have a small handle on the opposite side as well. Sizes range from 0.8 L to 4 L (½ quart to 4 quarts). Saucepans are usually made of metal or heatproof glass.

◆ **Pots.** Larger and heavier than saucepans, pots range in size from 3 L to 14 L (3 quarts to 20 quarts). Pots have two small handles, one on either side, which make it easier to lift a heavy pot. Most pots come with covers.

◆ **Skillets.** Sometimes called "frypans" or "frying pans," skillets are used for browning and frying foods. They vary in size and often have matching covers.

◆ **Double boiler.** A double boiler consists of two saucepans—a smaller one fitting into a larger one—and a cover. Boiling water in the bottom pan gently heats the food in the upper pan. This type of cookware is used for heating foods that scorch easily, such as milk, chocolate, sauces, and cereal.

◆ **Dutch oven.** This is a heavy-gauge pot with a close-fitting cover. This type of pot may be used on top of the stove or in the oven. Some Dutch ovens come with a rack to keep meat and poultry from sticking to the bottom.

◆ **Steamer.** This basket-like container is placed inside a saucepan containing a small amount of boiling water. Holes in the steamer allow steam to pass through and cook the food.

◆ **Pressure cooker.** This heavy pot has a locked-on cover and steam gauge. Steam builds up inside the pot, causing very high cooking temperatures that cook food more quickly than in an ordinary pot.

◆ **Be sure to choose cookware that can safely be used in a microwave oven.** What are some types of cookware that would not be suitable for microwave use?

Materials Used for Cookware

Material	Use and Care
Aluminum	• Cool before washing to prevent warping. • Avoid sharp tools like knives and beaters. • Do not use to store salty or acidic foods.
Anodized Aluminum	• Use non-abrasive cleaners and nylon scrubbers.
Stainless Steel	• Use non-abrasive cleaners and nylon scrubbers. • Use stainless steel cleaner to remove stains. • Do not use to store salty or acidic foods.
Copper	• Dry after washing. • Do not scour inside—the thin lining may be worn away. • Polish with copper cleaner or a paste of flour and vinegar.
Cast Iron	• Store in dry place. • Store cover separately—pan may rust if stored covered.
Glass	• May need a wire grid if used on an electric stovetop. • Use non-abrasive cleaner and nylon scrubbers. • Do not plunge hot pan into cold water or put into the refrigerator.
Glass-Ceramic	• Use non-abrasive cleaner and nylon scrubbers. • Dishwasher-safe. • Use manufacturer's care instructions.
Stoneware	• Dishwasher-safe. • Use non-abrasive cleaner and nylon scrubbers.
Enamel (glass baked on metal)	• Dishwasher-safe. • Use non-abrasive cleaner and nylon scrubbers.
Microwave-safe Plastic	• Dishwasher-safe. • Use non-abrasive cleaner and nylon scrubbers.
Non-stick Coatings	• Follow manufacturer's directions for use and care. Some cannot be washed in dishwasher. • Use non-metal tools to prevent scratching.

Stock pot

Pressure cooker

Dutch oven

Saucepan

Double boiler

Steamer basket

Non-stick skillet

Microwave Cookware

Microwaves are reflected by metal but pass through glass, plastic, and paper materials. These characteristics are important to remember when choosing and using containers for microwave cooking. Metal and foil are not generally used in microwave ovens. They can cause **arcing,** electrical sparks that can damage the oven or start a fire. Never leave metal tools, such as a spoon, in any food being microwaved.

When choosing containers for use in the microwave, look for a label that says "microwave safe" or "microwavable." Use only plastics that are marked with these labels in the microwave. Many glass, glass-ceramic, and stoneware containers are safe for use in the microwave. If in doubt, perform this simple test. Fill a glass measuring cup with water and place it in the oven next to the empty container that you are testing. Heat for two minutes at full power. If the empty container is too hot to touch, don't use it in the microwave.

Safety Check

For your safety, copper pans sold in Canada must be coated with another metal because ingesting large amounts of copper may be poisonous. Therefore, do not use badly scratched, pitted, or uncoated copper pans to cook or to store food.

The Safe Use of Cookware

Most of the cookware in Canada is safe to use for daily meal preparation, as long as you maintain it well and use it as intended. However, there are some potential risks in cookware materials.

Benefits and Risks of Cookware Materials

Aluminum: Aluminum has been associated with Alzheimer's disease, yet there is no definite link proven. The World Health Organization estimates that adults can consume more than 50 mg of aluminum daily without harm. During cooking, aluminum dissolves most easily from worn or pitted pots and pans. The longer food is cooked or stored in aluminum, the greater the amount that gets into food. Leafy vegetables and acidic foods, such as tomatoes and citrus products, absorb the most aluminum.

Copper: Small amounts of copper are good for everyday health. However, it is not certain how much can be safely taken each day. Large amounts can be poisonous. Because of this, copper and brass pans sold in Canada are coated with another metal to prevent the copper from coming into contact with food. Small amounts of the coating can be dissolved by food, especially acidic food, when cooked or stored for long periods. Don't use badly scratched or uncoated copper cookware to cook or store food in as it loses its protective layer if scoured. Nickel is one of the metals used in coating, so anyone allergic to nickel should avoid nickel-coated cookware.

Stainless steel and iron cookware: The metals used in stainless steel or iron cookware that may produce health effects are iron, nickel, and chromium. Most often North Americans lack iron, yet large amounts can be poisonous. Iron cookware provides less than 20 percent of total daily iron intake—well within safe levels.

Nickel is not poisonous in small quantities, but it can cause an allergic reaction. Again, if you are allergic, avoid stainless steel cookware.

Small doses of chromium are good for your health, but they can be harmful in higher amounts. One meal prepared with stainless steel equipment gives you about 45 micrograms of chromium, not enough to cause concern.

Ceramic, enamel, and glass: The minor components used in making, glazing, or decorating glassware or enamelware, such as pigments, lead, or cadmium, are harmful when taken into the body. Therefore, in Canada, glazed ceramics and glassware are regulated under the Hazardous Products (Glazed Ceramics and Glassware) Regulations. Cookware made of these materials cannot be sold, advertised, or imported if it releases more than trace amounts of lead and cadmium. Products having greater than the allowable leachable levels of lead and cadmium must be identified by a label indicating the presence of lead and/or cadmium, or by a design feature such as a hole or a mounting hook, and should not be used for food.

Some countries do not have the same strict lead and cadmium limits as Canada. If you bring in glazed ceramic cookware from abroad, be aware that it may not meet Canadian permitted levels for lead and cadmium.

Plastics and non-stick coatings: Many containers have been made for use in microwave ovens, where metal cookware is unsuitable. Using plastic containers and wrap for anything other than their original purpose can cause health problems. With wrap, the concern is that food may absorb some of the plasticiser, the material that helps make it flexible. This is most likely to happen at high temperatures, when microwaving, or with fatty or oily foods like cheese and meat. Don't use plastic bowls or wrap in the microwave unless they are labelled as microwave-safe. If you reuse items, such as dairy product containers, let the food cool before storing, then refrigerate it immediately. Avoid visibly damaged, stained, or unpleasant smelling plastics and containers.

Non-stick coatings are applied to metal utensils to prevent food from sticking and protect cookware surfaces. The only time these items are a risk is if they are heated to temperatures greater than 350°C (650°F). This might happen if an empty pan is left on a burner. In this case, the coatings can give off irritating or poisonous fumes.

Source: Health Canada (2003).

Bakeware

Most bakeware consists of pans of different sizes and shapes. Light-coloured pans transfer oven heat to food quickly and give baked products a light, delicate crust. Dark pans absorb more heat from the oven and can produce thick brown crusts in baked products, though not in other foods.

Glass pans absorb more heat than metal bakeware does. If you use a glass pan for baking, reduce the oven temperature by 14°C (25°F).

Here are some basic types of bakeware:

◆ **A variety of bakeware is available.** Compare and contrast the results achieved by cooking with shiny vs. darker metal pans.

- ◆ **Loaf pan.** A deep, narrow, rectangular pan used for baking breads and meat loaf.

- ◆ **Cookie sheet.** A flat, rectangular pan designed for baking cookies and biscuits. A cookie sheet has two or three open sides.

- **Baking sheet.** Similar to a cookie sheet, except with four shallow sides about 2.5 cm (1 inch) deep. Baking sheets are used for baking sheet cakes, pizza, chicken pieces, fish and other seafood.

- **Cake pans.** Available in assorted sizes and shapes.

- **Tube pan.** A variation on the standard cake pan with a central tube to help trap added air in angel food and sponge cakes.

- **Pie pans.** Shallow, round pans with slanted sides. Pie pans are used for pies, tarts, and quiches.

- **Muffin pans.** Used for baking muffins, rolls, and cupcakes. These pans are available in 6- and 12-muffin capacities.

- **Roasting pans.** Large, heavy pans, oval or rectangular in shape, used for roasting meats and poultry. Roasting pans may be covered or uncovered.

- **Casserole.** A covered or uncovered pan used for baking and serving main dishes and desserts. Various sizes are available.

- **Aluminum foil pans.** Disposable pans made of foil. These pans are useful for special, one-of-a-kind occasions and can be recycled.

Cooking Tools

A variety of tools are available for the many different cooking tasks. Here are some you might find helpful:

- **Turner.** Used to lift and turn flat foods, such as hamburgers and pancakes.

- **Tongs.** Used to grip and lift hot, bulky foods, such as broccoli spears.

- **Basting spoon.** Used to stir and baste foods during cooking.

- **Baster.** A long tube with a bulb on the end used for suctioning up juices for basting.

- **Ladle.** Has a small bowl and a long handle for dipping hot liquids from a pan.

- **Oven meat thermometer.** Used to measure the internal temperature of meat

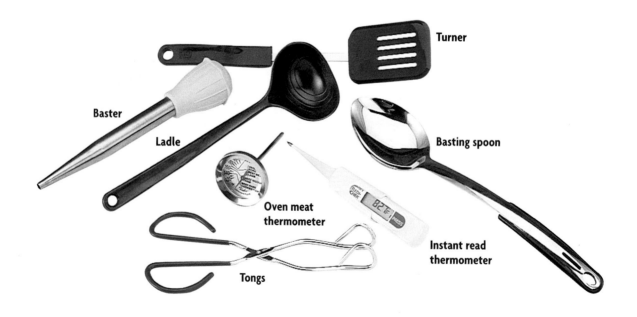

Baster

Ladle

Turner

Basting spoon

Oven meat thermometer

Instant read thermometer

Tongs

and poultry as it roasts in the oven. This type of thermometer cannot be used with thin food or in a microwave oven.

◆ **Pastry brush.** Used to brush hot foods with sauce or pastry with a glaze.

◆ **Skewers.** Long rods made of metal or bamboo, with one pointed end. Pieces of food are threaded onto skewers for cooking or serving.

◆ **Instant-read thermometer.** Used to measure the internal temperature of food at the end of cooking time, including foods prepared in a microwave or conventional oven. This type of thermometer cannot be used while food is cooking in the oven. To gauge the internal temperature of thin foods, insert the thermometer sideways.

Both digital and analog models of instant-read thermometers are sold, with the digital version being easier to read.

◆ **Baking racks.** Used for holding baked goods during cooling or hot pans when they are removed from the heat.

◆ **Potholders, oven mitts.** Thick cloth pads used to protect hands while handling hot containers. Oven mitts are also available in a silicone material.

INTERNET CONNECTS

www.mcgrawhill.ca/links/food
To learn more about ingredients and kitchen tools, go to the web site above for *Food for Today, First Canadian Edition,* to see where to go next.

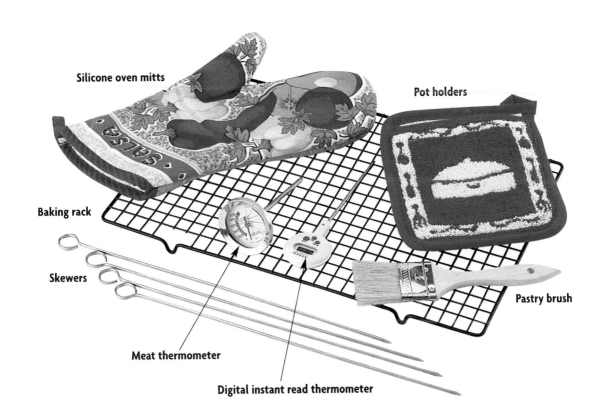

Silicone oven mitts

Pot holders

Baking rack

Skewers

Meat thermometer

Digital instant read thermometer

Pastry brush

How to Use a Meat Thermometer

A meat thermometer is an indispensable tool when cooking meat or poultry.

Look and Learn:
Explain the importance of inserting the thermometer into the thickest area of a cut or as close to the centre as possible.

Casserole

◆ Casseroles: Insert the thermometer into the thickest portion. If the dish is shallow, check the temperature at the end of the cooking time with an instant-read thermometer. Insert it about 1 cm (½ inch) into the mixture.

Ground meat—meat loaf

◆ Ground meat or poultry: Place the thermometer in the thickest part of the food.

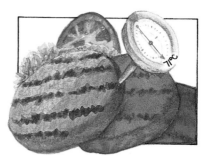

Ground meat—burgers

◆ Thin pieces: Insert the instant-read thermometer sideways until the tip is in the centre of the burger.

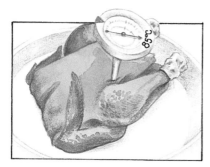

Whole poultry

◆ Whole poultry: Insert the thermometer into the inner thigh, near the breast. It should not touch the bone. If the bird is stuffed, take a reading of the stuffing at the end of the cooking time.

Ham

◆ Roast: Insert the thermometer into the centre of the thickest part, away from gristle, fat, and bone.

Preparation Tasks

Cutting Foods

Food preparation often involves a variety of cutting tasks. You may need to trim unwanted parts from food or cut food to the desired size. With practice, you can become a cutting expert. Knowing how to use cutting tools properly is the first step to succeeding in the kitchen as well as to preventing accidents.

Equipment for Cutting

Two key cutting tools for a well-equipped kitchen do no actual cutting. One of these is a cutting board, a specially designed surface to help protect kitchen counters. To reduce the risk of foodborne illness, choose a cutting board made of a non-porous material.

The second cutting tool, a **sharpening steel,** is a long, steel rod on a handle used to help keep knives sharp. Regular and correct use of a sharpening steel is an essential skill to learn. Here is what to do (reverse the directions if you are left-handed):

1. Hold the handle of the steel in your left hand. Place the point straight down, very firmly, on a cutting board. In your right hand, hold the knife by the handle, blade down.

2. Place the knife blade against the right side of the steel. The knife blade and steel should touch near the handles. Tip the knife away from the steel at a 20-degree angle.

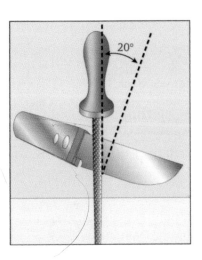

FYI

Garnishing

Small amounts of vegetables and fruit that have been cut into interesting shapes can be used as a garnish. A garnish helps to add colour and eye appeal to any plate. For example, slice lemon wedges, arrange on a leaf of lettuce, and place beside a fish entree. Or cut radishes into rosette shapes and add to a plate of meat.

3. Draw the blade down the steel and toward you, keeping it at a 20-degree angle to the steel. Use gentle pressure.

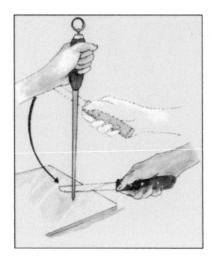

◆ From left to right: bread knife, slicing knife, chef's knife, utility knife, boning knife, paring knife, sharpening steel. Identify the task you would perform with a utility knife.

4. When the tip of the knife reaches the tip of the steel, repeat the process, holding the knife against the steel on the left. Draw the blade down along the steel four or five times, alternating right and left sides.

Knives

Many cutting tasks require the use of a knife. The basic types of knives include:

◆ **Chef's knife.** Also called a French knife. Has a large, triangular blade. Ideal for slicing, chopping, and dicing.

◆ **Slicing knife.** Used for cutting large foods, such as meat and poultry.

◆ **Utility knife.** Similar in shape to a slicing knife but smaller. Used for cutting smaller food items, such as tomatoes and apples.

◆ **Paring knife.** Used to **pare**—cut a very thin layer of peel or outer coating from—fruits and vegetables.

◆ **Boning knife.** Has a thin, angled blade, well suited to removing the bones from meat, poultry, and fish. May also be used to trim fat from meat.

◆ **Bread knife.** Has a **serrated**, or saw-tooth-patterned blade for slicing through coarse-grained breads.

Small Appliances

With its many speed settings, an electric blender can be used to chop, grind, and mix. A food processor is similar to a blender, but is often more powerful and versatile. This heavy-duty cutting machine comes with an assortment of blade attachments for various jobs, such as slicing and grinding meats. Some food processors have a tool for kneading bread dough.

Alternative Cutting Tools

Other simpler cutting tools and their uses include:

◆ **Vegetable peeler.** Has blade that swivels. Perfect for paring fruits and vegetables.

◆ **Poultry shears.** Scissors-like tool, capable of cutting through bone. May also be used for snipping, trimming, or cutting dried fruit, pastry, or fresh herbs.

Common Cutting Tasks

Recipes often use terms such as *cube, grate,* or *score* to indicate how foods are to be cut. To prepare food successfully and prevent accidents, you need to know what each term means and how to perform the technique correctly. Here is a guide to some common cutting tasks.

Look and Learn:

What are the safety precautions being taken in each of these diagrams?

Slice. To cut a food in large, thin pieces.

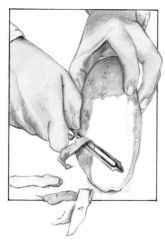

Pare. To cut off a very thin layer of peel. A peeler or paring knife works best.

Cube and dice. Both these terms refer to cutting food into small, squared pieces. Make the pieces about 1.3 cm (½ inch) on each side when cubing and 3 to 6 mm (⅛ to ¼ inch) when dicing.

Grate. Cut food into smaller pieces or shreds by pressing and rubbing the food against the rough surface of a grater.

Score. To score means to make shallow, straight cuts in the surface of a food, such as a flank steak. Scoring helps tenderize meat. A slicing knife is most often used to score meats.

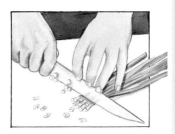

Chop and mince. Both these terms refer to cutting food into small irregular pieces. Minced pieces are smaller than chopped pieces. To use a chef's knife to chop or mince, hold the knife handle with one hand, pressing the tip against the cutting board. The other hand should rest lightly on the back of the blade, near the tip, as in the picture. Pump the knife handle up and down, keeping the tip of the blade on the board so that the blade chops through the food.

- **Food chopper.** Ranges in size from small hand-held nut chopper to large chopper with several blades.

- **Food grinder.** Grinds meat, poultry, nuts, and many other foods. Also good for grating, shredding, and other fine cutting needs.

Techniques for Cutting

Although some cutting tools only require the push of a button, using knives requires specific skills. When using most knives, hold the food firmly on the cutting board with one hand and hold the knife by its handle with the other. For rounded foods, such as some fruits and vegetables, first cut a thin slice from the bottom so the item will sit flat. Grip the knife firmly and use a back-and-forth, sawing motion while pressing down gently.

✚ Safety Check

Keep knives sharp. A dull knife is much more likely to slip and cut you because you will have to exert more pressure.

When using a knife, keep your fingers away from the sharp edge of the blade. Be sure the fingertips of the hand holding the food are curled under. Never hold the food in your hand while cutting, and never cut with the blade facing your body.

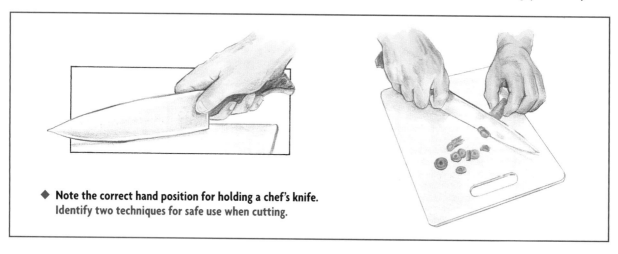

◆ Note the correct hand position for holding a chef's knife. Identify two techniques for safe use when cutting.

◆ Small appliances and other cutting tools include (from back left to right) food chopper, blender, grater, food processor, food grinder (in front) poultry shears, peeler. Name two advantages to owning a food processor rather than just a blender.

Mixing Foods

Another common recipe task is combining ingredients through mixing. You can use different mixing tools and techniques, depending on the food and the desired results.

Equipment for Mixing

Many kinds of mixing tools, from small hand-held utensils to electrical appliances, are used for mixing tasks. Two mixing appliances, the blender and food processor, were mentioned earlier in connection with cutting.

Other tools commonly used when mixing include:

◆ **Electric mixer.** Used to blend, beat, and whip ingredients. Lightweight, hand-held models are convenient. Heavy-duty models are attached permanently to a stand.

◆ **Rotary beater.** Used to mix and whip foods more quickly and easily than can be done with a spoon or whisk. Often used to beat egg whites.

◆ **Mixing bowls.** Come in many different sizes. May be of stainless steel, glass, pottery, or plastic.

◆ **Mixing spoon.** Used for many mixing tasks. Different sizes and shapes are available.

◆ **Sifter.** A container with a fine wire screen at the bottom and a blade that forces dry ingredients through the screen.

◆ **Wire whisk.** A **whisk** is a balloon-shaped device made of wire loops held together by a handle. Used for mixing, stirring, beating, and whipping.

◆ **Rubber scraper.** Used to scrape food from bowls, pans, and other containers. Helpful in moving thick ingredients from the sides of the bowl to the middle while mixing. Also used for **folding**, which is described on the next page.

◆ These are common mixing tools. In back (left to right): electric mixer (with extra attachments), sifter, hand-held electric mixer; in front: rotary beater, wooden spoons, wire whisk, rubber scraper. Why are rubber scrapers such an important tool to have when cooking or baking?

Techniques for Mixing

As with cutting, the techniques of mixing have a vocabulary all their own. Some of these terms found in recipes will be readily familiar to you. Others will not.

Look and Learn:

Name one recipe in which you would use each of the following mixing techniques.

Fold. Folding is a technique used to gently mix delicate ingredients, usually with a rubber scraper or wooden spoon. The technique involves cutting down through the mixture, moving the utensil across the bottom of the bowl, and bringing it back up to the surface along with some of the mixture from the bottom. The utensil is never lifted out of the mixture.

Mix, combine, blend. To thoroughly incorporate one ingredient into another, using a wooden spoon, wire whisk, rotary beater, electric mixer, or electric blender.

Beat. To thoroughly mix foods using a vigorous motion. Egg whites may be beaten to add air to them.

Cream. To beat together ingredients, such as shortening and sugar, until soft and creamy.

Whip. To incorporate air into a mixture to make it light and fluffy.

Stir. To mix by hand, using a wooden spoon or wire whisk in a circular motion. Can also be done while cooking to keep food from sticking to the pan and to distribute heat throughout foods.

Sift. To force one or more dry ingredients—for example, flour—through a sifter or strainer to add air, remove small lumps, or mix two ingredients.

Other Tasks

A variety of other tools and techniques are used in food preparation. Here are some additional terms you may find in recipes:

◆ **Strain.** To separate solid particles from a liquid, such as broth or juice. The liquid is poured through a bowl-shaped fine screen called a strainer or sieve (SIV).

◆ **Drain.** To drain liquid from a solid food, such as fruits, vegetables, or cooked pasta. This is done by putting the food in a colander—a bowl with small holes in the bottom—or a large strainer.

◆ **Purée (pyoo-RAY). Purée** means to make food smooth and thick by putting it through a strainer, blender, or food processor.

◆ **Baste.** To brush or pour a liquid over a food as it cooks.

◆ **Dredge.** To coat a food with a dry ingredient, such as flour or crumbs.

Many heating and cooking tasks are also involved in food preparation. These techniques and the equipment needed are explored next.

How Cooking Affects Nutrients

One of the goals of food preparation is to retain nutrients such as vitamins and minerals. You've already learned that proper storage helps retain nutrients. Another key is to choose cooking methods that minimize nutrient loss and to use those methods properly.

Some nutrients in foods can be destroyed by heat. These include vitamin C, thiamine, and folate.

When foods are cooked in liquid, water-soluble vitamins and some minerals dissolve into the liquid. Unless the cooking liquid is consumed, these nutrients are lost. Some minerals and fat-soluble vitamins may be lost as fats and juices drip from meat, poultry, fish and other seafood.

Although very little protein is lost during cooking, animal proteins are sensitive to high temperatures. Overcooking in dry heat toughens them, making them unpleasant to eat.

The exact effect of heat on food depends on both the food and the cooking method. The following pages discuss various basic cooking methods, ways to retain vitamins and minerals, and ways to reduce fat.

Basic Cooking Techniques

Choosing a Cooking Method

When choosing a cooking method, you must look at the type of food being cooked. Once the kind of food being cooked is determined, an appropriate cooking method is chosen to achieve the desired results—a nutritious and appetizing dish.

Moist-heat Methods

Moist-heat cooking includes methods in which food is cooked in hot liquid, steam, or a combination of the two. Moist heat may be used for a number of reasons. Applying moist heat to less-tender cuts of meats breaks down the collagen in them, making the meat tender. The long, slow cooking of moist heat will help develop the meat's flavour. If you choose this method when cooking tender cuts of meat, you should generally shorten the cooking time. Otherwise, the cut can be over-cooked easily and fall apart.

Some foods, such as rice or dry beans, must absorb liquid as they cook. Moist heat methods also give you an opportunity to add seasonings, sauces, and other foods to the dish. You can create many different combinations in this way.

Many cooking appliances, including the microwave and slow cooker, use moist heat. When using a conventional oven, you can choose any of these moist-heat methods: boiling, simmering, steaming, and pressure cooking.

Boiling

When a liquid reaches boiling temperature, it forms large bubbles that rise to the surface and break. Water boils at 100°C (212°F). Boiling is suitable for only a few foods, such as corn on the cob and pasta. Many other foods tend to overcook easily or break apart when boiled. Nutrient loss is higher with boiling than with other methods. Boiling also toughens foods high in protein, such as eggs.

When boiling foods, be sure to use a saucepan or pot large enough to hold the food and the boiling liquid. Bring the liquid to the boiling point, then add the food. Be sure the liquid continues boiling as the food cooks.

Boiling is also useful when you want liquid to evaporate quickly. For instance, you might boil a sauce to thicken it or boil a soup to concentrate the flavour.

Simmering

Simmering differs from boiling in that bubbles in the liquid rise gently and just begin to break the surface. Water simmers at about 86°C to 99°C (186°F to 210°F). Simmering is used to cook many types of food, including fruits, vegetables, and less-tender cuts of meat and poultry. Some foods that would break apart or toughen if boiled can be successfully simmered.

◆ Adding the cooking liquid from simmered vegetables to soup is one way of conserving nutrients. What are some others?

As with boiling, some nutrients, especially water-soluble vitamins, are lost during simmering. For this reason, it is wise to consume the cooking liquid from simmered foods, such as vegetables and dry beans, whenever possible.

To simmer food, bring the liquid to a boil and then add the food. After the liquid returns to a boil, reduce the heat so that the food simmers. A slow cooker can also be used to simmer some foods, such as meats and dry beans.

Two special cooking techniques that make use of simmering are stewing and poaching. **Stewing** involves covering small pieces of food with liquid and then simmering until done. **Poaching** refers to simmering whole foods in a small amount of liquid until done. Eggs, fish, and whole fruits can be poached.

 **Safety Check**

When adding food to boiling liquid, use tongs or a long-handled spoon to hold the food just above the surface of the liquid. Then ease the food in. Dropping the food from high above the liquid can cause the liquid to splash up and burn you.

Steaming

Steaming is a method of cooking food over, but not in, boiling water. The food is usually placed in a steamer basket that fits inside a saucepan. Steam is created by a small amount of boiling liquid in the bottom of the pan. The boiling liquid does not come in contact with the food. The pan is covered during cooking to trap the steam. You can also use an electric steamer to cook food.

Many foods can be cooked in steam, including vegetables and fish. Foods retain their colour, shape, and flavour well when steamed. Few nutrients are lost. Cooking time is longer with steaming than with boiling or simmering.

 FOR YOUR HEALTH

Full Steam Ahead

Steaming not only locks in flavour and nutrients but also is a simple way of cooking certain foods, such as rice, which can become sticky when simmered. Here are some healthful steaming suggestions:

- Steam chunks of boneless chicken breast with broccoli florets, carrot strips, and slices of onion, for a nutrient-rich alternative to stir-frying.

- When steaming vegetables or rice, steam them over seasoned, canned chicken or vegetable broth instead of water. This method adds flavour without adding fat.

◆ **Steaming foods locks in flavour and nutrients. Can you explain why?**

Pressure Cooking

A pressure cooker cooks food in steam under pressure. Because pressure makes temperatures above 100°C (212°F) possible, the food cooks 3 to 10 times faster than with other methods.

A pressure cooker is best used with foods that take a long time to cook. Examples are less-tender cuts of meat and poultry, dry beans, soups, one-dish meals, and vegetables. This method has all the advantages of steaming plus faster cooking times. Follow the manufacturer's directions and accident prevention guidelines carefully. The food in a pressure cooker is superheated and under high pressure.

Dry-heat Methods

Dry-heat cooking means cooking food uncovered without added liquid or fat. When cooked in dry heat, animal foods lose some juices, carrying off some B vitamins. For example, some thiamine is destroyed by cooking food at high temperatures. In general, however, few nutrients are lost unless the food is overcooked. Dry-heat methods include roasting and baking, broiling, and pan-broiling.

Roasting and Baking

Roasting and baking both involve cooking food uncovered in a conventional or convection oven. **Roasting** generally refers to cooking large, tender cuts of meat or poultry. **Baking** is the term used with foods such as breads, cookies, vegetables, and casseroles, though some meat, poultry, and fish preparations are also baked. Baked ham and baked chicken are examples.

Roasting gives tender meat and poultry a flavourful, crispy, brown crust. Use a shallow, uncovered roasting pan with a rack. The roasting rack allows fat to drain away from the food—a real benefit for those trying to reduce their fat intake.

For baked goods such as breads, cookies, and cakes, preheating is important. **Preheating** means turning the oven on about 10 minutes before using it so that it will be at the desired temperature when the food is placed inside.

◆ Roasting and baking are dry-heat cooking methods. Name two more foods that would be cooked using these methods.

Pan Placement in the Oven

When baking, placement and spacing of pans are important. The pans must be placed so the hot air in the oven can circulate freely. If pans touch each other or the oven walls, they create a **hot spot**—an area of concentrated heat. The food overcooks in these areas. When baking several pans of food at one time, place them diagonally opposite one another, as shown here.

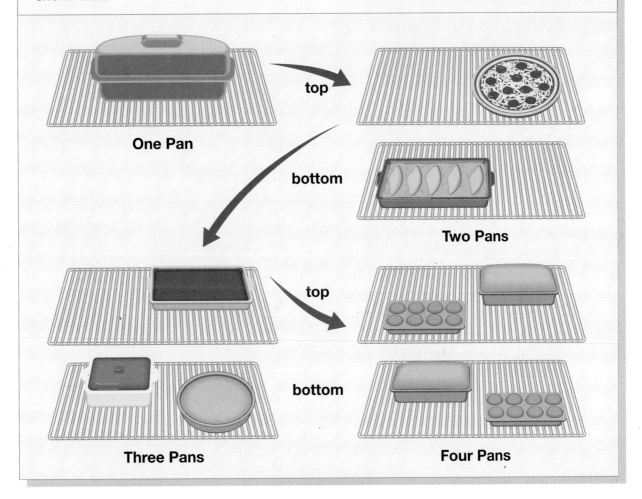

One Pan

top

bottom

Two Pans

Three Pans

top

bottom

Four Pans

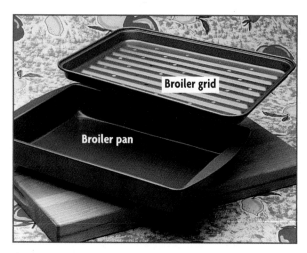

◆ **A broiler pan consists of two parts that fit together. What makes broiling a low-fat cooking method?**

Broiling

Broiling refers to cooking food under direct heat. The broiler pan is placed below a burner or heating element. The heat radiates down onto the food, cooking it quickly.

Broiling works well with tender cuts of meat and poultry as well as fish and other seafood, fruits, and some vegetables. Foods that are already cooked may be broiled for a short time to brown them. Broiling may also be used to melt cheese toppings.

A broiler pan has two parts. A slotted grid holds the food. The grid fits on top of a shallow pan that catches drippings. This allows fat to drain away during cooking.

Safety Check

Never cover the broiler grid with foil. Foil keeps drippings from falling through, which could cause a grease fire.

Never put your hands into the oven when broiling to turn or remove food. The intense heat can cause severe burns. Instead, take the broiler pan from the oven first. Remember to use potholders or oven mitts. Put the pan on a heatproof surface or wire rack, then turn or remove the food.

For broiling in most stoves, set the oven control on "broil." Usually you can't control the broiling temperature. To control the cooking, you can vary the distance of the pan from the heat source and the cooking time. For thicker foods, position the pan farther from the heat and increase the cooking time. This allows the food to cook all the way through without burning on the outside. Check a cookbook for guidelines about positioning specific foods for broiling.

Outdoor cooking on a grill or spit is similar to broiling except that the heat source is below the food. The food is placed on a wire grid.

Pan-Broiling

Pan-broiling is a stovetop method of dry-heat cooking. Foods such as hamburgers, tender cuts of steak, and some cuts of pork may be pan-broiled. The food cooks quickly and retains a minimum amount of fat.

To pan-broil, cook the food in a heavy skillet over medium heat. Don't add fat. As fat accumulates in the pan during cooking, pour it off or remove it with a baster.

FYI

Broiling Tips

Pat meat and poultry dry. Moisture can keep food from becoming brown and crisp. Don't salt foods before broiling. Salt draws moisture from foods, causing them to dry out. Brush fish, fruit, and vegetables lightly with oil or melted butter or margarine to keep them from charring. To prevent foods from sticking, always start with a cold broiler pan. Use tongs, not a fork. The fork pierces the food, making holes that allow juices to escape.

Frying

Frying involves cooking food in oil or melted fat. Keep in mind that frying in even a small amount of oil adds fat and calories to foods. Here are several different methods:

- **Sautéing.** To **sauté** (saw-TAY) means to brown or cook foods in a skillet with a small amount of fat. Low to medium heat is used. This method is often used for chopped vegetables, such as onions and peppers, and small pieces of meat and fish.

- **Pan-frying.** Pan-frying is similar to sautéing but usually involves larger pieces of meat, poultry, fish, or other seafood. The food may need to be turned several times during the cooking process for complete, even cooking. Pan-frying is often used to brown meat before cooking it in moist heat.

- **Deep-fat frying.** This method is also called "french frying." Food is immersed in hot fat and cooked until done. This method is used for tender foods, such as vegetables, and some breads, such as doughnuts. For best deep-fat frying results, use a deep-fat thermometer to keep the fat at the correct temperature.

Note that every fat has a **smoking point**— a temperature at which fats begin to give off irritating smoke and break down chemically. Oil that has reached its smoking point is no longer good for cooking. Animal fats, such as butter and lard, have low smoking points. Safflower, soybean, corn, and peanut oils have relatively high smoking points. They make the best choices for frying.

Combination Methods

Sometimes the best way to cook a food is by a combination of methods. Braising and stir-frying are two popular cooking methods that combine dry-heat and moist-heat cooking.

◆ **Braising combines frying and moist-heat cooking. What is another combination method of cooking?**

Braising

Braising combines browning food (pan-frying) with a long period of simmering to tenderize the food and enhance the flavour. It is often used for large, less-tender cuts of meat and poultry.

Use a Dutch oven or other heavy pot with a tight-fitting cover. Brown the food first on all sides. Then add seasonings and a small amount of liquid to the food and cover the pot. The cooking may be completed in the oven (usually at 180°C or 350°F) or on top of the stove. Vegetables are sometimes added to braised meat or poultry near the end of the cooking time.

◆ With stir-frying, a technique that began in Asia, a special bowl-shaped pan, called a wok, is traditionally used.

Stir-Frying

Stir-frying also combines frying and moist-heat cooking. In this method, small pieces of food are fried quickly in a small amount of oil at high heat. Stir the food constantly to keep it from sticking to the pan. During the last few minutes of cooking, add a small amount of liquid to the food and cover the pan, allowing the food to steam briefly.

Microwave Cooking Techniques

Microwave Oven Basics

Microwaving is a fast, healthy way to cook. Food cooks quickly with less fat and liquid than in most conventional methods. That means more of the water-soluble vitamins are retained, and fewer vitamins are destroyed by heat.

Microwave cooking isn't complicated, but it is different from conventional cooking methods. Start by reading the owner's manual. It will give specific directions for using your microwave oven. It will also help you understand how the microwave power settings work, the kinds of foods that can be microwaved, and the proper equipment to use.

Food Composition

A food's composition—what it is made of—affects the way it cooks in the microwave. The microwave oven may not result in even cooking. Therefore, proper food handling and cooking techniques are important when using the microwave oven to ensure the safety of the food that is to be served.

Foods high in water, such as vegetables, will cook faster than foods with a lower water content, such as meat.

Fat, sugar, and salt also attract microwaves; but be careful when heating these items. Concentrations of fat or sugar can create hot spots when exposed to microwaves. Serious burns on the skin or mouth could result. Food under salted areas will cook faster than that under unsalted areas. Therefore, don't sprinkle salt on food before microwaving—wait until after cooking.

Some foods—pasta and rice, for example—need time to absorb liquids as they cook. As a result, no real time is saved when cooking such foods in the microwave. Other foods, such as potatoes and winter squash, have a tough skin that keeps moisture from evaporating. Steam can build up inside the skin and cause the food to burst. Pierce foods like these with a fork to allow steam to escape. For the same reason, do not cook eggs in the shell in the microwave oven—they will burst.

Microwaving Successfully

Here are some additional principles and techniques to guide you in microwave cooking:

◆ **Food density.** The heavier a food feels for its size, the more dense it is. The denser a food, the longer the cooking time.

◆ **Shape and size of food.** Foods of a uniform thickness cook most evenly. If foods are unevenly shaped, the thinner parts will cook through before the thicker parts. Small pieces cook faster than large ones.

◆ **Starting temperature of food.** The colder the food is to start with, the longer it will take to cook. Thaw most frozen foods, except vegetables, before microwaving.

◆ **Amount of food.** The more food you're cooking, the longer it will take. The same number of microwaves are produced no matter how much food you put in the oven.

◆ **Types of food.** When cooking larger pieces of meat, debone them first. Cook them at 50 percent power and turn them at least once during cooking. This will allow more even heating so that the outer portion of the meat is not overcooked.

◆ **Reheating food.** When reheating food in the microwave, ensure that the centre of the food reaches 74°C (165°F). Never reuse containers that came with microwave convenience foods.

◆ **Covering food.** Covering food will allow steam to be trapped in the container, which will help to kill bacteria, keep food moist, and shorten cooking time. It also keeps food from spattering in the oven.

◆ **Placement of food.** The best arrangement of food for microwaving is a ring shape. When possible, leave space between pieces of food to allow better microwave penetration. You can also arrange foods like the spokes of a wheel. Food in the centre of the oven cooks more slowly. Therefore, arrange thicker, tougher pieces on the outside, and thinner, tender parts toward the centre.

◆ In a microwave that is not equipped with a turntable, it is important to rotate foods a half turn so they cook more evenly. What other measures can you take to ensure that microwave foods cook evenly?

Chapter 7   Review and Activities

Summary

- Major cooking appliances include the conventional stove, the convection oven, and the microwave oven.

- Small cooking appliances include the toaster, toaster oven, electric skillet, portable electric burner, slow cooker, broiler/griller, rice cooker/steamer.

- Cookware includes saucepans, pots, skillets, double boiler, Dutch oven, steamer, and pressure cooker. Materials used for cookware include metals, glass, ceramic, stoneware, enamel, plastic, and non-stick coatings.

- Microwave cookware includes items that are glass, glass ceramic, stoneware, plastic, and paper. Do not use any cookware or utensils containing metal in a microwave.

- Bakeware includes loaf pans, cookie sheets, baking sheets, cake pans, tube pans, pie pans, muffin pans, roasting pans, casseroles, and aluminum foil pans.

- Cooking tools include a turner, tongs, basting spoon, baster, ladle, pastry brush, skewers, oven meat thermometer, instant-read thermometer, baking racks, potholders, and oven mitts.

- Cutting equipment includes a cutting board, sharpening steel, and various knives.

- Small appliances, such as an electric blender or food processor, may also be used for cutting, slicing, and grinding.

- Other cutting tools include a vegetable peeler, poultry shears, food chopper, and food grinder.

- Common tasks for cutting different foods are slicing, paring, cubing and dicing, grating, scoring, and chopping or mincing.

- Mixing means combining ingredients. Equipment used for mixing includes an electric mixer or rotary beater, mixing bowls, mixing spoons, a sifter, a wire whisk, and a rubber scraper.

- Techniques used to mix ingredients are mixing, combining, blending, stirring, beating, creaming, whipping, folding, and sifting.

- Other food preparation techniques are straining, draining, puréeing, basting, and dredging.

- The type of food being cooked determines which cooking method to use. Retaining as many vitamins and minerals in the food is another factor to consider when choosing how to cook it.

- Moist-heat cooking means a food is cooked slowly in hot liquid, steam, or a combination of the two. Moist-heat methods include boiling, simmering, steaming, and pressure-cooking.

- Dry-heat cooking means cooking food uncovered and without liquid or fat. Methods are roasting, baking, broiling, pan broiling, and frying.

- Cooking methods combining dry-heat and moist-heat include braising and stir-frying. This method browns the outside of the food but retains its moisture and flavour

- Microwave cooking is a quick and healthy method of cooking. What a food is made of determines how it is cooked in the microwave. Other factors that affect microwave cooking include the food's density, size and shape, starting temperature, and amount.

Knowledge and Understanding

1. What are the key differences between the following pieces of cookware?
   - A saucepan and a pot.
   - A cookie sheet and a baking sheet.

2. How are conventional, convection, and microwave ovens alike? How are they different?

3. List the factors to consider when purchasing and/or using cookware, bakeware, and microwave ware. Remember to consider Canadian guidelines and standards in your list.

4. What does "beating" mean when used to describe a mixing technique? Name three tools that could be used to beat a mixture.

5. What are three basic categories of cooking methods? Which method could you use to make meats more tender?

6. List the methods of dry-heat cooking.

7. Rank these cooking methods from 1 to 6, according to how well they retain nutrients in food: frying, simmering, pressure cooking, roasting, boiling, steaming.

Thinking and Inquiry

8. Beatta's family recently moved to Canada. They need to purchase all new cooking appliances and tools, but they have a limited budget. What small cooking appliances might you advise them to buy or not to buy? Explain your answer.

9. What might happen if you tried to follow a recipe without understanding the meaning of food preparation terms and techniques? Discuss your answer.

10. Raina would like to make sure that she loses as few nutrients as possible when cooking. Describe at least four cooking techniques that Raina can employ to ensure minimal nutrient loss in her food.

11. Many families limit their use of microwave ovens to thawing frozen foods and heating leftovers. Describe at least three techniques that families could use to expand their cooking of different types of food in the microwave.

Communication

12. Develop a pamphlet that contains consumer information on what to look for when purchasing major appliances, cookware, and bakeware. Include information on how to use these items safely.

Application

13. Working in pairs, evaluate the cookware, bakeware, and microwaveable containers in your school's foods lab to ensure that each item is safe for use.

14. Develop a checklist for use in your school foods lab for which cutting equipment to use with which foods. Post your checklist on a wall in the classroom.

15. **a)** Find two recipes for each of the following:
    - An egg dish appropriate for dinner.
    - A vegetable side dish.
    - A ground beef dish.
    - Soup.
    - Chicken.

    b) What basic cooking method does each recipe use?

CHAPTER
8

A Cook's Book

While reading this chapter, you will:

- Use mathematical skills accurately in meal planning and recipe changes, employing both SI metric units and imperial measures.

- Demonstrate the ability to follow a recipe, make substitutions, and alter portions as necessary.

- Demonstrate accurate measuring skills.

- Show the useful information available in cookbooks.

- Demonstrate collaborative problem-solving, conflict-resolution, and planning skills, and be able to explain the need for these skills by referring to organization theory.

Cookbooks not only help you make tasty foods, but also provide a wealth of information. Browse through various cookbooks to discover some of the extra information available. What extra information do you find useful in a cookbook?

KEY TERMS

assembly directions
desired yield
equivalents
recipe
test kitchen
volume
yield

RESEARCH SKILLS

• roles in small groups

Whether you are a beginner cook or an experienced one, recipes act like a road map—they give you directions. Reading a recipe and applying proper techniques in measurement will help you produce consistent and appetizing results in the kitchen. In this chapter you will learn how to do this. In addition, you will learn how to alter, convert, and make substitutions in a recipe. You will also discover other useful information that is available in a cookbook. You will become familiar with the common features of a cookbook as you progress through the chapter.

Many cooks have a favourite cookbook. What would you look for in a cookbook?

Introducing a Cookbook

Cookbook Use

A cookbook means exactly what the word implies—a book for cooks. It is a book that provides suggestions to help a cook decide what to prepare and serve for many different parts of a meal. The cookbook then supplies directions, or a "map," for how to combine various ingredients to make a particular food or beverage. This is referred to as a **recipe**. Recipes are provided in a cookbook as a set of instructions for preparing a particular menu item in a meal.

Cookbook Varieties

Take a walk through any major bookstore in your community and you will discover that there are a large number and variety of cookbooks on the market. As you peruse the shelves, you will notice that many cookbooks are geared toward lifestyle and current trends. In today's market, cookbooks include those that are low-fat, have simple and quick recipes to prepare, are vegetarian, contain gourmet cooking recipes, or are produced in association with a Canadian Health Association, such as The Canadian Breast Cancer Society or The Heart and Stroke Foundation. There are also cookbooks that provide recipes that are made with only a particular staple ingredient, such as pasta, tofu, or chicken.

Cookbook Components

Even though there are as many varieties of cookbooks as there are ingredients, most basic cookbooks are divided into the courses of a meal. These major sections include:

◆ Appetizers.

◆ Soups.

◆ Salads.

◆ Main meals (this may be further divided into eggs, beef, fish, poultry, and vegetarian meals).

◆ Desserts.

◆ Beverages.

Many cookbooks, even the basic ones, provide not just recipes but also other information that may be useful to the cook. Extra information in a cookbook may include one or more of the following aspects related to food:

◆ What to look for when buying produce.

◆ Storage of food items.

◆ Preparation tips.

◆ Nutritional information.

◆ Special diets (such as low-fat or low-sodium diets).

◆ Historic information on the origins of food.

Some of this information may also be found in an appendix of the cookbook. Note the extra information that is available in the recipe for Cranberry-Orange Muffins on page 135 of this text. What extra information would you find helpful in a cookbook?

FOR YOUR HEALTH

Tips for Healthier Desserts

- **Keep the flavour, but not the fat.** Try to eat more fruit ices, sorbet, sherbet, frozen yogurt, frozen tofu, ice milk, and lower-fat ice cream.

- **Boost your calcium.** Good choices include milk pudding, yogurt, and rice pudding.

- **Fill up on fibre.** Some desserts contain more fibre than others. Try fruit crisps, cobblers, and bread puddings.

- **Be fruitful.** For refreshing, nutritious desserts, it's hard to beat fresh fruit. Try different combinations, such as melon and grapes, strawberries and pears, melon and blueberries, pears and kiwi, oranges and melon, blueberries and peaches. Have them plain or dress them up with vanilla yogurt, ice cream, frozen yogurt, custard sauce, vanilla pudding, or sweetened yogurt cheese. For special occasions, serve fruit, sorbet, or sherbet in meringue shells or chocolate cups.

Source: Callaghan and Roblin (2000).

◆ **This is one type of extra information that is useful in a cookbook.** What other tips for "healthier desserts" can you add to this list?

Recipe Information

Success with a recipe depends not only on the cook's skill but also on the recipe itself. Therefore, the producer(s) of a cookbook, whether the person is a chef, a dietitian, or a combination of people writing the book, should have tested all of the recipes in the cookbook to make certain that it is reliable.

Cranberry-Orange Muffins

Yield 12

These moist, high-fibre muffins are the best way I know to use up leftover cranberry sauce. It's even worth buying or making cranberry sauce just to use in these muffins.

175 mL	natural bran	3/4 cup
250 mL	whole-wheat flour	1 cup
125 mL	granulated sugar	1/2 cup
7 mL	cinnamon	1 1/2 tsp.
5 mL	baking powder	1 tsp.
5 mL	baking soda	1 tsp.
250 mL	cranberry sauce	1 cup
1	egg	1
125 mL	buttermilk or low-fat plain yogurt	1/2 cup
50 mL	vegetable oil	1/4 cup
5 mL	grated orange rind	1 tsp.

Ingredients and Amounts

In bowl, combine bran, flour, sugar, cinnamon, baking powder, and baking soda; mix well. Add cranberry sauce, egg, buttermilk or yogurt, vegetable oil, and orange rind; stir just until combined. Spoon batter into paper-lined or non-stick muffin tins. Bake in 200°C (400°F) oven for 25 minutes or until firm to the touch.

Directions

Equipment

Temperature

Time

Nutrition Information Per Muffin

Calories	156
g fat	5
mg cholesterol	23
mg sodium	126
g protein	2
g carbohydrate	27
fibre	Good

Variations

Apple-Raisin: Instead of cranberry, use 250 mL (1 cup) applesauce plus 125 (1/2 cup) raisins.

Banana Date: Instead of cranberry, use 250 mL (1 cup) mashed banana and 125 mL (1/2 cup) chopped dates.

Zucchini: Instead of cranberry, use 250 mL (1 cup) grated unpeeled zucchini and 125 mL (1/2 cup) raisins.

Source: Lindsay, Anne (1988).

◆ A good recipe contains all the information shown here in a logical, easy-to-follow format. Note the other information that is available for this recipe. Why are the variations useful to a cook?

Recipes are tested in what is known as a **test kitchen**. This is a kitchen where people devise a recipe, prepare it, taste it, and repeat the process until the recipe produces an appetizing food item consistently.

The components of a well-written and complete recipe include the following:

◆ **Ingredients.** The ingredients should be listed in the order in which they are used. This makes it easier to follow the recipe and not omit an ingredient. Amounts of ingredients are also given.

◆ **Yield.** The **yield** is the number of servings or amount the recipe makes. The yield of a recipe can be increased or decreased, as necessary.

- **Information about temperature, time, and equipment.** This may include pan size and type, oven temperature or power, and cooking time. A well-written recipe will also tell you if a conventional oven needs to be preheated.

- **Step-by-step directions.** The directions should be clear and easy to follow. Steps may be numbered so that you won't skip any or lose your place. Some recipes include more than one set of directions, such as a conventional method and a microwave method.

- **Nutrition information.** This information is not essential, but it can be useful in helping you choose recipes that provide vital nutrients and that fit in with your eating plan. Typical nutrition information tells you the number of calories and the amount of fat and sodium for each serving of food. Some recipes also include information about carbohydrates, fibre, protein, cholesterol, both saturated and unsaturated fats, vitamins, and minerals.

- **Other Information.** As discussed on page 134, all kinds of extra information is available in a cookbook. Although this information is also an unnecessary component of a sound recipe, it may be useful in helping the cook to plan, alter, or prepare a successful meal. Refer to the extra information that is available in the recipe on page 135.

Recipe Formats

The standard, or most common, format for a recipe lists the ingredients first, followed by the **assembly directions**, the step-by-step procedure that explains how to combine the ingredients in a recipe. The recipe on page 135 is in the standard format. This format allows you to easily determine if you have all of the ingredients on hand.

A less common recipe format combines the ingredients and assembly directions. You may see a recipe written this way on a food package, for example. This format takes less space than the standard format.

The most important thing to remember when using a recipe of any format is to make sure that you have all the ingredients on hand before you begin assembling them. If you don't have all the ingredients, check to see if you can substitute other ingredients. It is also important to follow the recipe in a step-by-step manner so that you have success with the recipe.

Collecting Recipes

A reliable recipe source is a basic cookbook that gives standard recipes for common foods. You probably have several in your classroom or school library. If you don't find one you like, ask your teacher for recommendations. Other reliable recipe sources are magazines, newspapers, package labels, and web sites.

How can you tell if a recipe is accurate and complete? When you first read a recipe, analyze it. Are basic ingredients missing? Are descriptions of ingredients clear? Is a direction included for each ingredient? Do you have all the information needed to prepare the recipe? If the answer to any of these questions is no, look for another recipe.

Once you have a reliable recipe source, you can expand a recipe collection in whatever direction you choose, depending on the kinds of food you enjoy. Why not start a collection of recipes that are tasty, healthful, and easy to prepare? After trying a particular recipe, decide whether to add it to your list of favourites. If you plan to use a new recipe on a special occasion, try it ahead of time first and evaluate the results.

Pita Spirals

When is a sandwich not like a sandwich at all? How about when it's rolled up into a spiral and cut into pieces to show off the beautiful food design on the inside? This recipe is not difficult, it's just a little bit messy. Keep plenty of paper towels nearby.

Note: You can use flour tortillas instead of pita bread. (You won't have to snip them in half.)

Ingredients
1 pita bread (or 2 flour tortillas)
125 mL (1/2 cup) cream cheese, at room temperature
4 chives, 1 sprig of dill, and/or 3 basil leaves (optional)
1 medium-sized ripe tomato, sliced into thin rounds
6 large, crisp spinach leaves, washed and dried

Yield: This recipe makes 2 or 3 servings.
Time: It takes about 20 minutes, start to finish.

You will also need:
- scissors
- cutting board
- small bowl for the cream cheese
- dinner knife for spreading the cream cheese
- sharp knife for cutting the tomato and the sandwich
- paper towels to wipe messy hands
- plates

Should you ask an adult for help?
That's up to you, but make sure there is an adult in the house who knows you are doing this and can help you set up. (And, of course, if there is any task you feel uncomfortable doing, ask for help.)

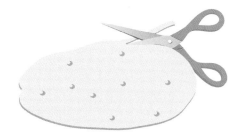

Snip around the edges of a **pita bread** with scissors to separate it into 2 halves. Put the circles down on the cutting board with the inside part facing up.

Put the soft **cream cheese** in a small bowl. Use scissors to snip tiny pieces of **chives**, **dill**, and/or **basil** over the bowl, if you'd like to add them.

Spread a thick layer of cream cheese onto each pita circle.

(continued)

Put 3 **tomato slices** in a row down the middle. They can be on top of each other a little.

Spread some cream cheese onto 2 or 3 **spinach leaves**. (This might be a little messy. Take your time.)

Lay the "frosted" spinach leaves on top of the tomatoes, with the cream cheese facing up.

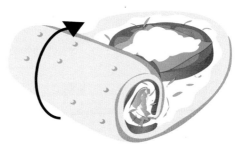

Roll up the circle, pressing the edges tightly closed. You will end up with a log shape.

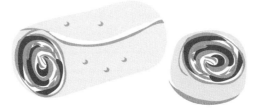

Cut the log crosswise into 3 or 4 pieces to show the lovely spiral design inside.

TIME TO EAT!

Source: Katzen, M. (1999).

◆ **Children's cookbooks are user-friendly for little chefs in the kitchen.**
   What changes are made in this recipe to make it fun and easy for a child to follow the recipe?

Organizing Recipes

Organizing recipes in your collection can help you find them when you need them. You can paste your recipes on index cards and use a card file box for storage. If you have access to a computer, you can use a word processor file or cookbook software to save recipes. You can then print a particular recipe and organize it into a binder. Divide the binder into sections according to the type of recipe it is; for instance, appetizer, poultry, and so on. You also may want to incorporate tips and techniques on aspects such as nutrition, food storage, or whatever else you need to help you plan and prepare successful menu items. Designing your own cookbook also can be a fun way to express your lifestyle, show your food preferences, and meet your nutritional needs.

┌─────────────────────────────────────┐
│ ▾   │
│ ⋮   **INTERNET CONNECTS**   │
│   │
│   www.mcgrawhill.ca/links/food   │
│ To learn more about basic information about cooking, including │
│ how to read a recipe, go to the web site above for *Food for* │
│ *Today, First Canadian Edition,* to see where to go next. │
└─────────────────────────────────────┘

Measuring Ingredients

Units of Measurement

In a recipe, amounts of ingredients can be given in several ways. Most ingredients are measured by **volume,** the amount of space an ingredient takes up. For instance, a pasta salad recipe might list "500 mL finely shredded cabbage." Some ingredients are measured by weight: 1.5 kg of mild Italian sausage and 75 g of semisweet chocolate are examples. A few ingredients may be measured by the number of items, such as one medium banana or two eggs.

SI Metric Units

In Canada, the measurement system that is used is the SI metric system, commonly referred to as "metric." Following are the most common metric units found in recipes, with their abbreviations in parentheses:

◆ **Volume:** millilitre (mL), litre (L).

◆ **Weight:** gram (g), kilogram (kg).

◆ **Temperature:** degrees Celsius (°C).

◆ **Food Energy:** kilojoules (kJ) or kilocalorie (commonly referred to as *calorie*).

Social Science Skills

Roles in Small Groups

Learning often involves working in small groups to complete a task or assignment. There are five common roles that are useful when working in small groups. If you work in the same group on all assignments, rotate group roles with every new assignment. This will allow you to have a chance to experience each role.

- **Manager.** Manages the group. Ensures that members understand the assignment, are fulfilling their roles, and that assigned tasks are being accomplished on time. If tasks are not divided up by the teacher, the manager may delegate various tasks to group members. The teacher responds to questions only from the manager, who approaches the teacher if there are any questions.

- **Recorder.** Records the names and roles of the group members at the beginning of each day. Records the group's answers and explanations, along with any other important observations, insights, and so on. The teacher considers the recorder's answers as the group response.

- **Technician.** Performs all technical operations for the group, including the use of a calculator or computer.

- **Encourager.** Observes the group's behaviour with regard to the task and encourages participation of members. The encourager may use statements such as, "We haven't heard your ideas yet, _____," or "What do you think, _____?" The encourager may be asked to assess how well the group is working together and participating. This may be reported to the group and/or to the teacher during a debriefing session at the end of the class. For example, the encourager may assess that all group members are participating but that the group needs to stay more on task the next day so that the assignments gets completed on time.

- **Presenter.** Presents oral reports to the class. If the presentation is long, other group members will assist the presenter.

- **All members.** It is each group member's responsibility to participate actively in the discussions, to stay on task, to be courteous to other members, and not to be overbearing in his or her role.

Sources: Adapted from Farrell, J.J., and R.S. Moog (1999).

Imperial Units

Canadians used the imperial system of measurement before we switched to the metric system. You may still see imperial units of measurement in recipes because many older cookbooks are still used today and people often use recipes that are old family favourites. Most new Canadian cookbooks have both metric and imperial units. It is important to be familiar with the imperial units because you may have measurement tools that are marked with this system.

Following are the imperial units and symbols most often found in recipes:

◆ **Volume:** teaspoon (tsp.), tablespoon (Tbsp.), cup (c), fluid ounce (fl. oz.), pint (pt.), quart (qt.), gallon (gal.).

◆ **Weight:** ounce (oz.), pound (lb.).

◆ **Temperature:** degrees Fahrenheit (°F).

Note that "ounce" is used to express both volume (in fluid ounces) and weight. To understand how the two are different, imagine a cup of popcorn and a cup of water. Both take up the same amount of space, but the popcorn is mostly air and, therefore, is much lighter. To find out how much each weighs, you would use a measuring scale, not a measuring cup.

Customary Measurements

If you are using a cookbook published in the United States, you will see the U.S. system of measurement, the customary system. There are some differences between customary measures and imperial measures. However, the approximate equivalencies for most of the units are the same. For more information regarding the customary system and conversions, refer to the Internet Connects on page 142.

Approximate Equivalents

You can express the same amount in different ways by using **equivalents,** different units of equal measure. For instance, 500 grams of ground beef is equivalent to approximately 1 pound. The table on page 143 shows equivalents in approximate amounts. These approximate equivalencies are the conversions that you will most likely find in recipes in Canadian cookbooks and in *Canada's Food Guide to Healthy Eating*.

◆ Accurate measurements are the key to successful food preparation. Why is accuracy important when cooking?

CONVERTING MEASUREMENTS

Paula has always enjoyed her grandmother's baked goods. Paula would like to bake some of these goodies on her own. However, her grandmother's recipes are in imperial units and Paula's measuring equipment is in metric units. Help Paula convert the following ingredients from imperial measurements to metric measurements for her grandmother's low-fat oatmeal muffin recipe.

Low-Fat Oatmeal Muffins

¾ cup	whole-wheat flour
¾ cup	all-purpose flour
1 cup	uncooked rolled oats
1 Tbsp.	baking powder
3 Tbsp.	sugar
¼ tsp.	salt
1	egg
1 cup	milk
¼ cup	applesauce
3 oz.	raisins

Bake at 400°F for 15 to 20 minutes.

INTERNET CONNECTS

www.mcgrawhill.ca/links/food
To learn more about metric conversion and equivalents, go to the web site above for *Food for Today, First Canadian Edition,* to see where to go next.

Equipment for Measuring

Now that you understand the different units for measuring ingredients, you'll want to be sure you have the right tools for measuring. A well-equipped kitchen includes the following measuring tools. Each has specific uses, as you will learn.

◆ **Dry measures** usually come in a set of several sized containers. Your kitchen may be equipped with a set of standard dry measures that come in sizes of 50 mL, 125 mL, and 250 mL. Suppliers have attempted to make measures closer to the actual conversion. Therefore, many metric dry measures sold today have the imperial system and a precise metric equivalency on them as well. A typical set includes 50 mL (¼ cup), 75 mL (⅓ cup), 125 mL (½ cup), and 250 mL (1 cup). You may even see dry measuring containers that have even more precise measurements on them, such as 59 mL or 78.5 mL.

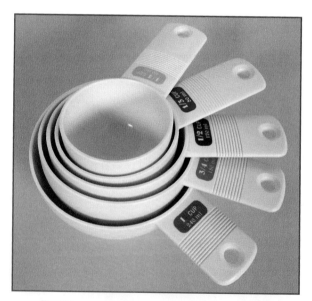

◆ Dry measures are used for accurate measuring of dry ingredients. Note that both metric and imperial units are shown on the measures.

Approximate Equivalents

Approximate Metric Equivalent*	Imperial Equivalent	Imperial Unit of Measurement
Volume		
5 mL		1 tsp.
15 mL	3 tsp.	1 Tbsp.
30 mL	2 Tbsp.	1 fl. oz.
50 mL		¼ cup
75 mL		⅓ cup
125 mL		½ cup
150 mL		¾ cup
250 mL	8 fl. oz. or 16 Tbsp.	1 cup
1000 mL or 1 L		4 cups
Weight		
30 g		1 oz.
500 g	16 oz.	1 lb.
1000 g or 1 kg	32 oz.	2 lb.
Temperatures		
−18° C		0°F
0°C		32°F
120°C		250°F
150°C		300°F
160°C		325°F
180°C		350°F
190°C		375°F
200°C		400°F

*Note: These equivalents are approximations in order to make metric conversion easier. For more information on metric conversion and equivalents, refer to the Internet Connects on page 142.

Source: Baird, Elizabeth, ed. (2001).

- **Liquid measures** are transparent measuring containers that have measurement markings on the side. Metric measures are marked in millilitres (mL) and may also contain imperial measurements on the other side of the container. A head space of about 1 cm (½ in) above the top mark makes it easier to move a filled measure without spilling. A spout makes pouring easier. Common sizes are 250 mL (1 cup) and 500 mL (2 cups).

- **Small liquid/dry measures** generally come in sets of four to six spoons. The standard metric measures come in 1 mL, 2 mL, 5 mL, 15 mL, and 25 mL. However, many metric sets sold today, as you'll notice in the photo on this page, include these four spoon sizes with the metric and imperial equivalents on them: 1.25 mL (¼ tsp.), 2.5 mL (½ tsp.), 5 mL (1 tsp.), and 15 mL (1 tbsp.).

Always use standard measuring equipment. A standard 250 mL liquid measure, no matter how it is shaped or designed, always holds the same amount. Coffee mugs, beverage glasses, soup spoons, and other non-standard items used for serving or eating food vary in size.

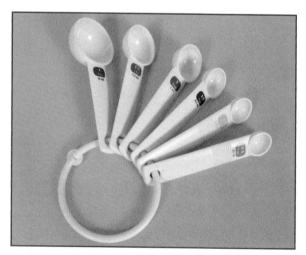

◆ Small liquid/dry measures come in sets of six spoons, as shown here. How would you measure 35 mL?

Other helpful measuring tools are a straight-edged spatula for levelling off dry ingredients, a rubber scraper for removing ingredients from measuring cups, and a food scale for measuring ingredients by weight.

Converting Recipes and Measuring Ingredients

Most Canadian recipes contain both metric and imperial measurements. However, you may notice a discrepancy between the equivalent units of measurement on a recipe and the equivalent units of measurement on some measuring equipment that you are using. An example of this is the following: A recipe calls for 50 mL or ¼ cup, yet your dry measure reads 60 mL or ¼ cup.

Therefore, when converting recipes and measuring ingredients, the following points are important to follow:

- **If converting a recipe from imperial units to metric units, you must convert all of the amounts.** For example, if you convert the dry ingredients, such as flour and baking powder, you must also convert the liquid ingredients, such as milk and water. This is especially crucial when baking items such as cakes, pastries, or cookies. Even small changes in the proportions of a recipe can cause the recipe to fail.

- **Once you have converted a recipe, test the recipe to see if the end product is acceptable.** If it isn't acceptable, some of the amounts of the ingredients may need to be adjusted.

(continued)

Converting Recipes and Measuring Ingredients (continued)

◆ When measuring, follow the recipe amounts and use the suggestions that are given in the "Using Combinations of Measures" section below.

◆ Baking requires precision and, to some extent, so does cooking. Therefore, measuring accurately is important until you learn how to approximate measures. Getting to know the consistency of your product, whether it is cookie dough, cake batter, or soup, will help you determine whether or not your ingredients are in the correct proportions.

Using Combinations of Measures

What do you do when you need a measurement and the measuring tools that you are using do not match the amount exactly? The answer is to use a combination approach.

Sometimes you may need to measure an unusual amount of an ingredient, such as 140 mL of sugar. How would you measure such an amount? First, use the measuring container that is closest to the amount you need (but not larger than that amount). For example, the closest measure to 140 mL is 125 mL. This leaves you with 15 mL, for which you can use the 15 mL small liquid/dry measure.

You can also remove small amounts from a measuring cup to get the exact amount called for in a recipe. To get 245 mL of milk, you would first measure 250 mL of milk in liquid measure and then remove 5 mL with a small liquid/dry measure.

Techniques for Measuring

In addition to the correct tools, the proper procedures are essential to accurate measuring and a successful recipe. The guidelines that follow will help you.

Measuring Liquids

Liquid measuring cups are used to measure all liquids, including oils and syrups. To measure liquids, follow these steps:

1. Set the cup on a level surface. If you try to hold it in your hand, you may tip it and get an inaccurate reading.

2. Carefully pour the liquid into the measuring cup.

3. Bend down to check the measurement at eye level for an accurate reading.

4. Add more liquid or pour off excess, if needed, until the top of the liquid is at the desired measurement mark.

5. Pour the ingredient into the mixing container. If needed, use a rubber scraper to empty the cup completely.

For small amounts of liquids, carefully pour into a small liquid/dry measure.

◆ Check the measurement of liquids at eye level. Explain why this is important.

Steak and Vegetable Fajitas

This recipe has "make it tonight" written all over it: it's quick, uses regular supermarket ingredients, and features family-pleasing tastes. Even better, it's easy enough for the first one in the door to prep and cook.

Test Kitchen Tip:
Use this recipe as a guide for making pork or chicken fajitas.

15 mL	vegetable oil	1 tbsp
375 g	beef stir-fry strips	12 oz
1	onion, sliced	1
2	carrots, halved lengthwise and sliced	2
1	sweet red pepper, sliced	1
1	zucchini, halved lengthwise and sliced	1
3	cloves garlic, minced	3
10 mL	chili powder	2 tsp
2 mL	salt	½ tsp
1 mL	ground cumin	¼ tsp
125 mL	salsa	½ cup
25 mL	lime juice	2 tbsp
Dash	hot pepper sauce	Dash
8	large flour tortillas	8

Makes 4 servings.

Per serving, about:

cal	577
carb	76 g
fibre	7 g
pro	31 g
total fat	16 g
chol	42 mg
sat fat	3 g
sodium	1010 mg

Percentage RDI:

calcium	9%
vit A	109%
iron	47%
vit C	102%
folate	19%

In large non-stick skillet, heat oil over medium-high heat; stir-fry beef in batches for 2 to 3 minutes or until browned but still pink inside. Transfer to plate.

Add onion and carrots to skillet; cook, stirring occasionally, for 5 minutes or until onion is softened. Add red pepper, zucchini, garlic, chili powder, salt, and cumin; cook for 3 minutes or until red pepper is tender-crisp.

Add salsa, lime juice, and hot pepper sauce. Return beef and any accumulated juices to pan; cook for 1 minute or until hot.

Meanwhile, stack tortillas and wrap in foil; bake in 180°C (350°F) oven for 8 to 10 minutes or until warmed. Wrap beef mixture in tortillas.

Source: Baird, Elizabeth, ed (2001).

◆ **How would the extra information on this recipe be useful to a cook when planning meals?**

Measuring Dry Ingredients

Dry measuring cups are used to measure flour, sugar, dry beans, and other dry ingredients. They can also be used for foods such as diced meat, chopped vegetables, and yogurt. Here are the steps to take when measuring dry ingredients:

1. Put a piece of waxed paper under the measuring cup to catch any extra ingredient. Don't measure an ingredient while holding the cup over the bowl in which you are mixing.

2. Fill the cup to overflowing with the ingredient. Some ingredients must be spooned into the cup lightly. Others can be packed down if specified in the recipe.

3. Level off the top of the cup using the straight edge of a spatula. Let the excess fall on the waxed paper. Put the excess back into the original container.

4. Pour the ingredient into the mixture. With semisolid foods, such as yogurt, use a rubber scraper to be sure the entire ingredient has been emptied from the cup.

As a general rule, spoon flour and sugar into the measuring cup lightly. If you shake the cup or pack it down, you will measure too much of the ingredient. Brown sugar contains moisture and tends to be fluffy, so pack it down with a spoon. When you empty the cup, the sugar should hold its shape.

Measuring Small Amounts

For amounts smaller than 50 mL or ¼ cup, use measuring spoons. Dry ingredients are usually measured by levelling them off evenly at the rim of the spoon.

Still smaller amounts of dry ingredients are measured as a dash or a pinch, the amount that can be held between the thumb and finger. These amounts are generally used for herbs, spices, and other seasonings.

Measuring Sifted Ingredients

Some recipes call for ingredients that have been sifted. Flour is an ingredient that is sometimes, though not always, sifted before use.

◆ Carefully level off the measure of dry ingredients with a straight-edged instrument, such as a spatula. Why has the cook set waxed paper on his work space?

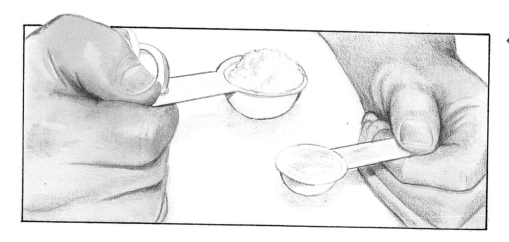

◆ It is important to level off a small liquid/dry measuring spoon. In what way could not doing this affect your recipe?

Be sure to sift ingredients *before* measuring them. Never sift whole-grain flours, which are too coarse to go through the sifter. Instead, stir whole-grain flour with a spoon before measuring.

Sift powdered sugar before you measure it. Granulated sugar can be sifted to remove lumps, if needed.

Measuring Fats

Fats, such as margarine or shortening, can be measured in several ways:

◆ **Stick method.** Use this method for fat that is packaged in sticks, such as butter and shortening. The wrapper is marked in millilitres and fractions of a cup. Simply cut off the amount you need.

◆ **Dry measuring cup method.** Pack the fat down into the cup, pressing firmly to fill in all spaces. Level the top. Using a rubber scraper, empty as much of the fat as possible. Use the same technique when using measuring spoons to measure fat.

◆ **Water displacement method.** This method, which requires some math, involves combining fat with water in a liquid measuring cup. First, subtract the amount of fat to be measured from 250 mL (1 cup).

The difference is the amount of water to pour into the measuring cup. (For example, to measure 75 mL (⅓ cup) shortening, use 175 mL (⅔ cup) of cold water.) After pouring in the water, spoon the fat into the cup, making sure it is completely below the level of the water. When the water reaches the 250 mL (1 cup) level, you have the right amount of fat. Pour off the water, and remove the fat with a rubber scraper.

◆ The water displacement method is a way of measuring fats accurately. What other technique could be used to measure fats?

Measuring by Weight

As you have read, the amounts of some recipe ingredients may be given by weight. Sometimes you can buy the exact weight of food you need, such as a 250 g (½ lb.) package of cream cheese. If that's not practical, a food scale, also known as a "portion scale," comes in handy.

To use a food scale:

1. Decide what container you will put the food in. Place the empty container on the scale.

2. Adjust the scale until it reads zero. Usually this is done by turning a knob.

3. Add the food to the container until the scale shows the desired amount.

Changing a Recipe

Why Change a Recipe?

From time to time, you may find that you have to change a recipe. Perhaps you don't have one of the ingredients and can't take the time to go out to buy it. You might want to substitute a more healthful or less expensive ingredient for one in the recipe. You might want to increase or decrease the recipe yield.

Changes are more likely to be successful in some recipes than in others. Mixtures such as salads, stir-fried foods, soups, and stews can usually be changed easily. On the other hand, recipes for baked products, such as muffins and custards, are like chemical formulas. Because each ingredient does a job in the recipe, the ingredients must be used in specific amounts in relation to each other. If one amount is changed or one ingredient is omitted, you risk having the recipe not turn out right.

When you change the ingredients in mixtures, you may notice a difference in flavour and texture. For instance, Paige sometimes substitutes cooked turkey for beef when making tacos. How might this change affect the flavour and texture of the dish?

◆ Always check to see if you have all the ingredients, before you begin preparing a recipe.

◆ **The success of a recipe depends on choosing appropriate substitutes and measuring them carefully.** What might be used in place of the apples in this loaf cake?

Changing the Yield

Recipes may need to be changed if the yield is not what you need. Most recipes, even those for baked goods, can be successfully doubled. Remember that larger equipment may be needed for mixing and cooking, and cooking times often need adjustment. For baked goods, it is best to use two baking pans of the original size rather than one larger one.

Many recipes for mixtures such as casseroles and soups can be not only doubled, but halved, tripled, and so on. The same process is used for both increasing and decreasing.

1. Determine the desired yield. The **desired yield** represents the number of servings you need.

2. Use the formula. To adjust the yield of a recipe, multiply the amount of each ingredient by the same number. That number is determined by using a simple formula:

desired yield ÷ regular yield = number to multiply by

Example: Your chili recipe serves eight and you need to serve only four: $4 ÷ 8 = 0.5$.

3. Multiply each ingredient amount by that number. This keeps all the ingredients in the same proportion as in the original recipe.

4. Make any necessary adjustments to equipment, temperature, and time. The depth of a pan affects how fast the food in it cooks. Use pans that are the right size for the amount of food, not too large or too small.

Making Ingredient Substitutions

If you don't have an ingredient you need for a recipe, you may be able to substitute another. The chart on the next page gives some common substitutions.

People who are concerned about healthful eating may have another reason to make substitutions. They want to reduce the fat and sodium in their eating plans.

◆ **Ground turkey meat was substituted for ground beef in this recipe.** What lower-fat substitution could you recommend for sour cream?

Ingredient Substitutions

If you don't have ...	Substitute ...
250 mL (1 cup) Sifted cake-and-pastry flour	250 mL (1 cup) all-purpose flour less 25 mL (1 tbsp)
5 mL (1 tsp) Baking powder	1 mL (¼ tsp) baking soda plus 2 mL (½ tsp) cream of tartar
Corn syrup	Equal amounts of maple syrup or molasses
30 g (1 oz) Unsweetened chocolate	50 mL (¼ tbsp) cocoa powder plus 12 mL (1 tbsp) butter
250 mL (1 cup) Buttermilk	250 mL (1 cup) milk mixed with 15 mL (1 tbsp) vinegar or lemon juice. Let stand 10 minutes to coagulate.
Superfine or berry sugar	Whirl granulated sugar in food processor until in smaller, finer crystals.
5 mL (1 tsp) Dry mustard	15 mL (1 tbsp) Dijon mustard (for wet mixture)
15 mL (1 tbsp) Soy sauce	15 mL (1 tbsp) Worcestershire sauce plus 10 mL (2 tsp) water plus pinch of salt
250 mL (1 cup) Tomato juice	125 mL (½ cup) tomato sauce plus 125 mL (½ cup) water
Garlic clove, 1 minced	1 mL (¼ tsp) garlic powder
15 mL (1 tbsp) Minced fresh ginger root	5 mL (1 tsp) ground ginger

Source: Baird, Elizabeth, ed. (2001).

Substitutions That Reduce Fat

Most recipes can be modified to reduce fat content. Changes in the ingredients used or the amounts of ingredients can make a significant difference. A change in the cooking method can sometimes also reduce the amount of fat.

Tony decided to try to reduce the fat in his favourite spaghetti sauce. First, he reduced the amount of beef from 750 g (1½ lb.) to 500 g (1 lb.). He also chose lean ground beef instead of the regular ground beef because it has less fat. Instead of cooking the onion and garlic in 30 mL (1 oz) of oil, he used a non-stick pan and cooking spray. He enjoyed the flavour and didn't miss the fat. He is still experimenting.

Tips for Reducing Fat

Here are some other suggestions that will help you cut the fat in recipes:

- Compare similar recipes and choose the ones with the least fat in their nutritional breakdown.

- Use fat-free or low-fat milk and milk products in place of all or part of high-fat dairy products. Instead of straight mayonnaise, try a mixture of half mayonnaise, half non-fat yogurt.

- Substitute chicken or turkey for high-fat cuts of meat. Use fresh, ground, skinless turkey breast in place of ground beef for meat loaf, for instance. You may want to increase the seasonings in the recipe because of the difference in flavour.

- Use lemon juice, flavoured vinegar, or fruit juice instead of salad dressings that contain oil.

- Substitute two egg whites for a whole egg or use egg substitutes.

Substitutions That Reduce Sodium

Most people take in far more sodium than the body needs. This excess can have harmful effects. Here are some ideas for reducing sodium in recipes:

- When shopping, reach for the lower-sodium versions of canned broth, soy sauce, and similar products.

- Use herbs, spices, lemon juice, or vinegar to enhance food flavours.

High-Altitude Cooking

Unless otherwise indicated, recipes are intended to be used at altitudes of 1000 m (3000 ft.) or below. If used at higher altitudes, they may not turn out right. Why? As the altitude gets higher, the air pressure gets lower. This affects food preparation in two main ways.

First, water boils at a lower temperature. This means that foods that are boiled, such as pasta, take longer to cook. Second, when the air pressure is low, bubbles of gas that form in liquids escape into the atmosphere more readily. As a result, baked goods are likely to rise too quickly then fall and be heavy. Sometimes reducing the amount of baking

FOR YOUR HEALTH

Adding by Subtracting

According to a mathematical principle, subtracting one amount from another yields a lower number. Nutritionists, however, are discovering that it is possible to add to the flavour of a recipe and *increase* its nutritional value, *while cutting down* on certain ingredients. Here are some examples of this new food math:

- Toast nuts before using them in dishes. That way, you can use fewer nuts to get the same nutty flavour.

- Add a pinch of cinnamon, nutmeg, or other sweet spice to a recipe and use less sugar.

- Add dried fruits or pureed dried fruits to a sweet recipe. They will pack in more nutrition while allowing you to cut down on the amount of sugar called for.

- Subtract heavy, fatty sauces on meats, vegetables, and other foods. In their place, add light, tangy salsas instead. You will be surprised at the boost in flavour.

Following Up

- Think of at least two ways to add flavour to foods while subtracting ingredients high in sodium, such as salt and ketchup. Be creative.

powder or soda and sugar and increasing the liquid can help.

People who live in high-altitude areas often can get helpful information about adapting recipes from their local newspapers or by searching the Internet. Many packaged foods include special directions for preparation at high altitudes.

Test Kitchen Worker

Joyce Parslow

What education is required for your job?

- An Honours Bachelor of Arts degree in Home Economics or Foods and Nutrition.

What skills does a person need to be able to do your job?

- Good writing and communication skills.

- A basic understanding of food science, nutrition, and cooking.

What do you like most about your job?

I like the variety and find the job interesting. The positions I've been in over the years have been constantly evolving, and have allowed my personal strengths to shape and develop the job.

What other jobs have you had in the past?

I have worked as a manager in Nestle Canada's Test Kitchen, and as a food stylist in a private business.

What advice would you give a person who is considering a career as a Home Economist?

Be sure to work on skills outside your academic training and stay connected with a network of colleagues and associates. Jobs are not often advertised in this field; they seem to come more by word-of-mouth.

Comment on what you see as important issues or trends in food and nutrition.

You need to be sensitive to where consumers are "at"—what their needs are within their lives—in order to provide information, communication, and services that are relevant and effective.

Chapter 8   Review and Activities

Summary

- Cookbooks provide suggestions and directions, in the form of recipes, to help a cook decide what to prepare for all different parts of a meal.
- There are many types of cookbooks available. Most are divided into sections following the courses of a meal.
- Recipe information contains ingredients; yield; information about cooking temperature, time, and equipment; directions; nutrition information; and "other" information.
- Ingredients are measured by volume or the number of food items.
- In Canada, the metric system of measurement is used today. The imperial unit of measurement was used before the metric system was adopted. Customary measurements are used in the United States.

- Equipment for measuring includes dry and liquid measures in large and small sizes.
- Recipes may be converted from imperial or customary units to metric units, but you must convert all the amounts of the recipe ingredients.
- You may change ingredients in a recipe by using similar substitutions.
- You may change the yield of a recipe by using the following formula: desired yield ÷ regular yield = number to multiply by.
- Recipes are intended to be used for altitudes of 1000 m. Cooking or baking at higher altitudes requires different cooking and baking times and temperatures to get the same results.

Knowledge and Understanding

1. What basic information should be found in a well-written recipe?
2. What information does a recipe's yield give?
3. Identify three things to look for when evaluating a new recipe.
4. How does a liquid measure differ from a dry measure?

Thinking and Inquiry

5. Discuss why accuracy is so important when converting a recipe and measuring ingredients.
6. What are the pros and cons of modifying favourite recipes to lower their fat content compared to buying a cookbook with low-fat recipes?

Communication

7. In the Social Science skills feature, the manager is in a position of authority. As a class, discuss how you could adapt the manager role to become a chef's role in the kitchen. Each time your food lab group works together in the kitchen, have someone be the chef/manager and perform the specific tasks that were discussed in class.

Application

8. Due to health concerns, Joel has been instructed by his doctor to lower his fat intake. Describe the extra information that may be found in a cookbook to help Joel cut down on fat in his diet.

9. Find a recipe with at least ten ingredients. List all the measuring tools you would need to measure the ingredients. Describe any special techniques needed.

10. Find a recipe in a magazine or newspaper that you would like to try. Adapt the recipe to make it healthier.

CHAPTER

9

CHAPTER EXPECTATIONS

While reading this chapter, you will:

- Demonstrate an understanding that providing for the food needs of family members can influence family relationships.

- Analyse the food needs of individuals of different ages.

- Demonstrate creativity in planning, preparing, and serving a meal.

- Demonstrate knowledge of correct mealtime etiquette.

- Plan meals that address factors such as nutritional needs, age, likes and dislikes, activity levels, special diets, and considerations related to time, money, and effort.

- Plan and budget for a family's meals for one week.

- Demonstrate an ability to schedule cooking times.

Meal planning can be easy and saves time in the end.

Meal Planning and Management

KEY TERMS

budget
cost per unit
cover
dovetailing
gratuity
meal appeal
place setting
pre-preparation
reservation
serving pieces
table etiquette
tableware
texture
unit cost
versatility
work plan

SOCIAL SCIENCE SKILL

- organizational skills

CHAPTER INTRODUCTION

Many families today have a busy lifestyle. In Serena's family, both she and her brother work after school and play organized sports and her mother works full time. It is always uncertain who will be home for dinner and who will prepare the meal.

Situations like this one are a real challenge for meal planning. A busy lifestyle, however, does not have to interfere with enjoying nutritious, tasty foods. In this chapter, you will learn ways to organize and prepare for the challenges of meal planning.

Planning meals for a busy family takes organization and flexibility.

Meal Planning Challenges

Sharing a meal with someone is an ancient custom that dates back thousands of years. Mealtime today is still an important time for friends and families to get together. Psychologist Tom Gardner says that mealtime is a natural time "to connect and share stories about the day's events" with the family (Pratt, 1999) and friends. It allows friends and families a time to discuss their day, make future plans, and simply enjoy one another's company. But remember, there is always some sort of planning and preparation involved in sharing a meal with others or when dining alone. Planning a meal involves making decisions about what foods to include and how to prepare them. When planning a meal, whether it is for guests, family members, or for yourself, it is important to take into consideration each person's special needs so that everyone at the table feels included. Respecting other people's special needs when planning a meal will show them that you feel they are important. Whether you are sharing a meal or a snack with family or friends, your consideration will help to strengthen your relationship with them.

Factors to Consider

As you begin to plan a meal, keep in mind a number of factors. A primary reason for eating is for nutrition. Another factor is how the meal fits in with the day's eating pattern. You would probably choose different foods for the main meal of the day than you would for a light lunch or supper. You would also consider your resources. Money and other factors might limit what you have to spend on food. It is also important to bear in mind the people who will be eating the meal. These factors may include one or more of the following considerations:

◆ Schedules.

◆ Likes and dislikes.

◆ Food allergies.

◆ Special diets, such as a low-fat diet or vegetarian.

◆ A person's activity level.

◆ Cultural or religious dietary laws.

◆ A person's stage in the life cycle, such as childhood.

It is important to know these special needs so that you can take them into consideration prior to preparing the meal. If, for example, you prepare a meal with an ingredient that one of your family members or guests is allergic to, this could be embarrassing, inconvenient, and possibly life-threatening to the allergic individual. Therefore, one of the most important things to do when meal planning is to find out the special needs of those for whom you are cooking and consider those needs. Regardless of whether it is a serious consideration, such as a food allergy, or a simple food dislike, this is an important point in meal-planning success.

All of these considerations may seem like an overwhelming challenge. However, there are many tools, such as cookbooks and Internet web sites, to help you plan meals that will meet your individual and family needs. The following pages contain important considerations to learn and remember when meal planning.

Nutrition and Energy Requirements

When meal planning, look at the meals that you and members of your family have eaten over the course of the day to ensure that they receive all of the essential nutrients in their diet. Use *Canada's Food Guide to Healthy Eating* to quickly check the number of servings in each of the four food groups that each family member has eaten throughout the day. Keep a copy of *Canada's Food Guide to Healthy Eating* posted on your refrigerator as a quick reference. Nutrition labelling and nutrition information boxes on recipes will also help you plan meals that meet nutritional needs.

◆ Involving children when you prepare a meal entices them to eat. What other entrees could you include in your meal plans to get children involved in meal preparation?

Nutrient needs also take into account energy requirements. In general, males have higher energy needs than females. An active person or athlete has higher energy needs compared to a person with a more sedentary lifestyle. A pregnant or breast-feeding woman also needs to increase her intake of food. Therefore, when planning meals, you need to take into account the energy requirements of people according to their stage in the life cycle and their activity level.

Toddlers and Preschoolers

Ask any parent to comment on the subject of planning meals for children and he or she will probably tell you that, at one time or another, it has been a challenge. When planning meals for preschoolers and toddlers, *Canada's Food Guide to Healthy Eating* is still an appropriate tool. For children, the portion sizes are smaller and the serving numbers differ from those in the regular guide. The following points are other suggestions to consider when planning meals for young children:

◆ Plan meals that are moist and easy to chew; for example, baked beans, meatballs, meat loaf, eggs, or macaroni.

◆ Get the children involved in planning meals. Allow them to look through a cookbook with you and grocery shop for the foods that you have chosen to cook and serve.

◆ Plan meals that are fun and interesting for children. For example, open-faced sandwiches. When it's time to serve the sandwiches, children could decorate them with vegetable pieces or condiments.

◆ When introducing a new food, plan to serve it with an old favourite. If the child doesn't like the new food, remember to plan a meal that offers it in a new way next time. It may take a while for the child to accept the food.

Older Adults

As people age, they often are required to alter their diet and eating habits. The following points take into account the normal physical changes that occur during later adult life. These suggestions will help plan meals for older adults.

◆ Plan meals that contain nutrient-dense foods. While older adults need less energy, they still need vitamins and minerals.

◆ Be aware that food needs vary with age and activity level.

- To help reduce the risk of osteoporosis, include meals that are high in milk and milk products.

- Plan meals that are colourful and well seasoned to help stimulate appetite, since there is a decrease in the senses of taste and smell as people age.

- Modify the texture of food by mincing or puréeing it or plan meals that are soft and moist so that they are easier to chew.

- Add fibre to the meal whenever possible. For example, serve unpeeled fruit, or soups and stews with lentils, beans, or barley.

Special Diets

Often people are required to make changes in their diet because of health concerns, such as diabetes or heart disease. Others may choose to follow a certain dietary regimen, such as vegetarianism, because of personal preference or ethical reasons. Religious or ethnic laws may require a certain food be eaten or abstained from at all times or during a certain time period. For example, Roman Catholics may give up a particular food during Lent; people of the Hindu religion refrain from eating beef; Muslims abstain from eating pork. As previously mentioned, it is also very important to avoid foods that contain ingredients that people are allergic to. Special diets also include the likes and dislikes of the people for whom you are planning a meal. Preparing nutritious foods that people like, or family favourites, is one way of ensuring that everyone is receiving essential nutrients. You can also adapt and combine family favourites to address many special diet concerns. For example, if you really enjoy chili and one member of your family is vegetarian and another is on a low-fat diet because of heart disease, you can prepare a low-fat vegetarian chili. Serve the chili with grated cheese on the side and plain whole wheat rolls. This compromise would consider all family members and make for an appetizing, nutritious meal.

INTERNET CONNECTS

www.mcgrawhill.ca/links/food
To learn more about guidelines and menu planning for people with various food allergies and special diets, go to the web site above for *Food for Today, First Canadian Edition,* to see where to go next.

Busy Schedules

When everyone is busy with work, school, and other activities, finding time for home-prepared meals may seem difficult. With planning and ingenuity, however, you can find ways to solve this problem.

Start by holding a family meeting to decide who will be responsible for food tasks, such as planning, shopping, cooking, and cleaning up. You may want to rotate these responsibilities from week to week. If family schedules are hectic but predictable, planning at least a week's worth of meals at a time can also help.

Here are some additional suggestions:

- Start a collection of healthful, quick recipes that fit your busy lifestyle. Put them where they can be found easily.

- Learn more about the microwave oven. It can be used for much more than heating leftovers and convenience foods.

- Make use of one-dish meals, which are often easier to prepare than a main dish with separate side dishes.

- Look for ways to combine convenience foods with fresh foods in recipes and meals.

◆ **A busy lifestyle can influence a person's cooking style.** What are some ways in which the skills of teamwork and leadership can be used to help organize family chores in the kitchen?

◆ Learn how to "cook for the freezer." When preparing a recipe, double or triple it and freeze the extra. Some families make cooking for the freezer a weekend project.

◆ Look for recipes with **versatility**—that can be adapted to many uses. For instance, Janice has a recipe for a basic seasoned meat-and-bean mixture, which can be used in a variety of recipes, such as chili, burritos, and taco salad. She prepares a large amount of the mixture and freezes it in recipe-size quantities to use in different ways.

Unpredictable Schedules

When family members have varied schedules, it's not always possible for everyone to sit down to a meal together. Here are some ideas for flexible meals:

◆ Plan meals that can be cooked early and refrigerated or frozen. Include instructions on how to assemble or reheat.

◆ Prepare one-dish meals in a slow cooker. Family members can help themselves as time permits.

◆ Set up a "breakfast bar" near the refrigerator with assorted cereals, bowls, spoons, and glasses. Keep milk, juice, and fresh fruit on one refrigerator shelf within easy reach.

Meals for One

Shopping for food and preparing meals for one person is another challenge that requires thought, planning, and creativity. Most recipes provide four, six, or even eight servings, and not all can be reduced easily. Small sizes of packaged foods may be hard to find or expensive. Buying and preparing large quantities of food can result in a person eating the same food day after day.

One suggestion for getting around this problem is buying bulk foods in just the quantity needed. Another option is sharing large food packages—or even meals—with a friend. Still another is storing as many

Simple one-dish meals such as arroz con pollo—a flavourful blend of seasoned rice and chicken—can save time. What are four other ways of working food preparation into a busy schedule?

foods as possible in single-serving packages. For example, a pound of ground meat might be divided into four patties that can be separately wrapped and frozen.

Some singles slip into poor eating habits because they neglect to plan for and prepare nutritious meals. Cooking and cleaning up a meal may not seem worth the effort for just one person. Here again, management skills can help. The suggestions already given for busy lifestyles can help make meal preparation easier for single people, too.

Even when dining alone, singles should attempt to make mealtime special. Setting an attractive table and enjoying a relaxing meal can be a satisfying and healthful end to a busy day.

Larger packages of meat, which are often more economical, can be divided into single-serving portions and stored in the freezer. Give two other suggestions that people cooking for one might use to plan meals.

Healthy Choices for When You Don't Want to Cook

Canadian households are spending more of their money than ever before on eating out (Statistics Canada, 2003). One reason for this may be that people do not always feel like cooking. Rather than skip a meal or grab something from a vending machine, try some of the suggestions below to help you make wise meal-planning choices if you do not always feel like cooking.

◆ Find restaurants in your area that offer healthy menu choices at a price range that suits your budget.

◆ Purchase foods from the prepared foods section of your local grocery store.

Many grocery stores have salads, rotisserie chickens, and casseroles that are prepared or cooked, and ready to take home.

◆ Take turns cooking by rotating cooking duties with other members of your household or with other groups of friends.

Source: Middlesex-London Health Unit, Nutrition Services (1999).

When Plans Must Change

Life can be unpredictable. Sometimes it becomes necessary to change plans. You may not get home in time to prepare the meal you had planned. Illness or last-minute schedule changes can also disrupt meals.

To prepare for these times, keep a supply of "back-up" foods on hand. Stock up on nutritious, quick-to-prepare foods that are shelf-stable or freezer-ready. Some basic items to consider are non-fat dry milk; canned chicken, tuna, and salmon; canned beans; and frozen portions of cooked dry beans, rice, and pasta. Set aside a few recipes or menus planned around your back-up foods. If the unexpected happens, you'll be prepared.

INTERNET CONNECTS

www.mcgrawhill.ca/links/food
To learn more about meal planning ideas for one person, go to the web site above for *Food for Today, First Canadian Edition,* to see where to go next.

Basic Meal Planning

Resources for Meals

What resources are involved in meal planning and preparation?

◆ **Time and energy.** If time or energy for meal preparation is limited, plan a meal that's simple to fix. You might look for a quick and easy recipe or think about using convenience foods along with fresh ones.

◆ **Food choices and availability.** Supermarkets offer an amazing variety of food. Still, your choices may be limited. Some foods are seasonal, especially fresh fruits. Your food store may not carry the items needed to prepare a special recipe. You might have to substitute an ingredient or choose another recipe.

◆ **Money.** Most people have a food budget, and with careful planning, you can stretch your food dollars. It is also useful to know the cost of ingredients so that you can find recipes that fit within your food budget. See details on food budgeting on page 166.

◆ **Preparation skills.** If you are just learning to cook, choose simple recipes that you can prepare with confidence. As you develop your skills, you can choose more complex recipes.

◆ **Equipment.** When you find a new recipe you think you might like, consider whether you have the necessary tools and equipment. If you don't, think about other equipment you might use. For example, a chicken stir-fry dish could be cooked in a skillet instead of a wok.

Using resources wisely often means making trade-offs. For instance, a microwave oven lets you use one resource (equipment) to save another (time). Cooking with convenience foods also saves time but may cost more than cooking meals from scratch. You must decide which is more important to you, time or money.

◆ **With practice, you can plan meals that are simple and delicious.** Identify two factors to think about when planning a meal.

Meal Appeal

Usually, meal planning begins with choosing a main course. Then you add side dishes that will complement it.

When selecting a main course, think about **meal appeal**—the characteristics that make a meal appetizing and enjoyable. In particular, consider:

◆ **Colour.** Think of your dinner plate as an artist's palette. Plan meals that include an array of colours. Colourful fruits and vegetables, for example, can help brighten any meal.

◆ **Shape and size.** Food is most appealing when the shapes and sizes vary. For example, cut carrots into strips and tomatoes into quarters. To vary the shape, chop, dice, cube, serve whole, or cut food with decorative cutters.

◆ **Flavour and aroma.** Try to avoid using foods with similar flavours or aromas in one meal. If all the foods are strongly flavoured—for example, spicy chili with garlic bread—the combination can clash. What type of bread would be better suited to this dish? Why?

◆ **Texture. Texture** is the way food feels when you chew it—for example, soft or hard, crisp or chewy. A meal should include a variety of textures. For example, with a soft main dish, such as pasta, you might serve a crisp tossed salad.

◆ **Planning for eye appeal is critical.** Which of these two meals would you rather eat?

◆ **Temperature.** If you were planning lunch for a cold winter day, steaming hot soup would be more welcome than a chilled salad. Keep meal appeal in mind when you serve the food, too. Hot foods should be piping hot and cold foods crisply chilled. To be sure they stay that way, serve hot and cold foods on separate plates.

Food Costs and Budgeting

Why Budget?

To plan meals, you need to have an essential resource—money. The amount of money you have to spend on food will determine what items you choose to buy. Unless you have an unlimited supply of money, you will need to budget.

A **budget** is a plan for managing your money in order to cover the costs of life's necessities. Budgeting involves looking at your income and deciding how much money to set aside for food, housing, clothing, transportation, health care, savings, and other uses.

Food expenses make up a significant portion of most family and personal budgets. For example, the average Canadian household spends about 11 percent of its budget on food (Statistics Canada, 2002). A lower-income family may spend a greater percentage on food simply because the total income is less. The challenge for any family is meeting nutrient needs without spending more than the budget allows.

Factors Affecting Food Expenditures

The amount of money spent on food varies according to your personal or family resources, goals, and priorities. Other factors that affect the amount of money a family spends on food include:

◆ Total family income.

◆ The number of family members. The larger a family is, the more it will need to spend.

◆ The age of family members. It costs more to feed growing teens than other members. By the same token, it costs less to feed aging relatives who may be part of the household.

◆ Knowing the cost of food items can help you choose recipes that suit your budget. Which foods are higher priced and which are lower priced?

- Food prices in your area at various times of the year.

- The amount of food eaten away from home.

- Time and skills available for food preparation.

- The amount of food wasted. Food waste may occur if a food was not stored or prepared properly.

- The type of foods or meals that are eaten. Meals that are based on higher priced menu items, such as steak, cost more than lower budget dishes, such as a lentil soup.

If someone in your family enjoys cooking, you might spend less money by eating more home-prepared meals. However, if busy schedules make convenience a family priority, you may spend more money on convenience foods. Every family has different priorities, so food budgets will vary.

Using a Food Budget

Whether you spend a little or a lot, you can benefit from following a food budget. It can show you whether you may be wasting money—or spending it wisely. It can also help you think about your food choices and determine whether they are wise ones.

Keeping a Spending Record

Setting up a food budget can be simple. To begin, analyse how much you spend on food now. Keep a record of all the food you buy for two typical weeks. Divide your record into food bought at the food store and food eaten out. Food eaten out includes take-out food, delivered food, and foods bought from vending machines. Do not include non-food supplies in your list, such as paper products, even if you buy them at the supermarket.

Add up the expenses for groceries and foods eaten out for the two weeks. Divide the total by two to get the average you spend per week.

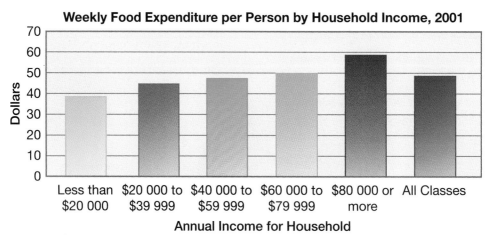

Weekly Food Expenditure per Person by Household Income, 2001

Source: Statistics Canada (2003).

1. Compare the amount of money that is spent on food per person for each income group.

2. Suggest reasons for the differences in the amount of money that is spent on food per person for each income group.

3. How much would it cost on average to feed a family of four if the family made $58 000 per year?

Setting a Budget Amount

Use the information from your spending record when you plan your budget. What percentage of your income are you spending on food? Are you comfortable with the amount you are currently spending? If so, plan to spend a similar amount in future weeks. If you want to plan on spending less, set an amount that's slightly lower. Be realistic. If you set an amount that's unrealistically low, you'll find it hard to stay within your budget. Use charts, such as the one opposite, as a guide to compare the amount of money that the average Canadian family spends on food in relation to the amount of money that your family spends on food.

Sticking with Your Budget

Once you've set an amount for your food budget, stay within those guidelines. Continue keeping records of how much you spend on groceries and foods eaten out. You will likely spend more some weeks than others, such as when you buy staples or special items. If you have any money left over, keep it as a reserve in your food budget for emergencies.

Evaluating the Food Budget

After you have used your budget for several weeks, take a look at what you've spent. On the average, were you able to stay within your budget? If you were not, you have two options —increase the amount budgeted or reduce your spending.

Use your spending record to evaluate your food purchases. If you made only basic purchases—with no "frills"—and you haven't eaten out, you may not be allowing enough money for food. Take a look at your budget again. Perhaps you can cut back in some other spending category to allow more money for food.

◆ Keeping track of your food spending for a period of time helps you decide on a realistic amount for your food budget. Why is it important to set a realistic food budget?

On the other hand, you may decide that you are spending more than you would like on food. If so, planning and money management can help you reduce your spending.

Reducing Your Spending

You can save money even before you begin spending it by planning your meals with your budget in mind. Here are some helpful tips to guide you:

◆ **Look for supermarket advertisements.** Newspaper ads and flyers can tell you about special prices on nutritious foods that your family can enjoy. Compare prices among stores.

- **Choose economical main dishes.** Meat can be an expensive part of a meal. You can save money by serving more beans with grains and other plant-based protein foods. If you want to include meat, fish, or poultry in meals, use a smaller amount in combination with vegetables, grains, and fruits.

- **Reduce food waste.** As you plan meals, think about how much your family eats. Prepare appropriate amounts of food for each meal. Safely store any leftovers for future use. Practise portion control when serving the food.

- **Prepare simple meals at home more often.** Homemade meals usually cost less than convenience meals or food eaten out. Your family may find it worthwhile to take the extra time needed to prepare meals at home. Sharing meal preparation tasks can cut down on preparation time and bring family members closer together.

- **Allow some flexibility in meal planning.** Be ready to take advantage of good prices on items such as seasonal fresh fruits and vegetables. When it's in season, fresh produce is often less expensive—and may taste better.

- **Choose less expensive forms of food.** Compare prices between different forms of foods (fresh, frozen, canned, dried) to find the best buy. Lower cost doesn't mean lower nutritional value or less flavour.

Careful shoppers find ways to get more for less.

Costing Menu Items

Once you have determined how much money you have to spend on food, you will need to cost menu items and recipes to find out if they are feasible to include in your menu plans. To determine the cost of a meal, you need to find out the cost of each item on the menu. This includes the cost of each ingredient that is part of a recipe. Follow the steps below to determine the cost of a meal or recipe:

- **Cost per serving versus the purchase cost.** When costing a meal, it is important to note that there will be some food waste. Fruits, vegetables, and meats are food items that have the most food waste. The amount that you pay for these items will differ compared to the actual portion of food that is edible. This will affect the cost per serving of your meal or recipe. An example is a recipe that asks for 500 mL (1 lb.) of cooked, diced chicken. You decide to use a whole chicken breast with the bone in. After cooking the chicken breast and dicing it, you find that it takes 1 kg (2 lb.) of uncooked whole chicken breast to get 500 mL (1 lb.) of cooked, diced chicken. Therefore, when costing a recipe, take into consideration the purchase price versus the amount of meat that is edible after cooking and removing the bone. In this particular example, if you chose to purchase boneless, skinless chicken, you will not have this consideration in your calculations. However, the cost per gram will be much higher. You need to decide then if you are willing to compromise money for time.

Use fruit, vegetable, and meat buying guides to assist you in determining how much product you need to purchase for a recipe. These guides will also help you convert the volume amounts into weight amounts. Buying guides are often in the appendix of a cookbook.

◆ **Converting measurements.** Finding the cost per serving requires converting the measurements because most fresh and frozen fruits, vegetables, and meats are sold by weight. You will need to convert the volume amount (typically in mL or actual number of items) into a weight amount (typically in grams). Once again, buying guides will help you convert volume to weight amounts.

One example shown in a Menu Costing Table is as follows:

The buyer's guide suggests that 1 whole mushroom = 50 mL (2 oz), sliced mushrooms =16.5 g (0.5 oz). If you require 300 mL (10 oz) of mushrooms, then divide this amount by 50 mL (2 oz), which equals 6. This determines that you need to purchase 6 whole mushrooms.

To convert the number of mushrooms into an amount by weight, perform the following calculation:

6 whole mushrooms × 16.5 g (0.5 oz) (unit weight/mushroom) = 99 g (3 oz) (number of mushrooms needed by weight)

◆ **Cost per unit.** For all ingredients, you will need to determine how much each menu item or ingredient in a recipe costs. To do this you must find out the **cost per unit**, often referred to as the **unit cost**. The unit cost or cost per unit is the amount of money that each unit of a particular food item costs. A unit may by a volume amount (mL or L), an amount by weight (g or kg), or the number of an item (1 bunch, 1 head).

purchase cost of the food item ÷ total quantity = cost per unit.

The following is an example from the Meal Costing Chart on page 171. Canned peaches are sold by volume. Therefore, the unit to be determined is mL. The cost of the canned peaches is $2.89 per 796 mL can. The calculation is $2.89 ÷ 796 mL = $0.0036 per mL.

◆ **Ingredient cost.** To determine the cost for each ingredient used in the recipe, multiply the cost per unit by the amount needed.

cost per unit × unit amount needed = total cost

For example, the canned peaches cost $0.004 per unit mL and you need 500 mL. The calculation is $0.004 × 500 mL = $1.80. Therefore, the total cost is $1.80.

Work Plan and Schedule
Get ready to cook
7:00   Set table
7:10   Mix juice and refrigerate
7:20   Turn on oven to preheat
7:25   Grease baking dish
       Mix batter; dip bread slices;
7:30   put in baking dish
       Put French toast in oven; set timer
       for 8 min. Start coffee
7:40   Start preparing cherry mixture
7:45   Turn French toast, set timer for 8 min.
7:48   continue preparing cherry mixture
       Remove French toast from oven, put on
7:56   platter; put cherry topping in serving dish
       Pour juice and milk
7:58   Serve coffee; breakfast is ready!
8:00

◆ **Ingredient cost total.** If one of your menu items is a recipe, then you must add together the cost of each ingredient to get the total cost of the recipe. It is important to determine the exact cost of each serving in a recipe. For example, if you are doubling a recipe then freezing the leftovers, you must take this into account.

To determine the exact amount of a recipe follow these formulas:

i) total cost of recipe ÷ recipe yield = cost/serving

Example: $7.48 (Total cost of recipe) ÷ 6 (Recipe yield) = $1.25 (Cost/serving)

ii) cost/serving × number of servings required = total cost of recipe

Example: $1.25 (Cost/serving) × 4 (Number of servings) = $5 (Total cost of recipe)

After you have determined the cost of the recipe required for this particular meal, add together the cost of all the food items in the menu. This will be the total cost of your menu for this particular meal.

Weekly Meal Planning

Most people find it helpful to plan meals for a week or more at a time. Long-range planning has several advantages. It cuts down on time spent deciding what to serve every day. It promotes a greater variety of meals and helps you get the most for your food dollar. It prevents extra trips to the supermarket for forgotten items. It also makes food preparation more organized and efficient.

When planning a week's worth of meals, use what you have already learned about planning menus. Here are some additional tips:

◆ Aim for balanced nutrition and variety in meals and snacks over the course of the week. Check to see that the menus for each day provide enough servings according to *Canada's Food Guide to Healthy Eating*.

◆ Set aside a regular time and place for meal planning.

◆ Ask family members about their plans for the week. Knowing when family members need to eat early, late, or away from home can affect the menus and recipes you choose.

◆ Check the refrigerator, freezer, and kitchen cabinets to see what foods you have on hand. Think of ways to use these foods (especially perishables, such as leftovers and fresh fruits and vegetables).

◆ Check newspaper ads to see what foods are on sale.

◆ Plan nutritious snacks as well as meals.

INTERNET CONNECTS

www.mcgrawhill.ca/links/food
To learn more about planning a meal that will meet all your nutritional needs, go to the web site above for *Food for Today, First Canadian Edition*, to see where to go next.

Once you have the menus for the week, you can use them to make your shopping list. A shopping list can help you manage money as well as time.

When you first try it, planning a week's worth of meals may seem time-consuming. However, it becomes easier with practice. Once you have planned meals for several months, you can use them over and over again. In the long run, weekly planning is well worth the initial investment of time.

Cost of a Meal for a Family of Four

Ingredients	Quantity of Item		Unit Purchase**		Cost Per Unit**	Cost of Item**
Item	**Quantity purchased to get the amount needed***	**Serving Amount Needed****	**Cost**	**Unit**		
Baked chicken	No waste—purchased boneless, skinless breasts	100 g × 4 = 400 g	$14.39	1000 g	$0.014	$5.60
Mushrooms,	sliced and sautéed 1 mushroom = 50 mL = 16.5 g; therefore, purchase 6 mushrooms = 300 mL = 99 g	75 mL/person × 4 = 300 mL	$6.59	1000 g	$0.007	$0.69
Canola oil	1 bottle = 1.89 L = 1890 mL	30 mL total for sautéeing	$4.59	189 mL	$0.0024	$0.07
Wild rice	325 mL uncooked rice = 1 L cooked rice = 300 g uncooked rice	250 mL × 4 = 1L	$1.99	450 g	$0.0044	$1.32
Seasoning Mix for rice	Use 1 package for making rice for 4 servings.	—	$1.99	—	—	$1.99
Steamed broccoli	1 bunch = 500 g = 1000 mL; therefore need 0.5 bunch = 250 g = 500 mL	125 mL/person × 4	$1.69	1 bunch	$1.69	$0.85
Sliced tomatoes	1 tomato = 4 thick slices = 210 g; therefore need 2 tomatoes = 8 slices = 420 g	2 slices of tomato /person × 4 = 8 slices	$4.39	1000 g	$0.0044	$1.85
Canned sliced peaches	1 can = 796 mL	125 mL/person × 4 = 500 mL	$2.89	796 mL	$0.0036	$1.80
Milk	4 L bag = 4000 mL	250 mL/person × 4 = 1000 mL	$5.89	1000 mL	$0.0015	$1.50

Total Cost of Meal $15.67 *

* Quantity purchased is the amount that is needed to get the serving amount or edible amount required. Refer to buying guides to get an estimate of amount needed and to convert volume amounts to amounts by weight.
** Serving amount needed × Cost per unit = Cost of item. Make certain that unit measurements match (for example, cost per unit is in grams, therefore serving amount needs to be in grams).

Source: Chart outline adapted from Johnson and Wales University Curriculum Committee (2002).

Sample Weekly Menu Plan

	Breakfast	Lunch	Dinner	Snacks	Memos
MONDAY	Bran Cereal Sliced Bananas Rye Toast Milk/Coffee	(Packed) Turkey Sandwich Carrot/Celery Sticks Pretzels Apple Milk (buy)	Spaghetti and Meatballs Tossed Salad Garlic Bread Milk/Coffee Italian Ice	Fresh Fruits or Vegetables Trail Mix Cranberry Juice	Krystal—not home for dinner, swim team banquet.
TUESDAY	French Toast Kiwi Halves Milk/Coffee	(Packed) Peanut Butter–Whole Wheat Sandwich Broccoli/Carrots Pear Milk (buy)	Vegetarian Chili Corn Tortillas Spinach Salad Milk/Coffee Sliced Fruit	Fresh Fruits or Vegetables Popcorn Vegetable Juice	Everyone home for dinner.
WEDNESDAY	Bagels with Non-fat Cream Cheese Orange Slices Milk/Coffee	Mom and Dad—lunch out Jason and Krystal— school lunch	Baked Chicken Brown Rice Broccoli Spears Whole Wheat Rolls Coleslaw Milk/Coffee	Fresh Fruits or Vegetables Pretzels	Dad—late for dinner, grocery shopping after work.
THURSDAY	Oatmeal with Raisins Whole Wheat Toast Milk/Coffee	(Packed) Leftover Chicken Sandwiches Carrot/Celery Sticks Banana Milk (buy)	Pork and Vegetable Stir-fry Rice Milk Canteloupe	Popcorn Strawberry Frozen Yogurt	Jason's basketball game—eat early.
FRIDAY	Assorted Cereals Bananas Whole Wheat Toast with Fruit Spread Milk/Coffee	(Packed) Leftover Chili Red and Green Pepper Sticks Corn Chips Mixed Fruit Cup Milk (buy)	Take-out Pizza Tossed Salad Mixed Fruit Juice	Fresh Fruits with Plain Yogurt Brownie	Jason—eating out with friends.

	Breakfast	Lunch	Dinner	Snacks	Memos
SATURDAY	Cheese, Vegetable, and Ham Omelet Whole Wheat Toast Orange Juice Milk/Coffee	Hearty Vegetable Soup Multigrain Rolls Fruit Milk	Grilled Burgers with Buns Potato Salad Sliced Tomatoes Milk/Coffee	Popcorn Flavoured Yogurt Mixed Fruit Juice	Rob and Kara coming over for dinner.
SUNDAY	Bran Muffins Grapefruit Milk/Coffee	Baked Ham Sweet Potatoes Broccoli Fruit Salad Milk Angel Food Cake	Sandwiches Tossed Green Salad Yogurt	Fresh Fruits or Vegetables Rice Cakes	Plan next week's menus.

Time Management and Teamwork

Time Management in the Kitchen

Once you have considered the special needs of the people you are cooking for, determined the resources you have, and devised a menu that is nutritious and pleasing to the eye, you are ready for the last step: preparing a work plan and schedule. Strategy, speed, and skill are the keys to time management in the kitchen. It is essential that prior to cooking and serving a meal, you are organized. Follow the suggestions on the next few pages to help you manage your time in the kitchen.

◆ Preparing a meal as a family is a great way to spend time together. Being organized is essential when working in the kitchen, especially when several people are working together. How can you use "Organizational Skills" (p. 177) to help organize the task of preparing a meal as a family?

Strategy: A Work Plan

Food preparation involves more than choosing a recipe and starting to work. Rather, it involves mapping out all the procedures and tasks that play a part in your recipe or meal. Do you have the ingredients and equipment you need? Are you familiar with the cooking techniques called for in the recipes? Can you complete the food preparation and clean-up in the time available?

A smart strategy is to always start with a **work plan**. Basically, this is a list of all the tasks required to complete the recipe and an estimate of how long each task will take.

Developing a Work Plan

Recipes and package directions often provide help in estimating time. The directions on a spaghetti package, for example, may tell you that the product requires nine minutes to cook. As an effective manager, however, you will need to draw on your ability to think critically to help you identify other tasks and find or estimate the time each requires—for example, boiling water for the pasta, chopping vegetables for the sauce, and cleaning salad greens. A good rule for beginning cooks is to allow more time than you think

Pizza Snacks

2 English muffins, split in halves
125 mL (½ cup) prepared pizza sauce
15 mL (1 tbsp.) chopped green pepper
15 mL (1 tbsp.) sliced mushrooms
15 mL (1 tbsp.) chopped onions
125 mL (½) cup shredded low-fat mozzarella cheese

1. Place English muffin halves, crust-side down, on broiler pan.
2. Spread each muffin half with 30 mL (2 tbsp.) pizza sauce.
3. Top with green pepper, mushrooms, and onion.
4. Sprinkle each muffin half with 30 mL (2 tbsp.) cheese.
5. Position broiler pan so the tops of the muffins are about 12 cm (4 inches) from the heat. Turn on broiler.
6. Broil until cheese is bubbly, about 2 to 4 minutes. Remove immediately and serve hot.
NOTE: Broiling time may vary.

Yield: 4 small pizzas

Work Plan—Pizza Snacks

Task	Approx. Time
Set table.	5 min.
Gather ingredients and equipment. Scrub hands.	8 min.
Split English muffins in half.	2 min.
Chop green pepper and onion. Slice mushrooms.	7 min.
Shred cheese.	3 min.
Put muffins on broiler pan and put on toppings.	3 min.
Broil until cheese is bubbly.	6 min.
Prepare to serve.	1 min.
	Total: 35 min.

you will need. As your skills improve, you will be able to work faster and make more accurate time estimates.

Look at the recipe for "Pizza Snacks" opposite and the work plan Naomi made for it above. Note that some of the first steps on the work plan come from the list of ingredients, not the assembly directions. Naomi saw from this list that the tasks would include halving the English muffins, shredding the cheese, and chopping and slicing the toppings.

Even before these steps comes the **pre-preparation**, tasks done before actual recipe preparation. In Naomi's case, these tasks included setting the table, washing the green pepper, peeling the onion and measuring out the other ingredients.

To cut down on last-minute tasks, consider whether foods can safely be prepared early. For instance, you could assemble a tossed salad (except for the dressing) and then put it in the refrigerator. Setting the table can also be done ahead of time, or you might plan on asking a helper to do it for you.

A successful work plan might even include important tasks like washing your hands and setting the oven temperature. Including such steps ensures that a new cook won't forget to do them.

Speed: A Schedule

Once you have a work plan, you can use it to make a schedule that shows when each task must be started. If you have developed a sound work plan, making a schedule should be a snap. Simply do the following:

1. Consult your work plan for the estimated time each task will take to complete.

2. Add these times to find the total preparation time.

3. Subtract the total preparation time from the time you want the food to be ready. This step tells you what time to start.

Naomi's estimated total preparation time is 35 minutes. She plans to serve the pizzas at 6:30, so she needs to start at 5:55. Naomi decides to chop and slice the vegetables first, shred the cheese next, and then split the

Schedule—Pizza Snacks

6:00   Get ready.
6:08   Split English muffins.
6:10   Chop and slice vegetables.
6:17   Shred cheese.
6:20   Assemble pizzas.
6:23   Broil pizzas.
6:29   Prepare to serve.
6:30   Serve pizzas.

English muffins. For this recipe, the remaining tasks match the order of the recipe directions.

Naomi has planned to use her time efficiently by cleaning up while the pizzas broil. Note that this is referred to as **dovetailing**, or fitting different tasks together smoothly. If you schedule duties simultaneously, remember to check on foods that are cooking or set a timer so that they do not overcook.

When you are learning to prepare food, it's a good idea to make a work plan and schedule every time. Eventually, you may need to do so only when you prepare a new dish or plan a special meal.

Skill: Working Efficiently

As you gain food-preparation experience, you will notice an improvement in your skills. You'll be able to complete some tasks in half the time they once took. Yet there is more to efficiency than just experience. Even a beginner can be efficient by knowing how to save time and energy. Here are some keys to efficiency:

- ◆ **Organize the kitchen.** Always store items in the same place so that you won't waste time looking for them.

- ◆ **Learn to use equipment properly.** Take the time to read the owner's manuals for the small and large appliances in the kitchen. Besides learning to use them safely, you may find they can be helpful in ways you didn't realize. Practise using your tools until you are comfortable with them.

- ◆ **Look for ways to simplify.** Could a different piece of equipment complete a task more quickly? Would a different cooking method be more efficient? Thinking through your options can help you save time and energy.

- ◆ **Gather all equipment and ingredients first.** Assembling everything you will need before you start has several advantages. First, you won't discover halfway through a recipe that you are out of an ingredient you need. Second, it will be easier to check whether you used every ingredient. Third, and perhaps most important, you will have everything you need right at your fingertips.

- ◆ **Dovetail tasks.** Not every preparation step needs your undivided attention. You could, for example, make a tossed salad while chicken pieces are roasting. Dovetailing is especially important when you are preparing a whole meal. If you plan to dovetail tasks, be sure to adjust your time schedule.

- ◆ **Clean up as you work.** Before you start work, fill the sink or a dishpan with hot, sudsy water. Whenever you have a few free moments, wash the equipment you have finished using. Also keep a clean, wet dishcloth handy to wipe up spills as they happen. Put away ingredients as you finish with them. Your final clean-up will take much less time.

Organizational Skills

Whether you are working in the kitchen, producing an assignment, or performing a household task, developing organization skills is a key ingredient to help your life run more smoothly. If you are organized, you are prepared. To develop good organizational skills, apply these five principles of organization to all your tasks.

1. Divide it.

Divide tasks into smaller steps. This will help you feel less overwhelmed about the assignment. For example, you have a Social Science research assignment that involves interviewing people from a different generation. Divide the assignment into the following parts: prepare interview questions, conduct interview, analyse interviewees' responses, and prepare written conclusions.

2. List it.

Make a list of all the tasks that you need to accomplish that day. Include school assignments, errands, household duties, and appointments to be made.

3. Cluster it.

Review the list that you made for the day and cluster similar tasks together. This will help you save time and energy. For example, if you are conducting an interview for your Social Science research assignment with someone who lives beside the mall, skim your list to see if any of your errands can be done at the mall.

4. Plan it.

Plan future commitments, such as appointments, assignments, meals, and social events, by jotting them onto a calendar or in an appointment book that displays the whole month. Being able to see a schedule of events for the whole month will help you prepare for busy times of the month. For example, if you have two assignments due on the same day, then you could adjust the calendar by moving up the due date for one of the assignments. This time-management strategy will prevent you from trying to rush and finish two assignments at once.

5. Organize it.

To minimize the mess of papers and clutter that can accumulate, use organizers such as binders with dividers, bins, and labels, to help you store similar items in one place. Using organizing equipment will help you know where to put things and where to find them. For example, group all of your tests from one subject into a section of your binder. Use a divider to separate them from the rest of the work in that subject. Label the divider "Tests."

Source: Adapted from Myers, Barbara (2003).

Teamwork in the School Kitchen

In the foods lab at school, you work as part of a team. You also work against the clock. Every lab activity needs to be completed—including clean-up and evaluation—within a limited period of time. Success depends on organization and co-operation.

◆ **Organizing the job.** As a team, you and your classmates need to start with a basic work plan. When you plan your schedule, decide not only when each task should start, but also who will do it. With every team member working, several tasks can be accomplished at the same time. You may want to use a schedule that has five-minute blocks of time down the left and columns with each person's name across the top. That way, the schedule shows what each person should be doing throughout the lab period. Be sure to consider work space and equipment as you plan your schedule.

◆ **Working together.** Foods labs, like many school and work situations, depend on everyone doing his or her job. Be responsible for the tasks you have agreed to take on. Work quickly and efficiently. Remember that accuracy is essential. If you have a question or a problem, ask another team member for help. Be willing to help out when someone else falls behind or makes a mistake. Keeping a sense of humour will help the work go more smoothly.

◆ **Cleaning up.** Cleaning as you go will make end-of-class clean-up easier and faster. Be sure all equipment is clean and dry. Most important, return everything to its proper place. Otherwise, you will slow down the next team using the kitchen. Be sure all work surfaces and appliances are clean and that you have disposed of waste properly.

◆ **Evaluating the results.** Labs usually involve the evaluation of both the finished product and the preparation process. Thoughtfulness and honesty are important for both. This is especially true if the food did not turn out as expected, if you experienced preparation problems, or if your

◆ Dovetailing tasks—for example, preparing a salad while boiling water to cook spaghetti—can help you streamline the preparation of a meal. What skill for food choices comes into play when you prepare a meal in this fashion?

team did not work together well. Think about what you learned from the experience and what you might do differently the next time.

Teamwork at Home

In many ways, teamwork in your kitchen at home is as important as it is in the foods lab. Organization, co-operation, and clean-up are again the watchwords of a successful effort.

Whether you are responsible for helping prepare family meals on a regular basis or just occasionally, you need to remember that these can be fun times. You might help a younger brother or sister learn a new cooking skill or just take time to talk with a family member. When you have more time, try out a new recipe together. Daily food preparation can be a chore or an opportunity to build togetherness. It all depends on your attitude.

◆ **Mealtime is an important event of the day for families.** What can you do to make the atmosphere at mealtime a positive experience?

Serving Family Meals

Family Meals

In today's fast-paced society, finding time to sit down and enjoy a meal as a family can be a challenge. The good news is that more and more families are meeting this challenge. Whether it is only once a week for dinner or each day at breakfast, eating together is important to a family's social health. Family meals are a time when everyone can relax, enjoy food, talk with one another, catch up on family news, and just have fun.

To make the most of family meals, you need to follow a few simple guidelines. These include keeping a positive mealtime atmosphere and paying attention to the table's appearance.

FYI

Mealtime Atmosphere

Sierra's family keeps the TV on during dinner. Dinner at Mark's house often erupts into complaints and accusations involving Mark, his sister, and their parents. What is wrong with these scenarios? Both families do not realize the importance of a positive mealtime atmosphere. An upbeat atmosphere can be as essential to your family's health as nutritious food.

Mealtime isn't the time to complain, criticize, or air the day's problems. Keep family meals fun. Focus on the pleasure of eating and of each other's company. What interesting topics can you think of to discuss with your family?

Even when you are eating alone, it is important to sit down and take time to enjoy yourself and your food. People who read or watch television as they eat pay little attention to what and how much they eat. They often eat more than they would if they relaxed, concentrated on the food, and enjoyed the meal.

Setting the Table

How the table looks at mealtime can be as significant as how the people around it behave. Start by making the eating area inviting. Be sure the table is free of papers and other clutter. Place a simple decoration on or near the table—for example, a vase with a single garden flower or a few interesting seashells.

◆ **Place settings can be formal or simple, depending on the meal to be served.** Devise a menu for a formal meal. Tell what would go on each serving piece shown in the illustration on the left.

Table settings include the following components:

- **Tableware. Tableware** includes any items used for serving and eating food. Types of tableware are dinnerware (plates, bowls, and cups), flatware (knives, forks, and spoons), glassware, and "linens" (anything from a cloth tablecloth and napkins to wipe-clean placemats and paper serviettes).

- **Place setting.** The pieces of tableware used by one person to eat a meal are called a **place setting.**

- **Serving pieces.** Platters, large bowls, and other tableware used for serving food are known as **serving pieces.**

- **Cover.** The arrangement of a place setting for one person is called a **cover.** The rules for this arrangement are based on both tradition and practicality.

Table-Setting Basics

Knowing how to set a table will help you serve family meals, entertain guests, and feel comfortable when you eat out.

The cover is usually on the table before people sit down to eat. The plate goes in the centre of the cover, about 2.5 cm (1 inch) from the edge of the table.

Arrange flatware in the order in which it is used, starting at the outside and working in toward the centre. Forks go to the left of the plate, knives to the right. Place spoons to the right of the knives. If you have both a soup spoon and a teaspoon, you'd probably use the soup spoon first. Place it to the right of the teaspoon.

Place a beverage glass just above the tip of the dinner knife. The cup and saucer or mug go to the right of the spoon, about 2.5 cm (1 inch) from the edge of the table. The napkin is usually placed under or to the left of the fork.

Settings for Family Meals

Most families choose simple table settings for everyday meals. For most meals, you need at least a dinner plate, fork, knife, teaspoon, and beverage glass. Add a cup and saucer or a mug if a hot beverage is being served. If salad is on the menu, add a salad plate or bowl. For soup, you'll need a bowl and a soup spoon.

At home, the same fork can be used to eat both a salad and the main dish. For a formal meal, separate forks would be used.

Serving Family Meals

In Ray's family, serving bowls are passed around the table, and everyone takes whatever she or he wants. Julie's dad prefers to dish food onto plates at the stove. These two most common styles of serving food are known as *family service* and *plate service*.

Family Service

In family service, the cover is set with the necessary tableware. The food is placed in serving dishes and passed around the table, with people helping themselves. It's less confusing if all the foods are passed in the same direction, generally to the right.

Sometimes, if a serving plate is too hot or a roast or ham is sliced at the table, a family member serves the food at the table. In that case, the dinner plates are stacked in front of the server. The food is placed on a plate and passed along to the diners, who then help themselves to other foods in the meal.

The main advantage of family service is that people can serve themselves the amount they want. This is especially helpful for those who are limited in the kinds or amounts of food they can eat. There are, however, several disadvantages. The hot food left on the table in serving dishes may cool to room temperature quickly. This allows harmful bacteria to multiply. Family service also can make it difficult to practise portion control, which can lead to overeating. A third disadvantage is that excess food left on a plate must be thrown away, which wastes food and money.

Plate Service

Plate service is generally used for family meals and in restaurants. The table is set without dinner plates, though space is left on each cover for the plate (and salad bowl if a salad is to be served). Food is placed on the plates directly from the containers in which it was cooked, and the plates are then brought to the table. The food remaining in pans can be kept hot on the stove or in the oven. The only exception is salad. This may be passed around the table in a serving bowl so that people can help themselves.

Besides cutting down on waste and bacteria build-up, and discouraging the tendency to overeat, plate service saves clean-up time. Because no serving dishes are used, there are none to wash.

General Guidelines

Place breads and rolls on a plate or in a basket, and pass it around the table. If a basket is used, line it with a napkin. Diners can place bread or rolls on the edge of their dinner plates. At more formal meals, provide a small bread-and-butter plate above the forks.

Serve salads either in individual bowls at each place setting or in a serving bowl to be passed around the table. If possible, serve salad dressing separately so that people can use the amount they want.

Serve dessert after the dinner plates, salad bowls, and serving dishes have been cleared from the table. If forks or spoons are needed, bring them to the table with the dessert.

◆ **Some families use plate service at home. How is plate service different from other ways of serving family meals?**

◆ Being invited to someone's home for a meal can be a real pleasure. However, you may not know the family's table etiquette. What basic rules of etiquette should you follow when in this situation?

Mealtime Etiquette

Table Etiquette

Aaron and Kayla are twins, but there is one important difference between them: table etiquette. **Table etiquette** is the courtesy shown by using good manners at meals.

Good table manners help put you at ease in social situations. They can also be an asset in the working world. Many business transactions take place over meals. Often, when companies consider an applicant for a job, the interview may include a meal. This gives the interviewer a chance to observe how the applicant would act during similar business situations.

Basic Etiquette

Here are some general etiquette guidelines:

Before Eating

◆ Place the napkin on your lap before you start eating. Don't tuck it into a belt or under your chin.

◆ If there are six or fewer people at the table, wait until everyone is served before you begin to eat. If there are more, wait until two or three have been served. Alternatively, take the host's lead and begin eating after he or she does.

◆ You may reach for serving dishes as long as you don't have to lean across your neighbour. If you can't reach the food easily, politely ask the person nearest the food to pass it to you.

While Eating

◆ Don't talk with your mouth full. Finish chewing, swallow the food, and then talk.

◆ If you're having problems getting foods (such as peas) onto your fork, push them on with a piece of bread. If you have no bread, use the tip of your dinner knife to push the food onto the fork.

- Break bread into smaller pieces before buttering or eating it.

- If you're dining at someone's home and aren't sure what to do, use your host's actions as a guide.

- Cut food into small pieces for eating. If you try to eat large pieces, you may have difficulty chewing and may choke.

- Sit up straight when you eat, and don't lean on your elbows.

- If you must cough or sneeze, cover your mouth and nose with a handkerchief or a napkin. If your coughing continues, excuse yourself and leave the table.

After Eating

- Never comb your hair or apply make-up while at the table.

- Don't leave a spoon in your cup. You might knock the cup over if your hand accidentally hits the spoon.

- When you have finished eating, place your fork and knife on your plate, pointing toward the centre.

Finally, remember that people from other countries and cultures have table manners that may be different from yours. Respect and accept people with other customs.

Restaurant Etiquette

Restaurant etiquette involves the same good manners that you use anywhere else. Still, there are a few basic guidelines that deal with situations found only in restaurants.

When You Arrive

When you enter a restaurant, you may be asked whether you have a reservation.

◆ **At the end of the meal, place your knife and fork on your plate as shown.** Give two other dos and don'ts of table etiquette.

A **reservation** is an arrangement made ahead of time for a table at a restaurant. When calling, give your name, the number of people in your group, and the time you plan to arrive. If you will be late or decide not to go, call and ask to change or cancel the reservation.

Near the entrance, you may see a checkroom. If you do, leave coats, umbrellas, packages, books, and briefcases. You are expected to tip the attendant.

Unless a sign states otherwise, never seat yourself. A restaurant employee will direct you and your group to a table.

The Meal

Jorge was puzzled by the term *á la carte* on his restaurant menu. Instead of ordering and possibly making a mistake and not getting what he wanted, he asked his server to explain it.

When dining out, don't be afraid to ask a few questions. This can be especially important

◆ When eating at a restaurant, be sure and look at the menu carefully and ask questions before placing an order. What types of questions might be good to ask?

when it comes to the restaurant's pricing policy. Sometimes the price of the entrée, or main dish, includes side dishes such as vegetables and salad. Other restaurants price each item individually (*á la carte*). Knowing the policy can help you avoid an embarrassing and uncomfortable situation.

On occasion, each person in a group will want to pay for his or her own meal. If the group is small, ask the server for separate checks before you order. Alternatively—or if the restaurant's policy is to make out only one check for each table—you might ask the server to figure out the cost for each person.

Restaurants may serve more food than some people can eat. If you have leftover food, such as part of a steak or chicken, ask to have it wrapped up so that you can take it home. Most restaurants have special containers and supply them for diners. This does not apply to all-you-can-eat buffets or salad bars.

In fast-food restaurants, self-serve restaurants, and some delicatessens, customers are expected to clear their own tables after they've eaten. Trays and disposable packaging are deposited in specified containers.

Communicating with Servers

Be polite to servers, whether in a fast-food or an elegant restaurant. Remember, they're working hard to serve you and a number of other people at the same time. Be considerate and patient, especially during busy periods.

To call your server, catch his or her attention by calmly raising your hand. If necessary, ask one of the other servers to get your server. Never call out or disturb other diners.

◆ If the server takes care of the payment of the cheque, the money or credit card should be given to the server. Name two ways the tip can be handled in this situation.

Paying the Cheque

At the meal's end, the server will bring you the cheque. In some restaurants you pay your server. In others you take the cheque to the cashier for payment. If you're not sure what to do, ask the server.

Look over the cheque carefully and add up the items. If there is a mistake, quietly point it out to the server. The server should correct any mistake or explain why the amount shown is right.

In most restaurants you are expected to leave a **gratuity** (grah-TOO-uh-tee). Also known as a "tip," this is extra money given to the server in appreciation for good service. Servers rely on tips as an important part of their pay. Sometimes the tip has been added in on the cheque. A standard amount to tip is 15 percent of the pretax food bill.

Methods of Payment

When paying for a meal in cash, leave the money, including the tip, on the table or in the tray on which the cheque was presented. If you use a credit card, the server or cashier will process the card and hand you the credit card slip. Again, go over the math to be sure the totals are correct. The slip has a space for a tip. Fill in the amount, add the final total, sign the slip, and hand it back to the server or cashier. Be sure to get your copy of the credit card slip for your records—and don't forget the credit card.

Complaints and Compliments

If you have any complaints about the food, tell the server. If nothing is done, complain to the manager. You can also complain to the manager if the service was poor.

While people rarely hesitate to voice their complaints, few remember to express their appreciation for exceptional food and service. Compliments are just as important to the management as are complaints.

Food Service Manager

Kathy Brown

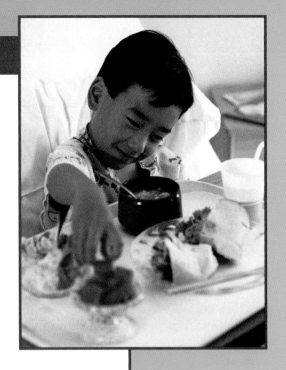

What education is required for your job?

- Bachelor's Degree in Applied Food and Nutrition and a Dietetic internship **or** a College Diploma in Food Service Management and three-to-five years of recent experience in food service.

What skills does a person need to be able to do your job?

- Demonstrated leadership and team building ability with excellent people skills.

- Excellent written and oral communication skills.

- The ability to organize and prioritize appropriately to meet demands and expectations.

- The ability to analyze, problem solve, make recommendations for change, and implement and evaluate programs.

What do you like most about your job?

I like the opportunity and challenge to be creative and innovative—to be continually working to develop new methods and models of delivering service to patients.

What other jobs/job titles have you had in the past?

I have worked as a dietetic assistant, food service supervisor, and administrative supervisor. I have always worked in a hospital.

What advice would you give a person who is considering a career as a Foodservice Manager?

Get as much practical experience as you can in the field. Begin by working as a food handler in an institutional foodservice operation. This is invaluable in helping to really understand the business from an operational perspective as a future manager. Be prepared to work long hours.

Comment on what you see as important issues/trends in food service and nutrition.

It is a challenge to provide high-quality service with shrinking resources. We are also seeing the redesign of the traditional meal service model to alternative meal service styles.

Chapter 9 Review and Activities

Summary

- Sharing meals with family and friends is an ancient custom.
- When planning a meal, take into consideration the individual needs of guests and family members.
- People have different nutrition and energy needs at different stages of life.
- Resources for basic meal planning include: time, food availability, money, preparation skills and equipment.
- The amount of money you have to spend on food will determine what you buy—this is your food budget.
- Cost menu items when planning meals, to make sure they will fit into your budget.
- Time management, teamwork and organizational skills are important for meal planning and preparation.
- A basic knowledge of table etiquette will put you at ease at mealtimes at home, in a friend's home, or at a restaurant.

Knowledge and Understanding

1. What does versatility mean in relation to recipes and meal planning?
2. Identify four factors that affect how much families spend on food.
3. List five suggestions for reducing food spending through wise meal planning.
4. Give three examples of ways to work efficiently in your kitchen at home or in the school foods lab.
5. Identify two benefits of a pleasant mealtime atmosphere.

Thinking and Inquiry

6. A friend of yours, who lives alone, has developed poor eating habits, such as buying food from vending machines and skipping meals. Give your friend meal-planning suggestions that will help him improve his eating habits.
7. Discuss factors that you think account for people spending more for food than they would like to spend.
8. In small groups, devise strategies for overcoming the following issues a family may face when meal planning. Share your strategies with the class.
   - Special Diets: One member is a vegetarian.
   - Stage of Life: One member is a preschooler.
   - Dislikes: One member does not like milk.
   - Schedules: At least one family member has to miss dinner one night of the week.

Review and Activities   Chapter 9

Communication

9. In small groups, write and perform a 5-minute skit demonstrating at least three dining etiquette errors and offer suggestions on how to correct them.

Application

10. You have $15 to spend on a meal for a family of four. Your family has 75 minutes to spend on preparing, serving, eating, and cleaning up after the meal. Plan the meal using the principles of meal planning. Cost out your entire meal using a "Cost of a Meal" chart like the one shown on page 171. Prepare a work plan and work schedule like the ones shown on pages 175 and 176.

Chapter 9 ◆ Meal Planning and Management   MHR • 189

Shopping Smart

While reading this chapter, you will:

• Produce general food-shopping guidelines that are efficient and economical.

• Demonstrate an understanding of Canada's food-grading practices and food-labelling regulations and terms.

• Describe how to identify fresh, ripe produce.

• Demonstrate an ability to calculate unit prices, decipher "best before" dates, read ingredient lists, and understand how comparatively expensive convenience foods are.

• Describe organic foods and explain their increased availability.

Inspecting and grading eggs is one way the government ensures foods are of good quality and safe for consumers to eat.

bulk foods
candling
comparison shop
convenience food
core list of nutrients
diet-related health claims
durable life
food co-operatives
generic
grade name
impulse buying
ingredient list
marbling
net weight
nutrient content claims
% daily value
rebate
single-serving sizes
staples
store brands

CHAPTER INTRODUCTION

Successful shopping begins with planning. To shop smart, you need to be an informed consumer. Knowing where to shop to get the best value and quality, how to compare prices, and how to decipher nutrition information and grades of meat are some of the skills you need when you go food shopping. The information in this chapter will guide you in becoming a smart shopper.

Before You Shop

Where to Shop

You can buy food at several kinds of food stores. Each has its value. Your choice will depend on your own needs and wants.

◆ **Supermarkets.** These are large stores that sell not only food but also many other items and services. Most supermarkets offer a variety of customer services. In a large, busy supermarket, you may find it difficult to buy just a few items in a hurry.

◆ **Warehouse stores.** They offer basic items with few customer services. As a result, prices are lower than in most supermarkets. Although most warehouse stores are large, they have a limited variety of items. Items are usually displayed in cartons rather than on shelves. Shoppers must bag their own groceries and carry them out.

◆ **Food co-operatives.** Another low-cost option, **food co-operatives** are food distribution organizations mutually owned and operated by a group of people. Members buy food in quantity and do the sorting, unloading, and other work themselves.

◆ **Outdoor markets like this one are cost-effective alternatives to shopping in more conventional settings. What factors besides cost need to be considered when shopping for food?**

These things help keep costs down. Some co-operatives are licensed to sell to the public as well as to members.

◆ **Health food stores.** They offer a wide range of foods, including items seldom found elsewhere. Foods are likely to be more expensive, however, than in other stores.

◆ **Specialty stores.** Although limited to specific items, such as fish, meat, baked goods, delicatessen foods, or ethnic foods, prices are usually higher than in supermarkets. In return, customers may get personal attention and fast service.

◆ **Convenience stores.** They give fast service and usually open early and close late. Some stay open around the clock. Their small size makes it easy to shop quickly, but they do not carry a full line of groceries. Prices are generally higher than in supermarkets.

◆ **Farmer's markets.** They specialize in fresh fruits and vegetables. The selection depends on the area and the season. You may find locally grown foods that are fresher and less expensive than those in the supermarket. Some markets are closed during cold-weather months.

◆ **Grocery stores are organized into departments.** How does a grocery store help consumers find items?

In the Supermarket

How Stores Are Organized

Some supermarkets are so big they may seem like food mazes. Understanding how stores are organized can help you navigate through them.

Most of the space in a supermarket is taken up by aisles lined with shelves stacked with shelf-stable foods in cans, jars, bottles, boxes, and packages. You might also find the following specific departments or sections:

◆ A produce department, where fresh fruits and vegetables are sold.

◆ A meat, poultry, and fish department.

◆ A refrigeration section. Often taking an entire aisle, this is where you will find milk and milk products, eggs, cured cold meats, and fresh pasta.

◆ A freezer section. Here you will find a variety of convenience foods and products meant to be consumed in their frozen state, such as ice cream.

Still other departments you might find include a meal centre, delicatessen, salad bar, or bakery, where you can buy fresh prepared foods. Some stores feature a department that specializes in **bulk foods**—shelf-stable foods that are sold loose in covered bins or barrels. You place as much food as you want in a plastic bag, tie it, and attach a tag or sticker to the bag so that the check-out clerk can identify the contents. Foods that may be sold in bulk include grain products, nuts, dried fruits, dry beans and peas, snack foods, flour, sugar, herbs, and spices.

Comparison Shopping

No matter what size your food budget, getting the most for your money should be one of your goals when shopping. When faced with so many choices—different types of products, brands, and sizes—how can you spot the best bargain? The answer is to **comparison shop**, that is, to match prices and characteristics of similar or like items to determine which offers the best value. Among the methods used in comparison shopping are calculating unit price, computing cost per serving, and trying store brands or generic items.

◆ **Most stores provide the unit price on a shelf tab for the convenience of consumers.** How is this helpful to consumers?

Unit Prices

Which is a better buy, a 398 mL can of pears for $1.79 or a 796 mL can of pears for $2.59? To find out, you need to know the cost per unit, or unit price. In many grocery stores, the unit price is shown on the shelf tab below the item, next to the total price. This gives you a quick and easy way to compare prices. If the unit price is not shown, you can calculate it yourself by dividing the total price of the item by the number of units. For the example given, the smaller can of pears costs $0.005 per mL ($1.79 ÷ 398). The larger can of pears costs $0.003 per mL ($2.59 ÷ 796), so it is the better value.

Cost Per Serving

Sometimes the unit price is not the best basis for comparison, particularly when you are shopping for fresh meat, poultry, or fish. These foods and packages are best compared by the cost per serving, the price of an individual serving.

Suppose that you were preparing a recipe that asks for 500 grams of uncooked boneless chicken. In this case, you have a choice whether to buy boneless chicken or to buy chicken with the bone in and debone it yourself. When comparing prices at the meat counter, you discover that the boneless chicken is $13.20 per kilogram and the chicken with the bone in is $7.80 per kilogram. At first, the chicken with the bone in may seem like a better bargain; however, because the bones, skin, and fat yield less meat, you have to purchase more.

To figure out the cost per serving, you need to determine how many servings a given amount will provide, then compare the prices to discover which item is the better value. Divide the price per kilogram by the number of servings it will provide. For this example, the calculations are as follows:

Chicken with bone:
$7.80 per kg ÷ 4 = $1.95 per serving

Boneless chicken:
$13.20 per kg ÷ 8 = $1.65 per serving

In this example, the boneless chicken is a better value.

◆ **Whether you choose convenience foods or the homemade versions, you may have to make some trade-offs.** What are the pros and cons of the convenience version versus the homemade version of one of your favourite foods?

Convenience Foods

In general, a **convenience food** is one that has been commercially processed to make it more convenient to store or use. Some convenience foods have been available for such a long time that they have become staples in the Canadian food supply. For example, you might not think of packaged sliced bread or bottled salad dressing as convenience foods. When they first appeared, though, these products were viewed as time-saving innovations.

Convenience foods help reduce meal preparation time. Food that is partially prepared when purchased, such as cheese that is already grated or vegetables that have been washed and pre-cut, can save time in the kitchen. However, convenience can be costly. Every additional step in processing adds to the price of a food. Before buying convenience foods, evaluate the cost per serving against other factors, such as time. Would you save money if you grated the cheese yourself?

You can use cost per serving to help you in meal planning, budgeting, and shopping.

◆ Foods can be purchased in large-sized packages or in single-sized servings. Identify three factors to consider when deciding which to buy.

For instance, you may want to compare the cost of a homemade food item with the cost of a packaged convenience food item. To do this, first you add the cost of the ingredients and then divide the total amount by the recipe yield. (See Chapter 9, for more information on costing recipes.) Next, find the cost per serving of a packaged convenience food by dividing the total price by the number of servings indicated on the label. To compare costs accurately, make sure that the serving sizes are equivalent for each item.

Convenience foods are also available ready-to-serve at deli counters, specialty food stores, take-out counters, and vending machines. Calculating the cost per serving will also help you to compare the cost between various convenience foods (for instance, pizza at the grocery deli counter versus pizza at a take-out restaurant or home delivery).

When grocery shopping, you may be tempted to buy items that are packaged in **single-serving sizes,** such as single-serving cans of juice or single-serving containers of yogurt, because they are more convenient. Compare the unit prices, or cost per serving, of the foods that are packaged in single servings with items that are packaged in larger servings or amounts. (Remember to compare servings of equal size.) You may find that buying the larger container is more economical. Larger containers also reduce waste, since there is not as much packaging. Single-sized servings are more convenient, especially for bagged lunches, picnics, and snacks on the go. However, when packing food for these purposes, you can be prepared by purchasing reusable plastic or glass containers. You can then use these containers again and again to store foods that come in larger containers. You will not only be saving money but also helping the environment.

Servings Per Kilogram of Meat, Poultry, and Fish

	Meat • Lean, boneless, or ground • Some bone or fat • Large amount of bone or fat	• 6 to 8 servings per kilogram* • 4 to 6 servings per kilogram* • 2 to 4 servings per kilogram*
	Poultry • Whole roasting chicken • Boneless or ground • With bones	• 3 servings per kilogram* • 8 servings per kilogram • 4 servings per kilogram
	Fish • Fillets or steaks • Dressed • Whole or drawn	• 8 servings per kilogram • 4 servings per kilogram • 2 servings per kilogram

*Amounts based on a 100–120 g serving.

Store Brands and Generics

A third strategy for saving money is to buy and try items other than commercial name-brand items. **Store brands** (also called private labels) are brands specially produced for the store. They are generally equal in quality to name brands but less expensive. **Generic** items, items produced without a commercial or store brand name, are usually even less expensive. The labels of generic products aren't as eye-catching as those of name brands, but your taste buds may not know the difference. Finding out which store brands and generics are good quality may take some experimenting, but the savings can make the effort worthwhile.

Other Money-Saving Ideas

Here are some additional suggestions for saving money at your food store:

◆ Use your shopping list, but be flexible. Look for sale items that you can substitute for the ones on your list.

◆ When using coupons, be sure you are really getting the best buy. Another brand may be less expensive even without a coupon.

◆ Try a warehouse store. Items can be bought there in large packages to save you money. Many of these types of stores carry only the basics and not a lot of choices. Some require you to purchase a membership card with an annual fee, so you must take into account whether or not you are saving money in light of this additional fee. Know your prices before shopping at this kind of store.

◆ Look for new products on the market. Compare the unit prices of these new products with other brands. Also look for products on lower shelves. More expensive

◆ **Many stores offer a choice between store brands and name brands.** Identify two factors to consider when deciding which to buy.

name brands are often placed at eye level on store shelves.

◆ Consider bulk foods. They cost less because they are not prepackaged. In addition, you can buy just the amount you want.

◆ Don't buy more food than you can store properly, or more than can be used before spoiling.

◆ Be aware of strategies designed to encourage impulse buying. Don't be tempted by small, high-profit items, such as candy and magazines, placed next to the check-out lanes.

◆ Take advantage of customer services provided by the store. You may find a coupon rack, for example, or brochures with tips on meal planning, food budgeting, and shopping.

◆ Surf your supermarket's web site, if it has one. Doing so enables customers with computers to communicate with the store. Customers can learn of future sales, send their suggestions through e-mail, print out coupons, and find other money-saving ideas.

How to Decide

What should you consider when choosing a place to shop? First, be sure the store is clean. Next, consider your priorities. What kinds of food do you shop for most often? How far will you travel to shop? Are you willing to give up some services in exchange for lower prices?

If time is a priority, you may want to do most of your shopping at one store. That way, you can become familiar with the location of the items and spend less time shopping.

Some stores use promotions, such as giveaways, special prices, or discount clubs for frequent shoppers, to attract customers. When choosing a place to shop, consider whether these promotions will actually save you money. You may find you can save as much or more by shopping at a store with low everyday prices.

✚ Safety Check

A safe shopping experience begins with a clean store. Here are some important qualities to consider:

• Check for cleanliness not just on the floor but also on the grocery shelves, in display cases, and in the check-out aisles.

• Self-serve areas, including bulk bins and salad bars, should be clean and, in some cases, covered.

• Fresh produce should look fresh—a sign of quality.

• Raw meat, poultry, and fish should look fresh, too. If you detect an odour when you pass by the seafood section, something's "fishy" about the freshness.

• Cold foods should be cold. Freezer sections should house solidly frozen foods, without signs of ice crystal formation or thawing.

When to Shop

The issue of when to shop involves answering three questions:

◆ **How often should you shop?**
The answer depends on several factors. One is the storage space you have, including the size of your refrigerator-freezer.

◆ **Which days should you shop?**
Depending on the grocery store and the area in which you live, the days on which sales prices are available will vary. Check the dates of grocery flyers and newspaper advertisements so that you know when the sale begins and ends. Shop in the evenings or late weekend afternoons. Items with a short shelf life, such as fresh fruits and vegetables and baked goods, are often marked down in price at the end of the day or business week. You can freeze items such as pies, breads, or baked goods to keep them fresh.

◆ **What time of day should you shop?**
One time of day *not* to shop is right before mealtimes (or any time you are hungry). Studies show that people spend as much as 15 percent more on food when they shop on an empty stomach. Other times to avoid are early evenings and weekends—when stores are generally the most crowded. Shopping when the store is free of crowds can save you time. You are also more likely to make better choices when you are not feeling pressured.

A Shopping List

A well-thought-out shopping list can save you both time and money. It helps you speed up your shopping time and saves you from making special trips for forgotten items. A shopping list can also help you avoid **impulse buying**—buying items you didn't plan on purchasing and don't really need. Impulse buying can ruin any food budget.

Making a Shopping List

Once you get in the habit of making a shopping list, you'll find it can be done quickly and easily. The first step is to plan the meals you will serve for that shopping period. Be sure to check the newspaper ads to see what's on sale—perhaps you can include some of those items in your meal plan.

Next, check your menus and recipes to see what ingredients you need to purchase. Be sure to include the amount or quantity of each item needed, increasing the number if you plan to cook for the freezer.

◆ A well-organized shopping list makes it easier to find needed items once you get to the store. What is the most logical order in which to shop for groceries? Explain your answer.

From time to time you will want to check your supply of these basic items:

- **Staples**, items you use on a regular basis, such as milk, bread, and peanut butter.

- Foods you keep on hand for emergencies: frozen entrees, canned foods, and other shelf-stable items.

- Cleaning supplies and paper products.

Many people keep a shopping reminder list handy in the kitchen. Whenever they notice that items are running low, they jot down a reminder to add those items to the shopping list.

INTERNET CONNECTS

www.mcgrawhill.ca/links/food
To learn more about food shopping guidelines regarding economics and safety, go to the web site above for *Food for Today, First Canadian Edition,* to see where to go next.

Organizing Your List

Organizing your list will help you shop more efficiently. When writing out your list, group items that are found in the same area of the store, such as dairy foods, meats, and frozen foods. This will help you avoid making several trips to the same area.

If you shop at one store regularly, make out your shopping list according to the way the store is arranged. Some stores provide a map or directory sheet showing which items are found in each aisle. Most have overhead signs above each aisle telling which foods are found there.

Some people keep copies of a basic shopping list that has the items they usually buy, arranged in the order those items are found in the store. Each week, they circle or check off the basic items they need and add any others. Alicia has her mother's basic shopping list stored in her computer. When her mother finishes the week's menus, Alicia adds the needed foods to the basic list and prints out the final one.

Coupons

Another consideration before you go shopping is whether you will use coupons. Coupons offer savings on the price of a specific product. Coupons are found in newspapers, magazines, product packages, and mailed advertisements. In some stores, a check-out computer automatically prints out coupons for future use on the basis of the purchases you have just made.

◆ Coupons can save money if used wisely. Name three types of information that should be looked at carefully before using a coupon.

There are two basic types of coupons:

- **Cents-off coupons.** These offer reduced prices on specific items. You present the coupon to the cashier when you make the purchase. The face value is subtracted from the total price of your purchases.

- **Rebate coupons.** A **rebate** is a partial refund from the manufacturer of a purchased good. You pay the regular price at the store. Later you fill out the rebate coupon and mail it, along with the required proof of purchase, to a specified address. The proof of purchase might be part of the package or a cash register receipt or both. A cheque for the coupon's face value is mailed to you.

Using Coupons

Clipping and sorting coupons takes time. For some people, the savings are well worth the effort. Others may find that they can save just as much by buying less expensive products without coupons.

Here are some suggestions for using coupons:

- **Be choosy.** Collect coupons only for items you usually buy or want to try. Otherwise, you may be tempted to buy an unnecessary item just because you have a coupon.

- **Read coupons carefully.** Some are good only on a certain size of a product or only in a specific store. Most coupons have a time limit. Stores cannot accept coupons after the expiration date printed on them.

- **Organize coupons so that they are easy to find and use.** For example, you might sort them alphabetically, by store aisle, or by food groups.

- **Swap coupons.** Some families and friends have coupon exchanges—they exchange coupons of food items they won't use for ones they will.

- **Go through your coupon collection regularly.** Pull out ones that expire soon so that you'll remember to use them. Throw away outdated ones.

Ready to Shop

Now that you've planned your shopping, you're ready to go to the store. Take along your shopping list and your coupons. Remember the environment, too. If you use cloth shopping bags or have paper or plastic bags to return to the store, take those with you.

Consider any errands you might want to do during your shopping trip. Do them before you shop for food. That way, you can bring food home immediately so that it can be properly stored.

◆ Cloth shopping bags conserve resources because they are reusable. **What items should you take to the store with you?**

◆ Food labels provide valuable information that is useful to the consumer.

Food Labelling

Even though food is inspected for safety and quality at various levels of government, you need to be a well-informed consumer so that you know what you are purchasing. Knowing how to read labels on packages and labels behind counters in the supermarket will help you determine what you are getting in terms of quality, nutrient content, and ingredients. Some of the information that you may see on a product includes the grade name of the product, nutrient information, ingredient lists, health claims, and "best before" dates. The following information will help you decipher labels and make informed food purchases when shopping.

Basic Information

There is basic information on food packages to help you determine what the product is. Information regarding the labelling of foods can be found in both the *Food and Drugs Act* and the *Consumer Packaging and Labelling Act*. The basic information on all food labels answers these questions:

◆ **Common name of the food.** What food is in the container? The label or package must identify the product.

◆ **Net quantity of the food.** How much food is in the container? The amount may be given in volume measurement, such as 398 mL, or as a **net weight,** the weight of the food itself, not including the packaging. Net weight includes the liquid in canned food.

◆ **Company responsible for the food.** Who manufactured, packed, or distributed the food? Where is the company located? This information is provided on the package or label.

◆ **Ingredient list.** Are all the ingredients listed? A list of all food products with more than one ingredient is supplied. They are listed in order from largest to smallest amount by weight.

Source: Canadian Food Inspection Agency 2002d.

INTERNET CONNECTS

www.mcgrawhill.ca/links/food
To learn more about the Government of Canada's role in food safety, go to the web site above for *Food for Today, First Canadian Edition,* to see where to go next.

The Government of Canada's Role in Food Safety

The government of Canada works with provinces, territories, municipalities, consumers and industry to protect our country's food supply and the health and well-being of all Canadians, from coast to coast.

Health Canada, through the *Food and Drugs Act*, is the federal department that establishes standards for the safety and nutritional quality of food sold in Canada. It is also responsible for assessing the effectiveness of the Canadian Food Inspection Agency's (CFIA) food safety inspection activities.

The CFIA inspects food produced at federally registered slaughterhouses and processing plants and carries out enforcement activities related to food. Canada's provincial and territorial governments are responsible for inspecting food processing establishments that distribute products provincially and territorially. In many cases, municipalities are responsible for inspecting restaurants.

Day in and day out, Government of Canada inspectors and scientists contribute to a rigorous and comprehensive food and safety system and help maintain the high standards Canadians rely on for food safety.

From the farm or the boat to the food processor, from the field or the sea right through to the family dinner table, from the greenhouse to the grocery store, there are thousands of Canadians working every day so that you and your family can be confident that the foods you eat are safe.

Sources: Canadian Food Inspection Agency. (2002b) and (2002c).

◆ **How does processing food affect its price?**

Grading Practices

Grade names are established for products so that consumers know what quality they are getting and so that producers and processors can get paid according to the quality of their products. The grade of a product often determines how the product is used. For example, only Grade A eggs are sold in the retail market for household use because they are of the highest quality. Grade C eggs are sent to processors to be used in commercial baking only. A **grade name** that may be seen on a food you purchase is a "prescribed name, mark, or designation of a category and includes a standard prescribed for an agricultural product" (Department of Justice, *Canada Agricultural Products Act*, sec. 2, 2002).

"Grade names and standards have been established for food products, such as butter and butter products, milk powder, eggs and processed eggs, fresh and processed fruits and vegetables, honey, maple products, poultry and beef carcasses, under the authority of the *Canada Agricultural Products Act*, the *Meat*

Inspection Act, and various provincial acts" (Canadian Food Inspection Agency, 2002). The standards that are established for grading are set out in the *Canada Agricultural Products Act*. This act deals with products that are imported, exported, and shipped from province to province. There are eight regulations in total under the *Canada Agricultural Products Act*. Each commodity, or food category, has its own regulation; for example, dairy products are referred to in the Dairy Products Regulations. The Canadian Food Inspection Agency is the federal agency that enforces the grading laws and inspection of facilities under this act and its regulations. There may be different grading policies and grade names regarding foods that are produced and sold within a province. For example, in Ontario, fruits and vegetables grown in Ontario and sold in Ontario may be graded with a grade name under the *Farm Products Grades and Sales Act*. Potatoes, for instance, may be graded as Ontario No. 1 and sold only in Ontario. For more information regarding provincial regulations, refer to the Internet Connects below.

INTERNET CONNECTS

www.mcgrawhill.ca/links/food
To learn more about provincial regulations and laws regarding the grading of various commodities, go to the web site above for *Food for Today, First Canadian Edition,* to see where to go next.

Labelling Products with a Grade Name

Following are some guidelines for labelling graded products according to federal law:

◆ Food products may be advertised with the price of the product included. However, if they include the price in the advertisement, then a grade name must be shown if there is more than one grade name available at retail. For example, if a grocery flyer is advertising canned corn, then the grade name of the corn, such as "Canada Choice," must be included in the flyer because there is more than one grade name for canned corn.

- A grade name must not be used in any way if that product does not have a grade designation in the regulations. For instance, if a store is selling ground pork, it cannot advertise it as cut from "Canada AAA" ground pork, since there isn't a grade name for ground pork in the regulations.

- Grade names can be used only on products that they are intended for. It is illegal to use grade names or symbols that are established under the regulations on any other product. For example, if a manufacturer wanted to name its line of pots and pans "Canada Choice," it couldn't, because this is a grade name legally established for certain processed fruits and vegetables.

- Imported food products can be advertised with the grade name from the country that they came from if the grade name is legally recognized by that country. For many products the word "Canada" cannot be used in the grade name of imported foods unless they undergo a percentage of processing in Canada. For example, apples imported from the United States may be sold as "Extra Fancy, Product of the U.S.A."; they cannot say "Canada Extra Fancy" because they are not produced in Canada.

Source: Adapted from Canadian Food Inspection Agency (2002e).

Labelling products with an appropriate grade name is a way to protect the consumer. A product must be labelled with the appropriate grade name and in an appropriate way according to the regulations set out for that particular product. Note that regulations vary and that there are exceptions. This is one way that consumers are able to know what they are getting.

Grade names differ from product to product. The following pages describe the grade names for some of the various products according to the *Canada Agricultural Products Act* and the regulations that are set out for each product. Look for these grade names in retail stores. They will help guide you in making informed food choices.

What to Look for When Buying Fresh Fruits and Vegetables

You may have noticed when shopping in a supermarket that some produce has a grade name on it while others do not. There are 31 fruit and vegetable commodities that have grade names established under the *Fresh Fruit and Vegetable Regulations*. It is necessary to declare a grade standard for fruits and vegetables that are listed in the regulation. There are exceptions; for instance, grade standards for strawberries and blueberries for processing are voluntary.

The table opposite identifies some common fresh fruits and vegetables and their grade names. Note that not all fruits and vegetables have a designated grade name; therefore, they do not need to be graded.

Grade Names of Fresh Fruits and Vegetables

Product	Grade name	When buying, look for ...
Fruit		
Apples	Canada Extra Fancy Canada Fancy Canada Commercial Canada Hailed Canada Commercial Cookers Canada No. 1 peeled Canada No. 2 peeled	Well-shaped, smooth-skinned fruit that is free of bruises. Brownish freckled areas do not affect flavour.
Apricots	Canada No. 1 Canada Domestic Canada Hailed	Plump, fairly firm fruit with as much golden orange as possible.
Bananas	No grade given for this item under this regulation.	Firm, unblemished bananas. Yellow with brown speckles indicate a sweet, tender fruit.
Blueberries	Canada No. 1	Firm, plump, dry, dark-coloured blueberries with a powder-blue bloom.
Canteloupe	Canada No. 1	Melon with a deeply netted, yellow-gold rind. Ripe fruit yields slightly to gentle pressure and has a musky fragrance.
Cherries	Canada No. 1 Canada Commercial Canada Orchard Run	Plump, bright-coloured fruit. The deeper the colour, the sweeter the fruit. Avoid very soft or shrivelled cherries.
Grapefruit	No grade given for this item under this regulation.	Firm, well-shaped fruit that is heavy for size.
Grapes	Canada No. 1 Canada Domestic	Plump grapes that are firmly attached to green stems. Avoid wrinkled or sticky fruit.
Kiwi fruit	No grade given for this item under this regulation.	Evenly ripe fruit, free of mould or soft spots that yield to gentle pressure.
Peaches	Canada No. 1 Canada Domestic	Fruit with yellowish (not green) background. Ripe fruit yields to gentle pressure when squeezed in the palm, not with the fingers.

(continued)

Grade Names of Fresh Fruits and Vegetables (continued)

Product	Grade name	When buying, look for . . .
Fruit		
Pears	Canada Extra Fancy Canada Fancy Canada Commercial	Firm, well-shaped, fruit. Use fully ripe fruit immediately. Minor scars and blemishes do not affect flavour.
Plums	Canada No. 1 Canada Domestic	Full-coloured smooth fruit. Ripe fruit yields to gentle pressure.
Strawberries	Canada No. 1	Firm, plump berries that are fully red with bright green caps. Strawberries do not ripen once picked.
Watermelon	No grade given for this item under this regulation.	A firm symmetrical melon with fully rounded sides and a yellowish underside. If cut, select a melon with bright red flesh.
Vegetables		
Asparagus	Canada No. 1 Canada No. 1 Slender Canada No. 2	Fresh, crisp, bright-green spears with tightly closed tips.
Beans	No grade given for this item under this regulation.	Bright, crisp, young beans of uniform size free of blemishes. Avoid mature beans with swollen pods.
Beets	Canada No. 1 Canada No. 2	(Only applies to beets that have no tops.) Firm, uniform beets free of cracks or blemishes. Attached leaves should be deep green and fresh looking.
Broccoli	No grade given for this item under this regulation.	Firm stalks with compact green bud clusters. Avoid yellow florets.
Cabbages	Canada No. 1 Canada No. 2	Firm, heavy head with fresh outer leaves and good colouring.

(continued)

Grade Names of Fresh Fruits and Vegetables (continued)

Product	Grade name	When buying, look for . . .
Vegetables		
Carrots	Canada No. 1 Canada No. 2	(Only applies to carrots that have no tops.) Firm, clean, bright orange carrots that are well shaped. If tops are attached, they should be bright green, fresh looking.
Cauliflower	Canada No. 1 Canada No. 2	Heavy, firm, creamy white heads with compact florets.
Celery	Canada No. 1 Canada No. 1 Heart Canada No. 2	Crisp, rigid green stalks with fresh leaves. Avoid limp or rubbery stalks
Corn, Sweet	Canada No. 1	Cobs with fresh-looking green husks and moist stems. Kernels should be juicy when pierced.
Cucumbers	Canada No. 1 Canada No. 2 (Applies to field cucumbers and greenhouse cucumbers.)	Firm, well-shaped, bright-green cucumbers. Avoid soft, over-mature, or yellowing ones.
Eggplant	No grade given for this item under this regulation.	Firm, purple eggplant that is heavy for its size, with glossy, unbroken skin.
Lettuce, Iceberg	Canada No. 1 Canada No. 2	A crisp head with fresh outer leaves, free of brown spots and yellow leaves. It should be springy firm to gentle pressure.
Mushrooms	No grade given for this item under this regulation.	Mushrooms free of blemishes or slimy spots.
Onions	Canada No. 1 Canada No. 1 Pickling Canada No. 2	Firm, small-necked onions with brittle outer leaves. Avoid dark-spotted or sprouted bulbs.
Peppers, red, green, or yellow	No grade is given for this item under this regulation.	Crisp, well-shaped, bright in colour with smooth skin.

(continued)

Grade Names of Fresh Fruits and Vegetables (continued)

Product	Grade name	When buying, look for . . .
Vegetables		
Potatoes	Canada No. 1 Canada No. 2	Clean, firm, smooth potatoes, without sprouts, green areas, or blemishes.
Spinach	No grade given for this item under this regulation.	Fresh crisp leaves with solid green colouring.
Squash, Winter	No grade given for this item under this regulation.	Heavy for its size with a hard rind that is not shiny.
Tomato	Canada No. 1 (Field) Canada No. 2 (Field) Canada No. 1 (Greenhouse) Canada Commercial (Greenhouse) Canada No. 2 (Greenhouse)	Smooth, well-formed, firm tomatoes, heavy for size and uniform in colour.
Zucchini	No grade is given for this item under this regulation.	Small, smooth-skinned, bright-coloured zucchini. Small ones are less seedy and more tender.

Sources: Adapted from Canadian Produce Marketing Association (2003) and Department of Justice Canada (2002).

Processed Fruits and Vegetables

The grade names and standards for processed fruits and vegetables that are sold in Canada are set out in the Processed Products Regulations. Canned fruits and vegetables are graded according to the following three grade names: Canada Fancy, Canada Choice, and Canada Standard. Some canned fruits and vegetables must be graded by law, but it is optional for others to be graded. For example, whole, diced, or sliced canned tomatoes are graded into one of the three categories, yet it is optional for tomato purée and tomato paste to be graded. In addition, some processed fruits and vegetables are not graded into all three categories. For example, apple sauce and apple juice have only Canada Fancy and Canada Choice grade categories.

INTERNET CONNECTS

www.mcgrawhill.ca/links/food

To learn more about what to look for when buying fresh fruit and vegetables, go to the web site above for *Food for Today, First Canadian Edition,* to see where to go next.

◆ Grade names and standards for processed fruits and vegetables— what do they tell us?

Frozen fruits and vegetables are graded into two categories, Canada A and Canada B. For some products, such as frozen concentrated orange juice, a third grading category, Canada C, may be used.

Other processed products under this regulation that are not graded include olives, pickles, relishes, chutneys, and more. For more information on food grading and regulations refer to the Internet Connects on page 203.

Safety Check

"The Meat Inspection Stamp indicates the product has been inspected and meets Canadian requirements for food safety. It does not indicate grading, nor does it mean the product was necessarily grown in Canada."

Source: Canadian Food Inspection Agency. (2002).

Beef Grading

Beef is inspected first to ensure that it is safe for people to eat. Once a beef carcass has been inspected and meets the standards of safety recognized in Canada, it may be graded into one of 13 categories set out in the Livestock and Poultry Carcass Grading Regulations. Grading of beef is voluntary in Canada, but provinces, such as Ontario, require the grade of beef to be acknowledged at the meat counter and in any advertisement.

Most beef is graded into the following categories: Canada Prime, Canada AAA, Canada AA, and Canada A. "It is important to understand the Canadian beef grades and their criteria so you can make informed decisions as a beef buyer. Grading groups beef of similar quality, yield, and value, into a grade category for product consistency. The Canada 'A' grades (Canada Prime, Canada AAA, Canada AA, Canada A) differ by the amount of marbling in the meat: Canada Prime having the most marbling and Canada A having the least. **Marbling** refers to the fine white streaks of fat running through the beef. Marbling increases tenderness, juiciness, and flavour."

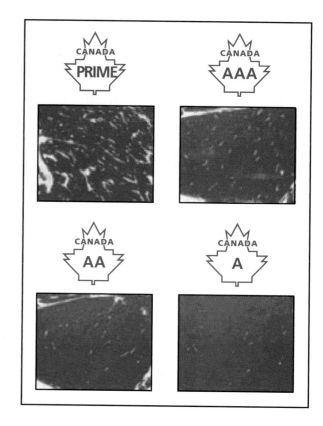

Most of the beef sold in Canada is graded. If you want to purchase a particular grade of beef, check store flyers or ask the staff in the meat department what grade of beef they sell. Some stores only sell one grade of beef.

Poultry Grading

Poultry grade names are set out in the Livestock and Poultry Carcass Grading Regulations. Poultry includes the following types of birds: chicken, capon, Rock Cornish hen, mature chicken, old rooster, turkey, duck, goose, and guinea fowl.

The three grade names for poultry are Canada A, Canada Utility, and Canada C. Poultry is also graded according to such factors as appearance. Others factors include:

◆ Conformation: bone shape of the skeleton and normal distribution of flesh.

◆ Amount of flesh and distribution of the flesh.

◆ Fat covering and its distribution.

◆ Dressing: presence of feathers, pin feathers, discolouration, dried-out parts.

Source: Siebart & Kerr (1994).

Poultry grading is voluntary. If a whole poultry carcass is graded, a grade name will appear on a tag that is placed on the breast of the poultry. The tag will show the common name of the poultry and the grade name in white letters inside a maple leaf symbol. You will also see the establishment number, the principal place of business, and the words "may contain kidneys."

◆ Like beef and eggs, poultry is strictly regulated through a grading process. Why is this process so important?

INTERNET CONNECTS

www.mcgrawhill.ca/links/food
To learn more about what to look for when purchasing various types of meat, such as pork, lamb, beef, and poultry, go to the web site above for *Food for Today, First Canadian Edition,* to see where to go next.

Egg Grading

Eggs are graded at registered egg-grading stations across Canada. All eggs sold are required to be graded and given a federal grade name. The four grade names, as determined under the Egg Regulations, are Canada A, Canada B, Canada C, and Canada Nest Run.

Part of the inspection of eggs is a process called candling. **Candling** is the process of passing a strong light over the egg so that the interior of the egg is visible. Grade A eggs are the only eggs that are sold in retail markets. When purchasing eggs, buy clean eggs with uncracked shells. Look for the Grade A name on egg cartons inside the Canadian Maple Leaf stamp. This will ensure that you are getting top-quality eggs that are clean, fresh, and safe. Other grades of eggs are sold for commercial baking or further processing.

The table on page 212 lists the criteria by which eggs are graded according to the three main grade designations.

Making the Grade—Eggs

Grade A	Grade B	Grade C
• Sold in retail stores for household use • The most commonly bought consumer egg	• Sold for commercial baking or further processing. • Can be sold at retail	• Sold to commercial processors for further processing only.
• Firm, white • Round, well-centred yolk • Clean, uncracked shell with normal shape • Small air cell (less than 5 mm deep)	• Watery white • Slightly flattened yolk • Uncracked shell possibly with rough texture • May be slightly stained or soiled	• Thin, watery white • Loose yolk • Possibly cracked shell and up to $1/3$ stained
	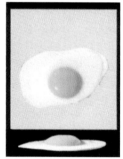	

Sources: Canadian Egg Marketing Agency. (n.d.) and Department of Justice (2002, August 31).

FYI

Sizing of Eggs

When purchasing eggs, look for the size that is indicated on the carton. Compare unit prices for each size of egg. Eggs are sized by weight. There is a weight range for each size. The most popular sizes are:

Peewee:	under 42 g
Small:	42–48 g
Medium:	49–55 g
Large:	56–63 g
Extra Large:	64–69 g
Jumbo:	Over 69 g

Source: Canadian Egg Marketing Agency (n.d.).

Milk Products

Even though fluid milk is not given a grade name, you can be certain that you are buying quality milk. All milk goes through several steps of inspection at processing plants. After these inspection steps, the milk is shipped to grocery stores, ready to be purchased by you and other consumers. You may see grade names on some milk products. The Dairy Regulations have grade names established for the following products.

Making the Grade: Butter and Cheese

Product	Grade Name
Butter	Canada 1
Butter products (such as light butter, dairy spread)	Canada 1
Cheddar cheese	Canada 1
Dry milk products (such as skim milk powder, whey powder)	Canada 1 or Canada 2

Source: Adapted from Department of Justice Canada (2002, August 31).

◆ **Which of these milk products are graded?**

Durable Life of Foods

The **durable life** of a food is the length of time that an unopened product will maintain the qualities that it is recognized as having if stored properly. Qualities include taste, nutritional value, and other qualities that the manufacturer may claim. Durable-life information is essential on the label of a package when a product has a durable life of 90 days or less after being packaged. Durable life information may be presented in the following ways on products:

◆ **"Best before" dates** must be on foods with a durable life of 90 days or less when packaged at any level of trade other than at a retail store. "Best before" dates indicate the date up to which the unopened product will keep its durable life. If a food item needs to be stored in another way besides at normal room temperature, information on how to store the food item must accompany the "Best before" date. For example, bread can be stored at normal room temperature and does not

◆ Why do these foods have "Best Before" dates?

require storage instructions. However, eggs must be kept cold, and therefore will be labelled "keep refrigerated."

◆ **"Packaged on" dates** tell the date on which a food was packaged. The "packaged on" date must be described on foods with a durable life of 90 days or less and that are packaged at a retail store. "Durable life" information must accompany the "packaged on" date as well. This can be on the actual label or on a poster next to the food. For example, a grocery store that packages its own meat, such as steaks, will be required to put a "packaged on" date and information about the durable life of the steak. You may see a package of steak stating information such as: "Packaged on April 8, 2003," "Best Before April 10, 2003," and "Keep Refrigerated."

There are products that do not need to have "durable life" information on them. Examples of these include fresh fruits and vegetables, donuts, and individual portions of foods that are sold by restaurants, automatic vending machines, and mobile canteens. Once a food has passed its "best before" date or "durable life" date that goes with the "packaged on" date, smell or taste the food. If in doubt, throw it out!

Nutrition Labelling

Nutrition labelling regulations are set out by Health Canada. These regulations are enforced by the Canadian Food Inspection Agency. Nutrition labelling is a consistent way of helping consumers make knowledgeable food choices. This can be done by looking for specific information on the package of a food product. A standard "nutrition facts" table and ingredients list are mandatory for most foods that are sold prepackaged. Nutrient claims regarding health claims and content of the product may be found on certain products, but this is up to the individual manufacturer. Here are some tips on how to use nutrition labelling so that you can make healthy food choices.

FYI

Nutrient Information on Food Labels

In a recent survey:

- 93 percent of Canadians indicated that they want nutrition information on food product labels.
- 70 percent of Canadians said they have used the nutrition information panel on food labels to make decisions about the foods that they buy.
- Canadians indicated they used the labels to:
- Determine if the product contained a great deal of the nutrient or ingredient that they were trying to increase in their diet.
- Find out if the product was low in a nutrient or ingredient that they were trying to decrease in their diet.
- Establish the amount of calories in a food product.
- Compare different and similar kinds of food.

Source: Adapted from Health Canada.

◆ **Nutrition facts** must be shown for most prepackaged food items. These nutrition facts are found in a table format, as in the example below. Look for the following points when using a nutrition facts table: specified serving size amount, energy shown in calories, the 13 nutrients in the core list, and the **% daily value** of a nutrient. There may also be other nutrients listed in the table that are not among the **core list of 13 nutrients**. For example, a product may list the amount of vitamin E that it contains. Refer to the sample table below for an explanation of these points and how to use them in making food choices.

◆ **Nutrition claims** can be a claim concerning the nutritional content of the product or a health claim that is related to diet. **Nutrient content claims** are a description of the amount of a nutrient in a food, such as "low in saturated fat," "a good source of iron," or "reduced calories."

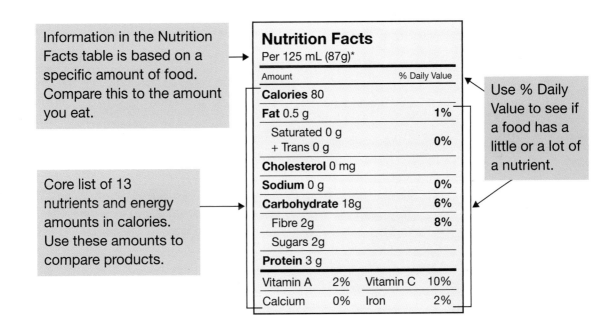

Information in the Nutrition Facts table is based on a specific amount of food. Compare this to the amount you eat.

Core list of 13 nutrients and energy amounts in calories. Use these amounts to compare products.

Nutrition Facts
Per 125 mL (87g)*

Amount		% Daily Value
Calories 80		
Fat 0.5 g		1%
Saturated 0 g + Trans 0 g		0%
Cholesterol 0 mg		
Sodium 0 g		0%
Carbohydrate 18g		6%
Fibre 2g		8%
Sugars 2g		
Protein 3 g		
Vitamin A	2%	Vitamin C 10%
Calcium	0%	Iron 2%

Use % Daily Value to see if a food has a little or a lot of a nutrient.

Diet-related health claims are scientifically supported recognitions that show a relationship between diet and a disease or condition. For example, "A healthy diet rich in a variety of vegetables and fruit may help reduce the risk of some types of cancer." Nutrition claims are usually found on the front of a food package. These claims help to guide people in making healthy food choices and to possibly reduce their risk of developing a health-related disease or condition.

◆ **Lists of ingredients** are shown on all prepackaged foods (assuming the food has more than one ingredient). Ingredients are listed by weight, from highest to lowest percentage weight of ingredients. People may want to limit or increase their intake of a particular ingredient; they could use this list to determine whether the ingredients are in a food.

Source: Health Canada, (2003).

425 g

INTERNET CONNECTS

www.mcgrawhill.ca/links/food
To learn more about how to use nutrition labelling from Health Canada, go to the web site above for *Food for Today, First Canadian Edition*, to see where to go next.

Organic Foods

Organic food products have increased in availability. They can now be purchased in many major supermarkets, health food stores, and markets. To be identified as an organic food in Canada, the National Standard for Organic Agriculture has established rules for organic agriculture products do not have to be certified in Canada. To label a product as "organic," the National Organic Standard of Canada requires that it be made up of at least 95 percent organic ingredients. To understand more about the standards and certification of organic foods, read the box opposite.

◆ **Does eating this food reduce your chances of getting heart disease?**

The National Organic Standard of Canada

This Standard holds the following six principles as the foundation of organic production:

1. Protect the environment, minimize soil degradation and erosion, decrease pollution, and optimize biological productivity.

2. Replenish and maintain long-term soil fertility using crop rotation, composting, and the use of permitted supplemental nutrients.

3. Maintain biological diversity for long-term sustainability including strategies for pest management that do not include synthetic pesticides.

4. Recycle materials and resources to the greatest extent possible within the enterprise.

5. Provide attentive care that promotes health and behavioural needs of livestock.

6. Maintain the integrity of organic food and processed products from initial handling to point of sale. Genetically engineered and/or modified organisms are prohibited.

Source: National Standard CAN/CGSBB–32.310– Organic Agriculture (1999).

Finishing Your Shopping

When you've selected all your items, it's time to head for the check-out lane. If you choose an express lane, be sure you have the right number of items. Don't choose a cash-only line if you intend to pay by other means.

Watch the display as the prices are rung up. The clerk could make a mistake. If the store has computerized check-outs, the incorrect price might have been entered into the computer. If you think you are being charged incorrectly, politely ask the clerk to check the price for you.

Food stores vary regarding what forms of payment they will accept. Some supermarkets accept credit cards or automated banking cards. Don't let the ease of using a card tempt you to go over your food budget.

Take your purchases home right away, and store them properly. Put frozen foods away immediately so that they don't thaw. Store refrigerated foods next, and finally, shelf-stable ones. Remember to repackage bulk foods in airtight, durable containers.

If you come home and discover a food you selected is spoiled or of poor quality, return it to the store as soon as possible. Do the same if you have any other problems with your purchases. Take the store receipt with you. Stores are interested in keeping their customers and will do their best to satisfy you.

INTERNET CONNECTS

www.mcgrawhill.ca/links/food
For more information about the Organic Standard, go to the web site above for *Food for Today, First Canadian Edition,* to see where to go next.

◆ Courtesy is important when shopping. Name three signs of a courteous shopper.

Chapter 10   Review and Activities

Summary

- To be a smart shopper you must be an informed consumer.
- Food stores offer different products and services, and are organized in different ways.
- Make the most of your food budget by comparison shopping.
- Shopping lists and coupons can save time and money.
- Become familiar with food grading and labeling practices.
- Use Nutrition Facts tables to help you make wise food choices.

Knowledge and Understanding

1. What is the advantage of shopping in a warehouse store? Name two drawbacks.

2. How can preparing a shopping list help you save money?

3. Identify three pieces of basic information found on most food labels.

4. What is the purpose of the % Daily Value information found in the Nutrition Facts tables on packages?

Thinking and Inquiry

5. Angelina clips every coupon in the Friday paper and then tries to use them all. Explain possible drawbacks to this approach.

6. Is it always wrong to buy on impulse? When is it most likely to be a problem? Write a newspaper article titled "Resisting the Temptation to Buy on Impulse When Grocery Shopping."

7. Describe the "durable life" information that is available on foods. What is the difference between a "best before" date and a "packaged on" date?

Review and Activities   Chapter 10

Communication

8. Working in pairs, write and perform a skit demonstrating at least three poor shopping strategies. Ask the class to identify them.

9. You and your group are dietitians from your local public health unit. Your current project is to teach families how to use nutrition labels on foods in making good food choices when shopping. In your presentation, demonstrate how family members may use labels if they are on a special diet or have a health concern; for instance, one family member might have low iron. Use posters, overhead transparencies, and other visual aids when giving your presentation to the class.

Application

10. Create a pamphlet for consumers to use to help them make informed decisions when shopping for food. Your pamphlet should include information on the following:

- How to comparison shop.
- How to save money.
- The grade names of various foods.
- How to read nutrition information on labels.
- How to determine the "durable life" of a food.

11. Choose one of your favourite homemade recipes to compare a similar convenience food product or mix to. Some good examples of foods to compare are banana bread, muffins, macaroni and cheese casserole, or another type of casserole. Prepare both the "homemade" recipe and the convenience food or mix. Evaluate the recipes for taste, quality, nutrient content, time and effort to make, and price. Write a summary of your evaluation.

UNIT 3

Nutrition,

UNIT EXPECTATIONS

While reading this unit, you will:

- Analyse the responsibilities involved in maintaining nutritional health and well-being.
- Identify consumer responsibilities in the investigation of current food issues.

Nutrients in foods are the keys to good health.

Health, and Well-Being

OVERVIEW

In this unit, you will explore nutrients and the role they play in maintaining good health throughout the life cycle. By doing this, you will gain an understanding of how *Canada's Food Guide to Healthy Eating* helps in the planning of nutritious meals. You will also explore factors affecting personal eating habits and dietary choices.

Nutrient Wise

While reading this chapter, you will:

- Identify nutrients, and their sources, required for maintaining good health at different stages of the life cycle.

- Correctly use food and nutrition terminology.

A balance of nutrients helps you to grow and gives you the energy to do the things you enjoy doing.

KEY TERMS

amino acids
antioxidants
basal metabolism
calorie
cholesterol
complete proteins
dietary fibre
Dietary Reference
Intakes (DRIs)
digestion
glucose
hydrogenation
monounsaturated fatty acids
nutrient deficiency
osteoporosis
phytochemicals
polyunsaturated fatty acids
saturated fatty acids

In this chapter you will examine nutrients and their function in the body. As a result, you will gain an understanding of how food choices affect energy, growth, and health during the life cycle. Discover how the six main nutrients play a major role in your health and well-being and that not all fats are created equal. Learn what nutrients protect your immune system and how good food choices can help you look and feel your best. Read about how your body extracts nutrients from foods and that you truly are what you eat.

Fruit and nuts—a winning combination and a nutritious snack.

Nutrients

Nutrients are found in the food you eat. They help you grow and they also provide you with the energy needed to stay healthy and enjoy your life. Nutrients keep your brain functioning, your skeleton moving, and your heart beating. You require about 50 nutrients to keep your body alive.

The nutrients your body uses are divided into six major types. All these types work together as a team, each one playing its own special role in your health and well-being.

◆ **Carbohydrates** (kar-boh-HY-drayts) are the body's main source of energy. One unique and important form of this major nutrient is **dietary fibre,** a mixture of plant materials that is not broken down in the digestive system. All forms of carbohydrates, except fibre, provide energy.

◆ **Fats** are a concentrated source of energy. You need fats in moderate amounts to perform important functions in your body, including transporting nutrients.

◆ **Proteins** are nutrients that help build, repair, and maintain body tissues. Proteins are also a source of energy.

◆ **Vitamins** are chemicals that help regulate many vital body processes and aid other nutrients in doing their jobs. Your body requires only small amounts of vitamins.

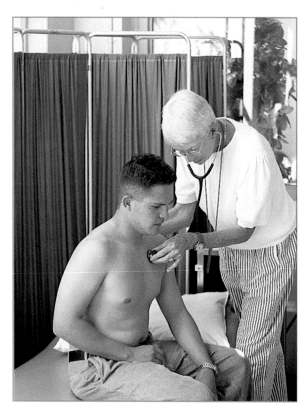

◆ Good nutrition is essential for good health. Name two other benefits associated with good nutrition.

◆ Just as a team relies on the contributions of each member, so the food you eat must include all vital nutrients for your body to function smoothly.

◆ **Minerals** are non-living substances that help the body work properly and, in some cases, become part of body tissues, such as bone. Like vitamins, minerals are needed in only small amounts.

◆ **Water** is a nutrient because it is essential to life. It makes up most of your body weight, too.

You will learn more about these nutrients later in this chapter.

Nutrient Teamwork

What would happen if a school's football team went out onto the field for a game without one or two of the players? To play well, a team must have all its members. Each has a specific job to do and needs to be present to do it.

The same is true of the key nutrients in your diet. No one nutrient can be substituted for any other. If any of the six main nutrients is absent, your entire body—and your health—suffers.

Effects of Poor Nutrition

When people make poor food choices or do not have enough to eat, serious health conditions can result. One such condition is a **nutrient deficiency**, a severe nutrient shortage. A nutrient deficiency can have far-reaching consequences. A lack of vitamin D, for instance, can keep children's bones from growing properly. Their bones become weak, and the children develop bowed legs. In adults, a lack of vitamin D results in brittle bones, which break easily. It may also cause muscle weakness and spasms.

◆ These children and their mother are enjoying a nutritious meal served to them by a group of teen volunteers.

Malnutrition refers to serious health problems caused by poor nutrition over a prolonged period. Generally, malnutrition occurs when people don't get enough to eat. Bad weather, inadequate transportation, political problems, or other factors can cause food shortages. Malnutrition usually results from poverty.

There is no internationally accepted definition of what poverty is. In Canada, there are low-income cut-offs (LICUs). Families who live below this income level have insufficient means to maintain a minimum standard of living. LICUs are not poverty lines and, according to Statistics Canada, should not be used for that purpose. Low-income cut-off families will likely use a larger part of their income on necessities such as food, shelter, and clothing than the average family would. How many children in these families go to school hungry every day? It is difficult to tell the exact number.

Low-income cut-offs show important trends. For example, 20 to 30 years ago, seniors were by far the largest group within the low-income category; more recently, lone-parent families headed by women have grown in significance. In 2000, there were 1 139 000 people under the age of 18 in low-income households before tax (Statistics Canada, 2003). Even though low-income cut-offs aren't an international definition of poverty, there are homeless children and adults on Canadian streets.

How have government cutbacks affected low-income families? Willingness to work does not save Canadians from poverty. The family incomes of the working poor are unstable and closely linked to the performance of the economy.

According to Statistics Canada (2003), low-income cut-offs identify those who are substantially worse off than the average. Approximately 57 000 Canadian families have experienced hunger.

◆ The families experiencing hunger are eight times more likely to be led by a single parent

◆ The children are in poorer health than those who have not gone hungry.

◆ Parents were skipping meals and cutting down on their own food intake when food was low.

◆ Primary caregivers in these families suffered more chronic health problems.

◆ Families found it necessary to visit food banks and to ask for help from family and friends.

◆ Mothers had less education than those in families who were not experiencing hunger (Holloway, Holloway, Witte, Zucker, 2003).

Children and families who are experiencing hunger in Canada face many problems, which are made worse when their health suffers because of a lack of nutritious food. It is difficult for young people to focus on schoolwork when they are continuously hungry. Food banks and breakfast programs are just some of the ways to help people in this situation. Foods and Nutrition courses in elementary and secondary schools and through social services are essential. Television programs focusing on good nutrition are another way to educate people.

It is especially important for children and families experiencing hunger to know how to shop and prepare foods to get the most nutrients out of their food dollar. These families need social workers trained in nutrition or dietitians to evaluate their situation and offer suggestions and assistance. Government funding is required to provide these types of educational programs, but they pay off with healthier citizens.

Poor nutrition can also occur among people who have an abundant food supply and can afford to buy enough food. Nutrition problems occur when people consistently choose foods that do not supply enough of the nutrients needed for good health. They may also get too much of some nutrients, such as fat.

The food choices you make have long-term effects on your health. An unbalanced eating plan can increase the risk of diseases that can shorten life or reduce the quality of life.

INTERNET CONNECTS

www.mcgrawhill.ca/links/food
To learn more about malnutrition and poverty, go to the web site above for *Food for Today, First Canadian Edition,* to see where to go next.

Although there are no "bad" foods, too much or too little of one food can create an unhealthy diet. Making balanced choices increases your chances of staying healthy, strong, and active throughout your life.

How Much Do You Need?

Everybody needs the same nutrients, although not necessarily in the same amounts. Females require more iron than males. Athletes and others who are physically active need more of most nutrients than inactive people. Older adults require less of many nutrients.

Canadian and American scientists have, with the help of the National Academy of Sciences, created a new set of standards for assessing the nutrient needs of people of different ages, genders, and with special needs, such as infants and pregnant women. Under the old system, Canadians used Recommended Nutrient Intakes (RNIs) and Americans used Recommended Dietary Allowances (RDAs). Together these scientists created new nutrition recommendations called **Dietary Reference Intakes (DRIs)** to help North Americans stay healthy.

What Is the Purpose of Dietary Reference Intakes?

◆ DRIs will be used by dietitians, nutritionists, and other health professionals as an important tool in shaping North American nutrition policy.

◆ The work being done by these scientists ensures that dietary guidance for Canadians is scientific and reliable.

- These standards will help in the planning and developing of Canadian educational programs and materials.

- They will set standards for assessing the nutrient intakes of Canadians.

- They will provide standards for decisions on food fortification.

- They will be considered when making safety regulations.

- They will also be used by the food industry for product development and nutritional labelling.

INTERNET CONNECTS

www.mcgrawhill.ca/links/food
To learn more about Dietary Reference Intakes (DRIs),
go to the web site above for *Food for Today,
First Canadian Edition,* to see where to go next.

How Nutrients Are Measured

Most nutrients are needed in relatively small amounts. It's easier to measure them using the metric system, the system of measurement used by scientists. The metric system includes small units of measure, such as the milligram (mg). For example, female teens need 15 milligrams of iron each day. That's equivalent to an amount about the size of a single dry bean.

Energy from Nutrients

Running, walking, sitting, and even reading this sentence all require energy. Your body gets this energy from carbohydrates, as well as protein and fats. The energy is measured in units called *kilocalories* (KIL-oh-KAL-uh-reez). A kilocalorie—or **calorie**—is the amount of energy needed to raise the temperature of one kilogram (a little more than 4 cups) of water one degree Celsius.

Your Energy Needs

The number of calories your body needs for energy in a given day depends on a number of factors. These include your activity level, age, weight, and gender. If you are still growing, the number is affected by increased energy demands for building muscles and bones.

The Dietitians of Canada recommend that instead of counting calories, you should focus on making healthy food choices and following *Canada's Food Guide to Healthy Eating.* They even provide a personalized nutrition profile that you can do on-line (see the Internet Connects feature on page 228). You might want to contact a registered dietitian as well.

Each of the four food groups in *Canada's Food Guide to Healthy Eating* contains important nutrients for you to stay healthy. If you only count calories, you can miss out on nutrients that your body needs to function properly. This may lead to fatigue and health problems. You will also miss the chance to taste many wonderful foods. Activity, portion sizes, and the foods that you choose from each food group, as well as how you prepare them, are all important. Try turning off the computer or TV and replace those activities with dancing or playing soccer. Does your energy level go up? Do you find yourself better able to cope with everyday problems?

INTERNET CONNECTS

www.mcgrawhill.ca/links/food
To learn more about *Canada's Food Guide to Healthy Eating*, DRIs, and personalized nutrition profiles, go to the web site above for *Food for Today, First Canadian Edition,* to see where to go next.

Recommended Sources of Calories

Scientists have determined that carbohydrates and proteins in their purest forms provide 4 calories per gram, whereas fat provides 9 calories per gram. Notice that fat has more than twice the number of calories per gram as either of the other energy-producing nutrients.

Health experts recommend that you get less than 30 percent of the calories you take in from fat, approximately 55 percent from carbohydrates, and at least 12 to 15 percent from protein. This ratio provides the healthiest balance of the three nutrients.

For instance, Julie, who needs about 2200 calories a day, should get less than 660 of those calories from fat ($2200 \times 0.3 = 660$). How many grams of fat will supply 660 calories? Since there are 9 calories in 1 gram of fat, divide 660 by 9. The answer is about 73 grams. If Julie eats a fast-food double cheeseburger and fries for lunch (about 47 grams of fat), she will need to eat lower-fat choices the rest of the day to stay under 73 grams of fat.

◆ Vigorous activity, such as running or swimming, uses large amounts of energy. Speak with a dietitian in your community about the calorie requirements of athletes. Share your findings with the class.

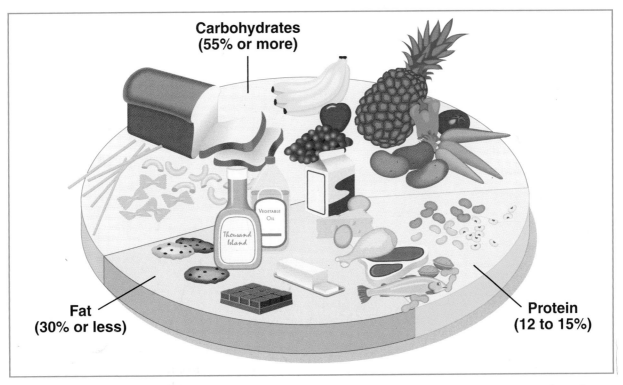

**Carbohydrates
(55% or more)**

**Fat
(30% or less)**

**Protein
(12 to 15%)**

◆ It is not just the number of calories you take in that is important but the sources of those calories. This drawing shows the recommended percentages for the healthiest balance of carbohydrates, protein, and fat. What percentage of your daily food intake should include fruits, vegetables, and grains?

Carbohydrates, Fibre, and Proteins

Carbohydrates

The body's main source of energy is carbohydrates. You may know them as starches and sugars. They are found mainly in foods from plant sources, such as fruits, vegetables, grain products, and legumes and peas. For good health, eat a variety of these foods every day. Generally, they are the least expensive form of energy you can buy.

If you don't eat enough carbohydrates, your body will use the other energy-producing nutrients for energy. When it does this, however, it keeps those nutrients from doing their specialized jobs.

◆ According to the Dietitians of Canada, there is a belief that the levels of serotonin, a hormone produced in the brain, increases when sweet or starchy foods are eaten. This is why breads and pastas are often called "comfort foods." As the serotonin levels increase, a calm feeling sets in.

◆ **Grain products, legumes and peas, and fruits and vegetables are important sources of carbohydrates. Explain the process by which starches and sugars provide energy for the body.**

Depending on their source, carbohydrates fall into one of two categories—complex and simple carbohydrates.

Complex Carbohydrates

Complex carbohydrates are broken down into two subcategories: starches and dietary fibre. Both are found in legumes, peas, and lentils; vegetables, such as potatoes and corn; and grain products, such as rice, pasta, and breads. Foods high in starch are usually good sources of proteins, vitamins, minerals, and dietary fibre.

Dietary Fibre

Dietary fibre is the only form of carbohydrate that does not provide energy. It consists of non-digestible plant materials. This complex carbohydrate is found only in foods from plant sources, such as fruits, vegetables, grain products, and legumes and peas.

There are two kinds of fibre, insoluble and soluble. Most fibre-containing foods provide both.

Insoluble Fibre

Insoluble fibre is fibre that will not dissolve in water. Insoluble fibre absorbs water, much like a sponge does, and contributes bulk. It helps food move through the large intestine at a normal rate. It promotes regular bowel movements and helps prevent constipation. This type of fibre appears to lower the risk of colon cancer. You can find it mainly in fruit and vegetable skins and in whole wheat or wheat bran products.

Soluble Fibre

Soluble fibre is fibre that dissolves in water. Soluble fibre increases the thickness of the stomach contents. Studies show that it may reduce blood cholesterol levels. You can find soluble fibre in fruits, vegetables, legumes, peas, lentils, and oat products.

Food Science ◆ L A B ◆

Connecting Fibre and Flavour in Cereals

Some people believe that high-fibre, whole-grain cereals may not be as tasty as low-fibre cereals made from processed grains. Is this always the case?

Procedure

1. Blindfold a classmate for a blind taste test.

2. Pour out 50 mL (¼-cup) portions of three cereals that are high in fibre (at least 5 grams of fibre per serving) and three that are not (2 grams of fibre or less per serving).

3. Have your subject taste each sample and record his or her reactions. Products are to be assigned a rating of 1 or 2, where 2 is high fibre and 1 is low fibre.

4. Compare the ratings for each cereal with the actual fibre content on the Nutrition Facts panel for the product.

Conclusions

◆ How did your subject's rankings compare with the actual fibre content of each cereal?

◆ How can this information help in your future purchases of cereal?

◆ How does cost correlate with flavour or fibre content?

How Much Fibre?

How much fibre do you consume? If you are like most other Canadians, you get only about half the recommended fibre intake. The Dietitians of Canada recommend 25 grams of dietary fibre a day for women and 38 grams a day for men. To compute your daily fibre needs during growth years (13 to 18 years) add 5 to your age. For instance, a 14-year-old needs 19 grams of fibre daily (14 + 5).

To get enough fibre, eat a wide variety of plant foods every day. Bean burritos, chili with beans, vegetable stir-fry dishes, and vegetable pizza are all excellent choices. Increase fibre gradually, and be sure to drink plenty of fluids to avoid digestive upset.

Simple Carbohydrates

Simple carbohydrates, or sugars, are a natural part of many foods. These sugars include *fructose* (FROOK-tohs), found in fruits; *maltose* (MALL-tohs), found in grain products; and *lactose* (LACK-tohs), found in milk products. Most foods that contain these sugars also provide other nutrients, such as proteins, vitamins, and minerals.

INTERNET CONNECTS

www.mcgrawhill.ca/links/food
To learn more about carbohydrates, go to the web site above for *Food for Today, First Canadian Edition,* to see where to go next.

Refined sugars are sugars that are extracted from plants and used as a sweetener. The most widely used refined sugar is *sucrose* (SOOK-rohs), or table sugar. Sucrose comes from plants such as sugar cane or sugar beets. Other refined sugars include corn syrup, honey, maple syrup, molasses, and brown sugar. Refined sugars do not supply nutrients other than simple carbohydrates. Eating large amounts of sweetened foods can lead to excess weight, which can contribute to health problems.

Proteins

When it comes to the energy they provide, complex and simple carbohydrates and proteins are all created equal. However, unlike their sweet and starchy counterparts, proteins have unique building roles in the body. They are used mainly to help the body grow and repair worn-out or damaged parts. About one-fifth of your body's total weight is protein. Your hair, eyes, skin, muscles, and bones are made of proteins. The proteins you eat help maintain them in good condition.

Proteins also regulate important body processes. For instance, they play a major role in fighting disease because parts of the immune system are proteins.

Proteins can do their job only if you consume enough carbohydrates and fats for your energy needs. If not, the body uses proteins for energy instead of for building and repairing.

◆ Good sources of protein include animal foods, which are called complete proteins, and plant foods, such as the ones pictured. Describe a meatless meal that would provide the protein your body needs.

Proteins are found in all foods from animal sources, including meat, poultry, fish and other seafood, eggs, and milk products. They are also found in foods from plant sources, especially legumes and peas, peanuts, vegetables, and grain products. Most Canadians eat more protein than they need. Excess amounts are broken down and stored by the body as fat.

Complete and Incomplete Proteins

Proteins are made of chains of chemical building blocks called **amino** (uh-MEE-noh) **acids.** Just as letters of the alphabet are arranged to make countless different words, so these chemical substances that make up body proteins can be arranged in numerous ways. Your body can make all but 9 of the 22 known amino acids. These nine are called *essential amino acids* because they must come from foods you eat.

Complete proteins—proteins that supply all nine essential amino acids—include meat, poultry, fish, eggs, milk products, and soy products. Except for soybeans, all foods from plant sources supply incomplete proteins, proteins lacking one or more essential amino acids. Although such foods by themselves fail to deliver all the essential amino acids, it is possible to obtain them all by eating a variety of foods and enough calories throughout the day. This is especially important for people who follow a vegetarian diet.

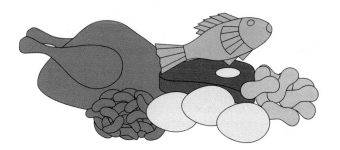

The Origin of "Upper Crust"

Have you ever wondered where the expression "upper crust," meaning to be of better quality or wealthier, came from? For pioneers in Canada, life was often very difficult. The women had to be very resourceful to provide their families with nutrients, such as carbohydrates and protein to help them survive the cold winters. When wheat was scarce for making pies, housewives had to find clever ways to feed their families and any guests that might arrive. These thrifty women learned to make the best of the resources they had. They often baked the pies using the more expensive wheat flour for only the top crust that could be seen. The bottom crusts were made from a less-expensive rye flour. By doing this, their families still obtained carbohydrates, but for a cheaper price. This is how the saying "upper crust" originated.

Source: O'Byrne, Lorainne (1977).

Most Canadians get the largest amount of their protein from animal sources. Health experts, however, recommend that people get more of their protein from plant sources. Why? Plant sources generally have less fat, and low-fat choices are now recommended.

INTERNET CONNECTS

www.mcgrawhill.ca/links/food
To learn more about complete and incomplete proteins, go to the web site above for *Food for Today,*
First Canadian Edition, to see where to go next.

Fats

Functions and Sources of Fats

Fats—or, more specifically, substances called *essential fatty acids,* found mainly in vegetable oils—are an essential nutrient with several important functions. Fats promote healthy skin and normal cell growth, and carry vitamins A, D, E, and K to wherever they are needed. In addition, fats stored in the body provide a reserve supply of energy and act as a cushion to protect your heart, liver, and other vital organs.

From a sensory standpoint, fats add flavour to food. Because they move through the digestive system slowly, they help you feel full longer.

What, then, is the problem with fat? Studies show that many Canadians eat too much fat—and the wrong kinds. Doing so can increase the risk of illness, such as heart disease and cancer. It can also create a health risk by contributing to overweight or obesity. Remember, fats have twice as many calories per gram as carbohydrates or proteins.

Although fats cannot, nor should not, be eliminated from one's eating plan completely, it is important to limit their use. One way of accomplishing this is to eat more complex carbohydrates. Another is to choose low-fat foods. Foods high in fat include butter, margarine, oils, cream, sour cream, salad dressing, fried foods, some baked goods, and chocolate. Moderate to large amounts of fat are also found in some cuts of meat, nuts and seeds, peanut butter, egg yolks, whole milk, and some cheeses.

◆ Although reducing fat in your diet is sound advice for most people, fat is not always the villain you may have been led to believe. In fact, you will see that you can't live without some fat.

◆ There are foods, such as margarine, butter, vegetable oils, and shortenings, that are obvious sources of fat. Can you name some foods that contain hidden sources of fat?

FYI

Confused About Fats?

If you look on a food package label you will not see the term *trans fatty* acids listed. Look for *partially hydrogenated* in the list of ingredients instead (Dietitians of Canada, (n.d.).

Cholesterol, Fats, and Health

"Is cholesterol the very same thing as fat?" "Do I need any cholesterol, or can I eliminate it from my eating plan?" Questions like these about cholesterol are common. You may have asked some yourself.

What Is Cholesterol?

Cholesterol (kuh-LES-tuhr-ol) is not fat. Rather, it is a fat-like substance present in all body cells, and needed for many essential body processes. It contributes to the digestion of fat and the skin's production of vitamin D. Adults manufacture all the cholesterol they need, mostly in the liver. Infants' and children's bodies, on the other hand, don't produce enough cholesterol. So they need it in their diet.

A certain amount of cholesterol circulates in the blood. It does not float through the bloodstream on its own, but in chemical "packages" called lipoproteins (LIH-poh-PROH-teenz). There are two major kinds of lipoproteins, LDL and HDL.

- LDL, which stands for "low-density lipoprotein," is a chemical that takes cholesterol from the liver to wherever it is needed in the body. However, if too much LDL cholesterol is circulating, the excess amounts of cholesterol can build up in artery walls. This build-up increases the risk of heart disease or stroke. Thus, LDL cholesterol has come to be called "bad" cholesterol.

- HDL stands for "high-density lipoprotein" and refers to a chemical that picks up excess cholesterol and takes it back to the liver, keeping it from causing harm. For this reason, HDL cholesterol has come to be known as "good" cholesterol.

Medical tests can determine the amounts of total cholesterol, LDL cholesterol, and HDL cholesterol in the bloodstream. The risk of heart disease may increase if LDL and total cholesterol levels are too high and if the HDL level is too low.

Making wise food choices can help reduce the amount of harmful cholesterol in the bloodstream. As you will see, both cholesterol and fat in foods may affect blood cholesterol levels. The good news is that cholesterol can't make you fat since it doesn't provide energy.

Cholesterol in Foods

Did you also know that all animals have the ability to manufacture cholesterol? This means that if you eat any animal product, including meat, poultry, and fish or other seafood, you will likely be consuming some cholesterol. Other foods high in cholesterol are egg yolks, and liver and other organ meats. Eating less of these foods may help reduce blood levels of LDL cholesterol.

Saturated and Unsaturated Fats

For most people, the amounts and types of fats eaten have a greater effect on blood cholesterol levels than does the amount of cholesterol eaten.

The fats found in food, such as butter, chicken fat, or corn oil, are made up of different combinations of *fatty acids*. There are three basic kinds of fatty acids. Each has a different effect on cholesterol levels. All fats include all three kinds of fatty acids, but in varying amounts.

- **Saturated** (SAT-chur-ay-ted) **fatty acids** are fats that appear to raise the level of LDL ("bad") cholesterol in the bloodstream. Foods relatively high in saturated fatty acids include meat, poultry skin, whole-milk dairy products, and the tropical oils— coconut oil, palm oil, and palm kernel oil.

- **Polyunsaturated** (PAH-lee-un-SAT-chur-ay-ted) **fatty acids** are fats that seem to help lower cholesterol levels. Many vegetable oils, such as corn oil, soybean oil, and safflower oil, are high in polyunsaturated fatty acids.

- **Monounsaturated** (MAH-no-un-SAT-chur-ay-ted) **fatty acids** are fats that also help lower LDL ("bad") cholesterol levels and may help raise levels of HDL. Foods relatively high in monounsaturated fatty acids include olives, olive oil, avocados, peanuts, peanut oil, and canola oil.

A simple rule of thumb is that fats that are solid at room temperature, such as butter, are made up mainly of saturated fatty acids.

Fats: What's in Them?

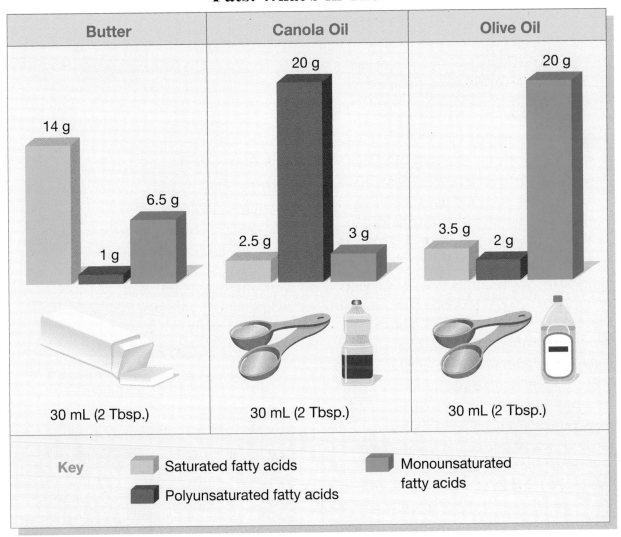

Butter	Canola Oil	Olive Oil

Butter: 14 g, 1 g, 6.5 g — 30 mL (2 Tbsp.)

Canola Oil: 20 g, 2.5 g, 3 g — 30 mL (2 Tbsp.)

Olive Oil: 20 g, 3.5 g, 2 g — 30 mL (2 Tbsp.)

Key
- Saturated fatty acids
- Polyunsaturated fatty acids
- Monounsaturated fatty acids

◆ **Butter, canola oil, and olive oil each contain all three types of fatty acids.** Identify the type of fat that is highest in each of the following: polyunsaturated fatty acids, saturated fatty acids, and monounsaturated fatty acids.

Fats that are liquid at room temperature, such as corn oil or olive oil, are composed primarily of unsaturated fatty acids.

Hydrogenation

If corn oil is high in polyunsaturated fats, then it would seem logical that margarine made from corn oil is likewise high in polyunsaturated fats. Unfortunately, this is not so. Margarine and vegetable shortening

are both examples of hydrogenated fats. **Hydrogenation** (hy-DRAH-juh-NAY-shun) is a process in which missing hydrogen atoms are added to an unsaturated fat to make it firmer in texture. Hydrogenation results in a type of fatty acid called *trans fatty acid*. Trans fatty acids have many of the properties of saturated fats. They can raise blood cholesterol levels. Partially hydrogenated vegetable oils, some margarines, and some

FOR YOUR HEALTH

cookies, crackers, and commercially baked products contain trans fatty acids.

For better health, many people are making a switch from saturated to unsaturated fats. You need to remember too that it's important to limit the total amount of fat eaten.

Micronutrients

Vitamins

Vitamins help keep your body's tissues healthy and its many systems working properly. They also help carbohydrates, fats, and proteins do their work.

Scientists are still learning about the functions of vitamins. One relatively recent discovery is that some vitamins have antioxidant (an-tee-OKS-ih-dunt) properties. **Antioxidants** are substances that protect body cells and the immune system from harmful chemicals in the air, certain foods, and tobacco smoke. Other recent studies suggest that some vitamins may protect against illnesses such as

heart disease and cancer. More research is needed, however, before scientists can say for certain what specific roles all the vitamins have in the body.

◆ You are what you eat. Vitamins and minerals play an important part in keeping your body healthy.

Types of Vitamins

So far, scientists have identified 13 different vitamins, only one of which—vitamin D—is manufactured by the body. The rest must be derived from food.

Vitamins are classified into two groups:

- **Water-soluble vitamins** are vitamins that dissolve in water and thus pass easily into the bloodstream in the process of digestion. Water-soluble vitamins include vitamin C and the eight B vitamins.

- **Fat-soluble vitamins** are vitamins that are absorbed and transported by fat. They include vitamins A, D, E, and K.

The charts on pages 240–242 list the functions and food sources of these nutrients.

If you eat more fat-soluble vitamins than you need, they will be stored in the body's fat and in the liver. Your body can draw on these stores when needed. In contrast, water-soluble vitamins remain in your body for only a short time. Therefore, you need them on a daily basis.

Vitamin Sources

Some vitamins can be found in a wide range of foods. Others are limited to just a few food sources. To be sure you are getting the vitamins your body needs, remember the following tips:

- **Eat plenty of fruits and vegetables every day.** These plants are the only naturally occurring source of vitamin C. In particular, eat plenty of dark green vegetables (such as broccoli and spinach) and deep yellow-orange fruits and vegetables (such as carrots, sweet potatoes, and cantaloupe). These foods can help meet your need for vitamin A.

- **Drink milk.** Milk is one of the best sources of vitamin D. The body can also make some vitamin D through the action of sunlight on the skin. That's why it's also called the "sunshine vitamin."

- **When you eat bread or pasta, choose enriched, whole-grain products.** These are excellent sources of folate, an important vitamin that builds red blood cells. Other sources include green leafy vegetables, legumes, and some fruits.

- ◆ **Foods high in vitamins usually contain substantial amounts of other nutrients as well.** Use the tables that follow to identify foods in this picture that are high in vitamin C. Which contain B vitamins?

Water-Soluble Vitamins

Vitamin/Functions	Food Sources
Thiamin (Vitamin B_1) • Helps turn carbohydrates into energy • Needed for muscle co-ordination and a healthy nervous system	• Enriched and whole-grain breads and cereals • Legumes and peas • Lean pork • Liver
Riboflavin (Vitamin B_2) • Helps your body release energy from carbohydrates, fats, and proteins	• Enriched breads and cereals • Milk products • Green leafy vegetables • Eggs • Meat, poultry, fish
Niacin (Vitamin B_3) • Helps your body release energy from carbohydrates, fats, and proteins • Needed for a healthy nervous system and mucous membranes	• Meat, poultry, fish • Enriched and whole-grain breads and cereals • Legumes and peas • Peanuts, peanut butter
Vitamin B_6 • Helps your body use carbohydrates and proteins • Needed for a healthy nervous system • Helps your body make non-essential amino acids, which then make body cells	• Poultry, fish, pork • Legumes and peas • Nuts • Whole grains • Some fruits and vegetables • Liver and kidneys
Folate (Folacin, Folic acid) • Teams with vitamin B_{12} to help build red blood cells and form genetic material • Helps prevent birth defects • Helps your body use proteins • May help protect against heart disease	• Green leafy vegetables • Legumes and peas • Fruits • Enriched and whole-grain breads
Vitamin B_{12} • Helps your body use carbohydrates, fats, and proteins • Teams with folate to help build red blood cells and form genetic material • Needed for a healthy nervous system	• Found naturally in animal foods, such as meat, poultry, fish, shellfish, eggs, and milk products • Some fortified food • Some nutritional yeasts

(continued)

Water-Soluble Vitamins (continued)

Vitamin/Functions	Food Sources
Pantothenic acid	
• Helps the body release energy from carbohydrates, fats, and proteins • Helps the body produce cholesterol • Needed for a healthy nervous system • Promotes normal growth and development	• Meat, poultry, fish • Eggs • Legumes and peas • Whole-grain breads and cereals • Milk • Some fruits and vegetables
Biotin	
• Helps your body use carbohydrates, fats, and proteins	• Green leafy vegetables • Whole-grain breads and cereals • Liver • Egg yolks
Vitamin C (Ascorbic Acid)	
• Helps maintain healthy capillaries, bones, skin, and teeth • Helps your body heal wounds and resist infections • Aids in absorption of iron • Helps form collagen, which gives structure to bones, cartilage, muscle, and blood vessels • Works as an antioxidant	• Fruits—citrus fruits (orange, grapefruit, tangerine), cantaloupe, guava, kiwi, mango, papaya, strawberries • Vegetables—bell peppers, broccoli, cabbage, kale, plantains, potatoes, tomatoes

Fat-Soluble Vitamins

Vitamin/Functions	Food Sources
Vitamin A	
• Helps protect you from infections • Helps form and maintain healthy skin, hair, mucous membranes, bones, and teeth • Helps you see normally at night • Works as an antioxidant	• Milk products • Liver • Egg yolks • Foods high in beta carotene (see phytochemicals, p. 245)

(continued)

Fat-Soluble Vitamins (continued)

Vitamin/Functions	Food Sources
Vitamin D	
• Helps your body use calcium and phosphorus • Helps your body build strong and healthy bones and teeth	• Fortified milk products • Egg yolks • Higher-fat fish—salmon and mackerel • Fortified breakfast cereals and margarine
Vitamin E	
• Works as an antioxidant	• Nuts and seeds • Green leafy vegetables • Wheat germ • Vegetable oils
Vitamin K	
• Necessary for blood to clot normally	• Green leafy vegetables • Fruits and other vegetables • Milk products • Egg yolks • Wheat bran and wheat germ

Minerals

Like vitamins, minerals are vital for good health. Most minerals become a part of your body, such as your teeth and bones. Others are used to make substances that your body needs.

Types of Minerals

Minerals can be divided into three groups:

◆ **Major minerals** are minerals needed in relatively large amounts. These include calcium, phosphorus, and magnesium.

◆ **Electrolytes** (ee-LEK-troh-lyts) are specific major minerals that work together to maintain the body's fluid balance. These include potassium, sodium, and chloride.

◆ **Trace minerals** are minerals needed in very small amounts, but they are just as important as other nutrients. They include iron, copper, zinc, iodine, and selenium. Scientists continue to research trace minerals and their functions.

✚ Safety Check

Since fat-soluble vitamins are stored in the body's tissues, an excess build-up of them is possible, leading to toxic or other damaging effects. An overdose of vitamin A, for example, can cause nerve and liver damage, bone and joint pain, vomiting, and abnormal bone growth. People who take vitamin supplements are advised to use caution.

Meeting Your Mineral Needs

Though your need for some minerals is small, getting the right amount is important to your health. For example, getting too much or too little iodine can cause thyroid problems. The thyroid gland, located in the neck, produces substances needed for growth and development. For certain individuals, getting too much sodium, or too little potassium, may be linked to high blood pressure.

Getting the right balance of minerals is not difficult. The key is to eat a wide variety of foods. However, you may need to pay special attention to whether you are getting enough calcium and iron—two major minerals especially important for teens.

Calcium and Strong Bones

Calcium has several important functions. One of these is to maintain bone strength. Lack of calcium throughout life is one of the factors that can lead to **osteoporosis** (AH-stee-oh-puh-ROH-sis). This is a condition in which the bones become porous, making them weak and fragile. As a result, posture may become stooped and bones can break easily. "One in 4 women and 1 in 8 men suffer from osteoporosis in Canada." "Women are at greater risk because they have

INTERNET CONNECTS

www.mcgrawhill.ca/links/food
To learn more about reducing the risk of osteoporosis, go to the web site above for *Food for Today, First Canadian Edition,* to see where to go next.

less bone tissue and because diminished estrogen at menopause accelerates bone loss." (Health Canada—Nutrition, 2002).

You can lessen your risk of osteoporosis, but you need to start now. Bone mass builds up during childhood, the teen years, and young adulthood. The more you do to build strong, healthy bones now, the less likely you will be to develop osteoporosis when you are older.

Here are some "bone-building" tips you can follow:

◆ Eat plenty of calcium-rich foods. These include milk and milk products, legumes and peas, and dark green, leafy vegetables.

◆ Follow other basic guidelines for healthy eating. Remember, nutrients work in teams. Like best friends on a team, vitamin D and many other nutrients work together with calcium.

◆ Play a sport, take part in some other vigorous activity, or exercise regularly. Weight-bearing exercise, such as walking or jogging, and weight training, help build and maintain strong bones.

◆ Avoid tobacco products, alcohol, and excess caffeine (found in coffee, tea, and soft drinks). All may contribute to osteoporosis.

◆ **Weight-resistance training, which includes the activity shown here, helps build and maintain strong bones. Name two foods you can eat that aid in this process. Identify the key nutrient in these foods.**

Iron and Red Blood Cells

Iron is essential for making hemoglobin (HEE-muh-gloh-buhn), a substance in your red blood cells that carries oxygen to all the cells in your body. If you don't get enough iron, your blood may not be able to carry enough oxygen to your cells. The resulting condition is called *iron-deficiency anemia* (uh-NEE-mee-uh). People with anemia are often tired, weak, short of breath, and pale.

Where can you find iron? Some sources are lean red meat, legumes and peas, dried fruits, grain products, and dark green, leafy vegetables. Eating foods rich in vitamin C at the same time as foods rich in iron helps the body absorb more of the iron from plant foods. Interestingly, the iron content of foods cooked in an iron skillet gets a boost. Researchers disagree, however, on how much iron can be absorbed from this source.

Major Minerals

Mineral/Functions	Food Sources
Calcium	
• Helps build bone and maintain bone strength • Helps prevent osteoporosis • Helps regulate blood clotting, nerve activity, and other body processes • Needed for muscle contraction, including the heart	• Milk products • Canned fish with edible bones • Legumes, peas, and lentils • Dark green, leafy vegetables—broccoli, spinach, and turnip greens • Tofu made with calcium sulfate • Calcium-fortified orange juice and soy milk
Phosphorus	
• Works with calcium to build strong bones and teeth • Helps release energy from carbohydrates, fats, and proteins • Helps build body cells and tissues	• Meat, poultry, fish • Eggs • Nuts • Legumes and peas • Milk products • Grain products
Magnesium	
• Helps build bones and make proteins • Helps nerves and muscles work normally	• Whole-grain products • Green vegetables • Legumes and peas • Nuts and seeds

Trace Minerals

Mineral/Functions	Food Sources
Iron • Helps carry oxygen in the blood • Helps your cells use oxygen	• Meat, fish, shellfish • Egg yolks • Dark green, leafy vegetables • Legumes and peas • Enriched or whole-grain products • Dried fruits
Iodine • Responsible for your body's use of energy	• Saltwater fish • Iodized salt
Copper • Helps iron make red blood cells • Helps keep your bones, blood vessels, and nerves healthy • Helps your heart work properly	• Whole-grain products • Seafood • Organ meats • Legumes and peas • Nuts and seeds
Zinc • Helps your body make proteins, heal wounds, and form blood • Helps in growth and maintenance of all tissues • Helps your body use carbohydrates, fats, and proteins • Affects the senses of taste and smell • Helps your body use vitamin A	• Meat, liver, poultry, fish, shellfish • Milk products • Legumes and peas, peanuts • Whole-grain breads and cereals • Eggs • Miso (fermented soybean paste)
Selenium • Helps your heart work properly • Works as an antioxidant	• Whole-grain breads and cereals • Vegetables (amount varies with content in soil) • Meat, organ meats, fish, shellfish
Fluoride • Helps strengthen teeth and prevent cavities	• In many communities, small amounts are added to the water supply to help improve dental health.

Electrolytes

Mineral/Functions	Food Sources
Sodium	
• Helps maintain the fluid balance in your body • Helps with muscle and nerve action • Helps regulate blood pressure	• Table salt • Processed foods
Chloride	
• Helps maintain the fluid balance in your body • Helps transmit nerve signals	• Table salt
Potassium	
• Helps maintain the fluid balance in your body • Helps maintain the heartbeat • Helps with muscle and nerve action • Helps maintain normal blood pressure	• Fruits—bananas and oranges • Vegetables • Meat, poultry, fish • Legumes and peas • Milk products

Safety Check

Rich in many vitamins and minerals, eggs can be a valuable contribution to your diet. However, if eggs aren't handled properly, a foodborne organism called salmonella can grow. Don't keep eggs and egg-rich foods at temperatures between 4 and 60°C (40 and 140°F) ("the temperature danger zone") for more than two hours.

Phytochemicals

If you look up **phytochemical** in a dictionary, you will find that this word (from the Greek *phyton,* or "plant") was coined over 150 years ago. Plants contain important disease-fighting nutrients.

It is estimated that every plant has at least 50 to 100 different phytochemicals. So far, most of the research has concentrated on identifying and classifying these substances, though early studies hint that many may play important roles in reducing the risks of cancer and other diseases. Some phytochemicals, like vitamins, are antioxidants.

One of the best-known phytochemicals is beta carotene (bay-tuh KAR-uh-teen), a substance that gives fruits and vegetables their bright yellow-orange and dark green colours. Beta carotene is an antioxidant believed to prevent certain kinds of cancer. The body uses beta carotene to produce vitamin A.

The following table lists just a few of the phytochemicals being studied.

Phytochemicals

Phytochemical	Food Source	Potential Health Benefits
Beta carotene	• Yellow and orange fruits and vegetables • Dark green vegetables	• May play role in slowing the progression of cancer
Allyl sulfides	• Onions, garlic, leeks, chives, shallots	• May play role in cancer prevention • May play role in lowering blood pressure and cholesterol
Indoles	• Cabbage, broccoli, kale, cauliflower	• May play role in cancer prevention
Saponins	• Soybeans, legumes, peas • Most vegetables	• May prevent cancer cells from multiplying
Lutein	• Kale, spinach, collards, mustard greens, romaine lettuce	• May protect against blindness
Phytosterol	• Soybeans and some soy products • Nuts • Whole-grain products • Many vegetable oils	• May play role in cancer prevention • May lower cholesterol

Water

Often called the "forgotten nutrient," water is actually the one most critical to our survival. You may be able to live for weeks without food, but you can live only a few days without water. About 50 to 60 percent of your body is water. Your blood is 80 percent water.

Water plays a role in many chemical reactions that constantly go on in the body. It also helps keep the body temperature normal. Think of what happens when you get too warm. You begin to perspire. As the perspiration evaporates into the air, it cools your body. Water also helps your body get rid of waste products.

On average, the body uses about 2 to 3 litres (quarts) of water a day. To help replace this lost fluid, be sure to drink at least 2 L (8 cups) of water daily. During strenuous physical activity or in hot weather, when you perspire heavily, you usually need even more. A good rule of thumb is to drink 250 mL (1 cup) of water for every 250 g (½ pound) of weight lost through perspiration.

Two litres (8 cups) of water daily may seem like a large amount. To make it easier to get the amount of water you need, keep bottles of water on hand. Carrying a bottle filled with water is one convenient way to help meet your daily need. If you like, flavour it with a little fresh lemon juice.

Other liquids, such as milk, fruit juice, and soup, can also help supply your body with water. So can fresh fruits and vegetables, most of which contain large amounts of water. Did you know that watermelon is over 90 percent water?

FOR YOUR HEALTH

Water, Water Everywhere

Don't wait until you are thirsty to drink water. By the time you feel thirsty, you may have already lost a litre (quart) of water or more. To stay well hydrated when water or other beverages are not handy, eat foods with a high water content. Here are a few:

Food	Percent Water by Weight
Lettuce	95
Watermelon	92
Grapefruit	91
Yogurt	75

◆ **Health experts highly recommend drinking at least eight glasses of water each day.** Name two foods that are good sources of this essential nutrient.

Food Science ◆ L A B ◆

How Much Water Is in Food?

Meeting daily fluid needs can seem challenging to many people. However, many foods contain a lot of water. Which foods have the most? You are about to find out.

Procedure

1. Weigh a raw potato, apple, and carrot, and record the weight of each.

2. Place one of the foods in a food processor, and process until it is a liquidy mash. Pour and scrape the food into a strainer, forcing out as much liquid as possible. Weigh the liquid, and measure it.

3. Calculate the percentage of water by comparing the liquid weight with the original weight.

4. Repeat with each of the remaining foods.

Conclusions

◆ Which food had the highest water content? Which had the lowest?

◆ Do you think it is possible to meet at least half (1L; 4 cups) of your water needs through solid food? Explain.

◆ Repeat the experiment using a slice of bread. Predict the percentage that is water. How close was your prediction?

How Your Body Uses Food

Digestion

The process of breaking down food into usable nutrients is known as **digestion**. It takes place in the digestive system, a long, hollow tube that extends from the mouth through the entire body. Here is what happens to food on its journey through the digestive system.

◆ While you are looking at this picture, your digestive system is busy breaking down the food you have eaten into nutrients so that your heart can beat and your brain can tell your eyes to focus on the book in front of you.

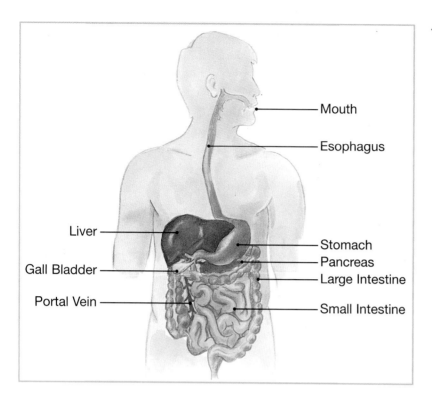

◆ Each part of the digestive tract has a specific role in breaking food down into nutrients. In what body organ does digestion begin?

Mouth

Esophagus

Liver

Gall Bladder

Portal Vein

Stomach

Pancreas

Large Intestine

Small Intestine

The Mouth

The digestive process starts before you even begin to eat the food. Just smelling and seeing food, or even thinking about it, can start saliva flowing in your mouth. Saliva is the first of many digestive juices that act on food to break it down chemically.

Food is also broken down physically as your teeth grind it into tiny pieces. Chewing food well is important. It mixes the food with saliva and makes it easier to swallow and digest. Solid food should be chewed until it is the consistency of applesauce.

The Esophagus

Once the food is swallowed, it passes into the esophagus (ih-SOFF-uh-gus), a long tube connecting the mouth to the stomach. The muscles of the esophagus contract and relax, creating a series of wave-like movements

that force the food into the stomach. This muscular action is called peristalsis (PEHR-uh-STAHL-suhs).

The Stomach

The stomach, the next stop on the digestive journey, is the widest part of the digestive system. It is a muscular pouch located on the left side of your body inside the rib cage. On the average, your stomach can hold about 1 L (4 cups) of food.

The walls of the stomach manufacture gastric juices—a combination of acid and enzymes that helps in the chemical breakdown of the food. In addition, the stomach breaks food down physically through peristalsis. The food is churned until it turns into a thick liquid called chyme (KIME).

Different kinds of food take different amounts of time to break down and leave the stomach. Think of your stomach as a holding tank. Carbohydrates take the shortest amount of time, usually one to two hours. Proteins take longer, about three to five hours. Fats take the longest time to digest, up to seven hours. That is why a food with fat will keep you from feeling hungry for a longer time.

The Small Intestine

From the stomach, chyme is released into the small intestine a little at a time. The small intestine is a long, winding tube between the stomach and the large intestine. Here, the chyme is acted on by three types of digestive juices:

♦ Bile, a substance that helps your body digest and absorb fats. Bile is produced in the liver and stored in the gall bladder until needed.

♦ Pancreatic (pan-kree-AT-ik) juice, which contains enzymes that help break down carbohydrates, proteins, and fats. It is produced by the pancreas (PAN-kree-us), a gland connected to the small intestine.

♦ Intestinal juice, produced in the small intestine. This digestive fluid works with the others to break down food.

When fully broken down, carbohydrates are turned into a simple sugar called glucose (GLOO-kohs). **Glucose** is the body's basic fuel supply. Fats are changed into fatty acids. Proteins are broken down into amino acids. Vitamins, minerals, and water do not need to be broken down—they're ready for action just as they are. They can be used by your body in the same form in which they occur in food.

Using the Nutrients

Once food has been broken down into nutrients, digestion is complete. However, your body still has work to do. It must absorb the nutrients and take them to where they can be used or stored.

Absorption

After digestion, the nutrients are absorbed into the bloodstream. Most absorption takes place in your small intestine. The lining of the small intestine is arranged in folds. It is lined with billions of tiny finger-like projections, called villi (VIL-eye). The villi increase the surface area of the intestine so that more nutrients can be absorbed.

After absorption, some waste mineral, including fibre, is left in the small intestine. This waste material is moved into the large intestine, also called the colon. The colon removes water, potassium, and sodium from the waste. The remainder is stored as a semi-solid in the rectum (REK-tum), or lower part of the intestine, until it is eliminated.

Processing and Storing Nutrients

After the nutrients are absorbed by the villi of the small intestine, they are carried through a blood vessel, called the portal vein, to the liver. One of the liver's many jobs is to turn nutrients into forms the body can use. For instance, it converts amino acids into different kinds of proteins. Then the proteins are carried by the blood to wherever they are needed.

Some nutrients, if not needed immediately, can be stored for future use. Extra glucose, for example, is converted by the liver into glycogen (GLY-kuh-juhn), a storage form of glucose. Glycogen is stored in the liver and the muscles. If there is more glucose than can

```
INTERNET CONNECTS

www.mcgrawhill.ca/links/food
To learn more about nutrients and nutrition,
go to the web site above for Food for Today,
First Canadian Edition, to see where to go next.
```

◆ **Even when you are asleep your body continues to work and renew itself. Name the type of energy your body uses during periods of rest.**

be stored as glycogen, the rest is converted to body fat. Fats are then deposited throughout the body as an energy reserve. Excess fatty acids and amino acids are also converted to body fat.

Minerals are stored in various ways. For instance, iron is stored in the liver and in bone marrow. Fat-soluble vitamins are stored mainly in the liver and in body fat.

Some nutrients, including most water-soluble vitamins, are not stored for long periods. If not needed, they are removed from the body with wastes.

How Nutrients Are Used

Nutrients and oxygen are carried throughout the bloodstream to individual cells, where they are used for specialized purposes. As you may recall, one of these is to provide energy. This is done by combining glucose with water. Such a process in which fuel is combined with oxygen to produce energy is known as oxidation (AHKS-ih-day-shuhn). Another example of oxidation is a log burning in a fireplace. The fuel in that case is wood. To keep burning, the wood must have oxygen from the air. Energy is produced as light and heat.

In your body, the fuel is glucose. When glucose reaches the cells, it is combined with oxygen. The result is energy as heat and power for the cells.

Your body uses energy for two basic purposes:

◆ *Automatic processes,* such as breathing, digesting food, and creating new cells. Even when you are resting or sleeping, your body is using minimal amounts of energy. This minimum amount of energy required to maintain the life processes in a living organism is called **basal metabolism** (BAY-zuhl muh-TAB-uh-lih-zuhm).

◆ *Physical activities,* such as work and exercise. The more active you are, the more energy you use. For instance, you would use more energy walking up a flight of stairs than riding in an elevator.

Generally, about two-thirds of the calories used by the body are for basal metabolism. However, this varies from person to person. It depends on factors such as age, body size, and body composition—the ratio of lean tissue to fat. The amount of energy used for basal metabolism is sometimes called the *basal metabolic rate,* or BMR.

As you can see, the human body is an amazing organism. Without even thinking about it, your body carries on thousands of complex processes every moment of your life.

Registered Dietitian in a Private Practice

Donna Weldon

What education is required for your job?

- Bachelor of Applied Science
- Dietetic internship
- Masters Degree in education (optional)

What skills does a person need to be able to do your job?

- Counselling, teaching, and interpersonal skills.
- Comfort with food and cooking.
- Oral and written communication skills, including public speaking.
- Sound understanding of nutrition and the ability to interpret scientific information.
- Research and organizational skills.

What do you like most about your job?

I like helping people make changes in their lifestyle and eating habits. I enjoy the variety of jobs that consulting allows me.

What other jobs/job titles have you had in the past?

I have worked as a clinical dietitian in a hospital, and a nutrition educator in the food industry.

What advice would you give a person who is considering a career as a registered dietitian?

Being a dietitian is very much about teaching, helping, and educating people. This is the kind of job that requires interpersonal skills and a sense of compassion. If you are interested in science and the function of food in the body, this is a fascinating field.

Comment on what you consider to be important issues or trends in food and nutrition.

With the research being done on the genome project, people will soon be able to determine what their genetic risks are for certain diseases and will be seeking very personalized information about what they should eat or avoid eating. In other words, while we have a food guide that covers all healthy Canadians, in the future we may be providing individual food guides to people based on their genetic makeup. It makes the science of nutrition look even more exciting in years to come.

◆ Good nutrition plays an important part in everyday life and at every stage of the life cycle.

Good Nutrition and the Life Cycle

The Life Cycle

Scientists refer to this constant progression from one stage of development to the next as the life cycle. The human life cycle is made up essentially of five developmental stages, each with its own growth and nutritional needs. These stages are the prenatal period, infancy, childhood, adolescence, and adulthood.

Prenatal Period

During the nine months of a normal pregnancy, a single cell divides and multiplies millions of times, ultimately developing into a being able to survive in the outside world. Proper development during the prenatal period depends on the right nutrients. Yet, the fetus (FEE-tus)—or unborn baby—is powerless to control its nutrient needs. Responsibility for meeting these needs falls to the mother.

Guidelines for Pregnant Women

A woman who suspects she is pregnant should see a doctor as soon as possible. Most women see an obstetrician (ob-stuh-TRISH-un), a physician who specializes in pregnancy. Increasing numbers of women are opting for the services of a midwife who, in addition to providing prenatal care, specializes in the delivery of healthy babies.

Nutrition During Pregnancy

A woman usually does not learn of her pregnancy until a month or more after she has become pregnant. Meanwhile, the food she has eaten has been the only nourishment for the unborn baby. Therefore, concern about good nutrition should begin before pregnancy. A healthy woman who has good eating habits before her pregnancy begins is more likely to have a safe pregnancy and a healthy baby. Poor eating habits can place the baby at risk for serious health problems.

Teen Pregnancy

Teen pregnancies are particularly at risk because teens need added nutrients for both themselves and the fetus. Poor eating habits can increase the risk of having a baby with a low birth weight (under 2.5 kg, or 5½ pounds) and also with physical or learning problems. Because most teens are not fully developed, they are also more likely to have difficult pregnancies.

◆ Eating right is essential throughout a person's life, but nutritional needs vary at different stages of the life cycle.

Nutritional Statistics on New Mothers

There are approximately 400 000 births every year in Canada. An estimated 10 percent of these births are at risk due to the mother's poor health and malnutrition. A woman's health from the beginning of a pregnancy is very important for the healthy delivery of a baby.

Health Canada also states that teens who get pregnant between the ages of 15 to19 years of age are more likely to deliver a baby with a low birth weight. The low birth weight rate among adolescents (6.5 percent) is almost a full percentage point higher than the national average (5.7 percent). Why do you think this is happening?

Cultural Diversity

Canada is made up of many different cultural groups. People's eating patterns are influenced by their culture. In some cases, according to Health Canada, social or religious beliefs may impose restrictions on food choices during pregnancy.

Nutrition for a Healthy Pregnancy

Pregnancy is a wonderful and exciting time of life for parents. Here are some basic nutrition tips for moms:

◆ Follow *Canada's Food Guide to Healthy Eating*.

◆ Choose a variety of foods.

◆ Consume a variety of iron-rich foods at each meal, such as meat, fish and other seafood, poultry, leafy green vegetables, enriched cereals, and legumes.

◆ Pick foods rich in folate, such as enriched breads and cereals; fruits, such as cantaloupe and oranges; dark green vegetables, such as asparagus, broccoli, and spinach; legumes, nuts, and seeds.

◆ Select three to four servings of milk products to ensure adequate calcium for both mom and baby. If milk is not included in the mother's diet, substitute calcium-rich foods, such as tofu, or calcium-enriched bread.

◆ Consult a doctor before taking a vitamin supplement that might be necessary during the pregnancy. A doctor can recommend appropriate amounts of vitamins and minerals suited to a mother's needs.

It is important for pregnant women to eat good food sources of folate, iron, calcium, vitamin D, and essential fatty acids every day.

Pregnancy and Weight Gain

Women should expect to gain weight during pregnancy. A healthy weight gain is usually 11 to 16 kg (25 to 35 pounds). A health professional may recommend a slightly different weight-gain range for underweight or overweight women. Women carrying twins may be advised to gain as much as 16 to 20 kg (35 to 45 pounds).

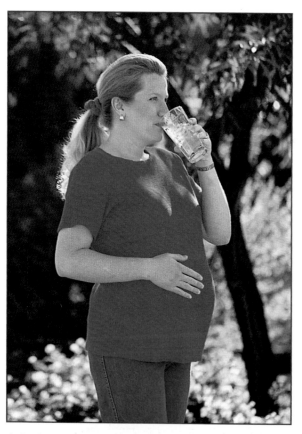

◆ During pregnancy, six to eight glasses of liquid, including water, juices, and milk, are needed daily. Identify three other specific eating guidelines a mother-to-be needs to follow.

Pregnant women should not go on weight-loss programs. Limiting food deprives the fetus of much-needed nutrients and can seriously affect the baby's health. Those who have made nutritious food choices should return to their prepregnancy weight within a few months after childbirth.

Infancy

Good nutrition plays a critical role during this period of unparalleled growth and development. The harmful effects of poor nutrition during infancy can last a lifetime.

Feeding Newborns

There are two choices for feeding newborn infants—breast-feeding or bottle-feeding. Both provide all the nutrients the baby needs for the first four to six months.

Breast milk has the right amount and type of fat for a baby. The protein in breast milk is more easily digested and absorbed than the protein in cow's milk.

For the first three days after birth, the mother's breasts produce a special form of milk known as colostrum (kuh-LAH-strum). This is a thick, yellowish fluid that is rich in nutrients and antibodies, substances that protect the baby from infection. Later, the colostrum changes to true breast milk.

A woman who is breast-feeding should eat the same kinds of foods recommended during pregnancy and should drink plenty of liquids. The right food choices will ensure that she produces enough milk to keep the baby well fed and healthy. She should not restrict calories while she is breast-feeding.

Bottle-feeding infant formula can also provide good nutrition. Infant formula is usually made of a cow's milk base. Vegetable oils and carbohydrates are added to make it similar to breast milk. Other types of formula are also available. For infants allergic to cow's milk, formulas with a soybean base are often used.

Adding Solid Food

After the first four to six months, the baby will be ready for solid food. The child's pediatrician, a physician who cares for infants and children, can offer sound recommendations. A baby's first "solid" foods are actually strained foods that are easy to swallow and digest. They should be introduced one at a

time. That way, if the baby has a reaction, the cause of the food allergy can be easily identified. The first solid food is usually baby cereal, followed by strained vegetables and fruits. More variety is added later.

During the last half of the first year, infants' eating skills improve. They can be given foods that need some chewing. They begin to learn to pick up some solid foods with their fingers. Healthy finger-food choices include pieces of fruit (without skins), cooked vegetables, cheese, and crackers. Babies also begin to use a spoon for self-feeding.

By the end of the first year, a baby usually can eat the same foods as the rest of the family, but in smaller amounts. Parents or caregivers should not try to limit the amount of fat eaten by children under age two. Babies and toddlers have high energy requirements and, thus, need more fat in their eating plans than do older children and adults.

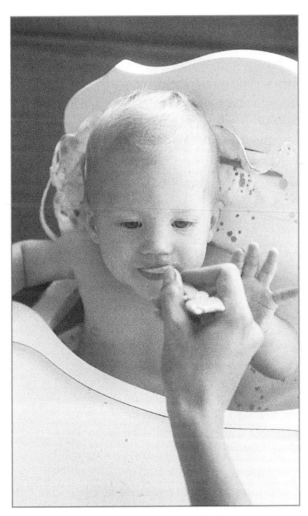

◆ Introducing solid foods one at a time makes it easier to pinpoint any food allergies. Which solid food is usually introduced first?

Safety Check

- Cow's milk should not be given to infants because their digestive systems are not fully developed. After 12 months of age, toddlers can be offered about 500 mL (2 cups) of whole milk (in place of breast milk or formula) each day to help assure that calcium needs are met.

- Do not add salt, sugar, fat, or spices to a baby's food. Babies do not need them because their taste buds are more sensitive than an adult's. Added salt, sugar, or fat may also lead to poor eating habits later on.

- Certain foods should not be fed to infants and small children because they can cause choking. These include nuts, seeds, raw carrots, hot dogs, hard candies, whole grapes, popcorn, powdered sugar, and peanut butter.

Young Children

Mealtime can be a happy time for toddlers, preschoolers, school-aged children, and parents. Never force children to eat everything on their plates when they are not hungry. This only creates friction between parent and child and can lead to weight problems in the future. As *Canada's Food Guide to Healthy Eating* suggests, a variety of foods is the key. Choose foods from each of the food groups. This helps children get the nutrients they need to grow and play. Mealtime, although it can be hectic, is an opportunity to spend time with children; pass on cultural, religious, and family rituals; and celebrate successes and special occasions, such as birthdays. Mealtime can be a good opportunity for parent and child to share the events of the day. Food is part of family life and customs.

Young children are active and growing. So it is essential that they receive a wide selection of nutritious foods from the four food groups in *Canada's Food Guide to Healthy Eating*.

At meals, food portions should be small. Many experts recommend beginning with 15 mL (1 tbsp.) of a food for each year of the child's life. That means the vegetable serving of a three-year-old should be about 45 mL (3 tbsp.). If the child is still hungry, he or she can be given more. The amount of food needed varies from child to child and from week to week.

During growth spurts—periods of very rapid growth—children may eat more than usual. At other times, they may want less food. Young children sometimes go through phases in which they insist on eating the same food at every meal or they hate a food at one moment and then love it the next. These food jags are usually temporary and shouldn't create long-term nutritional concerns.

Canada's Food Guide to Healthy Eating recommends that children four to nine years of age have two to three servings of milk products per day.

Children have very small stomachs that cannot hold very much food at one time. Therefore, they need between-meal snacks to help supply enough energy and nutrients. Healthy snacks include juice; yogurt; milk; pieces of fruit or vegetables; cooked meat, poultry, fish or other seafood; unsweetened cereal; and whole-grain crackers. Nutrient-dense foods should be encouraged.

Promoting Good Eating Habits

Do you have memories from early childhood of trying a food for the first time? Eventually, every child takes a chance with new foods. Introducing a young child to a previously untried food adds variety to the child's eating plan while simultaneously fostering good eating habits. Here are ways of making the most of this opportunity:

- Serve foods that vary in colour and texture. If the food has eye appeal, children will be more likely to eat it—and to meet their nutritional needs.

- Eat meals with children, and make the meals enjoyable. Be a role model for good eating habits and behaviour.

- Avoid using food as rewards or punishments. This practice gives young children the wrong impression about the purpose of food.

- Don't encourage children to become members of the "clean-plate club." Insisting that they finish all their food even after their hunger is satisfied can lead to overeating in later years.

- When possible, let children choose what foods they want to eat for some meals.

◆ Teaching children to prepare foods by themselves encourages good eating habits. What other benefits are there?

◆ Teach children how to prepare several simple, nutrient-rich foods by and for themselves.

◆ Invite children to help prepare part of a meal. Let them tear lettuce for a salad, make sandwiches, or aid with any other age-appropriate tasks.

INTERNET CONNECTS

www.mcgrawhill.ca/links/food
To learn more about nutrition at different stages of the life cycle, go to the web site above for *Food for Today, First Canadian Edition,* to see where to go next.

Adolescence

Next to infancy, the second most rapid growth period of life is the one you are going through now—adolescence. Because of the dramatic physical and psychological changes associated with this period, you, as a teen, have an increased need for almost all nutrients.

That is why you may feel constantly hungry or why you may often find yourself reaching for snacks. Do you eat a lot of junk food? Here are some healthy snack ideas that you might like to try instead.

◆ Savour popcorn with your favourite seasoning.

- Crunch into veggies when the munchies hit.
- Tasty fresh fruit might be perfect for you.
- Don't forget the milk and juice!

Many teens don't get enough calcium, zinc, iron, vitamin A, or vitamin C in their diets. One easy way to avoid this problem is to be sure you get the minimum number of servings suggested for people your age in *Canada's Food Guide to Healthy Eating*. Youth aged 10 to 16 years should have three to four servings of milk products per day. If you are highly active or still growing, aim for the maximum number.

◆ **With proper nutrition and other good health habits, many older adults remain very active.** Talk to an older relative, neighbour, or other senior citizen who is active to learn about his or her eating habits.

As a teen, you are assuming more responsibility for your life, including your food choices. Developing food skills and fitness habits during this period will help set the stage for a healthy and productive future.

Adulthood

Mr. Carstairs, who is 45, has a "spare tire" around his midsection, while his next-door neighbour, who is the same age, does not. The difference relates in part to the fact that Mr. Carstairs eats the same way he did when he was younger, even though most adults require fewer calories.

Despite their decreased need for calories, adults still need their full share of nutrients. They can meet this demand by choosing a variety of low-fat, low-calorie foods from *Canada's Food Guide to Healthy Eating*. Continuing to get regular physical activity throughout adulthood is important as well.

Many adults don't realize they have slipped into poor eating and exercise habits until they develop a health problem. Developing healthy habits now, while you are in your teen years, may help reduce future health problems. It will also make it easier to continue these habits throughout life.

Older Adults

As people age, they continue to need the same nutrients, although in smaller amounts. If they remain physically active, they can continue to eat as much as younger adults.

With maturity, the body's thirst signal often declines and people don't drink as much water as their bodies require. Older people, like all other adults, need to drink 2 L (8 cups) of water daily.

Special Problems for Aging Adults

Some aging adults face special challenges in meeting their nutritional needs. Many live on fixed incomes that are too low to provide enough nutrient-rich food. Those who live alone may dislike preparing a meal just for one—or may be too frail to cook. Some older people have health problems that create nutritional risks.

In many communities, social service programs are available to help aging adults in situations like these. Senior and community centres often offer meals for older citizens at reduced rates. These programs provide nutrient-rich meals as well as an opportunity for socializing.

Living alone or on a limited income can make meal planning challenging for people of any age.

Chapter 11   Review and Activities

Summary

- Nutrients in the food you eat help you grow and provide the energy you need for a healthy, active life.
- Nutrient deficiencies can cause serious health conditions.
- Vitamins help keep your body's tissues healthy and your systems working smoothly.

- Carbohydrates and proteins provide energy.
- Fats are essential nutrients with important functions in the body.
- Minerals are vital for good health.
- Nutritional needs change throughout the human life cycle.

Knowledge and Understanding

1. What are the six major types of nutrients? What are the main functions of each?

2. What are DRIs? How are they used by professionals or industry?

3. List three foods that supply simple carbohydrates and six foods that supply complex carbohydrates.

4. What is the difference between complete and incomplete proteins?

5. Name three types of fatty acids. Which is considered least healthy? Why? Where is it mainly found?

6. Why are good nutrition habits important for a woman even before she knows she is pregnant?

Thinking and Inquiry

7. Studies show that most Canadians eat less fibre than is needed for good health. Identify some possible reasons for this.

8. Suppose you are shopping for peanut butter. One brand claims "No Cholesterol" in large letters on the label. The kind you usually buy makes no such claim. Would you switch brands? Why or why not?

9. Cereal A is high in fibre (7 grams per serving) with 75 percent of seven vitamins and minerals. Cereal B is low in fibre (1 gram per serving) with 100 percent of the same seven vitamins and minerals. Which would you choose? Why?

10. If someone had a piece of the small intestine removed because of a disease, what nutritional problems could result?

Review and Activities   Chapter 11

Communication

11. View a nutrition-related TV show, movie, or cartoon (e.g., *Magic School Bus*). Would this program help children understand how food and nutrients are used in the body? Why or why not? Discuss your observations with the class.

12. a) Create a word search or crossword using 25 terms you have learned in this chapter. Include answers to the terms on a separate piece of paper.

b) Swap your word search/crossword with the person next to you so that you can do each other's.

c) When your puzzle is returned to you, check for correct responses using the answer sheet you created.

d) Put a total out of 25 on the top of the page and return it to the person who answered it.

Application

13. In groups, choose a nutrient out of a hat. You are sales people at a convention. Convince the class that your nutrient is the most valuable and important of all the six main nutrients. Create a visual aid to help you do this.

14. Think back to the last meal you ate. Which foods supplied carbohydrates? Fibre? Proteins? What types of carbohydrates, fibre, and proteins were they?

15. Create a vitamin and mineral checklist. Armed with your checklist, determine which vitamin and mineral needs can be met by the foods available in your home. Discuss your findings with an adult in your home. Sketch a design for a poster or bulletin board showing how food is broken down into nutrients and how nutrients travel through the body.

Nutritious Meals

CHAPTER EXPECTATIONS

While reading this chapter, you will:

- Explain the purpose of food guidelines.

- Use appropriate food guides or other material to plan nutritionally adequate meals in a group setting.

Select a variety of foods from each of the four food groups daily to maintain a healthy balance of nutrients.

KEY TERMS

Canada's Food Guide to Healthy Eating
Canada's Guidelines for Healthy Eating
combination foods
lifestyle diseases
moderation
nutrient-dense
reducing risk

How to plan nutritious meals is important. This chapter will focus on how to use *Canada's Guidelines for Healthy Eating* and *Canada's Food Guide to Healthy Eating* to help you select or prepare healthy meals.

A nutritious meal is a feast for the eyes and fuel for the mind and body.

Canada's Guidelines for Healthy Eating

Whether you are making lunch or packing food supplies for a two-week camping trip, planning nutritious meals can be a challenge. Just think of the thousands of foods and food products lining the shelves in your grocery store. How do you choose which items should go into your meals to give your body the nutrients it needs? This is why Health Canada developed **Canada's Guidelines for Healthy Eating** for Canadians over the age of two. The guidelines offer five main recommendations. These are listed here and are expanded on over the next few pages.

Canada's Guidelines for Healthy Eating

1. Enjoy a *variety* of foods.

2. Emphasize cereals, breads, other grain products, vegetables, and fruit.

3. Choose lower-fat dairy products, leaner meats, and food prepared with little or no fat.

4. Achieve and maintain a healthy body weight by enjoying regular physical activity and healthy eating.

5. Limit salt, alcohol, and caffeine.

1. Enjoy a *variety* of foods from each group every day.

You may have heard the expression "Variety is the spice of life." When it comes to choosing the foods you eat, variety is a good way of making sure you get all the nutrients your body needs. Scientists have identified about 50 different nutrients. By eating a variety of foods, you should get all the nutrients you need, as well as some that have not yet been identified.

No single food can supply all nutrients in the amounts you need. Consider the following examples. Sweet potatoes are packed with vitamins A and C and fibre, but have no calcium or phosphorus. Milk is a good source of calcium and phosphorus, but has no fibre and little vitamin C. Consequently, it is a good idea to eat some sweet potatoes and drink some milk. Eating a variety of foods is one of the main focuses of Canada's Food Guidelines. If you do this, you will not be bored with what you eat.

Eating many different kinds of foods, prepared in different ways, not only keeps you interested, but also gives you a chance to enjoy foods and cuisines from different ethnic and cultural groups. A wide variety of foods of various flavours, textures, and colours provides excitement for your eyes and your taste buds. Food then becomes not just something to be eaten, but a positive and pleasurable part of life that you share with others. Eating certain foods and sharing meals then become part of your memories. Do you remember a food that you enjoyed when you were a child? Does it still make you smile? Your favourite food could be quite different from someone else's, depending on their ethnic and cultural background and their experiences in life.

By eating a variety of foods from the different food groups, your body has a better chance of obtaining the essential nutrients it needs to function well and stay healthy. Each food group provides a set of key nutrients. Not all the foods in each group are created equal. The foods vary nutritionally because of natural differences and because of processing, enrichment, and preparation. Each food group is essential. As you can see, you need to eat a variety of foods for good health.

There Are No "Good" or "Bad" Foods

Keep in mind that there are no "good" or "bad" foods. Any food that supplies nutrients can be part of a healthy diet. But how much and how often you eat certain foods is important. Filling up on high-calorie and high-fat foods may cause health problems. The key is to balance your food choices so that they maintain your good health. Variety and moderation can help you do just that.

◆ **Enjoy your favourite foods but avoid eating them too often.** Why is this good advice?

Moderation

A concept that goes hand-in-hand with variety is **moderation**—avoiding extremes. Do you know someone who eats just a few favourite foods regularly and avoids other foods altogether? People who limit the variety of foods they eat can be missing out on essential nutrients. By eating moderately sized servings of many different kinds of foods, you get a wider variety of nutrients for good health.

INTERNET CONNECTS

www.mcgrawhill.ca/links/food
To learn more about *Canada's Guidelines for Healthy Eating*, *Canada's Food Guide to Healthy Eating*, and healthy eating in general, go to the web side above for *Food for Today*, *First Canadian Edition*, to see where to go next.

2. Emphasize cereals, breads, other grain products, vegetables, and fruits.

Most of the calories supplied by the food you eat should come from grain products, vegetables, and fruits. They are considered the foundation of a healthy diet. Choose whole-grain or enriched breads, cereals, and pastas. Eat dark green and orange vegetables and orange fruit more often. They will provide you with antioxidants, like beta carotene and Vitamin C, to keep you healthy. Remember that the fat content of vegetables varies, depending on how they are prepared. For example, French fries are higher in fat than plain baked potatoes.

◆ Grain products, vegetables, and fruits are key sources of carbohydrates that your body needs for energy. Carbohydrates should supply about 55 percent or more of your calories.

◆ Dietary fibre is found only in foods from plant sources. Because these foods contain different types of fibre, choose a variety of grains, especially whole-grain products, vegetables, and fruits to be sure you get the fibre your body needs.

◆ Grain products, vegetables, and fruits are excellent sources of many vitamins and minerals essential to health. Take another look at the vitamin and mineral charts in Chapter 11 on pages 240–242 and pages 244–245. Notice how many of the nutrients listed there are supplied by grain products, vegetables, and fruits. Some nutrients, such as vitamin C and beta carotene, are found only in fruits and vegetables.

◆ When planning meals, remember that you need more servings of grain products, vegetables, and fruits than you do of other foods. **Explain why this is recommended.**

- Most grain products, vegetables, and fruits are low in fat. Eating more of these foods can help you cut down on the amount of fat in your eating plan—as long as you don't add high-fat toppings, such as butter, sour cream, or rich sauces.

Get in the habit of eating more grain products, vegetables, and fruits. Think of them as central to your food choices rather than as extras to have "on the side." With so many flavourful choices available, you'll find it to be an enjoyable habit as well as a healthy one.

3. Choose lower-fat milk products, leaner meats, and food prepared with little or no fat.

Add legumes, beans, lentils, poultry, and fish and other seafood more often to your meals. Choose foods higher in fat or calories in moderation.

There are several reasons *Canada's Guidelines for Healthy Eating* encourage people to eat less fat. A high-fat eating pattern is linked with various lifestyle diseases. Regularly choosing foods high in fat or saturated fat can lead to being overweight or other medical problems.

Health experts have suggested the following goals regarding fat in your daily food choices:

- **Saturated fat:** 10 percent or less of your calories. Remember, the highest proportions of saturated fatty acids are found in animal fats and in tropical oils, such as coconut, palm, and palm kernel oil.

- **Cholesterol:** Limit the amount of cholesterol eaten. Only foods from animal sources contain cholesterol.

- **Total fat:** 30 percent or less of the calories you eat.

Visible and Invisible Fats

Some fat is called *visible fat* because it is easily seen. For example, you can see the butter on a baked potato or the layer of fat around a pork chop. People are usually aware of these sources of fats in foods.

Much of the fat people eat, however, is *invisible fat*. It is part of the chemical composition of the food and cannot be seen. Foods such as whole milk, some cheeses, egg yolks, nuts, and avocados are loaded with invisible fat. So are fried foods and some baked goods.

Lowering Fat

Controlling the amount of fat in your eating plan can help reduce your risk of lifestyle diseases and other health problems. It also allows you to eat more food without increasing your total calories. Remember, a gram of fat has 9 calories, while a gram of protein or carbohydrates has only 4 calories.

It's easier than you might think to cut down on fat. One way is by substituting low-fat food choices for high-fat ones. As you progress through this course, you will learn other ways of reducing the fat in the foods you eat and the cooking you do.

4. Achieve and maintain a healthy body weight by enjoying regular physical activity and healthy eating.

Have you or anyone you know ever tried to lose weight? Do you know someone who has been a yo-yo dieter—a person whose weight goes up and down every time he or she tries to maintain a healthy body weight? Self-image is an important part of the formula as well, allowing you to have a variety of foods in moderation. Walking, dancing, and skating are just some of the ways to have fun, enjoy time with your family and friends, and stay fit. Choose something you love to do, for instance, listening to music, and combine it with something you don't like to do as much, such as cleaning your room, at the same time, to make the activity more enjoyable. Physical activity takes many forms. Can you think of any other combinations that would work for you?

Healthy Body Weight

Generally, a few extra pounds don't do much harm. Being truly overweight, however, poses a serious health risk. It may contribute to one or more **lifestyle diseases,** illnesses that relate to how a person lives and the choices he or she makes. These diseases include high

◆ **Maintaining a healthy weight can help reduce the risk of lifestyle-related health problems, such as high blood pressure.** Analyze the statement "A person's eating patterns alone are not enough to ensure total health; even if the person is at an appropriate weight."

blood pressure, heart disease, stroke, diabetes, and certain kinds of cancer.

Being too thin can also be a problem. It may mean that you are not eating enough to meet your body's energy and nutrient needs.

Maintaining a healthy weight is a balancing act. Food provides energy. The key is to balance the energy supplied by the food you eat with the energy your body uses.

Be Physically Active Each Day

Being physically active will help you balance that energy. Everyone can improve their health and have fun by including some moderate activity in their lives.

5. Limit salt, alcohol, and caffeine.

According to Dietitians of Canada (2003), you should limit the caffeine you get to 400 mg per day, which equals about three to four cups of coffee. Did you know that caffeine is found in coffee, tea, cocoa, and cola drinks?

Table salt contains sodium and chloride, both of which are essential nutrients. Most people, however, eat more salt and sodium than they need for good health. Salt is added to most foods and beverages during processing. Many foods also naturally contain sodium. Here are some hints for cutting down on salt and sodium:

◆ Add little, if any, salt to food when cooking and at the table. When you must add salt, shake once—not twice.

◆ Choose salty snacks—chips, crackers, pretzels, and nuts—only occasionally.

◆ Go easy on processed foods. They generally have more sodium than fresh ones.

◆ Check labels for the amount of sodium in foods. Choose those lower in sodium most of the time.

◆ **Unsalted, air-popped popcorn is a healthy alternative to snack foods high in fat, sugar, and sodium.** Investigate other snack alternatives that help limit your intake of fat, sugar, and sodium.

FOR YOUR HEALTH

How Sweet It Is!

Because there are many different kinds of sugars, you may not be aware that a product you are buying has been sweetened. Examine the ingredients lists of products you buy. Any of the following terms that appear on the label will tell you that the product contains added sugar:

- Sucrose.
- Raw sugar.
- Dextrose.
- Maltose.
- Honey.

- Corn sweetener.
- High-fructose corn syrup.
- Fruit juice concentrate.
- Brown sugar.
- Glucose.

- Fructose.
- Lactose.
- Syrup.
- Molasses.

The Importance of Healthy Eating

Good nutrition is important for growth and development. It is also a key factor in reducing the risk of developing nutrition-related problems, including heart disease, cancer, obesity, hypertension (high blood pressure), osteoporosis, anaemia, dental decay, and some bowel disorders. **Reducing risk** means that the chances of developing a disease are lowered, but it does not guarantee that a disease will be prevented. Healthy eating can help you feel good about yourself and help you to do your best.

♦ **Let the rainbow be your guide to healthy eating.**

CANADA'S Food Guide
TO HEALTHY EATING
FOR PEOPLE FOUR YEARS AND OVER

Enjoy a variety of foods from each group every day.

Choose lower-fat foods more often.

Grain Products
Choose whole grain and enriched products more often.

Vegetables and Fruit
Choose dark green and orange vegetables and orange fruit more often.

Milk Products
Choose lower-fat milk products more often.

Meat and Alternatives
Choose leaner meats, poultry and fish, as well as dried peas, beans and lentils more often.

Canada

Canada's Food Guide to Healthy Eating

You probably know the expression "A picture is worth a thousand words." Health Canada decided to follow the wisdom of these words when it created a graphic tool to help people better understand how to plan healthy meals—a rainbow.

Understanding the Rainbow

The rainbow-shaped food-grouping system is designed to help you choose a variety of foods in moderate amounts, including plenty of grains, vegetables, and fruits. *Canada's Guidelines for Healthy Eating* were step one. The rainbow shows you how to eat healthy every day.

Key Nutrients in *Canada's Food Guide to Healthy Eating*

Grain Products	Vegetables and Fruits	Milk Products	Meat and Alternatives	The Food Guide
protein	—	protein	protein	protein
—	—	fat	fat	fat
carbohydrate	carbohydrate	—	—	carbohydrate
fibre	fibre	—	—	fibre
thiamin	thiamin	—	thiamin	thiamin
riboflavin	—	riboflavin	riboflavin	riboflavin
niacin	—	—	niacin	niacin
folacin	folacin	—	folacin	folacin
—	—	vitamin B_{12}	vitamin B_{12}	vitamin B_{12}
—	vitamin C	—	—	vitamin C
—	vitamin A	vitamin A	—	vitamin A
—	—	vitamin D	—	vitamin D
—	—	calcium	—	calcium
iron	iron	—	iron	iron
zinc	—	zinc	zinc	zinc
magnesium	magnesium	magnesium	magnesium	magnesium

Source: Health Canada (2002).

Who Is It For?

Canada's Food Guide to Healthy Eating meets the nutritional needs of all Canadians four years of age and over. It is not appropriate for those under the age of four because the number of servings and the serving sizes are too large for toddlers and preschoolers.

Using the Rainbow

Canada's Food Guide rainbow gives you advice on how to choose foods. It includes four food groups:

◆ Grain products.

◆ Vegetables and fruits.

◆ Milk products.

◆ Meat and alternatives.

Each group is important because it provides its own set of nutrients.

Foods are arranged in the rainbow according to the recommended number of servings. Grain products are at the top of the rainbow because you need more servings from this group than any of the others.

Within each food group is a wide assortment of foods. They differ in nutrients and calories—both naturally occurring and according to preparation methods. Spinach, for example, has more vitamins and minerals than iceberg lettuce. French fries have more fat and calories than a plain baked potato. Peaches canned in syrup have more sugar and calories than fresh peaches.

Choosing Nutrient-Dense Foods

In general, the greater the number of servings in a particular group, the larger the space it is given in the rainbow. The most space is given to foods that are **nutrient-dense**, low or moderate in calories yet rich in important

nutrients. As a rule, nutrient-dense foods are low in fats and added sugars and high in other nutrients, such as complex carbohydrates, fibre, proteins, vitamins, and minerals. Organizing the rainbow in this fashion is a way of helping you remember to eat more servings of grains, fruits, and vegetables than of any other foods.

The Purpose of Food Guides

Food guides are tools that are developed to help you make healthy food choices daily. *Canada's Food Guide to Healthy Eating* is not a rigid set of rules, but rather a flexible set of guidelines to help individuals or groups plan healthy meals.

◆ **Exercise and healthy eating can be fun.**

Meal Planning

Planning meals using food guidelines such as *Canada's Food Guide to Healthy Eating, Native People's Food Guide,* or health associations' food guides helps you to:

◆ Provide nutritious meals and snacks.

◆ Meet the special needs of family members.

◆ Include foods from different ethnic and cultural backgrounds.

◆ Prepare foods in different ways.

◆ Use money and time wisely when shopping for groceries.

◆ Provide interesting meals with variety in colour, flavour, and texture.

◆ Prepare many different kinds of food.

```
INTERNET CONNECTS

www.mcgrawhill.ca/links/food
To learn more about dietary guidelines from other
countries, go to the web site above for Food for Today,
First Canadian Edition, to see where to go next.
```

How Does the Rainbow Help?

The rainbow part of *Canada's Food Guide to Healthy Eating* suggests the kind of foods to choose for healthy living.

◆ **Enjoy a variety of foods from each group every day.** Try new foods, tastes, textures, and colours.

◆ **Choose lower-fat foods more often.** Everyone needs some fat in their diet, but only 30 percent of energy should come from fat, with 10 percent from saturated fat. Eating more breads, cereals, grains, vegetables, and fruits will help you cut down on fat. You can also choose leaner meats, poultry, and fish. Choose baking, broiling, or microwaving instead of frying. Have snacks such as chips and chocolate bars less often.

◆ **Choose whole-grain and enriched products more often.** Grains contain iron, zinc, and the B vitamins. Whole grains are also a source of dietary fibre. Try multi-grain breads, pumpernickel bagels, brown rice, or ready-to-eat bran cereals.

◆ **Choose dark green and orange vegetables and orange fruit more often.** Vegetables and fruit contain vitamin A and the B vitamin, folacin. Enjoy cantaloupe, salads, broccoli, squash, and oranges.

◆ **Choose lower-fat milk products more often.** Choose products with lower milk fat or butterfat content. They will still provide protein and calcium with less fat and calories.

◆ **Choose leaner meats, poultry, and fish, as well as legumes, and lentils more often.** Trim off visible fat before cooking and drain off extra fat after cooking.

To lower your fat and increase your intake of starch and fibre, try baked beans or split pea soup.

FYI

Are You Nuts?!

You may see a health program on TV or hear a news report that tells you to eat more nuts because they prevent certain diseases and do not contain as much fat as once believed. Consumer beware! A handful of nuts is fine, but a whole can is not, especially if they are high in salt. Nuts and seeds, like anything else, are good to eat as long as you are getting an appropriate amount of nutrients from all the other food groups and you balance them with physical activity.

Health programs and news reports may not tell you what sources they have used, so you can't tell what amount of a food they are referring to or what studies they have used. This makes it difficult to evaluate the information.

The Four Food Groups

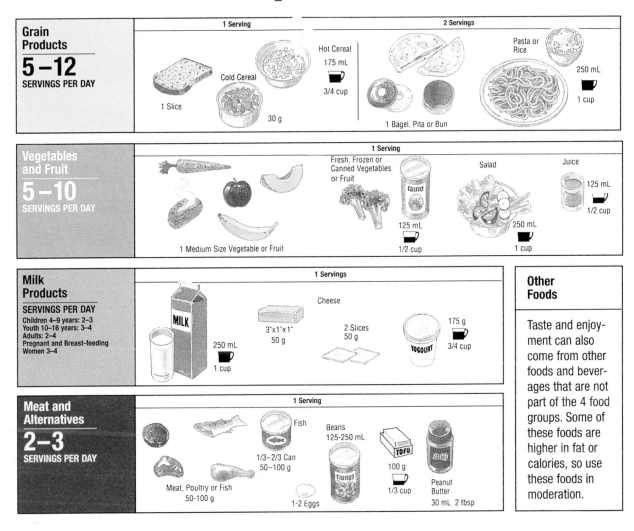

Grain Products
5–12
SERVINGS PER DAY

1 Serving

1 Slice

Cold Cereal
30 g

Hot Cereal
175 mL
3/4 cup

2 Servings

1 Bagel, Pita or Bun

Pasta or Rice
250 mL
1 cup

Vegetables and Fruit
5–10
SERVINGS PER DAY

1 Serving

1 Medium Size Vegetable or Fruit

Fresh, Frozen or Canned Vegetables or Fruit
125 mL
1/2 cup

Salad
250 mL
1 cup

Juice
125 mL
1/2 cup

Milk Products
SERVINGS PER DAY
Children 4–9 years: 2–3
Youth 10–16 years: 3–4
Adults: 2–4
Pregnant and Breast-feeding Women 3–4

1 Servings

MILK
250 mL
1 cup

Cheese
3"x1"x1"
50 g

2 Slices
50 g

YOGOURT
175 g
3/4 cup

Other Foods

Taste and enjoyment can also come from other foods and beverages that are not part of the 4 food groups. Some of these foods are higher in fat or calories, so use these foods in moderation.

Meat and Alternatives
2–3
SERVINGS PER DAY

1 Serving

Meat, Poultry or Fish
50-100 g

Fish
1/3–2/3 Can
50–100 g

1-2 Eggs

Beans
125-250 mL

TOFU
100 g
1/3 cup

Peanut Butter
30 mL 2 tbsp

◆ The bar graph of *Canada's Food Guide to Healthy Eating* shows the serving sizes for different foods and explains that different people need different amounts of food.

All four food groups are important to health. Each provides some, but not all, of the nutrients you need. One group cannot replace another. You need a variety of foods from the food groups each day.

Grain Products

This group includes all kinds of grain products. They supply complex carbohydrates, fibre, vitamins, and minerals. You need five to 12 servings from this group every day.

Examples of one serving are:

- 1 slice of bread.
- 30 g (1 oz.) of cold cereal.
- 175 mL (¾ cup) of hot cereal.

Examples of two servings are:

- 1 bagel, pita, or bun.
- 250 mL (1 cup) of pasta or rice.

To get the fibre you need, choose as many whole-grain foods as you can, such as whole wheat bread and whole-grain cereals. The grain products group includes many low-fat choices but also some higher-fat ones, such as croissants and other baked goods.

Grain Products
5–12 SERVINGS PER DAY

1 Serving

Cold Cereal
1 Slice
30 g
Hot Cereal 175 mL 3/4 cup

2 Servings

1 Bagel, Pita or Bun
Pasta or Rice
250 mL 1 cup

Vegetables and Fruit

Vegetables provide beta carotene, which your body uses to make vitamin A. They also supply vitamin C, folate (a B vitamin), and minerals, such as magnesium and iron. In addition, they contain fibre and complex carbohydrates, and are low in fat. Different types of vegetables provide different nutrients. For variety, include in your diet dark green and leafy vegetables, such as kale; dark yellow-orange vegetables, such as sweet potatoes; starchy vegetables, such as corn, peas, and potatoes, and legumes.

You should have five to ten servings of vegetables and fruit daily. Each one of the following foods counts as one serving:

- 1 medium-sized vegetable or fruit, such as a carrot, apple, banana, potato, or slice of cantaloupe.

- 250 mL (1 cup) of salad.
- 125 mL (½ cup) of fresh, frozen, or canned vegetables or fruit.
- 125 mL (½ cup) of juice.

Fruits provide important amounts of beta carotene, vitamin C, and potassium. Edible skins are good sources of fibre. Like vegetables, most fruits are low in fat and sodium. Be sure to have fruits rich in vitamin C regularly, such as citrus fruits, melons, and berries. Eat whole fresh fruits often for the fibre they provide. When choosing canned or frozen fruits, look for products without added sugar. Count only 100 percent fruit juices as a serving of fruit.

Vegetables and Fruit
5–10 SERVINGS PER DAY

1 Serving

1 Medium Size Vegetable or Fruit

Fresh, Frozen or Canned Vegetables or Fruit
125 mL 1/2 cup

Salad
250 mL 1 cup

Juice
125 mL 1/2 cup

Milk Products

Foods in this group are high in protein, vitamins, and minerals. They are also one of the best sources of calcium. Children four to nine years of age require two to three servings a day. Youth aged 10-16 years need three to four servings a day. Adults require two to four servings a day. Pregnant and breast-feeding women need three to four servings a day. One serving equals:

◆ 250 mL (1 cup) of milk.

◆ 50 g (2 oz) of hard cheese
7.5 × 2.5 × 2.5 cm (3" × 1" × 1") piece.

◆ 50 g or 2 slices (2 oz.) of processed cheese.

◆ 175 g (¾ cup) of yogurt.

Low-fat choices from this group include skim milk and non-fat yogurt.

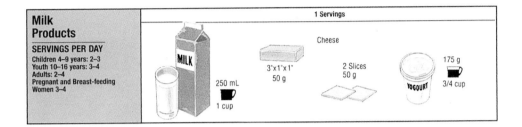

Meat and Alternatives

This group is an important source of protein, vitamins, and minerals. Two to three servings per day are recommended. One serving equals:

◆ 50–100 g (2–4 oz.) of meat, fish or other seafood, or poultry.

◆ 50–100 g (2–4 oz.) or ⅓–⅔ can of fish.

◆ 1–2 eggs.

◆ 125–250 mL (½–1 cup) of legumes.

◆ 100 g (⅓ cup) of tofu.

◆ 30 mL (2 Tbsp.) of peanut butter.

To limit the fat in your diet, select lean meats, fish, and poultry without skin. Have legumes and peas often. They are high in fibre and low in fat. Eat nuts and seeds in moderation because they are high in fat.

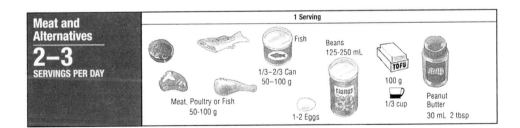

The Food Guide Rainbow

Keeping the Food Guide Rainbow in mind can help you balance your daily food intake.

Look and Learn

On the Food Guide Rainbow, find each food you have eaten so far today. How many servings from each group have you had? How do these foods stack up in terms of your nutrient needs?

Canada's Food Guide to Healthy Eating

◆ **Grain Products**

This group includes all kinds of grain products. They supply complex carbohydrates, fibre, vitamins, and minerals.

◆ **Vegetables**

Vegetables provide beta carotene, vitamin C, folate (a B vitamin), and minerals, such as magnesium and iron. They provide fibre and complex carbohydrates and are low in fat.

◆ **Fruits**

Fruits provide important amounts of beta carotene, vitamin C, potassium, and fibre.

◆ **Milk Products**

Foods in the milk group are high in protein, vitamins, and minerals, and are one of the best sources of calcium.

◆ **Meat and Alternatives**

This group is an important source of protein, vitamins, and minerals.

◆ **Choose foods from "other foods" wisely and in moderation.**
Why are these foods to be avoided as a regular part of your diet?

You may be used to eating amounts of food that are larger or smaller than what is considered a serving according to *Canada's Food Guide to Healthy Eating*. For example, if you eat 250 mL (1 cup) of cooked spaghetti, remember to count that as two servings, not one, from Grain Products.

Combination Foods

People often eat meals, such as casseroles, chili, moussaka, pizza, spaghetti, soups, stew, and sandwiches, that are made from the foods of more than one food group. These are called **combination foods**.

To help you figure out how many servings each food is:

1. List the main food items.

2. Estimate how much of each food item you ate.

3. Look at the bar graph on *Canada's Food Guide to Healthy Eating* to see roughly how many servings each food item provides.

For example, if you are eating tacos, you would probably have servings from Grain Products (taco shell), Meat and Alternatives (meat or bean filling), Milk Products (cheese), and Vegetables and Fruits (lettuce and tomatoes). Depending on the amounts of the different fillings, you might have full or half servings from the different groups.

"Other" Foods

Fats, oils, sugars, tea, coffee, alcohol, caffeine, herbs, and spices may provide calories from fat and sugar, but little or no vitamins and minerals.

Healthy eating habits are not created or destroyed by any one food, meal, or even a

day's meals. It is the average of what people eat over time, or the pattern of eating, that is important to health.

Canada's Food Guide to Healthy Eating makes it easy to plan for good nutrition. It is a valuable tool for getting all the nutrients you need in the proper balance.

Canada's Guidelines to Healthy Eating provide the following recommendations: Enjoy a variety of foods; emphasize cereals, breads, other grain products, vegetables and fruit; choose lower-fat milk products, leaner meats and food prepared with little or no fat; achieve and maintain a healthy body weight by enjoying regular physical activity and healthy eating; and limit salt, alcohol, and caffeine.

◆ Combination foods, such as pizza, spaghetti and meatballs, and sandwiches, help you enjoy foods from more than one food group. What could be a drawback of combination foods?

INTERNET CONNECTS

www.mcgrawhill.ca/links/food
To learn more about general nutrition, go to the web site above for *Food for Today, First Canadian Edition,* to see where to go next.

"Other" Foods

Category	Food Examples
Fats and Oils	butter, margarine, cooking oils, mayonnaise, oil-based salad dressings, shortening, lard
Sugar	jams, jelly, honey, syrup, candy, marshmallows, sherbet, popsicles
High-Fat and/or High-Salt Snack Foods	potato chips, pretzels, corn chips, cheese-flavoured puffs
Beverages	water, coffee, tea, soft drinks, fruit-flavoured drinks, alcohol
Herbs, Spices, and Condiments	oregano, pepper, salt, mustard, relish, ketchup, steak sauces, horseradish, chili sauce, pickles, soya sauce

Source: Health Canada (2002).

Cookbook Author and Food Writer

Anne Lindsay

What education is required for your job?

- A university degree in food and nutrition or food science.
- A journalism degree is helpful, but not necessary, for being a food writer.
- Cooking, food preparation, or chef's training.

What skills does a person need to be able to do your job?

- Extensive knowledge of food, food preparation, and cooking.
- Organizational skills.
- The ability to give presentations for consumers and the media.
- Excellent written and oral communication skills.

What do you like most about your job?

I love cooking and learning about food and food preparation. I like creating new recipes that taste delicious. I like the variety of work activities that I do, the people I meet, and the travelling involved. I like the independence and flexibility of working for myself.

What other jobs/job titles have you had in the past?

I worked as a county home economist for the Ontario Ministry of Agriculture and Food; food and nutrition instructor at Kemptville College of Agriculture and Technology; as a volunteer, on the Nestlé Canada Advisory Board; past Chair of the Nutrition Education Committee; present Chair of the Breakfast for Learning/Canadian Living Foundation.

What advice would you give a person who is considering a career as a cookbook author?

Get chef's training and experiment with foods and cooking. Try new recipes and restaurants. Read food magazines, newsletters, cookbooks, and information on the Internet. Travel outside Canada, taste all kinds of different foods, and learn all you can about foods and cooking in all cultures.

Comment on what you consider to be important issues or trends in food and nutrition.

I am concerned about the trend away from home cooking and its pleasures. Also a concern is the rampant rise in childhood and adolescent obesity, as well as the onset of Type 2 Diabetes among young people.

Chapter 12   Review and Activities

Summary

◆ *Canada's Guidelines for Healthy Eating* and *Canada's Food Guide to Healthy Eating* will help make planning a good, nutritious eating pattern easy.

◆ The key to maintaining a healthy body weight is to balance energy supplied by the food you eat with the energy your body uses.

◆ Good nutrition is important for growth and to prevent nutrition-related problems such as heart disease, high blood pressure, and some types of cancer.

Knowledge and Understanding

1. Why is eating a variety of foods important to good health?

2. What is meant by the term *invisible fat*? Name three foods in which it is found.

3. List five examples of different sugars that may appear on food labels.

4. List the four food groups in *Canada's Food Guide to Healthy Eating*. Give the range of recommended daily servings for each group.

5. What does the term *nutrient-dense* mean? How does it relate to choosing foods from the Food Guide Rainbow?

6. For each food group in *Canada's Food Guide to Healthy Eating*, give two examples of serving sizes.

Thinking and Inquiry

7. Why is it important to watch for follow-up reports on research findings?

8. Which of the five recommendations in Canada's Food Guidelines do you think is hardest for most people to follow? Why?

9. Research one dietary guideline from another country. Compare it to *Canada's Food Guide to Healthy Eating*. Note the similarities and differences. Present your findings to the class.

10. Do you feel the rainbow design is an effective way to get the desired nutrition message across? Why or why not?

11. Choose two combination foods (other than tacos). List the food groups that are represented by the combination foods' ingredients. How many servings would there be?

12. A friend tells you that honey and molasses are better for you than white or brown sugar. How can you decide whether this is true?

Communication

13. Your sister has learned that carrots are very nutritious. Therefore, she has stopped eating most other vegetables and eats large amounts of carrots at almost every meal. What would you tell your sister?

14. Research the dietary guidelines of other countries. What are the similarities and differences? Make a poster to communicate your findings.

Application

15. Choose one of *Canada's Guidelines for Healthy Eating*. List five suggestions for helping yourself and other people to follow it.

16. Find a newspaper or magazine article about a nutrition-related study. Identify the following information in the article:

- What was the purpose of the study?
- Who did the study and where?
- Who paid for it?
- What type of people or animals did the researchers study?
- How was the study carried out?

CHAPTER

13

CHAPTER EXPECTATIONS

While reading this chapter, you will:

- Analyse the relationship between eating breakfast and school performance and attitudes.

- Describe the effect of food habits on physical, emotional, and psychological well-being.

- Evaluate personal eating habits.

Personal Eating Habits

When it comes to eating, different families and individuals follow different patterns.

KEY TERMS

appetite
eating patterns
grazing
Rule of Hand

SOCIAL SCIENCE SKILLS

• data collection

CHAPTER INTRODUCTION

Food habits affect you physically, emotionally, and psychologically. This chapter will focus on the relationship between food habits and your life. You will also gain an understanding of the importance of eating breakfast. In the activities, you will practise the Social Science skills involved in collecting data.

A well-balanced meal can affect your growth, energy level, and overall health.

Daily Meals and Snacks

Eating Patterns

Have you ever visited or studied the homeland of another culture? If so, you may have been struck by differences in that culture's eating patterns. **Eating patterns** are food customs and habits, including when, what, and how much people eat. People have different schedules, so people often have different eating patterns. Some people eat the traditional three meals a day, while others prefer to eat five or six "mini-meals." Still others may follow different eating patterns from one day to the next.

FYI

How Old Is a Sandwich?

You may think of the sandwich as an invention of Western culture. The truth is that people of many cultures, East and West, have been enjoying foods on bread for over 2000 years!

Any eating pattern is acceptable as long as the food choices in it follow sound nutritional practices. It is also important to eat regularly. If you try to go too long without food, your body won't have the fuel it needs. Studies show that people who skip meals make up for it by overeating later. Usually, meal skippers eat more in a day than they would if they chose to eat at regular intervals.

◆ **Your daily routine is one of the factors that influence your eating pattern. Name some others.**

Traditional Meals

Despite the differences noted previously, traditional eating patterns in many cultures revolve around three main meals. These are breakfast, the midday meal, and the evening meal.

Breakfast

Breakfast is the most important meal of the day. Why? When you first awaken after seven or eight hours of sleep, your body's fuel gauge reads "empty." Breakfast gives you energy to get your motor running. A good breakfast also helps you feel alert during the morning hours. If you skip breakfast, it's harder to concentrate on your schoolwork. Research reveals that students who eat breakfast get to school on time and do better scholastically than those who don't eat breakfast.

Not all breakfasts are equal, however. A breakfast consisting of a complex carbohydrate, protein, and fruit—for example, whole-grain cereal or a muffin, milk, and a banana—gives you more lasting energy than a doughnut and a soft drink. You may feel fine after eating the doughnut and soft drink, but you will probably experience a mid-morning slump in your energy.

Some people skip breakfast because they are bored with standard breakfast fare. Any food, though, can be a breakfast food, as long as it provides some of the nutrients your body

◆ **Eating breakfast makes a difference in how you feel all morning. Any of these nutritious choices can give your body fuel for a morning of activity. List other tasty morning meal possibilities you might like to try to add variety.**

needs. Try having pizza, tacos, soup with crackers, or refried beans on toast for breakfast. Round out the menu with a serving of fruit and a glass of low-fat milk.

For a balanced breakfast, make sure to include foods from at least three out of four food groups from *Canada's Food Guide to Healthy Eating*.

The Effect of Food Habits

Food habits affect us physically, emotionally, and psychologically. Have you ever woken up with a headache? It could be because you did not eat enough the night before and have not yet eaten breakfast. Some people get grouchy and have headaches when they are hungry. It is their body's way of telling them they need fuel. Nutrients from food are the fuel that helps you enjoy the day's activities.

Skipping breakfast, for example, could cause you to overeat later in the day because your body is trying to make up for the nutrients it needed earlier. The eating pattern that is best for you helps you feel good physically, emotionally, and psychologically. What you eat today will affect your health tomorrow.

Good food habits help you physically. They enable you to:

◆ Get the nutrients you need for your brain and muscles to work.

◆ Feel alert.

◆ Concentrate and learn.

◆ Have energy.

◆ Fight off diseases more effectively.

◆ Sleep better.

◆ Grow and develop.

◆ Maintain a healthy body weight.

◆ Create strong bones and teeth.

FOR YOUR HEALTH

Beating the Breakfast Blahs

Are you a breakfast skipper? If time is your problem, begin by getting up a few minutes earlier. Make a meal out of foods such as these:

- Low-fat flavoured or plain yogurt, whole-grain muffin or bagel, and a banana.

- Peanut butter and jam sandwich and 1% or 2% milk.

- A breakfast drink made by blending 1% or 2% milk or yogurt, juice, and fruit.

Food habits affect you emotionally and psychologically as well. Have you ever noticed that some young children get very cranky and unhappy between four and five in the afternoon almost every day? They may be hungry and tired, and this is their way of letting people know it. These children need nutrients. Are you one of those people who get very crabby if they do not eat on time?

Having a fresh bowl of fruit on the table invites people to come in and spend time together. Food not only provides nutrients but also an opportunity for friends and relatives to get together.

INTERNET CONNECTS

www.mcgrawhill.ca/links/food
To learn more about nutrition information, assessing your own eating habits, and healthy eating, go to the web site above for *Food for Today, First Canadian Edition,* to see where to go next.

Midday and Evening Meals

Whether you call it lunch, brunch, or some other name, the midday meal gives you energy and nutrients to carry you through the rest of the day's activities. The evening meal is a good time to think about the food you've eaten that day. It's your chance to fill in any food group servings that you missed.

Dinner traditionally means the largest meal of the day. It may be eaten at midday or in the evening, depending on your personal preference and your schedule. In some cultures, people prefer to eat dinner at midday and a lighter meal, sometimes called supper, in the evening. The larger midday meal provides fuel for the day's activities. Some people find they sleep better if the evening meal is light.

The usual custom in Canadian culture is to have a light meal, or lunch, at midday, saving the largest meal for the evening—a time when all or most family members can eat together. On weekends or special occasions, some individuals and families may follow a different pattern.

Dinner

No matter when it is eaten, a dinner usually includes a main dish, a grain product, vegetables, a beverage, and sometimes dessert. With an increasing awareness of nutritional needs, more and more people are preparing main-dish meals that include smaller portions of meat, poultry, fish or other seafood, with the grain and vegetables mixed right in. Such a dinner might centre on stir-fried chicken with broccoli and water chestnuts, served over rice. Accompanied by a tossed salad, low-fat milk, and a whole wheat roll, and followed by fruit for dessert, such a meal follows *Canada's Food Guide to Healthy Eating*.

◆ **Some health experts are now recommending five or six smaller meals, as shown in the bottom picture, in place of three large ones.** Name some possible health benefits of this style of eating.

Snacks

If you enjoy between-meal snacks, here is good news: Snacking is not necessarily a bad habit. In fact, during the teen years, when your nutritional and caloric needs are at a high point as a result of rapid body growth, snacking can actually help you meet those needs.

Of course, what you choose to snack on can make all the difference. Many snack foods—such as candy, chips, granola, cookies, and other sweets—are high in fat, sugar, and calories.

For a nutritious snack, you can choose almost any nutrient-dense food. Try leftovers from the refrigerator, fresh fruits or vegetables, low-fat milk products, or whole-grain breads and cereals.

◆ **Snacks can be part of a healthy eating plan when you select wisely.** Analyze two or three foods you regularly snack on. Which are nutrient-dense? Which are not?

Remember, too, to pay attention to the *timing* of your snacks. If you snack too close to mealtime, you may not be able to eat the nutritious foods included in the meal.

Grazing

Some people prefer eating five or more small meals throughout the day instead of three large ones. This eating pattern is sometimes called **grazing.** Some health experts view grazing as a healthy alternative to conventional meal patterns.

If grazing is your eating pattern, think about your food choices toward the end of the day. Are you lacking any servings from any of the food groups? If so, eat those foods so that you'll be sure to meet the daily recommendations. At the same time, check to be sure you are not eating too much. The day's total servings and calories should be the right amount for you, just as if you were eating three traditional meals.

As you have learned, eating patterns vary from person to person and day to day. In the end, *when* you eat is less important than *what* you eat. The eating pattern that helps you get the nutrients you need and the right number of calories is the one that's best for you. Identifying your eating pattern can help you plan for good nutrition.

Data Collecting

Surveys

In surveys, the researcher asks a sample group questions and records the answers. This can be done using questionnaires or interviews. In questionnaires, the questions are written and given to the subject to answer in written form. Usually the questions are **closed questions**. The subject selects from answers provided (Holloway et al., 2003).

Interviews are usually done orally and contain **open-ended questions** that the subjects can answer freely. To discover how food affects people psychologically, you might conduct an interview about the "Other Foods" group; in particular, chocolate. A subject might be asked, "Why do you eat chocolate?" This is an open-ended question (Holloway et al., 2003).

Observation Research

In observations, the researcher watches and records the subjects' behaviour. This is one form of **primary research** (Holloway et al., 2003).

You may wish to discover, through observation, what people are eating for breakfast from the school vending machines. You would stand near the machines and watch what people are choosing for breakfast. You would then record your observations in a chart similar to the one below.

School Vending Machine Breakfast Purchases

Item	Quantity
srtny yulmo frmso mons rntri srtny yulmo frmso	*srtny yulmo frmso mons rntri srtny yulmo frmso*
srtny yulmo frmso mons rntri srtny yulmo frmso	*srtny yulmo frmso mons rntri srtny yulmo frmso*

Experiments

Data can be collected by working in the Foods and Nutrition lab. By controlling conditions in a taste test, such as using three types of one product (a beverage), you can determine personal food preferences.

Question-and-Answer Session

This is another method that can be used to collect data. This is often used in a classroom setting. A set of predetermined questions is used to start off the session. This is one way to discover if a group of subjects eats breakfast and if they believe it is important to eat breakfast. Possible questions could be:

1. Do you eat breakfast? Why or why not?

2. How many times a week do you eat breakfast?

3. Do you think breakfast is the most important meal of the day? Why or why not?

Content Analysis

In content analysis, the researcher examines and classifies the ideas presented in a sample group of communications, such as books, letters, movies, or television commercials (Holloway et al., 2003). This is secondary research. It can also include Internet information. Data-collection skills are an important part of research.

Keeping a Food Record

One way of becoming more aware of your eating habits is by keeping a food record. This is simply a list of all the foods you eat for a specific period of time—usually three consecutive days, including a weekend. A food record is not a test you have to pass. Rather, it is a way of letting you know the kind of food choices you are making now and how much you are eating.

INTERNET CONNECTS

www.mcgrawhill.ca/links/food
To learn more about meal and snack ideas,
and tracking and improving your own eating habits,
go to the web site above for *Food for Today,
First Canadian Edition*, to see where to go next.

Positive Food Habits

Analysing Your Current Habits

People sometimes aren't aware of how often and what they eat. Sometimes, they eat just to be sociable. Maybe you have found yourself making room for dessert at the end of a big meal. In such cases, you are eating not in response to hunger, but to appetite. **Appetite** is a desire, rather than a need, to eat.

Appetite is a learned, not an inborn response. It is shaped by social influences, such as friends, as well as personal influences, such as emotions.

◆ Keeping a food record makes it easier for him to identify ways he could improve his eating habits. Keep track of your own food intake for several days.

Whether you keep your food record in a diary, a personal journal, or just a page in your loose-leaf binder, it should include the following:

◆ The time you ate.

◆ The food eaten and the approximate amount.

◆ A brief description of the eating situation, including where you were, what you were doing, your mood, and any other information that could help you understand your food habits.

Reviewing Your Food Record

At the end of the allotted time, take a look at your food choices. For each day, count the number of servings you had from each group in *Canada's Food Guide to Healthy Eating* (page 271). Compare your totals with the recommended number of servings. Did you eat at least the minimum number of servings? If not, which foods did you miss? Were your food choices high or low in fats and added sugars?

Improving Your Eating Habits

Once you have identified any poor eating habits, think about why they occurred. Did you tend to make poor food choices in certain situations, such as while watching TV or when you were unhappy? Were you responding to appetite rather than hunger?

Next, think about how you can correct any problems you isolated. Don't just tell yourself, "I'll eat better from now on." That promise is hard to keep because it isn't specific. Instead, decide on specific changes you can make.

Remember, eating is an enjoyable part of life. Don't take the pleasure out of it. You can make changes in your food habits and have fun doing it.

◆ In settings like this one, it is possible to choose foods that are both satisfying and provide needed nutrients. Visit the food court of a mall near you, and make a list of the meal and snack possibilities that help you satisfy your nutrient needs.

FOR YOUR HEALTH

How Much Is One Serving?

Using *Canada's Food Guide to Healthy Eating* means understanding serving sizes and using this information in making food choices. Some serving sizes are easy, such as ½ bagel, 1 medium-sized fruit, or 1 egg. Others are more difficult to figure out. How much is 50–100 grams of fish? You don't have to weigh your food. Use the **"Rule of Hand"** and these visual aids as examples of serving sizes.

The "Rule of Hand"	The Size of . . .
A thumb is . . . 15 mL or 15 g (1 tbsp) *Example:* 30 mL of peanut butter or 2 thumbs of peanut butter is 1 serving. *Example:* 50 g of cheese or 3 thumbs of cheese is 1 serving. **A thumb-tip is . . .** 5 mL (1 tsp) *Example:* 5 mL (1 tsp) in your coffee is not 1 serving of milk! 1 serving of milk is 250 mL. **A palm is . . .** 1 serving of meat, fish, or poultry, or 50–100 g *Example:* A chicken breast that is the size of your palm is 1 serving.	**A deck of cards is the same as . . .** 50 g cooked meat, poultry, fish or other seafood **A large egg is the same as . . .** 1 average muffin **A golf ball is the same as . . .** 30 mL (2 tbsp) of peanut butter

FOR YOUR HEALTH (continued)

The "Rule of Hand"	The Size of . . .
A fist is . . . 1 cup or 250 mL *Example:* 250 mL or a fistful of salad greens is 1 serving. *Example:* 250 mL or a fist-full of rice, pasta, or hot cereal is 2 servings	**A computer mouse is the same as . . .** a small baked potato **A 10-cm (4-inch) CD is the same as . . .** a pancake or waffle **A baseball is the same as . . .** 1 medium apple or orange **Six dice are the same as . . .** 50 g of cheese

Sources: Health Canada (1992), Dairy Bureau of Canada (1994), and *Food Insight* (1999). Adapted from "How Much Is One Serving?" *Nutrition Matters,* Middlesex–London Health Unit, (n.d.)

INTERNET CONNECTS

www.mcgrawhill.ca/links/food
To learn more about starting a school breakfast program, go to the web site above for *Food for Today, First Canadian Edition,* to see where to go next.

Nourishment Program Co-ordinator

Cathi Moreau

What education is required for your job?

- Post-secondary education in any of the following areas: social work, nursing, humanities, or a related field.

What skills does a person need to be able to do your job?

- The ability to work with students, parents, and school administrators.
- Problem-solving skills.
- Sensitivity to people's differences and the ability to treat all people with dignity.
- Being flexible and able to adapt to changing demands of the job.

What do you like most about your job?

I like meeting new people, and I have met a lot of wonderful people whom I otherwise would not have met. It's great to see a new nourishment program start, and to know that I was a small part of its birth.

What other jobs/job titles have you had in the past?

I also work as a Family Home Visitor with the Healthy Babies/Healthy Children program. I teach first-aid courses at the Red Cross as well. I was a lifeguard/advanced instructor/aerobic instructor for 16 years, too.

What advice would you give a person who is considering a career as a nourishment program co-ordinator?

If you love kids and you want to make a difference in your community, then this job is for you.

Comment on what you consider to be important issues or trends in food and nutrition.

Poverty is an issue that needs to be addressed. Low-income parents are not bad parents; they simply cannot afford to buy nutritious food for their children.

I am also concerned about teen's preoccupation with weight. Girls want to be thin while boys are striving to meet weight limits for certain sports.

Chapter 13   Review and Activities

Summary

- Eating patterns vary with individual schedules, and cultures.
- Any eating pattern is all right as long as food choices provide sound nutrition.
- Food habits affect us physically, emotionally, and psychologically.
- Snacking is not necessarily a bad habit—it can actually help you meet your nutritional needs.
- You can make changes in your food habits and have fun doing it.

Knowledge and Understanding

1. Give three examples of different eating patterns.

2. Why is breakfast considered the most important meal of the day?

3. Divide a sheet of paper into two columns. In one column, list as many advantages of grazing as you can. In the second column, list as many disadvantages as you can.

4. What kinds of snack foods can help you meet your nutrient needs?

5. What is appetite?

6. What is data collecting? What is its purpose?

7. When keeping a food record, what information do you need to write down?

Thinking and Inquiry

8. Think about this statement: "Snacking during the teen years has the potential to help as well as the potential to harm." Write a short paragraph that explains your interpretation of the sentence.

9. How could you encourage a friend who is working on improved eating habits?

10. Alyssa was reviewing her food record. She noticed that when she ate alone or with her family, she usually made healthy food choices. However, her choices were less wise when she ate out with friends. Why might this occur?

11. Chris has been invited to the home of a friend for the evening meal. Chris knows that his friend's family eats a light meal in the evening because they have their big meal at noon. Because of his hectic schedule, Chris was able to have only a sandwich and piece of fruit a lunchtime. How can he satisfy his nutritional needs and hunger while at his friend's home?

Communication

12. Visit two fast-food restaurants or consult an Internet site that provides information about the number of calories, grams of fat, milligrams of cholesterol, and milligrams of sodium contained in their foods. Use this information to create a guide to fast-food dining in your area. Include the healthiest options on each of the menus.

13. Using recipe books or magazines, find three ideas for quick and easy foods that would provide needed nutrients according to *Canada's Food Guide to Healthy Eating*. As a group, prepare the foods in class for lunch. Working independently, evaluate the foods on the basis of cost, ease of preparation, taste, and the food groups that were included.

Application

14. Make a list of 15 nutritious snacks that require little preparation. Put a check mark by those you have already tried. Put a star by those you plan to try.

15. Using the instructions in the chapter, create a food record for yourself. After analyzing your current eating habits, make a list of specific changes you intend to make. Repeat the activity a month from now. Which new behaviours have become habits?

Diet, Lifestyle, and Health

While reading this chapter, you will:

- Identify different types of dietary regimens, and the reasons behind these dietary choices.

Today, there are many more food choices in restaurants to suit various dietary regimens.

KEY TERMS

cancer
diabetes
dietary supplements
food allergy
food intolerance
heart disease
HIV/AIDS
homocysteine
megadose
natural health products
vegetarians

SOCIAL SCIENCE SKILLS

- evaluating sources

Health issues and lifestyle choices affect your diet. In this chapter, forms of vegetarianism will be covered. You will also learn to identify health issues that require dietary modifications. Some examples of these are heart disease, diabetes, osteoporosis, cancer, and food allergies and intolerances.

Vegetarian recipes can have wide appeal.

The Vegetarian Lifestyle

Vegetarianism

Vegetarians are people who do not eat meat, poultry, fish or other seafood. Some vegetarians do not eat dairy foods or eggs. A vegetarian eating plan can supply complete nutrition. However, as with any other way of eating, the food choices require some thought and planning. According to the National Institute of Nutrition, about 4 percent of Canadians describe themselves as vegetarian (Teach Nutrition, n.d.).

Facts about Vegetarians

Some people are confused about what foods vegetarians eat. In fact, there are several kinds of vegetarians, depending on what foods they include in their eating plans:

- **Vegans** (VEE-guns or VEH-juns), also known as pure vegetarians, are people who eat only foods from plant sources, such as grain products, legumes and peas, fruits, vegetables, nuts, and seeds.

- **Lacto vegetarians** are people who eat milk products in addition to foods from plant sources.

- **Ovo vegetarians** are people who eat eggs in addition to foods from plant sources.

- **Lacto-ovo vegetarians** are people who eat foods from plant sources, milk products, and eggs.

- Some **semi-vegetarians** sometimes eat poultry and fish, but not red meat. Other semi-vegetarians include limited amounts of animal products, such as meat, fish and other seafood, poultry, milk products, and eggs.

Good Nutrition for Vegetarians

If they make wise food choices, vegetarians can get all the nutrients they need. As with any other eating pattern, the key to good vegetarian nutrition is variety. Although vegetarians choose to avoid some foods, they still have plenty of other foods from which to select.

For healthy vegetarian eating habits, plan balanced food choices from the food groups in *Canada's Food Guide to Healthy Eating*. It is especially important for vegetarians to get enough iron, zinc, vitamin B_{12}, and calcium.

Planning and good food choices are especially important for children and pregnant and nursing mothers. *Canada's Food Guide to Healthy Eating* identifies lentils, dried beans and peas, nuts, seeds, and eggs as alternatives to meat. The tools for a healthy vegetarian diet are planning, balance, variety, and meeting nutrient needs.

The dietary intake of people on special diets (for instance, diabetics, people with heart disease, and vegetarians) depends on such factors as current medical status and

FYI

The Vegetarian View

You may think of vegetarianism as a recent development, but in reality, it dates to antiquity. For over two millennia, vegetarianism has been a religious practice among people of certain Hindu and Buddhist sects, who consider all animal life to be sacred. Another religious group, the Trappist monks, embraced vegetarianism in 1666. More recently, the practice was adopted by Seventh-Day Adventists.

As a Western movement, vegetarianism got its start in Manchester, England, in 1809, among members of the Bible Christian Church. The first non-religious practice of vegetarianism took place in 1847, when the Vegetarian Society was founded.

INTERNET CONNECTS

www.mcgrawhill.ca/links/food
To learn more about vegetarian nutrition, recipes, and issues of concern to vegetarians, go to the web site above for *Food for Today, First Canadian Edition*, to see where to go next.

activity level. Health Canada suggests a health professional, such as a family doctor, community health nurse, or a registered dietitian, assess individual situations and make recommendations.

Specific Nutrients

It is helpful to take a look at how some specific nutrients are supplied in vegetarian food choices. Of particular interest are protein, fat, iron, calcium, and vitamins B_{12} and D.

◆ Grain products, legumes, nuts and seeds, and vegetables are all sources of protein. Identify three other nutrients provided by these products.

Protein

Obtaining enough protein on a vegetarian eating plan is not difficult, even for vegans. As you may recall, proteins are made up of amino acids. Proteins from plant sources do not provide all the essential amino acids, but eating a wide variety of foods from plants can provide complete protein over the course of the day. Dry beans or peas together with any grain products, nuts, or seeds are a good source of complete protein.

Fat

Some people who become vegetarians are surprised to find themselves putting on weight. Often, this is because their eating plans centre on whole milk, cheese, or eggs, all of which are high in fat. Nuts and seeds are also high in fat.

The solution to this problem is to choose a meal plan that emphasizes grain products, fruits, and vegetables. These foods provide many important nutrients but are low in fat.

Iron

Iron is essential in making hemoglobin, a substance in blood that carries oxygen to all body cells. This important mineral is found in many fruits, vegetables, and grain products, especially legumes and dried fruits. Since the iron in foods from plant sources is not easily absorbed, however, vegetarians run the risk of an iron shortage.

Because vitamin C aids the body in its absorption of iron, a sensible solution is to eat foods rich in vitamin C together with foods high in iron. If vegetarians eat a wide variety of foods, including rich sources of vitamin C, they will probably meet their iron needs. Another way to get iron is by using cast-iron cookware.

Calcium

Getting enough calcium is of particular concern for vegans as well as others who do not drink milk. As you have learned, a good supply of calcium is essential for healthy bones and teeth.

Calcium needs can probably be met by eating good plant sources of the nutrient. These include legumes and green, leafy vegetables, such as spinach, kale, and mustard greens.

Even so, it may be difficult for vegans to get enough calcium. They may be advised to drink fortified soy milk. Some health professionals recommend that vegans use calcium supplements.

Vitamins B₁₂ and D

Another concern regarding vegan eating plans is vitamins B_{12} and D. Vitamin B_{12} is not found in foods from plant sources. It can be gained through fortified food or a supplement. Vegans may also need supplements of vitamin D, which is found mainly in fortified milk. It may also be gained from sunlight.

Planning Vegetarian Meals

It is important that vegetarians find alternative sources for essential nutrients in their diets. Infants, children, adolescents, older adults, and pregnant or breast-feeding women who are vegetarians are most likely to be short of important nutrients.

INTERNET CONNECTS

www.mcgrawhill.ca/links/food
To learn more about vegetarianism, and modifications for vegetarians to *Canada's Food Guide for Healthy Eating*, go to the web site above for *Food for Today, First Canadian Edition*, to see where to go next.

◆ Even people who aren't vegetarians may want to collect tempting vegetarian recipes like the one pictured. Locate one vegetarian recipe either online or in a magazine geared toward the vegetarian lifestyle. Discuss trying out the dish with adults at home.

- Substitute products made from soybeans and wheat for foods from animal sources. Many of these items, including soy milk, bean curd (or tofu), and seitan (SAY-tan)—a wheat-based meat substitute—can be found in grocery stores or health food stores.

- Get acquainted with the many varieties of grain products, legumes and peas that are available. For instance, you might want to try grains such as millet, bulgur, and barley.

- Be sure to include good sources of vitamin C in your daily eating plan. Citrus fruits and melons are excellent sources.

- Use dark green, leafy vegetables, such as kale and mustard greens, liberally.

Vegetarian Recipes

Many vegetarian recipe books are available. They range from basic information on getting started with vegetarian foods to gourmet and ethnic recipes. Since vegetarian recipes are sometimes high in fat, choose them carefully. You can also adapt favourite non-vegetarian recipes, sub-stituting ingredients such as seitan or bulgur for meat.

Many ethnic cuisines, such as Asian and Central and South American, are based on vegetarian foods. They can provide you with a wealth of menu ideas and recipes as well as introduce you to new foods.

Eating Out Vegetarian-Style

Because of customer demand, many restaurants have begun offering at least one vegetarian meal on their menu. Except for vegans, most vegetarians should have no problems making food choices when eating out. They can usually find meatless meals made with milk, eggs, or cheese. Some food choices might include baked potatoes with cheese toppings, pizza, meatless lasagna, bean soup, and omelets.

Since vegans eat no animal products, their choices are more limited. Many restaurants offer salad bars or a selection of salads on the menu, but for those who eat out frequently, the limited choices can be tiresome.

Here are some suggestions for vegans to consider when eating out:

◆ Read the menu descriptions carefully. Sometimes the ingredients for each selection are listed. If not, and an item sounds as though it might be suitable, ask the server what it contains.

◆ Tell the server that you are a vegetarian, and ask whether the chef would be willing to make up a plate of cooked vegetables.

◆ Ethnic restaurants, such as Chinese, East Indian, Mexican, and Middle Eastern, usually offer some vegan meals.

◆ If a restaurant does not offer any vegan meals except salads, talk to the manager. Restaurants are always looking for ways to attract new customers and may be receptive to your ideas.

Managing Health Conditions

Illness and Recovery

Any type of illness puts a strain on the body. Whether you are fighting off a sore throat or have a broken ankle, a healthy, well-nourished body is better equipped to handle the problem. Even though a person who is ill may lose interest in eating, the body still has to have nutrients—often more of them than during healthy times.

If you are helping care for someone who is ill or recovering from an illness, follow these guidelines:

◆ Encourage fluids. The patient's physician or other health provider may specify how much is needed.

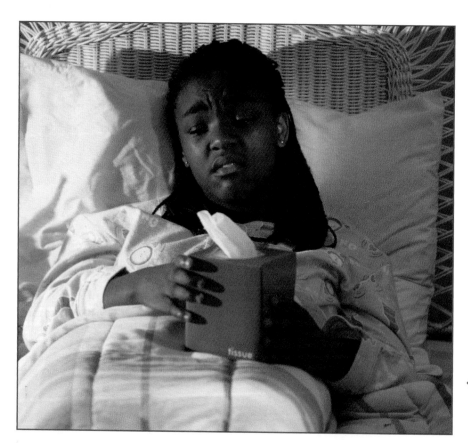

◆ Food can often help you to feel better by building your energy and therefore your body's ability to fight illness.

- Serve nutritious, eye-catching meals. Varying colours, shapes, textures, and temperatures can spice up any meal.

- Be sure the patient gets enough rest for the healing process to take place.

- Ask the physician or pharmacist whether the patient's medication affects the appetite or the way the body uses nutrients.

- Use disposable or plastic plates and cups if the patient has an illness that can spread to others.

Nutrients and Disease Prevention

After hearing that eating oatmeal might reduce the risk of heart disease, many people may begin having oatmeal each day for breakfast and lunch. Often, people jump on the bandwagon at the first report of a food or nutrient with supposed disease-fighting properties.

Two such classes of nutrients that have received much attention in the media are dietary supplements and herbal remedies. How can you as a consumer determine if these are for you?

Food Science
◆ L A B ◆

Comparing Antacids

One common food-related health problem facing most people at one time or another is indigestion. For relieving the discomfort of indigestion or heartburn, is one over-the-counter product better than another? You are about to find out.

Procedure
1. Gather several antacid products. Dissolve a standard dose of one of the products in 250 mL (8 oz) of water. Note the current time to the nearest second.

2. Begin adding vinegar to the cup, an eye dropper full at a time. After each addition, test the acidity of the solution with litmus paper. Keep track of how much vinegar you add.

3. Stop when the solution tests acidic, that is, when the litmus paper turns red.

4. Repeat the procedure for each product.

Conclusions
- Did one antacid neutralize the acid more quickly than the others? Did one neutralize more acid than the others?

- What ingredient or ingredients listed on the product's label do you think contributed to the antacid's effectiveness?

- What conclusions, if any, can you draw about the advertising of products as a whole?

Dietary Supplements

Dietary supplements are nutrients people take in addition to the foods they eat. Usually, these supplements take the form of pills, capsules, liquids, or powders.

Dietary supplements may be useful for people taking certain types of medication, pregnant and breast-feeding women, those recovering from illness, older people, and people with special nutritional needs. In such cases, these people may not be able to get enough nutrients from the foods they eat.

Women who have very heavy menstrual periods may need extra iron to prevent anemia. A doctor may recommend that a pregnant woman take a multivitamin that includes iron and folic acid.

Most people, however, do not need supplements. They can get all the nutrients they need by following a balanced and varied eating plan. People who rely on supplements to make up for poor food choices are only short-changing themselves.

Safety Check

Children often confuse vitamin and mineral pills with candy. Children can be harmed by large doses of supplements. If there are children in the home, be sure nutrient supplements are stored in child-resistant packages out of reach of children.

Nutrient Megadoses

Some people believe in taking megadoses (MEH-guh-dohs-es) of vitamins or mineral supplements. A **megadose** is an extra-large amount of a supplement thought to prevent or cure diseases. Excess amounts of some nutrients can accumulate in the body and cause harm. Excess amounts of those nutrients that are not stored by the body simply pass out of the body unused, making them a waste of money.

Your best choice is to try to get all your nutrients from food. If you decide to take supplements, avoid megadoses. Also, read the list of ingredients on the label of any supplement to be sure you know what you're getting. Avoid nutrients you cannot recognize.

Natural Health Products

Currently, there is no definition for natural health products. That is why Health Canada has created the Office of Natural Health Products. Its mission is "To ensure that all Canadians have ready access to natural health products that are safe, effective, and of high quality, while respecting freedom of choice and philosophical and cultural diversity."

Natural health products include traditional herbal medicines; traditional Chinese, Ayurvedic (East Indian), and North American Aboriginal Peoples' medicines; homeopathic preparations; and vitamin and mineral supplements.

The Office of Natural Health Products will:

◆ Set standards for natural health products.

◆ Assess safety, quality, and proper labelling.

◆ Develop standards for manufacturers and importers of natural health products.

◆ Conduct inspections.

◆ Research how natural products work.

◆ Research how natural products interact with each other and conventional methods. (Health Canada, 2003).

Special Eating Plans

Some people, because of long-term medical conditions, must be especially aware of their food choices. Their physicians may prescribe special eating plans to help manage their medical conditions. A dietitian may need to provide an assessment of the nutritional status of a patient with a condition, an illness, or an injury that puts her or him at risk.

◆ **People with health conditions need to take special care when eating out.** How can a person with diabetes use the skill of communication to ensure that he or she orders wisely from a restaurant menu?

Here are a few conditions that require special eating plans:

◆ **High cholesterol.** People with high cholesterol may develop heart disease. Lowering total fat and saturated fat intake as well as increasing soluble fibre is commonly recommended. Starting the day with oatmeal, strawberries, and non-fat milk would fit well in this plan.

INTERNET CONNECTS

www.mcgrawhill.ca/links/food
To learn more about family health history and cholesterol, go to the web site above for *Food for Today, First Canadian Edition,* to see where to go next.

◆ **High blood pressure.** High blood pressure is also a risk factor for heart disease and other medical conditions. A typical eating plan modification to help lower blood pressure may be to lower fat and sodium (including salt), while increasing potassium and calcium.

◆ **Homocysteine and heart disease.** Folate (folic acid), vitamin B_6, and vitamin B_{12} may play an important part in reducing heart disease and stroke. New evidence shows that high blood levels of the amino acid homocysteine, which is normally found in the body, may be linked to an increased risk of coronary heart disease. Low intake of folate, vitamin B_6, and vitamin B_{12} can affect the breakdown of homocysteine. High blood levels of homocysteine may damage blood vessels, cause increased blood clotting, and decrease the flexibility of blood vessels. These factors can increase the risk of heart disease and stroke. By following *Canada's Food Guide to Healthy Eating,* you can ensure you get enough of these vitamins.

FOR YOUR HEALTH

The Keys to a Healthy Heart

- If you smoke, quit or cut down.
- Be physically active every day.
- Cut down on saturated fat.
- Choose higher fibre foods, such as whole grains, vegetables, and fruit more often

---

INTERNET CONNECTS

www.mcgrawhill.ca/links/food
To learn more about homocysteine and heart disease, go to the web site above for *Food for Today, First Canadian Edition,* to see where to go next.

◆ **Diabetes.** Diabetes is a condition in which a person's body does not produce enough insulin, or the body can't use the insulin it produces. The body needs insulin to make energy from the sugar in food. There are three types of diabetes: Type 1, when the body makes little or no insulin; Type 2, when the body makes insulin but cannot use it; and Gestational diabetes, when the body is not able to use insulin properly during pregnancy. This type goes away after the baby is born.

About two million Canadians have diabetes. The rate is three to five times higher among Aboriginal Peoples.

Diabetes causes other health problems, such as heart disease, stroke, high blood pressure, blindness, kidney disease, and lower-limb amputations.

Good nutrition, regular physical activity, and maintaining a healthy weight can help prevent or delay Type 2 diabetes. Being overweight, especially around the mid-section, increases the risk for developing Type 2 diabetes.

INTERNET CONNECTS

www.mcgrawhill.ca/links/food
To learn more about diabetes, go to the web site above for *Food for Today, First Canadian Edition,* to see where to go next.

♦ **HIV/AIDS.** For people living with **HIV/AIDS**—a disorder that interferes with the immune system's ability to combat disease-causing pathogens—proper nutrition needs to be a priority every day. Maintaining or improving appetite is vital. Plenty of fluids and regular snacks are important. Often, nutritional supplements are needed.

♦ **Osteoporosis.** Osteoporosis causes bones to become weaker and break easily. You often don't know you have it until you break or fracture a bone. Osteoporosis can happen at any time and at any age.

To grow strong bones:

- Follow *Canada's Food Guide to Healthy Eating*.
- Include good sources of calcium (such as milk and milk products) in your diet as well as good sources of vitamin D (salmon, egg yolks).
- Eat a variety of foods containing protein.
- Limit your salt intake.

INTERNET CONNECTS

www.mcgrawhill.ca/links/food
To learn how to calculate your daily intake of calcium and to learn more about osteoporosis, go to the web site above for *Food for Today, First Canadian Edition,* to see where to go next.

♦ **Cancer.** There are many different types of cancer—uncontrolled cell growth. Cancer can spread from where it started to distant parts of the body. According to Canadian Cancer Statistics 2002:

- An estimated 136 900 new cases of cancer will occur in Canada in 2002.
- The result will be 66 200 deaths from cancer.
- The most frequently diagnosed cancer for women will be breast cancer.
- Prostate cancer will be the most frequent occurring cancer in men.
- The leading cause of cancer death for both sexes continues to be lung cancer.

There are many known risk factors for cancer:

- Thirty percent of all fatal cancers in Canada occur as a result of smoking.
- Twenty percent are linked to poor diet (including alcohol consumption).
- Workplace hazards.
- Family history.
- Infections related to unprotected sex. Human papillomavirus (HPV) can lead to cancer of the cervix. Hepatitis B and Hepatitis C can cause liver cancer.
- One of the main causes of skin cancer is exposure to the sun's ultraviolet rays.

Colon and prostate cancer have been linked to diets high in fat. A diet high in red meat, processed meat, and saturated fat has been noted as increasing the risk for several cancers. Most Canadians consume too much fat and not enough fresh fruit and vegetables. A diet including fruit and vegetables helps to protect against cancer.

INTERNET CONNECTS

www.mcgrawhill.ca/links/food
To learn more about cancer in Canadian children and teenagers, go to the web site above for *Food for Today, First Canadian Edition,* to see where to go next.

◆ **Food allergy.** For people afflicted with a **food allergy,** a physical response to certain foods by the body's immune system, a single bite of a particular food can cause symptoms. These range from itching, rash, and hives to abdominal pain, nausea, and even difficulty breathing. For adults, common allergy-causing foods are fish, shellfish, and nuts, especially peanuts. Common allergy-causing foods for children are cow's milk, eggs, peanuts, wheat, and soy. Special tests are used to determine which food or foods are responsible for an allergy.

◆ **Food intolerance.** Another sensitivity, **food intolerance,** is a physical reaction to food not involving the immune system. A food intolerance is most likely to cause digestive problems. One common example is an intolerance for lactose, the sugar found in cow's milk. Substituting lactose-reduced milk or soy milk for cow's milk is a typical solution.

Adjusting to a Special Eating Plan

It takes time for people who have been placed on a special eating plan to adjust to a new way of eating. Eating out and shopping for food pose special challenges. When in a restaurant, the person needs to learn to ask questions about how foods are prepared and to request special orders, when necessary. When at the grocery store, the individual needs to read food labels carefully, checking for ingredients to be eaten or avoided.

People on special eating plans are often surprised at the variety of flavourful foods that can be prepared within the guidelines of their plans. Many are delighted to discover the various herbs and spices that can be pressed into use to make mouth-watering low-fat, low-sodium marinades and sauces.

If you know of anyone who must follow a special eating plan, offer your support and encouragement. Try to help the person view the special plan as an opportunity to try new foods.

INTERNET CONNECTS

www.mcgrawhill.ca/links/food
To learn more about food allergies and food intolerances, go to the web site above for *Food for Today, First Canadian Edition,* to see where to go next.

◆ Adapting kitchens for easier use encourages independence and good nutrition among people with physical challenges. What are three differences you see between this specially built kitchen and others you have seen?

Physical Challenges

Sometimes a physical challenge requires that a person make adaptations in order to meet his or her nutritional needs. Generally, the nutritional needs of such an individual are no different from those of anyone else of similar age, gender, and activity level. However, physical limitations may affect how those needs are met.

People with limited mobility, limited use of the hands, or vision problems may find it difficult to use standard kitchen equipment. In this case, the solution is to adapt the kitchen and its equipment. Design innovations have helped many such people lead independent and self-sufficient lives.

Social Science Skills

Evaluating Sources

With so many pieces of information about food and nutrition bombarding you every day through advertising and the media, it is difficult sometimes to separate fact from fiction. When evaluating print or electronic resources on food and nutrition, it is necessary to consider several factors.

- **Who wrote the article**, book, web site, or media release?

- **Is the information reliable?** Is it based on dependable information, for example, scientific research into nutrients? Has it been repeated in other studies? The fact that being overweight, especially around the midsection, increases the risk for developing Type 2 diabetes can be classified as reliable information because it is backed up by Health Canada, which has based its observations on other studies.

- **Is there a bias?** Is the piece you are evaluating slanted in favour of one viewpoint? Are they trying to sell a product? What is it?

- **What credentials (education, job) does the author have?** Does the document come from a government source, such as Health Canada? Who paid for the study, report, or advertisement? In the case of natural health products, for example, there is information about products such as herbal medicines, homeopathic preparations, and vitamin and mineral supplements. Health Canada created the Office of Natural Health Products because more people were using these products and there was a need to ensure consumers' safety and provide scientific information about these products (Health Canada 2003).

- **When was the information published?** Is it still relevant to today's society, or is it outdated because there have been changes? For instance, the way cancer and diabetes are treated today differs from in the past. Also, the statistics have changed for cancer, diabetes, and heart disease. Researchers have discovered that for certain types of cancer, proper nutrition can reduce the risks. Unless you need historical information, periodicals and books published within the last 10 years are more reliable.

- **What is the relevance of the material?** What does it have to do with the course or the goal you hope to achieve, such as completing an essay on osteoporosis?

- **Where was it published?** This makes a difference in cases such as *Canada's Food Guide to Healthy Eating*. Some of the food additives and regulations are different in Canada than in other countries.

- **Is the source valid or logical?** Or is it based on unscientific theories?

- **How accurate is the information?** If *Canada's Food Guide to Healthy Eating* is being used as a basis for an article, are the serving sizes quoted correctly?

Remember to act like a detective and check your sources.

Sources: Adapted from Holloway, M., et. al. (2003) and Ontario Family Studies Leadership Council.

Career Profile

Nutrition Professor

Dr. Stephanie Atkinson, PhD., R.D.

What education is required for your job?

- An undergraduate degree in nutrition/dietetics combined with a dietetic internship.
- Graduate studies leading to a PhD in Nutritional Sciences.
- Two years of post-doctoral research training (with clinical involvement) in the endocrinology division of The Hospital for Sick Children.

What skills does a person need to be able to do your job?

- Research skills both for conducting clinical studies in humans and basic science research at the lab bench.
- Teaching skills.

What do you like most about your job?

I like the challenges of research and making a difference to treatment or knowledge of clinical problems in children. Teaching students about nutrition, particularly those training or practising in the health professions, is also satisfying. Interpreting scientific findings for application in clinical practice or policy setting, both of which have an impact on improving the health of our population, is also very rewarding.

What other jobs/job titles have you had in the past?

For the first five years after my dietetic internship and before returning to graduate studies, I worked as a pediatric dietitian, primarily with a dialysis-transplant team at The Hospital for Sick Children in Toronto.

What advice would you give a person who is considering a career as a research scientist/academic professor?

You need to work in a self-directed manner and to be creative. You must also be willing to work with others to accelerate the research process so that knowledge can be accumulated. It is important to be flexible in approaches to teaching and to choose an area of research that excites you and that you can focus on. Lastly, you must be prepared to dedicate enormous amounts of time to your career!

Comment on what you consider to be important issues or trends in food and nutrition.

Provincial and federal governments need to develop and implement policies and procedures that will ensure the best nutrition for health and prevention of disease for all Canadians.

Chapter 14   Review and Activities

Summary

- If they make wise food choices, vegetarians can get all the nutrients they need.
- There are different forms of vegetarianism.
- Health Canada has created the Office of Natural Health Products to help set standards and ensure the safety of natural remedies and supplements.

- Offer support and encouragement to people who are on special eating plans due to long-term illness or diseases such as heart disease and diabetes.

Knowledge and Understanding

1. What reason do the majority of people give for becoming vegetarians?

2. Name four types of vegetarians and the foods eaten by each.

3. Give three suggestions for planning and preparing meals to fit a medically prescribed special eating plan.

4. In general, how do physical impairments relate to nutritional needs?

5. What dangers are associated with megadoses of dietary supplements?

6. What is the main difference between a food allergy and a food intolerance?

Thinking and Inquiry

7. How might consumer complaints or suggestions affect menu items offered by a restaurant for vegetarians? What might happen if restaurant owners ignored consumer complaints and suggestions?

8. When Franco complained to his cousin Paul about a lack of energy, Paul told him he needed an herbal remedy to "detoxify" his body. Do you think Franco should follow Paul's advice? Why or why not?

9. Some people believe that certain foods can help cure certain illnesses; for example, that chicken soup helps cure a cold. Do you think there is any truth to such beliefs? Why or why not? How might a scientist try to test such theories?

Review and Activities   Chapter 14

Communication

10. Choose a food allergy or food intolerance and create an information brochure or commercial informing the public about the issue.

11. Eryka is writing a review of a recent nutrition study and has asked for your help in organizing her report. What questions would you suggest that Eryka ask herself about the study in order to evaluate it properly?

12. Find and prepare a simple recipe designed for a modified eating plan, such as a low-sodium or wheat-free plan. Rate the food for appearance, texture, and flavour.

Application

13. Prepare a simple meal, such as soup and a sandwich. Place it on a tray as if you were serving it to someone who was in bed recovering from an illness. Show how you would make the meal attractive as well as easy to eat.

14. Your 75-year-old neighbour has poor vision and no longer drives a car. He does his grocery shopping only when someone is available to drive him to the grocery store. You are worried that he isn't getting regular, nutritious meals. What solutions can you suggest for this problem?

15. Using library or Internet sources, research the connection between herbs and health. Possible topics:

a) What effect does echinacea have on colds?

b) What effect does ginseng have on energy?

c) Are there any herbs that help lower high blood pressure?

Report your findings to the class. Reports need to include positive and negative uses of the herbs, in addition to your overall evaluation.

Food Marketing and Advertising

While reading this chapter, you will:

- Describe the influence of marketing and advertising on personal food choices.

- Examine the relationship between consumer awareness and food marketing.

Evaluating competing health claims and information is an important skill to learn.

KEY TERMS

clinical trials
study design
food fad
food myth

SOCIAL SCIENCE SKILLS

• organizing information

The marketing and advertising of food influences people's food choices. In this chapter you will analyze different

information sources to gain an understanding of how to separate nutrition fact from fiction. You will also become aware of what constitutes food myths and fads, and learn where to get accurate information about nutrition.

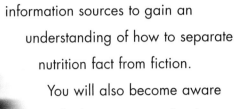

No product can guarantee good health or weight loss. Make your choices based on facts, not false promises. Which skill comes into play when evaluating product labels?

Separating Fact from Fiction

"Now, with less sugar!" a TV ad for a soft drink promises.

"Scientists Find That Fried Foods Are Good for You," announces the headline of a tabloid in the grocery store check-out line.

Each day, dozens of media messages about food and nutrition come your way. With this wealth of information, some of it conflicting, how can you tell what to believe and what to disregard?

Developing Consumer Skills

Part of the answer to the question is mastering two food-consumer skills—critical thinking and communication. Those skills constitute the first step in learning how to separate fact from fiction. As a critical thinker, you learn to look for the "angle" in a given message. When you see an ad, for example, you are alert to the fact that advertisers have something to sell and, therefore, may not be the most reliable information sources.

As an effective communicator, you learn to consider the source of the information. You become able to discriminate between legitimate sources and unsubstantiated claims.

Going to the Source

How often do you read articles or hear news stories about food that contain phrases such as "a recent study shows" or "scientists have found"? On the surface, such reports seem believable enough. How can you tell whether to accept the information at face value? Here are some tips:

◆ Check the original source, when possible. Credible research is carried out by qualified scientists and recognized institutions. The results are then reported in scientific and professional journals. Be wary of the results of research attributed to unnamed sources.

◆ Be alert for bias on the part of the people who performed or reported on the study. Which would you expect to be more objective, a study of the effectiveness of a food supplement paid by the supplement's manufacturer or one carried out by an independent research facility?

◆ Read past the headlines. Headlines are designed to get your attention and may be misleading. Don't jump to a conclusion before you have read or heard the whole report.

◆ Consider the body of evidence. Is the report based on preliminary findings? If so, it may be too early to make any changes in your eating habits. Wait until more evidence has been gathered. Remember, too, that different scientists interpret research results according to their fields of study, and that it takes time to review and adequately test early findings. Be on the lookout for follow-up reports.

◆ Consider the **study design,** that is, the approach used by researchers to investigate a claim. Some studies, known as **clinical trials,** are performed on human subjects. Others are designed around animal subjects. Findings involving animals aren't always reliable.

INTERNET CONNECTS

www.mcgrawhill.ca/links/food
To learn more about Canadian labelling and advertising requirements, go to the web site above for *Food for Today, First Canadian Edition,* to see where to go next.

◆ Valid scientific studies are done by professional researchers under controlled conditions. Name two sources to which you can turn for reliable results of such studies.

The Purpose of Food Marketing and Advertising

The purpose of food advertising and marketing is to sell a product. Whether it is a magazine about food, an actual food product, or a related product, such as toothpaste, the marketing company or ad agency wants to shape your beliefs and buying habits. Food advertisers and marketers want to influence how you spend your money.

Food advertisers and marketers attempt to convince you to buy their products in several ways:

♦ They entertain you with commercials with celebrities.

♦ They include free giveaways with their products; for instance, computer games in cereal boxes.

♦ They sell you an image or a lifestyle. One advertiser's purpose might be to make you believe your teeth are not white enough, so you need to buy its toothpaste to have a perfect smile. To sell its product, a snack food company tries to convince you that to be popular and to have a great party, you need to serve its potato chips. Models who are very young and thin are often made up to look older to promote everything from diet chocolate bars to fat-reduced cookies as healthy. Unfortunately, these factors can affect your self-image, your eating habits, and your personal food choices. The emphasis is seldom on real nutritional issues.

♦ They use phrases like "Preliminary studies show . . ." and dress up an actor in a white lab coat to say the words, creating

FOR YOUR HEALTH

Making Wise Food Choices

When you are examining food packages, flyers, or magazines, look for the following:

- **Bias.** Does the source stand to make a profit by convincing you to buy the product? Is the source really interested in your health?

- **Evidence.** How much research has been done, where, and by whom?

Be like a detective and look for clues that tell you whether the claim is fact or fiction.

the impression that she or he is a scientific researcher. Consequently, infomercials can often look like news reports.

Consumer Awareness and Food Marketing

Here are some shopping hints for you as a consumer of food and food-related products.

Read labels carefully to determine ingredients. How much salt or sugar has been added to the product? Does the cereal, for example, actually contain calcium, or is it in the milk that you add to the product? When you read the label, does the fruit-flavoured food actually contain fruit? Be label wise.

Make a grocery list to help you resist in-store marketing and advertising of products. That way, at the end of a shopping trip, you will find fewer items bought on impulse in your grocery cart that you really don't need. A grocery list will also help you resist the products you will find all around you as you wait in the store line-up. How did that chocolate bar sneak in there?

Check the reliability of the product's sources. Who is guaranteeing what and why? What must you do if you are not satisfied with the product? Is the company that is making the promises in this country?

Beware of free giveaways inside products. Is the advertiser trying to get you or a child to buy a product by including free games or contests? Are you buying the product because you want it, or has the free toy inside the box attracted you?

Free samples of food in grocery stores are another way advertisers tempt you to buy their products. If you go shopping when you are hungry, that free sample of sausage tastes very good. You may end up walking out of the grocery store with a box of them. That is what the advertiser is counting on.

Coupons are another method advertisers use to make their product more attractive. Is saving ten cents off the product really worth it? Ask yourself if you really need the product.

Two for the price of one may sound great, but this is another marketing technique used to get you to buy the product. Do you really need a second bag of cookies? Consumer beware!

Food Myths and Fads

When Margaret has a cold, her mother gives her a mixture of hot tea and fruit juice flavoured with cloves. Margaret's mother learned this remedy from her own mother. While this treatment might make Margaret feel better, it has no medicinal value. Its use as a cure for her cold is little more than a **food myth**.

INTERNET CONNECTS

www.mcgrawhill.ca/links/food
To learn more about nutrition information you can trust, and detecting and avoiding health frauds, myths, fads, and fallacies, go to the web site above for *Food for Today, First Canadian Edition*, to see where to go next.

Where do food myths originate? Some, like Margaret's grandmother's "cure" for the common cold, are handed down through generations of the same family. Others are spread by word of mouth. When a food or nutrition myth becomes so widespread as to be embraced by a fairly large group, it becomes a **food fad**.

◆ The spreading of health myths and quackery began long ago. Name some products today that make questionable health claims.

One weight-loss fad that was popular some years ago was the grapefruit diet. It was grounded on the myth that eating grapefruit at every meal could help a person shed pounds.

Consumer skills can help you avoid becoming the victim of food myths or fads. When you are confronted with a curious food or nutrition "fact," keep a healthy scepticism. Ask the individual who shares the information what his or her source is. Then investigate the source yourself and/or seek a qualified opinion.

Remember, your health is your responsibility. Separating nutrition fact from fiction is an important part of exercising that responsibility.

FOR YOUR HEALTH

Checking the Facts

If you are suspicious about any nutrition information you have received or if you just want to know more, you could contact one of the following professionals, associations, or institutions:

- A dietitian.
- Your doctor.
- Your local health department.
- Your Food Science or Foods and Nutrition teacher.
- A professional organization, such as Dietitians of Canada.
- A government department, such as Health Canada.
- The nutrition department of a nearby university or college.

Social Science Skills

Organizing Information

What do a recipe box and a daytimer have in common? They are both used to organize information. Just as you need to organize groceries so that the bags don't break and heavy cans don't end up on top of your bread or eggs, you can organize information to save time and energy. There are many ways to organize information, depending on what it is and what makes the most sense for easy access. For instance:

- Items, such as key nutrition terms, can be listed alphabetically or they can be organized in the order that they occur in the chapter or in your portfolio.

- To save time grocery shopping, a grocery list can be organized by where you will find the items in the grocery store or by similar items.

- A list of contents at the front of your portfolio or essay will help you to organize and find your material easily.

- Physical organizers of information are items such as dividers, tabs, folders, and plastic sheets. They help you locate the information you have gathered.

- Your computer can also help you organize information through the use of folders.

- Highlighting items in bold or in colour will assist you in finding, for example, key nutritional terms and important statistics in charts on marketing trends.

- Graphic organizers, such as pie graphs and tables, can help you record and organize statistics, such as the cost of convenience foods versus traditional recipes, and make information easier to understand.

There are many types of graphic organizers. Here are just a few.

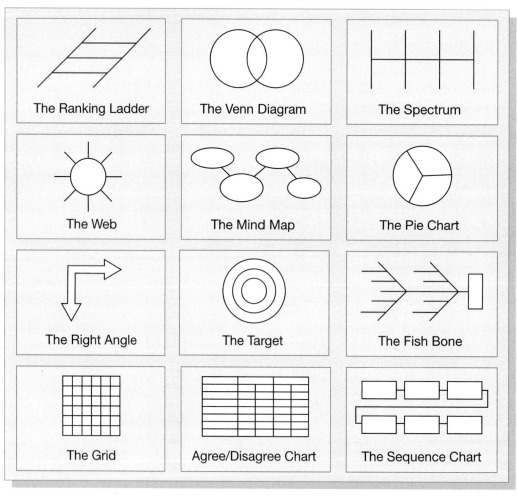

The Ranking Ladder	The Venn Diagram	The Spectrum
The Web	The Mind Map	The Pie Chart
The Right Angle	The Target	The Fish Bone
The Grid	Agree/Disagree Chart	The Sequence Chart

Source: Bellanca, J. (1990).

◆ **Try some of these organizing techniques. You may even end up inventing your own.**

Professional Home Economist

Teresa Makarewicz

What education is required for your job?

- A Bachelor's degree in foods and nutrition.

What skills does a person need to be able to do your job?

- Excellent written and oral communication skills.
- Public speaking; ability to give presentations/ food demonstrations.
- Research skills; teaching/training skills.
- Marketing and interpersonal skills.
- Need to be highly organized and able to multi-task.

What do you like most about your job?

I really like the flexibility my job allows me. I work from home and am able to take on a variety of different assignments/contracts. I mainly do food styling, recipe development and testing, and product promotions. I enjoy giving cooking demonstrations on television.

What other jobs/job titles have you had in the past?

I worked as a Professional Home Economist for a supermarket, where I did recipe development, ran a cooking school, and answered consumer questions about food and nutrition. I also worked in sales at a microwave store, for which I taught cooking classes and demonstrated their products.

What advice would you give a person who is considering a career as a Professional Home Economist?

Try to volunteer or assist someone who is currently doing what you are interested in. This will give you a feeling for the position and the industry. More importantly, it will show your eagerness to a prospective employer. Networking is very important. Become actively involved in organizations related to the field.

Comment on what you consider to be important issues or trends in food and nutrition.

People are more aware of the importance of healthy eating, but they are very busy and tend to rely more on convenience and fast foods. They are missing out on the pleasures of preparing healthy meals and they are also eating too much. The rising incidence of obesity in our population and the health consequences associated with obesity.

Chapter 15   Review and Activities

Summary

- Critical thinking and communication skills can help you learn to distinguish legitimate sources and information from unsubstantiated claims.
- Check sources, watch for bias, consider the evidence, and look for clinical trials involving human subjects when evaluating information about food claims.

- Read labels carefully, make a grocery list, and check reliability of product sources when at the store or supermarket.

Knowledge and Understanding

1. Why doesn't any one scientific study provide enough evidence from which to draw a conclusion?

2. Why is it important to watch for follow-up reports on research findings?

3. Name three techniques used by advertisers to persuade you to buy their products.

4. What makes an infomercial misleading?

5. How can you tell whether the author of a book on nutrition is a reliable source of information on the subject?

6. Where do food myths originate?

Thinking and Inquiry

7. Why do you think some people continue to believe false claims and myths when there is no evidence to support them?

8. "Scientists Say Miracle Vitamin Stops Aging." You have a friend who wants to start taking large doses of that vitamin. What advice would you give your friend?

9. Suppose that you are reading a magazine or newspaper and see a study on the effectiveness of vitamin C against colds. After reading the article, you discover that the study was financed by a company that makes vitamin C tablets. Why does this suggest a possible bias?

10. A friend tells you that honey and molasses are better for you than white or brown sugar. How can you decide whether or not this is true?

Communication

11. Find a newspaper or magazine article about a nutrition-related study. Identify the following information in the article:

a) What was the purpose of the study?

b) Who did the study and where?

c) Who paid for it?

d) What type of people or animals did the researchers study?

e) How was the study carried out? Present your findings to the class in an oral report.

Application

12. Choose three samples of well-known and advertised orange juices with and without pulp.

a) What claims are made on the containers?

b) Read the labels and compare the ingredients and nutrients.

c) What claims have been made in advertisements?

d) Taste each sample blindfolded. Record any differences in taste and texture. Which do you prefer? Why? Are all the product's claims true? Write up your conclusions in a one-page report.

CHAPTER

16

Food Additives

CHAPTER EXPECTATION

While reading this chapter, you will:

- Develop knowledge of the use and functions of food additives.

Food additives are found in a variety of food products.

326 • MHR   Unit 3 ◆ Nutrition, Health, and Well-Being

KEY TERMS

enrichment
food additives

SOCIAL SCIENCE SKILLS

• recording key ideas from research

Food additives are part of everyday life. In this chapter, you will gain an understanding of where and why food additives are used.

Cucumbers may look shiny and feel sticky to touch when displayed in grocery stores due to a coating of wax that prevents moisture loss and improves their appearance for sale.

A Safe Food Supply

Safeguarding the Food Supply

Government and industry make every effort to provide a safe food supply. In doing so, they face a number of challenges. One is testing food additives to be sure they will cause no harm. **Food additives** are chemicals added to food to preserve freshness or enhance colour or flavour.

Government Controls

In Canada, Health Canada officials control and evaluate food additives under the *Food and Drugs Act* and Regulations. Before any food additive can be used, a manufacturer is required to file a food additive submission that must contain information such as:

◆ Results of safety tests.

◆ How the additive will be used.

◆ Benefits of the additive to the consumer.

Health Canada officials evaluate tests done on laboratory animals and the results of clinical studies involving humans to see if there is any evidence that the additive would pose a health hazard to consumers.

They also study information from other scientific advisory groups, such as:

- Scientific Committee for Food of the European Community.

- Joint Expert Committee on Food Additives of the United Nations Food and Agriculture Organization.

- World Health Organization.

Scientists in the Food Directorate of Health Canada then establish an acceptable daily intake of the food additive. Even these substances must be retested as standards change.

Even though food additives are approved by Health Canada, consumers sometimes raise questions about their safety. In some cases, Health Canada undertakes a process of study and review.

◆ Shopping was easier when most food came from farms, but that is not today's reality. Factory-made foods and additives are here to stay. **How can you protect yourself from harmful food additives?**

INTERNET CONNECTS

www.mcgrawhill.ca/links/food
To learn more about Health Canada's Food and Drug Regulations, go to the web site above for *Food for Today, First Canadian Edition,* to see where to go next.

What Consumers Can Do

It is important that you, as a consumer, be educated and informed about food additives. What can you do?

- Read ingredients on food products.

- Keep up to date on reports about additives.

- Ask questions about them.

- Voice your concern if you have repeated side effects from them.

Why is it important to be educated and informed about food additives? If you have an allergy or a sensitivity, for instance to peanuts, it is very important to be aware of ingredients in food products. Some children are so allergic to peanut protein that a single bite of a food containing it can cause great difficulty breathing and even death. They must carry an epinephrine injection with them at all times. For others, the reaction to peanuts ranges from itching, rash, and hives, to nausea. Not only must you know if the food contains the allergy-causing item, you must also know if it has been produced in the same area as a product containing peanuts.

Peanuts are not food additives, but the same rule applies to additives. If you have an inherited metabolic disorder called phenylketonuria (PKU), you will not be able to break down or metabolize phenylalanine,

FOR YOUR HEALTH

Contacts for Information about Additives

If you want to find out more about a food additive:

- Look at the product's package or container. Many have phone numbers included on them. They may be able to tell you what the ingredient is used for.

- Contact Health Canada, the Canadian Health Network (part of Health Canada), and the Canadian Food Inspection Agency. They have web sites and publications with food facts listed.

- Groups, such as the Centre for Science in the Public Interest, provide information on additives and lobby the government for changes. Some information about additives that applies in the United States is not the same in Canada. For example, Health Canada has rejected Olestra as a food additive. It is an indigestible fat substitute found in some American cookies. It may cause abdominal cramping, gastrointestinal problems, and severe diarrhea. Canadians travelling in the United States should be aware of this and read ingredients on food products carefully.

- The Dietitians of Canada also provide information about frequently asked questions on their web site.

- Your Foods and Nutrition or Food Science teacher will be able to help you find information on food additives.

- Your school library or a local library is also a good source of information on food additives used in Canada.

an amino acid found, for example, in aspartame. Excessive use of aspartame, which contains phenylalanine, should be avoided by people with PKU because excessive phenylalanine in the blood can pose a hazard to them according to Health Canada. For this reason, all foods containing aspartame must state on the label that they contain phenylalanine.

It is important to read food labels and ingredient contents so that reactions to allergens don't occur.

Consumer concern can result in post-market surveillance programs, such as studies to monitor the actual consumption of an additive, such as aspartame, in Canada.

INTERNET CONNECTS

www.mcgrawhill.ca/links/food
To learn more about food additives to avoid, go to the web site above for *Food for Today, First Canadian Edition,* to see where to go next.

Food Additives

When you think of additives, you probably think of ingredients on food package labels with long, hard-to-pronounce names. Did you know that spices are considered additives? Currently, some 3000 food additives are in use.

There are many different viewpoints on additives, such as monosodium glutamate,

Food Science ◆ L A B ◆

Preservatives in Bread

Conduct an experiment using two loaves of bread—one homemade and the other a store brand with preservatives (one type of additive). You will observe that the breads will start to change in texture. Mould will start to appear after a few days. Note the difference in the rate of texture change and mould development in the bread slice wrapped in plastic.

Procedure

1. Place one slice of each bread on a plate, uncovered.

2. Wrap another slice of each bread in plastic wrap.

3. After two, five, and seven days, compare the slices for mould and other signs of spoilage.

4. What did you observe?

Conclusions

◆ Which slice changed texture first? How many days did it take?

◆ Which slice developed mould first? How many days did it take?

◆ Were there any other signs of spoilage? What were they?

◆ How did the plastic affect the results? Why?

◆ What conclusions can you draw from this experiment?

---

food dyes, hormones fed to cattle, butylated hydroxyanisole (BHA), and aspartame, to name a few. Most food additives are safe and provide people with many foods today, such as bread, which could not stay fresh for long without food additives to preserve their texture or flavour. There have been additives that were once considered safe but are now banned. It is your health and you must make the final decision. Consumers who are concerned about particular additives can avoid foods that contain them by reading ingredient lists carefully.

◆ Additives are used in many foods to improve the quality or lengthen the shelf life. What could happen without such additives?

FYI

Monosodium Glutamate

Monosodium glutamate (MSG) is produced from the fermentation of beets. North Americans consume more than 25 000 tonnes of it every year, mostly in the form of a food additive.

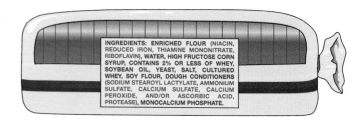

INGREDIENTS: ENRICHED FLOUR (NIACIN, REDUCED IRON, THIAMINE MONONITRATE, RIBOFLAVIN), WATER, HIGH FRUCTOSE CORN SYRUP, CONTAINS 2% OR LESS OF WHEY, SOYBEAN OIL, YEAST, SALT, CULTURED WHEY, SOY FLOUR, DOUGH CONDITIONERS (SODIUM STEAROYL LACTYLATE, AMMONIUM SULFATE, CALCIUM SULFATE, CALCIUM PEROXIDE, AND/OR ASCORBIC ACID, PROTEASE), MONOCALCIUM PHOSPHATE.

◆ A sweet tooth needs to be brushed often.

Sugar Substitutes and Sugar

Sugar substitutes sweeten food while adding few or no calories. They can benefit people who must restrict the amount of sugar they eat, such as those with diabetes. Critics are not certain how helpful they may be for weight loss. Common artificial sweeteners include aspartame (ASS-pur-tame), acesulfame-K (ay-see-SULL-fame—KAY), and sucralose (SUE-cra-lowse).

Foods that stick to your teeth, such as granola bars and caramels, as well as foods that are sipped, cause the most tooth decay because they stay on your teeth longer. So if you have a sweet tooth, make sure you brush often and use dental floss regularly.

Fat Substitutes

Fat substitutes are natural or artificial substances that replace fat in processed foods such as fried foods, baked goods, and ice cream. They are also used in reduced-fat foods, such as low-fat cheeses.

Some natural fat substitutes are based on proteins from ingredients such as low-fat milk or

FYI

No Sugar Added

"No sugar added" means that during processing, no sugar was added. However, the food itself may contain sugar, such as in fruit juices. This statement can cause confusion, so it is important to understand its true meaning.

egg whites. Others are based on carbohydrates from sources such as cornstarch and oat bran. Natural substitutes are considered safe.

Artificial fat substitutes have also been developed. Since they do not break down during digestion, they add no fat or calories to the foods containing them. Health Canada has rejected Olestra, a fat substitute, as a food additive. However, it is still used in the United States.

Some experts are concerned that fat substitutes will not help people learn healthful eating habits. An eating plan heavily weighted toward fat-free treats may lack the proper balance of foods from *Canada's Food Guide to Healthy Eating*.

◆ **Many people enjoy drinking a cup of coffee during a break.** Why is it recommended that people limit caffeine intake to three or four cups a day?

Caffeine

Health Canada recommends that the maximum caffeine intake for the average adult be 400–450 mg per day, which equals about four cups of instant coffee. The amount of caffeine differs, depending on the type of beverage you drink.

Caffeine is a stimulant and occurs naturally in coffee, tea, and cocoa. It is also an additive in soft drinks and gum. Caffeine keeps some people from sleeping and causes nervousness. Withdrawal may cause headaches and irritability. If you drink more than a couple of cups of coffee or pop containing caffeine a day and experience these symptoms, or if you are at a risk of getting osteoporosis or are pregnant, you may want to rethink your habit.

Food Fortification

Food fortification or **enrichment** means adding one or more vitamins or minerals to a food whether or not that food normally contains it.

Food fortification is under review because new scientific knowledge about nutrition and the role nutritious food plays in people's health has come to light. Canadian rules on fortification are different from those followed in the United States.

There are several reasons Canada has set rules for the addition of nutrients to foods:

◆ Random nutrient addition could cause too many or too few nutrients to be added. This might cause health problems.

◆ Rules protect the consumer from misleading messages about what certain nutrients can do.

◆ The quality of Canada's food supply is maintained.

Removing the Mystery from Additives

The Food Additives chart opposite will help you become familiar with the names of additives and better understand the purpose of the ingredients listed on packaging and contained in foods. The additives listed are just a few of those found in foods today.

INTERNET CONNECTS

www.mcgrawhill.ca/links/food
To learn more about food additives, go to the web site above for *Food for Today, First Canadian Edition,* to see where to go next.

Food Additives

Additive	Function	Used in These Foods
Beta carotene, ascorbic acid (vitamin C), sodium ascorbate, phosphates, dextrose	**Artificial colourings and colour stabilizers**: Used to make food appeal to the eye	Candy, pop, gelatin desserts, margarine, shortening, non-milk whiteners, cereals, fruit drinks, cured meats, cheese, breakfast cereals, marshmallows
Mannitol, aspartame, sugar (sucrose), dextrose, sucralose, acesulfame-K	**Sweeteners**	Baked goods, chewing gum, soft drinks, gelatin desserts, diet foods, low-calorie foods, frozen desserts, sweetener packets for restaurants, marshmallows, table sugar, sweetened foods
Alginate, propylene glycol alginate, carrageenan, corn syrup, gelatin, locust bean gum, xanthan, food starch-modified (corn)	**Thickeners, stabilizers**: Keep factory-made food mixed	Ice cream, cheese, candy, yogurt, pop, salad dressing, ice cream, drink mixes, chocolate milk, toppings, syrups, snack foods, imitation dairy foods, marshmallows, beverages, frozen pudding, cottage cheese
Alpha tocopherol (vitamin E), ascorbic acid (vitamin C), BHA (butylated hydroxyanisole), citric acid	**Antioxidants**: Slow down or prevent rancidity in fats, oils, and oil-containing foods, or browning when fruits or vegetables are cut and exposed to the air	Vegetable oil, cereals, chewing gum, potato chips, vegetable oil, ice cream
MSG (monosodium glutamate), HVP, salt, citric acid	**Artificial and natural flavourings, flavour enhancers**: Companies often keep the identity of flavourings a secret.	Pop, candy, breakfast cereals, gelatin desserts, soup, salad dressings, potato chips, restaurant foods, crackers, processed foods, popcorn seasonings
Ascorbic acid (vitamin C), vitamin A, E, D, ferrous sulphate (iron), niacin, riboflavin, calcium	**Nutrients**	Cereals, fruit drinks, cured meats, pasta, milk
Caffeine	**Stimulant**	Coffee, tea, hot chocolate, coffee-flavoured products, such as yogurt and frozen desserts, soft drinks, chewing gum

Food Additives (continued)

Additive	Function	Used in These Foods
Calcium propionate, sodium propionate	**Preservatives:** Extend the shelf life of food	Breads, rolls, pies, cakes
Calcium (or sodium) stearoyl lactylate, sodium bicarbonate	**Dough conditioner, whipping agent, and leaveners:** Strengthen bread dough so it can be used in bread-making machinery; help produce a more uniform grain and greater volume	Bread dough, cake fillings, artificial whipped cream, processed egg whites
Monoglycerides and diglycerides, phosphates	**Emulsifiers:** Keep oil and water mixed; make bread softer; prevent spoilage; make caramels less sticky; prevent the oil in peanut butter from separating	Baked goods, margarine, candy, peanut butter
Silica gel, cornstarch	**Anti-caking agents:** Prevent lumping of powder	Popcorn seasonings, icing sugar
glycerin	**Maintains water content**	Candy, baked goods, fudge

Note: Items considered additives in this chart might differ from other sources.

Source: Centre for Science in the Public Interest (n.d.).

Recording Key Ideas from Research

What is the best way to record key ideas from research so that you can find them when you need them? It can be difficult at first to know where to start and how to record points from research that you may intend to use in the future. With practice you will develop your own methods, but here are some basic steps to get you started.

School Librarian

Your school librarian can provide you with sheets of paper on which to record research notes. This is a good place to record the source you used in APA format.

Computer

You can create your own page for recording key ideas by producing a table on the computer. For example, for a book, the following table will enable you to record key ideas.

Research Notes

Book Resource

Author: _____

Publisher: _____

Copyright Date: _____

Title: _____

Place of Publication: _____

ISBN: _____

Page	Point-Form Notes

This type of form, with some minor changes, will work for books, periodicals (magazines, newspapers, journals), audiovisual resources (tapes, films, CDs, software, kits), encyclopedias, and Internet resources.

Charts are also useful to record key ideas when you have information you would like to see at a glance, such as the following one for food additives.

Additive	Function	Used in

Always remember to cite your sources.

Chapter 16   Review and Activities

Summary

- Health Canada has strict regulations as to how much and what types of additives can be used in foods.
- Health Canada is continuously studying and reviewing food additives.
- One single food won't fix poor eating habits.
- It is important to read food ingredient lists for many reasons.
- Through the investigation of food labels, web sites, and printed materials, you will gain a knowledge and understanding of food additives.

- By studying food ingredient lists you will recognize additives listed on labels and make educated choices as a consumer.
- Factory-made foods and chemical additives are a significant part of the Canadian diet.
- Sugar and salt are familiar additives that can pose a risk if people consume too much of them.
- Food additives have many functions.
- Additives used in the United States may not necessarily be used in Canada but may affect travellers.

Knowledge and Understanding

1. In Canada, what government agency controls food additives?

2. Before a food additive is used, what must a manufacturer do?

3. Why is it important to be informed about food additives?

4. Why does Canada set rules for fortification?

5. "An eating plan that relies heavily on fat-free treats may lack the proper balance of foods as outlined in *Canada's Food Guide to Healthy Eating*." Explain this statement.

6. Explain three functions of food additives.

7. How have additives affected the food supply?

8. Why does the statement "No sugar added" cause confusion?

Thinking and Inquiry

9. Brad had just bought a package of crackers from the school vending machine. He was about to take a bite when Serena, a classmate, stopped him. "I'm doing you a huge favour," she said. "Those crackers are loaded with additives. If you want a safe snack, I have an extra apple in my backpack. I'll be happy to give it to you." On the basis of information provided in the chapter, how would you advise Brad to respond? Explain.

10. Imagine that a respected scientist informs Health Canada that a certain additive is safe. Later it is discovered that the university where the scientist teaches receives large donations from the company that wants to use the additive. How might this affect your opinion of the scientist's findings?

11. Can you guess the following foods from the ingredients listed on their packages?

a)

> Torula Yeast, Dextrose, Sugar, Salt, Spice, Hydrolyzed Plant Protein, Onion Powder, Monosodium Glutamate, US Certified Colour, Extractives of Paprika & other spices, Garlic Powder, Disodium Guanylate, Natural Flavour, Silica Gel—Added as an Anti-caking agent.

b)

> Macaroni: Enriched wheat flour Cheddar Cheese Sauce: Modified milk ingredients, Cheese (Milk, Bacterial culture, Salt, Rennet and/or Microbial Enzyme, Calcium chloride, Lipase), Salt, Sodium Phosphates, Citric acid, Colour (Contains Tartrazine).

c)

> Partly skimmed milk, Sugar, Cocoa, Modified milk ingredients, Salt, Carrageenan, Artificial Flavour, Colour, Vitamin A, Palmitate, Vitamin D3.

Communication

12. Create a Food Additive Dictionary.

a) Include an alphabetized list of ten food additives. For example, one item in the list could be "antioxidant."

b) Include information about the additives and their functions.

c) Add pictures and labels showing where these additives are found.

13. Using library or on-line sources, investigate the history of a food additive that has been in use for at least 100 years. Write a short autobiography, in which you take the point of view of the additive. Discuss the reason you were "born" (your original purpose), what kind of popularity you have enjoyed, and any controversies that might lead to your untimely demise. Your autobiography may be humorous, but keep it informative. Read your work aloud to classmates.

Application

14. Compare various types of chocolate puddings.

a) How are they packaged and stored?

b) How does their taste, texture, and appearance compare?

c) What food additives do they contain?

d) How have the additives affected packaging, storage, texture, taste, and appearance?

15. Your friend wants to lose weight. She tells you that her weight-loss plan is based mainly on low-calorie foods and beverages made with artificial sweetener and fat substitutes. She asks for your opinion. What do you say to her?

Achieving

While reading this unit, you will:

- Analyse the concept of body image and its relationship to eating disorders and body-altering substance abuse.

- Demonstrate an understanding of how to make informed food decisions when dealing with stressful situations.

People come in all shapes and sizes, not just the male and female "ideals" shown in the media. Eating a well-balanced diet and exercising can help you achieve what is right for you.

Wellness

OVERVIEW

The way that society defines beauty affects how you feel about your body. In turn, this affects your eating patterns and your overall well-being. Eating habits and the image you have of your body are only part of your overall health and well-being. Maintaining a proper diet and good eating habits will help you achieve a healthy body weight for your size.

CHAPTER EXPECTATIONS

While reading this chapter, you will:

- Analyse information from several sources to determine society's changing perception of beauty.

- Demonstrate an understanding of the influence of role models in helping youth feel comfortable about their bodies.

Changing Perceptions of Beauty

How people spend time with their peers changes. Changing aspects of lifestyle, including social activities, have influenced how we perceive our bodies.

KEY TERMS

body image
direct comments
ectomorph
endomorph
evidence
fat talk
indirect influence
mesomorph
negative body image
opinions
positive body image
reflected appraisal
self-concept
self-esteem
social comparison

SOCIAL SCIENCE SKILLS

- differentiating between evidence and opinion

Body image is a topic of interest among many different age groups in Canadian society. In this chapter, you will discover how people define beauty in our society, how views about it have changed over time, and how these views affect the images people have of their bodies. Factors such as media, parental, and peer influence on body image will also be examined.

The way that society defines beauty has changed over time. Its definition of what is beautiful often affects how people feel about themselves and, in particular, about their appearance.

What Is Body Image?

Today's society has become very body-conscious. This means that many individuals have become very aware of their physical appearance, or simply how they look in the mirror. People have an image of what they think their body looks like, and what they think it looks like to others. This mental picture and the thoughts and feelings that a person has about her or his body is called **body image.** It is important to realize that body image is a very complex issue. How an individual views his or her body and judges himself or herself is different for every person because there are many factors that affect the person's viewpoint. Some of these factors include:

- Changes in the body, specifically during puberty.

- How the culture she or he lives in defines beauty.

- Parental, peer, and media influence.

- How good a person feels about himself or herself overall.

Chapter 17 ◆ Changing Perceptions of Beauty MHR • 341

Body Image and Self-Concept

Self-concept is the way you feel about yourself. This includes your characteristics and abilities. Part of self-concept is how you judge yourself or how worthy you feel. This part of self-concept is called **self-esteem**. Self-concept is often mistakenly centred around physical appearance. This is largely because of our culture's emphasis on weight and shape. Body image is only part of your self-concept.

Self-concept is formed at an early age and changes throughout life—your body image does as well. For example, as a child, you might have been fascinated by looking at yourself in the mirror. As an adolescent, you might become uncomfortable with the changes in your body and feel insecure about them. As you move into adulthood, you may accept your body and enjoy your overall appearance. As you grow into middle adulthood, your body will continue to change and so will your feelings about the way you look. Changes in your body and your feelings toward it will continue to vary throughout your life. How you view these bodily changes may be either positive or negative. This, in turn, will affect how you feel about yourself.

Positive or Negative Body Image

You may have a positive or a negative body image. The two extremes of body image are defined below:

- **Positive body image** is when you feel comfortable and satisfied with your body. You have positive thoughts and feel confident about your body.

- **Negative body image** means that you dislike your body, weight, hair, skin colour, or any particular part of your body.

Some of the factors that might lead to a negative body image and the impact of having a negative body image are discussed in the rest of this chapter.

Basic Body Types

The three basic body types are determined mainly by genetics. They are ectomorph, endomorph, and mesomorph. Most people have one or a combination of these body types. Which body type do you think you have?

Ectomorph

- Lean, usually thin, tall.

- Little muscle or fat.

- Long arms and legs, few curves.

- May be able to eat large amounts of food without gaining weight.

Endomorph

- Average to large frame.

- Usually wider at the hips.

- Higher percentage of body fat.

- May have trouble maintaining a healthy weight.

Mesomorph

- Muscular body.

- Broad shoulders and narrow hips.

- Large bones and heavy muscles may lead to higher body weights.

Source: Middlesex–London Health Unit (n.d.)

There may be a change in your proportions as you develop physically. This is a normal part of getting older. This, in turn, affects your body type. Several times in your life, it may seem that your body is out of balance. This may be especially true during adolescence. For example, as a child, you may have had chubby legs and a round, full stomach. As you grew into adolescence, your arms and legs became exceptionally long for your body weight and you felt out of balance. You are now characterized as an ectomorph body type.

Factors That Shape Body Image

Factors that influence body image include such things as the interactions you have with others, your parents' and peers' role in shaping your body image, the physical changes that occur in your body during adolescence, and the mass media. It can be difficult to understand how all these factors affect body image—every individual is exposed to different experiences daily and throughout life. This leaves us with some complex questions:

- What are some of the factors in your culture and in your relationships with others that influence your body image?

- What role do these factors have on influencing how you feel about yourself and, in particular, how you feel about your body?

Adolescents, Puberty, and Body Image

The way that males and females mature is different. During puberty, the male body usually grows wider in the chest and shoulders, whereas the female body tends to widen and round out at the hips. Females also develop breasts. As a result of these changes, adolescents may not know their exact body type until they finish growing. These physical changes may have an influence on body image for some adolescents. Some adolescents may feel uncomfortable about their bodies, since they are facing many changes in their lives at this time. Other factors may play a large role as well.

INTERNET CONNECTS

www.mcgrawhill.ca/links/food
To learn more about how to promote positive self-esteem in young men and women, go to the web site above for *Food for Today, First Canadian Edition,* to see where to go next.

What Is Beautiful?

Every person finds beauty in different things. Your parents may not approve of the clothes you wear or your hairstyle because they don't like the look of them, but you may think they look good. In this example, the old saying "Beauty is in the eye of the beholder" is true. However, Linda Jackson, a psychology professor at Michigan State University, has reviewed research that has been done on what people find attractive physically. She states that some of the research contradicts the saying "Beauty is in the eye of the beholder." Researchers have found that there is a lot of agreement worldwide, including in Western culture, on what characteristics people find beautiful. Jackson states that this is especially true of what people find beautiful in a face. Yet, there is less agreement among cultures about what body characteristics people find attractive. What is considered beauti-

ful in a body has also changed within cultures across time.

When discussing body image, it helps to look at what people in a society consider beautiful, since many people judge their bodies according to this ideal.

People have different ideas about what they find attractive in someone's face. For example, you may say to your friends that a particular someone is "so good-looking," while your friends may think that the person is "okay-looking." Even though everyone has particular preferences, researchers have found that the facial features in the photographs opposite are typical of what people find beautiful.

Researcher David Perrett found that people are attracted to faces that look like their own. They also find faces that are average appealing. This is encouraging, because many people have average-looking faces. People are attracted to a face with features that are associated with being young and healthy as well.

However, people must also remember that other characteristics, such as personality, abilities, and skills, are a major part of what makes up an individual. These are important aspects of beauty to focus on in yourself and in others.

A Beautiful Body

At one time or another, many of you have wanted to change your body, or at least a certain part of it. What is found attractive in a body varies among cultures. In addition, researchers have found that the qualities that people find attractive in a person's body are different for males and females. What constitutes an ideal body has also changed throughout time. Western culture has an ideal image of male and female bodies. At the present time, the ideal image of a man is to be strong, powerful, and muscular. A woman's ideal image is to be thin, but fit and toned. It is important to find out if you actually feel that these ideal images are what you find attractive in others and in yourself.

In Western cultures, including Canada, being physically attractive is valued. In addition, those who have a good body have more dating opportunities (Cash & Pruzinsky, 2002). Studies show what is desirable in men and women is close to the ideal image that the media portrays. Men want women to be slender and have small hips and large breasts. Women want men to be muscular and of average weight. In general, lean men and women are preferred. It is also important to note that both men and women look for physical attractiveness when choosing a partner. However, researchers have found that men value physical attractiveness much more than women do (Hoyt & Kogan, 2001). What effect do you think this has on a woman's body image? What effect do you think this has on a man's body image?

Judging Others by Their Beauty

Living in a culture where looking good is very important may cause people to judge others by their outward appearance. What their culture deems beautiful is noticed by people at a very young age. In one study, children considered peers who were goodlooking to be smarter, friendlier, happier, and more successful than unattractive peers (Health Canada, 2002). Professor Linda Jackson found that people judge both children and adults by their looks and they act differently toward those they find attractive. Both children and adults who are considered good-looking also

◆ Women with more feminine-looking faces are found to be attractive. Typical female features include a small lower face, a relatively flat middle face, full lips, high eyebrows, and a less prominent brow ridge.

◆ Male features that are found to be attractive vary somewhat. Studies have found some preference for masculine faces. Masculine features include a larger jaw and prominent cheekbones and brow ridge. Others prefer a "baby-faced" look in males.

get more attention and have more positive relationships. They are also more popular than those who are found unattractive. Even though people judge attractive individuals by their looks and act differently toward them, the nice-looking people may not necessarily see themselves that way.

The following scenario shows that how people are judged by others may not actually affect how they feel about themselves.

Emily is a good-looking teenager. People compliment her and often praise how she looks. Many boys she goes to school with want to ask her out. However, Emily doesn't feel this way about herself. She looks in the mirror and thinks that she is overweight and that she has a big nose. She doesn't feel good about her body and thinks that people are just being nice to her.

People judge others by their appearance. This can limit people by not giving them a chance because they do not fit the ideal image of what is physically attractive in society. People who are constantly teased about their bodies or are told over and over again that they are unattractive will usually begin to believe it is true and therefore begin to feel unhappy about their bodies.

This points out how important it is for adults and youth to be positive role models for children. One way to do this is to accept people with a variety of facial features and body shapes. Show children and others around you that it is important to get to know a person on the inside instead of judging him or her on appearance alone. In what other ways can you and others around you accept people for reasons other than their physical characteristics?

A Beautiful Face

Evidence shows repeatedly that babies are more attracted to a beautiful face. They demonstrate this by looking longer at pictures of people whom adults also rated as attractive or beautiful. These babies would look at people with big eyes, smooth skin, and full lips, no matter what their age, ethnic background, or gender.

◆ The features that our ancestors thought of as beautiful in a face, such as those shown in this bust of Egyptian Queen Nefertiti, dated 1350 BCE, are still considered beautiful by Western society today.

The Day I Figured Out That No One Is Perfect

By Ellie Logan, Age 9

Once there was a girl in my class that I thought was beautiful and smart. I believed that she was perfect. When it came time for my birthday, I invited her to my party, and she came.

A few months later, it was her birthday. I got a special necklace for her. Thinking about how happy she would be to receive my gift made me so excited. I asked her when her birthday party was going to be. She replied, "Why do you want to know? You're not invited. You're just a dork with glasses!"

I felt really bad when she said that. I just stood there looking at her. Everyone standing by her came to stand next to me. Then we all left.

That day, I figured out that even if someone looks perfect, there is a very good possibility that they aren't. When it comes to perfection, it's how someone treats you that is more important than how they look.

Source: Logan, Ellie. (1998).

◆ Being physically good-looking doesn't always mean the person has an attractive personality as well.

Personality

There are many other factors that people find attractive in a mate as well as in their friends. An individual's personality is the most important factor when choosing a mate (Penton-Voak & Perrett, 2000). Adolescent boys and girls also describe personality characteristics as being important factors of what they find attractive in their peers of the same and opposite sex (Carlson Jones, 2001). People who look only at physical appearance when choosing who they will marry or become friends with may be missing out on many opportunities to enjoy relationships with a wide variety of people.

Dangerous Obsession

By Sandy Naiman

Body dissatisfaction is becoming increasingly prevalent, almost a norm, in adolescence. Young women often grow up with a skewed self-image.

For too many young girls today, you are what you don't eat.

A new Canadian study of 1739 Ontario girls between the ages of 12 and 18 published last week in *The Canadian Medical Association Journal* confirms an alarming trend—27 percent have "disordered eating attitudes and behaviours," such as bingeing, self-induced vomiting, and abuse of diet pills.

Consumed by their own body-consciousness, inescapable in our Western "culture of thinness," many adolescent girls won't get into bathing suits, swim, or even eat in front of boys, one 14-year-old explained recently.

"None of my friends do—you just don't," she says. "I don't know why, but it's just not done. . . ."

Source: Retrieved April 19, 2003, from www.canoe.ca/LifewiseLiving01/ 0911_bodyimage-sun.html.

Interacting with Other People

Part of what makes people human is the daily interactions they have with one another. Many enjoy being social by playing sports on a team, talking with another person, or simply "hanging out" with others. There are two ways that interacting with other people can affect body image: reflected appraisal and social comparison.

Reflected appraisal is when we see ourselves as others see us, or as we think that they do. The way that we think others see us is affected by how we judge ourselves. However, how we think other people see us may be inaccurate. The following is an example of how we reflect on other people's views of us and, in turn, how this affects the way we feel about our body.

> Andrew got up this morning, dressed for school, and ate breakfast as usual. On the way out the door he stopped to look at himself in the mirror. He thought to himself, "I really like the way these new jeans look on me. My hours of working out at the gym have really paid off. I think I have enough guts to ask Mia if she wants to go to the school dance with me this Friday." Later that day, Andrew was in a hurry to get to math class because he was late. Upon entering the door of the classroom, he tripped and fell in front of his classmates, his teacher, and most importantly in front of Mia. The room filled with laughter. While walking home from school, a few classmates bantered at him, "Careful you don't trip on the cracks in the sidewalk!"
>
> When Andrew arrived home, he walked past the same mirror that he had looked at himself in earlier that morning. He stopped and said to himself, "I am such a klutz. Mia won't want to go out with me. I'm too tall and gangly. Forget the gym. It's not helping my body anyway."

In the example, Andrew changed how he felt about his body within the course of a few hours. It was affected by the way he felt other people viewed him and the way he measured himself. Andrew's body had not changed that day at all; just his image of his body and the way that he felt about it had changed. This also affected his confidence, since he didn't want to ask Mia out anymore.

Evidence versus Opinion

As part of a research paper, you will need to explore what experts have discovered about your topic. You will need to do some research. The discussion of issues, such as body image, in the area of Social Science tends to elicit strong feelings that are often based on personal experience and opinion. You will also form your own opinions about the topic that you are researching. It is important to find evidence that supports your opinions.

Opinions are statements that are based on judgments, beliefs, and estimations that people have on an issue, topic, or person. Many different factors affect people's opinions. These factors include family and friends, education, culture, religion, and social status. "People's backgrounds act as the filters through which they see the world around them. Their opinions become biased when they contain inaccurate and limited views of individuals and groups, or of situations and events" (Bain et al., 2002, p. 158).

There are opinions in many types of sources. A typical source in the media is an editorial. Here the writer is giving her or his opinion based on personal experiences and observations. Look for opinion statements in magazines, newspapers, and on the Internet, where people discuss a topic based on what they believe to be true.

Below are some examples of opinion statements:

- He has beautiful eyes.
- Joanne is too skinny.
- The city of Ottawa is overpopulated.
- Bobby has a negative body image because he has a poor relationship with his mother.

Evidence is giving proof of a statement. Evidence can be found in both primary and secondary sources. Statistics and the results of primary research are forms of evidence. Evidence from secondary sources, such as the Internet, magazines, or newspaper articles, may be given. However, if this evidence does not contain a source citing where the information originated, it may not be valid. For example, if you find a statistic on a web site that states, "Forty percent of females are dissatisfied with their bodies and 28 percent of males are dissatisfied with their bodies," these statistics need a reference within the text to indicate where they came from to be considered a valid source of evidence.

The following sources are good places to find evidence to support your opinions or to find out what research says about a research topic:

- Statistics Canada.
- Articles in a professional journal.
- Health Canada and other government web sites.
- Research-based organizations, such as universities.

Identifying Evidence versus Opinion

1. Read "Dangerous Obsession" on p. 348 and make a list of statements made that are opinions and a list of statements that are evidence.
2. Are the opinion statements backed up with evidence? If yes, what is the evidence?
3. Do you detect bias in the opinions? If yes, what is the bias?
4. Is the evidence in the article from a reliable source? If yes, what is it?

What we see when we look in the mirror is affected by the way we think other people see us. What are some of the factors that might affect how teenagers view their bodies?

Another person may have reacted differently in the same situation because he or she would have a different level of self-esteem and different life experiences.

The way that you interpret other people's opinion also depends on who it is. For example, you may not care about your younger brother's comments on the way you look in a new outfit, but you would care about your best friend's remarks on how the same outfit looks. Whose opinions matter to you also changes over time. During the seventh and eighth grades, friends are the most important influence, but by the first year of university, parents, friends, and teachers all become important influences (Health Canada, 2002).

Social comparison is when people rate themselves by comparing themselves to others. The standards used to rate oneself are based on popular culture. In Canadian society, and in many other societies, physical appearance is rated on the size and shape of a person's body. When individuals rate their bodies, they compare their shape and size to others who are popular in their culture.

Individuals may use models seen in the media to compare themselves to. This may be because many models fit the standard of popular culture. They are the ideal male—a muscular mesomorph—or the ideal female—slim (Health Canada, 2002). Peers may also be used for comparison. One study showed that adolescents may use peers to compare themselves to more than they use models. It has also been found that adolescents who compared themselves to peers and models or celebrities had a more negative body image (Carlson Jones, 2001).

Parents

Parents are the first people that you have contact with as a baby. For some children, their parent(s) is the primary person they interact with on a daily basis until they attend school. It is no great surprise, then,

◆ Teenagers may compare themselves to their peers. During this comparison, they often gauge themselves according to how their body shape and size looks in relation to others. **Identify two reasons people may compare their bodies to others.**

that parents play a part in shaping their child's body image. Parents may do this shaping by direct comments and indirect influence.

Parents might make **direct comments** about a child's eating, weight, or body. It has been found that parents in general are happy about the way their children look and believe their children are attractive. However, many parents make comments about their children's weight. They might even encourage their child to lose weight. Parents' comments about their child's weight affect how satisfied the child feels about her or his body. Even during adolescence, direct comments about eating or their bodies influence teenagers when these comments come from their parents (Cash & Pruzinsky, 2002). The following example demonstrates how a parent's comments may have an impact on a child's body image.

Joel, aged 8, was sitting at the kitchen table one day after school having a snack that consisted of bananas, orange juice, and peanut butter on crackers. Joel's mom

walked into the room and said, "That looks like a healthy snack. I like the food choices you've made. I've noticed how much you are growing lately, so you must be really hungry after school. Pretty soon you'll be as tall as I am!"

In this example, Joel is hearing good messages about his body and about his eating habits because he is being complimented. How would this contribute to the feelings and judgments that Joel makes about his body?

The behaviours and attitudes that parents demonstrate or model may have an **indirect influence** on a child's body image. A parent may be constantly trying to lose weight through dieting and exercising, or make comments about his or her own weight or body shape. It is difficult to prove whether or not parental behaviours such as these directly affect children's body image. Some studies show that there is a relationship between a parent's behaviours toward his or her own body image and their adolescent children's

◆ Since children learn from what they see and hear from others around them, parents act as role models for their children. Parents who participate in physical leisure activities with their children are showing them the importance of combining fun and fitness. How would this affect a child's body image?

body image (Cash & Pruzinsky, 2002). The situation below provides an example of how parents' behaviours and attitudes may influence a child's body image.

Eleven-year-old Sara lives with her two parents, who are very involved in sports. Her dad participates competitively in triathlons and her mom is constantly dieting and exercising. There are many fitness and health magazines around the house. Even though Sara's parents do not comment on her weight or body, they constantly comment about their own weight. Sara feels very aware of her own body because of her parents' actions.

Part of being a parent is teaching a child proper eating habits and how to maintain a healthy lifestyle. It is important for parents to give feedback on a child's eating habits and body. Positive feedback about body image

and modelling appropriate behaviours and attitudes will have a more favourable effect on a child's body image.

Peers

Peers influence one another in the same ways that parents do—either through comments or by the way they talk about or act toward their own bodies. Children and teenagers are often teased by their peers, usually about how a person looks. Adolescent girls often discuss weight and body shape. This is referred to as **fat talk**. Even girls who are of average weight or thinner and are happy with their bodies participate in these conversations. The peers of adolescents and children influence one another's body image. Girls seem to be more influenced by peers than boys do (Worell, 2001).

Barbie Dolls I'd Like to See

By Susan Jane Gilman

Most women I know are nostalgic for Barbie. "Oh," they coo wistfully, "I used to *loooove* my Barbies. My girlfriends would come over, and we'd play for hours. . . ."

Not me. As a child, I disliked the doll on impulse; as an adult, my feelings have actually fermented into a heady, full-blown hatred.

My friends and I never owned Barbies. When I was young, little girls in my neighbourhood collected "Dawns." Dawn dolls' hair came in different lengths and— although probably only a six-year-old doll fanatic could discern this—their facial expressions and features were indeed different. They were as diverse as fashion dolls could be in 1972, and in this way, I realize now, they were slightly subversive.

Of course, at that age, my friends and I couldn't spell subversive, let alone wrap our minds around the concept. But we sensed intuitively that Dawns were more democratic that Barbies. With their different colours and equal sizes, they were closer to what we looked like.

As a six-year-old, I remember gushing, "I want to be a ballerina and a bride, and a movie star, and a model, and a queen . . ." To be sure, I was a disgustingly girly girl. I twirled. I skipped. I actually wore a tutu to school. (I am not kidding.) For a year, I refused to wear blue. Whenever the opportunity presented itself, I dressed up in my grandmother's pink chiffon nightgown and rhinestone necklaces and paraded around the apartment like the princess of the universe. I dressed like my Dawn dolls—and dressed my Dawn dolls like me. . . . These dolls were part of my fantasy life and an extension of my ambitions. Tellingly, my favourite doll was Angie, who had dark brown hair, like mine.

But at some point, most prima ballerinas experience a terrible turning point. I know I did. I have an achingly clear memory of myself, standing before a mirror in all my finery and jewels, feeling suddenly ridiculous and miserable. *Look at yourself*, I remember thinking acidly. *Nobody will ever like you.* I could not have been older than eight. And then later, another memory: my friend Allison confiding in me, "The kids at my school, they all hate my red hair." Somewhere, somehow, a message seeped into our consciousness telling us that we weren't good enough to be a bride or a model or a queen or anything because we weren't pretty enough. And this translated into not smart enough or likable enough, either. . . .

Barbie is the only toy in the Western world that human beings actively try to mimic. Barbie is not just a children's doll, it's an adult cult and an aesthetic obsession.

It's true that, in the past few years, Mattel has made an effort to create a few slightly more P.C. versions of its best-selling blond. Walk down the aisle at Toys-R-Us (and they wonder why kids today can't spell), and you can see a few boxes of American Indian Barbie, Jamaican Barbie, Cowgirl Barbie. . . . Ultimately their packaging reinforces their status as "Other." These are "special" and "limited" edition Barbies, the labels announce; clearly *not* the standard. . . .

Now, I am not, as a rule, anti-doll. I once wore a tutu and collected the entire Dawn family myself. I know better than to claim that dolls are nothing but sexist gender propaganda. Dolls can be a lightning rod for the imagination, for companionship, for learning. And they're *fun*—something that must never be undervalued.

Continued on next page

Mass Media

Pictures, flyers, posters, billboards, music videos, and pop-up advertisements on the Internet are just some ways that you are bombarded with messages in today's society. These messages can range from the quite obvious, as when celebrities endorse products, to the more subtle. Subtle messages may include attractive people having fun while consuming a particular food or beverage, or simply pictures of people posed in a way that sends a message. These messages may influence body image because they present their audience with ideas of what is ideal. Statistics Canada (2001) has found that Canadians tune in to television for an average of 21.2 hours per week. One type of program that is popular is situation comedies. Gregory Fouts, a Canadian researcher, has found that more than 75 percent of the female characters in sitcoms are underweight and only 5 percent are above average weight (as cited in Media Awareness Network, 2003a.).

Changing Images of Beauty

It is difficult to say exactly what people viewed as beautiful about a body in the past, because it overlaps so much with fashion trends in clothing, hairstyles, and body adornment, such as tattoos and body piercing. There have been more changes in what is considered beautiful for women than there have been for men. This is best demonstrated by looking at who and what has been popular in the media in the past.

Female Changes in the Ideal Body

Early 1800s

Beginning in the Victorian Era, the corset was fashionable. This made a women's waist smaller and accentuated her hips and buttocks. The ideal body type for women was plump, fleshy, and full-figured.

1920s

The Victorian hourglass figure gave way to the thin flappers, who bound their breasts to achieve a flat profile.

Post–World War II

People became more active. Body fat was regarded negatively. It was believed to be unnecessary, since it would hold a person back from being active. The modified hourglass figure was the ideal image. Women used girdles to achieve this look.

1950s

A thin woman with a large bust was considered most attractive. Marilyn Monroe set the standard for women. She was a size 16.

1960s

Being thin was thought of as attractive. The model Twiggy was popular. She was a size 6 and looked like a young boy.

1960–1980

Over the next 30 years, being slim became the preferred body type. Models became thinner and thinner. During the 1980s, an emphasis on being toned and fit became popular. Everyone wanted a "hard body." Women wore shoulder pads to create an impression of power.

1990s

Women with large breasts and narrow hips became the ideal. People such as Pamela Anderson typified this trend.

2000+

Today, being thin is still considered the ideal. Sometimes this look is achieved through extreme measures, such as plastic surgery, liposuction, and breast implants. Women also use less invasive means to create the ideal body type, such as "miracle bras," control-top pantyhose, and girdles.

Sources: Adapted from TheSite.Org (n.d.); and Media Awareness Network (2002).

Male Changes in the Ideal Body

Pre-1900

The male body image was "manly." This meant that a man was not supposed to focus too much on his looks, since this was not considered masculine. Men wore top hats during this era to make them appear taller.

1920s

Men wore suits similar to those worn by men today. Charlie Chaplin, who was quite thin, was a popular character during this era.

World War II

Men's body image changed after World War II, when men focussed more on their appearance.

1950s

Men began to show more elegance and charm. Actor Cary Grant was the ideal example of this look. The rebel look, popularized by Elvis Presley and James Dean, was also adopted in the 1950s.

1980s

Being muscular and powerful became the ideal look for males in the 1980s. This look featured broad shoulders, narrow hips, and rippled abs, chest, and shoulders. Arnold Schwarzenegger, who typified this look, became popular. Bodybuilding gained more popularity and respect.

2000+

Today, men are shown in various forms in the media, from being fit and athletic to being very muscular and V-shaped.

Sources: Adapted from Media Awareness Network (2002); and L. Luciano. (2001) *Looking Good: Male Body Image in Modern America.*

Body Image Ideals Today

Body image ideals today are centred around fitness. Images of men and women show an ideal that is difficult for most people to meet. Think of what you see in fitness and fashion magazines. How many people do you know who look like the models in magazines? Many of the people you see in advertisements are "enhanced" with cosmetics, airbrushing techniques, and computer-generated images. For example, one picture may use one model's legs, another's face, and put them on another model's body. Even with dieting and hard work, many people's natural body shape will never look like those seen in the media. The ideal images that are promoted for males and females are shown in the pictures on page 358.

Attractive and famous people have been used to sell products and services for a long time. It is how the body is used in the media and how much clothing is worn that has changed. Can you think of an ad where a scantily clothed male is used to sell a product? How are the product and the image of the male associated? Is it realistic? It is in these ways that the media may be pushing the boundaries of the ideal body image.

Advertisements sometimes show women being dominated. How is that used to sell the product? Does this imply that violence against women is acceptable? Is that appropriate?

The media's portrayal of men is also exaggerated in some of its images. Many action-adventure movies show men with very large physiques. They are extremely muscular and can perform almost any stunt. Think of an actor who represents this ideal. How many people do you know who look like him? Is this an achievable body shape for most men?

◆ **What adjectives would you use to describe this male and this female?** What are some possible messages that are being presented in this advertisement?

Ethnicity in the Media

Until the 1970s, people of colour were not often seen in the media. "The progress made by the civil rights movement encouraged a new pride in people who were black. This also was adopted by many people of the white culture. 'Black is beautiful' became the trend, and afros as worn by the Jackson Five became popular, as well as the ethnic models that began to appear in advertisements and fashion magazines" (Media Awareness Network, 2002).

With the introduction of hip-hop and rap and influential actors from various ethnic backgrounds, there is more diversity seen in the media today. Nevertheless, some feel that "their bodies often fit the Western body ideal of tall, thin, and curved in the right places. Media fashion images tend to 'whitewash' or 'e-race' ethnic facial and body features, giving the models a very 'white' Western look. For most ethnic people this look is impossible to achieve." The lengths that some people will go to in order to achieve this look take a lot of time and effort (Media Awareness Network, 2002).

What lengths *do* people go to? Do the people you see today in the media fit the white ideal image of beauty, or *do* you see more diversity? Do the people who are seen in the media play a stereotypical role according to their ethnic or cultural background, or are their roles diverse?

◆ **Beauty comes in all ages and ethnicities.** What does your culture deem beautiful?

Youth Versus Aging

Looking young is also valued by our culture. We are constantly made aware of this because there are new products on the market every day to help people reverse the signs of aging in an attempt to stay young. Think of an advertisement you have seen that promotes staying younger. This trend began in the 1960s and continues today. Many models find themselves out of jobs once they reach a certain age. They are being replaced by younger and younger models. There has been some attempt in the media to change this. For example, some Canadian magazines will not allow models younger than 25 years to be in their publications. There are also more magazines for teen girls and women in which articles and advertisements do not focus on body image.

Because there is an increasing number of older adults in the Canadian population, more products and services are being advertised for this age group. Consider how this age group is being shown. Think of an advertisement that features an older adult. How is this person depicted? Are the images positive? Are they realistic, or do they show older people who look young and are exceptionally active and fit for their age?

Messages in the Media

Health Canada's Office of Nutrition Policy and Program (2002) is of the opinion that the media's message about these ideals is obvious: if a person works hard, he or she can achieve this image. But this message may be damaging to some people's body image and could have negative effects on an individual's health. Other organizations that make the following points promote media awareness about body image:

◆ Using thin, good-looking models to sell products and play glamorous characters on television programs encourages people to associate good looks with being successful, happy, and wealthy.

◆ The images of overweight men and women shown in the media label them as lazy, unhappy, and unsuccessful. Thin people are shown as more competent and popular. This sends the message that being thin is better.

◆ Using muscular young men and barely dressed young women in music videos says that if you are young and show off your body this way, you are cool.

◆ There is a mixed message in the media because it promotes thinness and being fit but also sponsors fast food, soft drinks, and candy.

INTERNET CONNECTS

www.mcgrawhill.ca/links/food
To learn more about media awareness go to the web site above for *Food for Today, First Canadian Edition,* to see where to go next.

"Ideal-Beauty" Message Now Also Aimed at Men

by Antonia Zerbisias

With men's health and fashion magazines proliferating, Calvin Klein producing more buff male ads, male movie stars pumping and liposucking, and good looks becoming career requirements in the toughened-up job market, men are being subjected to more and more impossibly physical ideas.

So it's no wonder that a recent issue of *Psychology Today* reports some people at war with their bodies are willing to die younger, if they can leave a thinner corpse.

The "1997 Body Image" indicates that 15 percent of women and 11 percent of men say they would sacrifice more than five years of their lives for the weight they want.

"Twenty-four percent of women and 7 percent of men say they would give up more than three years."

Tracing the survey results over the years (*Psychology Today* conducted similar surveys in 1972 and 1985), it quickly becomes clear that contradictions between the culture's thinning body ideals and the fattening of fast-food menus are making us very unhappy, indeed.

For example, "only" 49 percent of women who responded in 1972 hated their thighs. Today the percentage has shot to 61.

Twenty-five years ago, 36 percent of men were dissatisfied with their abdomens. Today, 63 percent think their pots have gone to pot.

Source: The Toronto Star Syndicate (2003).

Beauty in Other Cultures

Even though in Western culture thin is in, this is not the ideal in all cultures. In countries where food is in short supply and where there are many people living in poverty, people envy those who are overweight because they think they being large means being wealthy. In Nigeria, for example, young girls in some tribes are put into rooms called "fattening rooms" so they can fatten up. Because being overweight is seen as attractive, young women go through this fattening process to attract a husband.

Being fat is becoming less valued as the Western ideas about beauty and health are becoming known in Africa. This has also been the case in other areas of the world where researchers have reported that being fat was thought of as beautiful as well. In particular, one researcher reported that woman in Fiji were thought of as beautiful if they were big and round. After television and video were introduced to this culture in 1995, eating disorders among young girls aged 15 to 19 increased from 3 percent to 15 percent. There was also an increase in the number of girls dieting and believing that they were overweight. This researcher, however, denies that there is a direct relationship between eating disorders and television (Becker, as cited in Media Awareness Network, 2003b, 1999).

Other cultures in history have been known to use various devices to shape a particular part of the body. The results are considered beautiful in this culture. An example is the Long Necks of Burma. These women begin wearing rings around their necks at a very young age. More and more rings are added to the neck so that the shoulders are pushed down and the neck appears longer. Of course, the longer the neck, the more beautiful the woman is thought to be. This is reported as becoming a lost tradition among these women (Gluckman, n.d.).

Effects on Body Image

No one factor in our culture can be pinpointed as the one that affects body image the most. What we think is beautiful is connected to how we see others and how we see ourselves. In turn, this makes us behave in various ways toward our bodies.

◆ Long necks are believed to be beautiful in Burma, so the females of one tribe wear rings around their necks beginning at an early age to make them longer.

The value of being good-looking and the narrow way in which we define beauty in our culture puts pressure on people to look a certain way. This pressure, combined with factors such as personality and low self-esteem, may make people dissatisfied with their bodies. Problems associated with body image are increasing for both men and women—they are affecting people of many age groups and at a younger age than ever before (Health Canada, 2002).

Research has found that having a negative body image appears to be more of an issue for girls than for boys. The messages about how important it is to have the "right" kind of body seem to be stronger and more consistent for girls than for boys, especially messages from peers and the media (Cash & Pruzinsky, 2002). The Canadian Health Network reports that nine out of ten Canadian girls and women say that, in some way, they are

discontent with their bodies (Canadian Health Network, n.d.). Four out of ten adolescent boys report being unhappy with their bodies (Government of Saskatchewan, 2000).

Being unhappy about their bodies is affecting people's health because many are taking action to become more satisfied with their bodies. The concern is that people often resort to unhealthy and drastic measures to reshape their bodies or to lose weight. These measures include exercising excessively, dieting, forcing oneself to vomit, overusing laxatives, using steroids, and having plastic surgery. Being on a "diet," or restricting a certain food or the amount of food one eats, may be necessary for some people's health. Dieting can be a problem, however, because some people don't know when to stop, and this may lead to developing an eating disorder.

The Future of Beauty

What our culture finds beautiful affects how we feel about and act toward our bodies. This is true for both males and females. Our definition of beauty might focus more on what is beautiful within ourselves and look at the abilities, skills, and positive personality traits in ourselves and those around us. Some television programs, magazines, and advertisements are trying to shift our ideas of what is beautiful to a healthier picture, but they are still few. The media for the most part fails to recognize that unrealistic body shapes and weights are just that—unrealistic. Parents, peers, and the media can be positive role models for one another so that they can help children develop a healthy body image. This will help people in our society feel more positive about themselves and their bodies.

Career Profile

Counsellor

Susan Auckland

What education is required for your job?

- Masters degree in counselling, education, social work, or a related field.

What skills does a person need to be able to do your job?

- Strong interpersonal skills including ability to build relationships and to put others at ease.

- Critical thinking skills.

- Compassion and patience.

- Detective skills.

- Excellent communication skills including active listening.

- Knowledge of counselling theory and different strategies to assist clients in managing their problems.

- Thorough understanding of how eating habits and nutrition affect both mental and physical well-being.

- General knowledge of healthy eating acording to *Canada's Food Guide to Healthy Eating.*

What do you like most about your job?

I enjoy all aspects of my job, especially the opportunity to meet and work with many different people. Working with clients with eating disorders is challenging work because there is so much to know in this field. I have to be a kind of co-detective working with the clients to understand their eating-disordered behaviour—what it means to them and why it developed. I have to understand the change process and how to help someone move toward making changes.

What advice would you give a person who is considering a career in counselling?

Take advantage of volunteer opportunities—especially ones in which you get some kind of training. Explore the kinds of settings in which you think you would like to work. Ask yourself what kind of people you would like to work with. Talk to people working in jobs that interest you. Visit places in which you might like to work. Ask lots of different people about their career path into their job. This will not only give you lots of material for your résumé, but it will give you a clearer focus as you move forward in planning your career.

Chapter 17   Review and Activities

Summary

- People have become very conscious of their body image in today's society. How a person judges his or her body depends on many factors unique to that person.

- Self-concept is based on characteristics and abilities, not only physical appearance. How you feel about yourself is called self-esteem.

- You may have a positive or negative image of yourself, depending on how you feel about your body.

- There are three basic body types: ectomorph, endomorph, and mesomorph. Your body type changes at different points in your life. Some people are a combination of body types.

- What people find attractive in a human face is apparently universal. What people find attractive in a human body is different depending on the culture and the time period.

- People's idea of their own attractiveness is based on reflected appraisal, or how a person thinks others see her or him, and social comparison, or how a person rates himself or herself compared to others.

- Parents are the first people to shape a child's body image, through direct comments about the child's eating habits, weight, or body shape, through indirect influence, or through their behaviour. Peers and the media are also strong influences on a person's body image.

- Today's ideal body image has a lot to do with what is presented in the media, but the majority of people will never be able to attain that ideal. This can have negative effects on people's health and body image.

- The media are changing to include a wider variety of people in terms of ethnicity, age, and other factors.

- The ideal of beauty varies in different cultures; however, with the more recent exposure to television and videos in less-developed countries, these ideals are changing to conform more to Western ideals.

Knowledge and Understanding

1. What is body image?

2. Why is body image considered a part of your self-concept?

3. How are self-concept and self-esteem connected?

4. Explain what is meant by *reflected appraisal*.

5. What does it mean to have a negative body image?

6. What does having a positive body image refer to?

Thinking and Inquiry

7. Research various forms of the media— the Internet, magazines, film, and music videos—to find images of people from various ethnic backgrounds that were in the media 30 years ago and today. Discuss the difference between these images. What are the changes and the similarities?

8. Mark and Tonya are twin brother and sister. They are 15 years old. Tonya is not happy with the way that her body looks and is constantly dieting. Mark is quite satisfied with his body and takes pride in staying active. In groups of two, discuss some of the influences that may have accounted for the different attitudes that Mark and Tonya have about their bodies. Share your answers with the class.

9. When is the saying "Beauty is in the eye of the beholder" contradictory, and when is it true? Give examples from the text to support your answer. Also use your own anecdotal examples to prove your answer.

10. Does the media have a greater impact on some people than others? Explain your answer.

Communication

11. Choose a culture to research how beauty is defined in that culture. Answer the following questions in a one-page report:

- How does the culture define beauty in females?
- How does the culture define beauty in males?
- In what ways has the culture's idea of beauty changed throughout time?
- If it has changed or is changing, what factors have influenced these changes?
- What are the similarities and differences between the culture's ideal and the ideal of beauty for men and women in Western society?

12. Choose at least four advertisements from a current magazine that depict males, females, or both to sell their product. Write a one-page analysis of each ad that discusses the hidden messages used in each ad.

Application

13. Look at pictures of yourself at various ages and see how your body shape has changed. What body type, or combination of body types, do you have now and what type did you have in the past?

14. Prepare five questions on the changing views of beauty in society. Use these questions to interview an individual from an older generation. Write a 500-word report that expresses what you have discovered about this person's generation. Complete the report by adding pictures that show beauty trends from that generation. The pictures may be borrowed from the person you interviewed or found on the Internet, in books, or in magazines.

CHAPTER

18

CHAPTER EXPECTATIONS

While reading this chapter, you will:

- Describe unhealthy eating patterns and body-altering substance abuse.

- Identify strategies to remedy unhealthy eating habits and body-altering substance abuse.

Recognizing Unhealthy Eating Patterns

Establishing a healthy eating pattern enhances your appearance, energy levels, strength, and how you feel about yourself.

anabolic steroids
anorexia nervosa
binge eating disorder
bingeing
body distortion
bulimia nervosa
creatine
doping
eating disorder
eating patterns
grazing
health fraud
physiological help
pica
psychological help
purging
yo-yo dieting

CHAPTER INTRODUCTION

There is a lot of pressure on people today to look good. This preoccupation with appearance can have negative effects on some people, who will resort to supplements, "miracle products," steroids, or extreme dieting and exercise programs to achieve their ideal appearance or physical ability. Good looks and good health can be achieved naturally by establishing a healthy eating pattern, being active, and focussing more on people's inner beauty.

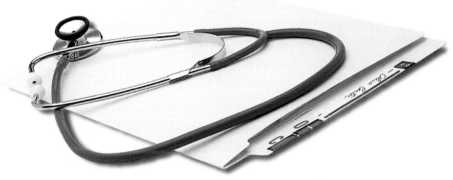

In an effort to achieve an ideal body, some people resort to extreme measures that may lead to serious health problems for them in the future.

Eating Patterns

Your **eating pattern** includes where, when, how, what, and why you choose to eat the foods you do. It is the overall pattern, not any one food or meal, that determines if an eating pattern is healthy or unhealthy. You must look at the total amount of food you choose to eat over a period of time.

Healthy Eating Patterns

Healthy eating patterns mean following *Canada's Food Guide to Healthy Eating* and choosing foods from the four food groups that are healthy choices. Many nutrition experts recommend having several small meals a day. If you have adopted an eating pattern that is healthy, you will usually eat meals at the same time each day and include nutritious snacks in between.

Healthy eating also means eating for the purpose of satisfying your hunger. Since food is often a focal point at social gatherings such as birthday parties, weddings, and holiday celebrations, there are always opportunities to overeat. It is natural to enjoy sharing food or a meal with others. A person with a healthy eating pattern will listen to her or his hunger cues and eat only enough to feel satisfied.

Unhealthy Eating Patterns

"Eating disorders have emotional, behavioural, and physical components, and can be life threatening"
— National Eating Disorder Information Centre (2002a)

There is a wide range of unhealthy eating patterns. They vary from eating too much at once or over a period of time, to eating too little, to eating substances that are not considered foods. The effect that an unhealthy eating pattern has on a person's body depends on the extent to which the person engages in this type of eating and the rest of the person's lifestyle. For example, it's okay to overeat once in a while, such as on special occasions, but to overeat continually and not exercise can lead to obesity. Obesity may lead to health problems such as heart disease.

The reasons for unhealthy eating patterns vary. People may eat because they are bored, lonely, depressed, or experiencing stress.

For those who have poor eating habits, adopting healthy ones is possible. The key is to make small changes to your food choices and make one change at a time. To help you better understand your eating patterns so that you can make changes toward healthier eating, see the For Your Health feature opposite.

Recognizing Unhealthy Eating Patterns

Grazing can be one type of unhealthy eating pattern. This refers to constantly snacking on unhealthy foods that are readily available when you are hungry. The problem with grazing is that the food choices you make may be poor because you are tempted to choose convenience foods. These foods are often high in fat, salt, and sugar, and do not contain a lot

of other nutrients. These foods may also become a habit and you may begin to graze when you are not hungry.

Pica is a craving for non-food items, such as clay, dirt, paper, or glue. Pica is usually found in pregnant women, people with mental disorders, or people whose family or ethnic customs include eating certain non-food substances. People may also eat these materials because they are actually lacking in a nutrient that the substance provides. Pica is considered an unhealthy eating pattern because eating such substances may be poisonous and can harm the body. Certain types of therapy are used to correct this behaviour.

◆ **Constantly weighing oneself is a sign that a person may be obsessed with his or her weight. This obsession affects males as well as females.** How would being obsessed with one's weight potentially affect a person's eating habits?

FOR YOUR HEALTH

Understanding Your Eating Patterns

By Swati A. Piramal

Who?

- With whom do you eat your meals?
- What foods do your eating companions enjoy?
- How much do they eat?

The habits of others, including dietary choices, exert a great influence on your own eating habits.

What?

- What foods do you usually enjoy?
- What foods that you eat regularly can be replaced with enjoyable, healthier choices?

You will be more satisfied and more likely to stick with a healthy diet when you choose foods you like and include them in your diet, in moderation.

Where?

- Where do you eat? (In your dining room, bedroom, kitchen.)

Eating food in many places can leave you tempted at every turn, because so many places become associated with eating. Taking a close look at where you eat can help you understand why you eat even when you are not really hungry.

When?

- When do you eat your meals and snacks?
- Do you eat when watching TV?

People are creatures of habit, and over time we train ourselves to become hungry at certain times of day, when exposed to certain stimuli. Becoming aware of the time you tend to eat your meals and snacks can help you plan for nutritious food substitutes, as well as stay in control of your eating.

Why?

- Do you eat in reaction to strong moods or emotions?

Perhaps you reach for food when you are depressed, tired, angry, or bored. Begin thinking of the feelings that lead you to eat. Are you really hungry or is a strong emotion eating you? Once you identify the moods that are associated with overeating or having unhealthy foods, you can plan ahead to control them.

How?

- How fast do you eat?
- Do you often rush through meals?
- Do you study, do homework, or read while eating?

Eating quickly and when you are preoccupied influences your diet pattern, as you tend to overeat or make unhealthy food choices. Take time to make mealtimes relaxed. Try not to work while eating, and be conscious of what you eat.

Start looking at your eating patterns objectively. See what makes you tick. These questions will start you thinking in the right direction. Armed with new knowledge, you will be well equipped to make the small changes in your eating lifestyle that add up to a healthy way of eating and permanent weight management.

Source: Adapted from Piramal S. (n.d.).

Dieting includes a wide range of behaviours. For example, some diets may cut out all of one particular kind of food or food group, such as foods high in protein; others may include taking diet pills or supplements. People may go on and off diets all the time and never establish healthy eating habits. **Yo-yo dieting**, or weight cycling, refers to a pattern of rapid weight gain and loss.

Dieting can cause health problems because a person who does not eat enough food over a period of time may become deficient in vitamins and other nutrients that the body needs to stay healthy. Many people who are constant dieters can benefit from nutritional education to help them understand how to make informed food choices that contribute to well-being.

People usually diet because they are unhappy with their bodies, although they may actually be at a weight that is healthy for them. It is reported that one-third of women who diet already have healthy weights (National Institute of Nutrition, 2001). Furthermore, dieting is not usually successful in keeping weight off—it is estimated that 95 percent of people regain most or all of the weight they lose. Some people go on and off diets continually, but diets do not work for many people because their bodies want to stay at a certain weight. If a body feels like it is being starved, it will slow down how much energy it uses. During a diet, a person will feel hungry. This may make the person feel cranky, extremely tired, and even depressed.

Dieting can actually backfire because it can make a person more likely to binge. For example, some dieters exclude a certain food or food group from their diet. On a low-carbohydrate diet, you would be restricting all breads, cereals, muffins, cookies, and so on. If you absolutely love cookies and are used to having one or two a day and are now excluding them from your diet, you may crave cookies, become frustrated with cutting them out, and consume many in one sitting.

Restricting foods is one way that dieting sets people up for failure. Dieting becomes a problem when a person becomes obsessed with food and with losing weight and is lost in thought about food. The Canadian Health Network (as cited in Government of Saskatchewan 2000) reports that 80 to 90 percent of eating disorders begin when a person has been dieting.

Situations like the one previously described may make a person feel guilty for losing control. This person begins to feel like a failure. When people feel they have failed at something, such as a diet, it can worsen their self-esteem and make them feel unhappier about how they look. This is why diets don't work and are actually unhealthy for people's bodies and minds. A better approach is to adopt a healthy eating pattern and engage in lifelong fitness to maintain a healthy lifestyle.

Eating Disorders

The term **eating disorder** describes an extreme, unhealthy behaviour related to food, eating, and weight. People with anorexia and bulimia are very unhappy with the way their bodies look. They also have a fear of putting on weight and losing control. Food is not a cause of the disorder but a symptom. In fact, the causes of eating disorders are very complicated. Research con-

FYI

Trends in the Health of Canadian Youth

Canadian Students' Responses to "Are you on a diet to lose weight?"

	Male			Female		
	No, because my weight is fine	No, but I do need to lose weight	Yes	No, because my weight is fine	No, but I do need to lose weight	Yes
Grade 6	81%	13%	6%	72%	21%	7%
Grade 8	79%	16%	5%	60%	27%	14%
Grade 10	82%	14%	4%	55%	28%	18%

Source: Health Canada. (2002).

tinues in this area to determine factors that contribute to eating disorders so that they can be prevented or treated appropriately.

There are three common types of eating disorders: anorexia nervosa, bulimia nervosa, and binge eating.

FYI

Eating Disorders and Athletes

Eating disorders are a big problem for many athletes.

- Gymnastics, ballet, figure skating, swimming, and distance running put athletes, especially females, at risk. These sports stress the importance of appearance or a thin body.
- Athletes who participate in bodybuilding and wrestling are connected with a higher risk, especially for male athletes (Powers & Johnson, n.d.).

Who Has Eating Disorders?

Eating disorders affect people from all age groups cultures, and income levels. They generally occur among teens and young adults, especially females. However, these disorders are occurring increasingly in males, older adults, and children as young as age ten. There is also a higher rate of anorexia and bulimia in athletes and in careers such as modelling and dancing. It is reported that between 15 and 62 percent of female athletes have an eating disorder (NEDIC, 2002a).

Even though there are statistics for eating disorders, it is difficult to determine how many people actually have this disease. People who have an eating disorder may not get help because they are embarrassed, don't realize they have a problem, or deny that they have a problem. This may be especially true for boys and men, because eating

◆ Statistics show that people in certain careers seem to suffer more from eating disorders than others. Why do you think this is so?

FYI

Quick Stats on Eating Disorders

- More than 5 percent of young Canadian women are affected by anorexia and bulimia. The percentage for males in the general population is unavailable.

- The number of males with eating disorders is on the rise. For adolescents, 20 percent of eating disorders occur in boys, and for adults, 10 percent of eating disorders occur in men.

- It is estimated that 15 to 20 percent of Canadian women have many of the symptoms of an eating disorder.

- Five times more people have bulimia than anorexia.

- Twenty-five percent of eating disorders last longer than 15 years, while 70 percent of eating disorders last more than five years.

Source: Canadian Health Network as cited in "Saskatchewan Health Canadian Health Network," (2000).

disorders are seen as being a "female thing" and it is not "manly" to have such a problem. There may be shame in admitting to having an eating disorder, and many people simply stay silent and deal with it on their own or try to ignore the problem. This is very dangerous because eating disorders have serious, long-term effects on your body and can even result in death.

The Dangers of Eating Disorders

Reasons for Eating Disorders

There is no easy way to describe who is a person with an eating disorder or who may be in danger of developing an eating disorder. In addition, there are differences between people who develop anorexia and those who develop bulimia. There is a combination of factors that may help to show who has an increased risk of developing such a disorder. The factors range from being a certain type of person to the family a person comes from to the culture and time period a person lives in. These are examined below.

◆ **Type of person**. In general, the types of people who may develop an eating disorder have a hard time making decisions because they do not know what they want, need to have structure in their lives, do not deal well with frustration, believe they cannot get things they want for themselves because it must come from someone else, and have a strong need to please others.

◆ **Low self-esteem**. People who do not approve of how they look or who they are have low-self esteem. People who lack confidence in themselves may try to change the way they look to make themselves feel more worthy.

- **Wanting to be perfect.** People who strive for perfection and want everything done right feel ineffective when they fail. This type of person also wants things to be in order, with rules and a structure. These people think that if changes are made to their bodies, their lives will also change. This, in turn, will make them able to cope with life, feel more effective, and make key decisions.

- **Control.** People who develop an eating disorder feel that having control over their bodies and lives is very important. They may feel this way because they have been overpowered or controlled by other people in their lives. If these feelings of being powerless are not resolved, these people may use food and weight as a way to manage the feeling of being overpowered. People affected with an eating disorder may think that they can control what goes in their mouths, even if they can't control other parts of their lives. They also think that having a healthy eating pattern means being out of control. Their way of eating—bingeing on a food they usually don't eat, then purging, or not eating at all—means that they are in control.

- **Fear of growing up.** Eating disorders often develop during adolescence because of the many changes that occur during this time in young people's lives. Some individuals don't know how to deal with these changes because they don't have the support of those around them. They may also not like the changes that they are seeing in their bodies because of the weight they have gained. The ideal of being thin puts pressure on them to diet and, in turn, makes them more at risk of developing an eating disorder.

- **The family that a person comes from.** Certain ways that family members interact and communicate with each other may make a person more at risk of developing an eating disorder. These ways include physical, sexual, or emotional abuse; depression or alcoholism; an overprotective parent; a child having to take on parental responsibilities because the parent is not around; families that do not deal with problems in a healthy manner; families that hide their feelings; and families with very strict rules.

- **The world that we live in.** This factor includes many reasons, ranging from what is popular at a given time to changes in the way we live as a society. Some main issues show how our world may cause conflict in what people expect and what is realistic.

Source: NEDIC (2002a).

In today's world, people are exposed every day to messages in the media that imply they should look a certain way. In North American culture, the message is that being thin is good and that being fat is being lazy and out of control. Some people may be more sensitive to this message than others and therefore may be at more risk for developing an eating disorder.

People are tugged in many directions. We are pressured to be "superheroes." For example, we spend long hours in school or at work every day. We go home to do homework, cook, clean, or take care of children, and are still expected to look good by staying thin and being active. In reality, there are not always enough hours in a day to do all the things that we want and have to do. People also live in a world that isn't perfect. Divorce rates are high, and some of our role models have eating disorders or drug and alcohol addictions. Many of us will never look like the ideal male or female because it is genetically impossible. This creates confusion for anyone who is trying to maintain a balance in his or her life.

Some people may be torn between trying to become Canadian at the same time as trying to keep some of the customs of their culture of origin. This creates conflict about who they are, and this may be expressed in their thoughts and actions toward food and weight.

No one reason can be pinpointed as causing an eating disorder. A traumatic experience or an incident in an individual's life, coupled with other changes in life and some of the factors just described, may trigger the beginning of an eating disorder in that person. Biology may influence who is at risk of developing an eating disorder as well (NEDIC, 2002b). Studies also have shown that athletes in sports that emphasize looks and weight are more at risk of developing eating disorders. These sports include figure skating, dance, gymnastics, wrestling, and rowing, to name a few (Anorexia Nervosa and Related Eating Disorders, 2002). The competitive nature of sports and the pressure from parents, coaches, and one's own personality to always strive for the best may actually be the reason why these athletes run a higher risk of getting an eating disorder. Being aware of who is at risk helps professionals, friends, and family members prevent these people from developing such a condition.

◆ Anorexia most often begins in early adolescence. Can you think of a few reasons why?

INTERNET CONNECTS

www.mcgrawhill.ca/links/food
To learn more about causes, impact, and treatment for people with eating disorders, go to the web site above for *Food for Today, First Canadian Edition,* to see where to go next.

Anorexia Nervosa

Anorexia nervosa is a type of eating disorder that involves an irresistible urge to lose weight through self-starvation and a refusal to maintain a minimally normal body weight. It is often described as "dieting out of control." No matter how thin anorexics—people with anorexia—become, they feel fat and see themselves as bigger than they really are. They have an obsessive fear of gaining weight.

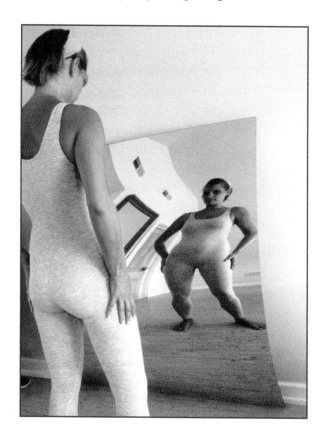

Symptoms and Effects

Anorexia is signalled by a large loss of weight. Weight loss alone does not mean that a person has developed anorexia, because there may be other reasons for the weight loss. However, significant weight loss in anyone should be cause enough for concern and to consult a family physician.

Anorexics will try to control their lives by controlling their weight and their eating patterns. Individuals with anorexia will do just about anything to lose as much weight as possible. They refuse to eat or eat very little. They feel hungry all the time. To transfer the feelings of hunger, they will often be very interested in food. For example, they may constantly look for recipes in cookbooks or want to prepare meals for other people but will not eat the meal themselves. The hunger they feel also makes them extremely tired. Despite feeling exhausted, some anorexics exercise strenuously every day for long periods of time.

It is difficult to understand how people with anorexia see themselves in the mirror. They are unhappy with their bodies and often criticize them. In essence, anorexics have a negative body image. They may see themselves as fat even when they are severely

Anorexia Nervosa

Signs and Symptoms	Effects on the Body
• A significant loss of weight, even though the person has not been ill.	• Lower heart rate and blood pressure.
• Eating noticeably less food, yet the person denies being hungry.	• Lower body temperature.
• Dieting, yet the person is not overweight.	• Menstrual periods become irregular or stop altogether.
• For females, missing menstrual periods.	• Body hair or "baby hair" grows on the face and back.
• Denying that being underweight is dangerous for a person's health.	• Hair loss on head.
• Saying that he or she "feels fat," even though the person is at or below normal weight. This is because an anorexic sees his or her body differently than it really is.	• Skin becomes dry and pasty-looking.
	• Swelling and puffiness around the ankles, fingers, and face.
	• Constipation.
• Developing strange eating habits, including always arranging food on a plate in a certain way, cutting food into tiny pieces, combining unusual foods, and preferring foods that have a certain texture or colour.	• Heart problems, osteoporosis, and brain damage may develop.
	• Children and teens may experience stunted growth.

Sources: Anorexia and Bulimia Association. (n.d.)

underweight. This is called **body distortion**. Some anorexics may be very happy with their bodies and be pleased with themselves for losing so much weight. Still, most anorexics deny having any problem and believe their behaviour is normal.

It is estimated that up to 20 percent of anorexics will die from the disease. Their deaths are often caused by heart problems, since the heart is a muscle and wears away from starvation or cannot function because of an imbalance in the body's electrolytes. There are some overlapping symptoms in people who have anorexia and those who have bulimia. In fact, many anorexics report that they also have symptoms of bulimia, such as purging. It is estimated that 30 to 50 percent of anorexics turn into bulimics (NEDIC, 2002a).

Binge Eating Disorder

Binge eating disorder involves eating huge quantities of food at one time, or **bingeing.** An eating binge usually lasts under two hours and often occurs when a person is emotionally upset or under severe stress. People may binge after being on a diet, to calm themselves, to distract themselves from something that is bothering them, or in response to feeling inadequate. Bingeing is sometimes referred to as compulsive overeating.

Symptoms and Effects

Individuals with binge eating disorder gain weight and develop the same health problems as overweight people. It is estimated that about one-fifth of people who are obese binge eat (NEDIC, 1997). These people are usually very distressed by their bingeing and

feel guilty and embarrassed about their behaviour. It is difficult to detect people who binge eat because it is usually done in private.

Binge eaters are unique because they don't always try to stay thin. Almost the same number of women as men are binge eaters. About 50 percent of binge eaters begin during adulthood (NEDIC, 2002a).

Bulimia Nervosa

Bulimia nervosa is an eating disorder that involves episodes of binge eating followed by **purging**—the use of self-induced vomiting, laxatives, or vigorous activities to prevent weight gain. Bulimics may also try to get rid of unwanted calories by fasting, going on a strict diet, or exercising to the extreme. Like people with anorexia, those with bulimia have a distorted sense of body shape and weight. Bulimics judge themselves according to how much they weigh and the shape of their bodies. Bulimia most often develops in later adolescence, when a person is moving into adulthood.

Symptoms and Effects

Bingeing usually begins when people do not allow themselves to have certain foods. A person may be very hungry from fasting or dieting, or may actually be starving. A person will then begin to binge on certain foods, usually those high in carbohydrates, and will consume a large amount in a short time. He or she will then feel guilty and ashamed for being so out of control. The individual also is afraid of gaining weight or feels uncomfortably full. A person will most often purge when "too much" food has been

◆ People with bulimia nervosa have frequent episodes of binge eating foods high in carbohydrates. What are five signs that indicate a person may be bulimic?

eaten that is considered "bad food." Purging may be a way of punishing herself or himself for being out of control.

People purge to relieve the guilt of binge-ing. But purging is dangerous to the body and is not a sure way to lose weight or to lose all the calories from a binge. Vomiting after a binge typically leaves behind about 1100 to 1200 calories that have been digested by the body. Vomiting also confuses the brain, making it difficult for it to tell the body when it is full or satisfied with the amount of food eaten. When people repeat-edly vomit, they cannot tell when they are full. They will then binge more often and be able to eat even more food at once. Laxatives are not very effective either. Only 12 percent of calories are purged from the body when laxatives are taken. Continual use of laxatives causes people to be constipated constantly and to have hemorrhoids and other digestive problems. Diuretics, or water pills, may cause

Bulimia Nervosa

Signs and Symptoms	Effects on the Body
• A preoccupation with food and eating. • Leaving the table immediately after eating (usually to go to the bathroom to vomit). • Variations in weight. • Physical changes, such as swollen glands under the jaw or unusual dental problems. • Often fasting (eating nothing or very little). • Overexercising and exercising excessively to lose weight, not just to stay fit. • Use of laxatives, diuretics (water pills), or diet pills. • Large amounts of food are missing, or money is stolen so the person can buy more food. • You may see the person binge eat or hear him or her talk about it.	• Very tired and low energy. • Headaches. • Dehydration. • Diarrhea. • Constipation. • Bloated and painful stomach. • Sore throat. • Teeth enamel becomes eroded. • Electrolytes (potassium, sodium, and chloride) become imbalanced. • Hands and feet swell (referred to as edema). • Liver and kidneys become damaged. • Bowels collapse. • Esophagus becomes torn. • Ulcers develop. • Heart attack and death are most probable.

Source: Adapted from NEDIC (2002a).

dehydration and damage to organs such as the kidneys. Those who purge by exercise are also putting themselves at risk. Overexercising and dieting put extra strain on the heart. Some bulimics die as a result of complications from their disorder.

Knowing when someone is suffering from bulimia can be challenging because bulimics are often successful at hiding their problem. Potential warning signs, symptoms, and effects of this eating disorder are described in the table above.

Helping Someone with an Eating Disorder

It is important to realize that people with an eating disorder have an illness. Most can't stop their self-destructive behaviours on their own. It's often up to others to recognize the problem and encourage the person to get help. This can be difficult, because many people with eating disorders become very defensive and deny that they have a problem. Individuals suffering from an eating disorder must realize that they have a problem, admit it, and take steps toward getting help.

One of the first steps in helping someone with an eating disorder is to do some background reading on the subject. You must first be able to recognize the signs of an eating disorder. This will help you determine whether or not you should approach the individual. A person who is recovering from an eating disorder will need support. You should be patient and understanding, because the path to recovery is long and painful. When helping an individual, keep the following points in mind:

♦ If the situation is an emergency, take the person to the nearest hospital or clinic. If she or he refuses to go, you may need to consult a family doctor or crisis line to direct you on what to do next.

♦ When approaching the person, do not verbally attack or blame him or her. Simply state that you are concerned about his or her health and would like to help.

♦ Realize that when you approach the person, she or he may deny what you say or get angry with you.

♦ If the person does not want to talk to you, accept this and let the person come to you when she or he is ready to discuss things.

♦ Realize that eating disorders are usually a response to other underlying problems and issues. Let the person know you care. He or she will appreciate your concern eventually.

♦ Be consistent and set limits. Make sure your limits are reasonable. For example, if the person with the eating disorder wants to skip a meal, tell the person that what to eat is up to her or him, but mealtime is family time and she or he must sit down and be part of the family conversation.

♦ Don't comment on how the person looks, even when it's a compliment.

♦ Focus on the person's abilities and skills, not on his or her appearance.

♦ Don't blame the person for the eating disorder. Realize it is the way the person copes with other problems and issues.

♦ Realize that you are not a professional therapist or counsellor and have limits as to what you can do.

Source: NEDIC (2002a).

Family members may want to look at their own attitudes about food and weight. Also be aware of what other family members are saying to the person with the eating disorder. Ensure that others are not acting in a way that feeds the disorder or makes the person feel worse. For example, a sibling may be teasing the person about her or his weight or appearance.

Eating disorders are difficult for family and friends to understand. At times, the disorder may become frustrating and scary for everyone. Outside support may help the family deal with a member who has an eating disorder.

Getting Help

A person with an eating disorder may be hospitalized in an eating-disorders clinic. How a person is treated is determined on an individual basis. Treatment usually includes physiological and psychological help.

Physiological help is help for the body. Medical and nutritional help regarding how to eat properly, achieve a healthy weight, and assess the physical condition of the person with the eating disorder are key. A dietitian who specializes in eating disorders, and a doctor, are both important professionals in this process.

FOR YOUR HEALTH

If You Have an Eating Disorder

If you think that you may have an eating disorder, it is important to get help from an experienced professional who specializes in these problems. You may feel uncomfortable admitting you have this disease. One way of seeking help is to go to someone you trust—a responsible friend, parent, family doctor, guidance counsellor, or teacher, and simply say, "I think I have an eating disorder and I want help." If you find it too difficult to say this, try writing a letter and delivering it to a trusted person in confidence. Once you have found help, there are other things that you can do that will help you recover:

- Break the rules that you have set for yourself about food. For example, if you eat only "diet" salad dressings and drinks, try introducing regular versions of these foods into your diet or eat small portions of the foods that you usually forbid, like cookies.

- Eat regular portions of food. Try going to a restaurant as a way of seeing what a normal portion is.

- Eat many small meals throughout the day. This will help you increase the amount of food that you can digest comfortably.

- Plan an activity after a meal. Get up from the table once you have eaten and go for a walk, call a friend, or give yourself a positive message, for example, "Eating this meal is part of getting better."

- Keep a journal. Write down your thoughts about eating and what foods you have eaten. Read your journal over to see if you need to eat more of a particular food.

- Join a support group.

- Be good to yourself. Focus on your abilities and positive characteristics. It is okay to slip up sometimes.

Source: Adapted from NEDIC, 2002a.

Psychological help is help for the mind. This includes counselling for the underlying problems that are at the root of the disorder. A counsellor may help an individual explore a traumatic event that happened in the past and discuss other attitudes and beliefs the person has toward his or her body and self.

◆ **Professional help is needed to recover from an eating disorder. Name some of the people and resources that an individual with an eating disorder can talk to or contact.**

◆ **Treatment for an eating disorder involves the help of a doctor, dietitian, and psychologist.** What contribution would each of these professionals make to help a person recover from an eating disorder?

People with eating disorders can recover, but the process is very slow. It usually takes at least one or two years of treatment for full recovery. The fact that such people are often resistant to treatment compounds the problem. As with any other illness, support from family and friends is an important part of the recovery process.

Treatment Options

Treatment may be a combination of individual therapy, group therapy, family therapy, and/or hospitalization. Individual therapy is used as a way of examining a person's behaviours and their consequences. This type of therapy offers strategies that help an individual deal with issues, changes, and worries in her or his life. Group therapy allows those with eating disorders to feel that they aren't alone in their struggle. Family therapy is a way of helping families work together as a team. Its goal is to help the family become healthy and happy by working on how each member acts and talks to other members.

Eating-disorder clinics are located in some hospitals. Patients may attend individual or group therapy sessions at the hospital, they may stay there during the day and go home in the evenings, or they may stay for an extended period of time. Support groups, although they are not therapy, are a good way for those with eating disorders and their family members to share their experiences.

Treatment involves using a team approach. The team may include health professionals, such as a physician to treat specific medical complications, a dietitian or nutritionist, psychologists, and social workers. Treatment ranges from nutritional education and changing eating habits to the use of drugs. Treatment approaches include, but are not limited to, the following:

◆ **Psycho-education** is often conducted in a group setting. People with eating disorders are given information about how an eating disorder starts. They look at the effects of an eating disorder, such as starvation and other complications that occur in the body. Nutrition and proper eating habits are also discussed. This type of approach helps shatter any myths about eating disorders. These myths are replaced with facts and knowledge. Although the sessions are short-term, this type of education helps some people stop bingeing and purging. It is also helpful for family members to attend so they learn what eating disorders are all about.

- **Cognitive-behavioural therapy** explores the patient's beliefs and attitudes. For example, people with eating disorders often think that being thin means being successful, happy, and loved by others. They often measure how worthy they are by how thin they are. They may also feel that adolescence is an extremely difficult time. This type of therapy looks at changing this unrealistic thinking. The therapist may suggest that the individual keep a food diary. This is used to record the food that he or she eats and the thoughts that he or she has about food. This diary is then used as a springboard for discussion about deep-rooted beliefs. This type of therapy can be used in a group or in an individual setting. It has been found to work quite well with those who suffer from bulimia and binge eating.

- **Psychodynamic therapy** examines traumatic experiences an individual may have experienced in the past. It looks at the types of relationships and conflict in a persons' life. This therapy also helps make a connection between past experiences and eating habits.

- **Drug therapy** may involve anti-depressant or anti-anxiety medication if a patient doesn't respond to other therapies. It may also be used in combination with other therapies (NEDIC, 2002a).

Substances for the Body

Many substances that claim to alter the way a body looks and functions are available to Canadians. Many people choose these substances either to alter the way they feel about their appearance or to enhance what their bodies can do. Two categories of substances that people use to change their looks or how they perform in athletics are supplements and hormones. Some of these substances are more harmful than others and have longer-lasting effects on the body. Most are costly and some are unnecessary because a healthy diet, a good exercise plan, and a realistic and positive body image are more likely to achieve a healthy body.

Supplements

There are many types of supplements on the market today that are meant to provide extra nutrients. In many cases, supplements are used in addition to the food a person eats. Some supplements are promoted as meal replacements or as a way of making up for skipped meals. Supplements may come in the form of pills, powders, liquids, bars, and ready-to-serve drinks or shakes.

INTERNET CONNECTS

www.mcgrawhill.ca/links/food
To learn more about getting help for an eating disorder, go to the web site above for *Food for Today, First Canadian Edition,* to see where to go next.

There are two important questions to explore before taking a supplement:

◆ **Should I be taking a daily supplement?** Taking a daily vitamin and mineral supplement is common among Canadians. Despite this, having a healthy eating pattern is more important than taking antioxidants, vitamins, and minerals in pill or powder form. Healthy foods have much more to offer than supplements alone. Besides, food tastes great! (Dietitians of Canada, 2003)

◆ **Is the supplement safe?** Many supplements that are on the market are not always necessary for the general population to consume. Many people can get all of the nutrients they need by eating a variety of nutritious foods. Of course, there are exceptions. Some people may be required to take a supplement, such as a vitamin or mineral pill, because their doctors advise them to. For example, a doctor may prescribe that a pregnant woman take a prena-

tal supplement throughout her pregnancy. This type of supplement is specifically designed for pregnant women because it contains a high amount of iron and other nutrients that may be required in addition to those the woman gets from her regular diet. There are also people who are prescribed high-calorie drinks because they need to gain weight lost due to an illness.

Certain people may add supplements to their diet to increase their athletic performance. Athletes may believe that supplements will help them sprint faster or enable them to do one more set of repetitions when lifting weights. The Canadian Centre for Ethics in Sports (CCES) (2002) states that research conducted on many supplements has not clearly demonstrated that taking any supplement will result in improved performance for an athlete. For many people, including athletes, a well-balanced diet can provide all of the nutrients that a person needs.

FYI

Government Regulations for Natural Health Products

As of January 1, 2004, new regulations about natural health products that have been established by Health Canada will come into effect. It will take from two to six years to fully implement these regulations. Natural health products that will fall under these regulations include herbal remedies, homeopathic medicines, vitamins, minerals, traditional medicines, probiotics, amino acids, and essential fatty acids (such as Omega-3). These products are sold without a prescription and may be purchased over the counter in stores.

Consumers will be able to identify a product as a "natural health product" because the label will have a licence number followed by the letters NPN. In the case of a homeopathic medicine, it will read DIN-HM.

The standardized labels will enable consumers to make informed decisions about the natural health products that they are considering purchasing. Among other things, the labels will contain the following information:

- Directions on how to use the product and how much to use.

- Recommendations on the purpose or use of the product.

- Medicinal and non-medicinal ingredients.

- Any known adverse reactions, any cautions, and any warnings of unsafe conditions for use associated with the product.

- Special storage information.

Health claims on these products will also be regulated. In order to make a health claim, there will have to be research evidence to support the claim.

Source: Health Canada, 2003a and b.

Many supplements sold in Canada have not been strictly regulated in the past. New regulations effective January 2004 will change this but will take a few years to implement. Until these new regulations are in effect, product labels may not always be accurate because they might not list all the ingredients. In addition, the ingredients may vary from batch to batch. The CCES does not support the use of dietary supplements for athletes. They may contain ingredients that are banned or restricted by various sports-governing bodies, and taking them may result in a positive drug test for an athlete. Ultimately, the decision is up to the individual.

Some supplements are promoted as "miracle products." As of January 2004, Health Canada's regulations for natural health products will help protect consumers against those who make false or misleading claims. Consumers often want the easy way out and will buy a "quick fix." They need to know how to determine which claims are true and which are misleading or fraudulent. Some companies may make false claims and prescribe unsafe substances or methods to treat a person's health. For example, some may recommend very high amounts of vitamins. However, some vitamins are toxic when taken in high doses and can have serious side

INTERNET CONNECTS

www.mcgrawhill.ca/links/food
To learn more about Natural Health Product Regulations, go to the web site above for *Food for Today, First Canadian Edition,* to see where to go next.

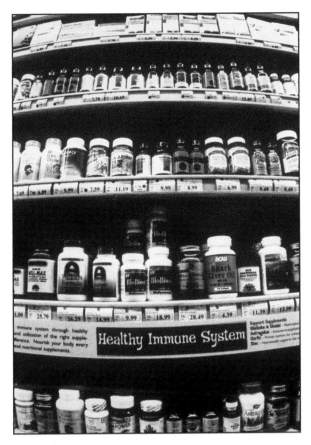

◆ **There are many different types of supplements sold in Canada. Taking a supplement may not be necessary. Certain supplements may actually be harmful to some people.** Where can you get reliable information about various supplements and products?

effects. These false claims and potentially harmful approaches are referred to as **health fraud** (Larson Duyff, 2000).

Weigh the pros and cons of taking supplements before using them. Consider what your goals are and how the substance can help you achieve these goals. For example, if a goal is to gain weight, how will the product help do this? Will consuming regular food be just as beneficial as using the product? Read the label carefully as well. Before using a supplement, ask for medical advice from a doctor or from a registered dietitian. It can be dangerous to use one of these products either to treat yourself for an ailment or to use a

supplement for other reasons without seeing a medical professional (Larson Duyff, 2000). Look at what the research says about any product before using it.

When you hear about a nutrition study in the news, often the report gives only a short summary of the results. This may oversimplify the results of the study. Nutrition information can be very confusing because the results of some studies may conflict with those of other studies. To decipher what is sound advice on nutrition, use your critical thinking skills. Some of the things you should ask are:

◆ Who conducted the research? What qualifications does the researcher have? Is she or he affiliated with a professional organization?

◆ Who paid for the study? Has this influenced the conclusions and recommendations?

◆ What was the study's design? Have the methods used been evaluated by other scientists?

◆ Have other studies come to the same conclusions? Has the study been repeated by others?

◆ What group of people was the study done on? Does this study apply to you? For instance, if the research was conducted on adults, the advice might not apply to children and adolescents.

Source: Larson Duyff, (2000).

How a product is advertised also may alert a consumer to false health claims. Although this will be stopped when the new regulations in Canada are enforced, ask the following questions in the meantime:

◆ Are the claims that the product makes actually true, or is it a sales gimmick?

◆ Does the claim sound too good to be true?

◆ If a product sounds too good to be true, it usually is.

◆ Does the advice mock what qualified nutrition experts say? If it does, the advice is probably unreliable. Nutrition experts may disagree, but they still have a high opinion of another scientist's work.

◆ Does the product use strategies such as testimonials or play on your emotions to sell itself? People who aren't experts may use these tactics as a way to influence others (Larson Duyff, 2000).

◆ What are the health risks versus the health benefits of using this substance? Look at the side effects. Some substances may pose significant health risks to certain people, especially if taken in large doses, or they may actually interfere with the consumers' lifestyle. For example, caffeine pills may have side effects such as diarrhea and nausea that may interrupt a person's daily routines. Other supplements have even caused death.

◆ Consider the cost of the product. Dietary supplements are often more expensive than their benefits warrant. (CCES, June 2002).

✚ Safety Check

It is a common belief that "natural" herbal products are safe and that the more you use, the better they are for you. This belief causes some people to take far more than recommended on the label. Some herbal products have ingredients like the herb ephedra that may be harmful to some individuals when taken in large amounts.

Ephedra has been sold as a way of losing weight, increasing energy, and helping people get results in bodybuilding. Health Canada has recalled certain products that contained ephedra or ephedrine because they posed serious health risks. Ephedra is contained in some products, such as nasal decongestants, as long as it meets approved requirements. Check with your pharmacist for more information.

Creatine

Creatine is a very popular supplement in today's market. Because of its popularity, there are many myths about it.

Creatine is an amino acid made naturally in the body from other amino acids. It can also be found in raw meat and fish, yet much of the creatine is destroyed during cooking. A person can get large amounts of creatine in his or her diet through supplements that are often sold as creatine monohydrate.

Although the results of studies are inconsistent and not all studies show improvement in these areas, creatine builds muscle and increases a person's performance in sports. Some studies have shown that increasing creatine in the diet may result in small changes in a person's performance under very specific exercise conditions. It is important to note that creatine will not build muscle beyond a person's natural limits for his or her body.

The effective use of creatine depends on how much of it people have stored in their bodies before taking the supplement, their regular diet, the sport they are involved in, the type of training program they are involved in, and their own bodies.

The side effects for adults using creatine include rapid weight gain—believed by scientists to be caused by fluid and not lean muscle tissue—and possibly diarrhea, stomach cramping, and muscle cramping.

Little research has been done on the effects on the body from long-term use of creatine supplements. Also, studies have been conducted only on adults who take creatine; the safety of creatine use by young people is unknown.

Anabolic Steroids

Many people are familiar with a type of hormone called anabolic steroids, often referred to as "steroids," "roids," or "juice." **Anabolic steroids** are fabricated versions of hormones that are found naturally in the body. To make them, the masculine effects of male hormones and the growth stimulation effects of female hormones are combined to produce imitation hormones. When a person uses anabolic steroids combined with physical activity, the result is the quick building of muscles. A person's muscle size and strength develops well beyond what could be achieved with training alone. However, the risk to a person's health is considered far greater than the gains (Sienkiewicz Sizer & Noss Whitney, 2003).

FYI

Steroid Use among Young Canadians

A survey reported that about 83 000 young Canadians between the ages of 11 and 18 admitted to using steroids at least once. Most of the users were male. The users reported that they took steroids to boost their performance in sports and/or to change the look of their bodies (Health Canada, 2002).

Source: Health Canada 2002.

Anabolic steroids are illegal in Canada if they are not used for medical reasons, under the authorization of a doctor. It is also illegal for a doctor to prescribe steroids for reasons other than a medical condition or illness. People may get steroids that are stolen and sold on the "black market." This makes steroids very dangerous because the ingredients are unknown and the substances may be unclean and unsafe. Steroids that are injected with a needle are also a health risk if people share needles. They may contract HIV, the virus that can lead to AIDS or other life-threatening illnesses, such as hepatitis C. The side effects and long-term consequences of using anabolic steroids make them very dangerous. Serious health risks include high blood pressure and liver disease. A more detailed list of the side effects of anabolic steroids appears in the table on page 388.

INTERNET CONNECTS

www.mcgrawhill.ca/links/food
To learn more about drug use and sports, go to the web site above for *Food for Today, First Canadian Edition*, to see where to go next.

Possible Physical Effects of Anabolic Steroids

In Males	In Females	In Adolescents
• Acne.	• Masculinization.	• Severe acne on the face and body.
• Shrunken testicles.*	• Abnormal menstrual cycles.	• Premature closure of the growth plates of the bones, leading to stunted growth.
• Decreased sperm production, which can lead to impotence.*	• Deepening of the voice.*	
• Enlarged prostate gland.	• Acne.	
• Breast enlargement.	• Excessive hair growth on the face and body.*	
• Premature baldness.	• Enlarged clitoris.*	
• Potential for kidney and liver dysfunction.	• Increased aggressiveness, mood swings.	
• Increased aggressiveness, mood swings.		

* These effects may be permanent with prolonged use.

Source: CCES. (2001).

Positive Body Image

Most young people who use steroids are male (Health Canada, 2002); however, the following points are applicable to females as well.

◆ **Set realistic and healthy goals.** When you participate in a sport or activity that gives you pleasure, it makes you feel good about your accomplishments. Sports and activities are a healthy way of spending time. They allow you to make friends, learn teamwork skills, and have fun. One activity that has become very popular is working out by using weight-lifting equipment. It may take awhile before you see the results you may want, but if you set goals and achieve them, you will feel very satisfied with the results. Weight lifting also helps you feel better and achieve a greater sense of accomplishment if you work hard naturally, without relying on steroids.

◆ **Feel good about yourself and help others feel good about themselves.** When you feel good about something that you have accomplished or when you have made a good decision, take credit for your efforts. Do the same for your peers, too. This will help to reinforce that you or a peer is good naturally and do not need to abuse substances. Compliment others on all areas of their personality, not just their looks. For example, compliment a person on his or her sense of humour, intelligence, skills, abilities, and talents.

Substance Restrictions in Sports

Canadian athletes who are affiliated with any national sporting organization are subjected to drug testing to determine whether they are using any banned or restricted substances to enhance their performance. When an athlete uses a substance or method that is banned, the practice is referred to as **doping.** Some of the banned substances for Canadian athletes include anabolic steroids and narcotics, such as painkillers. Restricted substances include caffeine and alcohol. The aim is to eliminate drugs in sports. Athletes are encouraged to rely on their own physical and mental abilities without the use of any such substances.

The Canadian Centre for Ethics in Sport oversees the testing of these athletes for banned substances. The primary list of banned substances is set out by the International Olympic Committee (IOC), although this is in the process of changing. An athlete who tests positive for one of these substances is subject to serious consequences. For example, an athlete who is caught doping for the first time is not allowed to compete in sports for four years and loses federal government funding permanently.

Why Substances Are Prohibited in Sports

When athletes compete, whether it's in an individual sport such as running or in a team sport such as soccer, the underlying principle is that everyone starts out even. For example, no runners are allowed to have a head start, nor do any teams begin a game with one team having a score of one while the other team starts out with zero. It is presumed that the winning person or team performed better without any unfair advantage. However, once someone cheats, the basic principle of competing on a level playing field has been taken away.

Using a performance-enhancing drug, such as anabolic steroids, gives an athlete an unfair advantage over other athletes who do not use these drugs. This is cheating. This is why many substances, such as anabolic steroids, are banned from use by athletes. Doping is also banned to protect athletes from using substances that may be harmful to their health, have the possibility of hurting others, and may be illegal.

"There are many other victims of drug abuse in sport but none is a greater victim than the athlete and coach who have competed drug free—who played the game by its rules."

—Robert Armstrong (Canada 1990, p. 448)

◆ Canadian athletes who are affiliated with a national sporting organization may be tested to see if they have used any banned substances. What advantage may athletes who use performance-enhancing drugs have over other athletes?

Chapter 18   Review and Activities

Summary

- An eating pattern includes where, when, how, what, and why you choose to eat the foods you do. It can be healthy or unhealthy.

- Unhealthy eating patterns include grazing, pica, and dieting.

- Eating disorders are extreme, unhealthy behaviours related to food, eating, and weight. People of all ages, cultures, and income levels can be affected; however, people in certain careers are especially at risk.

- Eating disorders often occur in people who believe they have little control over themselves or their lives, have low self-esteem, and want to be perfect. They want to be able to control what they eat, since they aren't able to control other areas of their lives. Physical changes during adolescence, negative family interactions, and the pressure of obtaining the ideal body image in today's society are also contributing factors.

- The main eating disorders are anorexia nervosa, or self-starvation; binge eating disorder, or eating huge quantities of food in a short time; and bulimia nervosa, or binge eating, then purging the body of the food through self-induced vomiting, using laxatives or diuretics, or overexercising. All of these behaviours create guilt and shame in people suffering from the disease, so the disease is often hidden and denied.

- To help someone with an eating disorder, read up on the disease, realize the behaviour stems from underlying problems, offer your support, and focus on the person's positive aspects.

- People with eating disorders need to realize they need help themselves. Physiological and psychological help are necessary, usually at an eating-disorders clinic in a hospital. Various therapies are available for the patient and the family.

- Many substances are available to Canadians to alter the way their bodies can look and/or function. These come in the form of supplements. Users should seek a doctor's advice to see if a supplement is necessary or harmful.

- Some natural herbal products, such as ephedra and creatine, are sold as ways to lose weight, increase energy, or get better results in bodybuilding. These can be dangerous if taken in excess and have not been proven effective.

- Fabricated hormones, or anabolic steroids, are taken by some athletes to increase their muscle strength beyond what they could naturally achieve by exercise and bodybuilding. Steroids are illegal in Canada except for medicinal purposes. Steroids have many health risks and serious negative side effects.

- To prevent substance abuse among their age group, adolescents need to learn to set realistic and healthy goals and acknowledge their own and others' accomplishments.

- Performance-enhancing steroids are banned among Canadian athletes in national sporting organizations so that all athletes have an equal opportunity to win.

Knowledge and Understanding

1. Make a list of unhealthy eating patterns.

2. Describe the difference between unhealthy eating patterns and healthy eating patterns.

3. Discuss several reasons dieting is not usually a successful way to lose weight.

4. Make a chart in your notebook titled "Types of Eating Disorders." Label the columns with the following headings:

- Definition
- Signs
- Physical Effects

Complete the chart with information you have learned in this chapter.

5. Briefly describe in your notes the treatment options available for someone who is suffering from an eating disorder.

6. What are two negative side effects that can arise from the use of anabolic steroids?

Thinking and Inquiry

7. The For Your Health feature "Understanding Your Eating Patterns" (page 369) looks at the who, what, where, when, why, and how of eating. Read the questions that are asked in this feature and analyse your own eating patterns. Write a journal entry that discusses the analysis of your eating patterns. What did you discover?

8. Your friend Amy is thinking about using a supplement because she often skips lunch. Where can Amy get advice on using a supplement? What questions should she ask?

9. How could you persuade a teammate to avoid using anabolic steroids? Discuss your answer with the class.

10. In recent years, a number of celebrities have admitted to struggling with eating disorders. Do you think such publicity has a positive or negative effect? Explain your answer.

Communication

11. Analyse the nutritional information on a package of protein powder. Compare the amount of protein in one serving with the amount of protein in a 100 g (3 oz) serving of steak. Compare the other nutrients, including the calories in each of the two items. Discuss your analysis with the class.

12. Choose a "natural" herbal product that is sold in Canada. Find at least two pieces of research that have been done on this product. Is the research reliable? What were the results of the research? How do the results compare to the advertising claims about the product? Weigh the pros and cons of using this product. Write a one-page report of your findings.

13. Find a song about eating disorders. Analyse the lyrics. Write a short report that discusses the message that the songwriter is trying to send to his or her audience.

Application

14. Imagine that you have a sibling with an eating disorder. Write a journal entry describing the signs that led you to suspect there was a problem. Explain how you plan to support your sibling.

15. Write a one-page newspaper article that discusses the following information about eating disorders:

- The prevalence of eating disorders in the Canadian adolescent population.
- The signs of someone with an eating disorder.
- Where people can go to get help if they suspect that they have an eating disorder.
- Treatment options available for people with eating disorders.

CHAPTER

19

Achieving a Healthy Body Weight

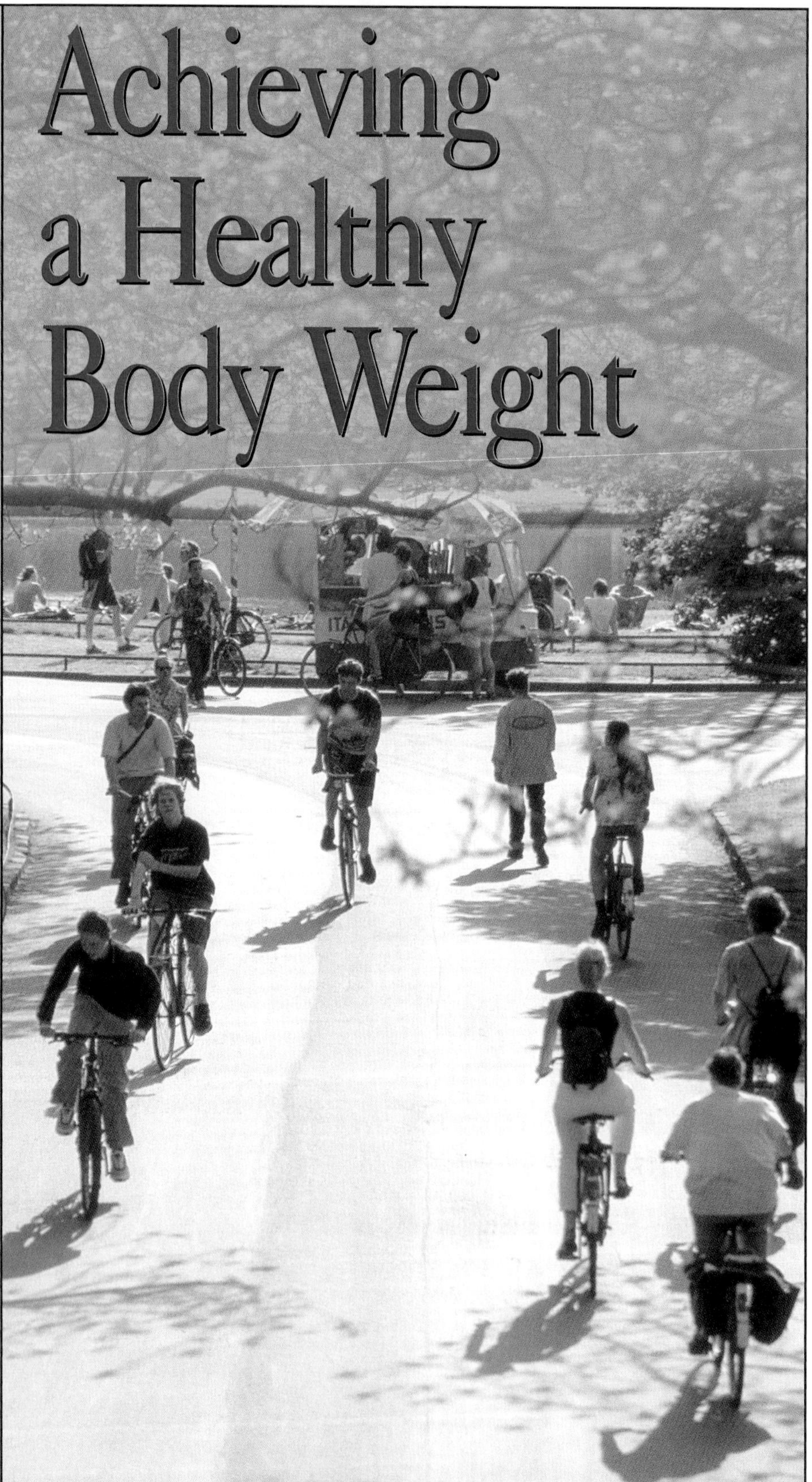

CHAPTER EXPECTATION

While reading this chapter, you will:

- Analyse weight-control programs to determine the characteristics of those most likely to help people reach and/or maintain a healthy body weight.

People have different body shapes and sizes. Accepting your own body and enjoying healthy food and physical activities are the key to well-being.

KEY TERMS

behaviour modification
body-fat percentage
Body Mass Index (BMI)
body-weight classification
system
fad diets
growth charts
over-the-counter drugs
set-point theory
skinfold calipers
skinfold measure
waist circumference
waist-hip ratio (WHR)

Many people have in their minds an ideal body weight. Some work very hard at achieving it through dieting. This is often very unhealthy and hard on their bodies. Other people seem to arrive at a weight that is right for them without much effort. What is most important is to maintain a weight that is healthy for you. This chapter looks at what a healthy weight means, how to achieve it, and how to maintain this weight. Strategies examined include accepting your body type, making informed and healthy food choices, and engaging in regular physical activity.

Participating in activities you enjoy is one way to maintain a healthy body weight.

Maintaining a Healthy Weight

Accepting Your Body

The human body comes in many different shapes and sizes. These differences have nothing to do with being too fat or too thin. Body shape is one of many traits passed down through heredity. Some people have wide shoulders or hips. Others are tall and thin; still others, short and stocky.

In spite of this, many people carry around in their minds an image of an ideal body—and they try desperately to reach that ideal. Usually, it's a losing battle. The tall, slender model you might see on TV inherited her shape, just as you did yours. You can change the amount of fat or muscle you have, but you can't change your body frame.

What Is a Healthy Weight?

Successful weight management starts with accepting the body you were born with. Then you can take steps to achieve a healthy weight within your body limits. You may never look like a model or famous athlete. Few people ever will. However, it's far more important to be fit and healthy, whatever your shape and size.

What is a healthy weight? It is one that will help you stay healthy throughout your life, within the framework of your own inherited shape, and minimizes your risk of lifestyle diseases.

It is also important to remember that body weight is affected by many factors. These factors include your age, height, body type, amount of food eaten, activity level, and genetics (Middlesex-London Health Unit, 2000). **Set-point theory** suggests that a body is apt to maintain a particular weight because of its own inner controls. Researchers have confirmed that after a person gains or loses weight, the body attempts to go back to its

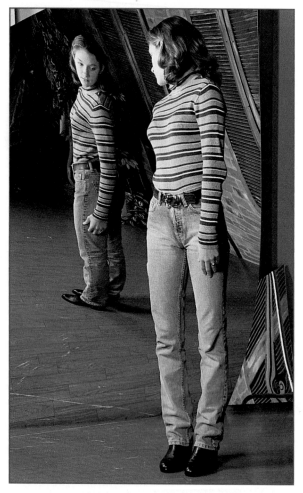

◆ Having a realistic perception of your appearance is a first step toward achieving and maintaining a healthy weight.

previous weight (Noss Whitney, Balog Cataldo, and Rady Rolfes, 2002).

Health professionals use a variety of methods to evaluate whether a person is at a healthy weight or above or below weight for his or her height. Common methods involve determining Body Mass Index (see opposite), waist circumference, waist-hip ratio, and body-fat percentage. The charts and ranges used for determining weight by these methods are most often used for adult men and women. Because children and adolescents are still growing, qualified medical professionals, such as physicians or nurses, monitor the changes in their bodies according to their age and sex and by referring to growth charts. Other criteria, such as food intake and health history, may come into play in assessing whether or not children are at a healthy weight.

Body-Weight Classification

In Canada, the **body-weight classification system** uses two methods to assess the risk that adults have for developing health problems if they are overweight or underweight. Qualified medical professionals also use the **Body Mass Index (BMI)** and **waist circumference.** This system is not suitable for people under the age of 18 or who are pregnant or breast-feeding.

Body Mass Index

Body Mass Index uses a ratio of weight to height. You can determine your BMI by using the Body Mass Index Nomogram graph (opposite) or by doing the following:

1. Record your weight in kilograms.

Body Mass Index Nomogram

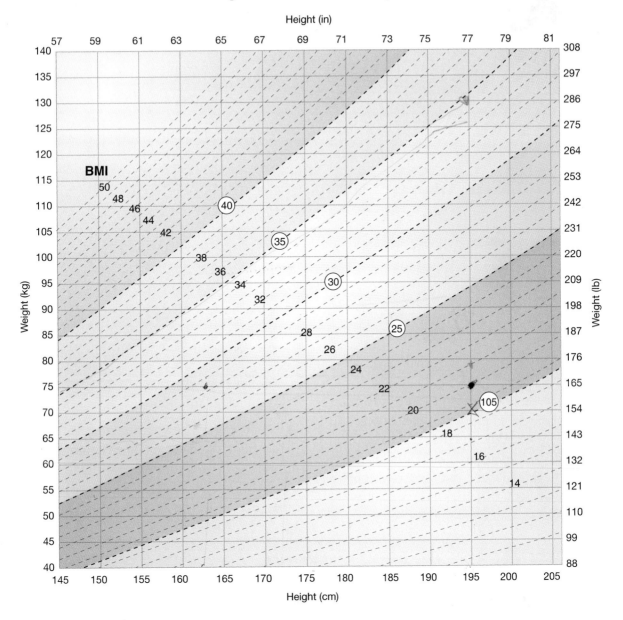

2. Measure your height in metres.

3. Divide your weight by your height squared (your height times itself). Use this calculation:

$$\text{BMI} = \frac{\text{weight in kilograms}}{\text{height in metres}^2}$$

By locating your BMI in the chart on page 396, you can determine if you are at risk for health problems related to your weight.

To estimate BMI, locate the point on the chart above where height and weight intersect. Read the number on the dashed line closest to this point. For example, if you weigh 69 kg and are 173 cm tall, you have a BMI of approximately 23, which is in Normal Weight range.

Having a normal weight on the BMI scale means you have the fewest weight-related

Health Risks Classification According to Body Mass Index

Classification	BMI Category (kg/m²)	Risk of Developing Health Problems
Underweight	< 18.5	Increased
Normal Weight	18.5 – 24.9	Least
Overweight	25.0 – 29.9	Increased
Obese Class I	30.0 – 34.9	High
Obese Class II	35.0 – 39.9	Very high
Obese Class III	> – 40.0	Extremely high

Note: For persons 65 and older the "normal" range may begin slightly above BMI 18.5 and extend into the overweight range.

Source: Health Canada. (2003).

health risks. Health problems that are associated with being underweight include infertility, osteoporosis, and a lack of nutrients. Being underweight could be the first sign that a person has an underlying disease. Being overweight is associated with health problems such as cardiovascular disease, some types of cancer, and type 2 diabetes.

Waist Circumference

Measuring waist circumference may also provide some information about who is at risk for health problems. To find your waist circumference, do the following:

1. Stand with your feet about 25 to 30 cm (10 to 12 inches) apart.

2. Have someone measure your waist—the area midway between your lower rib and the top of your pelvic bone. The measurer should stand beside you and place the measuring tape snugly around your waist.

Do not make the tape so tight that it compresses the skin.

Waist circumference measurement is based on a person's gender. A waist circumference of more than 102 cm (40 in) for males or 88 cm (35 in) for females is associated with increased health risks (Health Canada, 2003).

Limitations with the Body-Weight Classification System

Although it is more accurate than your weight alone, BMI and waist circumference are not foolproof indications of health or fitness. They don't take into account different body builds and body compositions, or the amount of fat versus lean tissue or muscle mass. For example, a bodybuilder may have a BMI of 30 or higher. Athletes and other individuals with large muscle masses are not necessarily at risk, even if they have high BMIs. Using BMI and waist circumference may not be suitable for the following groups of people:

◆ Young adults who have not stopped growing.

◆ Adults who are naturally very lean.

◆ Adults who have a muscular body build.

◆ Adults over 65 years of age.

◆ People of particular racial or ethnic groups. The BMI was devised using mostly Caucasian and European people. Therefore, African-Canadian people may not have the same health risks as Caucasian people at the same BMI.

These methods of weight measurement are definitely inappropriate for young people under the age of 18 and women who are pregnant or breast-feeding.

Looking at a person's Body Mass Index and/or waist circumference is only a snapshot in time. It doesn't take into consideration any weight loss or gain that a person has experienced. When assessing whether a person is at a healthy weight, medical professionals will also look at other factors, such as a person's level of activity and fitness, eating habits, any history of smoking, age, and family history. They may also look at the amount of body fat by using other measurements.

INTERNET CONNECTS

www.mcgrawhill.ca/links/food
To learn more about the body-weight classification system and weight-related health risks, go to the web site above for *Food for Today, First Canadian Edition,* to see where to go next.

Waist-Hip Ratio

You probably know the saying "You can't compare apples and oranges." A variation on this saying applies to body types. In this case, the comparison is of apples and pears. Some health professionals divide all individuals into one of two groups depending on their **waist-hip ratio** (WHR), a measure of how fat is distributed in the body.

Adults with pear-like shapes carry most of their fat on the thighs and hips. Those with apple-like shapes carry most of it over the abdomen. Research shows that "apples" may have a greater risk of health problems than "pears." Apples, however, seem to be able to lose excess weight more easily than pears.

Adults can check body shape very easily: Stand relaxed and measure the waist without pulling in the stomach. Then measure the hips where they are largest. Dividing the waist measurement by the hip measurement gives the waist-hip ratio.

Adult women should have a ratio no higher than 0.80; adult men should have a ratio no higher than 1.0. Ratios above these limits may increase the risk of health problems, even if the BMI shows that weight is at a healthy level.

Body-Fat Percentage

Some health and/or fitness professionals check the amount of body fat a person has in relation to muscle. Athletes may be concerned about their body fat and may have their **body-fat percentage** measurement taken by a qualified fitness and sports professional. In many instances, this gives a truer picture of healthy weight than BMI or just a number on a scale. Measuring body-fat percentage may show when extra weight is from muscle, not

FYI

Which Body Shape Are You?

◆ Pear-shaped people store fat on their thighs and hips. This fat does not necessarily pose a risk to their health. When pears lose weight, they do so in their upper body. This does not make their overall shape change very much.

◆ Apple-shaped people store body fat around their chest and stomach and also around internal organs, like the heart. They are more at risk for heart disease, diabetes, high blood pressure, and gall bladder disease. Diseases advance more quickly and become more severe in apple-shaped people, even when they are the same weight as pear-shaped people. When an apple-shaped person loses weight, it causes a reduction in upper-body fat. This makes them look different and decreases their risk of disease.

Source: Health Canada. (2002).

fat. There are various ways to measure body-fat percentage. One of the most common, inexpensive, and quick ways is the **skinfold measure**. This method assesses body-fat percentage by using **skinfold calipers**, a device that pinches the skin to measure body fat on various areas of the body. The measurements are then put into an equation. This method requires training, and a qualified professional should conduct the procedure.

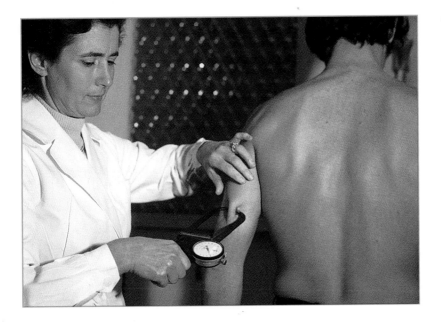

◆ Skinfold measurements are a quick and fairly inexpensive way of assessing a person's body-fat percentage. Do some research in your community and on the Internet to find other ways that body-fat percentage can be determined. What are the pros and cons of each method?

There are disadvantages to this method that may result in inaccuracies in the measurement of body fat. For example, the amount of tissue that can be pinched with the skin calipers may vary from person to person and results may not be consistent if a different person conducts the procedure.

Growth Charts

Growth charts are also used by medical professionals to assess healthy body weight. These are often the tools used by physicians when looking at healthy weights for children and adolescents. Growth charts show height and weight in relation to the age and sex of the individual. There are also growth charts that show Body Mass Index for children and adolescents. The height, weight, and/or Body Mass Index of young people are usually tracked by their physicians or by nurses throughout most of their childhood. Growth charts plot an individual's height and weight, beginning at birth. Plotting a person's growth on a chart shows how the individual is growing over time. These charts also indicate where an individ-

ual fits in relation to other children of the same age and sex. For example, Nathan's growth chart shows that he is growing within a normal range compared to other children.

◆ Physicians use growth charts to measure the height and weight of children and adolescents. Why would other weight measurement methods be unreliable?

If a change in his growth indicated that his weight and measurements suddenly fell well below or above the normal range for his age, the doctor may investigate further to find the cause of the difference.

The Healthy Weight for You

As you can see, there's more to evaluating a person's weight than meets the eye. If you're wondering about your weight, don't compare yourself to your friends or to a picture in a magazine. Instead, talk to a qualified health professional. He or she can use reliable methods to judge whether your weight is healthy for you.

While You Are Still Growing

Jonah was above weight for his age during different times throughout his childhood. However, when Jonah reached puberty, he grew much taller. Even though he gained weight over the next few years, by the time he was 18 he was of average weight and appeared quite lean.

Situations like Jonah's are common for children. Some children may be thin throughout childhood, yet gain a large amount of weight when they reach puberty. This is especially true for girls.

Growth will change the appearance of childrens' bodies. It is important to accept that young people come in many shapes and sizes. Dieting, or limiting your food intake, is not recommended while you are still growing. To diet during this time may have serious consequences because you may not get enough nutrients to help you grow and develop in a normal way. It is better to adopt a healthy lifestyle.

 **Safety Check**

No one weight measurement method is used to determine if a person is at a healthy weight. If you or someone you know are concerned about your health and/or weight, get advice from a qualified medical professional.

Weight Management

Being above Weight for Your Height

People who are above weight for their height may be at risk for developing health problems, including heart disease, diabetes, cancer, and high blood pressure. For some people, losing weight is a positive step toward better health. Even if you have finished growing, it is important to discuss any weight loss or weight-loss method with a qualified medical professional. He or she will assess your health and how your weight is affecting your health.

Evaluating Weight-Management Methods

With so much attention focussed on health and appearance, weight-loss methods are a big business. Everywhere you turn, you can find books, articles, and advertisements that claim to provide the answers to weight loss.

Some popular types of weight-management methods include:

- **Weight-management diets.** Eating plans that reduce calorie intake for weight loss.

- **Weight-management centres.** Organizations that provide both an eating plan and psychological support.

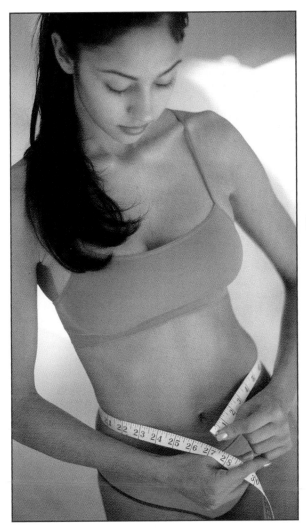

◆ Being above or below weight for your height may put you at risk for developing other health problems. The key to maintaining a healthy weight is to have a healthy lifestyle. What are some professional resources in your community that can assist you in adopting a healthy lifestyle?

◆ **Weight-management products.** Pills, shakes, prepared meals, and more, all sold with the promise of helping people lose weight.

Some of the weight-management methods that are promoted are based on sound nutrition principles. A counselling session with a qualified dietitian who provides you with an individualized eating plan is an example of a sound weight-management method. Consult your family physician or local public health unit to locate a registered dietitian in your area. These people can give you sound advice on achieving a healthy weight and can recommend strategies for a healthy lifestyle. Many methods, however, are not based on sound nutrition. Some methods can even be dangerous to your health.

⊕ Safety Check

Many Internet sites provide nutritional advice. Beware of those that offer "junk science." They may be a source of misinformation about nutrition. To get sound nutrition advice on the Internet, search for a professional organization such as your local public health unit, a registered dietitian organization (e.g., Dietitians of Canada), or Health Canada.

Fad Diets and Other Dangers

Every now and then, a scheme comes along that promises quick and/or easy weight loss. The best-known of these schemes become **fad diets**—popular weight-loss methods that ignore sound nutrition principles. Fad diets vary considerably but have one trait in common: They are risky.

Here are some other fad approaches to watch out for:

◆ **Very low-calorie diets (800 calories or less per day).** These may not provide enough energy or enough of the nutrients needed for good health.

◆ **Eating plans based on a single food, such as grapefruit or cabbage soup.** As you know, your body needs a variety of foods every day. These types of plans make it difficult to choose a variety of foods from the four food groups in *Canada's Food Guide to Healthy Eating.*

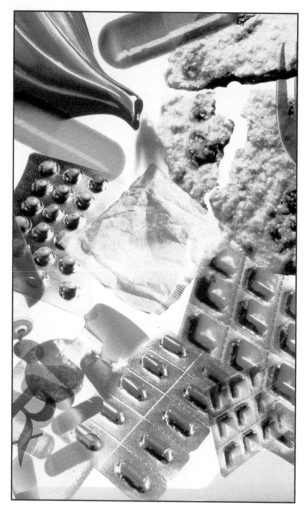

♦ There are no magic ways to lose weight.

- **Liquid diets that are low in calories.** Consequently, energy needs, fibre, and other important nutrients may be lacking in a person's diet. This may cause dangerous side effects and make a person feel sluggish and tired throughout the day. A person may also get tired of drinking the same thing.

- **Fasting—going without food.** This can be extremely damaging to your health.

- **Diet pills.** Some drugs can be obtained by prescription only and may play a small role in treating obesity. They're not for people with just a few pounds to lose.

Alternatively, some **over-the-counter drugs**—drugs that can be obtained without a prescription—may contain herbs or other ingredients that could create serious health problems.

- **Plans that promise quick weight loss (over 1 kg (2 pounds), per week).**

Even a weight-loss plan that would be acceptable for adults may pose problems for teens. At this point in your life, you are probably still growing. If you follow a weight-loss plan now, you might not get enough nutrients to grow into a healthy adult. If you are above the weight for your height and age, see a qualified health professional about your concerns.

Disadvantages to Consider

Certain weight-loss methods, although not dangerous to health, have other disadvantages.

Some methods simply don't work and are frauds. For instance, some products that claim to suppress appetite may use too little of an ingredient to actually have an effect.

Cost is another consideration. Weight-management centres and special diet products can be expensive. Think carefully about what you are getting for your money.

Some weight-loss plans offer very limited food choices. Favourite foods are denied and the diet becomes monotonous. As a result, people find it difficult to stay on the plan long enough to get the results they want. Imagine giving up your favourite food for a year or more. Could you do it? Would you want to?

Of those who do manage to lose weight by dieting, approximately 95 percent gain it back. The most likely reason is that weight-loss diets are seen as temporary ways of eating. Instead of learning to make healthful food choices, dieters often rely on printed menus or

Changing Your Attitude about "Diet"

Many people who hear the word "diet" think of a plan or strategy for losing weight. It is often viewed negatively because people say they are "going on a diet." This makes it sound like work, that it is "bad," or that it is a form of restriction. Diet actually means the foods that you eat on a daily basis. If you view "diet" in this way, you will enjoy it. Find ways to improve your eating habits to help you stay healthy.

Source: Middlesex–London Health Unit b, (n.d.)

prepackaged meals. As soon as they have lost the weight, they tend to go back to their old eating habits.

Successful Weight Management

If so many weight-management methods don't work, what does work? The most successful way to lose and manage weight is through **behaviour modification**, making gradual, permanent changes in your eating and activity habits. That is the key to keeping your weight at a healthy level throughout your life.

Be Realistic

Setting specific goals for weight loss can help motivate you and give you a way to see your progress. However, be sure your goals are reasonable.

First, be realistic about the size and shape of your body. Don't try to reach a weight or clothing size that's not right for you.

If you have a large amount of weight to lose, divide the task into a series of smaller goals. For instance, David's family physician recommended that he lose 15 kg (33 pounds), but his

first goal was to lose just 4.5 kg (10 pounds). The smaller goal was easier to reach and gave him the encouragement he needed to stick with his program.

Give yourself plenty of time to reach your goal. Excess weight isn't gained overnight, so it can't be lost overnight. It has taken you a lifetime to develop your eating and exercising habits. Aim for a weight loss of no more than 0.25 to 0.5 kg (½ to 1 pound) a week. The more slowly you lose weight, the better your body can adjust. Your weight loss has a greater chance of coming from body fat—and of being a long-term loss.

Be More Active

Inactivity is one of the basic causes of overweight. Just increasing your physical activity, even without cutting down on food, can often result in a leaner body. This doesn't mean you have to take up jogging. If you're not highly active, a good place to start is simply by increasing your physical activity. Taking the stairs instead of the elevator or walking the dog instead of simply watching it play outside are two examples. Just like setting reasonable weight-loss goals, setting reasonable activity goals is important.

Remember, the balance between energy in food and the energy you use for activities affects your weight. If you use up in activities about the same number of calories you get from food, your weight should stay at about the same level. If the food you eat provides more calories than you need for your activities, your body stores the extra as fat—and you gain weight. If you use up more calories in activities than you take in from food, you should lose weight.

In theory, you could change your energy balance just by eating less. In reality, however, it's better to increase your activity level as well.

Calories Burned in Activities

Degree of activity	Calories per minute
Sitting or standing quietly	1 to 2 calories
Light activity: cleaning house, playing baseball	4 calories
Moderate activity: brisk walking, gardening, cycling, dancing, playing basketball	6 calories
Strenuous activity: jogging, playing hockey, swimming	9 to 10 calories
Very strenuous activity: running fast, playing racquetball, skiing	12 calories

◆ **Vigorous physical activity is a key to successful weight loss.** In which of the activities above do you participate?

Why? Studies show that exercise not only burns calories during the activity, but also increases metabolism for a short time afterward. In other words, it increases the amount of energy used for basic body processes. Regular activity also helps ensure that the weight you lose comes from body fat, not muscle.

Whatever your level of physical activity, try to increase it or incorporate new types of activities into your life. Fitness can be fun and enjoyable. Having a physically active lifestyle will provide you with many health benefits as well as help you to maintain your weight.

INTERNET CONNECTS

www.mcgrawhill.ca/links/food
To learn more about Canada's Physical Activity Guides for various age groups, go to the web site above for *Food for Today, First Canadian Edition,* to see where to go next.

Change Your Eating Habits

Establishing new, more healthful eating habits will also help you reach and maintain a healthy weight. Be sure to follow a sensible eating plan that you enjoy and that allows you to eat a reasonable number of calories each day. You can get a reliable plan from a registered dietitian.

One key to successful weight management is to monitor your serving sizes. Too much food *of any kind* can result in weight gain. Another key is to eat fewer calories from fat. Remember, fat supplies more than twice as many calories per gram as do carbohydrates or proteins. Therefore, foods high in fat can make you gain weight more easily than other foods. In addition, studies suggest that fats in food are turned into body fat more easily than are excess carbohydrates and proteins.

By moderating portion sizes, eating less fat, and choosing nutrient-dense foods, you may find that you can eat more food instead of less and still lose weight.

◆ **By eating sensibly, you can maintain a healthy weight. What other measures can a person take to achieve a healthy weight?**

Refer to the strategies in the box below for ways to make healthy eating part of your healthy lifestyle.

Being below Weight for Your Height

People who are below the weight for their height have little body fat as an energy reserve and, possibly, less of the protective nutrients the body stores. This condition makes it harder for them to fight off infection.

Gaining weight can be just as challenging as losing weight. If you're concerned about being too thin, discuss the matter with a physician. There may be a medical reason for an inability to put on weight.

Healthy Eating as Part of a Healthy Lifestyle

- Plan your meals so that they are spaced apart. Good eating habits include eating three meals and two snacks on a daily basis.

- Listen to your body. Eat when you are hungry so that you don't overeat later. Learn to recognize your "just full" feeling. If you are uncomfortable then you've eaten more than you need.

- Pay attention to portion sizes — avoid the pitfalls of "supersizing".

- Choose a variety of foods from *Canada's Food Guide to Healthy Eating*. There are no "good" foods or "bad" foods. All foods can be part of healthy eating. For example, there's a difference between eating cookies every day for lunch with a sandwich, piece of fruit and glass of milk compared to eating a lunch of potato chips, pop, and snack cake every day.

- Chew food slowly and enjoy its flavours and textures.

- Rethink "dieting" — it can be dangerous, as it deprives you of important nutrients and leaves you tired and irritable. Instead, make healthy eating a part of your everyday life. Each small step, such as starting your day with a healthy breakfast or enjoying one more vegetable each day, adds up to a healthier you.

Source: Toronto Public Health (2003).

Toronto Public Health assumes no responsibility for any errors or omissions that may have occurred in the adaptation of its material.

◆ **An important key to gaining weight is to eat regular, nutrient-dense meals and snacks. Name some foods you enjoy that would fit this description.**

INTERNET CONNECTS

www.mcgrawhill.ca/links/food
To learn more about weight-loss programs, go to the web site above for *Food for Today, First Canadian Edition,* **to see where to go next.**

Here are some hints to help you gain weight without adding fat to your food choices:

◆ Go for larger portions of nutrient-dense foods from the four food groups.

◆ Eat regular meals.

◆ Enjoy nutrient-dense snacks, including yogurt and fresh or dried fruit.

◆ Don't forget to stay active. Exercise can help assure weight gained is muscle, not fat.

Maintaining a Healthy Weight

Whether someone has lost or gained weight, or has always been a healthy weight, maintaining a healthy weight is the goal to meet for better health. Once you achieve a healthy weight,

you should have no problem maintaining it as long as you continue to follow sound eating and activity habits. Still, if your weight starts to change, here are some suggestions:

◆ Keep a food record for a few days. Analyze the results to see if you are slipping into a poor eating pattern.

◆ Stay active. If you find your weight going up, increase your activity level.

◆ Keep a list of activities to do as alternatives to eating. If you find you're eating too much or too little because of stress, boredom, or some other reason, look to your list for healthy ways to cope with the situation. Try taking a hot bath, chatting with a friend, going for a walk, or simply brushing your teeth.

Accepting Your Natural Shape

Part of having a healthy weight involves being comfortable with your body. It is important to accept that every body is unique. Look at the positive aspects of who you are and praise yourself for them. If you are truly unhappy with your weight, then seek qualified medical advice. There may be underlying issues that are clouding your point of view. Simply accepting and enjoying your uniqueness is important. Don't focus just on weight loss or weight gain but on being healthy. This includes your overall well-being.

INTERNET CONNECTS

www.mcgrawhill.ca/links/food
To learn more about Health Canada's Vitality program, go to the web site above for *Food for Today, First Canadian Edition,* **to see where to go next.**

Physical Activity Specialist

Christa Costas–Bradstreet

What education is required for your job?

- A bachelor's degree in physical education or another health science.

What skills does a person need to be able to do your job?

- The ability to work on several projects at one time.

- Excellent time management and organizational skills, written and oral communication skills, presentation skills, and media and public relations skills.

- Experience in managing events.

- The ability to work with people of all ages.

- In-depth knowledge of current information in the field.

- Lots of energy to be able to grab opportunities that arise, since physical activity promotion is just gaining lots of attention.

- An excellent understanding of what the trends are in physical activity; the political climate; and historical perspective of physical activity promotion.

What do you like most about your job?

I love working with people in the community who we are trying to educate and the professionals in the community who also strive to get people to be more active. I love tackling some of the tough issues, like advocating for daily physical education classes for all grades in schools, and making physical education accessible and fun for everyone to encourage lifelong participation. It's a very high-energy job.

What advice would you give a person who is considering a career as a physical activity specialist/promoter?

Be passionate about promoting physical activity. Practise what you preach. Consider doing other certifications as well as a physical education degree. Get involved with a number of organizations and volunteer efforts that support the promotion of physical activity. Seek experience in the areas of advocacy and policy development.

Comment on what you see as important issues or trends in food and nutrition.

To achieve better health, everyone needs to balance physical activity with healthy eating daily!

Chapter 19   Review and Activities

Summary

- The human body comes in different shapes and sizes and depends on family traits.

- A healthy weight is determined by a person's age, body type, amount of food eaten, activity level, and family history.

- Set-point theory suggests that a body usually maintains a certain weight because of its own inner controls.

- Health professionals assess whether an adult is at a healthy weight by determining his or her Body Mass Index, waist circumference, waist-hip ratio, and body-fat percentage.

- Because children and adolescents are still growing, doctors and nurses determine whether their weight is appropriate by measuring their height and weight over a period of time and plotting it on a growth chart.

- The body-weight classification system is not a foolproof indication of a person's health or fitness because it doesn't take into account different body builds and the amount of fat compared to lean muscle mass.

- People are classified into two groups depending on their waist-hip ratio: pear-shaped or apple-shaped. "Pears" store fat on their thighs and hips, which doesn't pose a health problem. "Apples" store fat around their chest and stomach and have more health problems that tend to advance quickly.

- Athletes who are concerned about the amount of body fat they have can get their body-fat percentage measured by a qualified sports professional using a skinfold measure.

- Popular weight-management methods include reduced-calorie diets, centres that provide a healthy eating plan and psychological support, and weight-management products.

- Fad approaches to dieting that may be dangerous, give poor results, and/or are expensive include very low-calorie diets, diets based on a single food, liquid diets, fasting, diet pills, and quick weight-loss plans.

- The most successful method of losing weight is behaviour modification, or making gradual, permanent changes to your eating and activity habits.

- If you need to lose weight, make sure your goals are reasonable and divided into a series of smaller goals that you can manage. Give yourself a reasonable amount of time to reach your goals. Increase the amount of physical activity you get every day.

- To maintain your weight, continue with or establish healthy eating habits.

- To gain weight, eat three nutrient-dense meals and at least two snacks regularly every day.

- To be healthier and happier, focus on your overall well-being, not just gaining or losing weight.

Review and Activities   Chapter 19

Knowledge and Understanding

1. Why do people have different body shapes and sizes? Discuss as a class.

2. Describe the body-weight classification system that health professionals use in Canada to assess healthy weight in adults.

3. Describe the limitations of the various methods that are used to assess body weights.

4. Identify the differences and health risks associated with people who are pear-shaped compared to those who are apple-shaped.

5. What is a fad diet?

6. What is behaviour modification? How does it relate to weight management?

7. What are some of the risks associated with being above or below the weight for your height?

Thinking and Inquiry

8. How does the statement "You can't change your body because of genetics" apply to a person's weight goals? Discuss your answer with the class.

9. Why are fad diets popular? What can be done to teach people that adopting a healthy lifestyle is better in the long run? Discuss your answer in groups of three.

10. Paul calculated his BMI and found that it was 26.7. However, he doesn't look overweight. He eats a balanced diet and exercises regularly. What are some possible reasons for Paul being classified as overweight when he doesn't appear to be? What should Paul do if he is concerned about this weight measurement?

11. Is it possible for someone to gain weight by eating a low-fat diet? Explain.

Communication

12. You are a registered dietitian who works for the local public health unit. Part of your job is to run a program for adults called "Achieving a Healthy Weight." Prepare a pamphlet that promotes this program. Your pamphlet should include some of the information and topics that will be discussed in the program's sessions.

13. Create a poster that shows various ways you can maintain a healthy weight by healthy eating. Include as many visuals as possible. For example, show pictures that represent appropriate serving sizes for various foods, illustrate how to read nutrition labels on packages, and so on. Be prepared to discuss this in class.

Application

14. Your neighbour Joan, who is 30 years old, has been complaining about the weight that she has been gaining over the past few years. She does not enjoy exercising and has poor eating habits. She says that she thinks she will try cutting "junk food" out of her diet and will have only liquids for breakfast and lunch. What is your advice to Joan? Record your response in your notes.

15. Find ads for weight-loss methods in newspapers and magazines. Evaluate them on the basis of the information you have read in this chapter. Discuss what you find with the class.

CHAPTER

20

Reducing Fat in Your Diet

CHAPTER EXPECTATION

While reading this chapter, you will:

- Identify techniques for reducing the percentage of fat content in a person's diet to 30 percent.

Eggs are not just for breakfast. The centrepiece of this dinner is fluffy scrambled eggs accompanied by a broiled tomato, rice, grapes, and a green salad. How many food groups from Canada's Food Guide are represented in this meal?

KEY TERMS

au jus
blood cholesterol
dietary cholesterol
milk fat (m.f.)

SOCIAL SCIENCE SKILL

- writing a report

Fat is an essential nutrient that provides you with energy and contributes to overall health. However, consuming too much fat can lead to health problems. These health problems are a concern for many Canadians. Limiting certain types of fat and the total amount of fat in your diet is one way to achieve a well-balanced diet. This chapter will discuss types of fat and their associated health risks. In addition, suggestions for healthy eating will help you make wise food choices.

Cheese is a healthy food when eaten in moderation, but it contains a lot of fat.

Fat–An Essential Nutrient

Fat is an essential nutrient because it provides the body with energy and helps it perform vital functions. Fat helps transport fat-soluble vitamins in the body, promoting normal growth of cells and healthy skin. It also helps cushion vital organs, such as the heart and liver. Fat provides more than twice the amount of energy (calories) per gram as carbohydrates and protein. Fat has nine calories of energy per gram, whereas carbohydrates and proteins provide only four. Generally, foods high in fat are higher in calories.

Even though fat is essential to your health, you need to minimize your fat intake. High fat intakes have been linked to health problems such as certain types of cancer, obesity, and heart disease. As a result, Health Canada reports that 68 percent of Canadians over the age of 12 say that the amount of fat in the foods they eat is a concern to them (Health Canada, 2002). This concern has filled bookstore shelves, newspapers, magazines, and the Internet with "low-fat" recipes, and lined grocery-store shelves with "low-fat" and "fat-free" products. Still, you need some fat in your diet to help your body function.

Types of Fat and Their Effect on Health

Fat or fatty acids found in food belong in three main categories: saturated, monounsaturated, and polyunsaturated. Each of these categories can be broken down further. For example, you may have heard of omega-3 and omega-6 fatty acids. They are both part of the polyunsaturated family of fatty acids.

Cholesterol is a waxy substance found in some foods. There are two different types. The cholesterol in your bloodstream is referred to as **blood cholesterol;** the cholesterol found in animal products is called **dietary cholesterol**. Blood cholesterol levels need to be managed in the body to reduce the risk of heart disease and stroke. The way to keep blood cholesterol levels low seems to be by reducing all fats in the diet, especially saturated fats. For some people, dietary cholesterol has the effect of raising blood cholesterol levels. For other people, dietary cholesterol is not the major culprit in raising blood cholesterol levels. Some people just make too much cholesterol in their bodies and have normally high blood cholesterol levels. The table on page 413 reviews the various types and sources of fat and the potential effects of fat on your health, especially heart health.

Some fats may benefit your health, particularly your heart. To help reduce fat, look at the recommendations on the amount of fat healthy people should eat.

How Much Fat

Current nutrition recommendations for Canadians state that "the Canadian diet should include no more than 30 percent of energy as fat and no more than 10 percent as saturated fat" (Health Canada, 2002). This is for adults or young people who have finished growing. The following ranges of total fat that may be eaten are recommended for the future:

◆ 1 to 3 years old: 30 to 40 percent of total energy (calories) is the acceptable range for total fat.

◆ 4 to 18 years old: 25 to 35 percent of total energy (calories) is the acceptable range of total fat.

◆ Adults: 20 to 35 percent of total energy (calories) is the acceptable range of total fat.

Source: Food and Nutrition Board and Institute of Medicine, 2002.

Balance Your Fats

Even though a food may contain more than 30 percent of its total calories as fat, it may still contain other valuable nutrients, such as vitamins or minerals. Therefore, foods that are high in total fat should not necessarily be eliminated from the diet. They should be balanced with other foods that are lower in fat so that your total diet does not exceed 30 percent of calories from fat. For example, 30 percent of the calories in an avocado come from fat. However, avocados are a good source of other valuable nutrients. Remember, limiting fat intake to 30 percent or less of total calories refers to your overall daily intake, not the percentage of fat in individual foods. Dietary guidelines such as *Canada's Food Guide to Healthy Eating* can help you make informed decisions about food.

The main message is that healthy people should limit the overall amount of fat in their diets. It is especially important to reduce foods that are high in saturated and trans fats. This can be done by making informed food choices.

Types and Sources of Fat and Their Effect on Your Health

Type of Fat	State at Room Temperature	Food Sources	Effects on Health
Cholesterol (LDL "bad" cholesterol and HDL "good" cholesterol are the lipoproteins that carry cholesterol in the body.)	Waxy substance	• Manufactured in the body. • Food sources include meat, butter, eggs, shrimp. • Never found in plant foods.	• Little effect on risk for heart disease in healthy people.
Saturated	Solid	• Foods from animals— meat, poultry, whole milk products, butter, cheese. • Coconut, palm, and palm kernel oils.	• Raises both LDL and HDL cholesterol. • Linked to higher risk of heart disease.
Polyunsaturated	Liquid	• Vegetable oils, such as corn, soybean, safflower, cottonseed. • Omega-3 found in fish—salmon, mackerel, and swordfish.	• Lowers LDL and raises HDL cholesterol. • Linked to lower risk of heart disease.
Monounsaturated	Liquid	• Oils, such as olive, canola. • Cashews, almonds, peanuts, and many other nuts. • Avocados.	• Lowers LDL and raises HDL cholesterol. • Linked to lower risk of heart disease.
Trans ("Hydrogenated" on product labels)	Solid or semi-solid	• Shortening • Partially hydrogenated vegetable oils. • Most margarines. • Most commercial baked goods, such as cookies and crackers.	• Raises LDL cholesterol. • Linked to higher risk of heart disease.

Source: Adapted from National Institute of Nutrition (2001).

Comparing Fat and Cholesterol Content

Type of Food (84-g [3-oz.] serving)	Total Fat (g)	Saturated Fat (g)	Cholesterol (mg)
Fish and Shellfish			
Cod, cooked	1	0	45
Tuna, canned, in water	1	0	35
Red salmon, canned	6	2	45
Mackerel, cooked	13	2	60
Shrimp, cooked	1	0	166
Poultry			
Chicken, light meat, without skin, roasted	2	1	70
Chicken, dark meat, without skin, roasted	7	2	80
Turkey, breast meat, without skin, roasted	1	0	55
Meat			
Beef, top round steak, trimmed, broiled	4	1	70
Beef, ground, regular, broiled	18	7	76
Beef liver, pan-fried	7	2	410
Pork loin, trimmed, roasted	6	2	65

◆ **The fat and cholesterol content of different meats, poultry, fish, and shellfish vary.** Which item has the most saturated fat? Which has the least total fat? How many milligrams of cholesterol are in an 84-g (3-oz) serving of water-packed canned tuna?

People who are ill or recovering from an illness such as a heart attack or stroke should consult a qualified health professional to find out how much fat they need in their diets.

Reducing fat by too much in your diet or focussing too much on fat intake is not healthy either. For instance, people who are constantly counting the percentage or grams of fat that they eat may be so preoccupied that they take the pleasure and fun out of eating. This isn't a healthy approach and may contribute to poor eating habits.

INTERNET CONNECTS

www.mcgrawhill.ca/links/food
To learn more about fats and how to make lower-fat choices from the four food groups, go to the web site above for *Food for Today, First Canadian Edition*, to see where to go next.

Making Informed Food Choices about Fat

Whether you are purchasing, preparing, serving, or eating food, there are numerous ways to reduce the amount of fat that you eat. Having the tools to recognize foods that are high in total fat and specific types of fat will help you obtain a well-balanced diet. The suggestions on the following pages will help you reduce the amount of fat you eat.

Purchasing Food

When purchasing food, there are two ways to identify the amount of fat in an item.

- **Read the label.** Reading the label will help you find the amount of hidden fat (fat that is part of the ingredients) in a product. This can be done specifically by reading the ingredients list and by reading the nutrition facts table on the package. See the box on page 416 to determine what percentage of each fat is in one serving of a product. It also helps to look for other information on the label, such as "low in fat" or "fat-free." A label that reads "cholesterol-free" does not necessarily mean that a food is low in total fat.

When purchasing ground meats, such as beef or poultry, or processed meats, such as hot dogs, cold cuts, and deli meats, look for "lean" or "extra lean" on the packaging label. This way, you are getting less fat in meat and meat products.

When purchasing milk and milk products, read the label. Products such as yogurt, cheese, and milk have the percentage of **milk fat** listed on the label. For example, a container of sour cream may read 2% m.f. (m.f. is milk fat). The lower the percentage of milk fat shown on the label, the lower the fat content in the product.

FOR YOUR HEALTH

Go Easy on the Processed Meats

Cured meats are popular because of their smoky flavour. Unfortunately, the chemicals responsible for that flavour—nitrites and nitrates—have been linked with certain types of cancer. In addition, these meats are high in sodium, fat, or both. So enjoy an occasional hot dog or deli sandwich. Just remember to eat these foods in moderation.

Following Up

- Approximately 35 percent of the nitrites and 13 percent of the nitrates in food are added during the manufacturing process. The rest occur naturally in certain vegetables—such as spinach, lettuce, and beets—and in baked goods. Discuss how this information might affect your eating style in the future.

◆ **Visible fat.** Look for the visible fat in products that are packaged in clear containers, such as deli salads, entrees, and meat or poultry products. You can see the fat around the outside of a roast, pork chops, or steak. You can also see white flecks of fat (marbling) within the muscle tissue of meat. In poultry, most of the visible fat is located in the skin and in layers under the skin. Choose the leaner cuts of meat, purchase skinless poultry, and fresh or frozen fish that is not breaded or deep-fried.

◆ Because of the high fat and sodium content in conventional hot dogs, many people are switching to chicken and turkey franks, which are generally lower in both. Still, health experts advise eating such cured meat products only occasionally. Discuss possible reasons for the view health experts take toward cured meat products.

Finding the Percentage of Calories from Fat in a Single Serving

Looking at the percentage of calories that come from fat in a food is one way of comparing products. You may think that a product is lower in fat, but when you calculate the percentage, you may find that a major portion of the calories you are getting from this food are actually from fat.

To calculate this information, perform the following steps:

Amount of fat in grams × 9 calories = Number of calories from total fat

Number of calories from fat/Total calories × 100 = Percent of calories from fat

Use the fat information shown here from a fictitious box of crème cookies to calculate the percent of calories you are getting from fat.

Nutrition Facts

Total Calories per Serving: 180 calories
Serving Size: 3 cookies (60-gram serving)

Total Fat	6.0 g
Polyunsaturates	0.3 g
Monounsaturates	1.9 g
Saturates	1.3 g
Trans fat	2.5 g

Calculation using the above nutrition information:
6 × 9 = 54 calories
54/180 × 100 = 30 percent

Therefore, the percentage of calories that come from total fat in a single serving of these cookies is 30 percent.

Note: You can find the percent of each of the different types of fat by using the above calculation. Just replace the amount of fat in grams. For example, replace total in grams (6 g) with saturated fat (1.3 g), etc. Read the serving size when comparing various boxes of cookies. Is this the portion size you would usually consume?

◆ Check the labels on milk and milk products in your refrigerator or at your local grocery store. Identify the fat content of each product by percentage of milk fat. What other information is on the package to help you assess the fat content in each product?

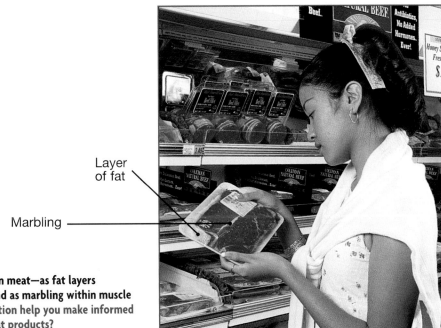

Layer of fat

Marbling

◆ Visible fat occurs in two ways in meat—as fat layers surrounding muscle sections and as marbling within muscle sections. How can this information help you make informed decisions when purchasing meat products?

Food Science ◆ L A B ◆

Making Invisible Fats Visible

Have you ever seen a magician make an object suddenly appear? You are about to do something similar. This isn't an illusion. You are about to make the invisible fat in foods visible!

Procedure

1. Start with a clean, dry work surface. Place five or six potato chips on a paper towel, and fold the edges of the towel over the chips. Press lightly to crush the chips.

2. Open the towel. Dump the solid contents into a waste receptacle, and brush away any crumbs that remain. Return the towel to its place on the work surface next to a sticky note or other piece of paper that identifies the food used.

3. Repeat steps 1 and 2 for small amounts of each of the following foods: pretzels, apple, snack crackers, muffin, and air-popped unflavoured popcorn.

4. Leave the paper towels undisturbed for 30 minutes. This will allow any water on the towels to evaporate. At the end of the 30 minutes, examine each paper towel by holding it up to a window or other light source. Any grease stains or other light spots indicate that the product contains some fat.

Conclusions

◆ Which foods produced stains? Which did not?

◆ Do you regularly eat any of the foods you tested?

◆ Were you surprised by any of your findings? If so, which?

◆ What changes in your eating habits might you consider making as a result of this experiment?

Planning Meals

You can cut down on your fat intake by planning meals and snacks that are lower in fat content. Fibre may have some effect on lowering blood cholesterol. To include high-fibre foods in your meals, serve vegetable and lentil or bean dishes as the main part of the meal. Other foods that are good sources of fibre include whole-grain products, such as whole-grain breads, brown rice, and whole-grain cereals. Meat does not have to be the focus of every meal. Tofu is another product that is a good substitute for meat, and so is fish, which is generally lower in fat. Remember to check the package for fat content, though, as amounts vary.

Foods that are often easy and convenient snack items, such as cookies, crackers, chips, and nuts are usually high in fat. When planning snacks, substitute fresh fruits and

◆ Soups based on legumes, such as lentils, peas, and beans, are very hearty. For variety, make them the focus of your meal. What other foods could you plan to serve with this lentil soup to make it a low-fat, high-fibre, yet well-balanced meal?

vegetables for these items. Planning meals and snacks around healthier choices will help reduce fat in the diet. Of course, even foods that start out low in fat may become higher in fat because of the way you prepare or serve them.

INTERNET CONNECTS

www.mcgrawhill.ca/links/food
To learn more about the nutrient value of some common foods, go to the web site above for *Food for Today, First Canadian Edition,* to see where to go next.

Preparation Methods

You may have planned a meal by choosing various foods that are relatively low in fat. But the meal may become quite high in fat, depending on how you prepare the foods.

For example, you may first choose to have salmon, rice, broccoli, and a vegetable salad for the main meal, and carrot cake for dessert. Then you decide you will pan-fry the salmon in butter, fry the rice, put a creamed cheese sauce on the broccoli, and make the vegetable salad by tossing it with a rich mayonnaise dressing. You also add cream cheese icing to the carrot cake. This has resulted in a significant increase in the fat and energy (calorie) content of each menu item, making the whole meal quite high in total fat. Can you identify what else is wrong with this menu?

Whether baking, cooking, or combining items, as in salads or sandwiches, there are ways to trim down the fat that is added to foods. When preparing foods, there are many methods of cooking that add little or no fat.

When cooking meat, choose a method that allows the fat to drain off the meat, such as broiling or roasting meats on a rack. White sauces and gravy are traditionally high in fat. Consider using seasoned non-fat yogurt in place of white sauce. Instead of serving roasts with gravy, try serving them **au jus**—with the pan drippings, from which the fat has been skimmed. The easiest way to skim fat is to wait until the drippings have cooled. The fat, which will rise to the top, may then be easily removed with a spoon.

To cook vegetables, steam, microwave, or bake them. Avoid frying or deep-frying your foods. Other ways to cut back on fat when preparing foods are:

- Use a non-stick frying pan and add little or no oil to the pan. Water may be used to help prevent foods from sticking to the pan.

- If using vegetable oil to sauté or fry foods, use a spray bottle to lightly coat the pan instead of pouring the oil directly onto it.

- Trim the visible fat from meat and remove the skin from poultry prior to cooking.

- Skim the fat off the top of soups and stews. This can be done more easily after chilling them.

- Think of creative ways of adding other ingredients besides oil, butter, or margarine to food. For example, top baked potatoes or grilled meats with salsa or chutney. Sprinkle vegetable dishes with herbs, spices, and lemon juice.

- Prepare your own marinades and salad dressings using fresh herbs, spices, and lemon or other citrus juices. Add water, not oil, to your marinades for the liquid. Use different kinds of vinegar instead of oil on salads.

Lower-Fat Gravy

To make lower-fat gravy:

- Shake a mixture of 30 mL (2 tbsp) of flour or cornstarch and 50 mL (¼ cup) of cold water in a covered container.
- Add it to 250 mL (1 cup) of broth.
- Heat the mixture to boiling, stirring constantly.
- Cook the mixture until it thickens, for about one minute.

INTERNET CONNECTS

www.mcgrawhill.ca/links/food
To learn more about cutting the fat in foods and low-fat recipes, go to the web site above for *Food for Today, First Canadian Edition,* to see where to go next.

- Substitute chicken or turkey for meats in recipes. For example, use lean ground chicken or turkey instead of ground beef.

- Look for ways to substitute ingredients in recipes by using the low-fat versions of products whenever possible. This works well for ingredients such as sour cream, yogurt, milk, and mayonnaise when making salads, sauces, and dips.

- When baking quick breads, such as muffins, loaves, or cakes, substitute half the oil in the recipe with unsweetened applesauce, or reduce the amount of fat the recipe calls for.

- Purchase a low-fat cookbook or search for low-fat recipes on the Internet.

Food Science
◆ L A B ◆

Taste-Testing a Reduced-Fat Product

According to an old saying, the proof is in the eating. You are about to test the truth of this by conducting a taste test of a full-fat dairy product and a lower-fat version made in the food lab.

Procedure

1. Place 250 mL (1 cup) of low-fat small-curd cottage cheese in a blender. Blend until smooth. Add 5 mL (1 tbsp.) of lemon juice and blend again.

2. Force the cottage cheese through a strainer. Remove as much of the solid contents as possible.

3. Have classmates taste small samples of both this cottage cheese blend and full-fat sour cream. Record their reactions in a chart.

4. Add commercial onion soup mix to both foods to make dips. Repeat step 3.

Conclusions

◆ How did the subjects rate the cottage cheese blend in comparison with the sour cream? Did all the subjects have the same reaction to the two samples? If not, explain.

◆ Did the results of the experiment differ when you added the onion soup mix? If so, how? What can you conclude?

◆ How can the results of this food science lab help you use recipes in the future?

◆ **Most of the fat in poultry is in or just under the skin. Removing the skin from poultry is a way of reducing the fat.**

FYI

Suggestions for Lowering Fat

High-Fat Food	Low-Fat Alternative	Fat Savings
Whole milk (250 mL/1 cup)	Fat-free milk	8 grams less fat
Fried chicken (84 g/3 oz.)	Baked chicken without skin	8 grams less fat
Regular salad dressing (15 mL/1 tbsp)	Flavoured vinegar, lemon juice, or fat-free dressing	9 grams less fat
Potato chips (28 g/1 oz.)	Plain popcorn, air popped (250 mL/1 cup)	10 grams less fat
Premium ice cream (125 mL/½ cup)	Low-fat frozen yogurt	20 grams less fat
Cheddar cheese (28 g/1 oz.)	Part-skim mozzarella	4 grams less fat
Sour cream on a baked potato (30 mL/2 tbsp)	Plain non-fat yogurt Salsa	6 grams less fat

Serving Food

What you add to your foods at the table can increase their fat content. There are many sensible choices for you and your guests that will help reduce fat in your diets.

When dining, leave the choice of how much fat to add to foods up to guests and family members. Sauces, salad dressings, and some condiments, such as mayonnaise, butter, and margarine, are typically items with a high percentage of fat. Serve these types of items on the side so that people can control how much they eat. For example, when serving sandwiches, arrange all the ingredients on the table and allow individuals to choose what they want on their sandwich. Some people may prefer to have only mustard and skip the mayonnaise, butter, or margarine.

There will be times when you serve higher-fat foods, such as a pepperoni and sausage pizza. Serve small portions of these kinds of foods. Accompany them with a fresh salad seasoned with herbs and topped with a low-fat salad dressing, and plain whole-grain rolls.

FOR YOUR HEALTH

Butter or Margarine—Which Is Better?

- Butter and margarine contain the same amount of fat, though the type of fat is different.
- Both butter and margarine are high in calories because of the high fat content.
- Both butter and margarine provide vitamin D.

Which Type of Fat?

Butter contains mostly saturated fat and a small quantity of naturally occurring trans fats. Saturated fat is solid at room temperature. Most saturated fats and trans fats raise total cholesterol as well as "bad," or LDL, cholesterol. Trans fats may also lower "good," or HDL, cholesterol. This increases the risk for heart disease and stroke.

Margarine varies in the types of fat it contains.

- Hard or "brick-type" margarine contains mostly saturated and trans fats that result from hydrogenation.
- Soft or "tub" margarines vary in the amounts of unsaturated, saturated, and trans fats, depending on the degree of hydrogenation.
- Non-hydrogenated soft margarine has 80 percent or more of its fat as unsaturated fats and contains almost no trans fat.

Choosing the Best Margarine

- Check the label for the words "non-hydrogenated."
- Choose a "tub" margarine that is readily "squeezeable"; that is, the container compresses easily when you squeeze it. The first ingredient will be liquid oil (corn, canola, etc.), not a hydrogenated oil.
- In addition to the previous two methods, and if a nutrition information panel is on the label, check:
  - Suggested serving size (standard is 30 mL or 2 tsp.) equals 10 g of margarine, of which 8 g is total fat.
  - At least 6 g (i.e., 75 percent) should be *unsaturated fats* (polyunsaturated plus monounsaturated).
  - No more than 2 g (i.e. less than 25 percent) is *saturated fats*.
  - If *trans fats* are listed, the amount should be almost none.

Example
Per 10 g (2 tsp.) serving:

Total Fat			**8.0 g**
Polyunsaturated	3.3 g*	Saturated	1.1 g
Monounsaturated	3.3 g*	Trans	0.1 g*

*Note in the examples that unsaturated fats (polyunsaturated and monounsaturated) add up to at least 6 g as recommended and there is virtually no trans fat.

The bottom line: Whether you choose butter or margarine or both, use all fats sparingly.

Source: Adapted from Middlesex–London Health Unit (2003).

Eating away from Home

It can be a challenge to limit your fat intake when eating away from home. The foods that are served in some restaurants are often high in fat and come in large portions. You can minimize your fat intake by making healthy food choices when ordering from the menu. There may be several clues that foods are high in fat. Look for the following words on a menu—they indicate foods that may be loaded with fat:

- Breaded.
- Creamy.
- In a cheese sauce (au gratin).
- Scalloped.
- Fried.
- Crispy.
- Parmigiana.
- Tempura.

When ordering from a menu, look for items described as *broiled*, *baked*, or *steamed*. These terms identify foods that are usually lower in fat. When in doubt about how a dish is prepared or what ingredients it contains, ask your server. You might also ask whether your food can be prepared differently from how it is described—for example, broiled instead of fried.

Be wary, too, of toppings, such as sauces, mayonnaise, salad dressings, and sour cream. Request either that your food be served without the topping or that the topping be served on the side so that you can use as little as you want. Another option is to ask for a substitute—for example, low-fat salad dressing or lemon juice instead of oil, or a tomato marinera sauce instead of a cream or oil-based sauce on pasta.

◆ **When preparing a salad, keep in mind that salad dressing isn't the only way to enhance the flavour.** Name some other low-fat possibilities for tossed salad.

Look for restaurants that offer a wide variety of salads or have a salad bar. This is one way of controlling how much fat you eat. You could make the salad bar your main course, since soup and bread are often included with it. When at the salad bar or selecting a salad from the menu, watch for high-fat foods that may be in the salad. If salad ingredients are coated with mayonnaise, as in potato or macaroni salads, they are quite high in fat, as are salads topped with bacon bits, cheese, and croutons.

Some restaurants specify choices on the menu that are low in fat or use symbols that indicate which items are low-fat. Other restaurants may have pamphlets that indicate the nutritional value of menu items, including the fat content of certain foods. Also look at the menu boards in fast-food restaurants, because they may tell how many grams of fat are in certain dishes. Be aware that this type of information may be the fat content of the food served *without* cheese, sauces, or dressings. Look for restaurants in your area that advertise healthy menu choices that are low in fat.

You probably eat most of your lunches either at work or at school. Packed lunches may become boring or inconvenient to pack. Your lunchtime may also be short. These factors may contribute to eating foods from fast-food restaurants, or convenience foods from vending machines or a cafeteria on a regular basis. Some people enjoy having a hot meal at lunch and are not interested in eating a lunch brought from home. In spite of these reasons, packing a lunch is a good way to save time and money, and can be flavourful and well balanced. They also allow you to know how much fat you are getting in your diet, because you have prepared and packed the food yourself. Follow the guidelines below and those examined earlier in the chapter to help you enjoy packed foods that are healthy choices:

◆ Purchase a vacuum bottle—a glass or metal bottle with a vacuum space between the outer container and the inner liner.

◆ Many fast-food restaurants now have information available on the nutritional content of the foods on their menu. **Explain** why this information is of value to their customers.

Vacuum bottles keep foods hotter than less-expensive foam-insulated bottles. This will allow you to pack leftover hot foods, such as homemade soups and stews.

◆ Pack fresh vegetables and fruits with low-fat salad dressing separately.

◆ Choose a variety of sandwich fillings that are low in fat, such as bean dips. Try them as dips for fresh vegetables, too.

◆ If you want to add to your lunch by choosing items from the cafeteria or a restaurant, choose a baked potato instead of fries. Dress it up with chives and low-fat yogurt or salad dressing. Or choose a broth-based soup, not a creamed soup.

Whether you eat your lunch at home, pack a lunch, or eat out at a restaurant, keep these suggestions on how to reduce fat in your diet in mind. They will help you to moderate your fat intake. This will permit you to splurge occasionally on higher-fat foods without feeling guilty.

Safety Check

What is the safest way to carry lunch to school? If you pack perishable food that's left at room temperature for more than two hours, the risk of foodborne illness increases. It's especially important to remember this if you typically store your lunch in a stuffy locker.

For the safest bet, use an insulated lunch bag. You can also freeze sandwiches and juice boxes to help keep cold foods cold. The foods will be thawed by lunchtime. Use ice packs or chilled, insulated vacuum bottles to help keep foods cool. Pack non-perishable foods such as dried fruit, boxed juice, and crackers.

Report Writing

Part of the process of doing Social Science research involves writing a final report. You will be ready to write your final report once you have done the following:

- Reviewed what the literature says or what other scientists have found out about your topic.
- Conducted, tabulated, and organized your own research from a survey, questionnaire, or interview.

Discussion and Interpretation

The next step is to discuss and analyse your research findings. This involves explaining the similarities and differences between what you found from doing your research and what you found from the review of the literature, and writing the following:

- **A summary of the findings from your research.** Look at the similarities and differences that you discovered while doing your research. Describe any trends you discovered. For example, when looking at the lunch habits of students in your school, perhaps you found there was a growing preference for bringing a certain kind of sandwich from home, or a trend toward buying pizza in the cafeteria. Discuss why this information is important.
- **An analysis and interpretation of the data collected** in the review of the literature and the research that you did. Look for contrasts between your research and other research.
- **An APA-style references list** when discussing any research conducted by other people.

Conclusions

In this section:

- Restate your goals for studying this topic. Did your study prove what you thought it would? If not, why didn't it?
- Were there any problems with the way you designed your study? For example, did you look at lunchtime eating habits on a very sunny Friday in June when more students than usual went out to eat, making the sample size too small?
- How would you do your study differently?
- What does your study suggest? Does it have implications for further studies and exploration of the topic? Is it a relevant topic of study?

Source: Adapted from Ontario Family Leadership Council (2002); and London District School Board (n.d.).

Chapter 20   Review and Activities

Summary

- Fat is an essential nutrient that provides the body with energy and helps it perform vital functions.
- Foods higher in fat are usually higher in calories.
- Fat in foods is divided into three categories: saturated, monounsaturated, and polyunsaturated.
- There are two types of cholesterol: blood cholesterol, found in your bloodstream, and dietary cholesterol, found in animal products. Blood cholesterol levels need to be kept low in the body to reduce the risk of heart disease and stroke.
- Health Canada recommends that Canadians include no more than 30 percent of calories as fat in their diets and no more than 10 percent as saturated fat.
- Foods high in fat should not be eliminated from the diet but balanced with other foods that are lower in fat or should be chosen less often.

- You can reduce fat in your diet by reading the nutrition facts on the label to find hidden fat content before you purchase the food; looking for visible fat in salads, entrees, or meat and poultry products and choosing items containing less fat; including more fibre in your meals; substituting healthier food choices for meals and snacks; preparing and cooking foods using less fat; serving high-fat items on the side so you can choose smaller amounts; and purchasing lower-fat versions of products.
- When eating away from home, packing your own lunch ensures that you will know the fat content of the food.
- When eating out, choose menu items that have been prepared using little or no fat and that have toppings and dressings served on the side if they are high in fat.

Knowledge and Understanding

1. What is the difference between blood cholesterol and dietary cholesterol? Share your answer with the class.

2. Which fats raise LDL cholesterol?

3. What recommendations have some experts made about the percentage range of fat for a 16-year-old?

4. Explain why foods higher in fat are often higher in calories.

Thinking and Inquiry

5. Record the foods and the amount of each food that you eat in a single day. Then revise each meal and snack so your menu will be lower in fat in the future.

6. Using the Internet Connects on page 419, about grams of fat found in common foods, and the information in the text, prepare a one-day menu that derives 30 percent of its content from fat.

7. You are a community dietitian who writes a column for the local paper. One of the questions that a reader sent you asks, "Should I use butter or margarine?" Write an answer to the reader in your notes.

8. a) Using the information in "Finding the Percentage of Calories from Fat in a Single Serving" on page 416, calculate the percentage of calories that come from fat for various products. Compare products that are similar, for example two types of crackers. Which one do you think is the better choice? Write a report in your notes.

b) After calculating the percentage of calories that come from fat, your classmate has decided that he or she shouldn't eat some of the foods, such as peanut butter, because more than 30 percent of calories come from fat in one serving. Write a letter to your classmate that explains what he or she should do rather than eliminating these types of foods altogether from his or her diet.

Communication

9. Create a bulletin board display of ways to reduce fat in your diet as a way of making healthier food choices. Bring it in and explain to the class.

10. Develop a lunch menu that is low in fat for a fast-food restaurant. Display your menu on Bristol board and discuss it with classmates. The menu should include the serving size of each food item, pictures of the food items, and the nutrient facts beside each item, including the total grams of fat per portion.

Application

11. Create a questionnaire/survey that will help you examine the lunchtime eating habits of students in your school. Questions should ask where the students usually eat lunch, what items they usually eat, and so on. Present your findings to the class.

12. Follow the Social Science Skills feature on page 427 to write a two-page report. In your report, include an analysis of the amount of fat that your peers consume in their diet at lunchtime. Use your own and your classmates' findings in the analysis of your report.

Strategies for Achieving Well-Being

While reading this chapter, you will:

- Demonstrate an understanding of the importance of achieving overall personal well-being.

- Identify personal food choices and how these choices affect your ability to cope with stress.

- Analyse the role of familiar foods in the management of stress.

Sharing a meal or snack with someone and engaging in physical activity are both enjoyable social activities. Getting pleasure from activities such as these is a great way to manage stress in your life.

KEY TERMS

aerobic exercise
anaerobic exercise
endurance activities
flexibility activities
hunger
lifestyle activities
satiety
strength activities
stress

Achieving overall health and well-being involves striving to be in the best possible physical, mental, and emotional health. Health and well-being is encouraged in this chapter through the practice of wellness. Wellness strategies include analysing the food choices you make to cope with stress, achieving a healthy body image, and communicating effectively in social relationships. An analysis of the benefits of physical activity and ways to increase your activity level are also presented.

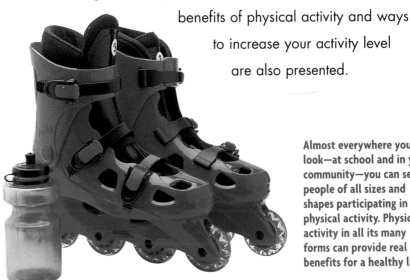

Almost everywhere you look—at school and in your community—you can see people of all sizes and shapes participating in physical activity. Physical activity in all its many forms can provide real benefits for a healthy life.

Factors Affecting Overall Health and Well-Being

When considering the factors that affect your health and well-being, you need to examine the whole self—both the mind and the body. You may decide on something that affects your body, which, in turn, may have negative or positive consequences for your health. The reaction that people have toward some situations in their lives may also have an impact on their health. Some of the factors that affect well-being are connected with the following:

- Foods that you eat.

- The amount of sleep that you get.

- The intensity and endurance of the activities you do.

- The lifestyle choices you make, such as consuming drugs or alcohol, or smoking, versus being physically active.

- Social relationships you form with others.

- Your response to stress and the management of stress in your life.

- The support you receive from family and friends.

- Your personality or what makes you unique.

Now consider how these things may have an impact on a person's health and well-being. Many of these factors are interconnected. For example, a child who is more social and outgoing may enjoy starting school and will adjust quickly, whereas a child who is shy and less confident may find starting school scary. There are other factors that you can't control, such as illnesses and events in your life.

Achieving Overall Health and Well-Being

To achieve overall health and well-being, take responsibility for your health and try to reach optimal overall health—mentally, emotionally, physically, and socially (Larson Duyff, 2000). To help you achieve this, include the following aspects of wellness in your life:

- Engaging in regular physical activity.

- Managing stress.

- Having a positive attitude about your body, those around you, and life in general.

- Developing good social and communication skills.

- Eating healthy foods and having a healthy attitude toward food.

Reasons behind Eating

Why do people eat? This seems like a very simple question, but the answer to this question is quite complex. We all know we need food to survive. Yet, we all sometimes eat when we aren't really hungry.

The Body

There are two basic reasons why we eat. The first is for physical reasons. Your body needs food for energy or to make it run. Following healthy eating habits helps you maintain your health and prevent certain illnesses.

The process and function of food in the body is a complex science. Basically, the human body has a physical need to eat. This is referred to as **hunger**. You learn to know when your body needs food or liquids by listening to internal signs. Some of these include a growling stomach that indicates it's empty, feeling thirsty, or having a dry mouth that warns you that you need to drink something to rehydrate your body. Some people may feel faint, dizzy, or nauseated when they are hungry (Larson Duyff, 2000).

The feeling of hunger disappears once you have eaten a fair amount of food. It takes about 20 minutes for the brain to receive the message from your stomach that you are full. Chewing food slowly, taking breaks while you're eating, and slowing down to enjoy your food will prevent you from overeating and leaving the table feeling uncomfortably full. The feeling of being satisfied after a meal is referred to as **satiety**. People may choose to continue eating for other reasons, such as the smell or sight of their favourite dessert, even though they are full.

The Mind

The second reason for eating is categorized as psychological, or having to do with human emotions, thoughts, and feelings. Psychological reasons for eating are complex because they

◆ **Your desire to eat can be triggered by the aroma and sight of food as well as by the taste. Is this hunger or appetite? What needs can it meet?**

are interconnected with many other factors, such as family, culture, and emotions. This is referred to as appetite. For instance, Graham and Connor went out for coffee one evening after dinner. Near the coffee shop, they could both smell fresh-baked cinnamon rolls. As they entered the shop, they could see them displayed behind the glass counter. They decided to share one to accompany their coffees. Why did Graham and Connor go out for coffee and then decide to indulge in a treat by sharing the cinnamon roll? Can you think of a time when you have chosen to eat for the very same reasons?

Eating for psychological reasons means taking pleasure from eating. Sharing food with family and friends, smelling the aroma of various foods, and thinking about food creates many memories. Having a good appetite contributes to choosing a variety of foods and getting enjoyment from eating them. In these ways, appetite contributes to wellness, since it is good for both the mind and the body (Larson Duyff, 2000).

Attitudes toward Eating

Eating is a normal part of human nature. Your attitude toward eating and food contributes to your overall health and well-being. To be able to relax and enjoy food without feeling guilty is what having a positive attitude toward eating is all about. Whether it's in a social atmosphere or while dining alone, food and eating should be a good experience. Cooking for others as an expression of love or celebrating a birthday party by taking pleasure in a piece of cake are also ways to enjoy food. Being able to relax and eat when you are hungry and feel comfortable about having a good appetite are part of having a positive attitude toward eating (Larson Duyff, 2000).

Some people view food negatively or use food in negative ways. They may be so preoccupied with food and/or their weight that it takes the pleasure out of eating. Other people may have a desire to eat because they are bored, stressed, anxious, depressed, feel unworthy or incompetent, or are sad about something. There are also people who use food to turn their thoughts away from an unsolved problem. Resorting to food in this way is using eating as an emotional outlet.

The Stress Connection

Have you ever lost sleep the night before a big exam or felt terribly nervous when you had to speak before a large audience? If so, you are not alone. Everyone at one time or another experiences these symptoms. Physical reactions like these are symptoms of stress. **Stress** is physical or mental tension triggered by an event or situation in your life. Physical stress is the result of an injury or illness in the body. Mental stress is caused by thoughts, feelings, actions, and other emotions that a person has toward experiences in his or her life. Not everyone finds the same situations stressful. Some people experience test anxiety, whereas others don't. At school, a teacher will experience types of job stress that differ from those experienced by a principal or a school guidance counsellor. Even going on a date, receiving an award, or experiencing some other positive event can be stressful.

To achieve wellness, you need to recognize how you manage stress. Do you turn to food in general or to certain foods? Do you exercise? Do you avoid the situation and run away? Are your stress-management strategies positive and healthy?

The Effect of Stress on the Body and Mind

Stressful situations can't be avoided. Tension may cause headaches, backaches, or other physical symptoms. It even plays a role in high blood pressure and heart disease. The effects of stress on the mind and body may also have an impact on personal nutrition. Have you ever felt too ill to eat? Have you ever been too upset to eat? Negative emotions resulting from stress can cause heartburn, diarrhea, and other digestive problems. In addition, the body needs nutrients during times of illness and injury to help the body heal. The mind-body relationship is powerful. When stress is not handled effectively, feelings of worry, fear, or anger may result, leading to depression and lack of energy. The solution is to learn how to cope positively with these situations through practising various aspects of wellness.

◆ **No two people react in quite the same way to what can be a stressful situation. How does your level of stress when taking a test compare with that of a friend?**

Recognizing your limits in all aspects of your life will help you balance work and leisure activities. It is important to take time for yourself, whether you spend time alone, reading a book, or taking a walk with a friend. Keep a positive attitude toward life—stay light-hearted by maintaining a sense of humour. Having a support network of family and friends can also help to reduce stress. Talk to people who are close to you. Ask their advice or simply use them as a sounding board. Remember to accept the things you can't change. Take control of your life and remember to believe in yourself. Don't forget to compliment and reward yourself for your accomplishments.

INTERNET CONNECTS

www.mcgrawhill.ca/links/food
To learn more about managing stress, go to the web site above for *Food for Today, First Canadian Edition*, to see where to go next.

Nutrition and Stress

The response to stress varies depending on the individual and the situation. Some people overeat when they feel tense; others lose their appetites altogether. People may be lonely, believe they have failed at something, or have simply had a bad day. All of these situations create mental stress in which some people turn to food as a way of helping them deal with or avoid their emotions, thoughts, and feelings.

Food may be mistaken or replaced with an emotion or a feeling. This is illustrated in the following example. Thomas is very worried about writing his math exam the next day. He decides to stay up all night to study. During the night, he becomes very tired. Instead of sleeping, he munches on potato chips to relieve his fatigue. The food gives him some energy and helps him to stay awake. He eventually falls asleep at the kitchen table with his head in his textbook. He awakens the next morning in a panic because he hasn't studied all of the material. His stress level is very high. He is too upset to eat, so he races off to school to do some last-minute studying for the exam. How has Thomas used food to replace his emotions? What should he have done to contribute to his overall health and well-being?

In contrast, good nutrition helps reduce stress. Eating right is one way to help prevent stress-related illnesses or manage their symptoms. By reacting to negative situations in a positive way, you can take control of your life and reduce your risk of illness.

Comfort Foods

People associate different foods or combinations of foods with memories they have of a certain occasion, a particular person, or a group of people. These foods fulfill an emotional need because they provide comfort, which is why these foods are referred to as comfort foods. Every person has a list of comfort foods that differs from another person's list, but, comfort foods all mean one thing— they provide us with a warm and soothing feeling inside. They also please our sense of taste, as they are delicious foods that we enjoy. Often the enjoyment of these foods stems from pleasant memories of home and family. They are foods that are familiar to us because they are part of our past.

People also enjoy certain foods when they are sick. You have probably heard of the soothing properties of chicken soup or hot lemon tea when you have a cold, or other home remedies that someone made for you while you were ill.

◆ Whether a certain food is unique to our heritage or simply a special dish that reminds us of family, foods that are familiar often provide us with comfort.

Comfort foods may also be foods that are part of your culture or heritage. They could be dishes that you had as a child only on special occasions or at a family function. They are foods you have loved and have learned to trust.

Comfort foods contribute to wellness because they provide people with something soothing after a busy day or provide some relief when they are sick. Part of what we enjoy about the foods that we turn to for comfort is that they are familiar. People find great comfort in familiarity. This may be why some people turn to certain foods when they are stressed. What are your comfort foods? What memories do they evoke for you?

Stress and Food Choices

When some people are faced with a stressful situation, they use food as therapy in the same way that other people use exercise or writing in a journal. Other people smoke excessively or drink alcohol as a way of relieving stress. It is important to recognize how stress affects your food choices and your lifestyle. The questions below will help you examine how physical and mental stress affect your food choices:

◆ Do you always resort to food as a way of managing stress?

◆ Do you find comfort in certain foods when you are tense?

◆ Do you find comfort in certain foods when you are ill?

A person who always uses food to escape problems, constantly overeats because of stress, or binges on food regularly, needs to learn how to manage stress without eating. Seeking the help of a qualified medical professional is recommended.

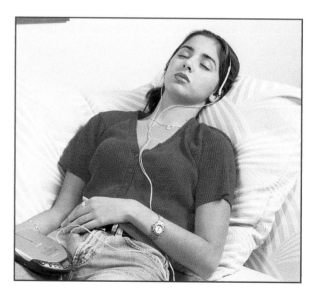

◆ Taking time to relax can help you manage the stress in your life. Record three activities that you do or could try to help reduce stress in your life.

FOR YOUR HEALTH

When the Pressure Is On

It's a vicious cycle that is all too common during the teen years: Pressures—from friends, from teachers, from family members—catch up with you. You begin to eat too much or too little, which takes a toll on your overall health and wellness.

How can you break the chain? Health experts offer a number of stress-busting solutions. Here are a few:

- Learn to manage your time. Keeping a daily planner can help. Be sure to set aside some time for you just to relax and enjoy yourself.

- If you're feeling angry or upset, listen to some calming music, read a funny book, or take your frustrations out by punching a pillow.

- Take positive action to solve a problem if you can. Share your feelings and problems with someone you trust.

- Stress can take the form of negative energy. Turn the negatives into positives. Try physical activity—run, walk, ride a bike, or clean a closet.

- Above all else, take time for eating well. Don't just grab whatever food is in sight. Include breakfast and exercise plans on your agenda for the day. Take care of your health.

Relationships with Family and Friends

Most people enjoy being social by spending time with family members and friends. When they are happy and having a good time, they feel better about themselves. The pleasure they get out of social activities contributes to their overall wellness. People are healthier if they have positive relationships with others. Try demonstrating the following behaviours and attitudes while interacting with others socially:

- Praise others and accept praise from them.

- Accept other people's differences and opinions. It's okay to agree to disagree.

- Enjoy having friendships with members of the same and opposite genders.

- Help other people and be considerate of their needs.

- Recognize that rules exist for a reason and abide by these rules.

- Manage conflict and criticism in a positive way.

- Use good communication skills.

- Remember your own values. Do not give in to peer pressure if it means going against your value system.

Source: Larson Duyff (2000).

You can make the most of your social relationships by enjoying the company of others. Healthy social relationships are a great way of enriching your life. A major part of having good relationships is communicating positively with the other person. By using good communication skills, you can change the way others act toward you in a positive way. These tips will help you communicate positively with family members and others and build solid relationships:

- **Show respect** for the other person. Remember that people need their privacy at times. Don't take this personally. Simply ask the person, "Would you like to be alone right now? Can I do anything for you?"

- **Greetings go a long way.** In the morning, it's nice to wake up to a greeting, even if it's short. A simple "Hello, did you have a good sleep?" or "Good morning" creates a positive tone for the rest of the day. On the flip side, when members arrive home at the end of the day, greet them with a "Hi," "Welcome home," or "How was your day?" Non-verbal communication, such as a hug or a high-five, is also a greeting. Try practising this with your siblings to see if it makes a difference in your relationship with them.

- **Communicate** both your positive and negative feelings. Don't let anger or frustration build. This can result in an explosion of pent-up emotions. Instead, use "I" messages when discussing your feelings. "I" messages state how you are feeling and the reason you are feeling a particular way. They don't attack or blame the other person. For example, "I get angry when you wear my clothes without asking. Some things are special and I don't want to lend them. I'd appreciate it if you would ask the next time."

- **Tell people that you appreciate their help.** Compliment them on their abilities, skills, and efforts. Ask for help as well. For example, "I need you to help me right now by keeping the noise level down so that I can study. Thank you. I appreciate your help."

- **Initiate activities.** Ask someone to spend time with you. Arrange an activity that you can do with a friend or a family member. This can mean going to a movie, walking in the park, or sharing a meal together.

- **Be a good listener.** Listen to a friend's or family member's problems. Let the person know that you are there for support. Also respond to his or her problems with empathy. You can do this by saying things such as, "That must have been difficult for you," or "I hear what you're saying." Communicate non-verbally by sitting face to face with the person and by making eye contact. Don't respond or interrupt until he or she has finished speaking.

- At times, it may be challenging to live with other family members because everyone has their own unique personality and opinions. Practising good communication skills when interacting with family members helps to reduce the stress and tension that may arise from conflicts. What communication techniques could you employ to help solve family issues in a harmonious manner?

INTERNET CONNECTS

www.mcgrawhill.ca/links/food

To learn more about developing good communication skills with your family, go to the web site above for *Food for Today, First Canadian Edition,* to see where to go next.

Attitude toward Your Body

The way you view your body also contributes to your wellness. If you are not happy or satisfied with the way you look, this will probably affect your attitude toward food and eating. This is because you will judge yourself according to how much you weigh or by the way you see yourself in the mirror. People often measure their self-esteem using the bathroom scales. Accepting yourself means accepting your whole self, including your body. Having a positive attitude about the way your body looks is part of achieving overall health and well-being. People who

have a healthy body image are more likely to treat their bodies with respect. This will contribute to the health of their mind as well as their bodies. The feature on page 440 suggests ways to respect and positively view your body as a way of achieving wellness.

Physical Activity

A major aspect of wellness is to have an active lifestyle. There are so many fun and simple ways to be active. Obesity levels in Canadian children are at an all-time high, and more than half of boys and girls in Canada are not considered active enough. Canadians are being urged to discover the benefits of physical activity by substituting some of the time they spend doing sedentary activities, such as watching television, playing computer games, or surfing the Internet, with more active pastimes, such as walking, biking, playing soccer, and so on. Developing a routine of being physically active young in life helps to reduce serious health risks later. Physical activity helps both the mind and the body.

◆ Combining social activities, such as a family birthday party, with activities that are centred around exercise, such as those at a park, is a great way to incorporate physical activity into your day. What other ways can you combine physical and social activities?

FOR YOUR HEALTH

Ten Steps for Building a Positive Body Image

1. Accept Yourself

Feeling good about yourself starts with accepting who you are and how you look. After all, healthy bodies come in all shapes and sizes. For some people, it may mean giving up the fantasy that being slimmer would lead to a happier life.

Focus on your good qualities and pass over any negatives. Feel what it's like to love your body unconditionally. Treat your body with a steaming hot shower, a massage, or a manicure.

2. Step off the Diet Roller Coaster—For Good!

Dieting brings temporary weight loss, but one-third to two-thirds of the weight is usually gained back in the first year. Almost all the weight is gained back within five years and sometimes much more.

The cycle of losing and gaining can be harmful to your health and lead to frustration, anger, and an even poorer body image. So stop dieting. Instead, eat well and enjoy being active.

3. Enjoy Eating Well

Eat for energy and for pleasure. Follow *Canada's Food Guide to Healthy Eating.* Choose more grains, pasta, legumes, fruits, and vegetables. Choose lower-fat dairy products, leaner meats, and foods prepared with little or no fat, and see how they taste.

Ask yourself if you are eating because of hunger or for some other reason. Learn to trust your body to tell you when to eat and when to stop.

Don't worry about having a chocolate once in a while. The trick is to only "indulge" once in a while! Think of balancing what you eat over the day or the week and remember that moderation is the key.

4. Enjoy Being Active

How about a noontime walk, a family hike, or a swim with friends? Physical activity lets you enjoy the outdoors and helps you deal with stress while making you feel more energetic. All this helps you feel good about yourself.

5. Create a Mental Spa

Right now, go ahead: breathe deep and relax. Think of a place where you feel peaceful, relaxed, and contented. Doesn't it feel good to slow down and let go of your responsibilities for a while? Experience the magic when you quiet your mind and let yourself enjoy the stillness.

6. Make Your Imagination Work for You

Everyone has 5000 thoughts every hour! And you can choose thoughts that encourage you or ones that drag you down. Use your imagination to practise attitudes you want in life. Act as if you like your body and feel what that's like.

(continued on the next page)

FOR YOUR HEALTH (continued)

7. Look Your Best Always

How you keep yourself shows how you feel about yourself. Wear clothes that fit and give away what you never wear. For fun, try a new hairstyle, indulge in a new pair of earrings, or buy a new hat. And remember to smile. It gives you and everyone you meet a real boost.

8. Get Support from Family and Friends

Ask for help when you need it. Organize a group of friends or find a buddy and help each other meet your goal to be the best you can be. Think of ways to create lots of fun and laughter for each other.

9. Be Thankful

To take your mind off negative thoughts, make a list of ten things that give you pleasure and keep this where you can see it. Make another list of the positive aspects of yourself—all the things your friends have complimented you on. This helps you realize how wonderful you really are.

10. Express Your Creative Self

Do things for fun—instead of competing or trying to be perfect! Have fun expressing your personality through drawing, sewing, singing, cooking, woodworking, or anything else that helps you feel happy. Know that you are unique and express it!

Source: Dietitians of Canada (n.d.).

Benefits of Activity

Being active improves your overall health. It helps to control weight, improves your fitness level, and increases your energy level. People who are inactive are at an increased risk of dying prematurely, experiencing depression, and developing heart disease, high blood pressure, osteoporosis, and colon cancer.

Why else should you be active?

◆ It helps keep your body mobile. If your muscles are not used regularly, they tend to stiffen, and movement eventually becomes painful and difficult. Regular activity can keep your muscles strong and flexible throughout life.

◆ It helps improve psychological health. Regular activity can help you feel better by reducing stress and anxiety. Studies show that active people have a brighter outlook on life.

Types of Activity

You probably already do some physical activity as part of your daily routine, such as biking or walking to school. Maybe you perform a regular chore at home, such as raking leaves or walking the dog. These are examples of **lifestyle activities**, forms of physical activity that are a normal part of your daily routine or recreation that promote good health throughout a lifetime.

◆ **Exercise includes more than running or lifting weights. Hobbies like gardening can reduce stress and increase physical activity.** Make a list of leisure activities that you enjoy. Use Internet or print resources to determine how much energy these activities expend.

A second type of activity is sports, which usually involve competition and are guided by a set of rules. When you think of sports, you may think of team sports such as football, soccer, and hockey, but other possibilities exist:

◆ **Individual sports.** Activities you can do by yourself, such as bicycling or golf. Many individual sports also are called lifetime sports because they are more likely than team sports to become part of a person's routine over a lifetime.

◆ **Partner sports.** Activities carried out with one other person. A benefit of partner sports is that they are easier to organize at a moment's notice than group events, such as a softball game.

◆ **Nature sports.** Activities in which there is some interaction with one of the forces of nature, such as surfing, rock climbing, sailing, orienteering, and swimming. A benefit of nature sports is that they can be relaxing and can promote good mental health.

✚ Safety Check

You may have heard the popular expression "No pain, no gain." Despite what you may already believe, pain during exercise is a sign that something is not right. If you experience pain, you should modify or stop the exercise you are performing.

Types of Exercise

Virtually all activities work one or more muscle groups and include some form of exercise. Some people, including teens, are beginning to rediscover so-called traditional exercises, such as doing crunches or working out with weights.

The many forms of exercise can be divided into two basic types. A well-rounded exercise program includes both.

- **Aerobic exercise** is vigorous activity in which oxygen is continuously taken in for a period of at least 20 minutes. During this time, the heart rate increases, sending more oxygen to the muscles to be used as energy to do more work. Aerobic exercises include walking, jogging, climbing stairs, bicycling, aerobic dancing, and swimming.

- **Anaerobic exercise**, which builds flexibility and endurance, involves intense bursts of activity in which the muscles work so hard that they produce energy without using oxygen. Running the 100-metre dash is an example of an anaerobic activity. Resistance training, another form of anaerobic exercise, builds muscles by requiring them to resist a force. The more work the muscles do, the stronger they become. Resistance can be provided by weights, machines, or your own body weight.

Amount and Type of Activity Recommended

Health Canada's physical-activity guidelines state that to stay healthy or to improve your health, you need 60 minutes of daily physical activity. This can be reached by adding up periods of ten minutes of continuous activity at a time, for instance, walking for ten min-

Finding Your Target Heart Range

Just as eating within a certain fat range is good for the heart, so aerobic exercise needs to be done within a prescribed range for maximum cardiovascular benefit. This range, which differs from person to person, is your *target heart range*. To find your target heart range:

1. First find your *resting heart rate* by sitting quietly for five minutes. Then take your pulse by placing two fingers (but not your thumb!) on the side of your neck just under the jawbone.

2. Subtract your age from 220.

3. Subtract your *resting heart rate* (the result of step 1) from the number you arrived at in step 2.

4. Multiply the number you arrived at in step 3 twice—first by 0.85 and again by 0.6.

5. Add each of the numbers you got in step 4 to your *resting heart rate*.

The resulting totals represent your target heart range.

---

utes, skating for ten minutes, dancing for ten minutes, and so on. Activities range in effort from being light to moderate to vigorous. The less effort you put into the activity, the more time you need to spend in total per day being active.

There are also separate guidelines for different age groups, such as children, youth, and older adults. For youth, it is recommended that you increase the time that you currently spend on physical activity every day and decrease the daily time you spend being inactive. Eventually, you should have increased the time spent on doing physical

◆ **Getting exercise by doing a physical activity that you can enjoy with friends is a way of increasing the likelihood of staying with the activity. Give other guidelines for choosing a physical activity that you will want to continue for the exercise benefits.**

activities by 90 minutes per day and decreased the same amount of time being inactive (Health Canada, n.d. "Canada's Physical...").

For all age groups, it is recommended that a combination of different types of physical activity should be done. This variety includes doing **endurance activities** that get your heart pumping and make you breathe deeper, such as dancing, tennis, or propelling a wheelchair ("wheeling"); to **flexibility activities** that help keep your joints and muscles moving, such as stretching exercises, bowling, or yoga; to **strength activities** that help keep your muscles and bones strong, such as push-ups, raking and carrying leaves, and climbing stairs. (Health Canada, n.d.; "Handbook for ..." 2002).

INTERNET CONNECTS

www.mcgrawhill.ca/links/food
To learn more about physical activity for youth 10 to 14 years of age, and for healthy active living, go to the web site above for *Food for Today, First Canadian Edition,* to see where to go next.

Getting the Activity Habit

The first step in starting an exercise or activity program should be to have a medical checkup. Once you get a clean bill of health, you can start planning.

Are you already physically active? If not, there is no better time than now to start.

Lifestyle activities taken up during the teen years are more likely to become lifelong habits than those acquired later in life. During the teen years, your energy level is also probably higher than it will be at any other period of your life.

What activity or sport should you choose? The possibilities are almost endless. Just be sure to pick something that holds your interest and that you can do—or at least learn to do—well. You're more likely to stick with an activity that you like doing and are good at. In addition, select an activity that fits in with your current lifestyle, including your schedule. Look for times in your day when you are not active. Try and fill some of this time with physical activity. Find out what programs are offered at your local community centre or through your local parks and recreation department. Based on this information, schedule activities that you know or think you may enjoy.

The benefits of staying active are well worth the time spent. Like good nutrition, regular activity is a habit that gives a lifetime of physical and emotional rewards. These all contribute to your overall health and well-being.

FOR YOUR HEALTH

Act Now!

You can easily work lifestyle physical activity into your everyday schedule. Here are some suggestions:

- Walk rather than ride to school.

- Get up to change the channel instead of using the remote.

- Play upbeat music while doing household chores.

- Plan social activities around physical ones. For example, turn a birthday party into a skating party.

- Schedule one night a week as family fitness night. This could be done as a replacement for television or movie night. Pick an outdoor activity like bicycling or skating. Check out your local community centre to find out what activities are available for the whole family.

- Look for other opportunities in your day where you could be active, such as taking the stairs instead of the elevator or escalator.

Chapter 21 Review and Activities

Summary

- To achieve overall health and well-being, you need to take responsibility for your health by getting regular physical activity; managing stress; having a positive attitude; developing good social and communication skills; and having a healthy attitude about food.

- People eat to satisfy hunger and thirst, to satisfy their appetites, and because it is enjoyable socially.

- Some people view food negatively because they are preoccupied with their appearance or weight; others eat when they experience negative feelings about themselves or a situation in their lives.

- Stress is mental or physical tension triggered by an event or situation in your life. Everyone reacts to different stresses in his or her own way.

- Stress has many negative physical and emotional side effects and needs to be managed effectively through healthy eating, physical exercise, and good communication with friends or people involved in a situation.

- Most people turn to comfort foods to fulfill an emotional need. These foods are usually associated with family, personal history, and culture.

- If a person constantly turns to food in times of stress, he or she may need to seek help to resolve personal issues that are causing the problem.

- Having positive social relationships is a good way to strengthen your sense of self-esteem and well-being.

- Having a healthy body image means treating your body with respect by eating well, being physically active, relaxing mentally, and looking your best. These enhance your sense of wellness.

- Obesity levels in children are on the rise. It is recommended that young people gradually replace some of their sedentary activities with hobbies and sports that will get their bodies moving.

Knowledge and Understanding

1. In groups of three, discuss the factors that affect overall health and well-being. Include examples of how each factor contributes to a person's health.

2. What is the difference between hunger and appetite?

3. What effect does stress have on the mind and the body?

4. What are comfort foods?

5. a) What are the benefits of being physically active?

   b) What are the risks associated with being inactive?

6. What steps will help get people into the activity habit?

Thinking and Inquiry

7. Kaley experiences a high amount of anxiety before final exams. She dreads them for weeks before they even begin. During this time, she usually eats very little, drinks a lot of coffee and cola beverages, and stays up late at night studying. As a result, Kaley feels very tired while writing an exam and usually experiences some kind of illness after exams are over.

   a) What factors may be contributing to Kaley's illness after exams?

   b) What advice would you give Kaley to help her experience less stress during exams and to help her stay healthy?

8. Evelyn and Bill have remained physically active throughout their lives. During their retirement years, they go for a brisk daily walk, swim once a week, participate in fitness classes at a local health club, and enjoy gardening in the summer months. Even though they are now well into their senior years, they remain independent by living in the same house they have lived in for most of their married life. How do you think staying physically active throughout their lives has helped them remain independent? Record your answer in your notes.

9. Explain the following in your notes:

   a) The role that good nutrition can play in helping you to cope with stress and stress-related illness.

   b) How stress may affect your food choices.

Communication

10. Write down what your usual routine is for one day during the week and for one day on the weekend. Look for times when you are inactive during the day. Think of ways in which you could incorporate physical activity into your day by replacing some inactive periods with more active ones. Revise your routine for these two days by making a schedule that incorporates more physical activity into them. Ensure that your new schedule includes a variety of moderate and vigorous activities.

11. As a class, prepare several scenarios of everyday situations that occur among family members or friends, such as getting ready for school in the morning, an issue that arises between friends, or a conflict among siblings. In groups of two, role-play the scenario. Your role-play must include the communication skills that were presented on page 438.

12. Write a one-page letter for the school paper giving advice on how to achieve wellness.

Application

13. Write a list of foods you find comforting. Explore why each of these foods makes you feel good. To help you with your analysis, answer the following questions:

   • Are these foods connected with memories of your family, friends, or culture? If so, describe the memories or occasions.

   • How often do you eat these foods?

   • How do you use these foods? As therapy for an illness, to warm you up on a cold day, or as a way of sharing a special dish with a special friend?

Food from Canadia

UNIT EXPECTATIONS

While reading this unit, you will:

- Demonstrate an understanding of our Canadian food heritage.
- Identify food supply and production industries in Canada.
- Complete an investigation of current global issues related to food using current Social Science research methods.
- Describe the relationship among family customs, traditions, and food, using current Social Science research methods.

No matter who we are or where we come from, we all have to eat to stay alive.

and Global Perspectives

OVERVIEW

In this unit you will learn about foods from Canada and around the world. The unit begins with a look at the foods of Canada's Aboriginal Peoples. Subsequent chapters will explore Canadian food sources, traditional and staple foods of Canada, and world food issues such as diversity of foods and world hunger.

Our Aboriginal Food Heritage

While reading this chapter, you will:

- Describe the diets and the characteristics of food-production methods of Aboriginal Peoples in various parts of Canada.

Many celebrations involve food. What food would you expect to be a part of this Cree celebration?

KEY TERMS

bannock
pemmican
potlatch
pow wow

In this chapter you will look at foods of Canada's Aboriginal Peoples. The chapter will begin with a look at foods that were, and, in many cases, still are traditionally used by the different Aboriginal Peoples across Canada. That will be followed by a discussion of foods and issues in Aboriginal Canadian nutrition today. Traditional recipes will also be included for you to try.

Aboriginal Canadians had many ways of adapting to and living in their environment. They taught the first European explorers how to find and store food for the harsh Canadian winters.

Canada's Original Peoples

Long before European explorers came to North America, Canada's Aboriginal Peoples lived in this country. They learned to live off the land and the fruits of the rivers, lakes, and seas. They were very resourceful people who learned to make the best use of the natural resources available to them.

In order to survive and thrive in Canada Aboriginal Peoples had to develop many skills. They were skilled hunters, learning the habits and habitats of the animals that they hunted on a regular basis. Skilled fishers, they knew

when to fish and how to manage their fishing so that the fish stocks they depended upon would not be depleted. Aboriginal people also knew a great deal about local plants, and how to use them to their best advantage. It was also essential that Aboriginal Peoples know methods of food preservation, since they needed to prepare and store large quantities of foods in order to feed themselves during the long, cold winters.

The Aboriginals Peoples of Canada belonged to distinct cultural groupings. These groupings were spread across Canada, with different peoples living in different areas of the country. There were ten different language families, and within each language family there were distinct cultural groups. Sometimes different cultural groups would have the same language. There are at least six distinct Aboriginal cultures in Canada: the Woodlands Peoples, the Plains Peoples, the Peoples of the Plateau, the Pacific Coast Peoples of the Mackenzie and Yukon River Basins, and the Inuit. Each had a different lifestyle and relied on different food sources that were native to the area in which they lived.

Woodlands Peoples

The Woodlands Peoples lived in what is now eastern Canada. They lived in the territory from the boreal forests of Newfoundland and Labrador in the east to the shores of Lake Superior in the west; from the shores of Hudson's Bay in the north, south to the Ottawa Valley and the north shore of the St. Lawrence River. The Woodlands Peoples included, among others, the Beothuk, Micmac, Maliseet, Montagnais, Naskapi, Ojibway, Algonquin, and Cree.

These groups of Aboriginal Peoples were experts in hunting, trapping, and fishing. They used the waterways in the area for travelling, and in the months when the waterways were flowing free of ice, they used lightweight canoes, which they crafted from local materials. In the winter months, Aboriginal Peoples travelled using snowshoes as they provided food for their families by trapping and ice fishing.

◆ During the winter months, the Woodlands Peoples were skilled trappers and fishers.

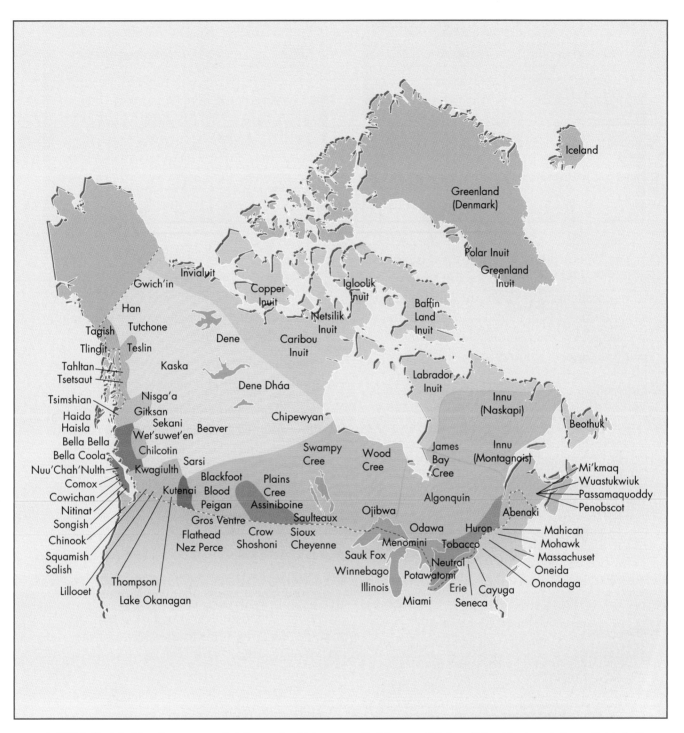

Iceland

Greenland
(Denmark)

Polar Inuit

Greenland
Inuit

Invialuit

Gwich'in

Copper
Inuit

Igloolik
Inuit

Baffin
Land
Inuit

Han

Netsilik
Inuit

Tutchone

Dene

Caribou
Inuit

Tagish

Teslin

Labrador
Inuit

Tlingit

Kaska

Innu
(Naskapi)

Tahltan

Dene Dháa

Tsetsaut

Tsimshian

Nisga'a

Chipewyan

Beothuk

Gitksan

Haida

Sekani

Haisla

Wet'suwet'en

Beaver

Swampy
Cree

Wood
Cree

James
Bay
Cree

Innu
(Montagnais)

Bella Bella

Chilcotin

Mi'kmaq

Bella Coola

Sarsi

Wuastukwiuk

Nuu'Chah'Nulth

Kwagiulth

Passamaquoddy

Comox

Kutenai

Blackfoot

Plains
Cree

Algonquin

Penobscot

Cowichan

Blood

Abenaki

Nitinat

Peigan

Assiniboine

Ojibwa

Songish

Gros Ventre

Saulteaux

Odawa

Huron

Mahican

Chinook

Flathead

Crow

Sioux

Menomini

Tobacco

Mohawk

Squamish

Nez Perce

Shoshoni

Cheyenne

Neutral

Massachuset

Salish

Sauk Fox

Potawatomi

Erie

Oneida

Thompson

Winnebago

Cayuga

Onondaga

Lillooet

Lake Okanagan

Illinois

Miami

Seneca

◆ **Which Aboriginal Peoples once occupied the area in which you now live?** Are any of their traditional foods part of your diet today?

Animals Hunted and Trapped by Woodlands Peoples	
Hunted	**Trapped**
• Moose	• Muskrat
• Deer	• Beaver
• Bear	• Hare
• Caribou	
• Geese	
• Ducks	

Fish and Sea Vegetables Eaten by Aboriginal Canadians	
Fish	**Sea Vegetables**
• Cod	• Dulse
• Lobster	• Irish Moss
• Oysters	• Kelp
• Eel	
• Atlantic salmon	
• Scallops	

The Woodlands Peoples also had access to many lakes, rivers, and streams. They were excellent fishers, and the waterways supplied them with abundant fish of many species. They rounded out their diet by using the greens and berries available to them in the wild.

Basic Fried Whitefish

1.5 kg	whitefish	3 lbs.
250 mL	cornmeal	1 cup
60 mL	bacon fat	4 tbsp.
5 mL	salt	1 tsp.
2 mL	lemon juice	½ tsp.
7 mL	Worcestershire sauce	1½ tsp.
2 mL	black pepper	½ tsp.

Mix cornmeal thoroughly with salt and pepper. Roll fish in the cornmeal mixture. Heat bacon fat in a heavy skillet. Brown fish 6 to 8 minutes on each side or until fish flakes easily with a fork. Mix lemon juice with Worcestershire sauce and pour over fish when serving.

Source: Lovesick Lake Native Women's Association. (1985). *The Rural and Native Heritage Cookbook (vol. 1.)* Burleigh Falls, ON: Lovesick Lake Aboriginal Women's Association.

Aboriginal Canadians dried meat, fish and berries, to preserve them for the winter. These dried foods, supplemented by the fresh catch of the day, supplied families with ample food for the long winter.

Woodlands Peoples who lived in Maritime regions enjoyed the bounty of the sea.

Woodlands Peoples also had agricultural skills and grew corn and potatoes; gathered wild fruits and vegetables, such as fiddle-heads (young wild ferns), blueberries, and cranberries; and cultivated and harvested a wide variety of plants, including:

- Sunflowers.
- Pears.
- Plums.
- Tomatoes.
- Squash.
- Cotton.
- Flax.
- Plants for medicinal use.

Aboriginal Peoples were also experts in plant breeding. Prior to the arrival of the Europeans, they grew over 86 varieties of corn in North America, and of those, 21 were grown in Canada. The Aboriginal Peoples taught the Europeans how to grow more than 29 different vegetables not found in Europe at the time. Among these were tomatoes, squash, cucumbers and corn.

Iroquoian tribes, who lived primarily in southern Ontario, were excellent farmers. They grew 15 different types of corn, including vari-

INTERNET CONNECTS

www.mcgrawhill.ca/links/food
To learn more about traditional Aboriginal food systems,
go to the web site above for *Food for Today,*
First Canadian Edition, to see where to go next.

ous sweet corns, popping corns, and bread or starchy corns. They also grew over 60 varieties of beans, which included broad beans and soup beans. Cucumber, squashes, melons, and sunflowers were some of their other crops. This success can be attributed to their extensive knowledge and understanding of plant breeding, planting techniques, and methods of fertilization. A good example of this is the way they grew corn, squash, and beans together. This is explained in the traditional Iroquoian story of the three sisters, told on page 456.

The Iroquoians were primarily vegetarian. They ate mainly corn, beans, and squash, and the seeds of sunflowers and squash.

They supplemented this with some fish and wild game as well as wild greens, berries, nuts, roots, and maple syrup. Corn was an important part of the diet of the Iroquoian people, and a key element of their religion and mythology. They mixed foods to create complete proteins from nuts, fruits, and vegetables, which others would get from meats. For example, crushed nuts and ground sunflower seeds were added to corn soup, thus creating a complete protein with all of the essential amino acids included. Cornbread was a staple prepared in many ways and dried for later use.

The Woodlands Peoples used a wide variety of berries in their diet. They had an annual longhouse celebration of thanksgiving on the arrival of the strawberry. This celebration was designed to thank the Creator for his gifts. Other berries eaten included raspberries, blackberries, chokecherries, and currants. Berries were eaten fresh, sweetened with maple syrup, dried, or made into a fruit drink.

Bacon Cornbread

325 mL	flour	1⅓ cups	1	egg, beaten	1
250 mL	cornmeal	1 cup	375 mL	evaporated milk	1½ cups
125 mL	sugar	½ cup	20 mL	vinegar	4 tsp.
7 mL	baking powder	1½ tsp.	75 mL	melted butter	⅓ cup
2 mL	baking soda	½ tsp.		bacon drippings	
5 mL	salt	1 tsp.	8 slices	cooked bacon, crumbled	8

Combine flour, cornmeal, sugar, baking powder, baking soda, salt and crumbled bacon. In a separate bowl combine egg, evaporated milk, vinegar, and bacon drippings. Add to flour mixture and stir just until moistened. Pour into greased 20-cm (8-inch) square pan. Bake at 160°C (350°F) for 40 to 45 minutes.
To serve: Serve warm with maple syrup.

Source: Lovesick Lake Native Women's Association. (1985).

The Three Sisters

The Three Sisters, corn, beans and squash, were a gift from the Sky-Woman. After her death, these vegetables grew from her side, as a promise to the Haudenosaunee that she would always provide food for their use. The Haudenosaunee believed that three spirit sisters guarded these three vegetables, and that the plants would not survive apart.

Corn, beans and squash were often planted in the same field. Beans climbed the corn stalks, using them for support, and the squash, which grew close to the ground, choked the weeds and kept the ground moist. Planting corn, beans, and squash together saved labour.

Most of the labour was done by women using digging sticks, and bone or stone hoes. They arranged the planting of seeds, hoeing and harvesting. Groups of men cleared the land using controlled fire and stone axes. In fall, husking bees took place at night. The women would work on husking the ears of corn and older men would tell stories for their amusement.

◆ **The Three Sisters of the Traditional Iroquoian Story — Squash, Beans, and Corn.**

Since dried and stored corn, beans, and squash guaranteed food supplies, more time could be devoted to ceremonies, hunting and trading.

Source: *Native Foods the Native Way.* (n.d.).

The Woodlands Peoples were also cultivating large orchards by the mid-1700s. They grew apples, peaches, and plums, and many areas of Southern Ontario where the Woodlands Peoples lived are still home to large orchards.

The Woodlands people collected many wild green plants to eat or for medicinal use. These included:

- Wild asparagus.
- Cattails.
- Milkweed.
- Wild dock.
- Mushrooms.
- Puffballs.
- Sorrel.
- Wild peas.
- Artichokes.
- Yellow pond lily roots.

Woodlands Peoples held the familiar maple tree in high esteem. Considered a gift from the Creator, the sap was boiled and made into maple syrup. The arrival of the sap was considered the first sign of spring, and each spring the chief would conduct a special ceremony at the base of the largest maple tree.

Since maple syrup was very important to the Woodlands Peoples, legends developed about how it came to them (see page 457).

Grandmother's Story

Many moons ago Nanabush's old grandmother took him into the forest in the spring of the year. She showed him how to make a hole in a maple tree and shape a short stick to place in the hole. The liquid that dropped onto his lips was very sweet and good. For a long time Nanabush thought about this beautiful golden liquid that was like the nectar in the summer flowers. Nanabush thought that it would be too easy for his people to gather this maple nectar so he climbed up to the top of the tree and scattered water over all the trees in the forest. Suddenly, the liquid that

dropped from the stick in the tree was not nearly as sweet. Grandmother asked him why he had done this. He explained that it would be too easy for his people and they would become lazy if he told them about this sweet nectar from the maple tree. This is why each spring the First Nations people had to go into the bush and collect buckets of sap and cut piles of wood to heat stones to boil the sap to make the sweet maple syrup and sugar.

Source: *Perfectly Natural Maple Syrup.* (n.d.).

The Plains Peoples

The people of the Plains included eight different tribes who spoke three distinct languages. In this group were Blackfoot, Blood, Peigan, Gros Venture, and the Plains Cree, all of whom belonged to the Algonkian language family. The Blackfoot, the Blood, and the Peigan all lived east of the Rocky Mountains in Central and Southern Alberta. The Tsuutina and the Chipweyan spoke Athapaskan and lived north of the Blackfoot. The Gros Venture lived east of the Blackfoot, while the Plains Cree lived in the northern part of the prairies and into Manitoba. The Assiniboine lived in what is now called Saskatchewan and Manitoba, to the south of the Cree. The Sioux, also called the Dakota, lived in scattered groups across the Canadian and American West.

The Aboriginal Peoples who lived in the central and southern plains were nomadic, following the buffalo herds. They travelled

◆ The Plains Peoples of the southern and central prairies were nomadic; they followed the buffalo herds across the plains.

with their teepees, hunting the buffalo as they moved across the plains. Plains Peoples used the buffalo for many things—food, clothing, and shelter. Buffalo meat was dried in the sun to be used throughout the winter months.

Pemmican is a mixture of powdered dried meat, fat, and sometimes berries. It was an important food for the nomadic Plains Peoples. Pemmican was made by adding melted buffalo fat and dried berries to dried, powdered buffalo meat. It was highly nutritious and lightweight, making it the ideal food to carry while travelling long distances.

Plains Peoples used a variety of berries to supplement their diet. The Saskatoon berry and choke berries were eaten by the Plains Peoples. They ate them fresh, or dried them for later use. Berries were dried in the sun; when people wanted to eat them, they would add water and cook the berries with a small amount of fat.

The Plains Peoples also ate birds and wild greens to supplement their diets. Those who lived closer to the mountains or in the northern plains ate moose and deer as well as buffalo. The Blood Peoples did not eat fish, but the people of the northern plains ate smoked and dried whitefish, pike, and pickerel.

The Plains Cree of northern Saskatchewan ate smoked and dried fish, as well as pemmican made from dried fish instead of buffalo meat. Other meats, which they ate as is or used in soup, included moose, deer, and bear, usually smoked or dried to preserve them. Bear fat was rendered and used for both cooking and as a hair treatment. The Plains Cree ate soups made from suckerheads or whitefish; sometimes fish eggs were added to bannock.

The Many Uses of the Buffalo

Skin (hides): clothing, bags and cases for carrying and storing, horseshoes, knife sheaths, drums, saddles, bridles, bedding, teepee covers, saddlebags

Sinew: threads, strings for hunting bows, games

Hair: braided into halters, stuffing for saddle pad

Tail: brush to kill flies and mosquitoes

Stomach: cooking pot; water bucket

Hoofs: boiled for glue, rattles

Bladder: food bag

Dung/chips: fuel

Bones: saddle horns, implements for dressing skins, needles, games

Meat: food (heart, liver, kidneys, and tongue were also eaten)

Ribs: arrow shafts

Shinbone: knives, fleshing tools for scraping hides

Shoulderblade: digging tool, hammer

Skull: painted and used in religious ceremonies

Bone marrow: fat, fuel for fires

Bone-ends: paint brushes

Hide from neck: warrior shields

Horn: spoons, drinking cups, ladles

Brains: for tanning skins

Teeth: necklaces

Beard: decorating a hunting bow

About Jerky

- 2 kg (4 lb.) slab of meat produces 0.5 kg (1 lb.) of jerky.
- Jerky is 75 percent protein.
- Recommended as a light source of protein for hiking and canoe trips.
- Nobody should go into the bush without it. It's a survival food and tastes delicious.
- Modern day recipes originated in the Ottawa Valley. The Aboriginal Peoples dried bear or moose meat with fat and berries pounded into it.
- Original jerky was rubbed down with salt and hung in tipis to smoke and dry.
- French explorers yanked and pulled at the meat while it was hanging to speed up the drying process, hence the translated name "jerked beef."
- To eat, simply chew like gum; keep going, the flavour improves.

How to Make Buffalo Jerky

1 pkg.	instant meat marinade	1 pkg	1 mL	onion powder	¼ tsp.
425 mL	cold water	1¾ cups	1 mL	black pepper	¼ tsp.
2 mL	liquid smoke	½ tsp.	0.75–1 kg	buffalo meat in strips	1½–2 lbs.
1 mL	garlic powder	¼ tsp.	15 cm x 3 cm x 3 cm (6"x1½" wide x ½" thick)		

Place meat in container and cover with marinade [all ingredients mixed], piercing meat slices deeply with fork. Marinate overnight in a covered container in fridge. Remove meat strips, drain slightly and place on rack making sure strips do not overlap. Place a cookie sheet under the rack in a 65–80°C (150–175°F) oven and bake 3–3½ hours. Remove from oven; cool, and store in a covered container in fridge. These larger pieces are not dried long and will be soft. Meat must be refrigerated to protect from spoilage.

Source: Lovesick Lake Native Women's Association. (1985).

Bannock is a flat, round bread originally made from oat, rye, or barley meal, and contains no leavening agent. Bannock originated in Europe, but was quickly adopted by the Aboriginal Peoples, since it was quick, easy to make, and nutritious. It became a staple food for North American Aboriginal Peoples.

My Bannock

500 mL	flour	2 cups
30 mL	baking powder	2 tbsp.
30 mL	sugar	2 tbsp.
2 pinches	salt	2 pinches
	water	

Mix with room-temperature water until mixture is dough. Form into hand-size patties. Fry in oil or bake in the oven.

Source: Armstrong, Terrance (2003).

Fruits and Berries Eaten by Aboriginal Peoples

 Crabapple	To be picked in the fall, after the first frost. White blossoms on trees turn to fruit of yellow-green. HOPA CRABAPPLE: Pink apple blossoms followed by fruit red all the way through. All recipes use the crabapple differently, so follow directions in recipe being used. Make sure to always remove blossoms and stems. Cut out any bruised or wormy parts.
 Cranberries	Gather this fruit in October. Cranberries will stay on stem all winter long. The fruit is scarlet red; the stems are trailing and wiry. There are many ways to use cranberries and they will keep for months and months. Wash well in cold water 2 or 3 times. Pack in sterilized jars and refrigerate. To freeze, lay out on tray and freeze for about 2 hours. When frozen, place in containers or in freezer bags. When needed, rinse out in cold water and use in any recipe calling for fresh cranberries.
 Elderberries	Pick in July to the middle of August. The berries are magenta-purple, almost black in colour and grow in a single cluster. During June and July, clusters of tiny, creamy-white flowers bloom. These flowers are called *elderblow*. Both the berries and the flowers are edible. The Aboriginal Peoples used the stems as well. They made maple spiles (spouts), pea-shooters, and whistles with them. The berries are best when dried. Excellent for use in pies, muffins, sauces, and juices. Always stew berries with a little sugar first; strain, and use in recipe. Elderberry has little acid and so is best mixed with other fruit. When using elderblow, simply remove any coarse stems and rinse. Use in favourite recipes.
 Huckleberries and Blueberries	HUCKLEBERRY: Is small and darker in colour than the blueberry and has a hard seed-like berry. Gather these in July and August. BLUEBERRY: These are gathered in July and August also. The fruits are blue-black in colour, with a waxy bloom and many soft seeds. PREPARATION: Simply pick through berries, removing all smashed or green berries. Place in pot filled with water and skim off whatever floats to the top. Use in favourite recipes.
 Wild raspberries	Pick in July or early August. The fruits are red (sometimes yellow) and juicy. Each is an aggregate of several tiny individual fruits. When the berries are ripe, they separate easily from the white central receptacle and fall off in a typical thimble form. Sort through berries carefully, removing any bruised or wormy fruit. Wash in cold water; drain, and let dry. Use in favourite recipes.
Stag sumac	EDIBLE BERRIES: Are hard and bright red in colour, covered with tiny hairs. POISONOUS BERRIES: Are white in colour and hang loosely. Sumacs are usually found in the same areas as the elderberry. They complement other less acidy fruits, such as the elderberry. PREPARATION: Break off fruit in whole clusters, gathering before hard rains wash out most of the acids. Put heads in a large container and cover with water. Using a potato masher, pound and stir for 10 minutes. Always strain juice through a cloth several times to remove tiny hairs.

Source: Lovesick Lake Native Women's Association. (1985).

The Aboriginal Peoples of the Plains collected many wild plant greens and roots, including:

- Pigweed.
- Dandelion.
- Cattail roots.
- Poplar cambium.
- Rosehips.
- Labrador tea.
- Mint.

Some of these were used to add to soups, others were used for tonics, and still others were brewed and used like tea.

Certain foods had symbolic value to the Plains Cree and other Aboriginal Peoples, and were an important part of celebrations and ceremonies. During the Abundance Ceremony and in the sweatlodge, dried chokeberry paste and Saskatoon berries were always served. The Flower Day Ceremony was held at the end of August, a tribute to the spirits of the ancestors, when people would burn sweetgrass and serve food at gravesides. After the graveside ceremony, the entire community would participate in a feast, where soup made with dried meat was served with herbal tea.

◆ **The Plateau Peoples relied heavily on salmon as a source of food.**

The Plateau Peoples

Six different tribes make up the Plateau Aboriginal Peoples in the interior of British Columbia: the Salish, made up of the Lillooet, the Thompson, the Shuswap and the Okanagan; the Kootenays, located in the southeast corner of the province; the three Athapaskan-speaking tribes, the Chilcotin, the Carrier, and the Tahltan, who were located in the northern part of the province; and the Tagish in the extreme north.

The Aboriginal Peoples of the Plateau relied heavily on salmon in their diet. The salmon was smoked and dried and stored in underground pits that were lined with birch bark. The Plateau Peoples made pemmican that included salmon oil and Saskatoon berries mixed in with the other ingredients. The Plateau Peoples also ate a variety of game, waterfowl, roots, greens, and berries, including Saskatoons, raspberries, blueberries, and salmonberries, as well as the inner bark of both evergreen and poplar trees.

◆ **Food was an important part of celebrations and ceremonies among Aboriginal Peoples.**

 Clover	RED: These plants should be picked in the spring. The rose-pink flowers are about 2.5 cm (1-inch) long and are formed in dense globe-shaped heads. WHITE: These flowers are white with pink bases and the leaflets are heart-shaped and formed in groups of three. The roots, stems, and flowers of the clover are all edible, but as wild flowers, should be cleaned and soaked in salted water for a couple of hours. Use in favourite recipes, as directed.
 Lamb's quarters	These plants should be gathered in spring or early summer. The leaves are diamond-shaped and toothed. A pale green flower grows at the top of the plant in clusters. The flavour of lamb's quarters suggests that of spinach and as with spinach, when preparing, do not drown; just wash leaves thoroughly and cook.
 Leeks	Leeks are best when picked in early spring. The leaves, when unrolled, are flat and lancehead-shaped. The flavour suggests that of onion with a hint of garlic. When cultivating, pull the entire plant and clean as you would a green onion (removing the outer skin). Eat raw or use for flavouring in cooking.
 Milkweed	The milkweed, when picked in early spring, is whitish-green colour. They may grow to a height of 1.7 m (5 feet). The seedpods grow from 8 to 12 cm (3 to 5 inches) long and are covered with soft spines and hair. The stalks emit a milky substance when broken. Pick stalks and seedpods and wash thoroughly. Boil for 1 minute; strain, and repeat at least 3 times. Boil once again for 10 minutes. Drain, season, and serve.
 Common morels	Common morels appear in May. In appearance they resemble long, tiny sponges and have hollow white stems. The cap has irregular pits like that of a honeycomb. To prepare, soak in cold salted water for 2 to 3 hours, before using in recipe.
 Stinging nettles	Gather these plants in spring or early summer, wearing gloves, as this plant releases an irritating oil, rich in formic acid, when touched. The stinging properties are eliminated through cooking and drying. Collect the young top leaves and steam until tender. Serve with butter. Do not overcook. They need only cook for about 1 minute. The leaves can also be dried and used for tea. The stinging nettle suggests the flavour of spinach.

(continued)

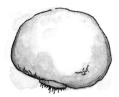

Puffballs

All puffballs with white flesh are good for eating. Avoid picking the ones that are over-ripe. These will fall apart when touched or, if cut open, the centre will appear yellow to greenish-brown. In preparing, if the puffball is small, simply scrape off the soil, rinse, and wipe with a damp cloth. Large puffballs should be peeled. The flavour suggests that of a mushroom.

Common purslane

This plant may be gathered all through the summer months. In appearance, the stems are a reddish colour, the leaves are small and paddle-shaped, and the flowers are small, 5-petaled, and yellow. When the leaves are used, first wash well then they can be used raw in salads or cooked. This is an excellent substitute for cucumbers. The seeds can be ground into meal and mixed with flour to bake breads or boiled and eaten as porridge.

Wild rose

This thorny plant grows in thickets 1.3 to 2 m (4 to 6 feet) tall and has oval-shaped, toothed leaves 5 cm to 10 cm (2 to 4 inches) long. The wild rose is a light red, 5-petaled flower. The fruit can be eaten raw and suggests the flavour of apples.

AS A SWEETENER: The seeds must be pulverized, boiled and strained through cheesecloth, to use as a syrup.

AS A TEA: Steep flowers for 5 minutes in boiling water and sweeten with wild honey.

Water cress

The plant should be gathered in the spring and summer. In appearance the leaves are shiny, dark green with rounded lobes, and the flowers are white, and grow in clusters. Water cress is popular because of its superior taste to any kind of lettuce. In taste it resembles spinach. To cultivate, snip or pinch off at the water's surface. Do not pull up the entire plant. Wash thoroughly and use in salads or as a fresh or cooked vegetable.

Wood sorrel

This plant should be picked in summer. The flower closely resembles the clover, as the flowers are compounded in 3s and close at night. Flowers vary in colour from yellow to purple and always have 5 petals. The stems are long and juicy. The wood sorrel has a delicate lemony flavour. Wash thoroughly and add to soups, stews, or mix in salads. The stems are full of moisture and make a good thirst quencher by simply nibbling.

(continued)

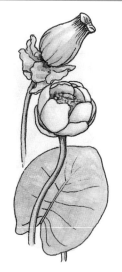

Yellow pondlily

This plant is gathered in the summer and fall, using a canoe or boat. The leaves are large and oval-shaped, with a deep curve at the heart-shaped base. The large and showy flowers are flattened globes made up of half a dozen thick golden sepals arching over the petals. The petals and sepals will rot away, leaving a large fleshy green capsule filled with numerous seeds. Eventually, the pulpy flesh of the fruit disintegrates to release these edible seeds. The taste of the seeds resembles that of the chestnut and the roots, the taste of potato.

PREPARATION: Remove outer shell that encloses the seeds; boil seeds to make gruel, or parch a hot frying pan until seeds swell and pop open slightly. These cracked seeds can be eaten as is or pounded into meal and used to make bread and porridge. The meal can also be used as a soup thickener. The seeds can be dried and stored in a cool, dark place. The potato-like roots are also delicious edibles. Their overpowering taste can be severed by boiling in two changes of water and seasoned.

Cattails

Cattails can grow to a height of 3 m (10 feet). They are found in any marshy areas.

CATTAIL SHOOTS: Are easily pulled and have a syrupy core which is eaten like celery, cooked or raw. The spikes taste similar to corn.

YELLOW POLLEN: When dried and sifted, can be used as flour, either alone or mixed half and half with conventional flour.

ROOTS and ROOTSHOOTS: Sprouts are good boiled and with butter or when cooked with meat. Cattail potatoes are found below the shoots, and when peeled can be used raw in salads or cooked as potatoes.

Dandelions

WINE: Flowers should be washed thoroughly and wine preparation begun immediately.

ROOTS: Can be used like chicory for a non-caffeinated coffee substitute.

The cooked leaves suggest a flavour of spinach. They should be picked before the flowers appear; otherwise they have to be boiled twice to remove the bitterness from them.

Fiddleheads

Fiddleheads gain their name because of their shape. The best time to cultivate this plant is before it reaches a height of approximately 15 cm (6 inches) and appears still curled and rusty in colour. When picking, pick close to the root. To prepare, remove rusty-coloured skin and wash in warm water. Let stand in cold water for 30 minutes.

Serving suggestions: Steam or sauté fiddleheads and serve with butter and bacon. The plant suggests a flavour of broccoli or asparagus.

Source: Lovesick Lake Native Women's Association. (1985).

◆ Due to the richness of resources in the area, the Aboriginal Peoples of the Pacific Coast were able to build permanent settlements.

Pacific Coast Aboriginal Peoples

The peoples of the Pacific Coast spoke five distinct languages. They included the Haida of the Queen Charlotte Islands; the Tsimshian, who lived along the coast of the mainland across from the Haida; the Nootka, who lived on the west coast of Vancouver Island; the Salish, who lived on the east coast of Vancouver Island on the Columbia River; and the Bella Coola (Nuxalk) and Kwakiutl, who lived along the central coastline of the mainland.

The peoples of the Pacific Coast had access to plentiful supplies of food that were right on their doorstep; this is why they did not have to live a nomadic life. The Pacific Coast Peoples were able to develop permanent settlements and sophisticated societies as a result.

The peoples of the Pacific Coast were excellent fishers and used a variety of methods to catch fish: nets, harpoons, and trolling.

They caught salmon, herring, flounder, and halibut, and did not waste any part of the fish. Salmon was most often smoked, dried, and then stored in cedar boxes.

The Pacific Coast Peoples are still famous for their traditionally prepared barbequed salmon. First, they soak the salmon in sea water for a short time, then dry it in the sun for about an hour. After that, it is stretched and threaded onto cedar sticks, which are set upright around a fire for two to three hours.

The Bella Coola People depended on the ooligan, a saltwater smelt that was highly valued for its oil. The oil was used for both flavour and as a preservative. The ooligan run began toward the end of March or early April. The Bella Coola People fermented the ooligan for seven to ten days, after which they would cook them and separate out the grease, which was then stored for later use. The Bella Coola People also ate a variety of shellfish, including mussels, clams, crab, and octopus. Once a year, they also hunted seal and preserved it with salt for use throughout the year.

The women of the Pacific Coast collected a variety of wild greens in the spring. Cow parsnip, which they ate raw or steamed, with ooligan grease, was an important part of their diet. Other wild greens and roots eaten by the Pacific Coast Peoples included:

◆ Sheep sorrel.
◆ Lamb's quarters.
◆ Shoots from salmonberries.
◆ Fireweed.
◆ Thimbleberries.
◆ Cama bulbs.
◆ Clobber.
◆ Silverweed.
◆ Riceroot.
◆ Fern.
◆ Seaweed.
◆ Cottonwood
◆ Mushrooms.

These were usually dried and stored for later use as flavouring in soups and stews.

The Bella Coola People cultivated berry patches; they burned trees and undergrowth

Wild Raspberry Bread Pudding

2.5 mL	wild raspberries, cleaned, dried	10 cups
500 mL	sugar	2 cups
12	slices homemade white bread	12
500 mL	heavy cream	2 cups

In a large bowl, sprinkle sugar over raspberries. Toss berries very lightly until all sugar has dissolved. Cover and set aside. Cut slices of bread to fit the bottom of a deep 10 cm (2 quart) bowl. Trim 8 or 9 slices of bread into wedges about 7.5 cm (4 inches) at the top and 1 cm (3 inches) across the bottom. Line sides of bowl with wedges, overlapping each one by about ½ inch. Pour fruit into the bowl and cover top completely with the rest of bread. Cover top of bowl with a flat plate and place a weight on top of plate. Place in refrigerator for at least 12 hours. Remove mold by quickly inverting it onto a chilled serving plate. The mold should slide out easily. Whip cream in a large chilled bowl until it hold its shape. With a spatula, cover mold on the outside and top. Serve chilled.

Source: Lovesick Lake Native Women's Association. (1985).

along the mountainside in order to make room for the bushes. They grew many varieties including raspberries, salmonberries, blueberries, huckleberries, soapberries, and elderberries. The berries were sun-dried or smoked, then formed into cakes, which were wrapped in leaves and stored in either cedar boxes or in ooligan grease.

Aboriginal Peoples of the Mackenzie and Yukon River Basins

There were 12 peoples who lived in the Mackenzie and Yukon River Basins; their language family was the Athapaskan Dene. The largest tribe in the area was the Chipewyan Dene, who lived in the area north of the Churchill River and west to Great Slave Lake. The Beaver People lived in the Peace River Valley, south and west of the Chipewyan.

The Slaveys Dene lived in the area west of Great Slave Lake as far as the Mackenzie River. Between the eastern end of Great Slave Lake and Great Bear Lake lived the Yellowknife, and the Dogrib lived to the southwest of the Yellowknife. Northwest of the Dogrib lived the Hare Dene. The Kutchen primarily inhabited the interior of Yukon, while the southern part of Yukon was inhabited by the Han, Tutchone, the Kaska, and the Mountain. The Sekani Dene lived on the eastern slopes of the Rocky Mountains.

The Aboriginal Peoples of this area were often faced with scarce food supplies. As a result, they had to adopt a nomadic way of life, following animals as they migrated. These Aboriginal Peoples followed moose, caribou, and mountain sheep, depending on where they lived. The northern groups were dependent upon caribou and the wood buffalo, while some peoples were more dependent on small game and fish. The Chipewyan Dene ate dried smoked moose, caribou, and

Rabbit Soup

	leftover rabbit meat and bones		1 mL	thyme	¼ tsp.
1	soup bone	1	1	bay leaf	1
125 g	salt pork	¼ lb.	1 L	chicken broth	4 cups
3	carrots, sliced	3	250 mL	potatoes, diced	1 cup
1	onion, quartered	1	125 mL	celery, diced	½ cup
1	clove garlic	1	125 mL	carrots, diced	½ cup
1 mL	parsley	¼ tsp.		salt and pepper	

Remove all meat from rabbit bones and set aside. In a kettle, combine bones and soup bones and salt pork. Add carrots, onion, garlic, parsley, thyme and bay leaf. Cover with water and simmer until almost dry. Add chicken broth and simmer 15 minutes. Strain broth and adjust the seasoning to taste. Add potatoes and simmer until tender. Add celery and carrots and cook 20 minutes longer. Then, add rabbit meat. Heat thoroughly and serve.

Source: Lovesick Lake Native Women's Association (1985).

buffalo. They also consumed whitefish, and many of these foods are still popular with the Chipewyan today. They also enjoy soups made with duck or rabbit.

Hunters travelled great distances in search of game. They travelled by birchbark canoe in the summer months when there was no ice on lakes and rivers; in the winter, they used dogsleds and snowshoes.

Game was held in high esteem, and there were very strict rules and rituals surrounding the killing and butchering of game. Bears were given great respect by the more northern tribes, and in the west, the lynx, the wolf, and the wolverine were of special ceremonial significance.

The Inuit Peoples

The Inuit Peoples occupy the Arctic region of Canada, from Labrador in the east to Yukon in the west. The Arctic region of Canada has

◆ The wolf played a significant part in the life and the ceremonies of the Aboriginal Peoples of the Mackenzie and Yukon River Basins.

very severe weather and difficult living conditions: winter and summer seasons are extreme opposites. The winters are cold, and the days are long and dark. In the summer, the sun never sets. A self-sufficient people, the Inuit managed to adapt to these severe conditions and thrive in a difficult land.

◆ **The Inuit lived in challenging conditions and learned to be self-sufficient.**

INTERNET CONNECTS

www.mcgrawhill.ca/links/food
To learn more about the diet of the Inuit Peoples,
go to the web site above for *Food for Today,
First Canadian Edition*, to see where to go next.

In the winter months, the Inuit hunt marine mammals such as seals, whales, and walrus. In the summer months, they travel inland in search of food, fishing, and hunting. They hunted caribou and birds to supplement their winter diet, and collected berries and wild greens. Seal or caribou were eaten raw, dried, or frozen.

The Inuit could eat only foods that were available in their region of the country. The Mackenzie Inuit had access to a large supply of meat and enjoyed caribou, musk-oxen, seal, whale, beaver, and muskrat on a regular basis. The Copper Inuit lived in the eastern Arctic, where in the summer they hunted caribou and musk-oxen, and in the winter they hunted seal. The Netsilik Inuit lived in

an icebound area of the eastern Arctic and were skilled hunters of marine animals. In the northern area of Baffin Island lived the Igloolik, who enjoyed walrus during the winter, and travelled inland in the summer in search of caribou and game birds. The Ungava and Labrador Inuit lived near the Atlantic Ocean. They hunted whale, seal, caribou, partridge, ducks, geese, and other small animals. They also fished off the coast of the Atlantic for salmon, cod, smelt, char, and trout.

Traditions of Aboriginal Peoples of Canada

Traditional attitudes toward health among Aboriginal Peoples have always embraced a wellness perspective. They teach that "health is not just freedom from disease but a healthy body, mind and spirit" (Government of Canada, 1994). Aboriginal Peoples strive for balance in the physical, emotional, intellectual, and spiritual health of themselves and others, and between themselves and the environment. Aboriginal Peoples learned to consume foods in amounts that provide their bodies with the nutrients they need.

Aboriginal Peoples did not waste food. Plants and animals were considered sacred— each part was used and very little waste was left. They believed that their Creator supplied the food, and it was their responsibility to share the food with others. The Iroquois, for example, planted enough crops to be able to feed another tribe, in case its crops failed. Aboriginal Peoples shared food, and would not see someone go hungry while they ate. Their spirit of hospitality was and is central to their culture, and they share this spirit through ceremonies like the potlatch and the **pow wow**. A **potlatch** is a ceremonial feast of the peoples of the northwest Pacific Coast. Traditionally, the host distributes lavish gifts to his guests, or sometimes destroys his own property to demonstrate his wealth and generosity. This is done with the expectation of eventual reciprocation. A **pow wow** is a large social gathering of peoples that usually includes competitive dancing and singing. Both of these were and are important social ceremonies to Aboriginal Peoples, and many celebrations included food.

Many legends of Canadian Aboriginal Peoples involved food. Some were about growing food, and the proper ways to plant and harvest it. Others involved fish and game, and how to slaughter and store the meat properly. Still other legends were about eating certain foods. When you study these legends, you can see how they guided food habits in order to provide a balanced, nutritious diet for the many different Aboriginal Peoples.

Foods and Nutrition among Aboriginal Peoples Today

Many of the traditional foods of Canada's Aboriginal Peoples are no longer as plentiful as they were in the past. Lifestyles have changed, and urban development has caused the movement of much of the game hunted by Aboriginal Peoples to more remote areas of the country.

As for everyone in Canada, changes in technology and access to food have had an impact on the food habits of Aboriginal Peoples. Food can now be stored without drying, in freezers, and fresh foods can be purchased year-round. Traditional foods are not as readily available as commercial food products are today. The introduction of high energy, low nutrient foods into the diets of Aboriginal Peoples has caused some nutritional and dental problems in the population.

There is an increased awareness of the health issues that arise from poor eating habits. The Government of Canada focusses on nutritional education for all Canadians and provides information to health care workers and individual citizens about nutrition. One of the most popular sources of information is *Canada's Food Guide to Healthy Eating*. Since many of the foods shown in this guide are not traditional foods of Aboriginal Peoples, special food guides based on more familiar, traditional foods have been developed. These allow Aboriginal Peoples to eat healthy diets that include traditional foods. Some of these food guides are a *B.C. Coastal and Interior Food Guide*, a *Cree-Ojibway Food Guide,* and an *Atikamekw/Montagnais Food Guide*.

The government has also developed recommended intakes of foods. It has created similar charts for traditional foods, and these are available to health care workers and Aboriginal Peoples to help them develop a better understanding of the contributions these foods make to their overall health.

Changing Food Habits and Nutritional Concerns

In many cases, Aboriginal Peoples no longer have easy access to their traditional foods. Lifestyles have changed and few continue to live a nomadic lifestyle. Large urban centres and towns now occupy land that used to be hunting grounds so Aboriginal Peoples have to travel further in order to hunt and fish for the foods they need.

A Food Guide for Aboriginal Peoples of Canada

EAT FOODS FROM EACH GROUP EVERY DAY FOR HEALTH

MILK & MILK SUBSTITUTES

MEAT & MEAT SUBSTITUTES

BANNOCK, BREADS & CEREALS

VEGETABLES, FRUITS & BERRIES

INTERNET CONNECTS

www.mcgrawhill.ca/links/food

To learn more about how supplies are provided to Aboriginal Peoples in the Far North, go to the web site above for *Food for Today, First Canadian Edition,* to see where to go next.

Changes in the food habits of Canadian Aboriginal Peoples have had an impact on their overall health. A traditional diet did not include candy, pop, and other snack foods high in energy and low in nutrition. Some of these changes have led to nutrition-related health problems.

Obesity

Obesity was not common among early Aboriginal Peoples, and was frowned upon. Overeating was considered bad, and in the Iroquoian community it was considered against religious teachings. Aboriginal Canadians were careful not to waste, and overeating was considered wasteful. The traditional diet contained mainly foods with high nutritional value.

Obesity is a major health issue among Aboriginal Peoples today, and a major risk factor for both diabetes and heart disease. Concerns about obesity and its long-term health consequences are being addressed by the government.

Diabetes Mellitus

Diabetes mellitus is the most common form of diabetes within the adult population of Canada. This disease begins gradually, usually after the age of 40, and is more common in families with a history of diabetes, and among people who are inactive and overweight. Before 1950, there were very few cases of diabetes in the Aboriginal Canadian population. Now it is a serious health issue—there is a higher incidence of diabetes among Aboriginal Peoples than in the general Canadian population.

The Canadian Diabetes Association is working to help individuals at risk for diabetes change their lifestyles to reduce their chances of getting diabetes. Adopting healthier eating and exercise habits reduces the risks for most people.

Cardiovascular Disease

Heart disease is a leading cause of death among Aboriginal Peoples. In these populations it is the second leading cause of death, while in the Inuit population it is the third leading cause of death. According to 1997 statistics from Statistics Canada, diseases of the heart are the second leading cause of death in the general Canadian population. The Aboriginal Peoples populations suffer from coronary heart disease, stroke, high blood pressure, and hardening of the arteries. Their risk of coronary heart disease and stroke is also higher than in the general Canadian population.

The risk factors for heart disease include family history and stress. Other important risk factors are in lifestyle—a poor diet, high in fat and sugar, little or no exercise on a regular basis, and smoking all increase the risk of heart disease. These factors, plus obesity, have been linked to high levels of heart disease and diabetes among Canada's Aboriginal Peoples.

There is also concern that with the change from a traditional diet of wild game, sea mammals, and fish, Aboriginal Canadians are now consuming more fat. Some store-bought meats, such as luncheon meats, contain more fat than the meats consumed in a traditional diet. There is also a concern that the fat purchased in stores contains less of the healthy fatty acids than those foods generally consumed in a traditional diet.

A reduction in the amount of high-fibre foods consumed is another concern. In the traditional diet, many wild greens were consumed, and these foods were high in fibre. Like the general Canadian population, Aboriginal Canadians are now eating more refined white flour and sugar and less of the raw foods that are higher in fibre.

The traditional diet did not include table salt. Aboriginal Peoples did use forms of salt, such as dried sea salt, but they did not use the refined table salt commonly used today. The traditional salts are believed to have contributed trace minerals such as iron, manganese, zinc, and copper to the traditional diet. It is estimated that Aboriginal Canadians are eating about ten times more salt than is necessary for good health. This salt comes in the form of added table salt, as well as in processed foods. Salt consumption is linked to both heart disease and high blood pressure.

Dental Disease

When the first Europeans came to North America, they remarked on the health of the teeth of the Aboriginal Peoples. The traditional Aboriginal diet was low in refined carbohydrates and high in protein. The diet of the Aboriginal Canadian population today is much higher in refined carbohydrates, and so a common health problem is dental disease. Many Aboriginal Canadians suffer from tooth decay, "baby bottle" caries, periodontal or gum disease, and other dental problems caused by missing teeth.

When the natural bacteria in our mouths act on the sugars we eat, an acid is formed. This acid attacks the enamel on our teeth and dissolves it, causing a cavity. Tooth decay is caused in part by frequent consumption of sugar.

"Baby bottle" caries occur when infants are given liquids in a bottle at bedtime, and are allowed to fall asleep with the bottle in their mouths. This allows the liquid to stay in their mouths, providing an ideal environment for bacteria to grow in and cause tooth decay.

Cost of Food

Only in the most northern areas of Canada do Aboriginal Canadians still have access to all of the foods in their traditional diet. The southern, more urban areas of the country, developed where traditional hunting and fishing grounds once were. The traditional methods of gathering food no longer exist. Large game has migrated north, and it costs more to travel in order to hunt. Many Aboriginal Peoples who traditionally relied on the hunt for their meat are now purchasing it in grocery stores.

Many Aboriginal Peoples live in areas remote from food distribution centres in cities and towns. When food is transported to these remote communities, it arrives with a higher price due to transportation and distribution costs. This increases the cost of providing food for the family, and a study done in Saskatchewan found that a nutritious basket of food cost two to three times more in the North than in the South. This makes it difficult to provide nutritious choices to families located in these isolated communities. Less expensive food choices tend to be of lower nutritional value, and eating them can add to the existing problems of a poorly balanced diet.

Aboriginal communities have worked together to find ways to reduce the costs of food to remote areas. Some make special arrangements with the local grocery store; some have formed co-operatives to purchase foods; and others have returned to traditional foods locally available. As times have changed so have the diets and lifestyles of Aboriginal Peoples, who look to the past for guidance and understanding of the importance of good nutrition to overall health, and work to ensure the best health for present and future generations.

INTERNET CONNECTS

www.mcgrawhill.ca/links/food
To learn more about projects to improve food security in the North, go to the web site above for *Food for Today, First Canadian Edition,* to see where to go next.

Canadian Aboriginal Chef

Bertha Skye

What education is required for your job?

- I am a self-taught chef with no formal training. I began cooking when I was 17 and sought opportunities to learn from those around me.
- To become a chef now, you need a chef's training program at a community college and an internship in a restaurant to gain practical experience.

What skills does a person need to be able to do your job?

- A love of food.
- Cooking skills, organizational skills, and creativity.
- Willingness to work hard, be flexible, and improvise.

What do you like most about your job?

I love good food and feel privileged to get paid for doing what I love. The freedom to choose what I want to do is a real plus. I also loved travelling. One of the highlights of my travels was an opportunity to cook Aboriginal foods for an event at the Canadian embassy in Germany. Wherever I travelled, I particularly enjoyed observing how people in different countries kept up their culture.

What other jobs/job titles have you had in the past?

Although I am "officially" retired as a chef, I still do consulting and catering. My son is also a chef and sometimes I assist and guide him in the preparation of Aboriginal food. I also provide workshops about healthy eating for Canadian Aboriginal youth. And because I love children, I provide childcare when I can. I have also worked as a counsellor in a women's shelter and a halfway house. I was a homemaker for many years as well. I have learned to make crafts, moccasins, and do beadwork.

What advice would you give a person who is considering a career as a chef?

Get an education. Complete high school and enrol in a chef's program at a community college. Seek out opportunities to further your education in this field.

Comment on what you see as important issues/trends in food and nutrition.

I am very concerned about the health of Aboriginal youth. We are seeing an increase in diabetes and obesity, which are secondary to poor eating habits and lack of exercise. Young people need to eat more fruit and vegetables and less junk food.

Chapter 22   Review and Activities

Summary

◆ Long before the arrival of Europeans, Aboriginal Peoples in Canada had learned to make the best use of the natural resources available.

◆ Aboriginal Canadians were skilled hunters and had extensive knowledge of plants for food or for use as medicine.

◆ Each of the distinct Aboriginal cultures had its own lifestyle and relied on different food sources that were native to the area in which they lived.

◆ Aboriginal traditional attitudes strive for balance in the physical, emotional, intellectual and spiritual health.

◆ Just as the rest of Canadians, changes in technology and access to foods have had an impact on foods habits of Aboriginal Canadians.

◆ Increased awareness of health issues among Aboriginal Peoples has led to programs that address nutritional needs and proper access to healthier foods.

Knowledge and Understanding

1. Describe three ways in which Aboriginal Peoples prepared foods for storage for the winter.

2. What is pemmican? How was it important to the early Aboriginal Peoples?

3. Define *pow wow* and *potlatch*. What do they have in common?

Thinking and Inquiry

4. What foods were common to all of the Aboriginal Peoples in Canada? Which of those are still eaten commonly today?

5. Many of the animals that Aboriginal Peoples hunted were considered sacred and included in special occasions and religious ceremonies. Give two examples. Why did the Aboriginal Peoples hold these animals in such high regard?

6. What are the three major nutrition-related health concerns of Aboriginal Peoples? How did changing eating patterns and eating habits have an impact on these issues?

7. How does the cost of food in remote communities compromise the health of the people who live there?

8. Compare the foods identified in *A Food Guide for Aboriginal Peoples of Canada* (see page 470) with *Canada's Food Guide to Healthy Eating* (see page 271). Make a chart like the one on the next page showing the differences and similarities between the two.

Food Group	A Food Guide for Aboriginal Peoples	Canada's Food Guide to Healthy Eating
meat	bear	beef

Communication

9. Choose one of the health issues related to nutrition discussed in this chapter. Create a pamphlet that could be distributed by public health officials to help people understand what impact nutrition has on their health.

Application

10. Make a comparison chart like the one below to show the different types of foods eaten by two of the different groups of Aboriginal Peoples in Canada. Use the headings of *Canada's Food Guide.*

Write a one-page summary indicating how geographic location influenced the types of food eaten by the different groups.

Food Group	Woodlands	Plateau
Meat		
Grains		

Canada's Regional Foods

While reading this chapter, you will:

- Determine the contribution of cultural and regional foods in the development of our Canadian food heritage and culture.

- Use a variety of tools such as books or search engines on the Internet to research and report on the emergence of a new Canadian cuisine.

- Select and use regional and seasonal foods to plan and produce a Canadian food product or meal.

Canadian regional foods vary with the geography of the land.

KEY TERMS

cabanes au sucre
chuck wagon
holubtsi
kolach
platz
pluma moos
tourtière

The foods of Canada reflect our country's natural resources and rich diversity of cultures. These natural resources include wild rice, beef, and more than 150 species of fish and shellfish. Apples and peaches lead fruit production. In this chapter, Canada's regional foods will be discussed, followed by a look at how regional differences in land and culture have had an impact on the foods commonly eaten in different parts of the country. This will lead to an understanding of how these factors combined to make a cuisine that is uniquely Canadian. Recipes are included so you can sample a taste of Canada.

Food in all its cultural and regional variety is celebrated all across this country. What kinds of cultural festivals happen in your area?

Origins of Canadian Foods

Canada is populated by people of many nationalities, who have retained their cultural identities. Because these different cultural groups settled in different areas of the country, the regional foods of Canada are influenced by the groups in each region. Each group brought favourite, traditional, and commonly eaten foods from their home country. These foods then became common in the areas in which the newcomers settled.

Another influence on regional foods is the natural resources of each area. Both coasts of Canada give the Canadians who live there access to the oceans' bounty. Other areas of Canada offer ideal growing conditions for many fruits and vegetables; two examples are the Okanagan Valley in British Columbia and the Niagara Peninsula in Ontario. Still other regions have natural resources that are found nowhere else in Canada, for example maple trees (the source of maple syrup) in New Brunswick, Nova Scotia, Quebec, and Ontario. These natural resources have shaped the regional foods in all areas of the country.

◆ When the first settlers came to Canada they had to learn to adapt to new foods and new methods of food preparation. Do you like to try new foods and cooking methods?

Early Foods

When the first Europeans came to Canada they brought their own food traditions and methods of food preparation with them. They had to adapt these to both the land and the natural resources available to them in Canada. The equipment and utensils for preparing foods back home were not available in this country, and much of the produce settlers were used to eating simply was not found in Canada; so settlers had to adapt and learn to substitute what they had.

Early Canadians learned from Aboriginal Peoples who lived in the areas where they settled. Without the help of Aboriginal Peoples, many of the early settlers would not have survived the extremes of the Canadian climate. Settlers learned methods of cooking and storing foods in order to have them during the long Canadian winters. Aboriginal Peoples taught the settlers which of the wild greens were safe to eat, and how to prepare them. Settlers learned how to grow and harvest the produce of their new land and about the fish and wild game that would support them through their early years in Canada. The settlers in turn passed on some of their culture to Aboriginal Peoples; for example, bannock, a staple of many Aboriginal Peoples, was originally a Scottish form of bread.

Scallop Chowder

2	onions, sliced	2
60 mL	butter	4 tbsp.
500 mL	scallops	2 cups
500 mL	boiling water	2 cups
250 mL	diced potatoes	1 cup
1 L	scalded milk	4 cups
	salt and pepper	

Sauté onions in butter. Remove onions from pan. Cut up scallops and sauté in butter. Add onions, scallops, and potatoes to boiling water. Simmer 30 minutes. Add scalded milk and simmer 15 minutes more. Add seasoning. Serves 5.

Source: McCann, Edna. (1996). *The Canadian Heritage Cookbook.* Scarborough, ON, Prentice Hall Canada.

A traditional dish of the early settlers was fish stew. Today we call this chowder. The name chowder is believed to come from the French word *chaudière*, which was a large iron cooking pot used in the early days. Chowder is believed to be French and Aboriginal in origin.

The early settlers had to adapt to very harsh conditions, without all of the support and equipment they were used to in their home country. Since they often had to cook meals in only one pot, over an open fire, settlers often made stews and thick soups. By making dishes like these, they could use fewer ingredients to feed more people. It was important to conserve food, especially during the long winter months.

Fresh fruits and vegetables were not available in winter, and stored root vegetables, such as potatoes and carrots, were used with care. Potatoes were a staple of the early settlers because they stored well and provided families with a good quality food supply over the winter. Potatoes were actually used for more than just food—they were grated and squeezed to produce starch for laundry, to make yeast for breads, and even to soothe headaches. Apples also winter well, and could be used year-round. In the early days, apples were Canada's most important fruit crop; they were grown in the Annapolis Valley in Nova Scotia and the Okanagan Valley in British Columbia. Peaches, grown in Ontario and British Columbia, were Canada's largest soft tree fruit crop, and rhubarb, which grows in the spring, was a popular springtime dish across the country.

A wide variety of berries grows naturally in Canada, and these were harvested and eaten by the early settlers. As well as jam, berries can be used to make pies, puddings, cobblers, and crumbles. Wild berries were very important to the first settlers: blueberries were popular in the Atlantic Provinces, Québec,

Mother McCann's Rhubarb and Raspberry Jam

1 L	rhubarb	4 cups
750 mL	raspberries	3 cups
1 L	sugar	4 cups

Put rhubarb in a pot with water to cover. Bring water to a boil and simmer until rhubarb is soft. Drain, rinse and drain again. Add raspberries and bring to a boil. Add sugar and cook until thickened, stirring all the time. Seal in sterilized sealer jars. Yields about 6 pints.

Source: McCann, Edna. (1996).

and Ontario; on the prairies, Saskatoon berries were a favourite; and other berries such as strawberries, elderberries, and raspberries were enjoyed as well.

Canada is well known for its maple syrup, which is produced only in New Brunswick, Nova Scotia, Québec, and Ontario, as well as the northeastern United States. For many early settlers, maple syrup and maple sugar were the only sweeteners available, and after the sugar was processed in the spring, it was stockpiled for use throughout the year. A favourite dessert, known as sugar pie, *tarte au sucre* in French, was made with maple syrup by the early settlers in Québec, and is still enjoyed today.

Ultimate Maple Syrup Pie

2	eggs	2
250 mL	brown sugar	1 cup
250 mL	whipping cream (35%)	1 cup
125 mL	maple syrup	½ cup
2 mL	vanilla	½ tsp.
1	9-inch (23-cm) pie shell baked and cooled	
	lightly sweetened whipped cream and/or toasted walnuts for garnish	

In a medium bowl, beat eggs lightly. Whisk in brown sugar, cream, maple syrup and vanilla. Beat long enough to dissolve the sugar crystals. Pour filling into pie shell and bake in preheated 180°C (350°F) oven 40 to 45 minutes or until centre is just becoming firm. Let cool before serving. Serve topped with whipped cream and sprinkled with toasted walnuts. Makes 8 servings.

Source: Stewart, Anita (2000).

Canada's Food Heritage

Since the early European settlers people have come to Canada from all over the world. Each group has brought traditions, and these have combined to create our Canadian food heritage. In Canada, we are lucky to be able to experience such a wide variety of foods— some that have been adapted from those of other countries, and others that are particular to a specific region of Canada.

Regional Foods of Canada

The Atlantic Provinces

Fish and seafood are the most important foods of this region. Cod has been the centre of the Newfoundland economy since the 1500s. Salt cod has helped many Newfoundlanders get through long hard winters.

◆ Those who live in Atlantic Canada have access to the bounty of the sea, fresh seafood at your doorstep. What challenges are Atlantic fishers facing today?

INTERNET CONNECTS

www.mcgrawhill.ca/links/food
To learn more about the culture and food of Newfoundland, go to the web site above for *Food for Today, First Canadian Edition,* to see where to go next.

A traditional dish in Newfoundland is fish 'n' brewis, which is soaked salted fish combined with soaked hard bread, all topped with scrunchions — bits of crisp, fried salt pork. Over the years, Newfoundlanders have had to replace cod fishing with other types of fishing, including tuna, herring, char, mackerel, turbot, ocean perch, lumpfish or roe, and varieties of shellfish such as snow crab, clams, shrimp, lobster, whelk, sea cucumber, and sea urchins. Scallops are also harvested from the seabed.

Atlantic Canada is especially famous for its shellfish, and lobster fests are put on by local groups on many summer weekends. Tourists flock to these festivals in order to experience real maritime cooking and culture. In New Brunswick, people fish for smelt and trout, while Nova Scotians fish for cod, eel, mackerel, and herring. Prince Edward Island offers lobster, as well as blue mussels, Malpeque oysters, clams, scallops, and fresh fish.

Fresh fruits and vegetables are grown locally, but the growing season is short because of the long periods of cold weather. Many different types of berries grow in the Atlantic Provinces. Partridgeberries (also known as mountain cranberries), rock cranberries, and lingonberries are a few examples. Blueberries are also an important crop. Maple syrup is an important product for both Nova Scotia and New Brunswick. New Brunswick is also famous for its fiddleheads, which are exported around the world. Fiddleheads are the young fronds of the ostrich fern, available in May and June and also enjoyed by Aboriginal Peoples in the region. When cooked, fiddleheads have a taste similar to asparagus. Potatoes are raised in Prince Edward Island and New Brunswick, showing the influence of the Irish, who settled the region.

Many other cultural groups have added to the cuisine of the Atlantic Provinces. In New Brunswick there is the influence of the early English settlers, who migrated north from the United States. Their diet is traditionally British. A traditional Saturday night meal in the Atlantic Provinces is homemade baked beans and steamed brown bread.

INTERNET CONNECTS

www.mcgrawhill.ca/links/food
To learn more about regional cuisine in Canada, go to the web site above for *Food for Today, First Canadian Edition*, to see where to go next.

Nova Scotia is home to a large French-speaking population, who are known as Acadians, after the name the French first gave to the area, *Acadie*. Acadian foods have a distinctive style, almost medieval. They are not fancy foods, just plain cooking, such as stews and soups. One popular dish is called *râpure*, a baked casserole made from grated potatoes, onions, and meat. Another favourite is *poutine*, which means pudding, and comes in various forms. This is not the same as the *poutine* served today—French fries, gravy, and cheese curds. Other popular meals include rich pea soup and a variation on *râpure*, called *râpée* pie, consisting of layers of cooked poultry and puréed potatoes.

Nova Scotia is also home to a large group of people of Scottish descent. They first arrived in Cape Breton in 1621. The Scottish heritage is seen in many traditional dishes that include oats. There is even a traditional wedding dish that is made with oatmeal, whipping cream, and sugar. Another dish, *colcannon*, came from Scotland and Ireland, and is made by mashing together potatoes, turnips, and cabbage.

Fiddleheads with Lemon Butter

500 g	fiddleheads	1 lb.
30 mL	melted butter	2 tbsp.
	juice of I lemon	
	salt and pepper to taste	

Wash the fiddleheads carefully so as not to break them. Place washed fiddleheads in boiling water. Boil 5–6 minutes or until tender. Drain. Place in serving dish. On the stovetop (or in a microwave oven) melt butter. Squeeze the juice of 1 lemon into the melted butter.

Pour lemon butter over the fiddleheads and toss them lightly until they are covered. Add salt and pepper to taste. Serve immediately.

Fiddleheads are an excellent addition to a salad. To use: wash fiddleheads, then place in boiling, lightly salted water. Cook until tender. Drain. Refrigerate until chilled. They add a flavour of broccoli or asparagus and are a delicious and different way to enhance a chef's salad or a jellied vegetable salad.

Source: McCann, Edna. (1996).

The Atlantic Provinces now ship their fresh seafood across the country and around the world. Due to changes in transportation, people in Ontario and the Prairie Provinces can now enjoy fresh seafood on a daily basis. Atlantic cuisine blends new cultures and foods from other parts of Canada and the world in order to create the new food of Atlantic Canada.

Québec

As a result of its cultural and linguistic ties to France, Québec shows the most European influence of any Canadian province. About one-quarter of the population of Canada resides in Québec. Québécois are proud of their language and heritage. It is not surprising then, that the food in Québec displays a distinctly French flavour. Common dishes include seafood soups, special cheeses, and

◆ **The influence of French culture is still strong in the province of Québec.** What types of French food have you enjoyed—besides french fries?

French breads and pastries. At the same time, there are foods that are unique to Québec. Among these is smoked meat, beef brisket smoked in a blend of spices and served thinly sliced. Back bacon, known in the United States as Canadian bacon, has far less fat and a milder flavour than streaky bacon.

INTERNET CONNECTS

www.mcgrawhill.ca/links/food
To learn more about French-Canadian cuisine, go to the web site above for *Food for Today, First Canadian Edition*, to see where to go next.

A pie made with ground pork, called **tourtière**, is another French-Canadian specialty. Ground pork is also a main ingredient in *cretons*, a popular spread made with kidney and lard. The early settlers made *cipate*, a pie made with game meats. Today, however, it is made with chicken, pork, veal, and beef.

In the spring, many Québécois and other Canadians travel to the countryside to enjoy the maple harvest. They go to the **cabanes au sucre** or sugar shacks, where the owners of the bush set up rustic restaurants each spring to cater to the visitors from the city. Visitors are treated to the foods of old Québec, while outside the sap boils to make maple syrup and sugar. Québec produces the vast majority of Canada's maple syrup. Some Canadians still prefer blocks of maple sugar to other sweeteners. Another Québec dessert made with maple syrup is *Grand-pères*, dumplings that are served with maple syrup.

The Québécois honour their patron saint on St Jean Baptiste Day, June 24, which is

Tourtière

In a pot mix together 250 g (½ lb.) each lean ground beef and ground pork.

Add:

1	onion, chopped	1
2 mL	salt	½ tsp.
2 mL	savory or thyme	½ tsp.
1 mL	celery salt	¼ tsp.
1 mL	ground cloves	¼ tsp.
125 mL	water	½ cup

Bring all ingredients to a boil. Turn down to simmer for 20 minutes. Add ½ cup bread crumbs spoon by spoon until the fat is absorbed. Cool mixture. Pour into uncooked pie shell. Add the top crust. Cook 25 minutes in a preheated, 230°C (450°F) oven.

Source: McCann (1996).

celebrated with unbridled enthusiasm in Québec. One of the most popular dishes enjoyed at this time is *tourtière*.

Québec has a rich heritage of cheese production, and its cheeses are famous worldwide. Oka cheese, for example, was first made by a Trappist monk in Québec in 1893. A large dairy co-operative, which maintains the original curing rooms used by the monks in the 19th century, makes the cheese today.

◆ Ontario is a province of vast differences, from Ottawa, our capital city, to rich agricultural lands, to the Niagara peninsula's unique growing conditions, to the northern regions rich in fish and game. What is the Niagara Peninsula most famous for?

The people of Québec have always had a love of food, which is one of the reasons Québec is known for its fine cuisine. Modern Québec cuisine reflects a desire for fine food, and there are many entrepreneurs in Québec who strive to bring unique culinary delights to the province. Some of their products include lavender flower jellies, herb *pestos*, exotic preserves, special sausages, apple vinegar, and fine wines and ciders.

Ontario

Over one-third of Canada's population lives in Ontario, making it the most heavily populated province in the country. Beef, dairy foods, maple syrup, and wild rice are among the chief products of Ontario. Poultry, eggs, fruits, and vegetables are also plentiful. Food customs in Ontario are as varied as the people who live there. The first settlers came from Scotland, Ireland, and England. Scottish shortbread, a sweet, buttery cookie, is a favourite in those communities and makes a common holiday

gift. Swiss Mennonites, who had landed first in Pennsylvania, settled in Ontario in the late 1700s. Immigrants from most European countries, as well as China, India, Sri Lanka, Vietnam, Ethiopia, Somalia, the West Indies and Caribbean, and countries of South and Central America, have enriched communities throughout the province. In addition, there are more Aboriginal Peoples in Ontario than in any other province.

Toronto, Canada's largest city, is also one of the most ethnically diverse cities in the world. In Toronto you can visit hundreds of ethnic restaurants and sample unique foods from around the world. You can visit Chinatown in the Dundas and Spadina area, or sample Greek cuisine on the Danforth, where every summer there is a festival of foods. Little Italy in Toronto boasts the largest Italian-speaking population of any city outside Italy. Not only can you taste these different cultures in restaurants, you can also buy fresh produce and other ingredients at stores and markets that cater to specific cultural groups.

FYI

The Best Dining the World Has to Offer!

As the world's most ethnically diverse city, Toronto's dining scene is accordingly extensive. Immigrants from the four corners of the world have brought their culinary skills with them, and Toronto's more than 5000 restaurants reflect the tastes, the cultures, and the ingredients available in this most sophisticated of cities. Toronto is blessed with 500 Chinese restaurants that offer cooking styles from the various provinces of China, including Szechwan, Hunanese, Mandarin, and Cantonese. Japanese, Vietnamese, Thai, and Korean cuisines are also in demand, and a number of other Southeast Asian cultures are creating their own niche in Toronto's food experience: Indonesian, Filipino, Malaysian, among others.

Indian and South Asian: This includes a diverse mix of cooking styles, including Tandoori, Sri Lankan, Madras, Bengali, and Afghani. A number of restaurants offer excellent vegetarian fare and can be the least expensive dining experiences available.

Italian: Romantic little cafes and upscale dining rooms dominate Toronto's two Italian neighbourhoods, Little Italy (College Street just west of Bathurst) and Corso Italia (St. Clair West just west of Bathurst).

Greek: Torontonians have for decades been flocking to Greektown (Danforth Avenue between Chester and Jones) to dine on souvlaki, moussaka, and baklava.

French: From traditional fare to contemporary innovative cuisine, Toronto has a wide assortment of French restaurants. A few also specialize in quality French-Canadian food, complemented with all-Canadian wine lists.

Afro-Caribbean: Most African restaurants are not located in the downtown core, though many can be found in the Bloor West area (between Dufferin Street and Dundas Street West). They tend toward East African cuisine (a combination of Arab, Indian, and African influences), and offer wonderful stews prepared with mild curries, saffron, and cloves. The Caribbean cuisine tends to reflect the foods of Jamaica (with its wonderful jerk spices) and Trinidad (a combination of South Asian and Chinese cooking).

Arab and Middle Eastern: The cooking is as diverse as its people and includes Lebanese, Turkish, Persian, and Syrian—chickpea-based salads, chicken with sesame sauce, spicy veal stews, eggplant casseroles, stuffed green peppers, and much more. Moroccan cuisine is also available, with its saffron sauces, grilled meats, and delicious wines.

Balkan-Albanian: A mixture of Italian and Greek flavours; **Croatian:** The coastal cuisine has Italian influences, while the mountain cuisine is more Germanic, along with Romanian, Serbian, and Slovenian foods.

British and Irish: With great traditional pub fare, the traditional afternoon tea and fine dining English-style.

German: One of the city's largest communities has its own share of eateries.

Jewish: From delis and dairy restaurants to Middle Eastern/Jewish restaurants.

Latin: Quite a number of Portuguese restaurants, with some that include Brazilian fare. The Hispanic community is also well represented; some restaurants specialize in one cuisine, or offer a combination of Argentinean, Chilean, Peruvian, Mexican, Spanish, and Cuban dishes.

Russian and Eastern European: Robust and hearty fare, it includes Polish, Ukrainian, and Latvian cuisine, among others.

Western and Central European: Belgium, Holland, Switzerland, Hungary, the Czech Republic, and Scandinavia are all represented in the city.

Canadian and American: From steak houses and oyster bars to regional specialties and contemporary fusion cuisines. A number also serve excellent wines from the Niagara region.

Source: Adapted from torontotourism.com.

Ontario has a rich agricultural heritage, beginning with the Aboriginals Peoples; the Iroquois planted corn as early as 500 CE, and by 1200, they had added tobacco, squash, sunflowers, and beans to their yearly harvest. The Scots and the Irish were the first settlers in Ontario, and farmed areas from the Grand River in the west to the Ottawa River in the east. They brought with them traditional recipes from their homeland, and grew traditional crops. The Scots grew wheat and oats. The Irish cleared forests and planted orchards that were handed down for generations; Ontario still has a large apple crop. The Mennonites, who settled in the Kitchener and Niagara regions, brought German traditions and cooking methods with them. Some examples are summer sausage and shoofly pie. Many traditional dishes are still served in the Mennonite community, and tourists travel to the Kitchener–Waterloo area to sample their cuisine.

Today, agriculture in Ontario is changing rapidly. The range of crops grown is much broader now than in the mid-20th century. Research, primarily directed by the University of Guelph, has produced new strains of fruits and vegetables, and many farmers now grow crops that used to be imported into Canada; ginseng and figs are good examples (Stewart, 2000).

Ontario's wide range of growing conditions allows for a variety of different crops in different areas of the province. Soft fruits—peaches, apricots, cherries and plums—grapes and melons are grown in the area extending from Niagara west along the Lake Erie shore. Southwestern Ontario grows an abundance of tomatoes, which are then processed in the area. Tobacco fields are being converted to peanut and ginseng fields, and soybeans and corn are also large crops. Many large beef operations are in Grey and Bruce counties to the east and south of Lake Huron. Access to many lakes and rivers offers Ontarians freshwater fish, like trout, herring, and pickerel, and aquaculture is also a growing industry. Wild blueberries are found in the area known as cottage country, or the Muskoka region. Cranberries are an important crop in the community of Bala, with a festival to celebrate their harvest every year. Eastern Ontario is known for its cheeses, apples, and maple syrup, and northern Ontario offers wild game and fresh fish.

◆ You may have seen fields like this—large crops of ginseng are now grown in Ontario. What is ginseng used for?

Cranberry-Apple Salad

1	medium thin-skinned orange, cut into eighths, with seeds removed	1
1	medium apple, cored and cut into eighths	1
500 mL	fresh or frozen cranberries	2 cups
300 mL	sugar	1¼ cups
1 small pkg.	orange or lemon JELL-O®	1
1 envelope	unflavoured gelatin	1
250 mL	cold water	1 cup
	grated peel and juice of 1 lemon	

Force orange, apple, and cranberries through fine blades of a food chopper or whirl in a food processor until chopped fine. Add sugar, mix well. Chill, stirring occasionally to dissolve sugar, for 2 hours or overnight. Prepare orange or lemon JELL-O® according to the package directions. In a small saucepan soften the unflavoured gelatin in 250 mL (1 cup) cold water. Cook over low heat, stirring until dissolved. Add to JELL-O® along with lemon peel and juice. Chill until it is the consistency of unbeaten egg whites. Fold in cranberry-apple-orange mixture until thoroughly blended. Pour into a 6-cup ring mould. Chill until firm. Unmould onto a plate. Garnish with Frosted Cranberries (below).

Frosted Cranberries

In a small bowl lightly beat 1 egg white. Dip 250 mL (1 cup) cranberries in egg, roll each cranberry in granulated sugar to coat. Dry at least 30 minutes.

Source: McCann (1996).

The Prairie Provinces

To the west of Ontario are the Prairie Provinces of Manitoba, Saskatchewan, and Alberta, famous for golden wheat fields and cattle ranching. The first settlers in the Prairies were European fur traders, whose settlements were around the trading posts of the Hudson's Bay Company. The homesteaders followed the fur traders and overcame extreme hardships to establish homes and farms in the harsh Canadian climate. The enormous expanses of land available were also ideal for cattle ranches, and huge herds of cattle were raised and then driven to market. During the cattle drives, workers depended

◆ **Canada's Prairie Provinces are famous for their wheat production and cattle ranching.** What famous celebration happens every summer in Alberta?

on the **chuck wagon,** literally a kitchen on wheels, for their meals. The wagon carried supplies of staple foods such as sugar, coffee, tea, beans, flour, dried fruits, syrup, and molasses. It also carried all the cooking utensils needed to prepare the food.

One million European immigrants came to the Canadian West just after Confederation. Then in 1904, Charles Saunders, a Canadian researcher, developed a new strain of high quality wheat that ripened enough to be harvested before the frost arrived on the Prairies. This wheat, called Marquis, made Canadian wheat famous throughout the world.

Canola, a more recently developed crop, is also grown in the West and harvested primarily for its oil, which is used in many products. Canadian blossom honey, made from canola blossoms, is also considered a delicacy. Different varieties of honey are produced on the Prairies and shipped worldwide. Honey produced in this region is of a fine quality, known for its clarity, colour, and uniformity. More than 75 percent of the honey produced in Canada comes from the Prairie Provinces (Siebert and Kerr, 1994).

There are many varieties of fish found in lakes throughout the Prairies. Fishing can go on all year long, with ice fishing in the winter. Fish from the Prairies are sold on world markets and better-known varieties include northern pike, pickerel, tullibee (a type of cisco, also called freshwater herring), whitefish, lake trout, and goldeye, which many consider a delicacy.

Farmers' markets are popular on the Prairies, where each market reflects the culture of the people in the area. Fresh produce, baking, and crafts are reminders of the diversity of cultures in the region. Ukrainian communities, famous for their special breads, sell *kolach*, braided Easter bread, and *holubtsi*, cabbage rolls. In Steinbach, Manitoba, you can experience Mennonite foods and crafts, including specialties such as cabbage soup, farmers' sausage, *pluma moos* (a fruit soup served cold) cottage cheese dumplings, and rhubarb *platz*—pie by the yard.

Many wild berries grow on the Prairies, especially in the northern areas. Varieties include strawberries, Saskatoons, red currants, raspberries, and blueberries.

Amy's Wild Rice Soup

50 mL	unsalted butter	¼ cup	50 mL	all-purpose flour	¼ cup
500 mL	thinly sliced mushrooms	2 cups	500 mL	warm chicken stock	2 cups
125 mL	chopped onion	½ cup	500 mL	cooked wild rice	2 cups
125 mL	chopped celery	½ cup	250 mL	milk	1 cup
50 mL	chopped sweet green pepper	¼ cup	250 mL	half & half cream (10%)	1 cup
50 mL	chopped sweet red pepper	¼ cup		salt and pepper to taste	

In a heavy saucepan, melt butter over medium-high heat. Cook mushrooms, onion, celery, green pepper and red pepper 6 to 8 minutes or until softened. Stir in flour; cook 5 minutes, stirring. Add chicken stock, stirring constantly to remove any lumps. Stir in rice, milk and cream. Reduce heat to medium and cook, stirring, until thickened and bubbling. Season with salt and pepper. Makes 8 servings.

Source: Stewart (2000).

People still eat wild greens too, for example dandelions, cattails, fireweed shoots, Labrador tea, wild onion, wild rice, wild mushrooms, and licorice root. These delicacies add zest and variety to the Prairie diet.

British Columbia

In British Columbia, on the North Pacific coast, salmon is a staple. Images of the salmon carved in stone reveal its significance to the Aboriginal Peoples of the West Coast since their earliest times. There are also many rituals surrounding the salmon in the spiritual life of West Coast Aboriginal Peoples. Other fish found com- monly in British Columbia are cod, halibut, tuna, and herring. All are consumed locally and exported to world markets. While British Columbia prawns, oysters, shrimp, clams, crabs, and mussels are among Canada's favourite seafoods, B.C. smoked salmon is a world-famous delicacy.

Thousands of Chinese immigrants came to British Columbia during the building of the railway in the mid-1800s and during the gold rushes. They worked on the railroad, often in very dangerous conditions and for little pay, to make money to help their families at home. Many eventually settled around Vancouver,

◆ The Pacific Ocean and mountain streams and rivers are a main source of food in British Columbia. What are some other natural resources in this province?

bringing their food customs and traditions with them. There is a large area of Vancouver called Chinatown where visitors can sample many Asian foods, both in restaurants and fresh from markets.

Fruit is an important crop in British Columbia, grown for local and Canadian use, as well as for export. Apples from the Okanagan Valley are especially famous, and other tree fruits grown in the region include pears, cherries, peaches, nectarines, apricots, and plums. Grapes are also grown in this region for a variety of purposes, including juices, jams, and British Columbia's flourishing wine industry.

Vancouver is known for its fashionable restaurants, and new and interesting food ideas. Edible flowers, for example, were first introduced to Canadians at Sooke Harbour House on Vancouver Island. Japanese sushi and sashimi were served in Vancouver long before they became popular in the rest of North America. In contrast to mainland, multicultural Vancouver, however, the city of Victoria on Vancouver Island maintains a strong British influence—tea is served, British style, in the afternoon.

◆ The Okanagan Valley is famous for its apples and other fruits. What is the most famous apple from British Columbia?

Cape Mudge (Quadra Island, B.C.) Halibut Chowder

25 mL	canola oil	2 tbsp.
5	medium carrots, peeled and cut in 5-mm (¼-inch) slices	5
3	large stalks celery, cut in 1-cm (½-inch) slices	3
2	large onions, coarsely chopped	2
4	large cloves garlic, minced	4
1.25 L	water or fish stock	5 cups
796 mL	can crushed tomatoes	1 28-oz. can
5 mL	dried oregano	1 tsp.
1 mL	sea salt	¼ tsp.
1 mL	coarsely ground black pepper	¼ tsp.
1	bay leaf	1
1	sweet red pepper, coarsely chopped	1
1	sweet green pepper, coarsely chopped	1
750 g	halibut, boned and cut in 2.5 cm (1-inch) cubes	1½ lbs.

Heat oil in a large saucepan over medium heat. Sauté carrots, celery, onion and garlic for 10 minutes or until softened. Stir in water, tomatoes, oregano, salt, pepper, and bay leaf. Bring to a boil, cover and simmer for 1 hour or until vegetables are very tender. Add red and green peppers; cook, covered, for 15 minutes. Gently stir in fish and simmer 5 to 8 minutes or until fish is cooked through and just beginning to flake. Discard bay leaf. Ladle into warmed soup plates. Makes 6 to 8 servings.

Source: Stewart (2000).

INTERNET CONNECTS

www.mcgrawhill.ca/links/food
To find out about traditional Canadian foods and recipes,
go to the web site above for *Food for Today,
First Canadian Edition,* to see where to go next.

Chapter 23 Review and Activities

Summary

◆ The foods of Canada reflect our country's natural resources and rich diversity of cultures.

◆ When the first Europeans came to Canada they brought their own food traditions and methods of food preparation with them.

◆ Early Canadians learned from Aboriginal Peoples about how to grow and prepare wild plants and game.

◆ Settlers passed on some of their food traditions to Aboriginal Peoples.

◆ Regional foods of Canada are influenced by the groups of immigrants who have settled in each region.

◆ Atlantic Canada is especially famous for its fish and shellfish.

◆ Québec cuisine has been strongly influenced by French culture.

◆ Ontario is the most ethnically diverse province with food traditions from countries all over the world.

◆ The Prairie Provinces are known for their golden fields of wheat and expansive cattle ranges.

◆ British Columbia, with its extensive fruit orchards, is also an important exporter of salmon worldwide.

Knowledge and Understanding

1. What types of things do you think the early settlers in Canada learned about food from the Aboriginal Peoples?

2. What foods would become staples for the early settlers?

3. On a map of Canada, make a list of foods that are particular to each region.

4. Name three dishes that exemplify Quebec cuisine. How do their ingredients reflect the foods available in Quebec?

5. How did access to natural resources, such as freshwater lakes and rivers, or the ocean, have an impact on the food habits of the people who live nearby? How has this situation changed, especially for people who do not live near water?

Thinking and Inquiry

6. Which region of Canada do you call home? What are the regional foods in your area? Which of these foods do you eat on a regular basis? List some foods you eat that come from other regions of Canada.

7. There are many different cultural food festivals that take place in Canada every year. Research a cultural food festival from a region of Canada. Explain the traditions and food customs related to the cultural celebration.

8. What influences from early Canadian food traditions do you find in your diet? How does the region of Canada you live in influence what you eat?

9. How has mass transportation and a more global world market influenced Canadian cuisine? What foods do you eat that you might not otherwise have been able to enjoy were it not for long distance and refrigerated transportation of food from other areas of Canada or the world?

Review and Activities   Chapter 23

10. How does the culture of the area in which you live influence the foods that are commonly eaten in your community?

11. How do the foods produced in your community influence the choice of foods commonly eaten?

Communication

12. Choose a province and prepare a pamphlet entitled Tasting [the province]. Include the following information in your pamphlet:

- Main food sources.
- Special foods.
- Cultural influences on food eaten in the province.
- Create a menu that highlights the food of the region. Describe lunch and dinner main courses, plus an appetizer and dessert.
- Include three recipes, one for an appetizer, one for a main course, and one for a dessert.

13. Compare the foods eaten and the cultures of two provinces in Canada. Make a poster showing the differences and similarities between the two. Present your poster to the class.

Application

14. On a map of Canada, make a collage of different cultural groups and foods from different regions of the country.

15. From this chapter, choose one of the recipes for a dish that you have never tried before. Prepare it for your family. Write a one-page summary of the experience.

Canadian Food Supply and Production

While reading this chapter, you will:

- Identify primary food sources in Canada.

- Complete an assessment of the influence of geography on food supply and production.

- Describe the role of co-operatives and marketing boards, including those of Aboriginal Peoples.

Canada's agricultural community provides Canadians with a wide variety of foods.

CHAPTER INTRODUCTION

In this chapter you will look at Canadian agriculture and learn about primary food sources in Canada. You will also find answers to questions such as, How does the geography of a region affect the range of foods that can be grown there? and What is the role of co-operatives and marketing boards, such as the Milk Marketing Board and the Egg Marketing Board, in food production and supply in Canada?

How does food get from the field to the supermarket?

Agriculture in Canada

The Canadian agricultural community produces a wide variety of **agricultural commodities**, the foods produced through agriculture. Our commodities are sold to both **domestic** and **export markets.** There are five major agricultural production sectors in Canada, and these make up 90 percent of the commodities produced in this country. These sectors are:

- Grains and oilseeds, including wheat, durum, oats, barley, rye, flaxseed, canola, soybeans and corn—34 percent.

- Red meats, including beef cattle, hogs, veal and lamb—27 percent.

- Dairy—12 percent.

- Horticulture—9 percent.

- Poultry and eggs—8 percent.

Source: Canadian Federation of Agriculture (n.d.). "Commodities..."

Canadian Agricultural Commodities

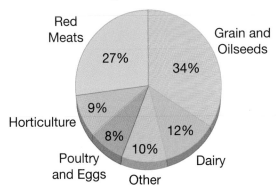

Source: Canadian Federation of Agriculture (n.d.). *Agriculture in Canada—Commodities.*

Grains and Oilseeds

Wheat is the largest crop in Canada, and the varieties include durum, spring, and winter wheat. In 1996, these accounted for 45 percent

FYI

Products That Use Corn

Below is a list of products that use corn. We tend to think of only very traditional uses for our agricultural crops; some of the products listed below may surprise you.

- Adhesives (glues, pastes, mucilage, gums, etc.).
- Aluminum.
- Antibiotics (penicillin).
- Asbestos insulation.
- ASA.
- Automobiles.
  - cylinder heads.
  - ethanol—fuel and windshield washer fluid.
  - spark plugs.
  - synthetic rubber finishes.
  - tires.
- Baby food.
- Batteries, dry cell.
- Beer.
- Breakfast cereals.
- Candies.
- Canned vegetables.
- Carbonated beverages.
- Cheese spreads.
- Chewing gum.
- Chocolate products.
- Coatings on wood, paper and metal.
- Colour carrier in paper and textile printing.
- Corn chips.
- Cornmeal.
- Cosmetics.

- C.M.A. (calcium magnesium acetate).
- Crayon and chalk.
- Degradable plastics.
- Dessert powders.
- Dextrose (intravenous solutions, icing sugar).
- Disposable diapers.
- Dyes.
- Edible oil.
- Ethyl and butyl alcohol.
- Explosives—firecrackers.
- Finished leather.
- Flour and grits.
- Frozen foods.
- Fructose.
- Fuel ethanol.
- Gypsum wallboard.
- Ink for stamping prices in stores.
- Insecticides.
- Instant coffee and tea.
- Insulation, fibreglass.
- Jams, jellies, and preserves.
- Ketchup.
- Latex paint.
- Leather tanning.
- Licorice.
- Livestock feed.

- Malted products.
- Margarine.
- Mayonnaise.
- Mustard, prepared.
- Paper board, (corrugating, laminating, cardboard).
- Paper manufacturing.
- Paper plates and cups.
- Peanut butter.
- Pharmaceuticals.
- Potato chips.
- Rugs, carpets.
- Salad dressings.
- Shaving cream and lotions.
- Shoe polish.
- Soaps and cleaners.
- Soft drinks.
- Starch and glucose (over 40 types).
- Syrup.
- Tacos, tortillas.
- Textiles.
- Toothpaste.
- Wallpaper.
- Wheat bread.
- Whiskey.
- Yogurts.

Of 10000 items in a typical grocery store, how many would you guess would contain corn in one form or another?

Source: Ontario Corn Producers Asociation (2003)

of the total production in Canada. The production of wheat has decreased in Canada in the past decade, while the production of other grains and oilseeds has increased. Barley was the second largest crop grown in Canada in 1996, with 24 percent of the total production. Corn, with 11 percent, was the third largest crop. Canola, a newer crop, was hardly grown at all in the 1970s, but it is now Canada's fourth largest crop and accounted for 8 percent of total production in 1996. The other grain crops produced included oats, soybeans, and flaxseed.

INTERNET CONNECTS

www.mcgrawhill.ca/links/food
To learn more about corn and soybean production in Canada, go to the web site above for *Food for Today, First Canadian Edition*, to see where to go next.

Grains and oilseeds grown in Canada are used for many things, including domestic food production and animal feeds. They are also used for industrial purposes, some of which would surprise many consumers (see FYI box on page 496). Grains and oilseeds can be used to make textiles, commercial paint sealers, varnishes, and other construction materials.

Domestic use of grain and oilseeds accounts for only half of the crops grown in Canada; the remainder is exported. As an important trader on the global market, Canada produces:

◆ 17 percent of the world's canola (rapeseed).

◆ 5 percent of the world's wheat.

◆ 9.9 percent of the world's barley.

◆ 14 percent of the world's oats.

◆ 1.4 percent of the world's corn.

Red Meat Production

Red meat production generated more than $7.6 billion of income for farmers in 1996. Cattle and calves represented 34 percent of the total livestock farm receipts, according to the 1996 Canadian Census of Agriculture. Hogs were second with 21 percent.

INTERNET CONNECTS

www.mcgrawhill.ca/links/food
To learn more about beef and pork production in Canada go to the web site above for *Food for Today, First Canadian Edition*, to see where to go next.

FYI

Farming and Recycling

Farming is the original recycling program.

Animals produce manure. Manure is put on the land to naturally fertilize the crops to help them grow. The crops and animals are used for food, and the whole cycle continues. It is the cycle of life.

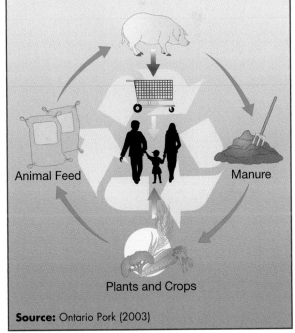

Animal Feed

Manure

Plants and Crops

Source: Ontario Pork (2003)

Our red meats are used both domestically and as exports. In the global markets, Canadian red meats account for 2 percent of the world's production, and in 1996, we exported 56 percent of our total production of cattle and calves. The value of these exports was $2.2 billion. Canadian-grown hogs are also being exported in greater numbers; in 1996, 41.5 percent of the total hogs produced were exported. That percentage is expected to increase in the coming years.

Dairy

The Canadian dairy industry is a **supply-managed system.** This means that the supply-management system limits the amount of a commodity that can be produced by any one producer during a given period of time. Producers buy **quota,** or the right to produce the product; the amount of quota sold for any given year is matched to the expected demand for the product. The level of milk products produced then remains fairly stable on a year-to-year basis. Canadian dairy farmers processed receipts of $3.7 billion in 1996.

There are two different sectors of dairy production. The fluid and liquid sector, those farms that produce milk and cream, provides for direct consumption. The other sector is the industrial sector; this milk is used to manufacture dairy products like butter, yogurt, cheese, ice cream, and powdered milk. Canada exports more milk products than it imports. Canadian cheese, for example, has been a valuable export for many years.

Horticultural Production

Canadian horticultural crops include apples and other tree fruits; strawberries, raspberries, and other berries; potatoes and many other vegetables; and sugar beets. Canada also has

◆ Canadian dairy farmers and manufacturers offer a wide variety of products that enrich our diet with calcium. How many different kinds of cheese can you name?

◆ Horticultural products account for 9.4 percent of all agricultural commodities produced in Canada. How many servings of these foods per day will keep us healthy?

◆ Canadians are eating more turkey today than ten years ago. Why are people increasing the amount of poultry in their diets?

a large floricultural industry, which grows flowers, trees, and nursery products for gardens and other types of landscaping. The wide variety of potatoes grown in Canada is our largest horticultural product, while apples are the second largest. White sugar from sugar beets is produced in the province of Alberta, and farm income from sugar beets accounted for $40.6 million in 1996 and 10 to 15 percent of total domestic sugar consumption. (Canadian Federation of Agriculture, n.d. "Commodities...").

Poultry and Egg Production

The fifth most important agricultural commodity in Canada is poultry and eggs. In the 1996 census of agriculture, these commodities were responsible for $2.1 billion worth of farm receipts. The production of poultry and eggs is also under a supply-management system.

With increased consumer demand for white meat, which is lower in fat than red meat, the production of chicken and turkey has increased in recent years. In the ten-year period between 1986 and 1996, chicken production increased over 50 percent, while turkey production increased by almost 40 percent.

The production of eggs in Canada has remained relatively stable over the past few years. Canadian egg producers sell their eggs on the domestic market. Most eggs, about 82 percent, are sold in their shells as table eggs (i.e., used as fresh eggs)(Canadian Federation of Agriculture, n.d. "Commodities...") The remaining eggs, about 18 percent, are sold as processed eggs. Processed eggs are found in a variety of manufactured goods. They are used not only in the manufacture of foods such as mayonnaise, noodles, and baked goods, but also in shampoo, pet food, and adhesives.

INTERNET CONNECTS

www.mcgrawhill.ca/links/food
For more information about egg production in Canada, go to the web site above for *Food for Today, First Canadian Edition,* to see where to go next.

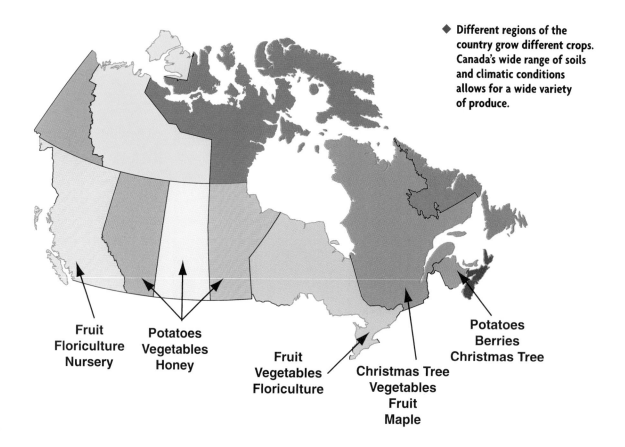

◆ Different regions of the country grow different crops. Canada's wide range of soils and climatic conditions allows for a wide variety of produce.

Fruit
Floriculture
Nursery

Potatoes
Vegetables
Honey

Fruit
Vegetables
Floriculture

Christmas Tree
Vegetables
Fruit
Maple

Potatoes
Berries
Christmas Tree

Regional/Geographic Influences in Agriculture

Canada is a country of many different geographic conditions, with an extremely broad range of climates, availability of arable land, and types of soil. All of these factors have an impact on the types of agricultural commodities that will grow in different parts of the country.

Even though Canada is such a large country, much of the land is unsuitable for agricultural production. In fact, 86.8 percent of the land cannot be cultivated. While much of this land is in the northern areas of the country, another 1.8 percent can be used only for grazing and will not support crops. Making

up another 3.7 percent is land suitable only for grazing and growing hay due to a short growing season, poor soil conditions, or other significant limitations. Another 5.4 percent is even further limited in its capacity to produce. Only 2.3 percent of the land in Canada is considered good or excellent for farming. Much of this land is in the southern areas of the country, where land is also being used for development of urban areas (Clark and Wallace, 1999).

INTERNET CONNECTS

www.mcgrawhill.ca/links/food
To learn more about agriculture in Canada go to the web site above for *Food for Today, First Canadian Edition,* to see where to go next.

The Earth as an Apple

1. Slice the apple into quarters. Set aside three quarters. These represent the oceans of the world. The fourth quarter roughly represents the total land remaining.

2. Slice the remaining quarter in half. This gives you two ⅛ pieces. Set aside one of the pieces. This represents the land that is inhospitable for us as humans—polar areas, deserts, swamps, high altitude, and too mountainous or steep in slope. The other piece of apple (⅛) represents the land where people live—not necessarily where the food is grown.

3. Now, slice this ⅛ of an apple into four sections; you will now have four pieces, each representing ¹⁄₃₂ of the earth. Set aside three of these pieces. These represent areas that are too rocky, too wet, too cold, too steep, or soil that has such limited quality that it cannot be used to produce food. Also included in these three sections are the areas that could be used to grow food but have been modified by humans for urban development.

4. This leaves us with a slice representing ¹⁄₃₂ of the earth. Carefully peel this slice. This tiny bit of peel represents the surface, the very thin skin of the earth's crust upon which humankind depends. Usually less than 5m (4 ½ feet) deep, it is a fixed amount of food-producing land.

Atlantic Canada

The rich soil of Prince Edward Island is ideal for growing potatoes, and PEI potatoes are recognized across the country. New Brunswick, Nova Scotia, and Prince Edward Island also produce apples in many varieties. Apples were introduced into this area of Canada by early European settlers, and have been a staple crop ever since. All of the Atlantic Provinces produce potatoes as well as mixed livestock. Dairy farms are concentrated in Nova Scotia and New Brunswick, where there is more space available for summer pasture. Fifty-six percent of the land in Atlantic Canada is considered poor to good for agricultural production. The remaining 44 percent is unsuitable for agriculture (Clark and Wallace, 1999).

Québec

Québec and Ontario are Canada's major producers of corn and soybeans. Québec, Ontario, and Alberta are the largest red meat producers in Canada, accounting for 74 percent of the total farm receipts in the 1996 Census of Agriculture (Canadian Federation of Agriculture, n.d. "Impact…"). Farms are smaller in Québec due to the smaller amount of land available for agriculture compared to that in Western Canada.

INTERNET CONNECTS

www.mcgrawhill.ca/links/food

To learn more about Canadian apples go to the web site above for *Food for Today, First Canadian Edition,* to see where to go next.

Dairy products from Québec and Ontario account for 70 percent of Canada's dairy production (Canadian Federation of Agriculture, n.d.

"Impact..."). Large dairy farms are located close to urban centres for easier access to processing facilities. Perishable goods are transported in refrigerated trucks to these facilities (Clark and Wallace, 1999).

Québec and Ontario also lead the way in the production of eggs and poultry, with over 61 percent coming from these two provinces (Canadian Federation of Agriculture, n.d. "Impact..."). Eggs are perishable, and must be transported to grading and packaging facilities, which are usually located a reasonable transportation distance from the egg producers.

Horticultural products from Québec lead the country in production (Canadian Federation of Agriculture, n.d. "Impact..."). The fertile soil near Montreal provides ideal growing conditions for lettuce, onions, celery, and carrots. Land near urban centres is very expensive, due to urban encroachment on agricultural lands, so farmers in these areas must produce high-yield crops to compensate. As perishable products, fruits and vegetables must be transported quickly to urban centres, their markets, to avoid spoilage (Clark and Wallace, 1999).

INTERNET CONNECTS

www.mcgrawhill.ca/links/food
To learn more about the produce industry in Canada go to the web site above for *Food for Today, First Canadian Edition,* to see where to go next.

The land in Québec and Ontario varies in quality; 4 percent of it is excellent, but 62 percent is unfit for agriculture. The remaining 34 percent ranges from good quality to poor. Much of the excellent and good quality land is around the major centres of Montreal and Québec City, with another large portion of agricultural land along the St. Lawrence Seaway and in the eastern townships. These are the areas of the province where urban development is occurring.

Ontario

Along with Québec, Ontario is a major producer of corn and soybeans. Grain farms in Ontario are not as large as those of the Prairies, but Ontario farms are specialized. The typically humid weather of Ontario summers helps produce a high yield, higher than in the Prairie Provinces (Clark and Wallace, 1999).

Along with Québec and Alberta, Ontario also shares the distinction of being the largest producer of red meats in Canada (Canadian Federation of Agriculture, n.d. "Impact..."). Again, the beef farms of Ontario are smaller than the huge cattle ranches of Alberta. Many of the large beef operations in Ontario are in Grey and Bruce counties to the east and south of Lake Huron.

The Niagara region and the apple orchards of eastern Ontario help to put Ontario in the top three horticultural producers in Canada. Québec, British Columbia, and Ontario produce 85 percent of Canada's horticultural produce (Canadian Federation of Agriculture, n.d. "Impact...").

Ontario's diverse growing conditions allow for a wide variety of crops in different areas of the province. Soft fruits, peaches, apricots, cherries, plums, grapes, and melons are grown in the area extending from Niagara west along the Lake Erie shore. Southwestern Ontario grows an abundance of tomatoes, which are then processed in the area. Tobacco fields are gradually being converted to peanut and ginseng fields.

Landforms in Ontario are as diverse as the quality of land in the province. Not surprisingly, the northern area of the province is largely unsuitable for agriculture. The land between the North and the South ranges in quality from poor to good. Factors that compromise the quality of the land in Ontario are rocky soil and rock formations found along the Canadian Shield, which lies across the province. There are pockets of land in these areas that are of very poor quality, but others that are good. Ontario and Québec share the distinction of having the most excellent quality land in the country, at 4 percent.

Prairie Provinces

The flat lands of the Prairies are the ideal place to grow field crops. The Prairie Provinces are responsible for the largest share of grain and oilseed production, with 82 percent of what was sold in Canada in 1996. These provinces produce not only wheat, but also oats, barley, canola, rye, and flaxseed. The farms in the Prairies are large, and use technology to its full advantage, specializing in single crops. The weather in the Prairies contributes to the quality of wheat grown there—springs are long and cool, while the summers are hot and dry.

INTERNET CONNECTS

www.mcgrawhill.ca/links/food

For more information on Canadian wheat go to the web site above for *Food for Today, First Canadian Edition,* to see where to go next.

The wide expanses of land available in the Prairie Provinces are ideal for cattle ranching. The dry grasslands provide ideal pasture for cattle in the summer months. The cattle are raised on ranches where the land is too dry for other crops. Alberta beef is well known for its quality, and Alberta is Canada's largest single beef-producing province. In 1996, Alberta produced 54 percent of the cattle and calves sold in Canada (Canadian Federation of Agriculture, n.d. "Impact..."). Hog production is increasing in the Prairie Provinces as well.

Only seven percent of the land in the Prairie Provinces is considered unsuitable for agricultural purposes, the lowest figure in the country. The amount of land considered excellent quality is 2 percent, with the remaining 91 percent ranging from good

◆ Alberta is known for its enormous cattle ranches.

to poor. Much of the pasture used for beef cattle is of lesser quality; the best land is used to grow grain.

British Columbia

The Peace River Valley produces wheat, oats, barley, canola, rye, and flaxseed. British Columbia also shares the lead for Canadian production of horticultural products, especially apples, other tree fruits, and grapes (Canadian Federation of Agriculture, n.d. "Impact..."). The valleys between the mountain ranges have rich fertile soil that is ideal for agricultural production. The climate of southern British Columbia, especially the Okanagan Valley, is very good for growing the tender fruits: peaches, sweet cherries, apricots, and grapes. Extremes of temperatures are less likely in this region, where winters tend to be less severe. Tender fruits are more likely to be damaged by low temperatures than apples, plums, pears, and sour cherries. The Fraser Delta, near the city of Vancouver, has well-drained soil, making this area ideal for growing lettuce, onions, celery, and carrots.

In British Columbia, 1 percent of the land is considered excellent quality for agricultural purposes, with 49 percent of the land ranging from good quality to poor. The remaining 50 percent is unsuitable for agriculture. Due to the mountainous terrain of the province, the good land suitable for agriculture is scattered around the province in pockets. Much of the best land is in valleys and along rivers, where soil is deposited.

Supply-Management Systems

There are five commodities that are supply managed in Canada: eggs, milk, turkey, chicken, and broiler-hatching eggs (the eggs from which broiler chickens will hatch). The supply-management system is unique to Canada. Commodities are managed in order to ensure that the volume of the commodity produced meets the demand for it by consumers. The system ensures that farmers get fair market value for their products; that is, the price farmers receive is consistent, and not subject to fluctuations of a market-driven economy. In non-managed markets, supply can exceed consumer demand, or not meet demand. If supply exceeds demand, farmers get less value for their crop; if supply does not meet demand, farmers get more value for their crop. Such fluctuation in pricing makes it more challenging for farmers to budget and manage their business.

The first supply-management system in Canada was established by the dairy industry in 1970. Egg producers were the first poultry-based group to adopt a supply-management system, when the Canadian Egg Marketing Agency was formed in 1972.

Marketing Boards

A marketing board for a commodity manages supply-management systems. The marketing boards were established on a provincial basis and monitor consumer demand on both a provincial and national level. Each commodity also has a national-level marketing board, which provides services to all of the provincial boards. The boards are responsible to federal and provincial supervisory bodies, which regulate their work.

The marketing agencies determine the amount of the commodity that will be used on a national and provincial level. Once the provinces know how much this is, they then issue quota to the producers in the province,

FOR YOUR HEALTH

Food Freedom Day

February 8, 2003 was Food Freedom Day in Canada. Food Freedom Day is the calendar date representing when the average Canadian has earned enough income to pay his or her grocery bill for the entire year. The date signifies that Canadians are fortunate to have access to a safe, affordable food supply. Canada's proud farmers are dedicated to providing this abundance of high quality food.

In 2001, Canadians spent 10.6 percent of their income on food. Average income per capita was $28 050 in 2001, while expenditures on food and non-alcoholic beverages (including restaurant meals) were $2970. In many other parts of the world, the cost of food is significantly higher. For examples of this, see the table below. The share of food expenditures in total expenditure has been declining for Canadians. In 1996, 10.6 percent of expenditures were on food, compared with 9.9 percent in 2001.

2000—Food and non-alcoholic beverages expenditures as a share of final consumption expenditure of households (%)	
Mexico	23.9
New Zealand	16.3
Spain	15.2
Japan	14.2
France	14.2
Belgium	13.0
Denmark	12.8
Finland	12.8
Germany	11.8
Australia	10.5
Canada	9.9
United Kingdom	9.8
United States	7.2

Source: Statistics Canada

What is the farmer's share of food revenue?

Between 1997 and 2001, the price Canadian consumers paid for food increased by 9 percent. In contrast, the average farm gate price increased by only 2 percent. This means the price paid by consumers for food increased almost five times more than the prices received as a return to farmers. Therefore, the farmer's share of revenue continues to drop while operating expenses (known as inputs) continue to rise.

Source: Canadian Federation of Agriculture (2003)

telling them how much of the commodity they can produce. This quota can be bought and sold by individual producers. Farmers who are retiring can sell their quota, and producers with quota are required to pay a levy to the marketing agency to fund its operations.

The National Farm Products Council (NFPC) regulates marketing agencies. This council acts as a public watchdog. It is responsible for ensuring that the marketing agencies are working for the benefit of consumers. The NFPC approves the national requirements for commodities, as well as any levies that the marketing agencies charge to producers.

INTERNET CONNECTS

www.mcgrawhill.ca/links/food
To learn more about the marketing boards for turkey, chicken and the diary industry go to the web site above for *Food for Today, First Canadian Edition,* to see where to go next.

The marketing agency sets the price paid to the producer for the commodity. This price is based on the cost to the farmer to produce the good. When the producer's costs go up or down, so does the price set by the marketing board. With this system, farmers can rely on a stable income, and plan accordingly (Canadian Egg Marketing Agency, n.d.).

Co-operatives

Co-operation means working together for a common goal or purpose. There are many different ways we co-operate with others. **Co-operatives** are formed by groups of people who have a common goal or purpose and agree to work for the good of all involved. Co-operatives play an important role in Canadian agriculture. They are critical in the processing and marketing of the following products:

◆ Grains and oilseeds.

◆ Honey.

◆ Maple products.

◆ Fruits and vegetables.

◆ Livestock.

◆ Marketing boards help market and manage a number of agricultural commodities in Canada.

The co-operatives perform a number of services for their members. There are two main types of co-operatives in agriculture. The first, marketing and processing co-operatives, provide many services to their members, such as:

- Marketing for the products that the members sell.

- Processing the products to get them ready for consumers.

- Transporting the products to market.

The other type of co-operative in agriculture is the farm-supply co-operative. This type of co-operative uses the buying power of a large membership to purchase supplies for the members including:

- Fertilizers, pesticides, and herbicides.

- Animal feeds.

- Farm machinery.

- Seeds.

- Building materials.

- Fuel.

Source: Canadian Federation of Agriculture, (2003 and n.d.).

Farmers have worked in co-operative groups for many, many years. In the earliest days, farmers shared the work of farming with each other in a co-operative way.

Food Co-operatives of Aboriginal Peoples

Northern Canada presents challenges in the delivery of goods. As a result of the difficulties in transporting goods, costs are higher in the North. Groups of Aboriginal Peoples have formed co-operatives in order to purchase supplies in bulk during the summer months when the transportation is less costly. During the summer shipping months the co-operatives purchase approximately 40 percent of the goods they will need during the coming winter months. There are 38 individual co-operatives in the North; they purchase goods for their members. There is also a larger group, which represents all 38 smaller co-operatives, called Arctic Co-ops Ltd. This larger group is owned by the smaller co-operatives. As with agricultural co-operatives, the buying power of many benefits all. The common goal of the members of a co-operative is to provide reasonably priced goods throughout the year.

Quantitative Research Methods

- **Experiments**   In an experiment, the experimenter manipulates an independent variable to observe the effects. Subjects in the sample group are assigned randomly to an experimental group, or a control group. The independent variable being studied is applied only to the experimental group and not to the control group, and the behaviour of both groups is observed. To be valid, the effects should occur only in the experimental group and not in the control group, and they should be observed when the experiment is repeated.

- **Surveys**   In surveys, the researcher asks a sample group questions and records the answers. In questionnaires, the questions are written and given to the subject to answer in written form. Usually the questions are closed questions that require the subject to select from the answers provided. Questionnaires can be used efficiently with very large sample groups. Interviews are usually conducted orally and contain open-ended questions that the subjects can answer freely. Interviews are suitable for smaller sample groups and for studies in which the answers cannot be anticipated.

- **Content Analysis**   In content analysis, the researcher examines and classifies the ideas presented in a sample group of communications, such as books, letters, movies, or television commercials. The researcher defines the variables before conducting the research. Although it can be difficult to obtain a reliable sample, content analysis is useful for anthropological and historical research.

Qualitative Research Methods

- **Observations**   In observations, the researcher watches and records the subjects' behaviour. Observations might be conducted in a laboratory setting; for example, a child psychologist might observe, from behind a two-way mirror, the interactions between a mother and child. Because the laboratory environment might influence the behaviour, a natural setting is preferred. The researcher can observe from a distance so that the subjects are unaware that they are being observed. In participant observation, the researcher is a participant in the group, and the subjects are aware that they are being observed.

- **Interviews**   In interviews, the researcher asks the subject to describe and explain his or her behaviour. As a method of qualitative research, interviews are useful for determining the motivation for the subject's behaviour, which might not be visible to the researcher. To be valid, the interview questions should ask subjects to discuss actions after they occur rather than to speculate about what they might do. Interviews are often combined with participant observation.

Federation of Agriculture Co-ordinator

Laurie Farquharson

What education is required for your job?

- At least a high school diploma and some university or college courses would be helpful.

What skills does a person need to be able to do your job?

- Organizational skills and the ability to multi-task.

- Excellent people skills, especially listening and speaking skills.

- Researching, writing, and basic bookkeeping skills.

- Some investment knowledge.

- The ability to plan and co-ordinate events.

- The imagination and creativity for designing displays, print materials, and events.

What do you like most about your job?

Teaching people about agriculture, where their food comes from, and how to prepare it.

What other jobs/job titles have you had in the past?

I worked as an intramural director for the Department of Athletics at the University of Guelph; a counsellor in a group home; a volunteer fundraising co-ordinator; and a camp counsellor/supervisor and director.

What advice would you give a person who is considering a career in the agriculture business?

Be involved with people, especially those in the agriculture industry. They are marvelous people who do amazing things and produce the food we eat.

Comment on what you see as important issues/trends in food and nutrition.

People need to learn and understand where their food comes from and how it is produced. Consumers must recognize the importance of maintaining Canada's high quality of food supply. Understanding and practising food safety is also beneficial. Lastly, I see a need to get back to eating basic food and learning how to make things from scratch.

Chapter 24   Review and Activities

Summary

- Canada's agricultural community provides Canadians with a wide variety of agricultural commodities.
- There are five major agricultural production sectors in Canada: grains and oilseeds, red meats, dairy, horticulture, and poultry and eggs.
- The supply-management system of managing agricultural commodities is unique to Canada
- Commodities are managed in order to ensure that the volume of a commodity produced meets the demand for it by consumers.
- The system also ensures that farmers get fair market value for their products.

- Marketing boards manage supply-management systems for a commodity.
- The National Farm Products Council regulates marketing boards.
- Marketing agencies set the prices paid to producers for commodities.
- Co-operatives are formed by groups of producers who have a common goal and agree to work for the good of all involved.
- Aboriginal co-operatives provide reasonably priced goods throughout the year for Aboriginal Peoples living in the North, where transportation of goods is difficult and costly during the winter.

Knowledge and Understanding

1. What are agricultural commodities? Name the five major agricultural commodity groups in Canada.

2. Define export and domestic markets. Which commodities are exported?

3. Define supply-management systems. Name three commodities that use this system in Canada.

4. Describe three different types of co-operatives discussed in this chapter. How are they different? How are they similar?

Thinking and Inquiry

5. What are the advantages and disadvantages of a supply-management system for producers? For consumers?

6. Describe three geographic factors that influence the food produced in the area of Canada where you live. What commodities are produced close to you?

7. What are the advantages of the Aboriginal co-operatives? What are the common goals of these co-operatives?

8. Given the amount of quality land available for agricultural purposes, should governments be limiting urban development on quality agricultural land? What will happen to Canada's ability to feed itself if there are no restrictions?

9. Why do you think the demand for white meat has increased in Canada over the past several years?

10. Look again at the list of uses of corn in this chapter on page 496. Choose another commodity and look on the Internet to find alternative uses for that product.

11. Describe the role of marketing boards. Visit the website of a Canadian marketing board to find out what it does for its members and the public. Print some examples from this site.

Communication

12. Prepare a 5- to 8-minute oral presentation on agricultural co-operatives. Address the following in your presentation:

a) Describe the role of commodity co-operatives in Canadian agriculture. What functions do they perform?

b) What are some commodities represented by co-operatives?

c) For a producer, what are the advantages of joining a co-operative?

d) What other kinds of co-operatives are there in Canadian agriculture?

e) What is the role of supply co-operatives?

f) What advantages do producers receive when they join a supply co-operative?

13. Read the For Your Health feature "Food Freedom Day" on page 505. Find out when Food Freedom Day will be in 2004. Write a news segment for either radio or television to explain Food Freedom Day to Canadians.

14. Do the activity described in the Earth as an Apple feature on page 501. Create a picture book for children to illustrate this concept.

Application

15. On a map of Canada, show five places where the five main commodities are produced. Point out the geographic features of the area that affect the production of each commodity in each area.

CHAPTER
25

CHAPTER EXPECTATIONS

While reading this chapter, you will:

- Identify the causes of hunger in Canada and the world and list some possible strategies for alleviating hunger.

- Determine how food-production methods can contribute to satisfying global food needs.

- Differentiate between the food-production methods of developed and developing countries and the impact of those methods on food security.

- Explain the importance of policy decisions as applied to global food issues.

As Canadians, we like to think that childhood hunger happens elsewhere, but unfortunately, a growing number of our children are hungry.

Investigating World Hunger

CHAPTER INTRODUCTION

In this chapter you will examine the issue of hunger in the world and strategies for overcoming it. You will look at how food production methods can help meet global food needs by comparing food production methods in developed and developing countries. The chapter will conclude with a look at policy decisions about global food issues.

Although many children in developing countries are going hungry, the United Nations and other charitable organizations are teaching the adults new farming techniques and introducing new grains that will flourish in their environments and help them in the near future.

Hunger

Hunger, as defined by Meriam Webster's Dictionary, is a craving or urgent need for food or a specific nutrient, and a weakened condition brought about by prolonged lack of food. As you read this chapter, think about the food that you consumed today and yesterday. Many more people in the world are hungry than are well fed. Have you ever been angry because your parents wouldn't buy you a favourite fast-food item? Think about the children whose parents can't afford to give them three meals a day. Can you imagine how they must feel?

If the World Were a Village of 100 People

There is no shortage of food in the global village. If all the food were divided equally, everyone would have enough to eat. But the food isn't divided equally. So although there is enough to feed the villagers, not everyone is well fed:

> *60 people are always hungry, and 26 of these are severely undernourished.*
> *16 other people go to bed hungry at least some of the time.*
> *Only 24 people always have enough to eat.*
> *— David J. Smith, (2002)*

Hunger in Canada

Issues about food security are becoming more and more of a concern for municipal governments in Canada. Canadians are also worried about persistent hunger and food-related health issues (Simpson, 2001). There has been a high level of public awareness of the issue of food insecurity in Canada since the late 1980s. The number of Canadians who are food insecure is estimated at 8 percent or 2.3 million households (McIntyre, 2003). Food-bank use has almost doubled since the Canadian Association of Food Banks (CAFB) first conducted the Hunger Count in 1989, increasing from 389 000 people in March 1989 to 748 000 in March 2002 (CAFB, 2003).

FOR YOUR HEALTH

A Food-Secure City

According to Toronto's Food Charter, 2001, a food-secure city strives to ensure:

- The availability of a variety of foods at a reasonable cost.
- Ready access to quality grocery stores, food service operations, or alternative food sources.
- Sufficient personal income to buy adequate foods for each household member each day.
- The freedom to choose personally and culturally acceptable foods.
- Legitimate confidence in the quality of the foods available.
- Easy access to understandable, accurate information about food and nutrition.
- The assurance of a viable and sustainable food production system.

Source: Simpson (2003).

Combating Hunger

In 1996, the World Food Summit developed the following definition of food security. "Food security exists when all people, at all times, have physical, social, and economic access to sufficient, safe, and nutritious food that meets their dietary needs and food preferences for an active and healthy life" (CIDA, n.d.).

People who need food subsidization can use a variety of methods to add to their food supply. Some of these include:

Food banks: Places where people in need can go to get free access to food that is donated by individuals and corporations.

Community gardens: Vegetable gardens grown by community members, with the produce shared among them. The number of community gardens in Toronto has risen from 50 in 1991 to 122 in 2001.

Good Food Box: Distributes boxes of affordable, regionally grown fruits and vegetables each month.

Food access grants: Provides grants to social service agencies for their food access programs to make good-quality food more easily available to people.

Diversion of food to food banks: Sometimes food that is not cosmetically perfect is not sent to grocery stores. Reclaim Ontario is working to divert this safe but not salable food to food banks.

Community kitchens: Groups of people come together to cook large quantities of food to reduce the overall costs for everyone.

◆ Working together helps people overcome hunger.

FYI

The Canadian Association of Food Banks (CAFB)

The CAFB contributes in the following ways to help solve the problem of hunger in Canada:

- Represents member food banks in every province in Canada.

- Co-ordinates donated food and transportation through the National Food Sharing System (NFSS) to ensure that products are distributed quickly and efficiently to member food banks.

- Meets with food banks, industry, and government to find short- and long-term solutions to Canada's growing hunger problem.

- Advocates on behalf of food-bank recipients with government representatives and through programs and activities, such as the Anti-Stigma campaign. The campaign attempts to reduce the stigma of using food banks and shows the variety of reasons why people use them.

- Conducts national research, including the Hunger Count, an annual survey of food-bank use in Canada.

- Produces food-bank facts about hunger in Canada.

- Partners with other groups to further the goal of ending hunger in Canada.

- Encourages people to get involved in CAFB activities.

CAFB member food banks uphold a Code of Ethics that promotes the personal dignity of food-bank recipients and the proper stewardship of donated food.

Seventy-four percent of Canadians surveyed in 2002 stated that they are seriously concerned about hunger in Canada. Ninety percent of those surveyed believe that the primary responsibility for solving hunger is that of the government (CAFB, 2003). These statistics suggest that food security needs to be discussed and addressed by all levels of government. Policies need to be put into place to provide all Canadians with safe food at a price they can afford. CAFB believes that it is up to the federal government to introduce a policy for affordable housing at the national level, to improve the National Child Benefit, and to provide a national childcare policy. All of these policies will reduce the pressure on family incomes and leave more money available to purchase nutritious food for families. On a provincial level, CAFB believes that social assistance and disability pensions need to be at a reasonable level, and that minimum wage should reflect the actual costs of the basic necessities of food and shelter (Orchard, Roberts, & Spencer, 2003).

Hunger in Rural Canada

When many people in Canada think of hunger, large urban centres come to mind. Nevertheless, hunger exists in rural Canada. Rural Canadians account for one-fifth of our population, or over six million people. Factors that influence a lack of food are:

- Changes to income and social support programs.

- Declining number of jobs that offer a living wage, or a wage that people can survive on.

- An increase in non-standard work.

- Social programs are not as accessible to rural Canadians as they are to urban Canadians.

- Rural Canadians are more dependent on cars because they don't have access to a transit system. This is an additional cost that they have to bear that urban dwellers may not have.

- The opportunities for employment are not as plentiful in rural Canada as they are in larger cities.

Due to the combination of some or all of these factors, there has been an increase in people's reliance on food banks in the rural areas of Canada (CAFB, 2003).

Child Hunger

Many Canadian children suffer from hunger, as shown in the following facts from the 1994 results of the National Longitudinal Survey of Children:

- 57 000 children under the age of 12 went hungry.

- 1.2 percent of all children went hungry in 1994.

- Most hungry children live in large urban areas.

- Aboriginal Peoples' children are four times more likely to go hungry than other children.

◆ **One of the great tragedies of hunger is when children suffer from malnutrition.**

◆ One-third of children who experienced hunger lived with two working parents. These are the children of the working poor.

◆ Families that use food banks are most likely to be headed by a lone mother and to live in Ontario.

Source: Turner, (1998).

How can we help find a solution to hunger in Canadian children?

The Global View of Hunger

One reason for variations in the food supply around the world is differing economic conditions. Countries are often categorized according to their economic progress. The industrialized nations, also called developed countries, are the richest. These are countries that rely on sophisticated, organized food industries to supply their citizens with food.

Developing nations are countries that are not yet industrialized or are just beginning to become so. People in such places cannot afford to buy food and must grow their own.

Some countries rank between industrialized and developing countries. As they progress economically, they are able to provide more food for their people.

Hunger in the Developing Nations

Food Shortages

It's estimated that about 800 million of the world's people don't have enough to eat. For some, that means going hungry for several days at a time. The most severe form of diminished food supply is famine—food shortages that continue for months or years. Many die of starvation during periods of famine.

◆ **Rice paddies like this one provide supplies of the staple grain throughout much of Southeast Asia.**

The problem of world hunger is a complex one. Some of the basic causes are economics, inefficient farming methods, fuel shortages, overpopulation, wars and politics, and natural disasters. These factors may affect food production, or they may cause problems in distributing or using the food.

Economics

In many developing countries, most people are too poor to buy food and live instead on very meagre meals consisting of home-grown foods. This practice of maintaining a small plot of land on which a family grows its own food is known as subsistence farming.

Some farmers have enough land to grow crops they can sell, or cash crops. However, when cash crops are exported, local food shortages often occur. Also, world food prices change so frequently that cash-crop farmers cannot depend on steady incomes.

In developing countries, good roads are rare. Villages are separated, with no modern transportation to connect them. As a result,

it's difficult to distribute food. One area may have a surplus of food, while a few kilometres away, people have nothing to eat. During famine, poor distribution keeps food aid from reaching starving people.

Food Production in Developing Nations

Subsistence farming makes use of ancient methods. Animals, instead of gas-powered machinery, supply the power. Farm tools are simple, having designs that date back hundreds of years. With such outdated tools and methods, food production is low. Modern farming equipment and methods may be costly and some may not be suited to the crops and conditions in developing countries.

Lack of understanding about irrigation, crop rotation, and other modern methods of producing crops limits the ability of farmers to produce large yields. Much of the farming knowledge that is used is often what has been passed down from one generation to the next. Many farmers in developing nations do not

◆ Subsistence farming relies on simple tools powered by people or animals.

have the advanced knowledge of the science of agriculture that farmers in developed nations do. Agricultural methods that cause erosion and affect the water table inhibit the ability to farm in the future. Lack of access to improved seeds leads to poorer crop yields. Agricultural practices in developed nations are becoming more and more scientific. There is a focus on stewardship, the careful and responsible management of their natural resources and maintaining a healthy relationship with the environment.

Fuel Shortages

Most food must be cooked before being eaten, which means that fuel for cooking is essential. In developing countries, wood is the most common cooking fuel. Many areas are experiencing serious shortages of wood. Without fuel for cooking, people may go hungry.

Overpopulation

The world population, which has been growing steadily, could increase to 15 billion people by 2010. The most rapid increase has been in developing countries. As population grows, so does the demand for food. At the same time, more land is taken for housing, leaving less land for farming. When people clear forests to get more farmland, they destroy their source of fuel.

Will the food supply keep up with the increase in population? Some experts think not.

Wars and Politics

Wars can have a devastating effect on food supplies. Animals are killed and crops destroyed. People are forced to abandon their farms. Fighting disrupts food distribution systems.

Food is also used as a political weapon. Opposing parties may interfere with food distribution or manipulate supplies. Food aid may never reach the needy because it is stolen and sold on the black market.

During the 20th century, millions of people in Africa died of starvation because of civil wars in many countries.

Natural Disasters

Natural disasters such as floods and earthquakes can destroy a region's food supply. Crops may be damaged and animals killed. If soil erosion occurs or roads are destroyed, food supplies can be affected for many years. Prolonged drought, especially in developing countries, can result in famine and starvation.

Ways to Reduce Hunger in Developing Nations

Many efforts are being made to increase the global food supply. The most common goal is to educate people in developing countries to help themselves because they cannot afford modern farming machinery and methods. Therefore, programs are designed to help people within the means available to them and in the conditions in which they live.

The United Nations, government agencies such as the Peace Corps, and private non-profit organizations such as the Canadian International Development Agency (CIDA) are involved in the education process. They show farmers how to improve their methods and equipment and how to increase water supplies.

INTERNET CONNECTS

www.mcgrawhill.ca/links/food
To learn more about the Food and Agriculture Organization of the United Nations, go to the web site above for *Food for Today, First Canadian Edition,* to see where to go next.

Research Improves Crop Yields, Farmer Income, and Nutrition

A few years ago, a widow in the Etheya District of Ethiopia hosted an on-farm trial of a new variety of wheat. When she realized the new variety made excellent bread and produced a high yield, she saved the seed to plant it in subsequent years. Once her neighbours saw the high productivity and quality of her seeds, they were in great demand.

"The widow doubled her income by selling the grain as seed to neighbouring farmers," says Doug Tanner, a Canadian agronomist who heads the Ethiopian office of the International Maize and Wheat Improvement Centre, a non-profit research and training institute headquartered in Mexico. The Centre has 20 regional offices globally, including Ethiopia and Kenya.

For more than 15 years, with support from the Canadian International Development Agency (CIDA), the Centre has been researching and developing new varieties of wheat and maize in East Africa, and encouraging farmers to use them. It has also helped researchers from the region develop new crop-management practices and strengthen maize and wheat research networking.

In Kenya, the International Maize and Wheat Improvement Centre has been a pioneer in controlling *Striga*, a weed that diverts essential nutrients from the roots of crop plants. It affects about 40 percent of Africa's maize crop, resulting in severe losses for subsistence farmers. Many experts consider *Striga* the greatest obstacle to food production in Africa, particularly in the Sahel region.

By rotating maize with legumes and improving soil fertility, researchers showed they could reduce *Striga* infestation over the long term. They have also developed novel

◆ After trying a new variety of wheat, an Ethiopian woman realized it not only grew better and larger crops, but also produced an excellent bread. Soon, her grain was in high demand from her neighbours and she doubled her income.

short-term solutions, such as new varieties of maize that can be seed-treated with a minute amount of herbicide before planting.

In Ethiopia, researchers such as Dr. Amanuel Gorfu have shown how rotating wheat with fava beans can improve wheat yields by as much as 65 percent in the first year. The beans improve soil fertility, enhancing the response of wheat to phosphorus fertilizer. What's more, fava beans are full of protein, which helps provide a more balanced diet.

"Farm families cannot afford to eat animal protein regularly, but they can incorporate legumes like fava beans, which are high in protein, into their diets," says Dr.Gorfu. "They boil them to make stews; sometimes they roast the seed of the fava bean and eat that as well."

(continued)

Research Improves Crop Yields, Farmer Income, and Nutrition (continued)

The international Maize and Wheat Improvement Centre is one of the Future Harvest research institutes established by the Consultative Group on International Agricultural Research (CGIAR). In keeping with Canada's pledge at the G8 Kananaskis Summit to double its support for CGIAR, CIDA approved a new research project in 2002. Researchers will help men and women farmers in Ethiopia, Kenya, Tanzania, and Uganda to adopt Quality Protein Maize (QPM), a variety developed by the International Maize and Wheat Improvement Centre over the past 35 years. The quality of the protein in QPM grain approaches that of milk protein.

"Quality Protein Maize has the potential to increase nutrition, improve health, and contribute to the food security of farming families in East Africa," says Mr. Tanner. "When you increase the quality of dietary protein, it's similar to raising income, since subsistence-farming families would benefit from enhanced protein nutrition without additional field work or spending scarce money. The increased protein quality may also strengthen immune systems and help people with HIV to better withstand related illnesses."

If past experience is any indication, African farmers will be only too happy to try the new variety. "Farmers are eager to participate in on-farm trials because they get new technology, improved varieties, and advice," says Dr. Gorfu. "Things are changing. When we first started research, the wheat yield was about eight-tenths of a tonne per hectare; now good farmers can get about three tonnes per hectare. That is tremendous progress!"

Source: Canadian International Development Agency (2003).

Addressing Food Security through Food Production

CIDA's policy is to work with developing nations to improve their agricultural production and methods. It believes that agriculture is the key to rural development in developing nations. If farmers are more successful, the overall health and well-being of their communities improves. The advances in agriculture have been linked to better education, water quality, and environmental practices. To achieve food security, developing nations need education and assistance in developing crops that will thrive in their natural environments and that will have a minimal impact on the natural environment and the quality of water.

Other Ways to Reduce Hunger

Many developing nations are working together and with countries like Canada to improve conditions for their citizens. Famine in Ethiopia made headlines worldwide in 1984–1985. Since then, the government of Ethiopia has worked in partnership with other countries to avoid a recurrence. The government developed early warning systems of food shortages and has striven to minimize the impact of them through supply-management systems. It is also working to improve water-collection systems, and conserving current water supplies. Improving agricultural production, as mentioned earlier, is the backbone of the plan.

FYI

Canadian International Development Agency (CIDA)

CIDA supports sustainable development activities in order to reduce poverty and to contribute to a more secure, equitable, and prosperous world.

Development is a complex, long-term process that involves all of the world's people, governments, and organizations at all levels. Working with partners in the private and public sectors in Canada and in developing countries, and with international organizations and agencies, they support foreign-aid projects in more than 100 of the poorest countries in the world. The objective: to work with developing countries and countries in transition to develop the tools to eventually meet their own needs.

Source: CIDA (2002).

The Role of Technology in Reducing Hunger

Food technology also has an important role in increasing the world's food supply. Through genetic engineering, scientists hope to produce varieties of grains and other plant foods that are resistant to drought and other environmental problems.

Nutritious products are also being developed. Because people in some developing countries cannot easily digest milk or milk products, an alternative product is being introduced around the world. This new product is made by grinding leaves into a paste, which is then made into a highly nutritious crumbly cake.

Solar energy offers much hope as a solution to the problem of fuel shortages. It has great potential where the climate is sunny and dry most of the year. Several types of solar cookers are available, including one made inex-pensively from cardboard, aluminum foil, and a plastic bag. These cookers can be used for most meal-preparation tasks, such as simmering rice, baking potatoes, cooking casseroles and stews, and even pasteurizing milk. The solar cookers are being used in various areas, including India, China, Africa, Central America, and the southwestern United States.

Nutritionists from non-profit organizations teach area residents how to use solar cookers. They also teach the basics of good nutrition.

Policy and Global Food Security

The member countries of the United Nations work together to achieve sustainable development and have formed a separate division that oversees issues and policies related to it. After the World Summit on Sustainable Development in 1996, this division took on more responsibility. Some of these include:

◆ creating partnerships and looking at food consumption and production patterns.

◆ Solar-powered cookers like this one provide a means of cooking food in areas where fuel is scarce.

◆ Food security is an important issue for the United Nations.

◆ Providing leadership and expertise to governments and other international organizations to implement sustainable development policies.

◆ Promoting an approach to sustainable development that is integrated, involves participation, and is implemented at local, national, regional, and global levels.

◆ Providing technical advice and assistance to countries that support sustainable development.

◆ Encouraging and promoting co-operation and sharing between the different agencies and organizations working for sustainable development.

◆ Promoting partnerships and encouraging dialogue on issues related to sustainable development.

Source: United Nations (2003)

INTERNET CONNECTS

www.mcgrawhill.ca/links/food
To learn more about international development through CIDA Youth Zone, go to the web site above for *Food for Today, First Canadian Edition,* to see where to go next.

Writing an Essay

Writing an essay is a basic Social Science skill that you will use often in Social Science courses. The purpose of an essay changes, but the basic steps in essay writing remain the same. The following are the basic steps to follow when writing an essay.

Step 1. Decide on your topic

You may have been given a topic by your teacher or you may have chosen a topic yourself after being given certain parameters. You may need to narrow your topic to a more manageable one. For example, the topic "Hunger" is too broad. Narrowing it down to "Hunger in school-aged children in Canada" will make it more manageable.

Step 2. Create a graphic organizer of your ideas.

The following graphic organizer can be used to help you organize your ideas for your essay.

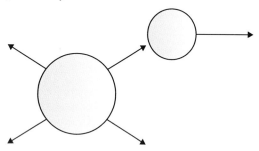

In the centre of the circle, write your topic. At the end of the arrows, write all of the main ideas relating to your topic. The second circle represents a subtopic of the main idea. These subtopics support the main ideas, which in turn explain your topic.

Step 3. Prepare an outline of your main ideas and subtopics.

Once you have decided on your subtopics, you can then organize the order of the subtopics in your essay. As well, you will know what you need to look for when conducting your research. This list of subtopics will form the outline of your essay.

Step 4. Write your thesis statement.

A thesis statement tells the reader what your essay will be about and what you will be saying about your topic. The outline of your essay will be set up to support your thesis statement.

Step 5. Write the body of your essay.

The body of your essay is made up of three basic components:

- The main ideas.
- Subtopics of the main ideas.
- An explanation of the subtopics.

Step 6. Write the introduction and the conclusion.

The essay's introduction should get the reader's attention. It is also designed to introduce the reader to your thesis statement. Write a few sentences of summary information that will lead to the thesis. Your thesis statement should be the last sentence of the paragraph.

   The conclusion brings the essay to a close. A few well-worded sentences that summarize your essay are all that are needed.

Resource Co-ordinator, Global Education

Adele Halliday

What education is required for your job?

- A Bachelor's degree in Social Sciences or international development.
- A Bachelor of Education is strongly preferred.

What skills does a person need to be able to do your job?

- Excellent interpersonal and oral communication skills, including public speaking ability and diplomacy.
- Good prioritizing and time management skills.
- Organizational and strategic planning abilities.
- Personal experience with justice and international development.
- Writing and editing skills, detail-oriented, and creative.
- Familiarity with non-profit organizations.

What do you like most about your job?

I like working with youth; teaching at conferences and workshops; facilitating social and global change; being creative; teaching about global issues, such as world hunger, poverty, international development, environment, and HIV/AIDS.

What other jobs/job titles have you had in the past?

I was a secondary school teacher for the Peel District School Board and the Toronto District School Board. I also taught mentally challenged children in Kenya, East Africa. I was an environmental education director in Belize, Central America.

What advice would you give a person who is considering a career in global education?

Spend some time in a developing country—this time could be voluntary or paid. Develop a broad understanding of a variety of global issues—not just food and nutrition— and how they are linked.

Comment on what you see as important issues/trends in food and nutrition.

World hunger is a growing crisis. Children die of hunger and preventable causes every day. Canadians need to realize that our nutritional habits affect others around the world.

Chapter 25   Review and Activities

Summary

- Food insecurity in Canada affects 2.3 million households.
- There are ways to address food security in Canada.
- Hunger exists in both urban and rural communities in Canada.
- Food shortages in developing nations are caused by a number of factors that affect food production and distribution.
- One way to help developing nations achieve food security is to help them learn to grow their own food.
- CIDA works with developing nations to help them learn to feed themselves.
- Developments in technology are helping to alleviate hunger in developing nations.
- The United Nations plays a role in working toward sustainable development for the people of the world.

Knowledge and Understanding

1. Define *hunger*.
2. Define *food insecurity*.
3. What is a *living wage*?
4. Identify five causes of food shortages in developing countries.
5. Explain what *food security* means.

Thinking and Inquiry

6. Explain two ways that technology is being used to address the issue of food shortages in the world.
7. Write an essay addressing the issue of food insecurity in Canada.
   a) Discuss how common food insecurity is in Canada.
   b) Discuss ways that the provincial government can address food insecurity.
   c) Discuss ways that the federal government can address food insecurity.

8. a) How does food production differ in developed and developing nations?
   b) How can developed nations help developing nations with their food supply through agriculture?
9. Use the Internet Connects on page 519 to locate the United Nations web site, and look under sustainable development. Search out a country and find out the following information under "poverty":
   - Programs and projects.
   - Co-operation (with other nations to reduce poverty).
10. Write a one- to two-page report on your findings.
11. Many people assume that hunger only exists in cities. Explain why people would think that. Discuss hunger in rural Canada and some of the causes of it.

Communication

12. Find out where the food bank is located in your local community. Ask a food bank representative the following questions:

- How many pounds of food do you distribute during the year?
- When is your busiest time?
- When is the slowest time for getting donations?
- Who are your main supporters?

13. Create a poster or Powerpoint presentation to educate a community group about food security and insecurity in Canada and around the world.

Application

14. Compare food security in Canada to that in a developing nation. Develop a poster to illustrate the similarities and differences between the two nations.

15. Go to the Internet Connects on page 523 to locate the web site for the Canadian International Development Agency (CIDA). Find out what Canada is doing for a developing country. Prepare a poster to explain Canada's role in helping that country achieve food security.

While reading this
chapter, you will:

- Prepare a global food
  product or meal using
  staple foods.

Staple Foods
of the World

Staple foods form the basis
of our food choices, and vary
from culture to culture.

CHAPTER INTRODUCTION

In this chapter you will learn about staple foods from around the world. You will see how they are prepared differently from culture to culture. Recipes are included so you can prepare some staple foods using different cooking methods.

Bread is called the "staff of life." In which cultures is this true?

A Brief History of Food

Growing food and agriculture began around 12 000 years ago. People came to realize that seeds planted and cared for would yield crops. These people settled down and began farming their food. The first people to do this were probably in the Middle East, where farmers grew earlier versions of wheat and barley. People in China and Central America are thought to have started farming next. Because of the differences in soil and climate, in northern China, people grew millet, and in the south, they grew rice. As the early farmers began to understand agriculture, they learned how to irrigate their crops by diverting water from streams, lakes, and rivers. Settlements began to develop around agricultural areas.

Animals began to be domesticated around the same time as settled farms began. The type of animal that was domesticated depended upon the area in which the people lived. Cows were uncommon in mountainous or rocky areas, where goats and sheep were better adapted to handle the terrain.

INTERNET CONNECTS

www.mcgrawhill.ca/links/food
To learn more about the history of food, go to the web site above for *Food for Today, First Canadian Edition,* to see where to go next.

Staple Foods

The food supply in any region depends on what foods can be grown there. These **staple foods** are foods that make up the region's basic food supply. Several factors determine the staple foods for a given area.

♦ **Geography.** Food is most easily grown where the soil is rich, such as valleys or plains. In mountainous areas, farming is more difficult. However, animals that can live on rocky slopes, such as goats, can be raised in these regions.

♦ **Climate.** Moderate temperatures make it possible to grow a wide variety of food. In some climates, temperatures vary and food can be grown only during the warm months. Extreme temperatures, high or low, limit the kinds of food that can be grown.

♦ **Rainfall.** Some crops thrive in areas that receive a lot of rainfall annually. Little, if any, food can be grown in totally dry areas such as deserts.

In many parts of the world, grains are the main staple foods. Each type of grain—wheat, rice, corn, or rye, is best suited to a particular climate. For example, rice grows best in warm, wet climates.

Staple Foods of the World

Wheat

Thirty-five percent of the world's population relies on wheat as its main staple food. Wheat is the primary cereal grain of the world's richest countries. New strains of wheat are being developed constantly, and now wheat is gaining ground in the developing world. The total amount of wheat grown in the world has doubled in the last few decades. Wheat is very high in nutrition and is easy to store and transport. The main producers of wheat are China, the United States, India, France, Canada, Turkey, Russia, the United Kingdom, and Pakistan.

♦ Wheat is the main staple for 35 percent of the world's population. In what forms do you eat wheat?

Preparing Foods Made from Wheat

Tabbouleh (Lebanon)

One Arab version has it that the tree of knowledge in the Garden of Eden was not an apple tree at all, but a huge stalk of wheat, so wide that the serpent placed on guard could not encircle it. In desperation the reptile persuaded Eve to prune the plant and, in passing, offer some of the grain to Adam. And in this way the couple incurred God's wrath. The tale has a twist though, for the wheat that caused their downfall inside the garden became their mainstay outside it, and the wheat berry is still highly regarded in the Arab world.

Ingredients

225 g	**bulgur** or prepared cracked wheat	1 cup
450 g	tomatoes, cubed	1 lb.
1	medium onion, finely sliced	1
	handful of fresh parsley, chopped	
	handful of fresh mint, chopped	
90 mL	olive oil	6 tbsp.
	juice of 2–3 lemons, to taste	
150 g	black or green olives	1 cup
	salt and pepper	

1. Take a salad bowl and put in the bulgur or cracked wheat, chopped tomatoes and onion together with the parsley and mint.
2. In another bowl, beat the oil and the lemon juice and season with salt and pepper. Then pour it over the salad and mix thoroughly.
3. Put the olives on top and then chill the salad in the refrigerator for about 2 hours before serving. Garnish with a little more parsley and chopped tomato, if desired.

Source: Wells, Troth. (1990). *The New Internationalist Food Book*. Toronto: Second Story Press, p. 14.

Irish Soda Bread

Since soda bread is a quick bread, not a yeast bread, it is quick and easy to make. It is rugged and grainy, perfect with meal-size salads, soups, and stews.

Ingredients

250 mL	all-purpose flour	1 cup
250 mL	whole wheat flour	1 cup
5 mL	baking powder	1 tsp.
5 mL	baking soda	1 tsp.
10 mL	granulated sugar	2 tsp.
2 mL	salt	½ tsp.
25 mL	butter	2 tbsp.
250 mL	sour milk or buttermilk	1 cup

1. In mixing bowl, combine flours, baking powder, baking soda, sugar and salt.
2. With pastry blender or 2 knives, cut in butter until mixture resembles fine crumbs.
3. Stir in sour milk, all at once, to make a soft dough (a little sticky).
4. Turn out onto lightly floured surface. Knead about 10 times. Form into ball. Place on nonstick baking sheet. Flatten into 7.5-cm (3-inch) thick round. With sharp knife, cut large X about 5 mm (¼ inch) deep in top of dough.
5. Bake in 190°C (375° F) oven for about 40 minutes or until golden brown.

Makes 1 large loaf, 12 pieces.

Source: Spicer, K. (1995). *Multicultural Cooking.* Campbellville: Mighton House, p. 175.

Corn

Corn is the second largest cereal crop in the world. When the Spanish explorers first came to Mexico they were astounded by the bountiful corn grown there by the Maya and Aztec peoples. Maize, another name for corn, is the only cereal crop of American origin. In many parts of Africa, corn is also a staple food. However, corn is low in protein and a heavy dependence on it can lead to nutritional deficiency. The main producers of corn include the United States, China, Brazil, Mexico, France, Argentina, and South Africa.

◆ Corn has been a staple in the Americas for thousands of years.

Preparing Foods Made from Corn

Cornmeal Tortillas

Ingredients

1 egg		1
250 mL	water	1 cup
125 mL	all-purpose flour	½ cup
75 mL	cornmeal	⅓ cup
2 mL	each baking powder and salt	½ tsp.

1. In a bowl, whisk egg and water. Beat in flour, cornmeal, baking powder, and salt. Set aside for 10 minutes.
2. Heat nonstick 17.5-cm (7-inch) skillet over medium heat. Brush very lightly with vegetable oil.
3. Stir batter, then pour batter, 25 mL (2 tbsp.) at a time, into skillet to make very thin pancakes. Cook just until dry on top. Do not turn. Stack until all pancakes are cooked. Stir batter as it is being used since cornmeal settles to the bottom.

Makes 12 tortillas.

Source: Spicer, K. (1995). *Multicultural Cooking*. Campbellville: Mighton House, p. 70.

Preparing Foods Made from Corn (continued)

Pastel de Choclo—Corn/Maize Pie with Chicken (Chile)

Variations of this pie are found in Bolivia and other Latin American countries. Corn or maize is the only major cereal grain native to the Americas. In North America, it was introduced to the colonists by the Iroquois Indians. Among the many varieties is the distinctively flavoured blue corn, grown in Arizona and New Mexico by the Hopi Indians.

Ingredients

For this recipe you can also use leftover cooked chicken, and miss out the first two steps in the method.

1.5 kg	chicken, skinned and cut into portions	3 lbs.
25 mL	oil	2 tbsp.
2	onions, chopped	2
5 mL	ground cumin	1 tsp.
5 mL	dried marjoram	1 tsp.
15 mL	flour	1 tbsp.
300 mL	stock or water	1¼ cups
50 g	raisins or sultanas	¼ cup
75 g	olives, cut in halves	⅓ cup
2	hard-boiled eggs, sliced (optional)	2
2	eggs, beaten	
180 mL	milk	¾ cup
1	medium can corn kernels	1
5 mL	sugar (optional)	1 tsp.
	salt and pepper	

Heat oven to 180°C (350°F)

1. First, place the chicken portions into a large pan and pour in just enough water to cover them. Put a lid on the pan and bring it to the boil. Then lower the heat and simmer for 30–40 minutes or until the chicken is cooked.

2. Lift out the chicken pieces, keeping the stock, and allow them to cool. Then remove the meat from the bones.

3. Now heat the oil in a pan and sauté the onions for a few minutes before adding the cumin and marjoram. Cook for 2 minutes before sieving in the flour, a little at a time.

4. After that, slowly add the stock or water, stirring constantly so that you get a smooth sauce. Bring this to the boil and then put in the chicken pieces, seasoning with salt and pepper.

5. Next, spoon the chicken mixture into an oven-proof dish and scatter the raisins or sultanas, sliced olives and hard-boiled eggs on top.

6. Then whisk the beaten eggs and milk together in a bowl, adding the corn. Pour this over the chicken and sprinkle the sugar on top. Bake in the oven for 45 minutes or until the topping is set. Serve with baked potatoes and salad.

Source: Wells, Troth. (1990). *The New Internationalist Food Book.* Toronto: Second Story Press, p. 10.

Rice

Rice is one of the world's oldest and most important staple foods. There are over 7000 varieties of rice grown around the world today. Most of it is produced in Asian countries. All rice is brown to start with; then the bran layer is stripped, and the rice is polished to make it white. It has less protein than most of the other cereal grains and provides mainly carbohydrates. The main producers of rice are China, India, Indonesia, Thailand, Vietnam, Japan, Brazil, and the Philippines.

INTERNET CONNECTS

www.mcgrawhill.ca/links/food
To learn more about rice and its nutritional value, go to the web site above for *Food for Today, First Canadian Edition,* to see where to go next.

◆ **Rice has long been a staple in China.** Why do you think rice is grown like this?

Preparing Foods Made from Rice

South Indian *Biryani*

This *biryani* uses cardamoms, which are native to the hills of South India and Sri Lanka. Cardamom is related to the ginger family and is now sometimes grown between rows of tea bushes or rubber trees on the plantations. First mentioned in European literature in the 12th century, cardamom has long been an important spice, the seeds from its dried pods lending delicate fragrance to curries and desserts. The meat should be marinated for 30 minutes.

Ingredients

900 g	beef, chicken, or lamb*, cut into small chunks	2 lbs.	40 g	oil	3 tbsp.
			40 g	margarine	3 tbsp.
5 mL	1 green chili, crushed or chili powder	1 tsp.	10 mL	2 sticks cinnamon or ground cinnamon	2 tsp.
1	large tomato, cut finely	1	2	seeds from 2 cardamom pods, crushed	2
10 mL	handful of fresh parsley or mint, chopped or dried	2 tsp.	5–10	curry leaves	5–10
			3	large onions sliced in rings	3
5 mL	turmeric	1 tsp.	10 mL	garam masala	2 tsp.
125 mL	yogurt	½ cup	110 g	black or other lentils, cooked until just tender but not too soft	½ cup
2.5 cm	ginger root, peeled and grated	1 inch			
5 mL	ground ginger or	1 tsp.			
2	cloves garlic, chopped finely or crushed	2			
900 mL	water	4 cups			
400 g	rice	2 cups			

*With lamb, you can use a half or whole shoulder and cook it as one piece, cutting the meat as you serve.

Heat oven to 160°C (325°F).

(continued)

Preparing Foods Made from Rice (continued)

South Indian Biryani (continued)

1. Put the meat in a bowl and add the chili, tomato, mint or parsley, turmeric, yogurt, salt, ginger, and garlic. Leave it to marinate for 1 hour.

2. Now, in a heavy pan, heat the oil and margarine together and cook the cinnamon, crushed cardamom, curry leaves and onions until they are golden brown. Keep some of the onion rings to use later to decorate the dish.

3. When it is ready, add the meat and its marinade and cook on a low heat until the meat is nearly tender — this will take about 30 minutes for chicken and up to 2 hours for lamb or beef, depending whether you are using a whole joint or pieces. It does not need to be completely cooked at this stage since it will cook some more in the oven (see below).

4. Meanwhile, bring the water to the boil in a large pan, adding a little salt, and cook the rice for 5 minutes if using white rice, 10 minutes if using brown. It is important that the grains are not completely cooked at this stage as they cook more later (see below) and the *biryani* should not be too wet. When the rice is ready, set aside.

5. Now put the garam masala and cooked lentils into the pan containing the meat and simmer for a further 10 minutes.

6. At the end of this time, transfer the mixture to an oven-proof dish and add the rice, stirring gently to combine the ingredients.

7. Garnish with the onion rings and place the dish in the oven for 30 minutes or so. This finishes the cooking of the meat, rice and lentils. It should end up fairly dry, but add more water if you wish. You can serve the *biryani* with side dishes such as cucumber raita, chutney, slices of banana, hard-boiled eggs, chopped apple, sultanas and desiccated coconut.

Source: Wells, Troth. (1990). *The New Internationalist Food Book.* Toronto: Second Story Press, p. 90.

Millet

Millet is the most ancient of the grains that are still grown today. It grows well in areas that are subject to droughts, and has sustained people who would otherwise have been victims of famine. Millet can grow in conditions of poor soil and very little rainfall. It is easy to store, and can even be stored for many years; this also helps to prevent food shortages in drought-ravaged areas of the world. Millet is usually cooked as porridge and made into a flat bread. It is one of the basic foods for over 400 million people in India, Africa, and China. The main producers of millet are India, China, Nigeria, Niger, Russia, Senegal, and Egypt.

Preparing Foods Made from Millet

Millet and Lentil Bake (Iran)

Ingredients

250 mL	red lentils	1 cup	5	cloves	5	
250 mL	millet, soaked	1 cup	3	seeds from 3 cardamom	3	
25 mL	oil	2 tbsp.		pods, crushed		
3	cloves garlic, crushed	3	2 mL	ground cinnamon	½ tsp.	
1	onion, chopped	1	2	bay leaves	2	
1.4 L	stock	6 cups		salt and pepper		

Heat oven to 150°C (300°F).

1. For this you need to use a large cooking pot that is suitable both for cooking on top of the stove and inside the oven too. Start by heating the oil in the pot and then soften the garlic and onion in it.

2. After that, add the millet together with the stock, cloves, cardamom seeds, cinnamon, and bay leaves and bring to the boil. Turn down the heat, cover the pot and simmer very gently for 1 hour or until the millet is soft.

3. Put in the lentils and cook for a further 15 minutes, until they and the millet are ready.

4. When this is done, pour off any remaining liquid. Replace the cover, put the pot into the oven and let it cook for 10–20 minutes until the moisture has been absorbed. This should be a fairly dry mixture and green salad makes a good accompaniment together with cucumber raita— simply dice cucumber and mix it with plain yogurt.

Source: Wells, Troth. (1990). *The New Internationalist Food Book.* Toronto: Second Story Press, p. 51.

Potatoes

The Irish were the first Europeans to use the potato as a staple food. They liked it because it was hardy, quick to grow, used less land, and was less labour intensive than growing grains. Since potatoes grew underground, they were less likely to be stomped on by their enemies. Since the potato was rich in nutrients and easy to grow, it became a staple food for the poor in Ireland and other parts of Europe in the 17th century. Unfortunately, the potato is also susceptible to disease, and the potato blight that hit Ireland in the mid-1800s led to the deaths by starvation of more than a million people. Today, the potato remains a favourite, nutritious, and still relatively cheap staple food all over the world. Main producers of potatoes are Russia, China, Poland, the United States, India, Germany, France, and the United Kingdom.

INTERNET CONNECTS

www.mcgrawhill.ca/links/food
For more information about the history and farming of potatoes, go to the web site above for *Food for Today, First Canadian Edition*, to see where to go next.

MISS KENNEDY DISTRIBUTING CLOTHING AT KILRUSH.

◆ When the potato crops were hit by blight, widespread famine occurred in 19th-century Ireland.

Preparing Foods Made from Potatoes

Curried Potato Fries (India)

With over 800 million people, India is the world's second most populous country, after China. About two-thirds of the people are farmers, growing a wide range of food from millet and rice to chickpeas, lentils, and, increasingly, potatoes, which are becoming an important staple.

Ingredients

4	medium potatoes	4
2 mL	turmeric	½ tsp.
15 mL	sesame seeds, toasted*	1 tbsp.
1–2	cloves garlic, crushed	1–2
	oil for frying	
	salt to taste	

1. To begin, cut the potatoes into French fry shapes and then soak them in water for 30 minutes. Drain them and leave to dry out a little.

2. After this, heat enough oil to shallow fry. Add the potatoes and salt. Cook for 15 minutes, stirring occasionally.

3. Next, add the turmeric and mix it well to spread the colour evenly.

4. When the potatoes are nearly done, put in the crushed garlic and toasted sesame seeds. Mix well and then serve with *dhal* (cooked lentils) or as a snack.

* To toast the seeds, put a heavy pan over a medium heat and when warmed scatter the seeds in without oil. As they cook they will jump and turn golden.

Source: Well, Troth. (1990). *The New Internationalist Food Book.* Toronto: Second Story Press, p. 15.

Latkes—Jewish Potato Pancakes

This potato mixture made into pancakes (*latkes*) and served with applesauce is a popular side dish served at Hanukkah. The same mixture is made by German cooks and becomes the German potato cake *kartoffelkuchen*, which is similar to Swiss *roesti*, when it is spread in a lightly greased 20-cm (8-inch) square nonstick pan and baked in a 210°C (425°F) oven for 40 minutes. These also resemble *ratzelach* (Polish potato cakes) and Irish *boxty*, which combines grated raw potato with mashed potatoes.

Ingredients

2	large potatoes, unpeeled and scrubbed	2
1	small onion (optional)	1
2	egg whites	2
15 mL	all-purpose flour	1 tbsp.
5 mL	salt	1 tsp.
2 mL	baking powder	½ tsp.
20 mL	canola oil	4 tsp.
125 mL	low-fat sour cream or yogurt	½ cup

1. Finely shred potatoes and onion, if using. Place in a sieve; press to remove excess moisture

2. In bowl, whisk together egg whites, flour, salt and baking powder until smooth. Stir in potato mixture.

3. In large nonstick skillet, heat 10 mL (2 tsp.) oil over medium high heat. When drop of water spatters on skillet, spoon potato mixture, about 45 mL (2 tbsp.) at a time onto skillet; form into 7.5-cm (3-inch) pancakes.

4. Cook for 4 minutes on each side or until golden brown. Remove to ovenproof plate. Keep warm in oven while remaining batch or batches cook, adding remaining oil as required.

5. Serve with applesauce, sour cream or yogurt.

Makes 12 *latkes* (pancakes), 6 servings.

Source: Spicer, K. (1995). *Multicultural Cooking.*
Campbellville: Mighton House, p. 68.

Sorghum

Sorghum is also a drought-resistant crop. It is very important as a staple food in Africa, India, China, Southeast Asia, and Latin America. The United States is the major producer of sorghum, where it is used to feed animals, not people. Sorghum is often eaten as porridge or pounded into a flour to make bread. Other main producers of sorghum are India, Mexico, Argentina, China, Australia, and Ethiopia.

Nutritional Content of Sorghum Compared to Corn

Nutrient per 100 g serving	White Food Sorghum	Corn
Total calories	370.5	357.1
Calories from fat	25.8	32.4
	Grams	**Grams**
Total fat	2.867	3.6
Saturated fat	0.506	0.22
Unsaturated fat	2.361	3.38
Protein	9.78	7.14

FDA– and USDA–certified laboratory results

Source: National Grain Sorghum producers (2003)

Preparing Foods Made from Millet and Sorghum

Mixed Cereal Stew (Lesotho)

Ingredients

110 g	wheat grains, soaked overnight	½ cup
110 g	sorghum or millet, soaked overnight	½ cup
950 mL	stock	4 cups
30 mL	oil	2 tbsp.
1	onion, chopped	1
500 g	mixture of potatoes, carrots, and cabbage, chopped	2 cups
	milk	
	salt and pepper	

1. Start the stew by draining the cereals, keeping the water they were soaked in. Now put them into a pan with the stock, cover, and bring to the boil. Then turn down the heat and simmer for 45 minutes or until the grains are soft, adding some of the retained soaking water if necessary to prevent them drying out.
2. Using another pan, heat up the oil and sauté the onion until it is golden. Add the potatoes and carrots and cook them for 10 minutes, stirring often so that they do not stick. Then put in the cabbage and the remaining soaking water and cook for a further 5–8 minutes.
3. When the vegetables are done, stir in the cooked cereals, add the milk and boil gently until the stew is the desired consistency for you. Then add the pepper and salt and serve with sliced tomatoes.

Serves 4.

Source: Wells, Troth. (1990). *The New Internationalist Food Book.* Toronto: Second Story Press, p. 120.

Other Staple Foods

The staple foods described in the preceeding pages are some of the main staples in the world today. However, there are other staples in use.

◆ Bananas and plantain are grown and eaten as a staple food in tropical regions.

◆ Cassava is a drought-resistant plant that is high in carbohydrates and low in protein, grown mainly as a subsistence crop.

◆ Yams are an important staple in Nigeria, the Caribbean, parts of Latin America, and Southeast Asia.

Preparing Foods Made from Sorghum and Yams

Yams with Spiced Sorghum Butter

250 mL	unsalted butter, room temperature	1 cup
135 mL	sorghum syrup* or 125 mL (½ cup) clover honey and	9 tbsp.
	15 mL (1 tbsp.) robust-flavoured (dark) molasses	
5 mL	ground cinnamon	1 tsp.
2 mL	ground cloves	½ tsp.
	large pinch of cayenne pepper	
280–300 g	yam (red-skinned sweet potatoes), 10–11 oz each	8

1. Beat butter, sorghum syrup, cinnamon, cloves and cayenne in medium bowl to blend; season with salt. (Can be prepared 5 days ahead. Cover and refrigerate. Bring mixture to room temperature before using.)
2. Preheat oven to 180°C (350°F). Rinse sweet potatoes; pat dry. Pierce each several times with fork; place on baking sheet. Bake potatoes until tender, about 1 hour.
3. Cut top of each potato lengthwise; press in ends to open top. Spoon some sorghum butter into opening of each potato and serve.

*Sorghum syrup (a juice extracted from cereal grass) is available at some natural foods stores. (If you cannot find sorghum syrup, the combination of honey and molasses works nicely)

Makes 8 servings.

Source: *epicurious.com.* (2003)

What are Yams?

Yams are a vegetable native to Africa. Grown in tropical regions around the world, Yams are a root crop. Though many think they closely resemble sweet potatoes, yams are not related to the sweet potato at all.

CLASSIFICATION

Yams belong to the family Dioscoreacea, and are tubers most often grown on a tropical vine. The word "yam" is an African word for the phrase, "to eat."

There are 150 different varieties of yams, including the air-potato, the only true yam cultivated in the United States.

GROWTH

Yam plants bear thick tubers, climbing stems, leaves, and flowers. The greater majority of yam plants are grown in warm regions of the tropics. In Africa and New Guinea, the yam is a staple, and the primary agricultural commodity. In the United States, sweet potatoes outnumber yam plants and consumption.

APPEARANCE

Yams vary in size, shape and flavour by species. The flesh of the yam can be white, yellow, pink or purple. Some yams are sweet, some are tasteless, and others are bitter. Some varieties of yams grow up to 7 feet in length, and can weigh up to 68 kilograms.

A VERSATILE VEGETABLE

Yams are a versatile vegetable that is easy to prepare and cook. All varieties of yams can be boiled, broiled, fried, roasted or baked.

BUYING YAMS

Yams are sold in Canada and the United States in chunks, sealed with a wrapping usually made of plastic. Because most varieties of yams are large in size, it is rare to find whole yams in any produce section in North America. Look for yams that are free of blemishes and bruises, and have tight, unwrinkled skins. The flesh of the yam should feel firm.

STORING YAMS

Yams should be stored in a cool, dark, dry area. They can be safely kept for up to two weeks. Uncooked yams should never be refrigerated. Cooked yams can be refrigerated up to for 3 days.

*WARNING

Unlike the sweet potato, yams cannot be eaten raw. Uncooked yams are toxic!

Chapter 26 Review and Activities

Summary

- Staple foods are foods that make up the basic food supply for people in a region.
- Staple foods vary from culture to culture.
- The staple food supply in any region depends on what will grow there.
- Geography, climate, and rainfall are factors that determine which staple foods will grow in a given region.

- Staple foods around the world include wheat, corn, rice, millet, sorghum, bananas, cassava, and yams.
- Staple foods are prepared by using a wide variety of cooking methods.

Knowledge and Understanding

1. What are staple foods? Give two examples.
2. Which staple grain is the primary staple for 35 percent of the world's population?
3. What is sorghum? Where is it a staple?
4. Why were potatoes considered a good staple crop? What is one of the problems with growing potatoes?
5. Why would rice be the staple food in southern China and millet the staple food in northern China?

Thinking and Inquiry

6. What are the staple foods in your diet? Which other countries tend to use them?
7. Explain how geography influences the production of staple foods in an area.
8. Explain how climate and rainfall influence the staple foods in a region.
9. Choose one of the staple foods discussed in the text. Find recipes for this food from five different countries or cultures. Explain the similarities and differences between them.
10. Research and find a staple food described in the chapter. In which country or countries is it a staple food? How is it eaten? Use a cookbook to find a recipe that uses it.

Communication

11. Choose one of the staple foods and design a recipe to use it. Try out your recipe and write a report on it.

12. Choose an area of the world to study. Find the following:

a) Which staple foods are produced in that area?

b) How does geography influence the staple foods produced?

c) How do climate and rainfall influence production of the staple foods?

d) Prepare a sample menu for a meal that includes an appetizer, main course, and dessert, featuring the area's staple foods, and find recipes to accompany your menu.

e) Prepare one of the recipes for your class to sample.

f) Do a presentation using PowerPoint, a poster, or a bulletin board to highlight these foods.

Application

13. Prepare two different recipes for the same staple food. Compare how the staple is used in both. What are the similarities? What are the differences? Write a one-page summary of your findings.

14. Consider the geography, climate, and rainfall in your area. Explain how that influenced the staple foods originally grown there. Is that influence still as strong?

CHAPTER EXPECTATIONS

While reading this chapter, you will:

- Present the results of an investigation into the foods, traditions, and religious laws of different cultures, including types of foods eaten and characteristic flavours.

- Plan and prepare food products, using a variety of cultural traditions.

- Identify the food customs and traditions of your own families.

Diversity in Food

Different cultures contribute their own food customs and preparation techniques to international cuisine to make it interesting.

In this chapter, you will learn about the foods, traditions, and religious dietary laws of different cultures. The types of foods eaten and the characteristic flavours of the different cultures will be discussed. With this information, you will be able to plan and prepare foods using a variety of cultural traditions. You will be asked to report on your family's cultural traditions and food customs as well.

Latin American cuisine has been influenced by the Aztec, Incan, and Mayan cultures that made up its early history.

Latin America

Foods of Latin America

Latin America stretches from Mexico and the islands of the Caribbean to the tip of South America. Because the area is so large, it includes climates and geographical features of all kinds—tropical rain forests, snow-capped mountains, arid deserts, and temperate zones. Foods vary according to the growing conditions. Nevertheless, many similarities exist among the cuisines—styles of food preparation and cooking associated with a specific group or culture.

Corn, or maize, is the staple grain in much of Latin America. Wheat and rice are also grown in some areas.

◆ **Dry beans, corn products, chili peppers, and avocados are common ingredients in Latin American cooking.**

Mexico

Mexico's cuisine developed out of both the Aboriginal Peoples' foods and the influence of the Spanish conquerors. Cornmeal, rice, cooked dry beans, and chili peppers are the basics of Mexican cooking. The bland taste of corn and beans provides a contrast to the spicy taste of the various peppers.

The bread of Mexico is the tortilla. You have probably eaten tortillas in tacos, burritos, and similar foods. This flat, pounded bread is usually made from *masa*—dried corn soaked in limewater and ground while wet. In some dishes, masa is made into a dough and cooked by steaming. The best known of such dishes is *tamales*, masa formed into various shapes and often filled with finely chopped chicken and other foods. The bundles are steamed in corn husks or banana leaves.

Much of Mexican cuisine is hotly spiced. One dish that often surprises visitors to the country is *pollo con mole poblano*, chicken in a thick, dark sauce of chili peppers and chocolate.

◆ *Pollo con mole poblano* is a delicious combination of braised chicken in a sauce of chili peppers, nuts, and chocolate.

Most Mexican meals include *frijoles*, cooked dry beans. *Frijoles refritos* are cooked dry beans that are mashed and fried in lard. Popular desserts include flan, a sweet baked custard topped with a sauce of caramelized sugar and preserved guava.

◆ Following centuries of tradition, this Mexican woman makes tortillas using the traditional tools—a *metate* to hold the dough and a *metlalpil* to roll it.

INTERNET CONNECTS

www.mcgrawhill.ca/links/food
To learn more about food festivals that celebrate different cultures across Canada, go to the web site above for *Food for Today, First Canadian Edition,* to see where to go next.

Central America

A bridge of seven small countries connects Mexico to South America: Belize, Costa Rica, El Salvador, Guatemala, Honduras, Nicaragua, and Panama. This region is where the Mayan empire flourished. People who live in these countries today are of Mayan, European, African, and mixed descent. The cooking has Mayan and Aztec roots with Spanish and Caribbean influences.

Corn and beans are the staple crops. Bananas, coffee, coconuts, and cacao (the bean from which chocolate is made) are exported to other countries.

Chicken is widely eaten in Central America. It might be prepared with pineapple or in a mixture of ingredients, such as pumpkin seeds, tomatoes, and raisins.

A favourite food is *chayote*, a crisp vegetable with a delicate flavour, which is often sliced and simmered. Costa Ricans mix it with cheese and eggs, whereas cooks in the Dominican Republic fry it with eggs, tomatoes, and hot peppers.

The Caribbean

The tropical islands of the Caribbean Sea are to the south and east of Mexico, between Florida and South America. Caribbean nations include Cuba, Jamaica, Haiti, the Dominican Republic, and Puerto Rico.

Columbus landed on these islands on his voyages to find spices and a shorter route to India. The Spanish came later, as did the Dutch, Portuguese, British, and French. All these cultures left their marks on the people who live there today, in the languages they speak, their customs, and their food.

Caribbean Cuisine

The staple food is the plantain, a starchy food that looks like a banana but is cooked as a vegetable. It can be roasted, fried, boiled, baked, or combined in dishes with meat and cheese. Abundant fish and shellfish are taken from local waters. Among these are flying fish,

◆ This buffet from Barbados includes beans, rice, plantain, fish, pineapple, and other locally available foods.

FOR YOUR HEALTH

Eating What Comes Naturally

Many of the staple foods of Latin America—such as grains, beans, and fresh fruits and vegetables—are rich in nutrients. The popularity of these foods in Latin American cultures is mainly a result of their ready availability.

conch, shrimp, cod, clams, grouper, and red snapper. In the warm climate, tropical fruits—including mangoes, bananas, coconuts, papayas, and pineapples—are also plentiful. So are sweet potatoes, pumpkins, and chili peppers.

The dishes of the Caribbean vary from country to country. Some are colourfully named. For example, *Moros y Cristianos* ("Moors and Christians") is a Cuban national dish made with black beans and rice. Jamaican "Saturday Soup" consists of hot peppers (originally from Africa), carrots, turnips, and pumpkin added to beef stock. The cuisine of Haiti, which includes a soup made of bread and pumpkin, reflects both African and French influences.

Islanders use coconut milk and fruit juice to prepare both main dishes and desserts, such as coconut custard. Ice cream made with papaya and other local fruits is also popular.

South America

Twelve nations make up South America, the southern half of the Western Hemisphere: Argentina, Bolivia, Brazil, Chile, Colombia, Ecuador, Guyana, Paraguay, Peru, Surinam, Uruguay, and Venezuela. South America also includes French Guiana, a European possession.

As in the rest of Latin America, the population is of Aboriginal Peoples, European, and African ancestry. The climate, culture, people, and growing conditions vary greatly from country to country and from rural area to city.

Brazil

Brazil, the largest country in South America, produces great amounts of beef, coffee, and cocoa. The people trace their ethnic roots to Aboriginal Peoples, Portuguese, and Africans. This blend of cultures can be seen in Brazilian food. From West Africa comes *dende,* or palm oil (which gives a bright yellow-orange colour to foods), *malagueta* peppers, and coconut milk. From the Portuguese comes a love of sausage and the use of kale as a soup ingredient.

Sausage appears in *feijoada,* the national dish of Brazil. Links of the smoked meat are simmered—along with beef short ribs, slices of dried beef, and pork—in a pot of black beans. Side dishes of rice, collard greens, sliced oranges, and manioc flour (a toasted breadcrumb-like grain) complete the rib-sticking stew. Brazil's long coastline accounts for the many fish recipes, including *mariscada,* a fish stew consisting of clams, mussels, cod, shrimp, and crab cooked with tomatoes and spices.

Peru

Peru is located on the Pacific coast of South America. When the Spanish conqueror Pizarro came to Peru in the 16th century, the Aboriginal Peoples were eating corn, potatoes, squash, beans, cassava, sweet potatoes, peanuts, tomatoes, avocados, and chili peppers. Although these foods are still popular, and the potato remains its staple food, Peru is also noted for its fishing industry. Popular meats include seafood and beef.

◆ Black beans are a staple in Brazil.

Peru was a Spanish colony for almost 300 years. The Spanish influence can be seen in foods such as *gazpacho,* a cold tomato-based soup of Spanish origin. *Ceviche* is a native Peruvian dish in which raw fish is marinated in lime juice. Other foods often eaten in wealthier areas include meat, poultry, vegetables, and grains, which are highly seasoned with onions, garlic, and hot peppers. Rice, potatoes, and bread accompany the main meals.

In poorer areas, meals include potatoes, corn, squash, and soups made of wheat and barley. The foods of those living in jungle areas consist of a variety of fish, small game, fruits, and nuts.

Argentina

South of Brazil, along the eastern coast of South America, lies Argentina. Today most of its inhabitants are of European descent.

Raising beef is one of Argentina's major industries, and as a result, most people eat beef. It is often grilled outdoors and served with spicy sauces. *Puchero* is a meat and vegetable stew. Another widely eaten dish is *empanadas,* turnovers of dough filled with vegetables, meat, fruit, or a combination of the three. Meats are also combined with fruits in local stews such as *carbonada criolla*—beef mixed with peaches.

Cuban Black Bean Soup

The variations on recipes for this Cuban signature dish are endless. This one has a creamy texture that makes it irresistible.

Ingredients

1	medium onion, chopped	1
1	rib celery, chopped	1
1	garlic clove, minced	1
20 mL	vegetable oil	1 tbsp.
250 mL	chicken or vegetable broth	1 cup
2 500-g cans	black beans, drained	2 1-lb. cans
Dash	cayenne pepper	Dash
20 mL	lemon juice	1 tbsp.
	salt and pepper	

4 servings

Equipment: Stock pot or Dutch oven

1. Sauté onion, celery, and garlic in oil until tender.

2. Add chicken or vegetable broth, black beans, and cayenne pepper.

3. Simmer mixture over medium heat, stirring occasionally, until heated through (about 5 minutes).

4. Carefully purée mixture in small batches in a blender or food processor. Return to stock pot.

5. Stir in lemon juice and simmer until thoroughly heated.

6. Season to taste with salt and pepper and serve hot.

Note: For a chunkier soup, purée only half the mixture before returning to stock pot.

Nutrition Information

Per serving (approximate): 286 calories, 17 g protein, 45 g carbohydrate, 5 g fat, 0 mg cholesterol, 206 mg sodium

Good source of: potassium, iron, zinc, vitamin E, B vitamins, phosphorus

Food for Thought

• Make a list of all the kitchen tools you would need to prepare and cook this soup.

• Discuss how and where in a meal you would serve this soup—for example, as an appetizer or as a main course. What would you serve along with it to make it a well-balanced, authentic Cuban meal?

◆ **A family in Afghanistan enjoys the evening meal.**
Name two differences between the dining customs in
the Middle East and those common in the United States.

Africa and the Middle East

Africa

The Sahara forms a natural east-west dividing line through Africa. It separates the five nations in the north, along the Mediterranean Sea, from the rest of the continent.

The people living south of the Sahara are mainly Africans. Those living north of the Sahara are mostly Arabs, with a culture similar to that of the Middle East.

Sub-Saharan Africa

The area south of the Sahara is sometimes known as the sub-Saharan region. The concept of society in this region is defined by kinship groups—centuries-old networks of clans and tribes numbering sometimes in the thousands. In the past, these clans often lived together in villages and jointly owned the surrounding farmland. Food traditions are linked more with these social groups than with political boundaries past or present.

Influence of Climate

Most of sub-Saharan Africa has a tropical or subtropical climate. However, there is a wide range of geographical features, including mountains, coastlines, river valleys, tropical rain forests, and desert. Consequently, different foods are raised in these various regions.

In western and central Africa, areas that are hot and humid, the chief crops include plantains, rice, bananas, yams, and cassava. In the grasslands in the east and south, corn,

◆ **At this market in the West African nation of Mali, peanuts and yams are among the foods sold.** Identify two ways in which yams are prepared and eaten in Africa.

millet, and sorghum are grown. Wheat is grown in many areas, along with foods such as onions, garlic, pumpkins, watermelons, cucumbers, chilies, dates, and figs.

Chickens, cattle, sheep, and goats are raised wherever possible. Small herds of animals have traditionally provided income, as well as food, for small farmers and herders. The eating of meat, however, is usually reserved for special occasions. People living along waterways, such as rivers, lakes, and seas, have an abundant supply of fish.

Influence of Settlers

Over the centuries, food crops introduced from other continents have been incorporated into African cuisines. Coconuts were introduced from Asia in the 1500s. In the same century, corn arrived from the New World. In the 1600s, cassava became an important food source. In the 1700s, peanuts were introduced, possibly from South America.

Yams have remained a staple starch throughout Africa. The traditional way to prepare them is to boil, peel, and slice or pound them until they form a paste, called *fufu*. In West Africa, cooks mash and deep-fry them, make them into croquettes, or slice and bake them. In some areas, cooks make *fufu* by mashing cassava and plantains.

South Africa was visited and also settled by many waves of Europeans looking for trade routes or escaping persecution. These French, Dutch, British, and German Europeans brought their own food preferences and preparation methods. African cooks modified them with local produce and techniques. *Bredie,* for example, is a stew made with meat or fish, vegetables, onions, and chili peppers.

The African Meal

Most Africans eat one large meal a day, generally in the evening. A typical meal may include a grain such as millet cooked into a porridge or a vegetable such as yams. This is served with a seasoned stew made with vegetables and flavoured with meat, poultry, or fish, if available.

The evening meal is always a social occasion. The food may be served in one large bowl, which is set on the ground. People sit around the bowl, using either pieces of bread or their fingers to scoop up the food.

In many areas of Africa, spicy foods are preferred. Cooks make their own seasoning mixes, based on the many kinds of hot chili and spices available. One blend, called *berbere*, is commonly used in Ethiopia in soups and stews. It is a spicy combination of garlic, red and black peppers, salt, coriander, fenugreek, and cardamom. Other spices may be added, depending on the cook's preference.

North Africa

The five main countries that make up North Africa are Algeria, Egypt, Libya, Morocco, and Tunisia. The population is clustered along the Mediterranean, in desert oases, or in irrigated parts of Egypt along the Nile. Because of its location along ancient trade routes linking Asia to Europe, this area has been well travelled. Its cuisine reflects the influence of those early travellers. The use of rice as a staple and the variety of produce are two legacies of foreign visitors. Two other staple starches grown in the region and still widely used are wheat and barley.

North African Cuisine

Although there are some differences among the cuisines of North Africa, all make use of olive oil, chickpeas, fava beans, lentils, lamb, and goat. Dried fruits and nuts play a role in the cuisine, as do chili peppers and cinnamon.

One notable dish of the region is *tajine,* a Moroccan specialty. The dish is a long-cooked stew of lamb, prunes, and almonds, sometimes flavoured with cinnamon. *Tajine* is often served with *couscous,* a fluffy steamed grain. *Couscous* is also the name of an entire meal featuring the grain and one of several stewed meats or poultry mixed with aromatic vegetables. Another dish that is both savory and sweet is *pastilla,* common in both Morocco and Algeria. This dish, which bears French influences, is a pigeon pie made with phyllo dough, eggs, vegetables, spices, and nuts. The finished dish is sprinkled with sugar.

The Middle East

The Middle East is located just east of North Africa, between Southeast Europe and Southwest Asia. The main countries of the Middle East are Iran, Iraq, Israel, Jordan, Kuwait, Lebanon, Saudi Arabia, Syria, and Turkey. Most people in this area are Arabs. Israel, which is a Jewish nation, is the exception.

Middle Eastern Cuisine

There are many similarities among the foods of the various nations of the Middle East and North Africa. The names and some seasonings may vary, but the basic ingredients and cooking methods are similar.

Fruits include apricots, pomegranates, dates, figs, grapes, and oranges. Vegetables include eggplant, peppers, olives, cucumbers, and tomatoes. Seasonings include parsley,

◆ Tabbouleh (in front) is a refreshing salad from the Middle East made with bulgur and accented with dill.

dill, mint, cinnamon, lemon juice, pine nuts, onion, and garlic. *Tahini,* a sesame seed paste, is popular. Lamb is commonly eaten; chicken and fish are also used when available. Chicken is sometimes an ingredient in stews made with lentils, beans, rice, and vegetables. Pork is a food forbidden by religious law throughout this region.

Staple Foods

Although rice and barley are eaten, the staple starch of the Middle East is wheat, especially in the form of bulgur. This grain is a featured ingredient in *tabbouleh,* a popular salad that also includes tomatoes, mint, parsley, onions, and olive oil.

Another important staple food is yogurt. Depending on where you are, you might find yogurt made from the milk of cows, goats, camels, or buffalo. In several countries, yogurt is called *leban. Leban* is often mixed with vegetables, especially cucumbers and dates, for a side dish or part of a main dish.

Here are some other dishes commonly found in this area:

◆ *Kubaybah* or *kibbi.* A mixture of ground lamb, bulgur, cinnamon, and allspice.

◆ **Stuffed vine leaves** are filled with a rice and meat mixture and served with a sauce made of yogurt, garlic, and mint.

◆ *Herrira.* A mutton and vegetable soup. Is eaten often during Ramadan, the month when Muslims fast during daylight hours.

◆ *Chelo.* Popular especially in Iran, Iraq, and Lebanon. Steamed rice accompanied by a meat or vegetable dish.

◆ *Koresh.* A stew of meat or poultry with vegetables, fruit, nuts, seasoning, and perhaps cereal. Most Iranians will eat a *chelo koresh* for one meal a day.

◆ *Hummus b'tahini* is a favourite in Israel and other Middle Eastern nations.

Desserts of the Middle East are often fresh, seasonal fruits. The people of the Middle East also enjoy sweet desserts, such as *baklava,* phyllo dough layered with nuts and honey syrup. *Halva* is a candy made of ground sesame seeds and honey.

For a feast, such as a wedding, it is common to roast a whole sheep and serve it with *couscous*. A salad of tomatoes, peppers, cucumbers, mint, melon, grapes, dates, and figs might be included.

Israel

Israel includes people who originate in the Middle East along with others from around the world. Consequently, its food customs embrace both Middle Eastern traditions and those of many other countries. Customs also reflect Jewish food traditions and laws, including a prohibition against mixing dairy foods and meat.

Traditional condiments, which find their way into most recipes, include *shatta, zhoug,* and *tahini*. *Shatta* is a red chili pepper mixture. *Zhoug* is a combination of green chili peppers, parsley, coriander, cumin, garlic, olive oil, and salt and pepper.

Some Israelis live in a *kibbutz* (kee-BOOTS), a communal organization, which raises its own food. Breakfasts at a *kibbutz* are substantial. They may consist of fresh produce, cold meats, cheese, fish, eggs, condiments, vegetable salads, and hot coffee.

Chicken and lamb are widely used. So are chickpeas, which are enjoyed both in *falafel*—patties of the ground legume seasoned with parsley and fried—and in *hummus b'tahini,* a spread of ground chickpeas, lemon juice, and *tahini*. Both dishes are served with pita bread, the pocket bread popular throughout much of the Middle East.

Couscous Tabbouleh

This refreshing salad combines a staple grain popular in North Africa and flavours of the Middle East.

Ingredients

250 mL	reduced-sodium chicken broth	1 cup
175 mL	couscous	¾ cup
50 mL	lemon juice	¼ cup
15 mL	olive oil	1 tbsp.
1 mL	salt	¼ tsp.
1 mL	pepper	¼ tsp.
125 mL	peeled, chopped cucumber	½ cup
1	tomato, chopped	1
125 mL	chopped green onion	½ cup
125 mL	chopped fresh parsley	½ cup
50 mL	chopped fresh mint	¼ cup
	mint leaves (for garnish)	

4 servings, ½ cup each

Equipment: Medium saucepan

1. In a medium saucepan, bring chicken broth to a boil.
2. Place couscous in a large bowl. Carefully pour hot broth over couscous. Let stand 5 minutes. (All liquid should be absorbed. Drain if necessary.) Cool to room temperature.
3. In a small bowl, whisk together lemon juice, olive oil, salt, and pepper. Set aside.
4. Add cucumber, tomato, green onion, parsley, and mint to couscous.
5. Drizzle lemon juice mixture over couscous. Toss to mix.
6. Serve, garnished with mint leaves, if desired.

Nutrition Information

Per serving (approximate): 183 calories, 4 g protein, 32 g carbohydrate, 4 g fat, 0 mg cholesterol, 339 mg sodium

Good source of: iron, vitamin A, vitamin C, B vitamins

Food for Thought

- Tabbouleh is traditionally prepared with bulgur wheat. Name two other grains you could use to prepare this recipe.
- What pre-preparation tasks could be done while the couscous is cooling to room temperature?

Europe

Western Europe

The cuisines of many world cultures, including our own, trace their roots to countries and regions of Western Europe, which include Austria, the British Isles, France, Germany, Greece, Italy, Portugal, Scandinavia and Spain.

The British Isles

The British Isles are an island group just off the European continent. The two largest islands are Great Britain—which includes England, Scotland, Wales, and Northern Ireland—and Ireland. The food of this region tends to be hearty and cooked by plain, simple methods. Beef, mutton (meat from older sheep), pork, and fish are favourite foods. Many Britons eat four meals a day: breakfast, lunch, tea, and dinner (or supper).

The habit in our own country of eating hearty breakfasts is a custom inherited from Britain. Today, breakfast in the British Isles still usually includes cereal, eggs, bacon or sausage, broiled tomatoes, toast, and marmalade. Tea is more common in the morning than coffee.

British Cuisine

Typical lunches and dinners in Britain revolve around meat, including:

◆ **Roast beef and Yorkshire pudding.** Beef baked in the oven, with a popover-like mixture cooked in the pan drippings. Roast beef is usually served with a horse-radish sauce or mustard.

◆ **Shepherd's pie.** Leftover ground lamb or beef cooked with onions, garlic, tomatoes, and seasonings. The dish is covered with mashed potatoes and baked.

◆ Despite differences in culture and customs throughout Europe, some foods and methods of food preparation transcend national boundaries. The shellfish stew shown here is a common sight all along the Mediterranean coast.

◆ Plum pudding, a Christmas tradition in England, is a dense cake made with raisins, nuts, and flavourings, steamed in cheesecloth. Despite its name, plum pudding is not made with plums. Can you name another food whose name includes an ingredient that is not present?

◆ **Cornish pasties** (PAS-tees). Popular in the south of England, these baked pastry turnovers—filled with steak, onions, chopped potatoes and carrots—were once carried to work by miners and eaten cold.

The British also enjoy a variety of game— pigeon, quail, pheasant, and deer. Fish is also common to British menus. *Finnan haddie,* a fish dish sometimes eaten for breakfast, is smoked haddock prepared with milk, onion, lemon juice, pepper, and parsley.

Tea

A meal that is uniquely British is four o'clock tea. Tea generally includes bread—either plain or in small finger sandwiches—and a dessert. Crumpets, which are similar to what Canadians call English muffins, might also be served. So might scones, a tasty variation of baking-powder biscuits. Scones are often served with jam and clotted cream—a thick spread skimmed from rich, whole milk. In Scotland, tea may be served with oatcakes or oatmeal biscuits.

Sometimes, Britons have their tea served with a non-sweet dish that is somewhere between an appetizer and a main course. This meal is called high tea. A typical dish served at high tea is *Welsh rabbit* (or *rarebit*), seasoned, melted cheddar cheese on toast. High tea often takes the place of supper.

France

The goal of French cooking is to maximize the flavours of all ingredients in a dish so that no one flavour overpowers another. Much of French cooking is fairly simple— and frugal. The practice of deglazing a pan— adding stock or another liquid to a defatted sauté pan to loosen the browned-on particles—got its start in French kitchens. Deglazing is an easy and economical way of making a sauce.

Haute Cuisine

The classic dishes of France are often grouped under the heading *haute cuisine.* Literally "high cooking," this is a method of food preparation that makes use of complicated recipes and techniques, often involving costly ingredients. Originally, great chefs

◆ *Cassoulet* is typical French country fare. What method of cooking do you think is used to make *cassoulet*?

prepared these time-consuming dishes for aristocrats. Food preparation was considered an art. Rich sauces, elegantly decorated dishes, and exotic ingredients characterize haute cuisine. Haute cuisine still exists today, usually in expensive restaurants.

Cuisine Bourgeoise

Outside of the aristocracy, a simpler form of cooking developed. *Cuisine bourgeoise* (boor-JWAHZ) is based on hearty, one-dish meals made from fresh ingredients from the local market. *Cuisine bourgeoise* varies from province to province. Examples include:

- ◆ *Ragout.* A flavourful stew made with vegetables and meat, poultry, or fish. It is often named after the region where it originated.

- ◆ *Pot-au-feu.* A soupy casserole of less-tender cuts of beef, along with sausage and poultry, simmered in an earthenware pot with aromatic and root vegetables.

- ◆ *Cassoulet.* A hearty blend of white beans, meats, preserved duck, and garlic sausage.

- ◆ *Bouillabaisse.* A hearty soup that combines several types of fish and shellfish, tomatoes, and herbs.

Meals in France

French people rarely eat between meals. A typical breakfast is light, consisting of coffee or hot chocolate and some kind of bread—toast, a croissant, or *brioche,* a round roll made from a rich yeast dough. Lunch or dinner might include an *hors d'oeurve* (appetizer), followed by a light fish course, then a main dish and vegetables. Next comes a salad of greens simply dressed with a vinaigrette. A meal concludes with either a sweet dessert or with bread and cheese. Such a menu sounds filling. Portions, however, are kept sensible, and food is eaten slowly.

Spain and Portugal

Spain and Portugal inhabit a peninsula, which provides both countries with thousands of kilometres of coastline. Many of the dishes of both nations are based on fish and seafood.

Meals in Spain

Breakfast in Spain, as in France, generally consists of coffee or hot chocolate and a bread. The bread might be *churros,* fried strips of dough.

Lunch often consists of a salad, fish, a meat course, and fruit or a light dessert. Supper at home may be a light meal, but at a restaurant, it may be another large meal. Spanish people eat out late, with dinner hour generally starting at 10:30 P.M.

◆ *Tortilla española* is one of numerous dishes featured among the selection of *tapas* in Spain. It is an omelet filled with green peppers, onion, and potato, served at room temperature.

A few dishes are enjoyed throughout the country. These include chicken with garlic, garlic shrimp, *gazpacho* (cold vegetable soup), and *paella*—a combination of saffron-flavoured rice, poultry, and shellfish. Another dish of Spain, *tortilla española,* is an omelet made with potatoes, onions, and green peppers. The dish, served in slices at room temperature, is popular in *tapas* bars—restaurants that specialize in small servings of foods ranging from main dish to salad items.

Portuguese Cuisine

Portuguese cooking is similar to Spanish cooking, except that the Portuguese prefer foods with more spices. The cuisine was greatly influenced by travellers to India, South Africa, and South America. Portuguese foods tend to be rich because they contain more cream and butter.

Germany and Austria

Generally speaking, German food tends to be rich and heavy. Sausages abound, with different combinations and seasonings in each region. Familiar favourites include *bratwurst* and *knockwurst*.

Veal and pork are the most popular meats. Germans also eat beef and poultry, but fish is not popular.

German Cuisine

Some German dishes are characterized by a blending of fruit, vegetables, and meat to achieve sweet-sour flavours. An example is *sauerbraten,* beef marinated for several days in a sweet-sour sauce, and then simmered in the same sauce. It is served with noodles, dumplings, or boiled potatoes. *Schnitzel,* means "cutlet" in German, usually of veal. In *wienerschnitzel*—or "Viennese cutlet"— the veal is dipped in egg, breaded, and fried.

Germans are noted for their rye and pumpernickel breads as well as *stollen,* yeast bread with raisins and candied fruit. Another favourite is *streusel-kuchen,* a coffee cake topped with a mixture of flour, sugar, butter, nuts, and cinnamon.

German desserts include cakes and cookies. Marzipan, a rich candy made of ground

◆ *Schnitzels* (veal cutlets) and *wursts* (sausages) are staples of German cuisine. Name a food commonly eaten with schnitzels and wursts.

◆ Pasta is eaten up and down the boot-shaped country called Italy. In the north, in Venice, it is served as "black pasta," deriving its dark colour from cuttlefish ink. In the south, in Sicily, it is served with local sardines, pine nuts, and raisins.

almonds and sugar, has its origins in Germany. So does *nürnberger lebkuchen,* which is better known as gingerbread.

Austrian Cuisine

Austria is a nation south of Germany. The people there share not only a common language with the Germans but also many of the same food customs. Austrian cooking, in addition, bears influences of the cooking of its other Eastern European neighbours.

Austrians are famous for their rich cakes, almost always served *mitt Schlag*—with thick, sweetened whipped cream. *Linzertorte,* a cross between a pie and a cake, has a crust made in part of ground nuts and a sweet jam filling. *Sachertorte,* another famous Austrian dessert, is a rich chocolate cake spread with apricot preserves and a dark chocolate icing.

Italy

Where did pasta come from? A popular explanation is that Marco Polo brought the recipe to Italy from China in the 1300s.

Whatever its origins, pasta is the dish most associated with Italy. It is usually eaten, however, as a first course, not as a main course.

Italian Cuisine

In the south of Italy, pasta is often—though not always—served with tomato sauce. On the southern island of Sicily, a local favourite is *pasta con sarde*. In some parts of northern Italy, rice is favoured over pasta, in both rice balls and *risotto,* short-grained rice simmered carefully in stock. Another grain common in the north is cornmeal, served as *polenta,* cornmeal mush that is sometimes cooled, sliced, and fried.

Along Italy's northwest borders, the cooking is similar to that of France and Germany. Butter is used in place of olive oil. Italians of this region also eat *speck* (SHPEK), a local sausage.

Seafood is popular along the coastal areas. In the south, fresh bass is served mariner-style, with tomatoes, onions, and fresh basil.

No Italian meal would be complete without a *contorno* (vegetable course). Served after the main course, a large plate of eggplant, string beans, artichokes, peas, potatoes, or other vegetable is passed around the table.

Salads may begin or end a meal. They are usually served with an oil and vinegar dressing. Salads, pickled vegetables, cheeses, and other appetizers are called *antipasto*, which means "before the meal."

Italy is famous for its cheeses, from hard parmesan and romano, which must be grated, to *ricotta* (or "recooked" cheese), which is similar to cottage cheese.

Greece

The history of Greece includes a period of nearly 400 years when it was ruled by Turkey. As a result, many Greek dishes, such as vine leaves stuffed with seasoned meat and rice, are similar to foods in the Middle East.

Greek Cuisine

Greek cooking often makes use of tomatoes, green peppers, garlic, lemon juice, and olive oil. Rice appears in many dishes. *Feta* cheese, made from sheep's or goat's milk and cured in brine, is widely eaten as an appetizer and in salads. It is also used in cooking.

Because of Greece's location on the Mediterranean, Greek cuisine makes use of fish and shellfish. Grilled octopus is eaten, and shrimp are sometimes baked with tomatoes and feta cheese. Lamb is the most popular meat, often served grilled. *Moussaka* is a layered casserole made with seasoned ground lamb and sliced eggplant. A rich white sauce is poured over the mixture before baking.

Northern Europe

Denmark, Norway, Sweden, and Finland make up the Scandinavian countries. Although these countries do not have a lavish cuisine, the people have used the foods available to them creatively and tastefully.

Foods of Scandinavia

Scandinavians rely heavily on fish for food. Dried and salted cod is a staple. Fish may also be fried, poached, or grilled, as well as used in soups and fishballs.

◆ Fish is a prominent part of this Swedish *smorgasbord*.

Dairy products are also important to Scandinavian cooks. Each country has a version of thick or sour milk, which may be eaten with sugar. Milk, butter, and cream are essential ingredients in many dishes. Scandinavians also bake an array of rye and white breads.

Because the local growing season is so short, Scandinavian meals rarely include an abundance of fresh fruits and vegetables. Root vegetables such as potatoes, carrots, onions, and rutabagas are used regularly. Fresh berries (lingonberries, raspberries, and strawberries) are often used to accent desserts. *Fruksoppa,* or "fruit soup," is a mixture of dried fruit and tapioca cooked in a sweetened liquid and served cold.

Scandinavian Cuisine

The Swedish *smorgasbord* is perhaps the finest example of a bountiful buffet. Originally, the word meant "sandwich board." Now it is a collection of assorted meats and fish dishes, raw vegetables, salads, and hot dishes.

Smørrebrød are open-faced sandwiches, which the Danes eat daily. Thin slices of buttered bread are topped with pickled herring, cooked pork, raw cucumbers, onion rings, apple slices, mustard, and horseradish. The Danes are also well known for their rich, flaky, buttery pastries with touches of sugar, almonds, or jam.

Eastern Europe

Russia

Russia is one of the many countries that once made up the Soviet Union. It covers a vast area, from Eastern Europe to the Pacific Coast in Asia.

Russian Cuisine

Food in Russia differs from region to region, as it does in most countries. National dishes are based mainly on available staple foods. One example is Russian black bread, a dark, heavy, moist bread of rye and wheat, flavoured with chocolate, caraway, coffee, and molasses.

Hearty soups are also common. *Schchi* is a soup made from sauerkraut. Other popular soups are made with fresh cabbage and potatoes. *Borscht,* or beet soup, is one of the best-known Russian soups. If available, meat or sausage is added. Most soups either contain sour cream or are served with it.

◆ This assortment from the Russian table includes borscht, *piroshky*, and *kasha a la Gouriev*. The latter is a custard-like dessert made with farina and served warm.

Scandinavian Marinated Cod

Cod is a staple food in Scandinavia. This recipe might be prepared for a midday meal or a light supper. The cooked cod could also be flaked and used in a salad.

Ingredients

454 g	cod fillets	1 lb.
50 mL	olive oil	¼ cup
30 mL	lemon juice	2 tbsp.
50 mL	finely chopped onion	¼ cup
5 mL	salt	1 tsp.
2–3 mL	pepper	½ tsp.
30 mL	butter or margarine, melted	2 tbsp.
30 mL	vegetable oil	2 tbsp.

4 servings

Equipment: Shallow baking dish, broiler pan

1. Wash cod fillets in cold water and pat dry. Place in shallow baking dish.
2. In a small bowl, whisk together olive oil, lemon juice, onion, salt, and pepper.
3. Pour mixture over cod fillets. Let marinade 30 minutes (15 minutes on each side). Drain marinade from fillets and discard.
4. In another small bowl, blend melted butter or margarine with vegetable oil.
5. Preheat broiler.
6. Brush cold broiler grid with 1 tablespoon of the butter and oil mixture.
7. Place cod fillets on broiler pan.
8. Broil fillets 10 minutes per 2.5 cm (1 inch) of thickness, turning halfway through cooking time.
9. Brush fillets with remaining butter and oil mixture after turning.
10. When done, the fish should flake easily with a fork.
11. Serve immediately.

Nutrition Information

Per serving (approximate): 300 calories, 20 g protein, 1 g carbohydrate, 6 g fat, 49 mg cholesterol, 260 mg sodium

Good source of: potassium, vitamin E, B vitamins, phosphorus

Food for Thought

- What other varieties of fish might you substitute for the cod?
- What other acids, herbs, or spices could be used in the marinade for this recipe?

Fish—including sardines, salted herring, and salmon—are common. Caviar is often served with *blini,* small buckwheat pancakes, and sour cream. Buckwheat is also eaten crushed and cooked as *kasha,* and is served as an accompaniment to meats.

Tea is the most popular beverage. On cold evenings, you might find a gathering of Russians drinking tea and enjoying good conversation.

Other Eastern European Nations

The food in some other nations of Eastern Europe has many similarities to that of Russia and, sometimes, to food of the Middle East. The use of wheat, *kasha*, and cabbage, for example, is widespread.

Poland. In Poland, the national dish, *bigos,* is a stew of game meat with mushrooms, onions, sauerkraut, sausage, apples, and tomatoes. *Krupnik* is a barley and vegetable soup to which sour cream and dill are added.

Hungary. Hungarians enjoy grilled skewered lamb or beef in addition to the dish for which they are most famous, *gulyas* or *goulash,* in Canadian culture. This souplike dish is made with beef, onions, paprika, potatoes, and perhaps garlic, caraway seeds, tomatoes, and honey.

Hungarians also enjoy sauerkraut, pork-stuffed cabbage rolls, strudels, and *dobos torta,* a chocolate-filled sponge cake with many layers, glazed with caramel.

Czech Republic. The people of the Czech Republic area rely on dumplings as the cornerstone of their meals. Dumplings may be made from a variety of foods and come in many shapes and forms. Pork, beef, and game are common, as are cabbage and sauerkraut with caraway. One of the most famous Czech dishes is *kolacky,* yeast buns filled with fruit, cottage cheese, poppy seeds, or jam.

Romania. Corn is the mainstay of cooking in the area of Romania. Cornmeal mush, the national dish, is served with melted butter, sour cream, or yogurt. Romanian cooks also use peppers in their dishes and are known for their richly flavoured stews.

Bulgaria. Grains, vegetables, fruit, nuts, and yogurt are mainstays of Bulgarian cuisine. Fresh vegetables are eaten widely in salads. Fruits, nuts, and herbs grow well in this region. The people prefer fish and lamb to other meats. A favourite dish is *potato musaka,* a casserole of vegetables, meat, potatoes, onions, garlic, tomato, eggs, cream, and grated cheese.

Asia and the Pacific

Asia

For purposes of discussion, the countries of Asia and the Pacific will be treated in four sections. The first will look at the world cultures of Japan, China, and Korea. The second will examine Southeast Asia. The third will cover the Asian subcontinent of India; the fourth, Australia and New Zealand.

Asian World Cultures

Asia is the world's largest continent in both area and population. Traditional Asian cooking emphasizes grains and legumes, and uses an abundance of fresh ingredients. The staple grain is rice, though wheat is widely used in parts of China, India, and Japan. Another staple is soybeans, which are used to make many products, such as soy sauce, tamari, and tofu. Soybean sprouts are used fresh and in cooked dishes.

The basic cooking methods include boiling, steaming, and frying. Main dishes are usually a mixture of fried or steamed vegetables, mixed with a small amount of meat, poultry, or fish. Foods are prepared and cooked in bite-size pieces, which allows them to be picked up with chopsticks. The custom of cutting foods in small pieces started centuries ago when fuel was scarce and expensive; small pieces would cook quickly.

Coastal areas enjoy an abundant variety of seafood. Seaweed is an important ingredient of Asian cooking. It is used in soups, sauces, and main dishes, and is also served as a side dish.

Japan

Japanese cuisine features foods that are economical, nutritious, and attractive in appearance. Traditionally, Japanese people have eaten mainly vegetables, seaweed, and fish, as well as some fruit. Popular seafood includes squid and eel.

The Japanese dietary guidelines recommend that a person eat 30 different foods a day. Accordingly, meals usually consist of small amounts of a variety of foods. Fish is consumed both cooked and raw. It is presented the second way as *sushi* or *sashimi*, bits of very fresh raw fish combined with vinegared rice. *Sushi* is additionally wrapped in sheets of *nori,* or pressed seaweed.

Cooked dishes include *sukiyaki*—a mixture of vegetables and meat cooked quickly in a wok—and *tempura*—crisp batter-fried vegetables and seafood. *Soba,* buckwheat noodles, are widely eaten for lunches and snacks.

◆ **The tea ceremony is a centuries-old Japanese custom. The tea is prepared and served in a ritual of grace and precision. Under what circumstances do you think this ceremony occurs?**

◆ *Sushi* and *sashimi*—assorted fish, usually served raw in combination with vinegared rice—are staples of Japan that have gained a following in Canada.

In addition to having a pleasing flavour, Japanese food must also appeal to the eye. Foods and table settings are carefully arranged.

China

Chinese cuisine dates back thousands of years and goes hand in hand with Chinese philosophy. In this philosophy, the universe is seen as an interplay of opposing forces. Food preparation, therefore, balances opposites. Ingredients are carefully selected and cut into pieces to retain a sense of harmony and symmetry. Whether for a banquet or a simple family meal, the foods blend simplicity and elegance.

A Chinese meal does not have a main dish or a specific serving order of dishes. Instead, many dishes are arranged in the centre of the table, the variety depending on the number of diners. Each person is served a bowl of rice, and then helps him- or herself to some of each food. Soup is eaten during the meal or at the end of it—sometimes, sweetened, as dessert—but never at the beginning. Hot tea is always served.

Chinese Cuisine

The foods of China, which vary from region to region, range from spicy to simple and nurturing. From the southern province of Canton comes *congee* (kahn-JEE), a "mother's-milk" dish of rice gruel flavoured with meat or poultry. *Congee* is usually served with fried bread. *Chow fun* is broad noodles stirfried with strips of meat, onions, and bean sprouts.

◆ A noodle maker in Hong Kong displays the noodles he has made by swinging the dough in his hands, a traditional Chinese method.

Noodle dough is known throughout China. In the northern capital of Beijing, it is made into *lo mein*—thin spaghetti-like strands—and dumplings of all shapes and sizes. The region is also home to a special-occasion dish that is one of the most complicated recipes of any culture. That dish, *Peking duck*, requires several days of preparation, during which the duck is air-dried. The meat and crisp-roasted skin are ultimately presented ceremoniously on separate platters, along with thin pancakes.

First introduced in Canada in the 1960s and 1970s, Szechwan cooking comes from the province of the same name in central China. This area is noted for its extremely hot peppers. Other ingredients that contribute to the zesty, spicy cuisine of this region include fresh ginger and garlic.

Korea

As in much of Asia, rice is essential in Korea. It is sometimes cooked with barley or millet, which adds nutrients, texture, and flavour to the rice.

Meals usually consist of a soup or stew plus a grilled or stir-fried dish. Fish and fish pastes appear regularly in Korean foods. Garlic, in many forms, is used in meals. In fact, some of the hottest foods in the world can be found in South Korea.

Pickles add interest and flavour to Korean dishes. They might be made from almost any foods, such as pumpkins, cabbage, or ginseng. They can be rich in minerals and vitamin C.

Southeast Asia

Southeast Asia includes Cambodia, Indonesia, Laos, Myanmar (formerly Burma), Thailand, and Vietnam. These countries are in the tropics and have a variety of tropical fruits and vegetables, as well as a huge assortment of spices. The cooking reflects the influence of Chinese and European settlers.

Thailand

Coconut milk, the juice from coconuts, is frequently used as a liquid in Thai cooking, from main dishes to desserts. Noodles are a favourite and appear in casseroles and in soups. They are also mixed with sauces made of oysters, black beans, or fish. Then they are topped with chopped peanuts, coconut, and green onions.

◆ Like many nations in Southeast Asia, Thailand is a blend of old and new, as this scene at the floating market shows. What can you assume about the geography of Thailand based on this picture?

◆ *Pad Thai* is made with the flat noodles characteristic of Thai cooking. Name another dish common to the Thai table.

Most food combinations in Thailand have four basic flavours—sweet, sour, salty, and spicy. They also meet four texture requirements—soft, chewy, crunchy, and crispy. Popular dishes include *pad Thai,* a mixture of rice noodles, shrimp, peanuts, egg, and bean sprouts. *Satays,* bamboo-skewered lengths of marinated and grilled chicken or beef, are served with a peanut dipping sauce.

Vietnam

Rice and fish are the staple foods in Vietnam. The Vietnamese eat rice every day, by itself and combined with other foods. Rice starch is used to make noodles and dumpling wrappers. Foods are usually seasoned with *nuoc-mam,* a strong fish sauce.

Fish has always been the main source of protein for the Vietnamese. Fish and other foods are commonly seasoned with fresh ginger, coriander, lemon grass, and sweet basil. Many foods are rolled in lettuce or rice paper wrappers, which are easily dipped into spicy sauces.

Indonesia

Indonesian foods are highly spiced. One of the most popular dishes is *nasi goreng,* a mound of fried rice surrounded by assorted meats, such as beef and shrimp, and vegetables. The diner mixes them to obtain a wide variety of flavour

◆ Terraced rice fields like this one in Bali, Indonesia, provide the island nation with an abundant supply of its staple grain.

combinations. *Gado gado* is a salad of lettuce, hard-cooked eggs, onions, and bean sprouts, topped with a peanut butter–based dressing.

The Philippines

The inhabitants of the Philippines are a blend of Chinese, Arab, and Indian people living on 7000 islands. The culture and food reflect the influences of those who have settled there, including the Spanish and Americans of the last few centuries.

The Chinese introduced foods such as cabbage, noodles, and soy to the Philippines. The Spaniards brought tomatoes, garlic, and peppers.

The staple foods are fish, pork, and rice, which is made into cakes, noodles, and pancakes. Fish sauces are also widely used. The national dish is *adobo,* which is pork marinated and browned in soy sauce, vinegar, garlic, bay leaves, and peppercorns.

Thai Chicken Satays

Satays can be eaten as an appetizer or as a main course served with rice.
Traditionally, satays are served with a peanut dipping sauce.

Ingredients

500 g	boneless, skinless chicken breasts	1 lb.
15 mL	lemon juice	1 tbsp.
15 mL	lime juice	1 tbsp.
30 mL	finely chopped onion	2 tbsp.
15 mL	garlic powder	1 tbsp.
8 mL	curry powder	½ tbsp.
15 mL	sugar	1 tbsp.
125 mL	coconut milk or plain, non-fat yogurt	½ cup
	vegetable cooking spray	

4 servings (20 satays, about 5 satays per serving)

Equipment: Bamboo or wooden skewers; broiler pan

1. Place about 20 bamboo or wooden skewers in water to soak. Set aside.
2. Slice the chicken breast into 2.5- × 10-cm (1- × 4-inch) strips.
   Place in a medium bowl.
3. In a blender or food processor, blend remaining ingredients until smooth.
4. Reserve 50 mL (¼ cup) mixture and set aside.
5. Pour remaining mixture over chicken strips and marinate 15 minutes.
6. Preheat broiler.
7. Spray the broiler pan with the vegetable cooking spray.
8. Thread each chicken strip onto a skewer and place on cold broiler pan.
9. Broil for about 5 minutes on each side until chicken is golden brown.
   Brush with reserved sauce while cooking to preserve moistness.
10. Serve hot.

Nutrition Information

Per serving (approximate): 229 calories, 37 g protein, 8 g carbohydrate, 4 g fat, 98 mg cholesterol, 104 mg sodium

Good source of: potassium, magnesium, B vitamins, phosphorus

Food for Thought

- What purpose does the coconut milk or the yogurt serve in the marinade?
- What foods could you serve with this recipe to complete an Asian meal?

India

Cooking in India varies from region to region, according to climate and culture. In the northern and central areas, wheat is the staple grain and lamb is the most common meat. In the south, rice is the staple grain and the food is much spicier. Very little, if any, meat is eaten—especially beef, since cows are considered sacred animals. Garlic, cardamom, cumin, coriander, cloves, and other fragrant spices are widely used.

Virtually all Indian recipes begin with complex blend of toasted and ground spices called *garam masala.* Most cooks grind and mix their own spice blends and keep several on hand in jars. Yogurt is used widely.

India boasts a wide variety of meatless main dishes; among these is *chana baji,* sautéed chickpeas and onions liberally flavoured with cumin. When poultry and fish are available, they are used sparingly in proportion to other ingredients. The dish *biryani* is a colourful plate piled high with flavourful *basmati* rice with almonds, raisins, and bits of either lamb, goat, or chicken.

As in Africa, breads are used as edible utensils. *Chapati,* a simple flat wheat bread, is used in some areas to scoop up rice and lentils. Breads are baked in a clay oven, or *tandoor,* which also lends its name to a famous Indian dish—*chicken tandoori.* The dish is made of chicken pieces that have been marinated in a blend of yogurt and garam masala before cooking at high heat in the tandoor.

Australia and New Zealand

The foods in Australia and New Zealand are very similar to those of the cultures who settled the coastal parts of these countries. Among these cultures are the English, the Scottish, and the French.

Menus vary according to location, from the outback of Australia, to the large cities along its coast, to the smaller cities and rural areas of New Zealand. Meals usually feature foods that are locally available. Meat and seafood are plentiful. Many people eat steaks and chops (beef or mutton) for breakfast. New Zealanders enjoy *toheroas,* which resemble clams.

One uniquely Australian dish is *pavlova,* a rich mixture of meringue, fruit, and cream. Pies and sweet rice dishes are common desserts.

◆ **This Indian feast includes *tandoori chicken, raita, dal, lamb vindaloo,* and *basmati* rice.**

Chapter 27   Review and Activities

Summary

- Latin American cuisine has been influenced by the Spanish and the Aboriginal Peoples. Their food staple is maize, but wheat and rice are also grown there.
- South American foods originate from the Aboriginal Peoples, Portuguese, and Africans. Their food staples are palm oil, peppers, coconut milk, sausage, and kale.
- Africa and the Middle East are divided by the Sahara desert.
- People living in South Africa eat plaintains, rice, bananas, yams, cassava, corn, millet, sorghum, and wheat. Chickens, sheep, and goats are also raised and eaten there.
- Those living in North Africa are mostly Arabs and follow Middle East cuisine. Their food staples are rice, wheat, and barley.
- In the British Isles, beef, mutton, pork, and fish are the favourite foods.
- French cooking is divided into *haute cuisine*, elegant dishes with exotic ingredients and rich sauces, and *cuisine bourgeiose*, based on hearty one-dish meals of meat and local vegetables.
- Spanish and Portuguese cuisine focus on fish and seafood dishes. The Portuguese prefer spicier food.
- German and Austrian foods are rich and heavy. Sausages, veal, and pork, and rye breads are popular. Austrians are famous for their rich cakes.

- Italians are famous for their pasta, tomato sauce, and cheeses.
- Many Greek dishes are similar to those of the Middle East. Rice, feta cheese, fish, octopus, and shellfish are common foods.
- Northern Europeans depend largely on fish, dairy products, root vegetables, and rye and white breads in their meals, and fresh berries in their desserts.
- Eastern European foods consist of grain products, fish, game meat, pork, beef, lamb, and hearty soups made from root vegetables.
- Asian foods emphasize grains, legumes, and vegetables, as well as fish served in bite-size pieces. Garlic and spices are used liberally.
- Southeast Asian cooking includes a variety of tropical fruits, vegetables, and spices. Noodles, rice, fish, and coconut milk are also common ingredients.
- Indian cooking varies according to the region. Wheat and rice are the staple grains. Meat is rarely eaten, though poultry and fish are.
- Australia and New Zealand follow similar eating habits as their English, Scottish, and French ancestors. Meat, seafood, and local foods make up their meals.

Review and Activities   Chapter 27

Knowledge and Understanding

1. Name two influences on Brazilian cooking and two foods reflecting these influences.

2. Name two foods introduced into Africa in the 16th century and their places of origin.

3. Name and describe three dishes often eaten in the Middle East.

4. List three traditional condiments used in Israel.

5. Name two foods usually served at British tea.

6. What is the basic philosophy behind cooking in France?

7. How is the Chinese cooking of the Szechwan province different from that of other regions of the country?

Thinking and Inquiry

8. Chinese foods are said to reflect the Chinese people's traditional philosophy of life. What philosophy of life would Canadian food reflect?

9. Choose two of the cultures studied in this chapter. For each one answer the following questions:

   • What are some common foods?
   • What factors influenced the choices of foods?
   • How are these foods prepared?
   • What factors influenced the method of preparation?

10. Explain how two different religions have influenced food habits in the world.

11. Describe how global travel and increased telecommunications have affected the exchange of food customs. How does this compare to the past?

12. Explain which cultures have influenced Caribbean foods. How did these cultures come to exert this influence? What other countries' foods have been influenced in a similar manner?

Communication

13. Plan a menu to serve at a food festival. Choose five different countries representing five different regions of the world. For each of the countries, choose an appetizer, a main course, and a dessert or beverage. Prepare a pamphlet to be distributed to participants at the festival.

14. You are hosting two exchange students this summer from the country of your choice. Design a food plan for the week that would incorporate some of their favourite dishes, and introduce the students to some of yours. Make sure that you balance your menu and follow *Canada's Food Guide to Healthy Eating*.

Application

15. Many of our food customs and traditions come from our culture. Prepare an oral report for the class answering the following questions.

   • What cultural background do you come from?
   • Are both your parents from the same background?
   • What are the food customs and traditions that you follow as a family?
   • What are the food customs and traditions that you follow as an extended family, on your father's side? On your mother's side?
   • Ask your parents or guardians how the food customs and traditions of your nuclear family differ from those of their nuclear family.

   Summarize what you have learned about your food culture.

UNIT 6

Issues and Trends

UNIT EXPECTATIONS

While reading this unit, you will:

- Plan, perform, and present the results of an investigation into the nutritional status of Canadians.

- Predict trends in the preparation of foods in the home and in the commercial sector.

- Describe noticeable trends in food-consumption patterns.

- Identify the components and foods that form the basis of various cuisines around the world.

- Identify the economic, political, and environmental factors that affect food production and supply throughout the world.

- Identify the factors that are critical to achieving and maintaining food security and eliminating hunger.

Food is an important part of our world for many reasons other than just satisfying hunger.

in Food and Nutrition

OVERVIEW

This unit has been designed to look at foods and nutrition based on expectations from the senior curriculum. By studying this unit, you will gain an understanding of the nutritional status of Canadians, current trends in food preparation, world cuisine, the factors affecting Canadian food production and supply, and issues relating to food security and hunger on a worldwide basis.

CHAPTER EXPECTATIONS

While reading this chapter, you will:

- Compile a body of core information on the nutritional status of Canadians and determine personal nutrient intake, using a variety of print and electronic sources and telecommunication tools.

- Demonstrate an understanding of how the findings of your nutritional survey apply to you and your family.

Nutritional Status of Canadians

Many Canadians are unaware of what nutrients they are getting from the food they eat.

KEY TERMS

macronutrients
micronutrients
oxidation

SOCIAL SCIENCE SKILL

- developing research skills using internet sources

CHAPTER INTRODUCTION

This chapter provides you with information on the nutritional status of Canadians. By studying their eating patterns, you will be able to identify what nutrients are lacking in Canadians' diets. Recording your own personal nutrient intake will help you better understand and analyse your own eating habits.

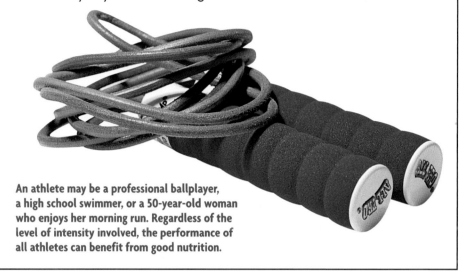

An athlete may be a professional ballplayer, a high school swimmer, or a 50-year-old woman who enjoys her morning run. Regardless of the level of intensity involved, the performance of all athletes can benefit from good nutrition.

Canadian Eating Habits

How Do Canadians Rate Their Eating Habits?

According to the National Institute of Nutrition's 2001 Tracking Nutrition Trends Survey, adult Canadians rated their eating habits as:

38%
Very Good/
Excellent

20%
Fair/
Poor

42%
Good

◆ **How do your eating habits compare to other Canadians? Why did you rate yourself the way you did?**

Source: Health Canada (n.d.).

Statistics like this provide an insight into the attitudes, eating behaviours, and nutritional knowledge of Canadians. This helps government agencies such as Health Canada, professional organizations such as Dietitians of Canada, and educational organizations such as schools shape a healthier future for Canadians. It also helps people understand the role nutrition plays in their lives.

It is valuable to record eating habits by age and gender because people at different life stages and males and females sometimes have different nutrient needs.

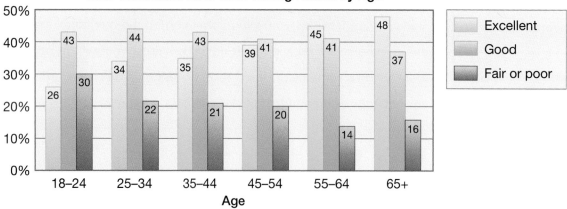

How Canadians Rate Their Eating Habits by Age

Legend: Excellent, Good, Fair or poor

Source: Health Canada (2002).

◆ **In one or two paragraphs, summarize the information that this graph provides.**

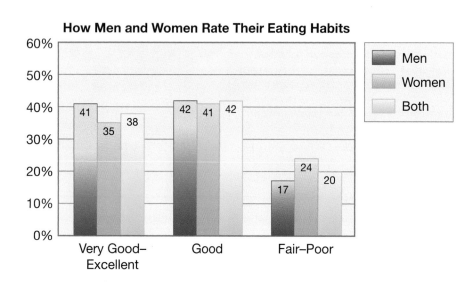

How Men and Women Rate Their Eating Habits

Legend: Men, Women, Both

Source: Health Canada (n.d.).

◆ **More women (42 percent) than men (35 percent) reported that they feel their eating habits are "very good" or "excellent." Only 17 percent of women rated themselves as having "fair or poor" eating habits compared to 24 percent of men.**

INTERNET CONNECTS

www.mcgrawhill.ca/links/food
To learn more about how Canadians rate their eating habits, go to the web site above for *Food for Today, First Canadian Edition,* to see where to go next.

How Aware Are Canadians of *Canada's Food Guide to Healthy Eating?*

◆ About 41 percent of Canadians are able to correctly name all four food groups from *Canada's Food Guide to Healthy Eating.*

- More women (54 percent) than men (35 percent) were able to name all four food groups in the food guide.

- Younger adults are more familiar with the food guide than older adults.

Source: Health Canada (n.d.).

Where Do Canadians Get Their Nutritional and Health Information?

According to the National Institute of Nutrition's report, *Tracking Nutrition Trends 1989–1994–1997: An Update on Canadians' Attitudes, Knowledge, and Reported Actions:*

- 71 percent of Canadians reported that they get their nutrition information from product labels more than any other source.

- Radio and television programs were the second most referred to sources of information, identified by 68 percent of Canadians.

- For 67 percent of Canadians, friends, relatives, and colleagues were reported as a nutrition information source.

- The use of magazines for nutrition information was reported by 65 percent of those surveyed.

- Books were referred to by 55 percent of Canadians.

Source: Health Canada (n.d.).

- Less than half of Canadians (46 percent) reported that they consult their physicians for nutrition information.

- 43 percent turn to materials offered by health associations.

Source: Health Canada (n.d.)

INTERNET CONNECTS

www.mcgrawhill.ca/links/food
To learn more about using *Canada's Food Guide to Healthy Eating,* go to the web site above for *Food for Today, First Canadian Edition,* to see where to go next.

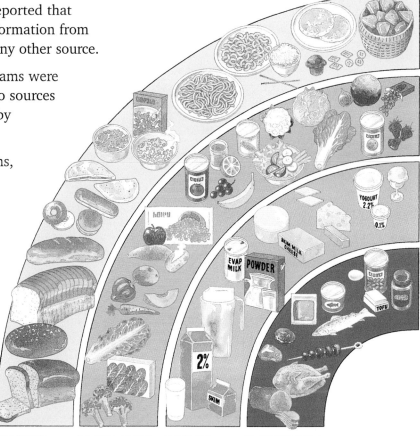

Grain Products
Choose whole grain and enriched products more often.

Vegetables and Fruit
Choose dark green and orange vegetables and orange fruit more often.

Milk Products
Choose lower-fat milk products more often.

Meat and Alternatives
Choose leaner meats, poultry and fish, as well as dried peas, beans and lentils more often.

Canadä

- **The Rainbow illustrates the different food groups in *Canada's Food Guide to Healthy Eating***

FOR YOUR HEALTH

Healthy Eating Survey

To determine your current eating habits, on a sheet of paper numbered 1–12, answer "yes" or "no" to the following questions:

1. I am happy with my eating habits.

2. I know what the four food groups from *Canada's Food Guide to Healthy Eating* are.

3. I eat a variety of foods from each of the four food groups.

4. I know where to find the suggested number of servings for all four food groups.

5. I choose foods within the suggested number of servings for the food groups.

6. I choose whole-grain and enriched-grain products more often.

7. I choose dark green and orange vegetables and orange fruit more often.

8. I am active every day.

9. I enjoy eating with my family and friends regularly.

10. Food is an important part of life's celebrations for me.

11. I choose "Other Foods" wisely.

12. I choose lower fat foods more often.

Source: Health Canada (2002).

- In groups, total the answers to each question. Post the totals.
- Total the answers to each question by gender. Post the totals.
- Using graphic organizers of your choice, record your findings.
- Draw conclusions about the eating habits of the class.
- What three conclusions did you draw about your own personal eating habits by doing this questionnaire?

INTERNET CONNECTS

www.mcgrawhill.ca/links/food
To learn more about your nutrition profile, go to the web site above for *Food for Today,* *First Canadian Edition,* to see where to go next.

Vitality

Vitality is enjoying eating well, being active, and feeling good about yourself. *Canada's Food Guide to Healthy Eating* is a tool to help individuals over the age of four make healthy food choices. Healthy eating is not about one food or one choice or one nutrient. It is the average of what is eaten over time. Choices may be balanced over a day, or even over several days.

To help you do this, Health Canada created the Rainbow. The Rainbow drawing contains the four food groups: grain products, vegetables and fruit, milk products, and meat alternatives. For each food group, there are recommendations for the size and number of servings per day, as shown in the chart below.

The lower number of servings is the minimum needed to get the basic level of nutrients and what would be appropriate for a four-year-old child. An active youth or adult may require the maximum level in the particular food-group range. That is why the Food Guide gives a higher and lower number of servings for each food group. *Canada's Food Guide to Healthy Eating* also contains an "Other Foods" section. Although taste and enjoyment can come from this group, some of the foods are higher in fat or calories. The food guide recommends using these foods in moderation.

The Flexibility of Canada's Food Guide

How can one food guide meet everyone's needs? Canada's Food Guide is meant to be a guideline. It is flexible in the number of servings and the size of servings. If you follow the Food Guide, you will get from 1800 to 3200 Cal (7500–13 400 kJ). You can choose the number of servings necessary for your nutrient and energy needs.

On the bar side of the food guide, under the heading "Different People Need Different Amounts of Food," factors influencing a person's needs for energy and nutrients are given. This shows that Canada's Food Guide is flexible. The number of servings you need every day from the four food groups depends on your age, body size, activity level, whether you are male or female, and if you are pregnant or breast-feeding.

Canada's Food Guide Rainbow

Food Group	Servings Per Day
Grain Products	5–12
Vegetables and Fruit	5–10
Milk Products	2–3 (Children 4–9 years) 3–4 (Youth 10–16 years) 2–4 (Adults) 3–4 (Pregnant and breast-feeding women)
Meat and Alternatives	2–3

◆ No two people are exactly alike. Different people need different amounts of food.

Factors Influencing Energy and Nutrient Needs

Age influences your food and nutrient needs. For example, a teen generally has higher energy and nutrient needs than a 35-year-old. A teen's body is growing and maturing. The amount of food preschoolers need depends on their age, body size, activity level, growth rate, and appetite. The Food Guide is flexible here. A child-size serving is anywhere from a half to full size for foods in each food group. Generally, the size of portion increases with age. A two-year-old may eat a half-slice of bread while a four-year-old may eat a whole slice. Both of

these can be counted as one child-size serving of grain products. Because preschoolers have both small stomachs and high requirements of energy, they may need to eat small amounts more often. Regularly scheduled meals and nutritious snacks are important at this age.

Girls between seven and nine years of age have about the same energy requirements as adult women. The Food Guide allows them to choose the lower to middle number of servings. Girls 10 to 12 and boys 7 to 12 need more energy to allow for growth spurts and are more likely to eat more servings. Females particularly need calcium and iron.

By having a range of servings in each food group, *Canada's Food Guide to Healthy Eating* is flexible enough to incorporate the

◆ Appetites for teens and preschoolers tend to increase during growth spurts and periods of intense activity.

different stages of the life cycle. The Food Guide promotes a flexible eating pattern that meets individual needs. People with a larger body size have greater nutrient and energy needs. Males with a larger body size and greater muscle mass generally have higher nutrient and energy needs.

Increased activity levels may also mean increased energy and nutrient needs. A competitive swimmer, wrestler, or jogger would choose the largest number of servings from each of the four food groups and add the "Other Foods" category. Athletes have higher energy needs than most people, and at times they may need to choose more servings.

A 35-year-old who is not very active will eat different amounts of food from day to day to satisfy his or her nutrient and energy needs. As appetite and activity level changes, he or she may adjust the number of servings and the amount of "other foods" consumed. This is another way that the Food Guide is flexible.

As small children grow and become more active, they may choose more servings from each of the food groups and add "other foods."

Gender also influences your energy and nutrient needs. Children's energy needs tend to increase through puberty, but the increase is not steady. Children grow at different rates. Girls tend to mature and stop growing earlier than boys. For this reason, boys' appetites will continue to increase and girls' energy needs will level off in the teen years.

Females who are pregnant and/or breast-feeding need to pay special attention to iron, folate, and calcium needs. Canada's Food Guide allows for all these differences through the ranges in servings.

INTERNET CONNECTS

www.mcgrawhill.ca/links/food

To learn more about the importance of nutrition by age and by gender, go to the web site above for *Food for Today, First Canadian Edition,* to see where to go next.

Cultural Diversity in Foods and Flexibility in the Food Guide

Canada's Food Guide to Healthy Eating encourages variety of food choices. A variety of cultural and ethnic foods adds spice to meal patterns. Perogies and cabbage rolls, for example, are combination foods. For cabbage rolls, the outside cabbage leaf would fit under the Vegetables and Fruit group. The rice and meat filling would fit under the Grain Products and Meat and Alternatives groups.

Special Occasions

Birthdays, holidays, and religious celebrations are some of the occasions that can bring special foods into our lives. We may overeat and feel guilty. Relax and enjoy these special times with family and friends when food plays an important part.

Serving Sizes

What is a child serving size? There is a wide difference in portions of foods eaten by preschoolers. While parents and caregivers determine the selection of foods offered, preschoolers to teens can determine how much to eat. By trusting hunger signs, preschoolers and young children especially can learn to respond to physical signs that indicate when they are hungry or satisfied.

◆ What foods from other cultures do you enjoy? What food groups would they fit under?

◆ *Canada Food Guide to Healthy Eating* gives examples of serving sizes. What would a serving size be for pizza?

Canada's Food Guide to Healthy Eating refers to serving sizes that are not large—250 mL (1 cup) of spaghetti, a bagel, or a hamburger bun each counts as two servings of grain products. A 250 mL (1 cup) juice box counts as two servings of vegetables and fruit. One medium-sized carrot is a vegetable serving. One sandwich made with two slices of bread counts as two servings of grain products. It is important to refer to the food guide to understand the serving sizes of various food groups.

Influences on Canadians' Eating Habits

In the 2001 Tracking Nutrition Trends (Health Canada, n.d.) survey, people were asked about "key motivators" to change or improve their eating habits. Their responses are shown in the graph at right.

The importance of each of these factors varied according to age. For adults under 25, the most important factor for 17 percent was "looking better." For adults over the age of 45, "maintaining health" and "preventing disease" were the most important factors. More

Key Motivators to Improve Eating Habits

Maintain Personal Health—58%

Lose Weight—22%

Needs of Family—10%

Prevent Disease—8%

Look Better—8%

Source: Health Canada. (n.d.).

women (74 percent) than men (64 percent) consider health maintenance to be very influential in their food choice decisions. For almost three-quarters (72 percent) of Canadians, "weight management" and "weight loss" were identified as "very" or "somewhat" influential.

Time appears to be a significant influence on Canadians' eating habits. According to the Food and Consumer Manufacturers of Canada's 1999 Consumerline Survey, Canadians are increasingly feeling more pressed for time. More than two-thirds of Canadians (68 percent) reported they are short of time. While many Canadians understand the importance of healthy eating, approximately 13 percent don't feel they have enough time to prepare nutritious meals (Health Canada, n.d.).

The biggest challenge facing women who want to eat well is time. Women reported that they don't have time to plan, purchase, and prepare healthy meals, especially when they are tired after a day at work (Dietitians of Canada, 2003).

INTERNET CONNECTS

www.mcgrawhill.ca/links/food
To learn more about healthy eating challenges facing women, go to the web site above for *Food for Today, First Canadian Edition,* to see where to go next.

Are Canadians Eating Enough from the Four Food Groups?

The following statistics from a recent study on the food habits of Canadians help us understand the nutritional status of Canadians:

◆ More than a quarter of the adult population did not consume the minimum number of servings from each of the four food groups.

◆ Almost half of all teenaged girls were not consuming the minimum number of servings from each food group.

◆ Almost half of adult women and almost 60 percent of female teens did not eat the minimum number of servings of meat and alternatives.

◆ Thirty percent of adults and male teens are not consuming the minimum number of servings of grain products.

◆ Forty percent of female teens are not consuming the minimum number of servings of grain products.

Source: Beef Information Centre (2001).

◆ More than half of all adult females and males are not consuming the minimum servings of milk products. Forty percent of teen males are not consuming the minimum servings of milk products. What is the main nutrient derived from the milk products food group?

◆ Almost half of female teens did not consume the minimum five servings of vegetables and fruit per day. More than half of the adults and male teens in the study did not consume the minimum five servings of vegetables and fruit per day.

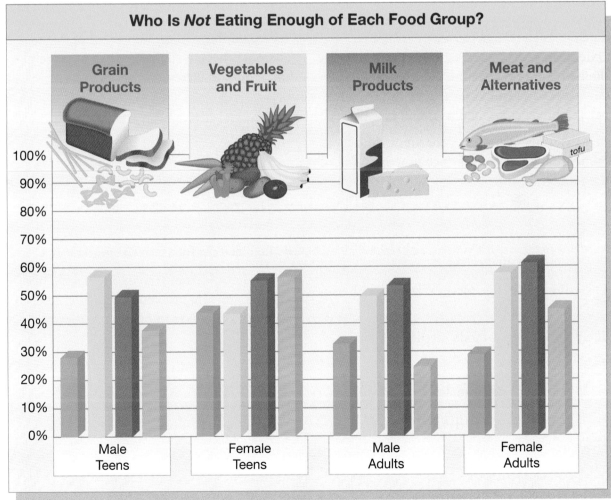

Who Is *Not* Eating Enough of Each Food Group?

Source: Pasut, L. (2001).

Vegetables and fruit reduce the risk of some diseases. Reducing risk means that the chances of developing a disease are lowered. It doesn't guarantee that a disease will be prevented.

Vegetables and fruit contain substances called antioxidants. Antioxidants prevent damage to your cells caused by oxidation. **Oxidation** occurs when oxygen reacts in the body to form harmful "free radicals." Vegetables and fruits contain the antioxidants beta-carotene and vitamins C and E.

Reasons people are not consuming the minimum number of servings from each of the food groups:

- Dislike the food.

- Health reasons.

- Vegetarian beliefs.

- Getting too much energy from the "other foods" category.

Energy from "other foods" accounted for:

- 27 percent in adult females.

- 29 percent in adult males.

- 27 percent in female teens.

- 33 percent in male teens.

The high level of intake from "other foods" is a concern because the minimum number of servings from the four food groups are not being met by a significant proportion of the population.

Macronutrient Intake by Adults

Macronutrients are the major nutrients in the diet. These are carbohydrates, protein, and fat, which provide energy.

The percentage of fat, protein, and carbohydrates in the diet has changed compared to almost 30 years ago. Fat in the diet has decreased from 40 to 30 percent of energy. There has been a slight increase in protein and a greater increase in carbohydrates.

Factors that have lead to the change in macronutrient intake are:

- Lower-fat versions of foods.

- Leaner cuts of meat.

- Changes in cooking methods (less deep-fat frying).

- Reduced-fat foods on the market.

Despite this change in eating habits, obesity is a growing problem in Canada, likely a result of a decrease in physical activity.

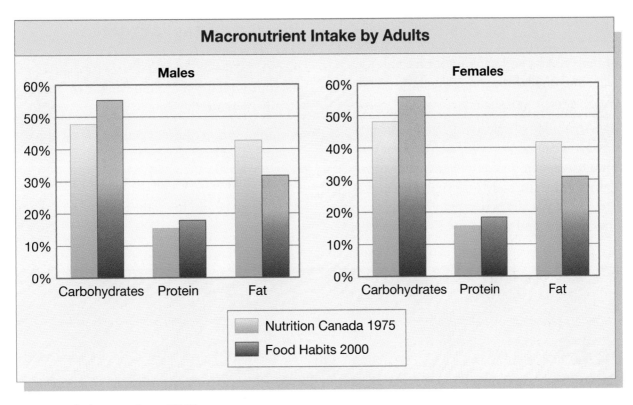

Macronutrient Intake by Adults

Males / Females

Carbohydrates — Protein — Fat

Nutrition Canada 1975
Food Habits 2000

Source: Beef Information Centre (2001).

Nutrition and Physical Activity

Being active means making physical activity part of your everyday life. It helps you to:

◆ Manage your weight.

◆ Strengthen your heart, lungs, and muscles.

◆ Gain self-confidence.

◆ Reduce stress.

How Physically Active Are Canadians?

◆ 57 percent of adults aged 18 and older do not get enough exercise for optimal health benefits.

◆ The majority of Canadians face increased risk of chronic disease and premature death due to physically inactive lifestyles.

◆ More women than men are physically inactive.

◆ Physical inactivity increases with age.

Source: Canadian Fitness & Lifestyle Research Institute (2002).

How Active Are Canadian Children?

◆ 58 percent of Canadian youth aged 12–19 are not active enough for optimal growth and development.

◆ Girls are significantly less active than boys.

◆ 64 percent of girls are considered physically inactive.

◆ 52 percent of boys are considered physically inactive.

Source: Canadian Fitness & Lifestyle Research Institute (2002).

An optimal level of activity would be reached, for example, by a child engaging in a half-hour of martial arts and walking for a total of at least one hour throughout the day.

You are awake about 15 to 19 hours per day. If you are physically active *one hour* a day (you can add up your activities in ten-minute segments), you will achieve your daily total. Your body is designed to move. Staying physically active regularly helps you stay healthy and reduce the risk of disease.

Ways to Stay Active

◆ Walk whenever you can.

◆ Start with a ten-minute walk then gradually increase the time.

◆ Join a group of friends and play pickup hockey or another game that you enjoy.

◆ Use the stairs instead of the elevator.

◆ Reduce TV or computer time.

◆ **Are you active at least one hour a day?** What are three new ways you can build physical activity into your life?

Micronutrients

In order to compile a body of core information on the nutritional status of Canadians, it is necessary to understand key terms, such as the following:

- **Micronutrients** are nutrients that are required in the diet in small amounts and include all the vitamins and minerals.

- **Recommended levels** are the amount of a nutrient needed by most people. They are found in the new Dietary Reference Intakes.

- **Fortification** is the addition of nutrients to a food, such as adding iron to pasta.

- **Dietary reference intakes** (DRI) are made up of four values for each nutrient, for every life stage and gender group: Estimated Average Requirement (EAR), the Recommended Dietary Allowance (RDA), the Adequate Intake (AI), and the Tolerable Upper Intake Level (TUIL). Mostly scientists and nutritionists who work in research or academic settings use DRI values.

FOR YOUR HEALTH

Keys to Good Health

1. **Eat a variety of foods**
   - Eat a variety of different foods daily through your meals and snacks.
   - Vary your choices from each food group.
   - Experiment with new varieties, flavours, colours, and preparation methods to add zing to your meals.
   - A variety of foods will provide you with many different vitamins, minerals, antioxidants, and fibre.

2. **Balance your food intake according to your age, gender, and activity level.**
   - Eating the right amount of food is as important as what you choose to eat.
   - *Canada's Food Guide to Healthy Eating* gives examples of serving sizes.

3. **Achieve and maintain a healthy weight by eating well and keeping active.**

Nutrient Needs of Athletes

Eating right can't improve an athlete's skills—only practice can do that. An athlete's daily food choices, however, can make a difference between a good performance and a poor one.

Generally, an athlete's nutritional needs can be met by following the recommendations in *Canada's Food Guide to Healthy Eating*. Nevertheless, the athlete does have two nutritional needs that far exceed those of the average person: the need for energy and the need for water.

Energy Needs

As noted earlier, during digestion, carbohydrates are broken down into the simple sugar, glucose, which is used for energy. Extra carbohydrates are turned into a storage form of glucose known as glycogen, which is stored in the liver and muscles.

During vigorous and extended periods of exercise, the body uses glycogen for fuel. When glycogen is used up, athletes run out of energy. Therefore, it's essential for athletes to eat plenty of carbohydrates to build up their glycogen reserves.

Mean Nutrient Intake of Teens (13–17 Years) Compared to Recommendations

	13–17 Years (n = 84)	Recommended DRI[a]
Males		
Calcium (mg)	1407	1300
Folate (mcg)	**299**	400
Iron (mg)	22.2	11
Zinc (mg)	15.8	11
Vitamin A (RE)	1888	900 mcg[b]
Vitamin C (mg)	173	75
Vitamin B12	6.1	2.4
Females		
Calcium (mg)	**1004**	1300
Folate (mcg)	**274**	400
Iron (mg)	15.1	15
Zinc (mg)	9.8	9
Vitamin A (RE)	1434	700 mg
Vitamin C (mg)	214	65
Vitamin B12	5.0	2.4

[a] All DRI values are Recommended Daily Allowances (RDA) except calcium, which is Adequate Intake (AI).

[b] DRI values for Vitamin A are in micrograms, not retinol equivalents.

[c] Bolded values indicate levels below Dietary Reference Intakes (DRI).

Source: Beef Information Centre (2001).

During training and competition, athletes may need two or three times as much energy as the average person. Complex carbohydrates are the best choice for supplying this additional energy. Carbohydrate loading, as this eating pattern is called, includes eating foods such as legumes and peas, breads, cereal, pasta, rice, and potatoes. Similar to non-athlete's calorie needs, about 60 percent of an athlete's calories should come from carbohydrates, about 25 percent from fat, and about 15 percent from protein. Individual needs vary. Note that health experts do not recommend carbohydrate loading for teen athletes.

◆ Successful athletes know that performing their best requires good nutrition. **After reading this section, list two do's and don'ts for teen athletes in training.**

Liquid Needs

Athletes lose a great deal of water through perspiration—as much as 3 to 5 litres (3 to 5 quarts) during a strenuous workout. If the water is not replaced right away, dehydration (dee-hy-DRAY-shun), or lack of adequate fluids in the body, can result. This condition can lead to serious health problems.

An athlete who is dehydrated may become weak and confused. The body can become overheated, especially when exercising in hot weather. Heat exhaustion or heat stroke can result. These are serious conditions requiring immediate medical attention.

To prevent dehydration, athletes should drink water before, during (about every 15 minutes), and after an event. They should drink water even if they do not feel thirsty. Thirst is a sign that dehydration has already begun.

One good way to gauge the amount of water to drink is to weigh in before and after the event. Loss of water usually shows up as a loss in body weight. For each 250 g (½ pound) lost during exercise, athletes should drink 250 mL (1 cup) of fluid.

In addition to water, juices and fruit drinks may be used. However, because they are high in sugar, they may cause stomach cramps, diarrhea, and nausea. To cut down on sugar, dilute juices and fruit drinks with an equal amount of water.

Sports drinks are also available. They are valuable mainly to athletes involved in exercise lasting longer than 90 minutes.

◆ Be sure to drink additional water whenever you exercise vigorously, even if you don't feel thirsty. **Why is drinking water important?**

Food Science ◆ L A B ◆

Calories to Burn

You know the expression "Seeing is believing." You are about to see the energy released when food is burned by your system.

Procedure

1. Press the eye of a needle into the narrow end of a cork. Mount a shelled walnut on the point of the needle. Weigh the resulting construction.

2. Remove both ends of a large can and one end of a small can. Punch holes in the large can near the bottom and in the small can near the top (the open end).

3. Pour 100 mL of tap water into the small can. Measure the temperature of the water.

4. Insert a glass rod through the holes in the side of the small can. Use the rod to balance the small can within the large can.

5. Place the nut on a non-flammable surface and light it with a match. Immediately place the large can over the burning nut so that the small can is above the nut. Allow the nut to burn for two minutes or until the flame goes out.

6. Stir the water with the thermometer. Record the water's highest temperature. Weigh the nut/cork/needle construction again, and record the result.

Conclusions

◆ How much did the weight of the nut change?

◆ How much did the temperature change?

◆ Repeat the experiment using a different kind of nut. Do you arrive at a different result? Why or why not?

Common Myths

Some athletes believe they need extra protein to build muscles because dietary protein is needed to build body protein. However, an athlete's protein requirements can be met easily through normal eating. Excess protein does nothing to build up muscles—only physical training can do that.

What about vitamin or mineral supplements? Almost all athletes who eat a wide variety of nutritious foods do not need vitamin or mineral supplements. The same is true of salt tablets. While some salt and potassium are lost through perspiration, these minerals can be easily replaced in well-chosen daily meals.

Timing of Meals

If you eat just before an athletic event, the digestive process competes with your muscles for energy. Instead, eat three to four hours before the event to allow time for proper digestion.

Follow these suggestions to get the most from your pre-event meal:

◆ Choose a meal that is low in fat and protein and high in complex carbohydrates. As you may recall, fat and protein take the longest to digest.

◆ Eat foods you enjoy and have eaten before. A pre-game meal is no time to experiment with a new food.

◆ Choose foods that you know you can digest easily.

◆ Have a reasonably sized meal (not too large) so that your stomach is relatively empty by event time.

◆ Drink large amounts of fluids with the meal.

After an athletic event or a hard workout, you need to refuel your body. In addition to replacing the water you have lost, be sure to eat nutritious food within one to four hours after the event—the sooner the better. Studies indicate that more carbohydrate (as glycogen) can be deposited in the muscles immediately after exercise than hours afterward.

Remember that there are no quick fixes to improving athletic performance. Careful training and sound nutrition, practised every day, are the surest ways to long-lasting top athletic performance.

A Healthy Body Image

A healthy body image means accepting who you are and how you look. It means having confidence in who you are. A healthy weight enables you to stay active and lowers the risk of health problems. It is not just a low weight. It means that you are getting the proper nutrient intake through a variety of foods to maintain a healthy, active lifestyle.

A Balanced Lifestyle

Food is one of life's greatest pleasures. Eating well by following *Canada's Food Guide to Healthy Eating* is just one way to get the most out of life. Spending time with family and friends is another way to achieve balance in life. Remember, healthy bodies come in a variety of shapes and sizes. Being positive about yourself helps you to stay healthy. It is also important to be active and feel good physically.

◆ **To perform your best, eat a pre-game meal three to four hours before the event starts.** Give two other pre-game tips for teen athletes.

Developing Research Skills
Using Internet Sources

When do you start your research?

Start as soon as you receive or determine your topic. In this chapter you will need information on the nutritional status of Canadians.

1. When looking for information on this topic, Health Canada is a good place to begin your research. Health Canada provides an index and search engine (a place where you can type in your topic) at **http://www.hc-sc.gc.ca/english/search/ a-z/p.html**. A search engine allows you to search the entire site for information on a topic. Some of the information is free and some of it you must purchase.

2. This is a federal government site, which will provide you with statistics and quick links to help you with your research. A link is a highlighted and underlined word. If you click on it, it will take you to other information or resources.

3. On the top left-hand corner, you can click on the appropriate language for your search. The information is available in both French and English.

4. There are a number of options that you can choose along the top and left-hand side.

5. In the top bar, there is a Contact Us link. You can e-mail a question to Health Canada or make a comment about the web site. You will receive an answer using this telecommunication tool.

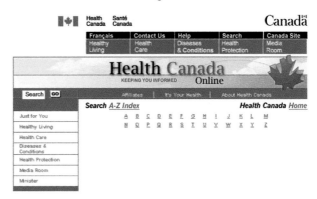

6. An interesting spot to visit on this web site is the Media Room on the top right. There is a link to a photo gallery. You can download pictures for the front of a binder cover or to use in your project.

7. If you click on the letter N in the index, it will lead you to the Food and Nutrition Index. Click on the link "Food and Nutrition."

8. From there click on the link "Office of Nutrition Policy and Promotion."

9. On the left you will find a bar called "FAQs," which has frequently asked questions about such topics as special diets, serving sizes, publications, and healthy weight.

10. The "Site Map" on the left is important. It provides you with quick links to such information as: *Canada's Food Guide to Healthy Eating*, *Canada's Guidelines for Healthy Eating*, and *Canada's Physical Activity Guide to Healthy Active Living*, among many others.

Source: Adapted from Health Canada (n.d.).

Nutrition Research Head

Danielle Brule

What education is required for your job?

- Bachelor of Science in applied science with a specialization in Dietetic or Nutritional Sciences.
- Masters Degree or Doctorate in Nutrition.
- Completion of a graduate dietetic internship or equivalent experience to be a dietitian in Canada

What skills does a person need to be able to do your job?

- Strong research skills, including knowledge of statistics, food analytical methodology, food consumption survey methodology, and food and nutrient databases.
- Ability to write for scientific publications and to evaluate scientific literature.
- Ability to plan, organize, and implement survey and research activities.
- Excellent written and oral communication in English and French.
- Supervisory and managerial skills.

What do you like most about your job?

I really like planning and developing food consumption surveys including the methodology, protocol, and questionnaires; training the personnel to conduct interviews; and providing advice to people on nutrition surveys and food composition databases.

What other jobs/job titles have you had in the past?

I worked as a nutrition survey officer at Health Canada.

What advice would you give a person who is considering a career as a dietitian in a research facility?

Dietitians can be found in many settings (clinical, administration, research, community practice, private sector, etc.). First and foremost, you must know your strengths and weaknesses, your abilities and skills. Secondly, do your research to ensure that you select the right type of job and work environment that will suit you by talking to and visiting people who are currently doing the type of work you would like to do. Make sure that you have a good and active network of people having some degree of influence because most jobs are often found by individuals who just happen to be there at the right time.

Comment on what you see as important issues/trends in food and nutrition.

A current major problem related to food is obesity in both children and adults. An important issue is the mandatory Nutrition Labelling on most foods and the need to educate people on the new regulations. We will also be seeing dietitians applying the new Dietary Reference Intakes in their practices.

Chapter 28 Review and Activities

Summary

◆ *Canada's Food Guide to Healthy Eating* is a flexible tool to help you make wise food choices.

◆ Vitality is enjoying eating well, being active, and feeling good about yourself.

◆ Healthy bodies come in a variety of shapes and sizes.

◆ A good weight is a healthy weight, not a low weight.

◆ A healthy weight helps you to stay active and lowers the risk of health problems.

◆ More than half of the Canadian population is not meeting the recommended minimum number of servings from *Canada's Food Guide to Healthy Eating*.

◆ "Other foods" are providing a quarter of the energy in the average diet, replacing foods from the four food groups.

◆ Canadians have reduced their total fat intake to 30 percent of energy, meeting the Nutritional Recommendations for Canadians.

◆ Many Canadians are not meeting the recommendations for the micronutrients calcium, folate, iron, and zinc.

Knowledge and Understanding

1. How do the nutritional needs of athletes differ from those of non-athletes?

2. Give three suggestions for planning meals before an athletic event.

3. Jill, an inactive student, and Mina, a swimmer, both weigh 54 kg (120 pounds). Do their protein needs differ?

Thinking and Inquiry

4. Why do you think some children receive more encouragement to participate in exercise than others do? How do you think such encouragement (or lack of it) affects children?

5. Helen's family are lacto-ovo vegetarians. They do not eat meat or fish, but they do eat milk products and eggs. How can Helen's family use *Canada's Food Guide to Healthy Eating* to meet their nutrient needs?

   a) Instead of meat, what other foods can the family use to meet the recommended number of servings from the Meat and Alternatives food group?

b) Helen is a preschooler. What nutrients does she need to get? Helen drinks at least 500 mL (2 cups) of milk every day and likes it on her cereal, in puddings, and in soup made with milk. What important nutrients does the milk supply?

6. You strain your leg muscle while jogging one day. The doctor tells you to try to stay off your feet for a few weeks. However, you want to continue with some type of exercise during that time. What can you do?

Communication

7. Refer to the table "Mean Nutrient Intake of Teens Compared to Recommendations" on page 596 to answer the following questions:

a) What micronutrients may teens be at risk of missing? Why?

b) Create graphs for the micronutrients, showing teen's mean intake and recommended DRI.

c) Do you find it easier to draw conclusions from the graph or the chart? Why?

8. Using the statistics in How Aware Are Canadians of *Canada's Food Guide to Healthy Eating* on page 582, design an advertising campaign to promote the food groups and *Canada's Food Guide to Healthy Eating.*

a) What is your target market? Why?

b) Where would you advertise? Why?

9. Write an article for a newspaper, Web site, or newsletter on one of the following subjects:

• Planning an exercise program.

• Nutrition for athletes.

Application

10. Find three recipes that would help a busy parent create a supper that would be nutritious, easy to make, and quick.

11. Use *Canada's Food Guide to Healthy Eating* and cookbooks to plan three meals for an athlete who is training for a sport of your choice.

CHAPTER
29

CHAPTER EXPECTATIONS

While reading this chapter, you will:

- Identify new developments in food preparation and service.

- Describe new foods and food products and analyse their role in the Canadian diet.

- Describe the appeal and uses of herbs and spices in food preparation.

- Use a variety of print and electronic sources and telecommunications tools to investigate and report on the technology behind some of the new food products.

- Prepare a menu using some new food products or recipes, and evaluate the results.

There are constantly new food products on the market. The way that these foods are prepared and are served also changes according to lifestyles, trends, and the technology of the day.

Trends in Food Preparation and Consumption in Canada

KEY TERMS

free radicals
functional foods
herbs
nutraceuticals
omega-3
seasoning blends
special purpose food

Even though it is still primarily women who do the grocery shopping in households today, there is a wide variety of Canadian consumers. This makes it very difficult for the producers of agri-foods, food processors, and those in the food service industry to predict consumer buying trends. To improve the chances that new products or businesses will be successful, companies must look at social and demographic trends, the total amount of money spent by a given consumer on food and on specific food groups, and other consumer demands.

Food labels can be confusing.

Factors That Affect Food Market Trends

Canadian Consumers Today

It is predicted that the Canadian population will continue to grow slowly until 2010. This means the total amount of food that Canadians consume will remain stable, and then decrease. This will create a great deal of competition among food companies and the food service industry, as they develop more new products for a market that is expanding very little. Companies in the food industry will each have to find a niche in order to survive (Ag Canada, 2001). A niche market is a specific subsection of a market. For example, a niche within the coffee shop market is the high-end coffee shop that prepares specialty coffees, such as lattes and cappuccinos, and sells coffees brewed from a variety of beans. In order to find a niche in a food market, a company must look at changing demographics and consumer demands.

Within the population of Canada, the fastest-growing group is made up of people over 50 years old, and food industries and services will have to focus on the demands of this aging market. Canada has also become very ethnically diverse, as people from all over the world have migrated here. This creates a demand for the introduction of various foods from particular cultures, specialized food products, and ethnic

restaurants. Although Canadians have shown an interest in adopting and adapting food products from other cultures, decreasing family size, the changing structure of the family, and the number of dual-earner couples (families in which both parents are employed) are also having an impact on food trends. A large proportion of Canadian families have both parents working outside the home, or are single-parent families. This puts time constraints on families, and thus creates a demand for more convenience foods, take-out foods, and restaurant meals.

Companies also track the spending habits of consumers. This allows them to cater to specific groups of consumers by finding out how they spend their money on food.

The size of the Canadian family, its structure, and who participates in the workforce are all factors that food-marketing companies look at to help predict food trends. See if you can name three things that a small family such as the one shown at bottom, might want in the way of food products and services.

Specific Consumer Demands

Health and Nutrition

What does the Canadian consumer want? Food producers and processors know that today's consumers are very knowledgeable

◆ Small families have their own special needs in terms of food products and services.

about food products and services, and have many concerns and demands. Canadian consumers are concerned about six basic but important aspects of the foods they eat: health and nutrition, convenience, quality and freshness, variety, impact on the environment, and food safety.

For manufacturers in the food industry, information on nutrition trends among Canadians is a good indicator of how successful potential new products likely would be when introduced into the market. In the Tracking Nutrition Trends 2001 survey, the National Institute of Nutrition (2002) has found the following nutrition trends among Canadians:

◆ 88 percent of Canadians stated that when making food choices, nutrition is of some importance (extremely, very, quite).

◆ 82 percent of consumers were either very or somewhat concerned about total fat in their diets.

◆ 58 percent of Canadians changed or improved their eating habits to maintain their personal health.

◆ 22 percent said they improved their eating habits in order to lose weight.

◆ When asked what changes people had made in their eating habits over the past year, the top three responses were 34 percent consumed less fat, 26 percent ate more fruits and vegetables, and 14 percent reduced their sugar intake.

These findings clearly show that health and nutrition are important to many Canadians. This trend is therefore a major driving force for introducing new food products. Let's examine the reasons some new food products have been introduced into the Canadian market.

Nutrition Labelling

In Canada, part of the role of government is to make sure that the public is educated about the link between what we eat and our health. Health and nutrition concerns of consumers have led Health Canada to make it mandatory (with a few exceptions) to put a standard table of Nutrition Facts on most food product labels. The Canadian Nutrition Facts table lists 13 components, including the amount of trans fat, in one standard-sized serving of a food. This is revolutionary, since Canada is the first country to include trans fat on food labels.

As a way of educating the public about the link between the foods we eat and their effects on our health, companies are allowed to choose among five general health claims to print on packages of their food products. The wording and circumstances are regulated as to what can be claimed. For example, a product containing calcium may state that calcium is linked to a reduced risk of osteoporosis.

In light of these nutrition concerns, it is not surprising that an increasing number of products make some nutritional claim. For example, *light, low in fat,* or *fat free*. There are specific requirements that a product must meet before it can state these claims on its package. It is up to the manufacturer to decide whether to highlight a certain nutritional feature of its product, and due to high consumer demand for health information, many manufacturers are choosing to do so. Consumers can use this information, along with nutrition tables and ingredient lists, in comparing products. Nutrition education, such as that provided on food labels, may have an impact on health if consumers use this information to make healthier food choices.

FOR YOUR HEALTH

Some Common Nutritional Contents Claims

Keyword	What they mean
Free	An amount so small, health experts consider it nutritionally insignificant
Sodium free	Less than 5 mg sodium*
Cholesterol free	Less than 2 mg cholesterol, and low in saturated fat (includes a restriction on trans fat)* Not necessarily low in total fat
Low	Always associated with a very small amount
Low fat	3 g or less fat*
Low in saturated fat	2 g or less of saturated and trans fat combined*
Reduced	At least 25% less of a nutrient compared with a similar product
Reduced in calories	At least 25% less energy than the food to which it is compared
Source	Always associated with a "significant" amount
Source of fibre	4 grams or more fibre*
Good source of calcium	165 mg or more of calcium*
Light	When referring to a nutritional characteristic of a product, it is allowed only on foods that are either "reduced in fat" or "reduced in energy" (calories) Explanation on the label of what makes the food "light". This is also true if "light" refers to sensory characteristics, such as "light in colour"**

*Per reference amount and per serving of stated size (specific amount of food listed in Nutrition Facts)

**Three exceptions that do not require an explanation are "light maple syrup," "light rum," and "light salted" with respect to fish. Note that a separate provision is made for the claim "lightly salted," which may be used when a food contains at least 50 percent less added sodium compared with a similar product.

Source: Health Canada. Retrieved from http://www.hc-sc.gc.ca/hpfb-dgpsa/onpp-bppn/labelling-etiquetage/te_background_08_table1_e.html

FYI

To assist you with your grocery shopping, the Heart and Stroke Foundation has created a program called Health Check.™

Health Check™ is based on *Canada's Food Guide to Healthy Eating*. The Health Check™ logo on the food package means that the product's nutrition information has been reviewed by the Foundation, and that it meets established nutrient criteria. Choosing Health Check™ products can contribute to a healthy diet for you and your family. Look for the Health Check™ logo at your local supermarket. Health Check™ ... tells you it's a healthy choice.

Source: Heart and Stroke Foundation.
www.healthcheck.org/english/about_sec.html

Scientific Terms in Food and Nutrition

Food and nutritional scientists have been looking at the health benefits of foods we eat and the possibility that some foods will reduce our risk of getting certain diseases or health problems. You may have already heard that foods such as broccoli, tomatoes, garlic, and blueberries contain naturally occurring substances that are beneficial to your health. Such foods and food products are referred to as functional foods and nutraceuticals, and there are various definitions for these scientific terms. The Bureau of Nutritional Sciences in the Food Directorate of Health Canada has proposed the following definitions for these two terms:

1. A **functional food** is similar in appearance to, or may be, a conventional food, is consumed as part of a usual diet, and is demonstrated to have physiological benefits and/or reduce the risk of chronic disease beyond basic nutritional functions. Examples of these foods include tomatoes, oats, garlic, and broccoli.

2. A **nutraceutical** is a product isolated or purified from foods that is generally sold in medicinal forms not usually associated with food. A nutraceutical is demonstrated to have a physiological benefit or provide protection against chronic disease. In Canada, evening primrose oil, garlic oil, and cod liver oil are some of the nutraceuticals available in stores.

Source: Health Canada (2003).

The research in food and nutritional sciences is advancing daily. You may have heard terms such as antioxidants and phytochemicals in recent discussions of nutrition and food. Phytochemicals are compounds that occur naturally in some foods, such as fruits, vegetables, whole grains, and legumes. Some phytochemicals operate as antioxidants in the body, while others help to enhance immunity. Some even trigger enzymes that can prohibit substances that cause cancer. Other phytochemicals act in ways that imitate the valuable properties of human estrogen. Antioxidants are substances that help to protect our bodies from free radicals. **Free radicals** are formed in the body as a result of normal metabolism, but then circulate in the body, damaging cells. This damage can lead to cancer. Free radicals may also be damaging to protein and fat molecules. Antioxidants help by soaking up free radicals before they cause damage. Food components containing antioxidants include vitamins C and E, and beta-carotene, which is converted to vitamin A in the body.

Research and New Food Products

Scientific advancements have made it possible to use familiar foods and ingredients in new ways. Scientists are also revealing the beneficial effects of certain substances that are already in the foods that we eat. This research may be contributing to a shift in the amount of certain foods that some Canadians consume. Research into food and nutrition is also helping to introduce new products to the market, and giving familiar old food ingredients a new twist by helping consumers to recognize their potential health benefits. Here are some examples.

Eggs

Eggs have made a comeback in recent years: there is even a new type of egg called omega-3. Scientists have found that foods containing polyunsaturated fats, such as omega-3 fatty acids, perform a function in the body that may help to reduce the risk of heart disease. **Omega-3** fatty acids, specifically, have been found to help lower triglyceride levels in the blood. The health benefits of these eggs may be felt if they are part of a diet that limits overall intake of dietary fats. Hens produce omega-3 eggs when their diet is enriched with ground flax seed. Omega-3 eggs are higher in omega-3 fatty acids and lower in saturated fats than other eggs.

Other research on eggs has shown their positive effect on vision, making eggs also a functional food. This is due to two natural antioxidants, lutein and zeaxanthin. Research has found that these chemicals can help enhance the health of eyes and protect them from ultraviolet rays. Both lutein and zeaxanthin are found in egg yolks.

Soy-Based Foods and Beverages

Soy-based foods and beverages have become popular additions to supermarket shelves,

---

Texturized Vegetable Protein (TVP)

TVP is a protein obtained from soybeans and other vegetables. It is a flavour enhancer used in many foods. It is made by breaking down soy protein into amino acids. TVP is sold dry and can be rehydrated with boiling water. TVP has a texture similar to ground beef, and chunk-sized pieces can be used like stewing meat. TVP also can be used to replace ground meat in recipes for lasagna, chili, or tacos.

Sources: Adapted from *The Soy Daily*. (2000–2003). The soy glossary or what is it? Retrieved June 14, 2003, from **http://www.fengshuitours.com/Glossary.asp** and Soyfoods Canada. (n.d.)*Soy: Always in Good Taste.* [Brochure].

---

cookbooks, and even restaurant menus. Soybeans come from a plant and are used in the manufacture of hundreds of products. The production and consumption of soybeans is not new in Canada, but the use of soy as an ingredient in many products has widely expanded. Products include tofu, soy margarine, soy milk, soy cheese, soy ice cream and yogurt, veggie burgers, and soy ingredients in cereals and breads among others. The health benefits of a diet rich in soy have been widely researched, and studies have found that a soy-rich diet is linked to both a reduction in the risk of heart disease and the lowering of blood cholesterol. In addition, research has shown that soy has the potential to help maintain the health of bones and may help to prevent some cancers. New research in the area of kidney disease and dietary interventions has been looking at ingredients that are found in soy protein isolates. There is the potential for even more soy-based

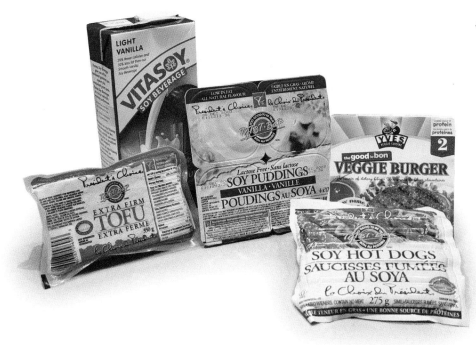

◆ A growing number of soy-based foods and beverages are on the market today. Choose two soy-based foods or beverages and compare them with two other similar traditional items. Use taste, quality, texture, convenience, and cost as criteria for your comparisons.

products (as functional foods) to be brought onto the market if further health benefits continue to be discovered.

Grains and Grain Products

Grains are the seeds of plants in the grass family. Common grains in North America include wheat, rice, corn, buckwheat, oats, rye, triticale, barley, and millet. Every seed, or kernel, of grain is composed of three main parts:

◆ **The germ**. The germ is a tiny embryo in a seed that will grow into a new plant.

◆ **The endosperm**. The endosperm is the food supply for a seed's embryo, made up of proteins, starches, and other nutrients. It takes up most of the inner part of the grain.

◆ **The bran**. The bran is the outer protective layer of a seed. It is edible.

Grains get a lot of attention in health news because they are naturally packed with nutrients. The endosperm is high in complex carbohydrates and proteins, with just a small amount of vitamins and minerals. The bran is rich in fibre, B vitamins, and some trace minerals. The germ provides B vitamins, vitamin E, iron, zinc, other trace minerals, some protein, and a small amount of saturated fat.

Whole grains give the body energy and are also high in dietary fibre. Researchers have found a link between a diet high in fibre from whole grains and a reduced risk of colon cancer. Whole grains may also act to prevent heart disease, stroke, and diabetes. Canadian scientists have investigated cereals, which include grains such as wheat, barley, and oats, to find their potential as functional foods. Oats, in particular, have been found to contain a particular soluble fibre, called β-glucan. Oat β-glucan helps to metabolize lipids and carbohydrates in the body. β-glucan is recognized as functional because it has been found to help lower blood serum cholesterol and have beneficial effects in the treatment of diabetes. In addition to β-glucan, oats contain many other components that benefit the body. Some of these components are potent antioxidants.

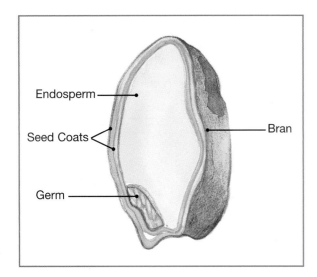

◆ All three parts of the grain kernel are nutritious. What is the function of each part?

Many grocery stores, markets, and bakeries are carrying artisan breads, some of which contain a variety of whole grains. Overall, there has been an expansion in the number of bread products containing whole grains and mixtures of whole grains. This has extended to restaurants, including fast-food establishments, as some now serve their sandwiches on whole wheat breads. High-fibre breakfast cereals and breakfast cereals sold as meal replacements are also becoming more popular. The increase in the number of whole-grain breads, cereals, and cereal products available may be a response to the health-conscious consumer's desire both to increase fibre intake, thus maintaining a healthy colon, and to benefit from phytochemicals and other nutrients. Figuring out which products and nutrients really are beneficial is a challenge.

When the whole grain—the entire edible kernel—is used, the resulting products contain most of the kernel's original nutrients. Very often, however, once grains are processed, they lose vitamins, minerals, and fibre content. When buying new grains and grain products, keep nutrition in mind. Choose whole-grain products as much as possible and aim for at least three of your daily servings of grain to be from whole grains. Try different grains for variety.

Yogurt

Yogurt is being purchased by more Canadians than ever before. According to Statistics Canada (2003 "Food..."), in 1996, 9 percent of households were buying yogurt; in 2001, this number rose to 22 percent. Yogurt is a probiotic food: it contains live organisms that, when eaten in sufficient amounts, help improve the balance of microbes in the human intestinal tract. The organisms include lactic acid bacteria such as *lactobacillus acidophilus*, *lactobacillus bulgarius*, and *bifidobacteria*. Probiotics are referred to as friendly bacteria. Moreover, people who do not drink milk or find that they cannot tolerate milk may find that yogurt is a good way to get their daily recommended intake of calcium. For these

◆ The health benefits of yogurt may be one of the reasons why it has become more popular. Read the labels, including the ingredients list, of various yogurts. Look for the names of bacteria and other ingredients that may have been added. Do some research on each of the ingredients unknown to you and find out what each one does.

people, yogurt is easier to digest than milk since the bacteria in the yogurt help to digest the lactose or milk sugar.

Calcium

Calcium intake is a health concern for many Canadians. Calcium is needed to help build bones and maintain bone strength, which helps to prevent osteoporosis, a potentially debilitating disease. Calcium-fortified orange juice is a new product that is responding to these concerns. There are various forms of calcium salts that can be used to fortify products with calcium. You may see names such as calcium carbonate, calcium phosphate, or calcium citrate on ingredients lists. As Canada's population grows older there may be more people in danger of developing osteoporosis. The result could be more food products fortified with calcium, as a preventive measure.

The addition of calcium to orange juice makes the juice a **special purpose food.** Special

purpose foods are those created in order to perform a function that is specific to certain groups of people. In this case, it is intended for people who do not drink milk and so need some other source of calcium in their diets.

"Under proposed changes, Canadians would gain access to an expanded range of special purpose foods — products formulated specifically for groups such as pregnant women, seniors or athletes, who have different nutritional needs. These special purpose foods would carry directions for use, including who should consume it, for what purpose, and how much."

INTERNET CONNECTS

www.mcgrawhill.ca/links/food
For more information on food fortification and regulation of food fortification go to the website above for *Food for Today, First Canadian Edition* to see where to go next.

◆ More and more products that have been fortified with calcium are appearing on the market as a result of Canada's aging population.

◆ Herbs and spices give many dishes an added dimension. One benefit of herbs and spices is that they add flavour to foods without adding fat or salt. **Why would this be appealing to many people?**

Herbs and Spices

Herbs and spices are seasoning ingredients that are used in small amounts to flavour foods. The extra flavour they provide can be helpful for health-conscious people who are limiting their use of salt and fat. **Herbs** are the flavourful leaves and stems of soft, succulent plants that grow in the temperate zone. Some familiar herbs used in cooking include basil, thyme, oregano, rosemary, sage, and bay leaf, most of which can be purchased fresh or in dried forms. Herbs may also be used for medicinal purposes and sold as supplements.

Spices are usually the buds, bark, seeds, stems, or roots of aromatic plants and trees, most of which grow in tropical countries. Many can be found both whole, such as nutmeg, peppercorns, cumin seeds, cardamom, and cinnamon sticks, and finely ground or in pieces. A few, such as ginger root, which is commonly used in Asian cooking, are sold fresh.

Seasoning blends

Seasoning blends are conveniently packaged combinations of herbs and spices. Most blends are used for specific purposes. Some examples are Italian seasoning, which combines flavours typical in Italian cooking, and curry powders, blends of spices typically used in South Asian cuisine. You can buy these blends or mix and grind combinations to your own taste.

The use of herbs and spices in cooking is limitless. Alone or blended, they are very appealing to our senses of taste, smell, and even sight. Experimenting with combinations of herbs and spices can enhance the flavour and degree of spiciness of many basic dishes, in a healthy way. Adding herbs such as basil, oregano, and thyme to a chicken and rice dish creates one flavour, while adding a combination of curry spices to chicken and rice creates an entirely different flavour. Spices and herbs are also placed on foods as a garnish, adding visual interest to a dish. A roast lamb garnished with a few sprigs of fresh rosemary adds both flavour and aroma, and enlivens the presentation of the meal. Herbs and spices appear in many convenience food products, atop breads and other baked goods, in herbal teas, and as part of menu items in restaurants.

Basic Herbs, Spices, and Seasoning Blends

		Flavour	Uses
Herbs	**Basil**	Mild licorice flavour with a hint of mint	Dishes containing tomatoes, meat, poultry, carrots, peas, rice
	Bay leaf	Strong, aromatic, pungent flavour	Braised meat, stews, soups, bean dishes (use leaf whole; remove before serving)
	Dill weed	Sharp flavour, similar to that of caraway seeds	Cruciferous vegetables, carrots, green beans, cucumbers, fish, poultry, breads
	Marjoram	Delicate, sweet, spicy flavour with hint of mint	Soups, stews, poultry, stuffings, salads, tomato sauces
	Mint	Strong, refreshing, aromatic flavour	Yogurt dishes, tomato dishes, rice, bulgur, vegetables, lentils, fruits, tea
	Oregano	Strong, clove-like flavour	Italian and Mexican dishes, bean dishes, pork, poultry, salads, green beans
	Sage	Strong, slightly bitter flavour	Poultry, pork, stuffings, potatoes, white beans, chowders
	Thyme	Strong, clove-like flavour	Poultry and stuffings, lamb, dry beans, stews, soups
Spices	**Cinnamon**	Sweet flavour	Meat dishes, desserts, legumes, sweet potatoes, squash
	Cloves	Strong, hot, pungent flavour	Meat dishes, grains, legumes, fruit desserts
	Cumin	Strong, musty flavour	Mexican and Middle Eastern foods, legumes, tomato sauces, soups, rice
	Dry mustard	Hot, sharp, spicy flavour	Meat, poultry, soups, stews, egg dishes, salad dressings
	Ground ginger	Hot, pungent, spicy flavour	Stir-fries, stews, soups, squash, sweet potatoes, grains, legumes, desserts
	Nutmeg	Mild, spicy flavour (best if purchased whole and grated fresh)	Cooked spinach, zucchini, carrots, sweet potatoes, soups, stews, ground meat, bulgur, fruits, desserts

		Flavour	**Uses**
Seasoning Blends	**Chili powder**	Spicy, hot, pungent flavour	Tex-Mex cooking, chili, stews, soups, barbecue sauces, dishes made with corn
	Curry powder	Pungent, spicy flavour	East Indian cooking, poultry, meats, fish, yogurt dishes, legumes
	Italian seasoning	Blend of basil, marjoram, oregano, rosemary, sage, savory, and thyme	Italian cooking
	Poultry seasoning	Blend of lovage, marjoram, and sage	Any dishes made with poultry, including stuffing

Food Service and Nutrition

The food-service industry is a large and ever-changing business sector in Canada.

In Canadian households in 2001, 30 percent of total food expenditures were on restaurant foods (Statistics Canada, 2003 "Household..."). In recent years, in both fast-food and full-service restaurants, there has been an increase in the number of menu items geared to healthier eating. To help customers identify and choose items that are lower in fat, some restaurants will provide nutritional information on request. Some provinces have programs that identify restaurants offering a variety of healthy menu choices; the *Eat Smart* healthy restaurants program in Ontario is an example.

Supermarkets and Nutrition

Supermarkets have also begun expanding their repertoire of nutrition services. Here are some examples:

◆ A dietitian on staff can answer nutrition-related questions and provide workshops on making healthy food choices. If your local supermarket doesn't offer this service your local health unit may give "supermarket tours" to teach shoppers how to read food labels, for example.

◆ Some supermarkets provide cooking classes that show how to cook low-fat meals or make healthy dinners fast.

◆ In the produce section, nutritional information may be found above fresh fruits and vegetables as a way of allowing shoppers to make more informed purchases.

FYI

Breakfast on the Go

According to *Foodservice and Hospitality* magazine, breakfast is the food-service industry's fastest-growing phenomenon. The number of restaurant-prepared breakfast meals has grown by 60 percent over the past eight years. Breakfasts sold at drive-through windows have also dramatically increased in number, from 6 percent of breakfasts in 1994 to 27 percent in 2002 being purchased at drive-through outlets. This increase may be due to two factors: Many Canadians have less time to spend on preparing and eating meals today, compared to in the past, and Canadians may actually be making a greater effort to eat breakfast because they believe it is the most important meal of the day.

Eating breakfast at a restaurant does not, however, necessarily mean eating healthier foods. At most traditional breakfast eateries, the eggs, bacon, home fries, toast, and coffee combination is still the most popular meal. But bagels are also a huge seller in the breakfast market—and they make a good breakfast choice because they are portable and lower in fat than the traditional bacon and eggs breakfast.

Source: Adapted from Campbell, Liz. (2003, April). "Scrambling for Breakfast" *Foodservice and Hospitality*, 36, 2, pp. 29–36).

Convenience Foods and Services

Demographic changes in Canada, such as an increase in the number of single-parent families and families in which both parents are in the workforce, can limit time spent in the kitchen preparing meals. This has prompted an increasing demand for quality convenience foods and services.

Supermarkets offer a wide selection of convenience foods in every department. In the produce department, for example, there are pre-washed and cut vegetables, including various kinds of lettuce in a bag. Some even come with the appropriate amount of salad dressing and other toppings—a complete salad in a bag. Shredded cheese in a bag is also another popular item. In the frozen-food section are many different microwavable entrees and side dishes. In the cereal aisle, there are breakfast bars, granola bars, and cereal bars that are easy to carry in a pocket or lunch bag. Individually packaged breakfast meal replacements and shakes are also ready to eat or drink and convenient, with little mess. Read the labels on some of these products to see how they are being presented to customers. Are they promoting convenience foods, a busy lifestyle, or good nutrition?

New lines of condiments, sauces, salad dressings, and marinades are appearing on more store shelves. These come in bottles, ready to use alone or on other foods. The variety has expanded to include tastes from many other cultures. What were once available only in small specialty kitchen and food shops are now taking up more and more room on ordinary grocery store and supermarket shelves.

Many supermarkets and delicatessens have increased their services by offering ready-to-eat prepared foods. These range from complete meals that can be taken home and re-heated, to individual, chilled foods such as salads, sandwiches, and wraps, and hot items such as pizzas, pastas, rotisserie chicken, barbecued meats, casseroles, and soups. The popularity of barbecuing, smoking meats and fish, and the introduction of the indoor electric grill, surged during the 1990s as a convenient and fun way of preparing food.

Grocery shopping on-line has also gained popularity: it is easy, convenient, and offers plenty of variety.

To provide convenience and meet the nutritional needs of specific groups, meal replacements and nutritional supplements are also readily available. Protein drinks, energy bars, and high-energy drinks designed for athletes can be purchased in corner stores, drugstores, supermarkets, and snack shops in sports facilities and gyms

In the food-service industry the takeout window, or drive-through, has also become popular. Many fast-food restaurants and even casual dining establishments are making it easier for consumers to take out food. Food service companies, fast-food restaurants, and street vendors are catering to customers' desires by expanding menus of hand-held foods that are easy to eat while on the move. One example of this is the introduction of wraps and pita sandwiches. Depending on

the ingredients and condiments added to this style of sandwich, they can be a healthier alternative to traditional fast foods, such as cheeseburgers and French fries.

Food-Packaging Technology

All packaging is designed to keep food safe from damage and contamination. Certain advancements in packaging technology have decreased the amount of preservatives and other chemicals that must be added to food during processing. However, packaging can create a great deal of waste. It is important to recycle packaging as much as possible, and to look for ways to reduce the amount of packaging when purchasing food. Packaging is often for convenience purposes. More and more products are sold in individual serving-size containers. Food products also can be sold in a package that contain several individually wrapped items for convenience. Microwavable foods come in microwavable packages that can be brought from the oven to the table. Quick-freeze or flash-freeze methods using liquid nitrogen have improved the quality, taste, and texture of frozen foods. Below are a few other notable developments in food-packaging technology:

- Resealable plastic bags are an added feature with more and more products.

- Gable tops with spouts on milk and juice cartons. This plastic spout on the top of a paperboard carton gives a new look and is designed to make pouring from cartons easier.

- Pouches are upright flexible packages used to hold beverages. They are made of thin flexible, clear plastic and coated with a thin aluminum coating.

◆ **New packaging has been created to accommodate convenience foods.**

◆ Condiment bottles that pour from the bottom make it easier to get the contents out without turning the container upside down.

Aseptic Packages

You probably know these as juice boxes. This type of packaging has become increasingly popular, as it is now used for foods such as soup broths, soy beverages, milk products, and whipping cream. Aseptic packaging refers to a process of pouring sterile food into sterilized packages made of paperboard, polyethylene, and aluminum foil. This filling is done under sterile conditions. Products in aseptic packages if unopened have a long shelf life without refrigeration.

Plastics

Many plastic packages, trays, and bowls are specially made for use in the microwave oven. These containers must be made of a material that has a higher melting point than the food it contains. Polypropylene, a type of plastic, has high tensile strength and a high melting point, making it ideal for containers for heating foods. As you may have noticed,

not all plastics are microwavable. Some plastic materials melt or warp when they are used to microwave foods or liquids. Check the directions on the package to determine whether the plastic is microwave safe.

INTERNET CONNECTS

www.mcgrawhill.ca/links/food
For more information on the technology and use of plastics in food packaging, go to the web site above for *Food for Today, First Canadian Edition,* to see where to go next.

Future Packaging

Scientists are constantly working to improve the safety of food and reduce the amount of packaging. Two advances in packaging technology that may appear on the market in the future are biodegradable packaging, and plastic wrap that reveals when a food is no longer fresh. One type of biodegradable packaging is a protein-based, edible coating that can be sprayed onto frozen foods such as pizza. The plastic wrap increases food safety because when the amount of certain bacteria in the wrapped food increases, a blue X appears indicating that the food is no longer fresh.

Food Safety and Environmental Concerns

Food safety and the environment are key concerns of Canadian consumers. Consumers want to be confident that the foods they eat are safe. Environmental concerns, especially among our youth, relate to how agricultural products are grown, processed, and packaged. These concerns may place challenging demands on the food industry in the future.

Irradiation

Many issues related to food safety are controversial. It is important to understand the facts as well as the opinions on both sides of each issue. Irradiation, the process of exposing food to an ionizing energy source, is one such issue. The sources of energy used in irradiation of foods may include gamma rays, x-rays, and electron beams. The purpose of irradiation is to increase the shelf life of foods and kill harmful micro-organisms. Irradiation does not make foods radioactive. It can cause minor changes in flavour, and at permitted levels, it does not decrease the nutritional value of food.

Health Canada currently permits irradiation of wheat, flour, whole wheat flour, onions, potatoes, whole and ground spices, and dehydrated seasoning preparations. Health Canada has proposed regulations to allow for the irradiation of fresh and frozen

◆ This symbol on food packages indicates that it has been irradiated to increase shelf life and kill harmful micro-organisms.

ground beef; fresh and frozen poultry; prepackaged fresh, frozen, prepared and dried shrimp and prawns; and mangoes. Irradiation of products is not mandatory, and foods that are irradiated must be labelled with the *Radura* irradiation logo, shown above.

Bottled Water

Sales in the bottled-water industry began to increase dramatically in the 1980s and continue to do so. A wide variety of bottled water is sold in supermarkets, and it is also readily available in vending machines and from food-service establishments. Canadians may be turning to bottled water because they feel that it is a safer, more pure alternative to drinking tap water. Others may simply prefer the taste of bottled water.

INTERNET CONNECTS

www.mcgrawhill.ca/links/food
For more information on the consumption, safety, and regulation of bottled water in Canada, go to the web site above for *Food for Today, First Canadian Edition*, to see where to go next.

FOR YOUR HEALTH

Is bottled water safer than tap water?

Manufacturers and importers of bottled water are required to ensure that their products continually meet Canadian health and safety standards. Quality standards for bottled water and municipal water service are similar. Both bottled water and municipal water services that meet or exceed their required health standards are considered safe. At the present time, no waterborne disease outbreaks have been associated with drinking bottled water in Canada.

Health Canada recommends that populations particularly susceptible to illness or disease should consider either boiling their water prior to use or using only sterile water. This recommendation applies to infants, pregnant women, frail seniors, and those whose immune systems have been weakened by disease, surgery, or other therapy.

What should I consider before purchasing bottled water?

Examine the bottles closely before purchasing and buy only bottles where the seal is unbroken. Make sure the water is clear and free of debris. Consumers should avoid refilling old bottles unless they have been properly cleaned and sanitized (Canadian Food Inspection Agency, 2003).

Organic Foods

There has been an increase in the availability of organically produced foods in grocery stores and markets. Some restaurants boast that the ingredients in their dishes are grown organically. People may be choosing to eat organically grown foods because they believe that these foods are safer and more nutritious. They may be concerned about harmful effects of commercial pesticides, fertilizers, hormones, or other chemicals on the environment and on their bodies. Organic farmers use composted matter and manure as a way of fertilizing their crops, rather than commercial chemical fertilizers. Some experts maintain that foods that are organically produced do not have greater nutritional value compared to foods that are grown using conventional methods (Piche, personal communication, June 4, 2003). Organically grown foods are usually more expensive than conventionally grown foods, as you will see when you are shopping and comparing prices.

Chapter 29 Review and Activities

Summary

- Canada has a wide variety of consumers, whose buying trends are studied by food producers.
- Companies must use niche marketing to be successful.
- Consumer demands in food selection include health and nutrition, variety, convenience, and food safety.
- Omega-3 eggs, soy-based products, and TVP are among new foods now on supermarket shelves.
- Herbs and spices add flavour, aroma, and visual appeal to prepared foods.
- The food-service industry is a large and changing business sector in Canada.
- Food-packaging technology is designed to protect food from damage and contamination.
- Irradiation, bottled water, and organically grown foods are among current issues related to food safety and the environment.

Knowledge and Understanding

1. Make a list in your notes of the factors that may affect what new food products are introduced into the market.
2. Explain the difference between a nutraceutical and a functional food.

Thinking and Inquiry

3. How has our aging population affected the introduction of new food products and services to the market today? What effect will this population have on the future of new products and services?
4. Do you think the increasing demand for convenience food products and services will continue? Why or why not?
5. Look for research regarding various functional foods, including the ones that you learned about in this chapter. Write a one-page report that summarizes the potential effect that these foods could have on the health of Canadians.
6. Look for new food products in your local supermarket. Research the packaging technology behind at least two food items. Include in your one-page report an analysis of the audience to whom you think this product is marketed. Explain your answer.

Communication

7. Compare a new food product such as a frozen entree or a commercially prepared meal with a homemade meal of your own. Compare cost, quality, and taste, and weigh the pros and cons. Write a one-page report giving your opinion.

8. Tour your local supermarket. Map out the location and approximate percentage of shelf, freezer, or refrigerated space devoted to displaying the following foods:

- Organic fruits and vegetables in the produce section.
- Bottled water in the beverage section.
- Convenience frozen entrees in the frozen-food section.
- Breads, rolls, buns, bagels in the baked-goods section.
- Convenience items in the dairy section.
- Convenience food items in the produce section. How do you think the location of these foods affects their sales?

9. Prepare a menu using some of the food products that you learned about in this chapter.

Application

10. Conduct a survey on people who attend your school. Ask them if they are eating any new food products, trying a new restaurant, or preparing their food in a new way. Analyse the effects that these new products or services could have on their health.

11. Prepare a basic tomato sauce (marinara sauce) without herbs and prepare a marinara sauce using fresh and/or dried herbs. Compare this to a new brand of canned or jarred basic tomato sauce. Make a chart in your notes that compares all three tomato sauces with respect to quality, taste, cost, and convenience.

12. Choose one of the new food products that you learned about in this chapter. Read the ingredients list on the item. Research and describe any ingredients that are unfamiliar to you. Why do you think the producer added these ingredients to the product?

CHAPTER

30

World Cuisines

CHAPTER EXPECTATIONS

While reading this chapter, you will:

- Identify the components of a cuisine.

- Describe a selection of the wide variety of tastes and food preferences displayed by societies around the world.

- Demonstrate an understanding of the scientific principles of a variety of types of food preparation.

- Conduct and present the findings of an analysis of the nutritional value of a variety of cuisines from around the world.

- Plan, prepare, and serve specific foods prepared in the style of a variety of ethnic and/or Aboriginal Peoples' cuisines, and draw comparisons among them.

The manner in which foods are prepared is a key factor in the nutritional value of ethnic dishes.

al dente
cerviche
dal
dim sum
Dublin coddle
enchiladas
gumbo
hors d'ouvres
matambre
pho
rosti
soufflé
sushi
Tandoor

CHAPTER INTRODUCTION

This chapter presents an overview of cuisines from around the world. You will also discover some of the customs, cooking and eating utensils, and styles of preparation and service associated with different types of foods. A summary of the nutritional content of the foods is also provided. The scientific principles behind cooking foods—baking bread, browning meat, making yogurt, boiling eggs, and thickening soups and stews are studied as well.

During food preparation, both chemical and physical changes occur to food. These changes affect colour, taste, appearance, and texture of foods.

Components of a Cuisine

The components of a cuisine—the staple foods, and ways of preparing, cooking, serving, and eating food in a given country or culture—vary enormously around the world. Factors that cause these variations in a cuisine include such things as availability of agricultural products grown or imported, natural resources, climate, economics, religion, and, of course, the people themselves. In the past, the staples eaten in a country and the way in which these staples were prepared allowed people to identify various dishes as unique to a specific culture. However, the foods that are considered staple ingredients, preparation methods, and kitchen tools have changed dramatically as a result of globalization and technological achievements. Globalization means expanding businesses into new world markets. International demand for large multinational food companies, such as McDonald's, have largely replaced local food vendors in many countries. This chapter gives an overview of cuisine components in some of the countries around the world, and how these have been affected by globalization.

Africa

Africa is the second largest continent in the world and one of the most diverse in climate, geography, languages, and cultures. It is not surprising, then, that we also find a wide variety of staple foods and cuisines in Africa.

Sub-Saharan Africa

This is the area south of the Sahara Desert including West Africa, East Africa, the Horn of Africa, Central Africa, and down into South Africa. Rural and urban cuisines in these regions not only differ but also are changing from the traditional ways in which food is prepared, cooked, and served. Changing technology, education, and a growing middle class are a few of the factors contributing to changes.

In this part of Africa, the traditional diet is generally loaded with carbohydrates, and high in fibre. Only a small portion of the diet comes from protein and fat. People in some parts of Africa live in severe poverty, have little or no formal education, and do not have an adequate and safe water supply. This contributes to poor nutrition and disease, which affects the overall health of people in these regions.

Staple Foods

The staple fruits and vegetables in this part of the continent include mangoes, bananas, plantain (a tropical fruit that belongs to the banana family), okra, yams, fresh corn, and cocoyams, a type of wild yam. Important proteins come from pulses such as peas, beans, and lentils. Meat is not eaten often in rural areas but would more likely be a part of the urban person's diet. In certain tribal cultures, beef may not be eaten, since owning cattle is seen as a symbol of wealth and high status. Animals that live in the forest, such as oxen, goats, sheep, elephant, and even mice, and certain insects, may be part of the diet for some people. Fish and other forms of seafood are usually eaten only in areas where they can be caught. This includes coastal areas and wherever there is a nearby lake, river, or stream. A variety of plants are used to make flour for breads and other products. These staples include sorghum, corn or maize, cassava, which is also referred to as manioc, millet, wheat, and rice.

◆ Outdoor markets are still the norm in many African countries.

Cassava/Manioc Scones

Ingredients

250 mL (1 cup) cassava/manioc
250 mL (1 cup) flour
5 mL (1 tsp.) baking powder
25 mL (2 tbsp.) margarine, melted
25 mL (2 tbsp.) oil
salt

1. To begin with, put all the ingredients except the oil into a bowl and knead until you have a ball of dough.
2. Now sprinkle some flour onto a flat surface or board and roll out the dough to a thickness of 1 cm (½ inch). Then cut into scone-sized rounds using a cutter or glass.
3. When this is done, heat up the oil in a shallow pan and cook the scones on each side until they are light brown. Serve right away, with main dishes.

Serves 4.

Customs and Cuisine

In the rural parts of the sub-Saharan region, cooking methods may be both indoor and outdoor. Foods are cooked over open fires or in pits that contain heated stones. Equipment used for cooking and preparing includes perforated clay steamers, jugs and jars for storing food and drink, a mortar and pestle for grinding, knives, and heavy iron and clay pots. Eating utensils are rarely used. This may be why it is customary to wash and clap one's hands prior to eating.

A key staple that makes up 80 percent of the calories for the day is called *fufu* or *ugali*. The western regions refer to this starchy mixture as *fufu*, while the eastern parts of the sub-Saharan call it *ugali*. It is made from any starchy plant such as rice, yams, cassava, manioc, plantain, corn, millet, or cocoyams. To make this mixture, a starchy vegetable, root, or cereal is mashed into a paste. It is then cooked in water. Once cooked, the mixture is eaten with the fingers by making it into a ball and dipping the ball into spicy sauces and condiments. *Fufu* or *ugali* may also be made into cakes or fritters and then fried. It can be served as a side dish in the same way as dumplings are.

Safety Check

Cassava contains a substance that is poisonous until cooked. Therefore, cassava is usually peeled and boiled before eating.

Source: Adapted from Wells, Troth. (1990). *The New Internationalist Food Book.* Toronto: Second Story Press.

Staple foods prepared and eaten in other regions include plantains, which are eaten cooked in many ways, or used as an ingredient in other cooked foods in Eastern Africa. Plantains may be fried to make them into crispy plantain chips, or made into a thick, smooth plantain soup, called *mtori*. A dish called *Nyama Ne Nyemba* is eaten in Zimbabwe. It consists of a hearty portion of beans, to which diced beef, chilies, curry spice, and garlic are added to give it more flavour. Food in South Africa is largely influenced by the Dutch settlers. A common dish, called *sambal*, is a salad made from grated fresh vegetables sprinkled with vinegar or lemon juice, chilies, and cayenne pepper.

Ethiopia, located on the Horn of Africa, is known for a type of stew called *wot*. A base ingredient, such as chicken, *doro wot, or beef, beg wot*, is added to sliced onions that are cooked in butter. Tomato paste and spices such as chilies or black pepper are added. This stew is served with *injera*, a thin pancake-like bread that is torn into pieces and used to scoop up the food.

Western Africa, which includes Nigeria, is home to a soup called *okro* soup. It contains a base of vegetables and seafood. Okra thickens this soup and chilies make it hot and spicy. *Okro* soup may be the ancestor of a dish that is a cross between a stew and a soup, known as **gumbo,** a spicy, popular dish that is part of the Creole cuisine of America.

North Africa and Southwest Asia

This is the area of the world where Europe, Asia, and Africa meet. The northern part of Africa includes countries such as Egypt and Morocco. The southwest part of Asia is called the Middle East. Countries in this area include Turkey, Iran, and Saudi Arabia. The cuisines in these areas are in many ways quite similar.

FYI

How Do Starches Thicken Food?

Starches are used to thicken sauces, gravies, soups, salad dressings, and desserts. The most common sources of starch are cereal grains (corn, wheat, and rice) and tubers (potatoes and cassava).

To thicken a food, you heat a starch such as wheat flour or cornstarch in water. The starch molecules absorb water in a process called gelatinization. Starch molecules do not dissolve in water because they are too large. However, when starches are cooked in water, the energy from the water molecules loosens the bonds between the starch molecules. Clusters of starch called *granules* then absorb water and swell— gelatinization. Once a starch mixture is thickened, or gelatinized, and begins to cool, the starch can become rigid, forming a gel. A gel can be cut with a knife and will not spread out to take the shape of the container it is in. You see this in the cornstarch-thickened lemon filling of a lemon meringue pie. When the filling cools, it becomes firm—the starch has gelled.

Egypt

In the northern areas of Africa, there is a definite influence from the cuisine of the Middle East. In Egypt much of the food is vegetarian.

Staple Foods

Bread is a major staple regardless of economic or social class. Bread made from corn, millet, or sorghum is typical in the peasant class. *Bettai,* or *bettawa*, is a flat circular Arabian yeast bread. It is broken into sections and used to pick up food. It is often flavoured with fenugreek, which tastes similar to anise or black licorice. Protein sources include legumes, such as lentils, chickpeas, and *mish*, a strong cheese made from skim milk. Egypt also produces and consumes a lot of dates.

Customs and Cuisine

Some popular Egyptian foods include *meushti*, or stuffed vegetables that show the influences of nearby Greece and Turkey. Vegetables may be stuffed with bulgur, a cracked wheat staple used in many ways. *Moulighia*, or *millokhia*, is a green leafy vegetable similar to spinach and used primarily in *moulighia* soup, where it acts as a thickener. Chicken or rabbit are used to make stock and flavoured with tomato paste, coriander, pepper, and garlic. Raw onion may be sprinkled on top. A dish called *ful* or *ful medamis* is often served for breakfast or lunch. It consists of boiled beans and oil.

Turkey

Turkish cuisine is influenced by the food traditions of both its neighbour Greece and Middle Eastern countries. The staple ingredients in Turkish food are rich and varied. Eggplant, also called *aubergine*, is sliced or cubed and fried. It is often a part of a casserole in which *bamya* (okra), zucchini, or peas are added. It may be served with a cucumber, tomato, and onion salad. Arabian flat, round bread, called pita, is a staple at meals as well. Turkish figs and peaches often end a meal. Olive oil and butter are widely used in many dishes, as are beef, mutton, and lamb as protein sources. Lentils, peas, and beans are eaten in many

◆ Open markets are regularly set up in villages in Turkey. They are a place to sell all kinds of foods and spices, coffees and teas. Local farmers also come to sell their cheeses and yogurt. The taste of milk products may vary, depending on the region.

FYI

How is Yogourt Made?

You can make your own yogurt at home by adding certain friendly bacteria, called lactic acid bacteria (*lactobacillus*) to milk that has been heated. Heating the milk first kills unwanted bacteria. It also changes the structure of the whey proteins in the milk, increasing their capacity to bind water and promoting the growth of the friendly bacteria that ferment the milk.

Fermentation is a chemical reaction that splits complex compounds into simpler substances. Usually fermentation involves breaking down sugars into carbon dioxide and alcohol. In dairy foods, a sugar is broken down into lactic acid, which is very sour and gives foods such as plain yogurt and sour cream their sour taste.

The bacteria used to make yogurt grow best at temperatures between 41°C and 45°C (106°F and 113°F). When making yogurt at home, you must keep the yogurt at that temperature for about eight hours to produce a smooth consistency. During that time, the bacteria produce acid and flavours that give yogurt its characteristic taste. After the yogurt is done, you can add fruit and sweetener, if you want.

dishes, with rice and bulgur used to make a pilaf or stuff a variety of meats and vegetables. Yogurt, or *yought*, accompanies many dishes, including soups and casseroles, and a variety of flavourful local cheeses also accompany meals.

Customs and Cuisine

Depending on which part of Turkey you are exploring, the fare may differ slightly. In the coastal regions near the Aegean Sea, breakfast may be tomatoes, a boiled egg, goat's milk cheese, and thick slices of white bread or pita. Strong Turkish coffee or tea is taken with the meal. Apple tea, also a common hot drink, is served in a small, clear glass.

Other Turkish favourites include dolmas—stuffed leaves, usually grape leaves, filled with a mixture of meat, rice, and seasonings. As a treat there is Turkish Delight, a cubed sugar and flour-covered confection made from a syrup thickened with cornstarch and flavoured with orange flower water, rosewater, or mastic, a resin from a Mediterranean tree.

South Asia

This area includes Nepal and the island of Sri Lanka, and extends over to India and into Pakistan. What sets this cuisine apart from the rest of the world is the blending of spices cooked with vegetables and meats. These combinations are generally referred to as curry, while *masala* is the name for the mixtures of spices in India. Families will have their own, cherished masala recipes. **Tandoor** is a style of cooking popular in some areas of East India, and uses a special clay oven with sloping sides to bake breads and chicken.

Roti is the common name for all breads in this region, and they are prepared in many different ways. Breads are usually made from wheat flour but can be made from chickpea or other flours as well. Rice is also a staple here and comes in many different varieties. It is used in specific ways according to which dish is being prepared.

FYI

Comparing Food Guides from around the World

Food guides are a good way to learn about the indigenous foods of a particular region. While devising a food guide, the government or other organization within a country can look at the nutritional status and food consumption patterns of the people. This process can also take into account national food supply and nutritional standards. Here are some interesting similarities and differences among the basic food categories presented in an international group of food guides. Compare these to *Canada's Food Guide to Healthy Eating*.

Milk and Milk Products. The Philippines is the only country that does *not* have a Milk and Milk Products group in its food guide. Traditionally, Filipinos do not include milk in their diet. Milk was, however, put in as part of the major protein group. Mexico grouped milk under foods of animal origin. Korea and China recommend a smaller number of servings of the milk group in their guide. The Chinese food guide, designed to be like a pagoda, has placed legumes into the Milk and Milk products group.

Fluids. Germany has a separate group for fluids, to stress their importance. In its guide, Puerto Rico includes a recommendation for the amount of water to be consumed and shows a picture of water in the guide. In a place such as Puerto Rico, with its hot, tropical climate, maintaining the proper balance of fluids in the body is crucial.

Potatoes. It is interesting to note that in the food guides of Korea, the United Kingdom, Portugal, Germany, and Mexico, potatoes are *not* presented as part of the vegetable group, but are included in the grains category.

Root Vegetables. These vegetables, including potatoes, have their own separate category in the Swedish food guide. This is because they are what the Swedish call a "base food." Root vegetables provide the foundation for an inexpensive and nutritious diet, and amounts consumed can remain the same every day. The Swedes recommend that this group be supplemented with other vegetables.

Overall, food guides are similar in that they all recommend that people consume large amounts of grains, vegetables, and fruits, and that they consume meat, milk, and milk products in moderation.

Source: Painter, J., Jee-Hyun, R. and Yeon-Kyung L. (2002). "Comparison of International Food Guide Pictorial Representations." *Journal of The American Dietetic Association* (102), 483–4 (pp. 89).

In this region, vegetarianism is very common, usually as part of religious observances. Hindus, for example, do not eat beef, and sometimes other meats as well. Moslems, including most of the people in Pakistan, do not eat pork. In fact, the cuisine of South Asia is a good example of a diet that uses foods other than meat, poultry, and fish to obtain, protein. *Dal*, a dish of lentils prepared in many ways, serves as a major source of protein and is used daily. Lentils, chickpeas, and other dried beans and peas are excellent sources of protein that also supply complex carbohydrates, fibre, and certain

vitamins and minerals. Rice supplements the protein and also provides complex carbohydrates. Yogurt provides complete protein, as well as calcium, phosphorus, and magnesium.

East and Southeast Asia

As we travel to Eastern and Southeast Asia, the cuisine changes significantly. This area of the world includes Japan, China, Taiwan, Cambodia, Korea, the Philippines, Vietnam, Thailand, Singapore, Malaysia, and Indonesia.

Staple Foods

Rice is the main staple in these countries, although noodles are another staple served daily with many meals. Noodles made from rice flour may be as thin as hair or formed into flat, thick, long sticks. Chinese egg noodles are made from wheat flour and eggs, while cellophane noodles, also called vermicelli

INTERNET CONNECTS

www.mcgrawhill.ca/links/food
For more information about international cuisines go to the web site above for *Food for Today, First Canadian Edition,* to see where to go next.

Many people in the northern parts of Thailand live in small villages, including this young girl. They often are subsistence farmers, living on only whatever foods they can grow. Traditionally, they process any foods that are eaten. This job may be left up to women and children. **How do you think this lifestyle affects their nutritional state?**

The carefully arranged fruits, vegetables, and other items on top of this Balinese woman's head show just a few of the varieties of fruits that are available in Southeast Asia. Research to find out why she is carrying this food on her head?

or glass noodles, are made from the starch of ground mung beans. Asian fruits are eaten frequently. These include *durian*, *rambutan*, and persimmons. Usual vegetables include Chinese long beans, bok choi, and water chestnuts. Coconuts and coconut milk are widely used in dishes and beverages. Other staples include bean sprouts, cabbage, green beans, onions, peaches, pears, peppers, and soybeans or soybean products, such as tofu.

Many of the countries in Southeast Asia are islands or have long coastlines that allow good fishing. Shellfish and finfish are both popular, as well as pork, chicken, and duck, all raised as sources of protein. Traditionally, the foods, and thus the diet in these parts of Asia, are lower in fat. A wide variety of vegetables and fruits are generally consumed, and grain-based foods such as noodles and rice are eaten daily.

Customs and Cuisine

In this part of the world, people generally use chopsticks to eat, although hands, forks, and spoons for eating soups are all also used. Some varieties of East and Southeast Asian cuisine include:

◆ **Dim sum.** These are tiny Chinese dumplings and other foods filled with different meats and vegetables. The dough is made from wheat flour. Once prepared, these Chinese delicacies are steamed and served hot with various sauces.

◆ **Sushi.** From Japan, sushi is the general name for a variety of small cakes or balls made of cold rice. The rice is vinegared and wrapped or molded around small bits of food, such as raw or cooked fish and vegetables. It may be wrapped or rolled with edible seaweed as well. Sushi are traditionally served with condiments such as grated horseradish, called *wasabi*, ginger, and Japanese soy sauce pickled.

◆ **Pho.** This Vietnamese dish is served in a large bowl. It consists of a generous portion of noodles mixed with broth and strips of meat, vegetables, green herbs, chilies, and garlic arranged on top. *Pho* is eaten with chopsticks and a porcelain spoon. Sauces, such as *nuoc mam*, a salty fish sauce, are served in little dishes on the side so that people can dip their food into them according to taste.

Europe

European culture has created a rich array of cuisines and food traditions. Many of these cuisines made their way from Europe to North America along with the early explorers and settlers, and later with the waves of European immigrants to Canada and the United States.

◆ In these regions of Asia, meals may be served with small dishes that contain a variety of sauces. They range from salty fish sauces to oyster, peanut, and other spicy sauces. Why do you think this is customary?

Food Science ♦ L A B ♦

How Does Temperature Affect Egg Whites?

In this experiment you will discover what effect, if any, temperature has on beaten egg whites.

Procedure

1. Place three refrigerated egg whites in a quart-size glass bowl that is clean and free of grease. With a rotary beater or electric mixer, beat the whites until they form peaks that bend over slightly when the beaters are lifted out of the whites.

2. Scoop the contents into a clean measuring cup, then measure and record the results.

3. Repeat the procedure above with three egg whites that have been at room temperature for at least 30 minutes.

Conclusions

◆ Which egg whites produced the greater volume?

◆ How might this information help you if you were preparing meringue for a pie or a cake that called for beaten egg whites?

Northern and Western Europe

In northern regions of Europe, the staple for making breads and cereals is wheat. Rye is quite popular in many areas as well. Along with wheat, oatmeal has traditionally been a staple in Scotland, and, as you have learned, potatoes historically provided people in Ireland with the complex carbohydrates they needed to survive.

Germany is well known for its sausages and other smoked meats, while in Norway, Sweden, and Finland fish and seafood are an important part of the diet. France has long been known for its rich variety of cheeses and pastries.

Though food habits are changing in Europe, as they are in North America, many of the traditional foods in these regions are high in fat, since they owe their flavours to a variety of rich sauces and plenty of butter.

Customs and Cuisine

In England, since the seventeenth century, tea accompanied by cakes, biscuits, or bread with butter has been served as a snack, especially in the late afternoon. In other parts of Europe such as France and Spain, coffee is preferred. The Swiss enjoy *milchkaffe*, a blend of hot milk and coffee, and in Finland, people drink coffee in the morning with *pulla*—a braided yeast dough often flavoured with cardamom. A few other foods that are popular in Western Europe include the following.

- *Rosti* is a traditional Swiss pancake made from potatoes. It is often served with liver and bacon. Rosti are prepared using shredded potatoes formed into a large pancake and fried in butter.

- **Soufflé** is a baked, egg-based dish traditional in French cuisine. It is prepared using thick, creamy sauces mixed with beaten egg whites. The sauce can be sweet, with chocolate or fruit, or savoury, using cheese or salmon.

- **Dublin coddle** is, of course, from Ireland and is a type of stew. It consists of ham, sausages, onions, and potatoes cooked together slowly. Coddle can be served with Irish soda bread—a buttermilk and flour bread leavened with soda.

◆ French cuisine is known for classic dishes such as this cheese *soufflé*—a rich mixture of cheeses that uses the chemistry of beaten egg whites to make it rise. What does the French word *soufflé* mean?

FYI

What Makes Baked Goods Rise?

Baked goods rise because of *leavening*. To leaven means to make light and porous. In baked goods, leavening involves producing a gas that expands as the batter or dough is heated, leaving holes as the batter or dough sets during baking.

Some baked products are also leavened by carbon dioxide. This gas is produced by leavening agents such as baking soda, baking powder, and yeast. Baking soda (bicarbonate of soda) is a chemical agent for producing carbon dioxide. Baking soda is a base. When it is mixed with an acid, a chemical reaction occurs:

Baking soda + Acid + Heat
= Carbon dioxide + water

Acids and Bases

Acid is the name for a group of chemicals that share certain characteristics. Weak acids taste sour. The acetic acid in vinegar and the citric acid in fruits such as oranges and lemons give these foods their sour taste. *Base* is the name for another group of chemicals that react with acids. Bases are the chemical opposite of acids. When a recipe calls for baking soda, an acidic food such as vinegar, buttermilk, molasses, honey, fruit juice, or yogurt is also added. Together, the base and the acid react to give off carbon dioxide. The carbon dioxide leavens the baked product.

Southern Europe

This region may also be referred to as the Mediterranean region. Spain, Portugal, Italy, and Greece all have borders on the Mediterranean Sea. The sunny, warm climates of these countries are perfect for growing the staple foods of the region.

Thick, crusty loaves of white bread are the staple here. Cornmeal is also used to make some breads and a food called *polenta* in Italy. This is a thick cornmeal porridge that is formed into patties and then fried or grilled. These patties become the base for other foods, such as tomato sauces. Pasta, in many varieties, is also an Italian staple. Most of the region makes extensive use of olive oil, both in cooking and cold with other foods. Cheese, made from both goats' and cows' milk, is used as an ingredient in many dishes or enjoyed alone. Feta cheese, made from goat's milk, is a staple in Greece, as is *tzatziki*, a thick yogurt with shredded cucumber, garlic, and salt.

Since they border on the sea, the Mediterranean countries consume a great deal of fish and shellfish, both good sources of protein. Lamb, poultry, and beef are used for protein as well. Foods are often seasoned with garlic and other vegetables, such as tomatoes, eggplant, peppers, zucchini, and onions. All these ingredients contain many important nutrients, such as vitamins and antioxidants. Grapes and olives also grow well in the warm rocky areas of Southern Europe and are enjoyed frequently. The cuisine of the Mediterranean region provides the people with nutrient-dense foods, even though many dishes are high in fat and calories.

◆ Mediterranean foods are nutritious and flavourful, though often high in calories.

Scientific Principles of Cooking Meat, Poultry, and Fish

Tenderness

When cooking meat, poultry, or fish you want your end product to be uniformly tender. The factors that affect tenderness are explained here.

Connective Tissue

The amount and type of connective tissue in the meat will affect its tenderness. The main tissue in meat is skeletal muscle. These muscles have long fibres that are held together in bundles by connective tissue. Cuts from shoulders, legs, and other parts of the animal that do the work contain more connective tissue. This makes them tougher cuts of meat. Both shellfish and finfish do not have these muscular areas so they have little connective tissue, making them tender by nature.

Elastin

Elastin and collagen are two types of connective tissue. These tissues are made up of protein molecules that resemble a coiled spring. These coils make a strong rope-like fibre that helps to bind and support other tissues. Elastin is also called gristle, and does not break down throughout the cooking process. Collagen, on the other hand, disperses in heated water and forms gelatin when cooled. Collagen is tender connective tissue and helps meat appear plump.

Heat

Heat applied when cooking meat and poultry unwinds the proteins in the muscle. These proteins then join with other proteins. If meat is overcooked using dry heat, the proteins shrink and the meat becomes drier and tougher. Controlling the amount of heat is the key to tender and juicy meat. Alternatively, tougher cuts of meat can be cooked in liquid by a slow cooking method that will help to soften and dissolve connective tissue. Most meat and poultry will then be made more tender.

Acids

Acids are chemicals that share common characteristics. Citrus fruits, such as limes, oranges, and lemons, contain citric acids that are considered weak acids. Because of this mild quality, citrus juices are used to marinate meat. The juices from lemons, limes, and oranges help to tenderize meat, poultry, and fish, and add flavour.

(continued)

Scientific Principles of Cooking Meat, Poultry, and Fish (continued)

Enzymes

Enzymes are protein substances that cause chemical changes to occur. When a plant or animal is processed into a food, some of the enzymes remain active. Unless foods are heated to destroy these enzymes, chemical changes continue, destroying the cells and causing the food to spoil. However, enzymes in fruits such as papaya, figs, and pineapples attack the connective tissue in muscle fibre. This makes the meat more tender. Enzymes can be used as ingredients in commercially prepared meat tenderizers, and these work best when in direct contact with the meat. Injecting the liquid enzyme directly into the meat is the best way to ensure that the tenderizer will work.

Physical Techniques

Meat may also be tenderized by cutting the long fibres against the grain. This is done by slicing the muscle fibres and connective tissue at a right angle. You can also shorten the muscle fibres to make the meat more tender and easier to chew by pounding meat with a mallet, grinding it up, or scoring it (making shallow cuts in the surface of the meat).

The Browning Process

You may have noticed the rich brown colour and intense flavour of the outside of a roast of meat or poultry. Food cooked in dry heat or in fat goes through a browning process. As food browns, the colour, flavour, and texture are altered as the result of complex chemical changes. One of these changes is called the *Maillard reaction*, which occurs when carbohydrates (either sugar or starch) and amino acids combine on the surface of roasting meat. The reaction occurs only when the surface of the food cooked in dry heat or fat reaches temperatures over 150°C (300°F). With moist heat, the temperature cannot rise above the boiling point of water, 100°C (212°F). This is why foods cooked in moist heat do not brown. The Maillard reaction also does not occur in foods cooked in a microwave oven because the air inside does not get hot enough.

Source: Adapted from Larson Duyff (2000).

Customs and Cuisine

Appetizers, **hors d'oeuvres**, and snacks are also traditional in parts of these regions. In Spain, they are referred to as *tapas*, while in Greece these tidbits are called *meze*. In Portugal, lunch and dinner meals are taken leisurely, and may take as long as two hours to complete. Children are included in both conversation and the drinking of wine during meals. Popular Mediterranean dishes include:

◆ **Spaghetti alla carbonara** is a rich Italian dish that consists of pasta tossed with salt pork or crisp bacon, grated cheese, and beaten raw eggs. In Italy pasta is properly cooked **al dente** (to the tooth) so that it is slightly chewy, not soft.

◆ **Spanokopita** is a rectangular Greek pie made with *phyllo* pastry. This paper-thin pastry is buttered and used to hold the filling of the pie—a mixture of chopped spinach, onions, and feta cheese.

◆ *Massa sovada* is a rich sweet bread made in Portugal. This bread is leavened with yeast, made with eggs, and flavoured with cinnamon. *Massa sovada* is often served at festive occasions.

INTERNET CONNECTS

www.mcgrawhill.ca/links/food
For more information about food customs and culture, go to the web site above for *Food for Today, First Canadian Edition,* to see where to go next.

Latin America

This cultural and geographical designation embraces Mexico, the countries of Central America, such as Costa Rica and Guatemala, parts of the Caribbean, and all of South America.

Staple Foods

Corn or maize is one of the most important ingredients in making breads such as tortillas and tamales, both staples of Latin American cuisines. Tamales are a traditional Mexican food made of corn dough wrapped in corn husks or banana leaves and then baked or steamed. Wheat flour is more popular in some areas than others, and rice accompanies dishes eaten in certain regions including Mexico and Central America.

◆ Tortillas are the staple food in many parts of Latin America. They are versatile and can be filled with many ingredients. Plan a one-day menu around tortillas. Use tortillas to make as many different combinations as possible.

An important source of protein in the Latin American diet is beans (*frijoles*), especially among poorer people. Red beans, kidney beans, pinto beans, and black beans are all consumed and often combined with rice to make a complete protein. Beans may be boiled or fried in lard. Beef, another source of protein, is eaten in parts of Mexico, and is the foundation of the diet of people in parts of Argentina, Brazil, Paraguay, and Uruguay. Fish and seafood are eaten in coastal areas of Latin America.

These parts of the world produce many tropical and subtropical fruits. Avocados, bananas, lemons, limes, guava, mango, papaya, and pineapple are all popular. Fruits are also used to make juices and other refreshing drinks. Peppers, tomatoes, and chilies are abundant. Potatoes and sweet potatoes are thought to have originated in the mountain regions of Peru and Ecuador. Much Latin American food is seasoned with cilantro (leaves from the coriander plant) and cinnamon. Of course, chilies and citrus fruits such as lemons and limes also flavour foods and some beverages.

INTERNET CONNECTS

www.mcgrawhill.ca/links/food
To learn more about the diets of people around the world, go to the web site above for *Food for Today*, *First Canadian Edition*, to see where to go next.

Customs and Cuisine

Mexican people use earthenware casserole dishes to cook and serve food. The main meal in Mexico is at midday. This leisurely lunch can last for three hours, as it is too hot to do much else during this time of the day.

A substantial lunch, served hot, is also the customary main meal of the day in most of South America. Coffee is popular throughout much of this part of the world, and is often served with hot milk (*cafe con leche*). In Brazil, it is hospitable to serve coffee to guests, and it concludes both lunch and dinner. Other Latin American foods include:

♦ *Ceviche* is a popular appetizer in Peru and Mexico. It consists of raw white fish that is marinated in lemon or lime juice and served with onions.

♦ **Enchiladas** are tortillas filled with meat, chicken, cheese, or vegetables, and rolled with the ends open. They are covered with a sauce, such as tomato sauce, and baked. When tortillas are fried flat they may be topped with ground meat, *frijoles*, cheese, or shredded lettuce. These are referred to as *tostados*. In Central America, tortillas may be served open-face and topped with pickled vegetables such as carrots, beets, or cabbage. In Guatemala, people first spread the tortilla with guacamole and top with sausage and pickled cabbage. This is referred to as *mixtas*. In El Salvador this type of sandwich is changed slightly by filling a tortilla with cheese, *chiccarones* (fried pork rinds), or black beans. Another tortilla is placed on top and the edges are sealed. This tortilla sandwich, called a *papusa*, is then fried. Pickled cabbage is served as a side dish.

♦ *Matambre* is an Argentine national dish. It consists of flank steak seasoned with herbs. The steak is filled with spinach, carrots, and whole hard-boiled eggs. It is then rolled, tied, and baked or poached in broth. It may be served as a main course or sliced cold and served as an appetizer.

Ceviche (Peru)

In the 1430s the Incas, the last of the indigenous conquerors, began to create their empire in Peru. The Spanish took over in 1532, but kept the Incas' exploitative structures, with the added twist of outlawing local culture and demeaning the Aboriginal Peoples as inferior. With its extensive coastline, Peru has a long connection with the sea and fishing. It was the leading fishmeal exporter in the 1970s but the depletion of *anchoveta* (anchovies) led to today's emphasis on increasing pilchard and mackerel catches for local consumption. The ceviche is not cooked, but it needs to marinate for 20–40 minutes before serving.

Ingredients

900 g	white fish fillets (sea bass or hake are best)	4 lbs.
4–6	juice of limes or lemons	4–6
1	large onion, sliced finely	1
½–1	chili, chopped finely, or 5 mL chili powder	½–1 tsp.
75 g	sweet potato, sliced and cooked	⅓ cup
150 g	cassava/manioc, sliced and cooked	½ cup
3	tomatoes	3
75 g	olives	⅓ cup
	salt and pepper	

1. To begin, cut the fish fillets into small pieces. Then place them in a bowl or dish and pour on enough lime/lemon juice to cover them.

2. Now add the other ingredients and mix them in gently. Squeeze on more lemon or lime juice if necessary to make sure everything is covered. Leave the fish to marinate for 20–40 minutes.

3. After that time, drain off some of the liquid, keeping it, and transfer the fish and other marinade ingredients to a serving bowl. The ceviche is now ready to be eaten.

Serves 4 to 6

Executive Director

Judy Murphy

What education is required for your job?

• a Bachelor's degree in business or management

What skills does a person need to be able to do your job?

• Business management skills

• Strong interpersonal skills and the ability to interact with a diverse group of people

• Strong written and oral communication skills and the ability to deal effectively with the media

• Marketing, sponsorship, and financial management skills

• Ability to deal effectively with a board of directors

What do you like most about your job?

I enjoyed the variety in my job, the interaction with the people, and the excitement of the Folklorama festival.

What other jobs/job titles have you had in the past?

I have worked as a professional musician, as an auditor, and as a director of finance and operations.

What advice would you give a person who is considering a career as an executive director?

Find an area of expertise such as sponsorship, fundraising, marketing, or finance in order to enter the industry. Broaden your skill set and learn all you can, then move into an executive director position.

Comment on what you see as important issues/trends in food and nutrition.

Folklorama remains true to its roots with authentic food. Food is always an integral part of any festival. People often come to Folklorama to experience foods from different cultures. Folklorama offers an opportunity for people to pass down recipes to new generations.

Chapter 30   Review and Activities

Summary

- Components of a cuisine include staple foods and ways of preparing, cooking, serving, and eating food in a given country or culture.

- In some areas of the world, these components have changed dramatically as a result of globalization.

Knowledge and Understanding

1. Describe various ways that meat can be tenderized.

2. Explain the scientific principle behind two methods of tenderizing meat.

3. Why will meat cooked in a microwave oven or in moist heat not turn brown on the outside? Record your answer in your notes.

4. How does the process of fermentation help make yogurt?

5. Describe the effect of temperature on the process of beating egg whites.

Thinking and Inquiry

6. Research the effect that globalization has had on the way that staple foods are prepared and consumed around the world. Report your findings to the class.

7. Different countries have different names for the small tidbits or appetizers that may be consumed prior to a meal or as a snack. Research some of the popular items that are part of several countries' appetizers. Write a one-page report that compares the different ingredients and style of preparation and presentation of the appetizers from the individual countries.

8. In your notes, list some of the popular dishes from each region. Beside each item, list any ways that we have adapted these dishes in Canada.

9. Answer the following questions in your notes:

   a) Using the feature "Comparing Food Guides from around the World," analyse what we can learn from comparing food guides from different countries.

   b) What professionals would benefit from knowing about the recommendations and contents of food guides from various countries around the world? Why would this knowledge benefit these people?

Communication

10. There are parts of the world that were not included in this chapter. Research some of the staple foods, popular dishes, and common ways that foods are prepared from these countries. Compare these countries with the information regarding staple foods, customs, and cuisines from other countries that you read about in this chapter. Present your findings in chart form, using illustrations.

11. a) Make a chart in your notes that lists the staple foods common to each part of the world described in this chapter. You can further subdivide each part of the world into countries. Beside this column, write down the major nutrients that are found in each staple ingredient. In the next column, record how these nutrients affect the body. For example, Southern Europe—Greece—olive oil—monounsaturated fatty acids—may help to reduce bad cholesterol in the body.

   b) Using the information in the chart, write a summary for each area of the world that gives an analysis of the general nutritional content in their diets. Your analysis may include a discussion regarding the differences between people who are from urban versus rural parts of each region or are wealthy versus poor.

Application

12. In your foods lab, prepare a variety of different appetizers from the various countries that you researched in question number 8 of this chapter.

13. Plan a one-day menu using various ingredients and dishes from each region. Prepare some of the dishes that are included in your menu.

14. Choose one main dish that you read about in this chapter that is unfamiliar to you. Prepare this dish at home for your own family.

While reading this chapter, you will:

- Describe the effects of various economic factors on food production and supply.

- Investigate the impact of a variety of political factors on food supply, and present the results of your investigation.

- Demonstrate an understanding of the effects of different environmental factors on the production and supply of food.

- Describe policies necessary to protect the health and safety of food producers.

- Identify the impact of biotechnology on food production, supply, and safety.

- Identify legislation governing pesticide and fertilizer use, and the labelling of biogenetically engineered foods.

Only one percent of the Canadian population now lives on a farm. Why is it important that Canadians produce their own food?

Factors Affecting Food Production and Supply

KEY TERMS

aquaculture
bioengineering
fertilizers
inputs
Integrated Pest
Management (IPM)
low tillage
no tillage
pesticide
sustainable development

In this chapter you will explore many issues related to Canada's food supply and come to understand the agricultural community in Canada today. What economic and political factors influence Canada's agriculture? What is the impact of agriculture on the environment, and how does the agricultural community try to reduce that impact? You will consider these questions and also look at the use of technologies in agriculture and the impact biotechnology can have on food production, food supply, and food safety. You will explore government action and legislation regarding food labelling as well as the use of pesticides and fertilizers in agriculture today.

As Canadian citizens and educated consumers, we need to be aware of modern Canadian agriculture.

Profile of Agriculture in Canada

Many of us have an old-fashioned view of agriculture and the people who work on farms. We fail to realize that changes affecting all Canadians have had an impact on those involved in agriculture too. New technologies increase efficiency on the farm. Some technologies that have industrial appli-

cations also have agricultural applications. The cost of this new technology is high, and farmers have to be more efficient to break even or make a profit. While the size of farms is increasing, the number of people involved in farming is decreasing (Agriculture and Agri Food Canada, n.d.).

The Changing Farm

While the total population of Canada is steadily increasing, the farm population has been on a steady decline since the 1930s. The steady exodus from the countryside to the city by young people seeking employment and the increase of rural, non-farm families has changed the lifestyle of rural Canada. As technology changes, farm size increases. As a result, we now have a small number of farmers producing food for the Canadian population. The chart below shows the relationship between the growing Canadian population and farming since 1931.

While the number of farms has decreased, the amount of land being farmed has been relatively stable in the last two decades. Farm size in Canada varies from province to province, with the larger farms on the prairies, and the smaller farms in the Atlantic Provinces. Another change to farming is in the amount of land being rented or leased. More farmers are renting land now than 20 years ago; almost 30 percent more farmland was leased in 1996 than in 1976. Part of the reason for this change is the cost of farming. Some farmers prefer to rent land and put their capital expenditures into equipment or buildings.

The Changing Farm

Canada	Canadian Population x 100 000	Farm Population x 100 000	Total Number of Farms x 1000	Average Farm Size in Hectares
1931	104	33	729	91
1941	115	32	733	96
1951	140	29	623	113
1961	182	21	481	145
1971	215	16	366	188
1981	243	12	318	207
1991	272	9	280	242
1996	288	9	277	246
2001	311	3	247	273

Source: Ontario Agri Food Education (2003). *Update: The changing farm face.* Milton: Ontario Agri Food Education.

Even though farms are larger, 98 percent of all farms in Canada are owned by families (Agriculture and Agri Food Canada, n.d.). The legal structure of farms is changing too. Even though families own most farms, more and more farms are being registered as partnerships or family corporations. In 1996, 37 percent of all farms were registered in this manner (Canadian Federation of Agriculture, n.d.).

Who is farming is changing as well. The average age of farmers is increasing. The number of farmers under the age of 35 has decreased from 19.9 percent in 1991 to 11.5 percent in 2001. The median age of farmers rose from 47 in 1996 to 49 in 2001 (Statistics Canada, 2002b). In 1996, men ran almost two-thirds of farms. Farms run by women accounted for only 5 percent. The other 30 percent of farms were run by male/female partnerships (Canadian Federation of Agriculture, n.d.).

INTERNET CONNECTS

www.mcgrawhill.ca/links/food
To learn more about agricultural statistics, go to the web site above for *Food for Today, First Canadian Edition*, to see where to go next.

Skills and Education of Farmers

Computer use on the farm has increased just as it has in the rest of society. The computer is becoming an essential tool for business management on Canadian farms. Between 1996 and 2001, computer use on farms increased by over 65 percent (Statistics Canada, 2002a).

Farmers' skills are becoming increasingly diverse. A farmer must be able to manage a small business and perform a variety of other tasks, including recognizing an ill animal, fixing machines, using high-tech equipment, and surfing the Internet for information on markets and the newest technologies available. As a result of these new demands, farmers, like other Canadians, are attaining higher levels of education now than ever before (Canadian Federation of Agriculture, n.d.).

Farm Income

As costs continue to rise, more and more farmers must find off-farm work to supplement their farm income. Both men and women report off-farm income. Women tend to work off the farm slightly more than men (45.6 percent of women compared to 44.2 percent of men) (Statistics Canada, 2003). More than half of an average farmer's income comes from off-farm sources. This money can also be used to cover the times in farming when no income comes in. Farm income fluctuates during the year, depending on the season, and from year to year. The reasons for this include weather patterns, such as drought or too much rain; cost of farm inputs, such as equipment, seed, or feed for animals; and changes to world commodity prices due to overproduction or underproduction of a commodity in the world. The off-farm income provides a base income for the family. Farm families make 3.3 percent less income than the average Canadian family (Canadian Federation of Agriculture, 2003).

The Farmer's Share

The Canadian Federation of Agriculture (CFA) hosted an outdoor lunch on Parliament Hill to celebrate Food Freedom Day. CFA calculated the amount farmers would earn for their products, based on the ingredients used, if this meal were sold at a retail outlet.

The Farmer's Share
Chicken Soup

Chicken	$0.15
Onions	$0.01
Carrots	$0.01
Potatoes	$0.01
Celery	$0.01
Mushrooms	$0.08
Milk	$0.07
Parsley	$0.01
Flour (Wheat)	$0.00
Butter	$0.01
Roll	
Wheat	$0.01
Butter	$0.05
Milk	$
Total—The Farmer's Share	**$0.45**
Retail Price for Consumers	$7.50
Total (Retail + Tax)	$8.63

Source: Canadian Federation of Agriculture (n.d.).

◆ **The costs associated with farming continue to rise. A tractor can cost as much as 20 mid-size cars.**

Costs of Farming

Inputs

Inputs is the term used to describe the cost of what is put into farming. There is a variety of inputs, depending upon the type of farming operation. Some farmers have crops only; some have crops and animals; some grow horticultural produce; some own land; some rent land; some own machinery; and some rent machinery or have their crops harvested by someone else. All of these different ways of farming require different inputs.

One of the major costs of farming is land. The cost of farmland varies from province to province: the closer farmland is to a large, growing urban centre, the more expensive it is. As the number of people wanting to own a home increases, demand for land around cities makes the price rise. Some of the best agricultural land is around these urban centres. Historically, urban centres grew around industry; in many parts of the country that industry was farming. Southwestern Ontario

◆ As urban areas continue to encroach upon valuable farmland, the cost of that land increases. **What impact could this continuing reduction in available farmland have on our future food supply?**

is home to some of the richest farmland in Canada, but it is also an area seeing increased urban development.

The cost of land around urban areas is a vicious circle for the agricultural community and for Canadians in general. It is difficult for farmers to afford the land in these areas. Young farmers starting out may not be able to purchase land in urban areas, and farmers who already own land around cities are under pressure from developers to sell. The more land that is developed, the less is available for agricultural purposes. Land is finite, and once it is developed, it is no longer available for farming. Reducing the amount of farmland available causes the price to rise. As Canadians, we need to consider the impact of this on our food supply.

The input costs of farming are rising at a quicker pace than the amount of money returning to the farmer. Between 1986 and 1996, the cost of inputs rose by 25.2 percent, but during the same time period, the farm gate prices, i.e., income, rose by only 16.7 percent. In other words, costs are outweighing income (Canadian Federation of Agriculture, n.d.).

Farmers face large debt loads due to the costs of inputs to their businesses. Agriculture is an industry that is capital intensive, meaning much of the farmer's money is tied up in capital assets.

Where is the money tied up?

◆ Real estate (land)   54%
◆ Machinery   18%
◆ Inventories   8.4%
◆ Production quotas   6.8%

Changing interest rates, even a 1 percent drop or increase, can have a major impact on the cost of farming. A 1 percent drop in interest rates

FYI

Farming Facts 2002

Whether or not a farm's gross farm receipts exceed, meet, or fall short of its operating expenses, differs according to the receipts category it falls into.

The smallest farms, those with receipts less than $25 000, spent $1.68 in operating expenses for every dollar in receipts. Many farms in this category are hobby farms. Those in the largest receipts category ($250 000 and over) spent $.85 for every dollar they received. However, farmers in all receipts categories spent more to earn a dollar in 2000 than they did in 1995.

In terms of farm numbers, only farm operations with receipts of $250 000 and over were more numerous in 2001 than in 1996. They represented 34 139 farms, an increase of 32 percent from 1995. They accounted for only 14 percent of all farms in Canada.

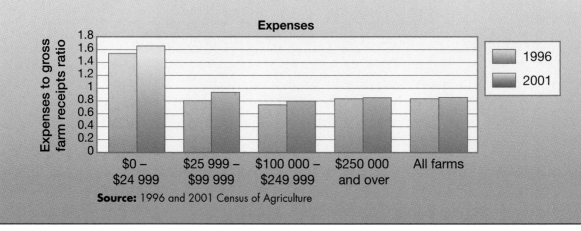

Source: 1996 and 2001 Census of Agriculture

could put an additional $270 million into the hands of Canadian farmers (Canadian Federation of Agriculture, n.d.).

Safety Nets and Government Support

In the agriculture business, there are good times and bad times, and much depends on things beyond the farmer's control. In times of crisis, the federal and provincial governments put support plans called *safety nets* in place. These support and stabilize farm incomes so that farmers can make it through the bad years. Widespread drought in the summer of 2002 caused a loss of income to many farmers in Western Canada. Drought-starved crops

produced smaller yields. Livestock producers had to provide feed which was in short supply for their animals. Pastures dried up, and farmers had to feed the animals hay, which is usually stored for the long winter months.

The Net Income Stabilization Account (NISA), is similar to a savings account. Farmers deposit money into it in the good years, and withdraw from it during the bad years when their incomes fall below a certain level. Federal and provincial governments match a producer's contributions. There are different triggers for withdrawal, but anytime the farmer's income falls below $35 000 from all family sources, he or she can make a withdrawal.

In the Canadian Farm Income Program (CFIP), both federal and provincial governments share cost. Farmers can apply to this program in tough times. Governments also contribute to crop insurance programs. The farmer pays a deductible, and receives the balance of the policy if the crop fails. Historically, farmers have received about 80 percent of their historical annual yield. Farmers can choose to buy insurance that offers a lower level of compensation, with lower premium costs. Other safety-net programs are offered on a province-by-province basis. These programs are designed to suit the needs of farmers in each particular province.

The financial situation many farmers face can be summed up by this fact: Between December 1997 and December 2001, the price Canadian consumers paid for food increased by 11 percent. In contrast, the price received at the farm gate—that is, the farmer's income—increased on average by 2 percent. (Statistics Canada, 2002).

What are Pesticides?

A **pesticide** is any product used to manage, destroy, attract, or repel a pest. A pest can be any unwanted organism, such as an insect, weed, rodent, bacterium, fungus, algae, or mite. Pesticide is a general term used to describe the following products: insecticides — to kill insects; herbicides — to kill weeds; fungicides to kill fungi; rodenticides — to kill rodents; and algaecides — to kill algae.

Why Farmers Use Pesticides

Around the world, billions of dollars worth of food are lost each year due to pests — by either reducing the crop yield or consuming the crop. All farmers rely on a variety of pest-control methods, including:

◆ Mechanical	→	Through cultivation of certain crops.
◆ Cultural	→	Through crop rotation.
◆ Biological	→	By adding beneficial insects or causing pest diseases.
◆ Genetic	→	Cultivating crops that are naturally pest resistant.

When these methods are insufficient to control pests, farmers will use pesticides. Farmers use pesticides because they are highly effective, energy efficient, fast acting, broad spectrum, (i.e., may control more than one type of pest), safe, economical, and less labour intensive, when chosen and applied properly.

The chart on page 654 shows the types of damage caused to crops by pests, and which type of pest is the cause.

Regulation of Pesticide Use in Canada

The use of pesticides is regulated by Health Canada through the Pest Management Regulatory Agency (PMRA). The PMRA has the following responsibilities regarding pesticide use in Canada:

◆ Performs a scientific assessment of all pesticides, developed in Canada or elsewhere, before they are allowed on the market in Canada.

◆ Re-evaluates pesticides that are currently on the market.

◆ Sets maximum residue limits under the *Food and Drug Act*.

◆ Enforces pesticide legislation.

◆ Provides education on the use of pesticides.

◆ Provides information about pesticides.

Types of Damage by Crop Pests

Damage	Cause
Death of crop plants	Insects, diseases, severe weed competition
Reduced growth or yield	Insects, diseases, nemotodes, and weeds
Spread of crop or livestock diseases	Insects
Reduced quality and appearance	Insects, diseases, and weeds
Increased difficulty with harvesting crops	Insects, diseases, and weeds
Damage or spoilage of crops in storage	Insects, diseases, and rodents
Human health risk	Diseases
Damage to meat or hides	Insects
Reduced growth of livestock	Insects, diseases

Source: (AGCare, n.d.).

Safety Check

Mandate of the Pest Management Regulatory Agency

The Pest Management Regulatory Agency (PMRA) of Health Canada has the mandate to protect human health and the environment by minimizing the risks associated with pest-control products, while enabling access to pest-management tools (PMRA, 2003).

The Health Division of the PMRA is responsible for looking at and protecting the health of Canadians. This division consists of three sections:

1. **The Toxicological Evaluation Section** identifies the possible human health effects of pesticides and establishes the levels at which humans can be exposed to a product without any harm. These limits account for differences in people, specifically for age. This section performs long-term and short-term research studies to ensure the health of Canadians.

2. **The Occupational Exposure Section** is responsible for performing tests and assessments on the amount of exposure individuals can have to pesticides during the course of a day. It looks at different groups, such as those who work directly with pesticides, such as farmers or applicators, and bystanders, those who work or live near where pesticides are used. They also look at the effectiveness of protective gear for those who work directly with pesticides.

3. **The Food Residue Exposure Assessment Section** evaluates where a pesticide could come into contact with food, including crops, meat, and milk products, as well as processed foods. It sets maximum limits of pesticide residue. It takes into consideration

Government Responsibilities for Pesticide Use

Federal (PMRA)	Provincial/Territorial	Municipal
Pest Control Products Act and regulations	Transportation, sale, use, storage, and disposal	Local by-laws regarding use
Pesticide registration and re-evaluation	Training, certification, and licensing of growers (farmers), applicators, and vendors	
Human health and safety	Issuance of permits to use pesticides	
Environmental impact	Posting of signs where pesticide has been used	
Value assessment	Spills and accidents	
Alternative strategies	Permits and use restrictions	
Compliance and enforcement	Compliance and enforcement	
(PMRA, 2003).		

the potential daily intake of the residue from all possible food sources and the different eating patterns of different groups of people, adults, children, teens, etc. It performs these assessments on both domestic and imported foods.

Other levels of government also have responsibilities related to the use of pesticides. The chart above shows the different levels of government and their responsibilities.

Integrated Pest Management Practices

Integrated Pest Management (IPM) is a process for planning and managing sites to prevent pest problems and for making decisions about when and how to intervene when pest problems occur. It is a sustainable approach, combining biological, cultural, physical, and chemical tools to manage pests so that the benefits of pest control are maximized and health and environmental risks are minimized.

The goals of IPM are:

- ◆ To meet society's needs for human health protection, food and fibre production, and resource utilization.

- ◆ To conserve or enhance natural resources and the quality of the environment for future generations.

- ◆ To be economically viable.

IPM practices include:

- ◆ Managing crops to prevent pests from becoming a threat; for example, rotate crops between fields.

- ◆ Identifying potential pests.

- Monitoring environmental conditions, pest and beneficial organism populations, and pest damage.

- Deciding whether treatment is needed based on the population of the pest and the amount of damage caused by the pest.

- Using a variety of pest-management practices, including biological, mechanical, and behavioural control methods to reduce pest populations to acceptable levels.

- Using targeted applications of pesticides when needed.

Source: PMRA (2003).

What are Fertilizers?

By definition, **fertilizers** are substances that provide plants with nutrients. They can be added to soil or water, or applied in other ways. Some soils are low in the necessary nutrients for plant growth, and fertilizers are added to increase the nutrient levels of the soil. Fertilizers can be thought of as foods for plants.

Why Farmers Use Fertilizers

When crops grow or bear fruit, they use up nutrients in the soil. In order to get good crop yields, there must be enough nutrients in the soil. Each crop takes nutrients from the soil, which must be replaced if the next crop is to be successful.

The amount and type of fertilizer applied depends on several factors. The farmer uses the following information to determine the best type of fertilizer to apply:

- **The requirements of the crop to be grown.** Different crops have different needs. Farmers learn which crops require which types of nutrients in order to use only the necessary amount and type of fertilizer.

- **Climate.** A lot of rain can wash away necessary nutrients for the crop.

- **The nature of the soil.** Soils naturally contain different amounts of nutrients. Farmers do soil tests to see which nutrients are present at what level. Then they know which type of fertilizer and how much to apply. It is recommended that farmers test soil annually, as soil composition changes.

- **Tissue tests.** Tests are performed on the plants that have been grown to find out which nutrient deficiencies the plant has. This analysis will determine which fertilizers must be applied for the next season.

There are many different types of fertilizer available, although when most people think of fertilizers they think of chemical fertilizers. These fertilizers come in two main types, dry and liquid. Dry fertilizers are produced as pellets or granules and are generally spread on the soil. Liquid fertilizers can be mixed with water and sprayed on the soil. Other types of chemical fertilizers, such as anhydrous ammonia, are gases that are injected into the soil. Fertilizer can be applied before planting, with planting, or after planting, depending on the crop.

Regulation of Chemical Fertilizers

Health Canada and the Canadian Food Inspection Agency (CFIA) are responsible for the regulation and registration of fertilizer and supplemental products. With respect to fertilizers, CFIA's activities include:

◆ Registration of fertilizers, fertilizers/ pesticides, and supplements.

◆ Review of product safety and efficacy and labelling.

◆ Monitoring of active ingredients and contaminants in the marketplace.

◆ Administering the Canadian Fertilizer Quality Assurance Program.

◆ Inspection and enforcement of legislation and regulations.

Source: CFIA, (n.d.).

Farmers are working to reduce the use of fertilizers on their land. They are carefully monitoring soils to add only the nutrients that are lacking, and necessary to the crop being grown.

The chart below compares fertilizer usage of Canada and other countries. As you can see, Canada is becoming a world leader in reducing fertilizer use.

Changing Practices in Providing Nutrients for Plants

Farm practices are changing, and as with Integrated Pest Management, farmers are using a variety of tools to provide nutrients for plant growth as well. Many farmers are using new technologies to predict the types and amounts of fertilizers to apply. Fields are plotted and data are kept on each individual plot. The information is fed to a Global Positioning Satellite (GPS). Specialized equipment reads data from the GPS system, and applies only the correct amount of fertilizer needed for each individual plot on the farm. This way, excess fertilizer is not spread on the soil.

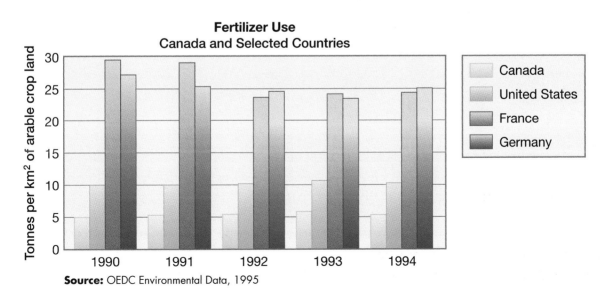

**Fertilizer Use
Canada and Selected Countries**

Legend: Canada, United States, France, Germany

Y-axis: Tonnes per km² of arable crop land

X-axis years: 1990, 1991, 1992, 1993, 1994

Source: OEDC Environmental Data, 1995

Another way of providing nutrients to plants is through crop rotation. This is an agricultural practice that has been used for more than 1000 years, among the great civilizations in Asia, Europe, and Africa, as far back as Ancient Rome. Farmers practise crop rotation by planting crops that use different nutrients, at different times. This practice conserves soil fertility by not using the same nutrients season after season and by returning nutrients to the soil. Corn and soybeans are a common combination for crop rotation. Many farmers also use the crop residue from one crop to provide nutrients for the next crop. As the crop residue decays, it forms humus, which feeds the next crop.

Agriculture and the Environment

Canadian farmers have long considered themselves stewards of the earth. They have great respect for the land since without the land, they would have no farm. Like other Canadians, farmers' awareness of environmental issues and concerns is increasing. Canadian farmers have invested millions of dollars to improve their practices and make significant changes in an effort to reduce the environmental impact of farming. Over 20 years ago, a plan was developed to reduce the use of pesticides in Ontario by 50 percent by 2002. That goal

◆ Three percent of Canadians are farmers. Their stewardship of the land is critically important to them, as they and their families are the first to be affected by the environment of the farm. As they have learned more and more about environmental issues, farmers have been working to improve their practices to reduce environmental impact. What have you done to reduce your environmental impact?

was exceeded, and the use of pesticides has been reduced by 60 percent. In 1992, Ontario developed an environmental farm plan that focussed on water quality, soil management, and improving streams and wildlife habitats. Between 1993 and 2000, the farmers who worked over half of the agricultural land in Ontario developed environmental plans with the assistance of the program. Grants were given to 8600 projects. For each grant dollar received the farmer had to give an additional three dollars. The farmers are committed to developing sustainable agriculture, with minimal impact on the environment.

Across the country farmers are working to reduce the amounts of pesticides and fertilizers they apply to the land. Statistics Canada reports reductions for the period from 1995 and 2000 in the box below.

Pesticide Reductions in Canada

Application	Reduction
Herbicides	7.5%
Insecticides	29.0%
Commercial fertilizer	17.3%
Irrigation	19.8%

Source: Statistics Canada (2003).

Soil Conservation

The soil is the most important agricultural asset. The structure of the soil is improved by increasing the amount of organic matter within it, and by decreasing the amount of erosion. Changing tilling practices in Canada are addressing these two issues.

With conventional tillage, most of the residue from the crop is tilled back into the

soil, usually back after harvest. Practices that have become more widely used in the past 30 years include:

◆ **Low tillage**, where most of the crop residue is left on the surface of the field for the winter months. This protects the soil against erosion, and increases the organic matter content of the soil.

◆ **No tillage**, where the soil is undisturbed between the harvesting of one crop and the planting of the next crop.

These new methods are made possible by new technologies that have been developed for farm use. Another benefit of these methods is the fact that less fossil fuel is being used as tractors drive up and down fields less often.

Manure Management

The management of animal waste — manure — is of great concern to Canadian farmers. Manure is a natural byproduct of livestock farming. It plays an important role in the sustainability of agriculture by providing an economical source of nutrients for crops and organic matter for soil enrichment. It also protects the soil from erosion. The two environmental concerns regarding manure are run-off to the water table and odour.

Canadian farmers are well aware of these issues and have been taking steps to address them. They are using new technologies, and adopting the best practices in manure management to reduce the problems. With input from farmers, provinces are introducing legislation to better manage manure. Farmers are working with the federal government's Department of Agriculture and Agri Food Canada to find new ways to reduce the negative effects of manure.

To combat odour, farmers are building inground tanks or grass-covered lagoons to store manure, and studies are being done on animal feeds to see how food affects the odour of manure. New equipment gets manure to the fields and injects it directly into the soil, which releases little if any nitrogen into the air, reducing any odour. Spreaders are equipped with GPS technology, so that only the correct amount of manure is put on each plot. Spreading only what will be utilized by the soil reduces run-off.

An innovative new technology is the manure digester. Manure is put into a closed tank, oxygen is removed, and the mixture is basically fermented. The end products are a methane-rich biogas, which can be used as fuel on the farm, or sold as solid and liquid fertilizer.

Governments and farm groups across the country are working to ensure that farming practices support sustainability of the land. Work is underway to develop a countrywide action plan to address environmental issues. The proposed common goals for this plan are:

◆ Reduce agricultural risks and provide benefits to the health and supply of water, with key priority areas being nutrients, pathogens, pesticides, and water conservation.

◆ Reduce agricultural risks and provide benefits to the health of soil, with key priority areas being soil organic matter and soil erosion caused by water, wind, or tillage.

◆ Reduce agricultural risks and provide benefits to the health of air and the atmosphere, with key priorities being particulate emissions, odours, and emissions of gases that contribute to global warming.

◆ Ensure compatibility between biodiversity and agriculture, with key priorities being habitat availability, species at risk, and economic damage to agriculture from wildlife.

Food Safety

In the past, food-safety efforts in Canada have focussed on food processors. Canada is known for its stringent standards after foods leave the farm gate. In the past few years, Canadian agriculture has begun an initiative focussing on food-safety measures on the farm. Chicken producers, for example have developed a system that focusses on production methods aimed at achieving optimum health, cleanliness, and safety at every stage of production. Egg producers have a similar plan, called Start Clean, Stay Clean. Both of these programs include strict safety and cleanliness standards. The careful records kept allow farmers to trace all aspects of the care and production of the product.

In the cattle industry, both dairy and beef, each calf is tagged at birth. This tag is its identification. It allows the industry to trace where the calf has been through its lifetime. The barcode on the tag stays with the animal until it is slaughtered, so it can be traced back to its original herd.

INTERNET CONNECTS

www.mcgrawhill.ca/links/food
To learn more about food safety, go to the web site above for *Food for Today*, *First Canadian Edition*, to see where to go next.

Safety Check

• Invented in the 1960s for NASA to provide safe food for astronauts, HACCP is the acronym for Hazard Analysis at Critical Control Points.

• HACCP is an internationally recognized system that implements checkpoints along the production line to produce safe food.

Other producers are following the HACCP guidelines too; they track both what the animals are fed, and the health of the animals. HACCP recognizes key points in production where problems could occur. Some examples are the introduction of germs, chemicals, or other dangers. Producers then introduce production methods that avoid or control the risks. Cleanliness standards are high: tracking of rodents and their control, feeding schedules, and even whether cats or dogs are allowed in the barn are some of the types of information recorded. Care is taken to find problems and address them before they get into the food chain.

Another way to maintain the safety of Canada's food supply is to stop diseases and pests from entering Canada from foreign countries. Inspectors check that products or produce brought into the country meet our standards. Animals that are imported into Canada are checked for parasites and other diseases.

The government and farmers are working together to improve food safety on and off the farm. Proposed common goals include:

♦ Protecting human health by reducing exposure to hazards.

♦ Increasing consumer confidence in the safety and quality of food sold in Canada or exported from Canada.

♦ Increasing industry's ability to meet or exceed market requirements for food safety and food quality.

♦ Providing value-added opportunities through the adoption of food-safety and food-quality systems.

Research in Agriculture

The agricultural community has been striving to improve practice and production for many years. An early textbook for farmers, *The Young Farmer's Manual*, published in 1867 in New York, had the following message under the heading "Progressive Agriculture":

The present is an age of improvement. The minds of all good farmers are being turned to the subject of better stock, and more abundant crops, from year to year, without incurring any unnecessary expense in the labors of the farmers.

Farmers and the agricultural community still strive to improve agricultural products and methods. Research is being done worldwide to improving agricultural practices and products. The University of Guelph in Ontario is one of the most research-intensive universities in Canada, and is internationally renowned for its research. There are numerous research stations across the province currently conducting projects in the following areas:

♦ Agricultural researchers strive to improve agricultural production in order to maintain a safe, secure food supply.

- **Animal programs.** Research involves beef, dairy, equine, fish, poultry, sheep, and pork production.

- **Plants.** Research on plants focusses on developing and applying life sciences technologies, food safety, pest management, and primary production. All of these objectives are applied to field crops, horticulture, and pest management.

```
INTERNET CONNECTS

www.mcgrawhill.ca/links/food
To learn more about agricultural research,
go to the web site above for Food for Today,
First Canadian Edition, to see where to go next.
```

- **Food programs.** Food research focuses on safety and improvement of quality of Ontario food products, development of value-added components in Ontario-grown food products, and design of innovative technologies to manufacture traditional and new food products.

- **Resources management and the environment.** Some priorities are efficient nutrient management, climate change, threats to water resources, management practices, and waste management.

- **Sustainable rural communities.** Objectives include economic development, response to change and restructuring, capacity building and information technology (University of Guelph, n.d.).

Biotechnology

Bioengineering

Bioengineering is the scientific process of altering the genetic make-up of an organism.

The Cell Switch

Most of us have purchased a quart of strawberries only to find them spoiled by the time we get to the bottom of the package. Now researchers have discovered a cell "switch" that will change everything. When fruit ripens, this switch turns on, and the plant begins to die. When this indicator is turned off, plants continue to live.

That means the shelf life of perishable produce that all consumers buy every day can be dramatically increased.

The genes involved in cell aging are virtually identical in plants and humans. As a result, the technology is now showing promise in the treatment of heart disease, glaucoma, and cancer. Many diseases are attributable to cell death occurring when it should not occur. In this case doctors may be able to use the technology to turn on the aging switch in those cancer cells and cause them to die.

This process changes the inherited traits of the original organism. Changing the inherited traits of plants and animals has actually been going on for hundreds of years, in the form of selective breeding. Farmers work toward breeding the most desirable traits into a wide range of plants and animals.

Plants have long been crossbred to produce new plants with more desirable characteristics. This is a slow process because plants must be bred again and again in order to get the desired results. The other problem with crossbreeding is that undesirable traits get passed on along with desirable traits.

Bioengineering, the science used to crossbreed now, is much more complex and sophisticated than the older practices. Scientists can isolate the exact gene that controls a desirable trait. They then use this knowledge to transfer the desirable gene from one organism to another, or even from one species to another. Bioengineering is not only more precise, but also transfers only the desirable traits, plus it takes less time.

Goals of Bioengineering and Biotechnology

♦ **To increase the quantity and quality of food.** One important goal of biotechnology as applied to agriculture is to increase the amount of food produced in the world. The ability to produce more food per hectare of land reduces the costs of food to the consumer, as well as the cost of production to the farmer. Biotechnology is developing pest-resistant strains of grain seeds as well as disease-resistant fruits and vegetables.

Improving the quality of food means that more of the food that is produced makes it to market. Less spoilage will reduce cost-sto consumers, as well as feed more people. Consumers demand good-quality produce that is fresh and free of spoilage. Biotechnology is being developed to slow the rate of spoilage and reduce waste.

♦ **To enhance the nutritional value of foods.** For years foods have been fortified by adding nutrients. For example, vitamin D has long been added to milk in Canada to help prevent vitamin D-deficiency diseases, such as rickets. Now, biotechnology is developing ways to enhance the nutritional value of foods by adding nutrients, or increasing their levels, in grains, fruits, and vegetables. For example, a new strain of tomato has been developed containing more beta carotene, which is transformed into vitamin A in the body.

♦ **To prevent disease.** Scientists are investigating ways to attach disease fighters to foods we commonly eat. These are called edible vaccines, and there is hope that they will replace vaccine injections in the future. One study is attempting to develop goats' milk that carries a vaccine against malaria.

Biotechnology and Developing Countries

Biotechnology is seen as a way for developing countries to begin to move forward by having more control of their food supplies. Through biotechnology, seeds are being developed that can grow and thrive in adverse conditions, and be resistant to disease and pests. Increased productivity will help feed more people. Dr. Florence Wambugu, a scientist from Kenya, founder of A Harvest Biotech Foundation, is working on developing a strain of maize that will be hardier than the ones currently grown. She and her team have gathered samples of maize that have natural resistance to pests, and are attempting to build these characteristics into a single crop that will grow well all over the country. She hopes to help solve the problem of world hunger by developing crops through biotechnology.

INTERNET CONNECTS

www.mcgrawhill.ca/links/food
To learn more about biotechnology, go to the web site above for *Food for Today*, *First Canadian Edition*, to see where to go next.

Safety and Biotechnology

There is concern among some consumers about the safety of foods produced through biotechnology. The federal government in Canada regulates biotechnology through Health

Canada and the Canadian Food Inspection Agency (CFIA). Before a new agricultural or food product can be produced or marketed in Canada, it has to go through a safety assessment. The assessment is designed to protect the health of humans, animals, and the environment. Products derived through biotechnology are called *novel products*, which simply means they have not previously been available for sale in Canada. The assessment process is based on principles developed in consultation with a broad range of concerned groups, including the World Health Organization and the Food and Agriculture Organization of the United Nations.

Health Canada, under the *Food and Drugs Act*, has also established a stringent process for evaluating the safety of foods derived from biotechnology. Each food is thoroughly assessed before it enters the Canadian marketplace to ensure that it brings no health or safety concerns. There are just over 50 foods developed by biotechnology approved for use in Canada at this time.

CFIA regulates products derived from biotechnology under five different acts of legislation: the *Feeds Act, Fertilizers Act, Seeds Act, Health of Animals Act*, and the *Plant Protection Act*. Through these acts CFIA regulates all seeds, plants, animals, fertilizers, and feeds, including those that are derived from biotechnology. The guidelines used to test these products are published on the CFIA web site. CFIA also does inspections after the approval of a product. The inspections consider labelling, field trials, and the licensing of manufacturing facilities. Currently there are 36 biotechnology-derived plants approved for environmental release in Canada. All of these have been approved for use as livestock feed. Another three plants have been approved for livestock feed usage only. Among the crops approved in Canada are corn, soybeans, cottonseed, potatoes, flax, tomatoes, sugarbeets, squash, and canola.

When assessing the safety of a new product derived from biotechnology, a detailed scientific study is conducted, taking the following factors into consideration:

◆ How the food crop was developed.

◆ The molecular data that characterize the change in genetics.

◆ Composition of the novel food compared to the non-modified food.

◆ Nutritional information of the novel food compared to the non-modified food.

◆ Potential for new toxins.

◆ Potential for causing allergic reactions. (CFIA, n.d.).

Under the *Food and Drugs Act*, the Novel Foods Regulation controls foods that are derived from biotechnology. This regulation requires that notification be made to the Health Products and Food Branch (HPFB) by any company that wants to sell a product derived from biotechnology, prior to the marketing or advertising of a novel

"The Government of Canada is committed to the ongoing process of ensuring that its regulations of biotechnology-derived foods are appropriate for the state of the science and the types of food and plant products that are being developed through research. As part of this commitment, Health Canada has been engaged in formal consultations over the past seven years regarding the assessment and approval of genetically modified foods. This has resulted in Health Canada strengthening the assessment system for novel foods by making mandatory a practice of pre-market notification and assessment that has been accepted and observed by the food industry over the last eight years. As the science continues to evolve, so will we" (CFIA, 2003).

food. This pre-market notification gives the scientists at Health Canada time to conduct a thorough safety assessment of all biotechnology-derived foods. This assessment is done to demonstrate that a novel food is safe and nutritious before it can be sold in the Canadian marketplace.

Labelling of Genetically Engineered Foods in Canada

Food labelling in Canada is governed under the *Food and Drugs Act*. Health Canada is responsible for setting the policies on food labels with respect to health and safety matters, nutritional content, allergens, and special dietary needs. This responsibility is the same for all foods. CFIA is responsible for developing policy for non-health and safety regulations and policies. Examples include misrepresentation and fraudulent claims on packages, advertising, and labels. CFIA regulates the manner in which ingredients are listed, product claims, and mandatory information. This applies to all foods equally.

The guidelines for labelling of genetically modified foods in Canada:

- Require mandatory labelling if there is a health or safety concern — from allergens — or a significant nutrient or compositional change.

- Ensure labelling is understandable, truthful, and not misleading.

- Permit voluntary positive labelling on the condition that the claim is not misleading or deceptive and that the claim is factual.

- Permit voluntary negative labelling on the condition that the claim is not misleading or deceptive and the claim itself is factual.

These policies are consistent with the policies for all foods in Canada.

Aquaculture

Aquaculture is the science of farming in water. It is one of the newest areas of agricultural science, and involves both plants and animals. At present, animal aquatic crops are more popular than plant crops. Types of animals produced through aquaculture include finfish, such as trout; and shellfish, such as oysters, clams, and shrimp. Some examples of plants that are grown through aquaculture are water chestnuts and watercress.

Aquaculture is one of the world's fastest-growing food-production industries. Between 1984 and 1998, aquaculture's share of the global fish and seafood production rose from 11 percent to 31 percent. Canada's aquaculture industry is growing as well, as shown in the chart on page 666.

The West Coast of Canada has many fish farms where salmon are raised in pens. More salmon from fish farms are now sold than salmon from the wild, and the fish-farmed salmon are cheaper. The federal Department of Fisheries and Oceans, (DFO) is the lead federal agency responsible for aquaculture in Canada.

The DFO is working toward sustainable aquaculture and has developed policies to regulate it. The DFO supports the concept of

◆ **What impact do you think large-scale fish farming will have on people employed in existing fisheries?**

Canadian Fisheries and Aquaculture Production 1984–2001

(per thousand metric tonnes)

	1984	1988	1991	1994	1998	2001
Fisheries	1234	1651	1509	1034	1017	1031
Aquaculture	8	21	44	54	91	153
Total	1242	1672	1553	1088	1108	1184
% Aquaculture	0.6	1.3	2.9	5.2	8.9	14.8

◆ **Do you think that aquaculture will continue to grow? Why or why not?**

Source: Department of Fisheries and Oceans, 2003

sustainable development as defined by the World Commission on Environment and Sustainable Development, which states "development that meets the needs of the present without compromising the ability of future generations to meet their own needs." The DFO states that in order to have sustainable development, aquaculture must:

◆ Maintain the quality of life and the environment for present and future generations.

◆ Adopt an ecosystem approach and respect the interests and values of all resource users and consider those interests and values in decision-making.

◆ Identify, plan, develop, operate, harvest, process, and when necessary dispose of aquacultural products in the most efficient, competitive, and environmentally responsible manner, using the best practices.

◆ Respect constitutionally protected Aboriginal and treaty rights.

◆ Create and share knowledge to promote innovation, continuous learning, and efficiency.

◆ Secure the participation of stakeholders, individuals, and communities in decision-making to ensure the best use of aquatic space.

◆ Make decisions in a fair, transparent, and inclusive manner.

Although aquaculture has the potential to be a valuable food resource for Canadians, the government realizes that it must carefully consider a number of issues. Those include the consequences of farmed salmon escaping into the wild, food safety, habitat interactions, water quality, navigational safety, aquatic animal health, and aesthetics. As a result of these concerns, the DFO is conducting research on aquaculture, which is providing the basis for conservation and protection of fish and their habitats as well as the protection of marine ecosystems. This biological science research seeks a sustainable way to expand aquaculture in Canada.

INTERNET CONNECTS

www.mcgrawhill.ca/links/food
To learn more about other interesting topics in agriculture, go to the web site above for *Food for Today, First Canadian Edition,* to see where to go next.

Associate Professor of Plant Agriculture

Doug Powell

What education is required for your job?

- A Bachelor of Science degree and PhD in a related field (I have a BSc in molecular biology and genetics and a PhD in food science)

What skills does a person need to be able to do your job?

- Critical thinking skills
- Strong written and oral communication skills

What do you like most about your job?

I like the freedom and independent work.

What other jobs and job titles have you had in the past?

I have been the editor of several newspapers; a freelance science writer and columnist for magazines and newspapers; the manager of the Information Technology Research Centre at the University of Waterloo; and a consultant for several government agencies.

What advice would you give a person who is considering a career as a professor/researcher?

Get a science background but expose yourself to a variety of other topics and activities.

Comment on what you consider to be important issues or trends in food and nutrition.

Consumer anxiety and a rejection of evidence-based approaches to producing safe, nutritious food. With respect to foodborne illness, there is a tendency to focus on the exotic and forget the basics, which could have a significant impact on overall public health. And this is not all about consumers. Everyone in the farm-to-fork food-safety system has a responsibility to reduce risk.

Chapter 31   Review and Activities

Summary

- While the total population of Canada is increasing, the farm population has been steadily decreasing since the 1930s.
- Farm size in Canada varies from province to province.
- The computer is becoming an essential tool for business management of Canadian farms.
- As farming costs rise, farmers and their families are turning to off-farm work to supplement their incomes.
- As urban areas encroach upon valuable farmland, the cost of buying that land is increasing.

- Farming is a risky business, depending on factors often beyond the farmer's control.
- Sustainable, environmentally safe use of pesticides and fertilizers is increasing.
- Governments and farmers are working together to improve food safety on and off the farm.
- Changing agriculture practice in Canada includes the use of biotechnology and aquaculture to increase both quantity and quality of Canadian-produced foods.

Knowledge and Understanding

1. Define aquaculture. Give some examples of animals and plants that are grown using aquaculture.

2. What is a pesticide? Why would a farmer use a pesticide?

3. What three areas of health does the Pest Management Regulatory Agency consider?

4. What is a fertilizer? What are three ways to replace nutrients in the soil?

Thinking and Inquiry

5. What are three things the agricultural community is doing to reduce environmental impact? What are three things you can do to reduce environmental impact?

6. What are three different ways in which farmers are working to increase food safety on the farm? What can you do to improve food safety in your home?

7. Canadian agriculture is responsible for the production and export of agricultural commodities around the world. With increasing pressures on farmers today, how can we as consumers and Canadian citizens, support farmers?

8. Explain how pesticide use is regulated in Canada. How do the roles of the various levels of government?

9. How does the PMRA determine pesticide residue levels for our food? Are imported foods subject to the same regulations?

10. The average age of farmers is increasing. What factors are keeping younger people out of farming? How can this have an impact on our food supply? What can we do to support young farmers?

11. What is the impact of urban development on the price of agricultural land? How does that affect the cost of getting into farming? How could that influence the prices we pay for food? What is the impact on our ability to grow our own food in Canada?

12. List and describe three different ways in which Health Canada strives to ensure that the food produced in Canada is safe to eat. How important is it that the government take a role in maintaining a safe food supply?

13. Why are safety nets important to support agriculture in Canada? What would happen to our food supply if more Canadian farmers went out of business?

Communication

14. Based on what you learned in this chapter, complete one of the following activities

a) Write a letter to your local newspaper stating your concerns about the shrinking farm population. What are the implications for the future Canadian food supply?

b) Write an article for a newspaper to explain the changes in Canadian agriculture and the impact they may have on the future of the Canadian food supply.

c) Write a script for a news report outlining the changes in the number of farmers and the size of farms in the past 70 years.

15. Research the type of safety nets available to farmers in your province. Prepare a pamphlet explaining your findings.

Application

16. Refer to the chart called The Changing Farm on page 648. Make a graphic presentation of the relationship between the Canadian population and the farm population. Based on your graph, answer the following questions.

a) What trend do you see in the Canadian population?

b) What trend do you see in the farm population?

c) What is the relationship between the two?

d) How does this trend affect Canada's ability to feed its citizens?

e) How does this trend affect Canada's ability to help provide food for the rest of the world?

17. Refer to the chart called The Changing Farm on page 648. Make a graphic presentation of the relationship between the number of farms and the size of farms since 1931. Based on your graph, answer the following questions:

a) What trend do you see in farm size?

b) What trend do you see in the number of farms?

c) What is the relationship between these two factors?

d) What factors have contributed to this trend?

CHAPTER

32

CHAPTER EXPECTATIONS

While reading this chapter, you will:

- Investigate the extent of hunger in the world today and present the results of your investigation.

- Describe micro-nutrient deficiencies prevalent in Canada and throughout the world.

- Summarize the causes of food insecurity.

- Identify economic and social policies that influence food security.

- Describe the social and cultural traditions that account for inequality among peoples of the world.

- Identify the ways in which the local community is responding to hunger and food security.

Food Security and Hunger

One of the ways to improve food security in developing countries is to teach the people how to be self-sufficient. Their future food security will come with their ability to produce their own food.

CHAPTER INTRODUCTION

In this chapter you will explore the issues surrounding food security around the world. The extent of hunger in the world today, types of micro-nutrient deficiencies, malnutrition, and the causes of food insecurity will all be discussed. What are the economic, political, and social policies, and cultural traditions, that account for the inequity of food supplies among peoples of the world? Most importantly, how can we rid the world of hunger and the circumstances that cause malnutrition?

Food aid is distributed for two reasons: as relief in times of crisis and to encourage and support social and economic development.

The Extent of Hunger in the World

Hunger afflicts one in every seven people on Earth.
(World Health Organization, 2003).

Food Security

Food security means all people, at all times, have physical and economic access to safe and nutritious food sufficient to meet their dietary needs and food preferences for an active and healthy life. The definition of food security recognizes that access to food includes not only the availability of food but also the resources to acquire the food. Achieving food security means ensuring that sufficient food is available, supplies are relatively stable, and that people can obtain it. Over 800 million people, that is approximately 20 percent of the world's population, are chronically undernourished (Food and Agriculture Organization, 2003).

Causes of Hunger and Food Insecurity

Efforts to reduce hunger in the mid-1900s were not as successful as world leaders hoped they would be. It seemed that every effort to increase production did not necessarily reduce the level of hunger in a given country. Production of food increased, yet people were still hungry. Even though there was more food available in developing countries, many people—landless labourers, small tenant farmers, and deficit farmers — were still hungry because they did not have economic access to food. In other words, they were too poor to buy the food that was available. Poverty among specific groups of people is the underlying cause of hunger in developing countries. The laws, customs, conventions, and structure of the society determine people's access to food. Entitlement to food is dependent upon a person's labour, trade, production of food, gift or transfer, or as a return on assets. The poor do not have enough of these assets to purchase sufficient food.

FYI

Percentage of Net National Disposable Income spent on food and non-alcoholic beverages in 1999.

Mexico	19.03%
Italy	10.58%
France	9.21%
Australia	8.75%
Germany	7.73%
Sweden	7.28%
U.K.	6.9%
Canada	6.73%
U.S.A.	5.49%

◆ **As Canadians we benefit from the hard work of our farmers through reasonably priced food.** What do you think would happen to the price of our food if the majority of it came from another country?

INTERNET CONNECTS

www.mcgrawhill.ca/links/food
To learn more about food security programs in Canada, go to the web site above for *Food for Today, First Canadian Edition,* to see where to go next.

Lack of food security in developing countries is due to the following circumstances:

◆ Low agricultural productivity caused by one or a combination of political, institutional, and technological constraints.

◆ High seasonal and year-to-year variability in food supplies caused by one or a combination of lack of rainfall and insufficient water for crops and livestock.

◆ Lack of off-farm employment opportunities contributes to low and unstable incomes in both urban and rural areas.

We now know that the causes and problems of food insecurity and poverty are linked. In order to affect either one, it is necessary to address both.

One of the ways in which the world community is working to reduce poverty in developing countries is by increasing agricultural production. Emphasis is on the small farmers who are among the poorest people in developing nations. Teaching these farmers sustainable methods of agriculture can increase production to benefit them, their families, and their communities.

As well, the Food and Agriculture Organization (FAO) aims to improve and increase employment opportunities in rural areas, and improve the stability of supplies. These two measures will result in more rural people having access to food supplies.

To do this, the FAO focuses on the countries that are least able to meet their own food needs: ensuring that the people can produce and access food, increasing food production, increasing the role of trade, investing in food security, and dealing adequately with disaster. The increase in food production must also be sustainable, adequate to feed the people, and culturally appropriate.

◆ One of the ways to achieve food security is through entitlement. Being able to produce enough by their own labour entitles these people to food.

The Special Programme for Food Security (SPFS) believe that changes in food security come from two areas: teaching farmers new ways of working, and institutional and policy changes. The SPFS works with different levels of government to institute the necessary changes and bring about food security. At the local level, the SPFS works with governments and other groups in order to ensure farmer participation. At the national level, the SPFS works to involve influential people who can bring about policy and institutional change.

The SPFS encourages co-operation between countries in the developing world. The organization brings people from a developed country to help people in one that is less developed. These experts from other countries work directly with farmers for two or three years. They teach farmers the knowledge and skills to improve their farms. The type of expert brought in depends on the needs in the area.

Social and Cultural Considerations

An important aspect of food security is an understanding of the social and cultural implications of food. The definition of hunger is also locally defined: for some it may mean a lack of rice in the diet; for others it may mean inadequate food supplies. There must also be an understanding of the cultural value of foods. In some cultures certain foods are considered inferior. If such food is given as food aid, how will it be accepted? Will it be eaten because that is all there is? Or will it be fed to animals because that is all it is considered fit for?

Micronutrient Deficiencies

Many people in developing countries suffer from micronutrient deficiencies. The main deficiencies are of vitamin A, iodine, and iron.

They are called micronutrients because the body needs only small amounts of these nutrients. Even though the amounts needed are small, the role these nutrients play in the overall health of an individual is critical. These substances allow the body to produce enzymes, hormones, and other substances essential to proper growth and development. The adverse effects of a **deficiency,** or lack of micro-nutrients are worse for pregnant women and children in developing countries.

◆ **Iron Deficiency.** Between four and five billion people, or 66–80 percent of the world's population, is thought to have iron deficiency. This makes iron deficiency the world's most common nutritional disorder. Iron deficiency leads to poor school performance, ill health, maternal hemorrhaging, premature death, and lost earnings. People with iron deficiency have a reduced capacity to work. When a large percentage of the population of a country is anemic due to lack of iron, the development of the country is in jeopardy. The people who are most affected are the poorest and the least educated. They are also the people who stand to gain the most from treatment and improved dietary levels of iron.

Treatment for iron deficiency includes:

◆ Increased iron intake through supplements and iron-rich diets.

◆ Infection control through public health.

◆ Improved overall nutritional status by reducing overall nutritional deficiencies and consuming a more diversified diet.

The World Health Organization (WHO) has developed guidelines to help countries work to reduce the impact of iron deficiency and anemia.

INTERNET CONNECTS

www.mcgrawhill.ca/links/food
To learn more about the World Health Organization (WHO), go to the web site above for *Food for Today, First Canadian Edition,* to see where to go next.

◆ **Vitamin A Deficiency.** Vitamin A is essential for the proper functioning of the immune system. The most recognized result of vitamin A deficiency is blindness, but children who are vitamin A deficient also have a 25 percent higher risk of dying from measles, malaria, and diarrhea.

Adding adequate vitamin A to a child's diet increases his or her chance of survival. Improving the health of children and their families improves the health and well-being of the communities in which they live. Improving the vitamin A status of pregnant women reduces maternal and infant mortality rates, reduces their risk of infection, and helps to reduce the number of cases of anemia.

Natural sources of vitamin A include milk, liver, eggs, red and orange fruits, red palm oil, and green leafy vegetables. Staple foods, such as sugar, flour, and margarine are fortified

---

FYI

Vitamin A Deficiency

• Between 100 and 140 million children are vitamin A deficient.

• An estimated 250 000 to 500 000 vitamin A deficient children become blind every year. Half of them die within 12 months of losing their sight.

◆ **World leaders have vowed to reduce the number of children affected by vitamin A deficiency disorders. Which foods might have prevented this child's blindness?**

with vitamin A in some parts of the world. At least 100 million children under the age of five are vitamin A deficient.

Treatment for vitamin A deficiency includes:

◆ High-dose vitamin A capsules for children aged six months to five years.

◆ Encouraging mothers to breast-feed their infants.

◆ Vitamin A supplements for mothers who are breast-feeding.

◆ Fortification of foods.

◆ Encouraging home gardens where vitamin A–rich foods can be grown.

In 1990, the World Summit for Children vowed to eliminate vitamin A deficiency. By 1997, little progress had been made and efforts to improve were undertaken. Countries with mortality rates of children under the age of five at over 70 deaths per 1000 were advised to begin immediate distribution of vitamin A

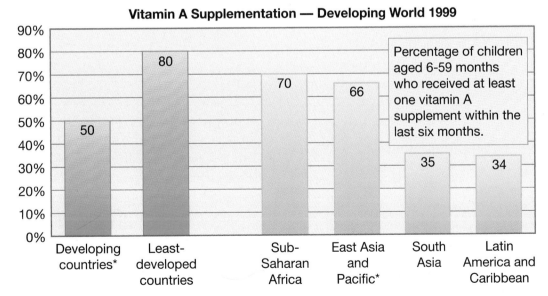

Vitamin A Supplementation — Developing World 1999

Percentage of children aged 6-59 months who received at least one vitamin A supplement within the last six months.

- Developing countries*: 50
- Least-developed countries: 80
- Sub-Saharan Africa: 70
- East Asia and Pacific*: 66
- South Asia: 35
- Latin America and Caribbean: 34

*Not including China

Regional averages are not calculated when the available country data cover less than half the region's births.

Source: UNICEF (2001)

supplements. Progress is now being made, and the number of developing countries supplementing children has gone from 11 in 1996 to 43 in 1999.

It is estimated that between 1998 and 2000, at least one million deaths of children were prevented through vitamin A supplementation (WHO, 2003, and UNICEF, 2003).

◆ **Iodine Deficiency.** The world is on the verge of eliminating iodine deficiency, the world's leading cause of brain damage. Iodine deficiency is also the most preventable cause of brain damage. The elimination of iodine deficiency will equal other medical landmarks such as the elimination of smallpox and polio.

Iodine deficiency has a big impact on the lives of children. It can cause developmental problems during pregnancy, which can result in spontaneous abortions, stillbirths, and congenital abnormalities. One abnormality is called cretinism, an irreversible form of mental retardation that affects people living in iodine-deficient areas of Africa and Asia. Other mental impairments are more prevalent, including impaired intellectual functioning. Iodine deficiency also impairs psychomotor development.

Since the 1980s the WHO has been working to eliminate iodine deficiency and has led an initiative to reduce the impact of the disease by providing guidelines and strategies. In 1993, iodized salt was chosen as the method to combat the deficiency. Salt is universally available, widely consumed on a regular basis, and inexpensive. It costs approximately five cents U.S. per person per year to iodize salt. Iodized salt has been used routinely in developed countries since the 1920s.

FYI

Iodine Deficiency Disease (IDD)

- IDD affects over 740 million people, 13 percent of the world's population; 30 percent of the remainder are at risk.

- IDD preys upon poor, pregnant women and preschool children, posing serious public health problems in 130 developing countries.

- Iodine-deficient people may forfeit 15 IQ points.

- Nearly 50 million people suffer from some degree of IDD-related brain damage.

- We have the means to prevent IDD by using small quantities of iodine at low cost.

INTERNET CONNECTS

www.mcgrawhill.ca/links/food
To learn more about the health of the World's Children, go to the web site above for *Food for Today, First Canadian Edition,* to see where to go next.

Between 1993 and 2003 the number of countries that iodize salt has increased from 46 to 93. Now approximately 70 percent of people living in countries with iodine-deficiency diseases have access to iodized salt. More than two out of three people now consume adequate amounts of iodized salt; prior to 1990 that figure was less than one in five people. As a result, 90 million newborns are now protected from a significant reduction in intellectual ability.

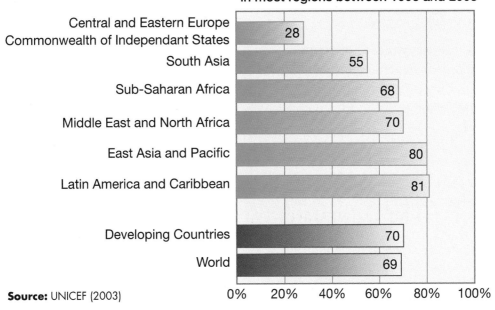

Significant Gains
Iodized salt consumption increases
in most regions between 1993 and 2003

Region	Value
Central and Eastern Europe Commonwealth of Independant States	28
South Asia	55
Sub-Saharan Africa	68
Middle East and North Africa	70
East Asia and Pacific	80
Latin America and Caribbean	81
Developing Countries	70
World	69

Source: UNICEF (2003)

Malnutrition

Good nutrition, especially among children, is the cornerstone to development. Children who are well nourished perform better in school, grow up to be healthier adults, and then give their children a healthier start in life. Women who are well nourished experience fewer risks during pregnancy and childbirth, and have children who fare better in both physical and intellectual development than do undernourished women.

More than half of child deaths worldwide are related to malnourishment. These children have lower resistance to infection, which makes them more likely to die from common childhood conditions, such as diarrhea and respiratory conditions, than other children. Children with malnutrition live in a cycle of illness because their undernourished status never allows them to build up their strength fully between illnesses.

The major factors contributing to malnutrition are poverty, low levels of education, and poor access to education. In order to deal with malnutrition, UNICEF and other world organizations are working on a number of different initiatives including:

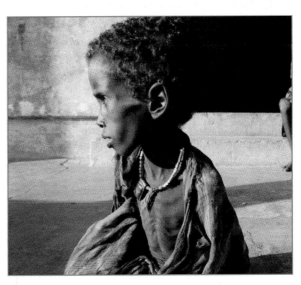

◆ **Children who are malnourished are more susceptible to illness and do not perform well in school.**

- Ensuring food security for poor households, which means both enough of and the right kinds of food.

- Educating families to help them understand the special nutritional needs of young children, especially regarding breast-feeding and the introduction of complementary foods at the right age.

- Protecting children from infection through immunization programs and ensuring that there is safe water and proper sanitation available.

- Ensuring that ill children receive proper care.

- Reducing micronutrient deficiencies.

- Improving the nutritional status of girls and women in order to ensure that the next generation has a healthy start to life.

The Downward Spiral of Malnutrition

Malnutrition is the single most important risk factor for disease. When poverty is added, the result is a downward spiral that may end in death. At the personal level:

- Poor people may eat and absorb too little nutritious food, making them more disease-prone.

- Inadequate or inappropriate food leads to stunted development and/or premature death.

- Nutrient-deficient diets provoke health problems; malnutrition increases susceptibility to disease.

- Disease decreases people's ability to cultivate or purchase nutritious foods.

- The downward spiral of poverty and illness can end in death.

A downward spiral that ends in death

4 Sickness and loss of livelihoods

Death

3 Malnutrition and increased susceptibility to disease

1 Poverty and illness

2 Inadequate food/ inappropriate diet

Turning the tide of malnutrition

This need not be so. Better nutrition ends malnutrition. Better health means stronger immune systems, which means less illness. Healthy people feel stronger, can work better, and may have more earning opportunities to gradually lift them out of both poverty and malnutrition. Healthier, more productive societies are a potential outcome.

In 1990, a goal was set to reduce child malnutrition by 50 percent. At that time approximately 174 million children under the age of five were malnourished (UNICEF, 2003).

Making the most of opportunities for better health and well-being

2 Better health, growth and development

1 Better nutrition

and the cycle continues

3 Better earnings

4 Better quality of work

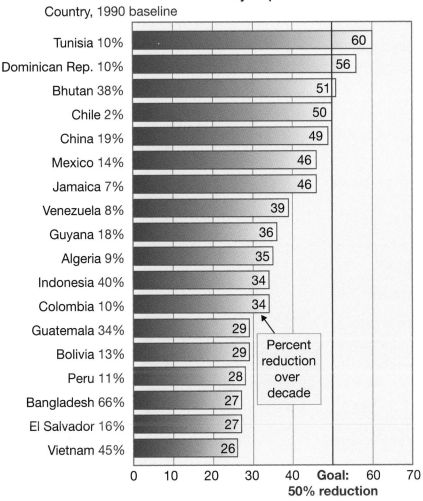

Progress During the 1990s
Countries where underweight prevalence declined by 25 percent or more

Country, 1990 baseline

Country	Percent decline
Tunisia 10%	60
Dominican Rep. 10%	56
Bhutan 38%	51
Chile 2%	50
China 19%	49
Mexico 14%	46
Jamaica 7%	46
Venezuela 8%	39
Guyana 18%	36
Algeria 9%	35
Indonesia 40%	34
Colombia 10%	34
Guatemala 34%	29
Bolivia 13%	29
Peru 11%	28
Bangladesh 66%	27
El Salvador 16%	27
Vietnam 45%	26

Percent reduction over decade

Goal: 50% reduction

Percent decline

◆ Overall, significant progress has been made in the reduction of child malnutrition, with underweight prevalence declining from 32 to 28 percent in the developing world as a whole. The largest decline was achieved in East Asia and the Pacific, where underweight levels decreased by a third (from 24 percent to 16 percent).

Responses to Food Insecurity

Food Aid

The United Nations and the World Health Organization see two distinct reasons for distributing food aid. The first reason is in times of crisis, the second is to support economic and social development.

Crisis or Emergency Food Aid

The complex nature of food emergencies makes providing food aid a challenging task. Some food emergencies are due to natural disasters, such as hurricanes, monsoons, floods, drought, and earthquakes. Other crises are created by humans and result from political turmoil and conflict, social unrest, and wars. After an emergency occurs, the victims are more susceptible to malnutrition due to unstable food supplies and thus are more at risk for disease and death.

The World Health Organization works with humanitarian agencies and the United Nations to provide food aid during times of crisis. It provides:

◆ Assessment and management of nutrition needs during the crises.

◆ Manuals and guidelines to help agencies deal with the crises.

◆ Collaboration with other agencies to provide assistance to people in need.

Source: WHO (2003).

Food Aid for Economic and Social Development

For countries with large numbers of people suffering from hunger, it is next to impossible to move forward socially and economically. For this reason, the United Nations, the World Health Organization, and other aid groups provide food aid to countries. With the ultimate goal of helping people to help themselves, food aid is given to improve people's health. Hungry people spend most of their energy trying to find food. They cannot attend clinics or demonstrations, nor can they take full advantage of opportunities presented to them. They have neither the energy nor the good health to think about development.

In order to eliminate hunger, conditions that promote self-reliance must be created. Food aid is seen as a bridge to development. Approaching food aid as part of the overall improvement of the health of communities means also considering disease control, environmental health, and promotion of healthy habits and good nutrition. Food aid is organized through the World Food Program (WFP).

World Food Program in 2002: A Quick Glance

Food distributed to 72 million of the poorest people in the world

• 14 million people in development programs.

• 44 million beneficiaries in emergency operations.

• 14 million people in rehabilitation operations.

Operations in 82 countries around the world

• 130 relief operations in 75 countries.

• 55 development projects and 33 country programs in 55 countries.

Total food distributed: 3.7 million tonnes

• 2.244 million tonnes for emergency operations.

• 580 979 tons for development projects.

• 918 435 tons for protracted relief and recovery operations.

Total expenditure: US$1.59 billion

• 88 percent on relief aid.

• 12 percent on development aid.

Total number of employees: 2684

Source: World Food Programs (2003).

World Food Program

The WFP is the food aid section of the United Nations. Its mission is to eradicate global hunger and poverty. WFP uses food to meet emergency needs and to support economic and social development. It also provides support in getting the right food to the right people in the right place at the right time. WFP helps victims of natural disasters, displaced people, hungry poor people, and women, since they bear the responsibility of providing food for their families. In many developing countries women eat last and the least.

The WFP fights hunger in the following ways:

◆ Rescue—ready to help and provide food aid in the event of an emergency, such as a natural disaster or war.

◆ Rapid reaction—plans to move food and humanitarian aid quickly into disaster areas.

◆ Rehabilitation—helps to get disaster-affected areas back to normal.

◆ Deterrence—by providing food aid, combats one of the largest roadblocks to development — the malnutrition of children and workers. In this way food aid acts as a deterrent to poverty and hunger.

Source: World Food Program (2003).

There are over 300 million chronically hungry children in the world. More than half of these children do not receive meals while at school; the other 130 million do not attend school at all. Children who go to school on empty stomachs are easily distracted, and have problems concentrating. Many children who suffer from malnutrition are developmentally stunted, both mentally and physically.

Research has shown that a basic education improves the economic well-being of a country by improving literacy and creating self-reliant individuals, and thus a healthy society. As a result, the WFP provides meals for school-children in order to combat malnutrition in developing countries. The meals also help the children to perform better at school and improve their overall nutritional and health status. In 2001, over 15 million children in schools in 57 different countries were fed by

◆ These children have a nutritious lunch each day at school, part of the United Nations goal of improving the nutritional status of the world's children.

the WFP. This program attracts children to school. The WFP focuses on areas where the enrolment ratios are low, and provides children with a hot lunch and nutritious snacks. When children can get food at school, their attendance improves. Studies have shown that when meals are added, enrolment can double within one year. Studies have also shown a 40 percent improvement in academic performance within two years (World Food Program, 2003).

INTERNET CONNECTS

www.mcgrawhill.ca/links/food
To learn more about food insecurity and hunger, go to the web site above for *Food for Today, First Canadian Edition*, to see where to go next.

Food Security in Canada

Food security for everyone in Canada is approached from two different perspectives. The first is the development of a sustainable food system, and the second is the elimination of poverty.

The Anti-Poverty Approach

The anti-poverty approach to food security assumes that we produce enough food for everyone in Canada. Nevertheless, many poor people do not have access to that food. The poor lack the income to buy enough nourishing food. From the 1930s, after the Great Depression, until the 1980s, there was no evidence of large-scale hunger in Canada because of the social welfare system developed in response to the Depression. The social welfare system was developed to provide income security for all Canadians. It was based on an equitable division of income and services, while recognizing social responsibility and concern for the individual. This is called the social safety net.

In 1981 signs indicated that the safety net was leaving people hungry. At this time, the first food bank was established since the Depression. Food banks have become the predominant response to hunger since then. Food banks are now well established across the country. In 1997 there were 501 food banks in Canada. By 1996, almost three million Canadians used food banks.

The anti-poverty approach cites social policy as the cause of poverty and hunger. It blames high rates of unemployment, the polarization of the job market into good jobs and bad jobs, minimum wages that are below the poverty level, inadequate welfare levels, high housing costs, policies of taxation, moving the responsibilities for social programs from the federal and provincial governments to local governments, and the unequal distribution of wealth.

The anti-poverty movement wants to see income security restored to Canada. The movement believes that income security will lead to food security. Anti-poverty activists want to raise awareness of poverty and work to reduce poverty and improve the lives of all poor people.

The Sustainable Food Systems Approach

This approach looks at changes to the food system over the past 60 years. Some of those changes include:

- Marginalization of small-scale food producers and processors.
- Urbanization and loss of rural ways of life.
- Changing packaging to increase profit.
- Alienation of consumers of food from the producers of food.

This approach believes that food has changed from an integrated part of life to a series of products that are made by global production chains. It blames corporate control of the food system for food insecurity.

FYI

The WFP believes that providing a nutritious meal at school is a simple but concrete way to give poor children a chance to learn and thrive. For nearly 40 years, WFP has become the largest organizer of school feeding programs in the developing world.

Source: World Food Program (2003).

◆ Are food banks a permanent solution to the problem of food security and poverty?

Environmentalists have joined this movement by saying that the corporate ownership of the food system disregards its environmental and human costs, and is therefore unsustainable. Environmentalists have focused on the production side of food security, calling for sustainable agriculture.

Recently, some limits of the environmentalist approach to sustainable agriculture have been noted. If all parts of the food system are not working, then food production, food distribution, preparation, preservation, consumption, and recycling of food and food waste must improve in order for the whole system to become more sustainable. This brings responsibility for food to all people, not just those who produce it.

The sustainable food systems approach looks at different ways of distributing food and food marketing, such as farmers' markets and community-supported agriculture.

This approach also looks at activities that help people supply their own foods—growing food, preserving food, and preparing their own food. Projects such as community gardens and community kitchens help poor people provide their own food. Such activities promote self-reliance and develop transferable skills.

Finding a Balance

Community-development projects like the ones mentioned above are seen as viable alternatives to food banks in Canada. Helping the poor learn to provide their own food preserves their dignity more than taking food from a food bank does. The solution to food-security issues in Canada must involve both anti-poverty and sustainable food systems approaches. Finding a way to bring together both initiatives is a challenge for Canadian policy-makers now and in the future.

Chapter 32   Review and Activities

Summary

- The definition of food security recognizes that access to food includes not only the availability of food but also the resources needed to acquire food.

- Efforts throughout the last century to reduce hunger were not as successful as world leaders had hoped.

- More than 20 percent of the world's population is chronically undernourished.

- Major nutritional disorders include iron deficiency vitamin A deficiency, iodine deficiency, and various forms of malnutrition.

- As well as increasing food production, organizations such as the Food and Agriculture

Organization (FAO), The World Health Organization (WHO) and UNICEF are working to improve employment opportunities in rural areas of developing countries so people can earn money to buy food.

- In order to eliminate hunger, conditions that promote self-reliance and sustainable food systems must be created.

- Research has shown that a basic education improves the economic well-being of a country by improving literacy and creating self-reliant individuals, and thus a healthy society.

- Food security in Canada is based on development of a sustainable food system and the

elimination of poverty.

Knowledge and Understanding

1. What is food insecurity?

2. What are micro-nutrient deficiencies? Why is it important to address them?

3. What do North Americans do to protect their citizens from iodine deficiency?

Thinking and Inquiry

4. Define food security and hunger. How are these two issues dealt with differently?

5. What are three problems caused by iron deficiency? Who is most vulnerable to iron deficiency? What are three ways to combat iron deficiency in developing countries? How can you ensure that you do not

develop an iron deficiency?

6. What are the two main reasons the United Nations, through the WFP, operates food aid programs? What is the difference between the two? Why are they both important?

7. Why is increasing the nutritional status of women and children important to improving economic and social conditions in developing countries?

8. What are the two different approaches Canada is taking to food security? What are the benefits of each? What are the problems of each? How would you tackle the issue of food security in Canada?

9. How does culture have an impact on food

Review and Activities   Chapter 32

Communication

10. Create a pamphlet about vitamin A deficiency. Include the following:

  a) Problems created by vitamin A deficiency.

  b) Who is most affected by it?

  c) Prevalence of vitamin A deficiency.

  d) What are the sources of vitamin A?

  e) How is the impact of vitamin A deficiency in the developing world being reduced?

  f) What progress is being made?

11. Compare school feeding programs run by the United Nations under the World Food Program in developing countries with those run in Canada, such as Breakfast for Learning. How are they similar? How are they different? Create a poster to illustrate your findings.

12. Go to the web site for the Canadian International Development Agency (CIDA) to find out how Canada is helping another country achieve food security. Make a poster to show what you have learned. Explain your poster to the class.

Application

13. Cook 60 mL of rice. Put it on a plate. Imagine that this is all of the food that you have to eat in a day. Write a reflection on how this makes you feel.

14. Have a hunger pizza demonstration. With a group of 24 people, get three different colours of paper, 12 pieces of green, 8 pieces of blue, and 4 pieces of purple. Each person will get one coloured piece of paper. Make or buy a pizza. Consider the whole pizza to be the world's food supply. Divide it and distribute the pizza in the following ways:

  a) The people who had the purple paper will get $\frac{1}{2}$ the pizza; they are the 17 percent of the world's population who has access to the most food and energy.

  b) The people who had the blue paper get $\frac{1}{3}$ of the pizza; they are the 26 percent of the world's population who are middle class.

  c) The people who had the green pieces of paper get the rest; they are the 57 percent of the world's population who live in poverty.

  d) Have a discussion about the feelings that each individual had as he or she received a share of the pizza.

  e) Write a reflection about the division of the world's food supply.

Chapter 32 ◆ Food Security and Hunger   MHR • 685

Appendix

Choose a variety of activities from these three groups:

Endurance

4-7 days a week
Continuous activities for your heart, lungs, and circulatory system.

Flexibility

4-7 days a week
Gentle reaching, bending and stretching activities to keep your muscles relaxed and joints mobile.

Strength

2-4 days a week
Activities against resistance to strengthen muscles and bones and improve posture.

Starting slowly is very safe for most people. Not sure? Consult your health professional.

Eating well is also important. Follow *Canada's Food Guide to Healthy Eating* to make wise food choices.

Get Active Your Way, Every Day—For Life!

Scientists say accumulate 60 minutes of physical activity every day to stay healthy or improve your health. As you progress to moderate activities you can cut down to 30 minutes, 4 days a week. Add-up your activities in periods of at least 10 minutes each. Start slowly... and build up.

Time needed depends on effort

Very Light Effort	Light Effort 60 minutes	Moderate Effort 30-60 minutes	Vigorous Effort 20-30 minutes	Maximum Effort
• Strolling	• Light walking	• Brisk walking	• Aerobics	• Sprinting
• Dusting	• Volleyball	• Biking	• Jogging	• Racing
	• Easy gardening	• Raking leaves	• Hockey	
	• Stretching	• Swimming	• Basketball	
		• Dancing	• Fast swimming	
		• Water aerobics	• Fast dancing	

Range needed to stay healthy

You Can Do It—Getting started is easier than you think

Physical activity doesn't have to be very hard. Build physical activities into your daily routine.

- Walk whenever you can—get off the bus early, use the stairs instead of the elevator.
- Reduce inactivity for long periods, like watching TV.
- Get up from the couch and stretch and bend for a few minutes every hour.
- Play actively with your kids.
- Choose to walk, wheel, or cycle for short trips.

- Start with a 10 minute walk—gradually increase the time.
- Find out about walking and cycling paths nearby and use them.
- Observe a physical activity class to see if you want to try it.
- Try one class to start—you don't have to make a long-term commitment.
- Do the activities you are doing now, more often.

Benefits of regular activity:

- better health
- improved fitness
- better posture and balance
- better self-esteem
- weight control
- stronger muscles and bones
- feeling more energetic
- relaxation and reduced stress
- continued independent living in later life

Health risks of inactivity:

- premature death
- heart disease
- obesity
- high blood pressure
- adult-onset diabetes
- osteoporosis
- stroke
- depression
- colon cancer

Physical Activity Guide
to Healthy Active Living

The U.S. Food Guide Pyramid
A Guide to Daily Food Choices

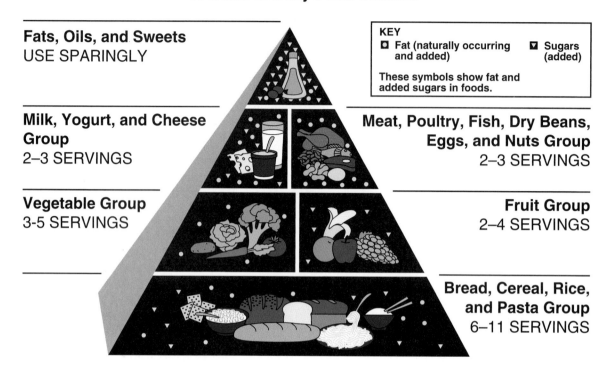

Fats, Oils, and Sweets
USE SPARINGLY

KEY
☐ Fat (naturally occurring and added)   ✓ Sugars (added)
These symbols show fat and added sugars in foods.

Milk, Yogurt, and Cheese Group
2–3 SERVINGS

Meat, Poultry, Fish, Dry Beans, Eggs, and Nuts Group
2–3 SERVINGS

Vegetable Group
3-5 SERVINGS

Fruit Group
2–4 SERVINGS

Bread, Cereal, Rice, and Pasta Group
6–11 SERVINGS

◆ The Food Guide Pyramid shows the types of foods you need and in which amounts in order to balance your daily food intake.

The Food Groups

All five food groups are important to health. Each provides some, but not all, of the nutrients you need. One group cannot replace another. You need a variety of foods from the food groups each day.

Bread, Cereal, Rice, and Pasta Group

This group includes all kinds of grain products. They supply complex carbohydrates, fibre, vitamins, and, minerals.

You need 6 to 11 servings from this group every day. Some examples of a serving are:

◆ 1 slice bread.

◆ 28 g (1 ounce) ready-to-eat cereal.

◆ 125 mL (½ cup) cooked cereal, rice, or pasta.

To get the fibre you need, choose as many whole-grain foods as you can, such as whole wheat bread and whole-grain cereals. This group includes many low-fat choices, but also some higher-fat ones, such as croissants and other baked goods.

Vegetable Group

Vegetables provide beta carotene, which your body uses to make vitamin A. They also supply vitamin C, folate (a B vitamin), and minerals such as magnesium and iron. They provide fibre and complex carbohydrates and are low in fat.

You should have three to five servings of vegetables daily. Each of the following counts as one serving:

◆ 250 mL (1 cup) raw leafy vegetables.

◆ 125 mL (½ cup) other vegetables, cooked or chopped raw.

◆ 175 mL (¾ cup) vegetable juice.

Different types of vegetables provide different nutrients. For variety, include dark green, leafy vegetables, such as kale; deep yellow-orange vegetables, such as sweet potatoes; starchy vegetables, including corn, peas, and potatoes; dry beans and peas; and others.

Fruit Group

Fruits provide important amounts of beta carotene, vitamin C, and potassium. Edible skins are good sources of fibre. Like vegetables, most fruits are low in fat and sodium.

You need two to four servings of fruit every day. One serving equals:

◆ 1 medium fruit, such as an apple, a banana, or an orange.

◆ 125 mL (½ cup) chopped raw, cooked, or canned fruit.

◆ 175 mL (¾ cup) fruit juice.

Be sure to have fruits rich in vitamin C regularly, such as citrus fruits, melons, and berries. Eat whole fresh fruits often for the fibre they provide. When choosing canned or frozen fruits, look for products without added sugar. Count only 100 percent fruit juices as a serving of fruit.

Milk, Yogurt, and Cheese Group

Foods in this group are high in protein, vitamins, and minerals. They are also one of the best sources of calcium.

Most adults need two servings of milk products daily. Three servings are recommended for pregnant or breast-feeding women, teens, and young adults up to age 24. One serving equals:

◆ 250 mL (1 cup) milk or yogurt.

◆ 42 g (1½ ounces) natural cheese.

◆ 56 g (2 ounces) processed cheese.

Low-fat choices from this group include skim milk, non-fat yogurt, and non-fat dry milk. Go easy on high-fat cheese and ice cream. Remember, too, that some milk products, such as flavoured yogurt, contain added sugar.

Meat, Poultry, Fish, Dry Beans, Eggs, and Nuts Group

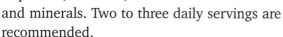

This group is an important source of protein, vitamins, and minerals. Two to three daily servings are recommended.

- 56 to 85 g (2 to 3 ounces) of cooked lean meat, poultry, or fish equals one serving. This is about the size of an average hamburger or the amount of meat in half a medium chicken breast.

- Each of the following portions is the equivalent of 28 g (1 ounce) of meat: 125 mL (½ cup) cooked dry beans; one egg; or 30 mL (2 tablespoons) peanut butter.

The total of your daily servings should be the equivalent of 140 to 196 g (5 to 7 ounces) of cooked lean meat, poultry, or fish. For instance, you might eat an egg for breakfast, 250 mL (1 cup) of cooked dry beans in bean soup for lunch, and a lean hamburger for dinner. These foods would give you the equivalent of 168 g (6 ounces) of meat.

To limit the fat in your diet, select lean meats, fish, and poultry without skin. Have dry beans and peas often—they are high in fibre and low in fat. Go easy on eggs, nuts, and seeds. Eggs are high in cholesterol; nuts and seeds are high in fat.

Crossover Foods

Some foods in the Food Guide Pyramid have been identified by the authors of the guide as "crossover" foods. These foods, which include dry beans and other legumes, may be considered as belonging to more than one food group. For example, dry beans may be considered as one serving from either the Meat, Poultry, Fish, Dry Beans, Eggs, and Nuts Group or the Vegetable Group. Note that any crossover food can be used to satisfy a serving requirement from *either* group it is classified in, but not *both*.

Methods

Muffin Method

Muffins that are properly mixed have a rounded, pebbly top with a coarse but tender texture inside. To mix ingredients for muffins:

1. *Sift* together or mix all dry ingredients (flour, sugar, baking powder, spices) in a large bowl. Using the back of a spoon, make a well in the centre of the dry ingredients.

2. *Beat* all liquid ingredients (eggs, milk, or water, oil or melted fat, liquid flavourings) together in a small bowl until they are well blended.

3. *Pour* the liquid into the well you have made in the dry ingredients. Mix just enough to moisten the dry ingredients. A few floury spots can remain, and the batter should be lumpy.

4. *Fold* in ingredients such as chopped nuts and raisins gently.

Take care not to overmix the batter. Overmixed muffins will have peaks on top and be tough and heavy. The insides will have long, narrow tunnels.

◆ Mix the dry ingredients and make a well in the centre.

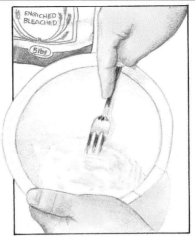

◆ Beat the liquid ingredients together.

◆ Add the liquids to the dry ingredients all at once. Stir briefly—do not overmix.

Pastry and Biscuit Method

In the pastry and biscuit method, the fat is cut into the flour. To *cut in* means to mix solid fat and flour using a pastry blender or two knives and a cutting motion. This technique leaves the fat in fine particles in the dough. During baking, the fat melts between layers of flour, giving a flaky texture.

◆ A pastry blender is a tool designed for cutting fat into flour. Why is this tool preferable to using the hands when making baked goods?

Handle the dough as little as possible. If the shortening and flour are overmixed, the texture will be mealy, not flaky. Mixing ingredients for biscuits is easy.

1. Sift together or mix the dry ingredients in a large bowl.

2. Cut the shortening into the flour until the particles are the size of peas or coarse bread crumbs.

3. Make a well in the centre of the dry ingredients, as in the muffin method, and add the liquids. Stir just until the ingredients are blended and form a soft dough.

Rolled Biscuits

Once you have mixed the dough, you can proceed with your recipe for either rolled or drop biscuits. Rolled biscuits are made by rolling out dough to an even thickness and cutting it with a biscuit cutter. If you don't have a biscuit cutter, you can use the rim of a water glass.

Begin by turning the dough out on a lightly floured board and kneading about ten strokes. Knead as much as possible with the tips of

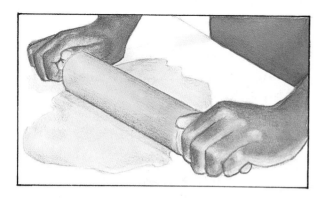

1. For rolled biscuits, roll the kneaded dough out to an even thickness.

2. Cut the biscuits out, being careful not to pull or tear the dough.

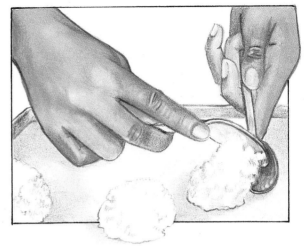

3. For drop biscuits, just drop the batter from a spoon in mounds onto a greased cookie sheet.

your fingers, since warmth from your hands may melt the shortening, causing the biscuits to be tough. Overkneading results in tough, compact biscuits.

Next, roll the dough out to a uniform thickness of about 1.3 cm (½ inch). Cut the biscuits out with a biscuit cutter that is lightly dusted with flour. Press the cutter straight down so that the biscuits have straight sides and even shapes. Do not twist the cutter. Otherwise, the dough might tear. You can reroll any leftover dough to make more biscuits.

Place the biscuits on an ungreased baking sheet, about 2.5 cm (1 inch) apart. Bake according to recipe directions.

Beating Egg Whites

When egg whites are beaten, air is incorporated into them. Beaten egg whites can be used to add volume and lightness to baked products. For example, they can be used to prepare soufflés. A soufflé (soo-FLAY) is a dish made by folding stiffly beaten whites into a sauce or batter, then baking the mixture in a deep casserole until it puffs up.

Here are some guidelines for beating egg whites:

◆ When separating the yolks from the whites, be careful that no yolk mixes with the whites. Yolks contain fat, and even a drop of fat can keep whites from reaching full volume.

◆ Before beating, let egg whites stand at room temperature for 20 minutes. This will allow them to reach the fullest volume when beaten.

◆ Use beaters and bowls that are clean and completely free of fat. Plastic bowls tend to absorb fat, so use only glass or metal bowls.

Forming Peaks

As you beat egg whites, you will notice them turning white and foamy. Eventually, they begin to form peaks. There are two different stages of peaks that eggs can reach. The terms for these stages frequently appear in recipes involving beaten eggs.

- **Soft-peak stage.** The peaks bend over slightly when the beaters are lifted out of the whites.

- **Stiff-peak stage.** The peaks are glossy and hold their shape when the beaters are lifted out of the mixture.

Stop beating egg whites as soon as they reach the stage called for in the recipe. Never try to beat past the stiff-peak stage. If you overbeat the whites, they will turn dry and dull and begin to fall apart. Since they have lost air and moisture, they can no longer be used.

When using beaten egg whites in mixtures, fold them in. If stirred or beaten, the whites lose air and volume. To fold beaten whites into a mixture, add them to the bowl containing the mixture. Use a flat tool, such as a rubber spatula, for folding.

Grain Measurements and Cooking Times

Grain (250 mL, or 1 cup, dry)	Amount of Liquid	Cooking Time	Cooked Yield (approximate)
Barley (pearl)	625 mL (2½ cups)	40 minutes	750 mL (3 cups)
Cornmeal	1 L (4 cups)	25 minutes	750 mL (3 cups)
Grits (regular)	1 L (4 cups)	25 minutes	750 mL (3 cups)
Kasha	500 mL (2 cups)	20 minutes	625 mL (2½ cups)
Millet	625 to 750 mL (2½ to 3 cups)	35-40 minutes	875 mL (3½ cups)
Rice (long- or medium-grain)	500 mL (2 cups)	45 minutes (brown) 15 minutes (white)	750 mL (3 cups)
Bulgur	500 mL (2 cups)	None	625 mL (2½ cups)

Dry Pasta Quantities

Type of Pasta	Dry Weight	Dry Volume	Cooked Yield (approximate)
Small pasta shapes—macaroni, shells, spirals, twists	120 g (4 ounces)	250 mL (1 cup)	675 mL (2½ cups)
Long, slender pasta strands—spaghetti, angel hair, vermicelli	120 g (4 ounces)	2.5-cm (1-inch) diameter bunch	500 mL (2 cups)

Wholesale Cuts for Four Major Meat Animals

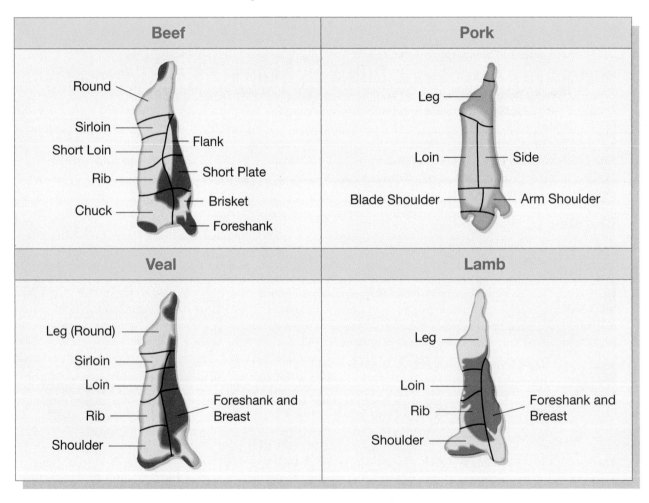

References

Chapter 3

Government of Canada. (2002). *Trends in the Health of Canadian Youth*. Retrieved April 22, 2003, from www.hc-sc.gc.ca/dca-dea/publications/hbsc

Krebs, Nancy. (2000, January). Guidelines for healthy children: Promoting eating, moving and common sense. *Journal of the American Dietetic Association*. Retrieved April 22, 2003, from findarticles.com

Moscovitch, Dr. Arlene. (1998). *Electronic Media and the Family*. Vanier Institute of the Family. Retrieved April 22, 2003, from www.vifamily.com

Ontario Ministry of Health. (2002). Lost at sea? The perils of childhood obesity. Retrieved April 22, 2003, from HealthyOntario.com

Partridge, Katharine. (1998, April). The healthy heart: What's happening on the cardiac beat? *Today's Parent*. Retrieved April 22, 2003, from todaysparent.com

Sandler, Adrian D. (2002, June). Eating disorders. *Journal of Developmental and Behavioral Pediatrics*. Retrieved April 22, 2003, from findarticles.com

Chapter 4

Moscovitch, Arlene. (1998). *Contemporary Family Trends: Electronic Media and the Family*. Ottawa: Vanier Institute of the Family.

Chapter 5

Dietitians of Canada. (n.d.). How to Become a Dietitian. Retrieved July 25, 2003, from www.dietitians.ca/career/i4.htm

Chapter 6

Lambton Health. (2002, November 1). *Health Information: Food Safety*. Community Health Services Department.

Recycle Plus. *Welcome to Recycle Plus*. Retrieved March 12, 2003, from www.recycleplusltd.com/#

Environment Canada. (2003). Resource Recovery: Around the House Trivia. Retrieved April 11, 2003, from www.rdkb.com/recover/house_trivia.html

Waste Reduction Week Canada. (2002). *Too Good to Waste: Volunteer and Classroom Handbook*. Retrieved March 23, 2003, from www.wrwcanada.com/handbook02e1mb.pdf

Chapter 9

Middlesex London Health Unit, Nutrition Services. (1999, March). *Nutrition Matters: Cooking for One or Two*, 2. Middlesex-London Health Unit.

Pratt, Laura. (1999, September). Stay organized in the kitchen. *Canadian Living*. Retrieved March 31, 2003, from www.mochasofa.ca/food/program/howto/02march18a.asp

Statistics Canada. (2002, December 11). The Daily: *Household Spending, 2001*. Retrieved March 27, 2003, from www.statcan.ca/Daily/English/021211/d021211a.htm

Chapter 10

Canadian Food Inspection Agency. (2002, October 30). *Guide to Food Labelling and Advertising, sec. IV: Claims as to the Composition, Quality, Quantity and Origin*, (sec. 4.2.6 to 4.2.17). 4.2.9 Organics (Revised 2000). Retrieved April 7, 2003, www.inspection.gc.ca/english/bureau/labeti/guide/4-0-1be.shtml

Department of Justice. (2002, August 31). *Canada Agricultural Products Act. Egg Regulations. Part 1. Sec. 3*. Retrieved April 7, 2003, from laws.justice.gc.ca/en/C-0.4/C.R.C.-c.284/23187.html#rid-23242

Health Canada. (2003, January 2). *Nutrition Labelling Toolkit for Educators. Background Factsheet 1: Nutrition Labelling: A Description*. Retrieved March 6, 2003, from www.hc-sc.gc.ca/hpfb-dgpsa/onpp-bppn/labelling-etiquetage/te_background_01_e.html

Chapter 11

Holloway, M., Holloway, G., Witte, J., and Zuker, M. (2003). *Individuals and Families in a Diverse Society*. Toronto: McGraw-Hill Ryerson.

Statistics Canada. (2003, March 5). *On Poverty and Low Income*. Retrieved March 5, 2003, from www.statcan.ca/english/concepts/poverty/pauv.htm

Chapter 12

Dietitians of Canada. (2003). *How Do I Know If I Am Eating Well Enough?* Retrieved February 22, 2003, from www.dietitians.ca/english/faqs/faq_34.html

Chapter 14

Health Canada. (n.d.). *Welcome to the Natural Health Products Directorate*. Retrieved March 30, 2003, from www.hc-sc.gc.ca/hpfb-dgpsa/nhpd-dpsn/index_e.html

Health Canada. (n.d.). *Centre for Chronic Disease Prevention and Control—Cancer.* Retrieved March 25, 2003, from www.hc-sc.gc.ca/pphb-dgspsp/ ccdpc-cpcmc/cancer/index_e.html

Teach Nutrition. (n.d). *Nutrition Quiz: Vegetarian Eating.* Retrieved March 8, 2003, from www.teach nutrition.org/cgi-bin/quiz-vegetarian_eating.pl

Chapter 17

Canadian Health Network. (n.d.). *Healthy Body Image, Healthy Girls.* Retrieved April 19, 2003, from www. canadian-health-network.ca/html/newnotable/ mar1b_2003e.html

Carlson Jones, Diane. (2001, November). Social comparison and body image: attractiveness comparisons to models and peers among adolescent girls and boys. *Sex Roles: A Journal of Research.* Retrieved April 18, 2003, from findarticles.com/cf_0/m2294/2001_ Nov?87080429/print.jhtml

Cash, Thomas F. and Thomas Pruzinsky (Eds.). (2002). *Body Image: A Handbook of Theory, Research, and Clinical Practice.* New York: Guildford Press.

Gluckman, Ron. *Stretching One's Neck.* Retrieved April 17, 2003, from gluckman.com/LongNeck.html

Government of Saskatchewan. (2000). *Fast Facts about Eating Disorders.* Retrieved April 19, 2003, from health.gov.sk.ca/rr_eating_disorders.html

Health Canada. (2002, November 14). *The Vitality Approach. Positive Self/Body Image.* Retrieved February 27, 2003, from www.hc-sc.gc.ca/hpfb-dgpsa/ onpp-bppn/leaders_image_e.html

Hoyt, Wendy D. and Kogan, Lori. (2001, August). Satisfaction with body image and peer relationships for males and females in a college environment. *Sex Roles: A Journal of Research.* Retrieved April 14, 2003, from www.findarticles.com/cf_0/m2294/2001_August/8278 2446/print.jhtml

Middlesex-London Health Unit. (n.d.). Adapted by Huron County Health Unit. *Every Body Is Different.* Retrieved April 14, 2003, from www.healthunit.com/ searchengine/find.asp?id=1227

Media Awareness Network. (2002, December 7). *The Way We Look.* Retrieved April 19, 2003, from www. media-awareness.ca/english/resources/educational/ teaching_backgrounders/body_image/way_we_look_ pdf.cfm

Media Awareness Network. (2003a). *Beauty and Body Image in the Media.* Retrieved April 11, 2003, from www.media-awareness.ca/english/issues/stereotyping/ women_and_girls/women_beauty.cfm

Media Awareness Network. (2003b). TV makes Fijian girls sick. *Ottawa Citizen,* May 20, 1999. Retrieved April 22, 2003, from www.media-awareness.ca/ english/resources/articles/body_image/ body_image_fijian_girls.cfm

Penton-Voak, Ian, and Perrett, David I. (2000, Spring). Consistency and individual differences in facial attractiveness judgements: An evolutionary perspective. *Social Research.* Retrieved April 23, 2003, from www.findarticles.com/cf_0/m2267/1_67/62402556/ print.jhtml

Statistics Canada. (2001, Fall). *Average Hours per Week of Television Viewing.* Catalogue no. 87F0006XPE. Retrieved April 14, 2003, from www.statcan.ca/ english/Pgdb/arts23.htm

Worell, J. (Ed.). *Encyclopedia of Women and Gender. Sex Similarities and Differences and the Impact of Society on Gender.* (Vol. 1, pp. 201–210).

Chapter 18

Anorexia Nervosa and Related Eating Disorders, Inc. (2002, February). *Athletes with Eating Disorders: An Overview.* Retrieved May 5, 2003, from www.anred.com/ath_intro.html

Canada. (1990). *Report of the Commission of Inquiry in the Use of Drugs and Banned Practices Intended to Increase Athletic Performance.* Ottawa: Minister of Supply and Services, Canada.

Canadian Centre for Ethics in Sport. (2002, June). *Should You Use Supplements?* Retrieved May 5, 2003, from www.cces.ca/forms/index.cfm?dsp=template&act =view3&template_id=129&lang=e

Dietitians of Canada. (2003, February 25). *FAQ's and Fact Sheets: Should I Be Taking a Vitamin and Mineral Supplement?* Retrieved June 9, 2003, from www. dietitians.ca/english/faqs/faq_42.html

Government of Saskatchewan. (2000). *Fast Facts about Eating Disorders.* Retrieved April 19, 2003, from www.health.gov.sk.ca/rr_eating_disorders.html

Health Canada. (2002, October 5). *What Can You Do About It?* Retrieved May 1, 2003, from www.hc-sc.gc. ca/hppb/hiv_aids/youth/roids/what/index.html

Larson Duyff, R. (2000). *Nutrition & Wellness.* Peoria, IL: Glencoe/McGraw-Hill.

National Eating Disorders Information Centre. (1997). *Eating Disorder Glossary.* Retrieved on April 21, 2003, from www.nedic/glossary.html

National Eating Disorders Information Centre. (2002a). *Eating Disorders: An Overview* [booklet]. Toronto, ON: National Eating Disorders Information Centre.

National Eating Disorders Information Centre. (2002b). *An Introduction to Food and Weight Problems* [booklet]. Toronto, ON: National Eating Disorders Information Centre.

National Institute of Nutrition. (2001). *Obesity— Exploding Some Myths.* Retrieved April 21, 2003, from www.nin.ca/public_html/Publications/HealthyBites/hb4_95en.html

Sienkiewicz Sizer, Frances and Noss Whitney, Eleanor. (2003). *Nutrition: Concepts and Controversies*, 9th ed. Belmont, CA: Wadsworth/ Thomson Learning.

Chapter 19

Health Canada. (2003, March 13). *Canadian Weights for Body System Classification in Adults* (Table of Contents). Retrieved May 21, 2003, from www.hc-sc.gc.ca/hpfb-dgpsa/onpp-bppn/weight_book_tc_e.html

Noss Whitney, E., Balog Cataldo, C. and Rady Rolfes, S. (2002). *Understanding Normal and Clinical Nutrition*, 6th ed. Belmont, CA: Thomson Learning, Wadsworth Group.

Chapter 20

Food and Nutrition Board (FNB), Institute of Medicine (IOM). (2002). *Dietary Reference Intakes for Energy, Carbohydrate, Fiber, Fat, Fatty Acids, Cholesterol, Protein, and Amino Acids (Macronutrients).* Pre-publication edition.

Health Canada. (2002, October 31). *National Population Health Survey. Canadians and Healthy Eating—How are We Doing?* Retrieved May 25, 2003, from www.hc-sc.gc. ca/hpfb-dgpsa/onpp-bppn/national_health_survey_ e.html#2

Chapter 21

Health Canada. (n.d.). Handbook for Canada's Physical Activity Guide to Healthy Active Living. Cat # H39-429/1998-2E. Retrieved June 6, 2003, from www.hc-sc.gc.ca/hppb/paguide/pdf/handbook_eng.pdf

Health Canada. (n.d.). *Canada's Physical Activity Guide to Healthy Active Living: Family Guide to Physical Activity for Youth 10–14 Years of Age.* Cat. # H39-646/2002-2E.

Retrieved June 5, 2003, from www.hc-sc.gc.ca/hppb/paguide/guides/en/pdf/YthFamilyGuideEnFinal.pdf

Larson Duyff, Roberta. (2000). *Nutrition and Wellness.* Peoria, IL: Glencoe/McGraw-Hill.

Chapter 22

Government of Canada. (1994). *Native Foods and Nutrition: An Illustrated Reference Manual.* Ottawa: Minister of Supply Services Canada.

Statistics Canada. (n.d.). Selected leading causes of death by sex. Retrieved May 17, 2003, from www.statcan.ca/english/Pgdb/health36.htm

Chapter 23

Siebert, M. and Kerr, E. (1994). *Food for Life.* Toronto: McGraw-Hill Ryerson.

Chapter 24

Canadian Egg Marketing Agency. (n.d.). *Supply Management.* Retrieved June 12, 2003, from www.canadaegg.ca

Canadian Federation of Agriculture. (n.d.). *Commodities.* Retrieved June 10, 2003, from www.cfa-fca.ca/english/agriculture_in_canada/commodities.html

Canadian Federation of Agriculture. (n.d.). *Impact of Agriculture on the Economy.* Retrieved June 10, 2003, from www.cfa-fca.ca/english/agriculture_in_canada/agriculture_and_the_economy.html

Clark, B. and Wallace, J. (1999). *Making Connections: Canada's Geography.* Toronto: Prentice-Hall Ginn.

Chapter 25

Canadian Association of Food Banks. (2003, March). *Hunger in Rural Canada.* Retrieved June 29, 2003, from www.cafb.ca

Canadian International Development Agency. (n.d.). Overview. Retrieved June 23, 2003, from www.acdi-cida.gc.ca/index-e.htm

McIntyre, Lynn. (n.d.). *Social Inclusion and Food Security.* Retrieved June 23, 2003, from www.ccsd.ca

Orchard, L., Roberts, W., and Spencer, B. (n.d.). *Three Conflicting Perspectives on Food Insecurity in Canada.* Retrieved June 23, 2003, from www.ccsd.ca

Simpson, Ann. (2001, October). *The Toronto Food Policy Council.* Caledon Institute of Social Policy. Retrieved June 29, 2003, from www.caledonist.org

Smith, David. (2002). *If the World Were a Village*. Toronto: Kids Can Press.

United Nations. *About the United Nations Division for Sustainable Development*. Retrieved on June 29, 2003, from www.un.org

Chapter 28

Beef Information Centre. (2001). *Food Habits of Canadians—Changing Nutrition Issues*. www.beefinfo.org

Canadian Fitness and Lifestyle Research Institute. (2002, June–October). 2001 *Activity Monitor*. Retrieved April 18, 2003, from www.cflri.ca/cf/ri/pa/surveys/2001survey/2001survey.html

Dietitians of Canada. (2003, March). *2003 Report on Healthy Eating: Challenges Facing Women*. Retrieved April 24, 2003, from http://www.dietitians.ca/english/pdf/Report_on_Healthy_Eating_Challenges_facing_Women.pdf

Health Canada. (n.d.). Office of Nutrition Policy and Promotion. Retrieved April 28, 2003, from www.hc-sc.gc.ca/hpfb-dgpsa/onpp-bppn/

National Institute of Nutrition. (2002, April). *Canadians Losing Interest in Healthy Eating Says Nutrition Survey*. Retrieved March 10, 2003, from http://www.nin.ca/public_html/En/media_latest.html

Chapter 29

Health Canada. (2003, October 4). *Nutraceuticals/Functional Foods and Health Claims on Foods*. Retrieved June 14, 2003, from www.hc-sc.gc.ca/food-aliment/ns-sc/ne-en/health_claims-allegations_sante/e_nutra-funct_foods.html

National Institute of Nutrition. (2002, April). *Tracking Nutrition Trends IV. An Update on Canadians' Nutrition-Related Attitudes, Knowledge and Actions, 2001*. Ottawa: National Institute of Nutrition

Statistics Canada. (2003, February 21). *Food Expenditure in Canada 2001*. Catalogue No. 62-554-XIE. Retrieved June 25, 2003 from 80-dsp-psd.pwgsc.gc.ca.proxy.lib.uwo.ca:2048/Collection-R/Statcan/62-554-XIE/0000162-554-XIE.pdf

Statistics Canada. (2003, February 21). Household spending on food. *The Daily*. Retrieved April 4, 2003, from www.statcan.ca/Daily/English/030221/d030221a.htm

Chapter 31

AGCare. (n.d.). *Welcome*. Retrieved July 5, 2003, from www.adcare.org

Agriculture and Agri Food Canada. (n.d.). *Overview*. Retrieved June 11, 2003, from www.agr.gc.ca/index_e.phtml

Canadian Federation of Agriculture. (n.d.). *Agriculture in Canada: Agriculture and the Environment*. Retrieved June 10, 2003, from www.cfa-fca.ca/english/agriculture_in_canada/agriculture_and_the_economy.html

Canadian Food Inspection Agency. (n.d.). *Introduction*. Retrieved July 6, 2003, from www.inspection.gc.ca/english/toce.shtml

Statistics Canada. (2002). *Overview*. Retrieved July 7, 2003, from www.statcan.ca/start.html

Todd, E. S. (1867). *The Young Farmer's Manual*. New York: The American News Company.

University of Guelph. Retrieved June 20, 2003, from www.uoguelph.ca

Chapter 32

Food and Agriculture Organization. *The Special Programme for Food Security*. Retrieved July 10, 2003, from www.fao.org./spfs

World Health Organization. (2003). *Nutrition*. Retrieved July 10, 2003, from http://www.who.int/nut

Unicef. *Progress since the World Summit for Children*. Retrieved July 10, 2003, from www.childinfo.org

World Food Programme. (2003). Introduction. Retrieved August 26, 2003, from www.wfp.org/index/asp?section=1

Glossary

A

adult modelling. Since children imitate familiar adults' behaviours, it is important for these adults to be aware of the behaviours they display in front of children.

aerobic (uh-ROH-buhk) exercise. Vigorous activity in which oxygen is continuously taken in for a period of at least 20 minutes. Activities including walking, jogging, bicycling, etc.

agricultural commodities. Foods produced through agriculture.

al dente (ahl DEN-tay). Term meaning firm to the bite, often referring to cooked pasta.

amino (uh-MEE-noh) acids. Chains of chemical building blocks from which proteins are made.

anabolic steroids (AN-uh-bahl-ik STEHR-oydz). Prescription medicines used to help build muscle strength in patients with chronic diseases. When used illegally, dangerous side effects can occur.

anaerobic (AN-uh-ROH-buhk) exercise. Exercise that builds flexibility and endurance, involving intense bursts of activity in which the muscles work so hard that they produce energy without using oxygen.

anorexia nervosa (an-uh-REK-see-yuh ner-VOH-suh). A type of eating disorder that involves an irresistible urge to lose weight through self-starvation.

antioxidants. Substances that protect body cells and the immune system from harmful chemicals in the air, certain foods, and tobacco smoke.

antipasto. Italian for "before the meal"; referring to appetizers.

appetite. A desire to eat.

aquaculture. A method of growing fish or seafood in enclosed areas of water.

arcing. Electrical sparks produced when metal is used in a microwave oven; can damage the oven or start a fire.

aromatic vegetables. Vegetables that add flavour to soups and other recipes; includes onions, garlic, celery, and green peppers.

assembly directions. The step-by-step procedure that explains how to put the ingredients in a recipe together.

au jus. Serving food with the pan drippings from which the fat has been skimmed.

B

bakeware. Equipment for cooking food in an oven.

baking. The term used for cooking with foods such as breads, cookies, vegetables, and casseroles, though some meat, poultry, and fish preparations are also baked.

bannock. A flat, round bread originally made from oat, rye, or barley meal that contains no leavening agent.

basal metabolism (BAY-suhl muh-TAB-uh-lih-zuhm). Minimum amount of energy required to maintain the life processes in a living organism.

behaviour modification. Making gradual, permanent changes in your eating and activity habits.

berbere. A spicy combination of garlic, red and black peppers, salt, coriander, fenugreek, and cardamom.

bias. A tendency to be swayed toward a particular conclusion.

binge eating disorder. A type of eating disorder involving a lack of control while eating huge quantities of food at one time.

bingeing. Eating huge quantities of food at one time.

bioengineering. The scientific process of altering the genetic make-up of an organism.

biryani. A spicy South Indian dish made from beef, chicken, or lamb and rice.

blanching. Partial cooking of food, usually vegetables, to kill enzymes.

blood cholesterol. The cholesterol found in your bloodstream.

body distortion. A person with a negative body image sees him- or herself as fat even when severely underweight. This is especially true of people with eating disorders.

body-fat percentage. The amount of body fat a person has in relation to muscle.

body image. The mental picture and the thoughts and feelings that a person has about her or his body.

body mass index (BMI). Uses a ratio of weight and height.

body weight classification system. A Canadian system that uses body mass index and waist circumference to assess the risk that adults have for developing health problems if they are overweight or underweight.

bouillon (BOOL-yon). A simple, clear soup without solid ingredients.

bran. The edible, outer protective layers of a seed.

budget. Plan for managing money in order to cover the costs of life's necessities.

bulgur. A Middle East cereal food made from cracked wheat.

bulimia nervosa (byoo-LIM-ee-yuh ner-VOH-suh). A type of eating disorder that involves episodes of binge eating followed by purging.

bulk foods. Shelf-stable foods that are sold loose in covered bins or barrels.

C

cabanes au sucre. Sugar shacks, where the owners of the bush set up rustic restaurants each spring to cater to the visitors from the city.

calorie. The amount of energy needed to raise the temperature of 1 kg of water 1°C.

Canada's Food Guide to Healthy Eating. A food-grouping system designed by Health Canada to help Canadians choose a variety of foods in moderate amounts that will satisfy their nutritional needs.

Canada's Guidelines for Healthy Eating. Five recommendations for Canadians over two years of age outlined by Health Canada about what the body needs to maintain good health.

cancer. Uncontrolled cell growth that can spread from where it started to different parts of the body.

carbohydrates (kar-boh-HY-drayts). Nutrients that are the body's main source of energy.

career. A profession or a life's work within a certain field.

ceviche. An appetizer in Peru and Mexico consisting of raw white fish marinated in lemon or lime juice and served with onions.

cholesterol (kuh-LES-tuhr-ol). A fat-like substance present in all body cells that is needed for many essential body processes.

chuck wagon. A "kitchen on wheels" used by workers on cattle drives during Canada's early years.

clinical trials. Studies performed by researchers on human subjects to investigate a health claim concerning a product.

coagulate. To become firm.

colostrum (kuh-LAH-strum). A special form of thick, yellowish milk that is produced by the mother three days after childbirth and is rich in nutrients and antibodies.

combination foods. Meals that are made from the foods of more than one food group in *Canada's Food Guide to Healthy Eating*.

comfort foods. Foods often associated with childhood that people believe make them feel better.

complete proteins. Proteins that supply all nine essential amino acids.

composting. A process by which organic materials are converted into a soil-like product called *compost* or *humus*. Kitchen waste that can be composted includes fruits and vegetable scraps, egg shells, tea bags, coffee grounds and filters.

conduction. Heat transfer by direct contact.

conservation. Concern about and action taken to ensure the preservation of the environment.

contaminants. Harmful substances that accidentally get into food as it moves from the farm to the table.

continuous cleaning. An oven that has special rough interior walls that absorb spills and splatters.

convection. Transfer of heat by the movement of air or liquid.

convection current. A circular flow of air or liquid resulting from uneven heating.

cookware. Equipment for cooking food on top of the stove.

co-operatives. Groups of people who have a common goal or purpose and agree to work for the good of all involved.

cost per unit. The amount of money that each unit of a particular food item costs by volume or weight.

cover. The arrangement of a place setting for one person.

CPR. Stands for cardiopulmonary resuscitation (KARD-ee-oh-PUL-muh-nayr-ee ree-SUS-uh-TAY-shun), a technique used to revive a person whose breathing and heartbeat have stopped.

creatine. A supplement that is popularly believed to build muscle and increase a person's performance in sports, though studies have not proven this to be true.

cross-contamination. Letting micro-organisms from one food get into another.

cruciferous (kroo-SIH-fur-uhs) vegetables. Vegetables in the cabbage family.

crustaceans. Shellfish that have long bodies with jointed limbs, covered with a shell; includes crabs, crayfish, lobsters, and shrimp.

cuisine. Styles of food preparation and cooking associated with a specific group or culture.

culture. The shared customs, traditions, and beliefs of a large group of people which defines a group's unique identity.

cultured. Fermented by a harmless bacteria added after pasteurization.

cut. A particular edible part of meat, poultry, or fish.

cut in. To mix solid fat and flour using a pastry blender or two knives and a cutting motion.

D

Dal. A dish of lentils prepared in many ways in South Asia.

danger zone. The temperature range at which bacteria grow rapidly. This range is above 4°C (40°F) and below 60°C (140°F).

deficiency. A lack or absence of something needed, such as micronutrients in the body.

deglazing. Adding stock or another liquid to a defatted sauté pan to loosen the browned-on particles.

dehydration (dee-hy-DRAY-shun). Lack of adequate fluids in the body.

desired yield. Number of servings you need.

developing nations. Countries that are not yet industrialized or are just beginning to become so.

diabetes. A condition in which the body cannot control blood sugar levels.

dietary cholesterol. Cholesterol found in animal products.

dietary fibre. A mixture of plant materials that is not broken down in the digestive system; necessary for good health.

Dietary Reference Intakes (DRIs). Nutrition recommendations created by scientists to help North Americans stay healthy.

dietary supplements. Nutrients taken in addition to foods eaten.

digestion. Process of breaking down food into usable nutrients.

dim sum. Tiny Chinese dumplings and other foods filled with different meats and vegetables.

direct comments. Parents may negatively influence their child's thoughts about body image at an early age by making comments about his or her weight, eating, or appearance in general.

domestic markets. A market whose buyers are in the country of origin.

doneness. Having cooked food long enough for the necessary changes to take place so that a cut tastes good and is safe to eat.

doping. When a professional athlete uses a substance, such as a steroid or narcotic, or method of performance improvement that is banned.

dovetailing. To fit different tasks together smoothly.

drop biscuits. Biscuits made by dropping dough from a spoon.

dry-heat cooking. Cooking food uncovered without added liquid or fat.

Dublin coddle. A type of Irish stew made from ham, sausages, onion, and potatoes.

E

eating disorder. An extreme, unhealthy behaviour related to food, eating, and weight.

eating patterns. Food customs and habits, including when, what, and how much people eat.

ectomorph. A male or female body type that is lean, usually thin, and tall, with little muscle, fat, or curves.

electrolytes (ee-LEK-troh-lyts). Specific major minerals that work together to maintain the body's fluid balance; includes sodium, potassium, and chloride.

emulsion. An evenly blended mixture of two liquids that do not normally stay mixed.

enchiladas. Tortillas filled with meat, chicken, cheese, or vegetables, and rolled with the ends open. They are covered with a sauce and baked.

endomorph. A male or female body type that includes an average to large frame, is usually wider at the hips, and has a higher percentage of body fat.

endurance activities. Activities that get your heart pumping and make you breathe deeper, such as dancing or tennis.

Energy Guide label. Label on a large appliance that gives consumers information about estimated yearly energy costs.

enrichment. A process in which some nutrients lost as a result of processing are added back to the product.

entrée (AHN-tray). The term used for main dishes on many restaurant menus.

entrepreneur (AHN-truh-pruh-NOOR). A person who runs his or her own business.

entry-level job. A job that requires little or no experience.

equivalent. The same amount expressed in different ways by using different units of measure.

esophagus (ih-SOFF-uh-gus). A long tube connecting the mouth to the stomach.

ethnic group. A cultural group based on common heritage.

evidence. Giving proof of a statement using primary and/or secondary sources.

export markets. Buyers in countries other than where a product is produced.

F

fad diets. Popular weight-loss methods that ignore sound nutrition principles.

famine. Food shortages that continue for months or years, frequently resulting in starvation.

fats. A nutrient that provides a concentrated source of energy.

fat talk. When adolescent girls talk to their peers about weight and body shape.

fertilizers. Substances that provide plants with nutrients, usually by adding them to soil or water.

flexibility activities. Activities that keep your joints and muscles moving, such as stretching, bowling, or yoga.

foam cakes. Cakes that are leavened with beaten egg whites, which give them a light texture.

folding. A technique used to gently mix delicate ingredients.

food additives. Chemicals added to food to preserve freshness or enhance colour and flavour.

food allergy. An abnormal, physical response to certain foods by the body's immune system.

food fad. When a food or nutrition myth becomes widespread. This is especially common with diets.

Food Guide Pyramid. A pyramid-shaped food grouping system in the U.S. that is designed to help people choose a variety of foods in moderate amounts.

food insecurity. When people do not always have physical, social, and economic access to sufficient, safe, and nutritious food that meets their dietary needs and food preferences for an active and healthy life.

food myth. Remedies handed down through generations of the same family as "cures."

food safety. Following practices that help prevent foodborne illness and keep food safe to eat.

food science. The scientific study of food and its preparation.

food security. Exists when all people, at all times, have physical, social, and economic access to sufficient, safe, and nutritious food that meets their dietary needs and food preferences for an active and healthy life.

food tolerance. A physical reaction to food not involving the immune system.

fortification. A process of adding 10 percent or more of the Daily Value for a specific nutrient to a product by the manufacturer.

franchise. An individually owned and operated branch of a business with an established name and guidelines.

free radicals. Formed in the body as a result of normal metabolism, but then circulate in the body, damaging cells. This damage can lead to cancer.

freezer burn. A condition that results when food is improperly packaged or stored in the freezer too long; food dries out and loses flavour and texture.

frying. Cooking food in oil or melted fat.

functional food. Similar in appearance to, or may be, a conventional food that is consumed as part of a usual diet and is demonstrated to have physiological benefits and/or reduce the risk of chronic disease beyond basic nutritional functions.

G

garam masala. A complex blend of toasted and ground spices that most Indian recipes begin with.

garnish. Any small, colourful bit of food that is used to enhance the appearance and texture of a dish.

generic. Items produced without a commercial or store brand name which are less expensive and have a plain label.

genetic engineering. A method of enhancing specific natural tendencies of plants and animals.

giblets (JIB-luhts). Edible poultry organs such as the liver, gizzard, and heart.

glucose (GLOO-kohs). The body's basic fuel supply.

glycogen (GLY-kuh-juhn). A storage form of glucose that is stored in the liver and the muscles.

gratuity (grah-TOO-uh-tee). Extra money given to a server in appreciation of good service; also known as a tip.

grazing. An eating pattern in which people eat five or more small meals throughout the day.

growth charts. Used by medical professionals to assess healthy body weights for children and adolescents in terms of height and weight in relation to age and sex of the individual.

gumbo. A cross between a soup and a stew that is spicy and part of American Creole cuisine.

H

haute cuisine. Literally means "high cooking"; a method of food preparation that makes use of complicated recipes and techniques.

HDL. Stands for "high-density lipoprotein"; a chemical that picks up excess cholesterol and takes it back to the liver, keeping it from causing harm.

health fraud. When a company makes false claims or sells unsafe substances or methods to treat a person's health.

heart disease. High blood levels of the amino acid homocysteine, not normally found in the body, may damage blood vessels, cause increased blood clotting, and decrease the flexibility of blood vessels, increasing the risk of heart disease.

heating units. Energy sources in ovens used to heat foods.

Heimlich manoeuvre. Technique used to rescue victims of choking.

herbal remedies. Non-standardized products containing herbs known to have medicinal-like qualities.

herbs. The flavourful leaves and stems of soft, succulent plants that grow in the temperate zone, such as basil, thyme, oregano, rosemary, sage, and bay leaf.

high tea. A meal when tea is served with a non-sweet dish that is somewhere between an appetizer and a main course; originated in England.

HIV/AIDS. A disorder that interferes with the immune system's ability to combat disease-causing pathogens.

holubtsi. Ukrainian cabbage rolls.

homocysteine. An amino acid not normally found in the body that may damage blood vessels, increase blood clotting, and decrease flexibility of blood vessels if present in high amounts.

hors d'oeuvres. Appetizers or light foods served before the main course.

hot spot. An area of concentrated heat.

hunger. A craving or urgent need for food or a specific nutrient.

hydrogenation (hy-DRAH-juh-NAY-shun). A process in which missing hydrogen atoms are added to an unsaturated fat to make it firmer in texture.

hydroponic (high-druh-PAH-nik) farming. Using nutrient-enriched water to grow plants without soil.

I

incomplete proteins. Proteins lacking one or more essential amino acids; foods from plant sources provide incomplete proteins.

indirect influence. The behaviours and attitudes that parents demonstrate or model for their children to imitate.

industrialized nations. Countries that rely on a sophisticated, organized food industry to supply their citizens with food. Also called "developed countries."

inputs. The cost of what is put into farming.

insoluble fibre. A type of fibre that will not dissolve in water but will absorb water; helps move waste through the digestive system.

Integrated Pest Management (IPM). A process for planning and managing sites to prevent pest problems and for making decisions about when and how to intervene when pest problems occur.

inventory. Ongoing record of the food stored in the freezer.

J K L

julienne. Long, thin strips of food.

key issues. The issues that are critical to the understanding of a topic.

kibbutz (kee-BOOTS). An Israeli communal organization that raises its own food.

knead. To work dough with your hands to thoroughly mix ingredients and develop gluten.

kolach. Braided Easter bread of Ukrainian origin.

lacto-ovo vegetarians. People who eat foods from plant sources, milk products, and eggs.

lacto vegetarians. People who eat milk products in addition to foods from plant sources.

latkes. Jewish potato pancakes.

LDL. Stands for "low-density lipoprotein"; a chemical that takes cholesterol from the liver to wherever it is needed in the body.

leavening agent. A substance that triggers a chemical action causing a baked product to rise.

legumes. Plants whose seeds grow in pods that split along both sides when ripe; includes dry beans and peas, lentils, and peanuts.

life span. Constant progression from one stage of development to the next. Stages include prenatal period, infancy, childhood, adolescence, and adulthood.

lifestyle. A person's typical way of life, which includes how you spend your time and what is important to you.

lifestyle activities. Forms of physical activity that are a normal part of your daily routine or recreation that promote good health throughout a lifetime.

lifestyle diseases. Illnesses that relate to how a person lives and the choices he or she makes. Examples include high blood pressure, heart disease, stroke, diabetes, and certain kinds of cancer.

living wage. An income or salary that people can survive on.

low tillage. When most of a crop's residue is left on the surface of the field for the winter months.

M

macronutrients. The major nutrients in the diet, including carbohydrates, protein, and fat, that provide energy.

maize. Corn; a staple crop in many countries.

major appliance. A large device that gets its energy from electricity or gas.

malnutrition. Serious health problems caused by poor nutrition over a prolonged period of time.

marbling. Small white flecks of internal fat that may appear within the muscle tissue of meat.

marinades (MAR-uh-nayds). Flavourful liquids in which food is steeped.

marinating. A method of tenderizing and adding flavour to foods before you cook them by steeping the foods in a liquid.

matambre. An Argentine dish of flank steak seasoned with herbs that is filled with spinach, carrots, and whole hard-boiled eggs, then baked or poached in broth.

meal appeal. Characteristics that make a meal appetizing and enjoyable.

media. A multitude of communication sources, including television, radio, movies, newspapers, magazines, advertisements, and the Internet.

megadose (MEH-guh-dohs). An extra-large amount of a supplement thought to prevent or cure diseases.

meringue (muhr-ANG). A foam made of beaten egg whites and sugar.

mesomorph. A male or female body type that is muscular, broad in shoulders and hips, and has large bones and heavy muscles.

micronutrients. Nutrients that are required in the diet in small amounts and include all the vitamins and minerals.

micro-organisms. Tiny living creatures, such as bacteria, visible only through a microscope.

milk fat (m.f.). The percentage of fat in milk products such as sour cream, yogurt, cheese, and milk.

millet. A grain that is able to grow in poor soil with little water and has been used since ancient times to make porridge or flat bread.

minerals. Non-living substances that help the body work properly and may become part of body tissues.

moderation. Avoiding extremes, such as eating adequate amounts of a variety of foods.

moist-heat cooking. Method in which food is cooked in hot liquid, steam, or a combination of both.

mollusks. Shellfish with soft bodies that are covered by at least one shell such as clams, mussels, oysters, scallops, and squid.

monounsaturated (MAH-no-un-SAT-chur-ay-ted) fatty acids. Fats that appear to lower LDL cholesterol levels and may help raise levels of HDL.

mulled. Beverages that are served hot and flavoured with sweet spices.

N

natural health products. Include traditional herbal medicines; traditional Chinese, East Indian, and North American Aboriginal Peoples' medicines; homeopathic preparations; and vitamin and mineral supplements.

negative body image. Not liking your body, weight, or specific parts of your body. It may also include dissatisfaction with hair, skin colour, or facial features.

neutraceutical. A product isolated or purified from foods that is generally sold in medicinal forms not usually associated with food.

no tillage. When soil is undisturbed between the harvesting of one crop and the planting of the next crop.

nutrient deficiency. A severe nutrient shortage.

nutrient-dense. Foods that are low or moderate in calories yet rich in important nutrients.

nutrients. Chemicals from food that your body uses to carry out its functions.

nutrition. The study of nutrients and how they are used by the body.

O

obese (oh-BEESE). A term that means having excess body fat.

obesity. Being overweight to the point that medical complications occur.

omega-3. A polyunsaturated fat, or fatty acid, that helps lower triglyceride levels in the blood. This helps to reduce the risk of heart disease.

opinions. Statements based on judgments, beliefs, and estimations that people have on an issue, topic, or person.

osteoporosis (AH-stee-oh-puh-ROH-sis). A condition in which bones lose their minerals and become porous, making them weak and fragile.

over-the-counter drugs. Drugs that can be obtained without a prescription.

overweight. Weighing more than 10 percent over the standard weight for one's height.

ovo vegetarians. People who eat eggs in addition to foods from plant sources.

oxidation (AHKS-ih-day-shuhn). A process in which fuel is combined with oxygen to produce energy.

P

pare. To cut a very thin layer of peel or outer coating of a food.

pasteurized. A heat treatment that kills enzymes and harmful bacteria.

peers. People who belong to the same societal group, especially those of the same age, grade at school, or status.

pemmican. Dried meat, pounded into a paste with fat and preserved in cakes.

peristalsis (PEHR-uh-STAHL-suhs). A series of wave-like movements that force food into the stomach.

pesticide. Any product used to manage, destroy, attract, or repel a pest.

pho. A Vietnamese dish made of strips of meat, vegetables, green herbs, chilies, and garlic, arranged on top of a generous portion of noodles.

physiologial help. Help for the body via a medical professional or a dietitian.

phytochemicals. Disease-fighting nutrients contained in plants.

pica. A person's craving for non-food items, such as clay, dirt, paper, or glue.

place setting. Pieces of tableware used by one person to eat a meal.

platz. "Pie-by-the-yard" made by Mennonites.

pluma moos. A cold fruit soup of Mennonite origin.

poaching. Simmering whole foods in a small amount of liquid until done.

polarized plugs. Electrical plugs made with one plug wider than the other and designed to fit in the outlet in only one way as a safety measure.

polenta. A cornmeal mush that is sometimes cooled, sliced, and fried.

polyunsaturated (Pah-lee-un-SAT-chur-ay-ted) fatty acids. Fats that seem to help lower cholesterol levels.

positive body image. When you feel comfortable and satisfied with your body.

potlatch. A ceremonial feast of the northwest Pacific Coast Aboriginal Peoples. Traditionally, the host distributes lavish gifts to his guests, or sometimes destroys his own property to demonstrate his wealth and generosity. This is done with the expectation of eventual reciprocation.

pow wow. A large social gathering of Aboriginal Peoples that usually includes competitive dancing and singing. The pow wow is an important social ceremony that includes food.

preheating. Turning the oven on about 10 minutes before using it so that it will be at the desired temperature when the food is placed inside.

pre-preparation. Refers to tasks done before assembling the actual recipe.

primary research. The collection of *original* data on a specific research topic.

primary source. An *original* document or account that is not about another document or account but stands on its own.

proteins. Nutrients that help build, repair, and maintain body tissues; also a source of energy.

psychological (sye-kuh-LODGE-ih-kuhl). Having to do with the mind and emotions.

psychological help. Help for the mind through counselling.

purée. To make food smooth and thick by putting it through a strainer, blender, or food processor.

purging. Getting rid of unwanted calories by self-induced vomiting, laxatives, or vigorous activities to prevent weight gain.

Q

quiche (KEESH). A pie with a custard filling that contains foods such as chopped vegetables, cheese, and chopped cooked meat.

quick-mix method. A bread-making method that combines active dry yeast with the dry ingredients.

quota. The purchased right to produce a product.

R

recipe. A set of directions for preparing a food or beverage.

recommended level. The amount of a nutrient needed by most people. Nutrient amounts can be found in Dietary Reference Intakes.

reconstitute. To add back the liquid in a food that was removed in processing.

recycling. The treating of waste so that it can be reused; an awareness of such practices.

reducing risk. Lowering the chances of developing nutrition-related problems, such as heart disease, cancer, obesity, hypertension, osteoporosis, and anaemia, by eating nutritiously. This does not guarantee that the disease will be prevented, however.

refined sugars. Sugars that are extracted from plants and used as a sweetener.

reflected appraisal. When you see yourself as others see you, or as you think they do.

reservation. An arrangement made ahead of time for a table at a restaurant.

resource. An object and quality that can help you reach a goal; includes time, money, skills, knowledge, and equipment.

roasting. Cooking large tender cuts of meat or poultry using a shallow, uncovered pan with a roasting rack. Roasting results in a crispy, flavourful, brown crust.

rolled biscuits. Biscuits made by rolling out dough to an even thickness and cutting it.

rosti. A traditional Swiss pancake made from potatoes.

roux (ROO). A blending of equal parts of flour and fat.

Rule of Hand. Guidelines for estimating the serving sizes of various types of foods.

S

saturated (SAT-chur-ay-ted) fatty acids. Fats that appear to raise the LDL cholesterol in the blood stream.

sautéing (saw-TAYing). To brown or cook foods in a frypan with a small amount of fat.

scalded milk. Milk that is heated to just below the boiling point.

scones. A variation of baking-powder biscuits; popular in parts of Britain.

score. To make shallow, straight cuts in the surface of a food.

seasoning blends. Convenient combinations of herbs and spices; examples are chili powder and Italian seasoning.

secondary research. Researching information and/or data that someone else has collected.

secondary source. Sources that interpret primary sources or are otherwise a step removed, such as a journal article or book about a poem, novel, or play, or a commentary about what an interview signifies.

self-cleaning. An oven with a special cleaning cycle using high heat to burn off food stains.

self-concept. The way you feel about yourself, including your characteristics and abilities.

self-esteem. How you judge yourself or how worthy you feel.

serrated. Refers to a knife with sawtooth notches along the edge of its blade.

serving pieces. Platters, large bowls, and other tableware used for serving food.

set-point theory. A person's body is likely to maintain a particular weight because of its own inner controls.

sharpening steel. A long, steel rod on a handle used to help keep knives sharp.

shelf life. The length of time food can be stored and still retain its quality.

shelf-stable. Foods that will last for weeks or even months at room temperatures below 29°C (85°F).

shirred eggs. Baked eggs.

shortened cakes. Cakes usually made with a solid fat.

skinfold calipers. A device that pinches the skin to measure body fat.

skinfold measure. A method of assessing body-fat percentage by using skinfold calipers to pinch the skin and measure the body fat on various areas of the body.

small appliance. A small electrical household device used to perform simple tasks such as mixing, chopping, and cooking.

smoking point. A temperature at which fat begins to smoke and break down chemically.

soba. Buckwheat noodles.

social comparison. When you rate yourself by comparing yourself to others.

soluble fibre. Dietary fibre that dissolves in water; may help lower blood cholesterol levels.

sorghum. A drought-resistant corn-like plant that is a staple food in Africa, India, China, Southeast Asia, and Latin America; eaten as porridge or made into bread.

soufflé (soo-FLAY). A dish made by folding stiffly beaten egg whites into a sauce or batter, and then baking the mixture in a deep casserole until it puffs up.

special purpose food. Foods created in order to perform a function that is specific to certain groups of people. For example, the addition of calcium to orange juice aids people who do not drink milk and need another source of calcium in their diets.

spores. Cells that will develop into bacteria if conditions are right.

standing time. Period during which heat build-up in a microwaved food completes its cooking.

staple foods. Foods that make up a region's basic food supply.

staples. Items used on a regular basis such as flour and honey.

steep. To brew in water just before the boiling point.

stewardship. In developing nations, the careful and responsible management of natural resources and maintaining a healthy relationship with the environment.

stewing. To cover small pieces of food with liquid, then simmer until done.

stock. A clear, thin liquid made by simmering water flavored with the bones of meat, poultry, or fish, plus aromatic vegetables and seasonings.

store brands. Brands specially produced for the store; also called "private labels."

strength activities. Activities that help keep your muscles and bones strong, such as push-ups, raking and carrying leaves, or climbing stairs.

stress. Physical or mental tension triggered by an event or situation in your life.

study design. The approach used by researchers to investigate a claim.

subsistence farming. Practice of maintaining a small plot of land on which a family grows its own food.

supply management system. A system that limits the amount of a commodity that can be produced by any one producer during a period of time.

supporting issues. Issues that reinforce and help define the key issues in research on a topic.

sushi. A variety of small Japanese cakes or balls made of cold rice that are wrapped or molded around small bits of food, such as raw or cooked fish or vegetables. It may be wrapped or rolled in edible seaweed as well.

sustainable development. Development that meets the needs of the present without compromising the ability of future generations to meet their own needs.

sustainable farming. The cutting back on, or elimination of, chemicals in farming.

T

tabbouleh. A Lebanese salad made from bulgur, tomatoes, and onions.

tableware. Includes any items used for serving and eating foods.

Tandoor. A style of cooking popular in East India in which a special clay oven is used to bake breads and chicken.

task lighting. Bright, shadow-free light over specific work areas.

technology. The practical application of scientific knowledge.

test kitchen. A commercial kitchen where people create a recipe, prepare it, taste it, and repeat the process until the recipe produces an appetizing food consistently.

texture. Way food feels when you chew it.

tolerance levels. Maximum safe levels for certain chemicals in the human body.

tourtière. A ground pork pie that originated in French Canada.

toxins. Poisons produced by bacteria.

trace minerals. Minerals needed in very small amounts.

tuber. A large underground stem that stores nutrients.

U

underweight. Weighing 10 percent or more below the standard weight for one's height.

unit cost. The amount of money that each unit of a particular food item costs by volume or weight.

unit price. An item's price per millilitre, litre, kilogram, or other unit of measurement.

unripened cheese. Cheese made from curds that have not been aged.

UPC. Universal Product Code. A bar code on food labels and other products; it carries coded information that can be read by a scanner.

utensils. Tools or containers used for specific tasks in food preparation. Examples include measuring cups, peelers, and cookware.

V

vacuum bottle. A glass or metal bottle with a vacuum space between the outer container and the inner liner; used to keep food hot.

variety meats. Edible animal organs.

vegans (VEE-guns or VEH-juns). Also known as pure vegetarians. People who eat only food from plant sources, such as grain products, dry beans and peas, fruits, vegetables, nuts, and seeds.

vegetarians. People who do not eat meat, poultry, or fish; some do not eat milk products or eggs.

versatility. Capability of being adapted to many uses.

vitality. Enjoying eating well, being active, and feeling good about yourself.

vitamins. Chemicals in food that help regulate many vital body processes and aid other nutrients in doing their jobs.

volume. The amount of three-dimensional space something takes up.

W

waist circumference. A measurement based on a person's gender that provides information about his or her risk for health problems.

waist-hip ratio. A measure of how fat is distributed in the body.

water-soluble vitamins. Vitamins that dissolve in water and pass easily into the bloodstream in the process of digestion; include B vitamins and vitamin C.

watts. Units by which electrical power is measured.

wellness. A philosophy that encourages people to take responsibility for their own physical, emotional, and mental health.

whisk. A balloon-shaped device made of wire loops held together by a handle which is used for mixing, stirring, beating, and whipping.

white sauce. A milk-based sauce thickened with a starch.

whole grain. The entire grain kernel.

wok. A special bowl-shaped pan used for stir-frying.

work centre. An area in the kitchen designed for specific tasks; includes equipment needed for the task and adequate storage and work space.

work plan. A list of all the tasks required to complete a recipe and an estimate of how long each task will take.

X Y Z

yield. Number of servings or the amount a recipe makes.

yo-yo dieting. A pattern of rapid weight gain and loss.

Index

bulimia nervosa, 376–378
bulk foods, 193, 197
busy schedules, 160–161
butter, 423

C

cabanes au sucre, 483
caffeine, 269, 332
cakes, 564, 565
calcium
    during pregnancy, 255
    health concern, 613
    sources, 244
    and strong bones, 243
    vegetarians, 302
calories, 227, 228, 598
    burned in activities, 404
    from fat, 416
    good sources, 228, 229
Canada's Food Guide to Healthy Eating,
    227, 228, 271–279, 300, 584
    awareness of, 582–583
    bar graph, food groups, 275
    Canadian habits, 590–592, 596
    healthy eating patterns, 367
    key nutrients in, 272
    nutrition life cycle, 255, 258, 260
    rainbow, 271, 273, 278, 583, 585
    use in meal planning, 158, 159
Canada's Guidelines for Healthy Eating,
    265, 279
Canadian Farm Income Program, 652–653
Canadian Food Inspection Agency, 202,
    214, 657, 664, 665
Canadian International Development
    Agency, 519–522
cancer
    eating plan, 310
    types and risks, 309
candling, 211
canola, 488, 497
carbohydrates, 223, 229–232, 267
    complex, 230
    as energy source, 228
    loading, 596
    simple, 231–232
careers, food-related, 54–65
    definition of "career," 55
    entrepreneurs, franchises, 61
    family and consumer studies, 57,
      59–60
    food production, marketing, 60–61
    food service, 56–57
    health and safety rights, 60
    successful workers, 58
    TAP strategy, 62
Caribbean cuisine, 551–552, 554
cattle industry, 660
cell death and "aging switch," 662
Central American cuisine, 551

cereals
    fibre and flavour, 231
    nutritional value, 611, 612
ceviche, 553, 641
cheeses, 566, 635, 637
chemical reaction in baking, 636
chemicals, hazardous, 74
chicken, 551, 558, 574
childhood
    and adult health, 35–36
    eating disorders, 35
    family eating habits, 29–30
    healthy habits, 32, 258–259
    marketing food to children, 44
    meal planning for infants, 159
    obesity, 32–33, 34
    physical activity, 33–34
    problems from poor eating, 27–28
    safety, 76–77, 306
Chinese cuisine, 571–572, 634
chloride, 245, 269
cholesterol
    blood or dietary, 412
    and childhood eating habits, 28
    eating plan to lower, 308
    in foods, 236, 268, 412, 414
    LDL and HDL, 235–236, 413
chopping appliances, 116, 118
chopsticks, 570, 634
chowder, 479
chuck wagon, 488
chyme, 250
cleaning up, 82, 176
    clean-up appliances, 81
    cleaning substitutes, 74, 75
cleanliness in the kitchen, 80–83
    personal hygiene, 80
    safe work methods, 80–81
cleanliness in the store, 197
clinical trials, 318
co-operatives, 191, 506–507
coffee, 332, 635, 641
coil elements, 104
cold storage, 90–95
    chart, 90–91
    cold storage centre, 70
    freezer storage, 93–94
    refrigerator storage, 90, 92
    see also frozen food
collagen, 638
colon (large intestine), 251
colostrum, 256
combination foods, 279
comfort foods, 5, 435–436
communication of information, 59
community gardens, 514, 515, 683
comparison shopping, 193–194
complete proteins, 233
complex carbohydrates, 230
composting, 98
condiments, 422

conservation
    energy, 95–96
    soil, 659
    water, 96
consumer changes, 605–606
consumer demands, 606–616
    basic concerns and trends, 606–607
consumer skills, 317, 318, 319–320
    food additives, 328–329
content analysis, 290
convection oven, 105
convenience foods, 195, 617–618
convenience stores, 192
converting measures, 142, 144–145, 169
cookbooks, 133–134
cooking and serving, 84, 121–128,
    179–182
    see also cooking techniques; serving
      family meals
cooking appliances, 103–106
cooking centre, 71
cooking techniques
    baking, 124, 125, 636
    boiling, 122, 123
    broiling, 126
    choosing a method, 121
    combination methods, 127–128
    dry-heat methods, 124–126
    effect on nutrients, 121
    frying, 127
    microwaving, 128–129, 619
    moist-heat cooking, 122–124
    reducing fat, 420
    tenderizing meat, 638–639
cooking tools, 112–114
cookware, 106, 107–111
    common items, 107
    materials, 108, 110–111
    microwave cookware, 109
copper
    body functions and sources, 245
    cookware, 108, 109, 110
core list of 13 nutrients, 215
corn (maize)
    products using, 496
    staple, 532–534, 549, 551, 640
cornmeal, 535, 565, 569, 637
cost per serving, 168–169, 194
cost per unit, 169, 194
costing meals, 168–170, 171
coupons, 196, 199–200, 320
couscous, 557, 559
cover (place setting), 181
CPR (first-aid technique), 78
creatine, 386–387
crop rotation, 658
crop yields, 520–521
cross-contamination, 80
crossbreeding, 662
cuisine bourgeoise, 563
cuisines, 549
    components, 625
    see also specific cuisines

Photo Credits

t=top; c=centre; b=bottom; l=left; r=right

xiii Joe Mallon Photography; xv Joe Mallon Photography; xvii Joe Mallon Photography; xxvi (t) Denis Scott/Getty Images, (b) Tim Fuller Photographers; xxvii Jerry Kobalenko/firstlight.ca; xxviii (t) Health Canada web capture. Reproduced with the permission of the Minister of Public Works and Government Services Canada, 2003, (c) Courtesy of Adele Halliday, (b) Tim Fuller Photographers; xx-1 Paul Rico Photography; 2 Tim Fuller Photographers; 3 (t) Joe Mallon Photography; 4 www.comstock.com; 6 (l) Tim Fuller Photographers; 7 Morgan Cain & Associates; 10 ©SuperStock; 12 Dick Hemingway; 14 Jack Clark/www.comstock.com; 16 Joe Mallon Photography; 17 © R.W. Jones/CORBIS/Magmaphoto.com; 18 (l) Tim Fuller Photographers, (r) Tim Fuller Photographers; 19 (t) Erik Svenson/Getty Images, (b) Richard Passmore/Getty Images; 21 © Chuck O'Rear/CORBIS/Magmaphoto.com; 23 Courtesy of Judy Creighton; 26 Jerry Kobalenko/firstlight.ca; 27 Patty Pappas; 29 Ron Chapple/Getty Images; 31 Courtesy of Diana Matovich; 32 Kevin Beebe/Index Stock; 33 Donna Day/Getty Images; 34 Photodisc Red/AA051770; 34 © Richard T. Nowitz/CORBIS/Magmaphoto.com; 36 Photodisc Green/LS011918; 40 © Mug Shots/CORBIS/Magmaphoto.com; 41 (t) CP(Lethbridge Herald/ David Rossiter), (b) China Tourism Press/Getty Images; 42 © Jennie Woodcock; Reflections Photolibrary/CORBIS/Magmaphoto.com; 43 (t) © Will & Deni McIntyre/Magmaphoto.com, (b) Dick Hemingway; 45 CP(Toronto Star/ Tony Bock); 46 © John Henley/CORBIS/Magmaphoto.com; 49 Joe Mallon Photography; 54 Digital Vision/dv436044; 55 (t) Joe Mallon Photography, (b) Paul Rico Photography; 56 Tim Fuller Photographers; 57 Morgan-Cain & Associates; 59 © Chuck O'Rear/CORBIS/Magmaphoto.com; 61 Paul Rico Photography; 62 Tim Fuller Photographers; 54 Digital Vision/dv436044; 55 (t) Joe Mallon Photography, (b) Paul Rico Photography; 56 Tim Fuller Photographers; 57 Morgan-Cain & Associates; 59 © Chuck O'Rear/CORBIS/Magmaphoto.com; 61 Paul Rico Photography; 62 Tim Fuller Photographers; 63 Courtesy of Calvin Knight — satec@w.a. porter C.I.; 66-67 Paul Rico Photography; 68 © Bart van Leeuven/ZEFA; 69 ©Gary Jochim/SuperStock; 70 (b) Tim Fuller Photographers; 71 Joe Mallon Photography; 72 (b) FotoKIA/Index Stock; 73 (bl) Joe Mallon Photography, (br) Joe Mallon Photography; 75 Tim Fuller Photographers; 76 Joe Mallon Photography; 77 Paul Rico Photography; 78 Joe Mallon Photography; 80 Paul Rico Photography; 81 Joe Mallon Photography; 82 FightBAC!® logo. Used by permission of the Canadian Partnership for Consumer Food Safety Education; 83 Morgan-Cain & Associates; 84 Tim Fuller Photographers; 86 (t) Joe Mallon Photography; 87 Tim Fuller Photographers; 89 Dick Hemingway; 92 ©David Forbert/SuperStock; 93 Joe Mallon Photography; 95 (t) © Ariel Skelley/CORBIS/Magmaphoto.com; 97 (l) Dick Hemingway, (r) © Alan Towse:Ecoscene/CORBIS/Magmaphoto.com; 98 Joe Mallon Photography; 99 © Images.com/CORBIS/Magmaphoto.com; 102 Rob Melnychuk/firstlight.ca; 104 (l) Joe Mallon Photography, (r) Joe Mallon Photography; 105 (t) Morgan-Cain & Associates/Carol Barber, (b) Natural Resources Canada. Reproduced with the permission of the Minister of Public Works and Government Services Canada, 2003; 106 Tim Fuller Photographers; 107 Tim Fuller Photographers; 109 Tim Fuller Photographers; 111 Tim Fuller Photographers; 112 Tim Fuller Photographers; 113 Tim Fuller Photographers; 114 Mary Moye-Rowley; 115 (t) Joe Mallon Photography; 115 (br) Morgan-Cain & Associates; 116 (l) Morgan-Cain & Associates, (r) Morgan-Cain & Associates; 117 Mary Moye-Rowley; 118 (c) Mary Moye-Rowley, (b) Joe Mallon Photography; 119 Joe Mallon Photography; 120 Mary Moye-Rowley; 121 Joe Mallon Photography; 122 Paul Rico Photography; 123 Paul Rico Photography; 124 Paul Rico Photography; 125 (t) Morgan-Cain & Associates/Carol Barber; 126 Joe Mallon Photography; 127 Tim Fuller Photographers; 128 © BRANDX/Magmaphoto.com; 129 Paul Rico Photography; 132 P.D. Joiner; 133 Photodisc Green/AA006864; 139 (t) © Claude Charlier/CORBIS/Magmaphoto.com; 141 Joe Mallon Photography; 142 Dick Hemingway; 144 Dick Hemingway; 145 Tim Fuller Photographers; 147 Joe Mallon Photography; 148 Mary Moye-Rowley; 149 (b) P.D. Joiner; 150 (tl) Joe Mallon Photography, (b) Paul Rico Photography; 153 Courtesy of Joyce Parslow; 156 Photodisc Green/BU002293; 157 © Tom & Dee Ann McCarthy/CORBIS/Magmaphoto.com; 158 Lisa O'Leary-Reesor; 159 Bob Thomas/Getty Images; 161 Paul Rico Photography; 162 (t) ©Imagemore/SuperStock, (c) Tim Fuller Photographers; 164 (tl) Tim Fuller Photographers, (cr) Paul Rico Photography, (br) Paul Rico Photography; 165 © Steve Prezant/CORBIS/Magmaphoto.com; 167 Tim Fuller Photographers; 169 Mary Moye-Rowley; 173 Photodisc Green/AA006858; 178 Paul Rico Photography; 179 (t) © Catherine Karnow/CORBIS/Magmaphoto.com; 180 Joe Mallon Photography; 182 Paul Rico Photography; 183 © Ariel Skelley/CORBIS/Magmaphoto.com; 184 Tim Fuller Photographers; 185 V.C.L./Getty Images; 186 Photodisc Green/FD002840; 187 Photodisc Green/FD002689; 190 © Layne Kennedy/CORBIS/Magmaphoto.com; 191 © Jeff Zaruba/CORBIS/Magmaphoto.com; 192 © Paul A. Souders/CORBIS/Magmaphoto.com; 193 © Jeff Zaruba/CORBIS/Magmaphoto.com; 194 (t) Joe Mallon Photography, (b) P.D. Joiner; 195 P.D. Joiner; 197 Joe Mallon Photography; 198 Paul Rico Photography; 199 Joe Mallon Photography; 200 Tim Fuller Photographers; 201 Michael Krasowitz/Getty Images; 203 © CORBIS/Magmaphoto.com; 209 (t) P.D. Joiner, (b) Canadian Food Inspection Agency; 210 Beef Information Centre and Canadian Beef Grading Agency; 211 P.D. Joiner; 212 Agriculture and Agri-Food Canada. Reproduced with the permission of the Minister of Public Works and Government Services Canada, 2003; 213 © Michael Mahovlich/Masterfile; 214 P.D. Joiner; 216 (l) General Mills Canada Inc., (r) Photodisc Green/AA026341; 217 Mary Moye-Rowley; 220-221 Tim Fuller Photographers; 222 Digital Vision/dv556079; 223 Photodisc Green/AA033456; 224 (l) Tim Fuller Photographers, (r) © Ed Bock/CORBIS/Magmaphoto.com; 225 Joe Mallon Photography; 227 Morgan-Cain & Associates/Carol Barber; 228 Steve Chenn/CORBIS/Magmaphoto.com; 229 (t) Morgan-Cain & Associates/Carol Barber, (b) © A. Inden/Masterfile; 230 Joe Mallon Photography; 232 Joe Mallon Photography; 233 (cr) Mary Evans Picture Library; 234 Brian Hagiwara/FoodPix/Getty Images; 235 © BRANDX/Magmaphoto.com; 237 Morgan-Cain & Associates/Carol Barber; 238 © CORBIS/Magmaphoto.com; 239 Joe Mallon Photography; 243 Joe Mallon Photography; 248 Tim Fuller Photographers; 249 Joe Mallon Photography; 250 Mary Moye-Rowley; 252 Paul Rico Photography; 253 Photodisc Green/AA010236; 254 Larry Dale Gordon/Getty Images; 255 Paul Rico Photography; 256 Tim Fuller Photographers; 257 Adam Smith Productions/CORBIS/Magmaphoto.com; 259 Fotografia/CORBIS/Magmaphoto.com; 260 © Anthony Redpath/CORBIS/Magmaphoto.com; 261 Photodisc Green/MD002273; 264 © G. Biss/Masterfile; 265 Photodisc Green/FD005201; 266 ThinkStock LLC/Index Stock; 267 Paul Rico Photography; 269 Tim Fuller Photographers; 270 Tim Fuller Photographers; 273 © Richard Cummins/CORBIS/Magmaphoto.com; 278 Paul Rico Photography; 280 D. Miller; 281 Douglas Bradshaw Photography Inc.; 284 Tim Fuller Photographers; 285 Joe Mallon Photography; 286 (t) Paul Rico Photography, (b) Joe Mallon Photography; 288 Joe Mallon Photography; 289 Paul Rico Photography; 290 (t) Joe Mallon Photography, (b) Tim Fuller Photographers; 292 Tim Fuller Photographers; 295 Courtesy of Cathi Moreau; 298 Benelux Press/Index Stock; 299 Joe Mallon Photography; 301 ©Francisco Cruz/SuperStock; 302 (b) Paul Rico Photography; 304 Photodisc Green/AA020372; 307 © Jose Luis Pelaez, Inc./CORBIS/Magmaphoto.com; 311 Tim Fuller Photographers; 313 Courtesy of Dr. Stephanie Atkinson, PhD, R.D, Professor of Nutrition, Dept. Pediatrics, McMaster University, Hamilton, Canada; 316 Joe Mallon Photography; 318 Rene Sheret/Getty Images; 320 © Bettmann/CORBIS/Magmaphoto.com; 323 Courtesy of Teresa Makarewicz; 326 Photodisc Green/AA033483; 327 Joe Mallon Photography; 328 Dave Miller; 330 Morgan-Cain & Associates; 331 © Gail Mooney/Masterfile; 332 © John Henley/CORBIS/Magmaphoto.com; 338-339 Chabruken/Getty Images; 340 Kindra Clineff/Index Stock; 341 (l) © CORBIS/Magmaphoto.com, (r) © Reuters NewMedia Inc./CORBIS/Magmaphoto.com; 342 © CORBIS/Magmaphot.com; 343 (t) © Jose Luis Pelaez, Inc./CORBIS/Magmaphoto.com, (b) © CORBIS/Magmaphot.com; 345 (t) ©

Text Credits

13 Ontario Family Studies Leadership Council (n.d.). *Inquiry and Research*. Retrieved July 22, 2003, from http://www.ofslc.org/teachers/Index1.html; 27-28 Problems Caused by Unhealthy Eating Habits — Adapted from Ontario Ministry of Health (2002, p. 1). *Lost at sea? The perils of childhood obesity*. © Queen's Printer for Ontario, 2002. Retrieved April 21, 2003 from HealthyOntario.com; 34 Obesity in Children — Ontario Ministry of Health (2002, p. 1). *Lost at sea? The perils of childhood obesity*. © Queen's Printer for Ontario, 2002. Retrieved April 21, 2003 from HealthyOntario.com; 47 Table: "Average Hours per Week of Television Viewing (Fall 1996)", adapted from the Statistics Canada publication *Canadian culture in perspective: a statistical overview*, Catalogue 87-211, December 1997; 47-48 Table: "Television Viewing Time". Adapted from the Statistics Canada publication *Television viewing data bank*, Catalogue 87F0006, January 2001; 50-51 Primary and Secondary Research — Ontario Family Studies Leadership Council and Ontario Family Studies Home Economics Educators Association (2002). Adapted from *Social science research skills in the family studies classroom: Overview*, p. 11; 58 Conference Board of Canada, *Employability Skills*, 2003; 60 Your Basic Health and Safety Rights — Ontario Ministry of Labour (2003). "My basic health and safety rights from WorkSmartOntario.gov.on.ca. © Queen's Printer for Ontario, 2003; 82 Four Steps to FightBAC!™ © Canadian Partnership for Consumer Food Safety Education. All rights reserved; 90-91 Cold Storage Chart — Canadian Partnership for Consumer Food Safety Education. *Food Safety for Older Adults*. © Canadian Partnership for Consumer Food Safety Education. All rights reserved. Retrieved March 11, 2003, from http://www.canfightbac.org/english/calss/pdf/fs_adults.pdf; 110-111 The Safe Use of Cookware — Health Canada (2003). *The Safe Use of Cookware*. Retrieved from http://www.hc-sc.gc.ca/english/iyh/products/cookware.html; 134 Tips for Healthier Desserts — Callaghan and Roblin (2000), *Dietitians of Canada: Great Food Fast*, Toronto: Robert Rose Inc., p. 137. © 2000 Dietitians of Canada; 135 Cranberry-Orange Muffins — Lindsay, Anne (1988). *The Lighthearted Cookbook*. Toronto: Key Porter Books Limited., p. 148.© 1988, 2003; 137-138 Pita Spirals — Katzen, M. (1999). *Honest pretzels: And 64 other amazing recipes for cooks ages 8 & up*. Berkeley, California: Tricycle Press, pp. 48-49. Copyright © 1999 Tante Malka, Inc.; 140 Adapted from Farrell, J.J., and R.S. Moog (1999). Roles for small groups. *Journal of Chemical Education*, 76, 570-574, University of Massachusetts Physics Education Research Group. Collaborative group techniques, 3. Used with permission from the *Journal of Chemical Education*, Vol. 76, No. 4, 1999, pp. 570-574; copyright © 1999, Division of Chemical Education, Inc. Retrieved March 12, 2003, from http://umberg.physics.edu/stories/storyReader$91; 143 Extracted from *The Complete Canadian Living Cookbook* by Elizabeth Baird and the Canadian Living Test Kitchen. Copyright © 2001 by Transcontinental Media Inc. Reprinted by permission of Random House Canada; 146 Extracted from *The Complete Canadian Living Cookbook* by Elizabeth Baird and the Canadian Living Test Kitchen. Copyright © 2001 by Transcontinental Media Inc. Reprinted by permission of Random House Canada; 151 Ingredient Substitutions — Extracted from *The Complete Canadian Living Cookbook* by Elizabeth Baird and the Canadian Living Test Kitchen. Copyright © 2001 by Transcontinental Media Inc. Reprinted by permission of Random House Canada; 166 Table: "Weekly Food Expenditures per Person by Household Income, 2001", adapted from the Statistics Canada publication *Food Expenditure in Canada*, 2001, Catalogue 62-554, February 2003; 171 Chart outline adapted from Johnson and Wales University Curriculum Committee (2002). *Culinary essentials*. New York: Glencoe/McGraw-Hill; 177 Adapted from Myers, Barbara (2003). *Getting organized saves time. 7 organizing secrets of successful people*, p. 1. Retrieved March 28, 2003, from http://ineedmoretime.com/success.htm. Free "50 Ways to Manage Your Time" tips booklet. Visit http://www.ineedmoretime.com. Copyright 2002-03 Barbara Collins-Myers. All Rights Reserved; 180 Excerpt: "Mealtime Brings the Family Together", adapted from the Statistics Canada publication *Canadian Social Trends*, Catalogue 11-008, Summer 2000, p. 28; 201 Adapted from Canadian Food Inspection Agency. (2002). *Guide to Food Labelling and Advertising*, Section II: Basic Labelling Requirements; Sections 2.1 to 2.15; 202 Adapted from Canadian Food Inspection Agency, *Food Safety and You*, "Why is Canada's food supply one of the world's safest? p. 2 (Retrieved June 4, 2003 from http://www.inspection.gc.ca/english/corpaffr/publications/fsydas/page1e.shtml) and Canadian Food Inspection Agency, *Food Safety and You*, "What is the Government of Canada's role in food safety?" May 17/02 (Retrieved June 4, 2003 from http://www.inspection.gc.ca/english/corpaffr/publications/fsydas/page2e.shtml); 203-204 Labelling Products with a Grade Name — Adapted from Canadian Food Inspection Agency (2002), *Guide to food labelling and advertising*. Section IV: claims as to the composition, quality, quantity and origin. Retrieved February 27, 2003, from http://www.inspection.gc.ca/english/bureau/label./guide/4-0/bc.shtml; 209-210 Beef Grading — Adapted from Beef Information Centre (2002). Buying and Cooking. Retrieved April 6, 2003, from http://www.beefinfo.org/specs_grading.cfn; 210 Poultry Grading — Siebert & Kerr. (1994). *Food for Life*, Toronto, ON: McGraw-Hill Ryerson. Reprinted by permission of McGraw-Hill Ryerson, p. 204; 212 Making the Grade — Canadian Egg Marketing Agency. The extraordinary egg: Making the grade. (n.d.). Retrieved April 6, 2003 from http://www.canadaegg.ca/english/educat/making-grade.html; 213-214 Durable Life of Foods — Canadian Food Inspection Agency, Retail Food Bulletins, Durable Life Dating of Foods. Sept. 11/99 (Retrieved May 5, 2003 from http://www.inspection.gc.ca/english/bureau/retdet/bulletins/dure.shtml) and Canadian Food Inspection Agency Fact Sheet. Durable Life Information on Food Products. Sept. 2001(Retrieved April 9, 2003 from http://www.inspection.gc.ca/english/corpaffr/foodfacts/lifee.shtml); 214-215 Adapted from "Nutrition Labelling Toolkit for Educators," Health Canada, 2003 (Retrieved January 2, 2003 from http://www.hc-sc.gc.ca/hpfb-dgpsa/onpp-bppn/labelling-etiquetage/toolkit_educators_e.html) and Nutrition Facts — To Help You Make Informed Food Choices, Health Canada, 2003 (Retrieved January 2, 2003 from http://www.hc-sc.gc.ca/hpfb-dgpsa/onpp-bppn/labelling-etiquetage/toolkit_educators_e.html). Adapted and reproduced with the permission of the Minister of Public Works and Government Services Canada, 2003. Health Canada assumes no responsibility for any errors or omissions that may have occurred in the adaptation of its material; 217 The National Organic Standard of Canada — National Standard CAN/CGSB-32.310 — Organic Agriculture, http://www.pwgsc.gc.ca/cgsb/032_310/standard-e.html, Canadian General Standards Board, 1999. Reproduced with the permission of the Minister of Public Works and Government Services (2003); 265 *Canada's Guidelines for Healthy Eating*, Health Canada (http://www.hc-sc.gc.ca/hpfb-dgpsa/onpp-bppn/food_guide_guidelines_e.htm). Reproduced with the permission of the Minister of Public Works and Government Services Canada, 2003; 271 *Canada's Food Guide to Healthy Eating*, Health Canada, 1997. Reproduced with the permission of the Minister of Public Works and Government Services Canada, 2003; 272 *Key Nutrients in Canada's Food Guide to Healthy Eating* (chart), Health Canada, 2002. Adapted and reproduced with the permission of the Minister of Public Works and Government Services Canada, 2003. Health Canada assumes no responsibility for any errors or omissions that may have occurred in the adaptation of its material; 275-277 The Four Food Groups — *Canada's Food Guide to Healthy Eating*, Health Canada, 1997. Reproduced with the permission of the Minister of Public Works and Government Services Canada, 2003; 280 Other Foods — *Food Guide Facts: Background for Educators and Communicators*, Health Canada. Adapted and reproduced with the permission of the Minister of Public Works and Government Services Canada, 2003. Health Canada assumes no responsibility for any errors or omissions that may have occurred in the adaptation of its material. Retrieved March 12, 2003 from http://www.hc-sc.gc.ca/hpfb-dgpsa/onpp-bppn/food_guide_background_6_e.html; 293-294 Adapted from "How Much Is One Serving?" *Nutrition Matters*, Middlesex-London Health Unit. While the information contained in the materials is

believed to be accurate and true, no responsibility is assumed by MLHU for its use; **321-322** Organizing Information — Bellanca, J. (1990). *Organizers from the Cooperative Think Tank*. IRI SkyLight; **342-343** Basic Body Types — *Every Body is different*. Middlesex-London Health Unit. (n.d.) While the information contained in the materials is believed to be accurate and true, no responsibility is assumed by MLHU for its use. Retrieved April 14, 2003 from http://www.healthunit.com/ searchengine/find.asp?id=1227; **347** Logan, Ellie. (1998). The day I figured out that no one is perfect. (1998) *Chicken Soup for a Kid's Soul: 101 Stories of Courage, Hope and Laughter* (p. 314). Deerfield Beach, Florida: Health Communications Inc.; **348** Sandy Naiman, "Dangerous Obsession," Sun Media. Retrieved April 19, 2003 from http://www.canoe.ca/LifewiseLiving01/0911_bodyimage-sun.html; **353-354** Barbie Dolls I'd Like to See — Gilman, S.J. (1998). "Klaus Barbie and other dolls I'd like to see." From the book *Body Outlaws* edited by Ophira Edut. Copyright © 2000 by Ophira Edut. Reproduced by permission of the publisher, Seal Press; **354-355** Female Changes in the Ideal Body — "Body Image timeline," TheSite.org (Retrieved April 11, 2003 from http://www.thesite.org/magazine/specials_body_image/distorted body_image/body_image_timeline.html). © Copyright YouthNet UK; **360** "Ideal-Beauty" Message Now Also Aimed at Men — Source: Antonia Zerbistas, " 'Ideal-beauty' Message Now Also Aimed at Men," The Toronto Star Syndicate. Reprinted by permission of the Toronto Star Syndicate; **369** Adapted from S. Piramal (n.d.). *Understanding Your Eating Patterns*. Retrieved May 24, 2003, from www.nicholaspiramal.com/nutrition/eatingpatterns.htm; **371** *Trends in the Health of Canadian Youth: Health Behaviours in School-aged Children* (Table 7.7), Health Canada. Reproduced with the permission of the Minister of Public Works and Government Services Canada, 2003. Retrieved April 21, 2003 from www.hc-sc.gc.ca/dca-dea/publications/hbsc_07_1.html; **386** Safety Check: Ephedra – Health Canada, 2002; **388** Possible Physical Effects of Anabolic Steroids – Canadian Centre for Ethics in Sport. (2001). *Guide to Drug-Free Sport*, p. 16; **395** Body Mass Index (BMI) Nomogram, Health Canada. Reproduced with the permission of the Minister of Public Works and Government Services Canada, 2003. Retrieved May 19, 2003 from http://www.hc-sc.gc.ca/ hpfb-dgpsa/onpp-bppn/bmi_chart_java_e.html; **396** Health Risks Classification According to Body Mass Index — Canadian Guidelines for Body Weight Classification in Adults, Health Canada. Reproduced with the permission of the Minister of Public Works and Government Services Canada, 2003. Retrieved May 19, 2003 from http:www.hc-sc.gc.ca/hpfb-dgpsa/onpp-bppn/bmi_chart_java_e.html; **398** Which Body Shape Are You? — Are You an Apple or a Pear? Health Canada. Reproduced with the permission of the Minister of Public Works and Government Services Canada, 2003 from www.hc-sc.gc.ca/hpfb-dgpsa/onpp-bppn/apple pear_e.html; **405** Healthy Eating as Part of a Healthy Lifestyle — Adapted from Toronto Public Health (2003). Healthy Weights Creative Brief. Toronto Public Health assumes no responsibility for any errors or omissions that may have occurred in the adaptation of its material; **413** Adapted from National Institute of Nutrition (2001); **453** Brune, Nick et al. (2003). *Defining Canada: History Identity, and Culture*. Toronto, ON: McGraw-Hill Ryerson. Reprinted by permission of McGraw-Hill Ryerson; **454** Basic Fried Whitefish — Lovesick Lake Native Women's Association. (1985). *The Rural and Native Heritage Cookbook (vol. 1.)* Burleigh Falls, ON: Lovesick Lake Native Women's Association; **455** Bacon Cornbread — Lovesick Lake Native Women's Association. (1985). *The Rural and Native Heritage Cookbook (vol. 1.)* Burleigh Falls, ON: Lovesick Lake Native Women's Association; **456** The Three Sisters — Reprinted from *Native Foods the Native Way* with permission of Ontario Agri-Food Education Inc.; **457** Grandmother's Story — Reprinted from *Perfectly Natural Maple Syrup* with permission of Ontario Agri-Food Education Inc.; **458** The Many Uses of the Buffalo — Brune, Nick et al. (2003). *Defining Canada: History Identity, and Culture*. Toronto, ON: McGraw-Hill Ryerson. Reprinted by permission of McGraw-Hill Ryerson; **459** Buffalo Jerky — Lovesick Lake Native Women's Association. (1985). *The Rural and Native Heritage Cookbook (vol. 1.)* Burleigh Falls, ON: Lovesick Lake Native Women's Association, My Bannock — Armstrong, Terrance (2003,

May) "My bannock." *Canadian Living*, p. 170; **460** Lovesick Lake Native Women's Association. (1985). *The Rural and Native Heritage Cookbook (vol. 1.)* Burleigh Falls, ON: Lovesick Lake Native Women's Association; **462-464** Lovesick Lake Native Women's Association. (1985). *The Rural and Native Heritage Cookbook (vol. 1.)* Burleigh Falls, ON: Lovesick Lake Native Women's Association; **466** Wild Raspberry Bread Pudding — Lovesick Lake Native Women's Association. (1985). *The Rural and Native Heritage Cookbook (vol. 1.)* Burleigh Falls, ON: Lovesick Lake Native Women's Association; **467** Rabbit Soup — Lovesick Lake Native Women's Association. (1985). *The Rural and Native Heritage Cookbook (vol. 1.)* Burleigh Falls, ON: Lovesick Lake Native Women's Association; **470** The North West Co. Winnipeg www.northwest.ca; **478** Scallop Chowder — McCann, Edna. (1996). *The Canadian Heritage Cookbook*. Scarborough, ON, Prentice Hall Canada; **479** Mother McCann's Rhubarb and Raspberry Jam — McCann, Edna. (1996). *The Canadian Heritage Cookbook*. Scarborough, ON, Prentice Hall Canada; **480** Ultimate Maple Syrup Pie — Stewart, Anita. (2000). *The Flavours of Canada*. Vancouver: Raincoast Books; **482** Fiddleheads with Lemon Butter — McCann, Edna. (1996). *The Canadian Heritage Cookbook*. Scarborough, ON, Prentice Hall Canada; **483** Tourtière — McCann, Edna. (1996). *The Canadian Heritage Cookbook*. Scarborough, ON, Prentice Hall Canada; **485** Adapted from Top Ten Reasons to Visit Toronto. Toronto Convention & Visitors Association. Copyright © 2001 The Toronto Convention & Visitors Association. All rights reserved. Retrieved May 24, 2003, from http://www.torontotourism.com/about/ top10.asp; **487** Cranberry Apple Salad — McCann, Edna. (1996). *The Canadian Heritage Cookbook*. Scarborough, ON, Prentice Hall Canada; **489** Amy's Wild Rice Soup — Stewart, Anita. (2000). *The Flavours of Canada*. Vancouver: Raincoast Books; **491** Stewart, Anita. (2000). *The Flavours of Canada*. Vancouver: Raincoast Books; **495** Canadian Agricultural Commodities — Canadian Federation of Agriculture (n.d.). Agriculture in Canada — Commodities. Retrieved June 10, 2003, from http://www.cfa-fca.ca/ english/agriculture_in_canada/agriculture_and_the_ecomonmy.ht ml; **496** A zillion uses for corn, Ontario Corn Producers Association. Retrieved June 16, 2003 from http://www.ontario-corn.org/classroom/products.html; **497** Farming and Recycling — Ontario Pork. Retrieved June 6, 2003 from http://www.porkpeo-ple.com/edu_farming.html; **500** Horticultural Industry Production Map, Agriculture and Agri-Food Canada. Reproduced with the permission of the Minister of Public Works and Government Services Canada, 2003. Retrieved June 12, 2003 from http://www.agr.gc.ca/ misb/hort/map_e.html; **505** Food Freedom Day — Canadian Federation of Agriculture. Retrieved June 10, 2003 from www. cfa-fca.ca; **508** Holloway, Maureen, et al. (2003). *Individuals and Families in Society*. Toronto, ON: McGraw-Hill Ryerson. Reprinted by permission of McGraw-Hill Ryerson; **513** Quote from Smith, David J. (2002). *If the World Were a Village: A Book About the World's People*. Toronto, ON: Kids Can Press Ltd.; **514** A Food-Secure City — Excerpted from *Toronto's Food Charter*, 2001 (Simpson, The Toronto Food Policy Council, 2003); **515** Canadian Association of Food Banks. Retrieved June 29, 2003 from http://www.cafb-acba.ca/about_e.cfm; **520-521** Research Improves Crop Yields, Farmer Income, and Nutrition, Canadian International Development Agency. Reproduced with the permission of the Minister of Public Works and Government Services. Retrieved June 23, 2003 from http://www.acdi-cida.gc.ca/ CIDAWEB/webcountry.nsf/vLUDocEn/C0C278C938EEA03E85256C FE004CF416?OpenDocument; **522** What we do, Canadian International Development Agency. Reproduced with the permission of the Minister of Public Works and Government Services, 2003. Retrieved June 23, 2003 from http://www.acdi-cida.gc.ca/ whatwedo.htm; **531** Tabbouleh — Wells, Troth. (1990). *The New Internationalist Food Book*. Toronto: Second Story Press, p. 14. Copyright © Troth Wells/New Internationalist 1990; **532** Irish Soda Bread — Spicer, Kay (1995). *Multicultural Cooking*. Campbellville: Mighton House, p. 175. Copyright © 1995 Kay Spicer; **533** Spicer, Kay (1995). *Multicultural Cooking*. Campbellville: Mighton House, p. 70. Copyright © 1995 Kay Spicer; **534** Wells, Troth. (1990). *The New Internationalist Food Book*. Toronto: Second Story Press, p. 10. Copyright © Troth Wells/

New Internationalist 1990; **536-537** South Indian Biryani — Wells, Troth. (1990). *The New Internationalist Food Book*. Toronto: Second Story Press, p. 90. Copyright © Troth Wells/New Internationalist 1990; **538** Wells, Troth. (1990). *The New Internationalist Food Book*. Toronto: Second Story Press, p. 51. Copyright © Troth Wells/New Internationalist 1990; **540** Wells, Troth. (1990). *The New Internationalist Food Book*. Toronto: Second Story Press, p. 15. Copyright © Troth Wells/New Internationalist 1990; **541** Spicer, Kay (1995). *Multicultural Cooking*. Campbellville: Mighton House, p. 68. Copyright © 1995 Kay Spicer; **542** Nutritional Content of Sorghum Compared to Corn — What is Sorghum? National Grain Sorghum Producers. Retrieved July 2003 from http://www.sorghumgrowers.com/whatis.htm; **543** Mixed Cereal Stew — Wells, Troth. (1990). *The New Internationalist Food Book*. Toronto: Second Story Press, p. 120. Copyright © Troth Wells/New Internationalist 1990; **544** Yams with Spiced Sorghum Butter — Epicurious.com. © 2003 CondéNet Inc. All rights reserved. Retrieved June 30, 2003 from http://www.epicurious.com/run/recipe/view?id=104296&action=filtersearch&filter=recipe-filter.hts&collection=Recipes&ResultTemplate=recipe-results.hts&queryType=and&keyword=yams&x=7&y=7; **545** What are Yams? — VeryBestKids.com. © Nestlé. Retrieved August 15, 2003 from http://ohoh.essortment.com/yams_rytw.htm; **581** Pie Graph — *What Do Canadians Do About Nutrition?*, Health Canada, 2002. Adapted and reproduced with the permission of the Minister of Public Works and Government Services Canada, 2003. Retrieved April 9, 2003 from http://www.hc-sc.gc.ca/hpfb-dgpsa/onpp-bppn/factsheet_canada_does_e.html; **582** *What Do Canadians Do About Nutrition?*, Health Canada, 2002. Adapted and reproduced with the permission of the Minister of Public Works and Government Services Canada, 2003. Retrieved April 9, 2003, from http://www.hc-sc.gc.ca/hpfb-dgpsa/onpp-bppn/factsheet_canada_does_e.html; **583** *Canada's Food Guide to Healthy Eating*, Health Canada, 1997. Reproduced with the permission of the Minister of Public Works and Government Services Canada, 2003; **589** Key Motivators to Improve Eating Habits — *What Do Canadians Do About Nutrition?*, Health Canada, 2002. Adapted and reproduced with the permission of the Minister of Public Works and Government Services Canada, 2003. Retrieved April 9, 2003, from http://www.hc-sc.gc.ca/hpfb-dgpsa/onpp-bppn/factsheet_canada_does_e.html; **591** Source: Laura Pasut, M. Sa, RD (2001). *Food Habits of Canadians. Changing Nutrition Issues*. Beef Information Centre. Retrieved April 22, 2003, from http://www.beefinfo.org/pdf/FHC.pdf; **593** Graphs — Laura Pasut, M. Sa, RD (2001). *Food Habits of Canadians. Changing Nutrition Issues*. Beef Information Centre. Retrieved April 22, 2003, from http://www.beefinfo.org/pdf/FHC.pdf; **596** Table — Laura Pasut, M. Sa, RD (2001). *Food Habits of Canadians. Changing Nutrition Issues*. Beef Information Centre. Retrieved March 22, 2003, from http://www.beefinfo.org/pdf/FHC.pdf; **608** Table providing a list of some of the more common nutrient content claims and what they mean, Health Canada, 2003. Reproduced with the permission of the Minister of Public Works and Government Services Canada, 2003. Retrieved June 14, 2003 from http://www.hc-sc.gc.ca/hpfb-dgpsa/onpp-bppn/labelling-etiquetage/te_background_08table1_e.html; **621** *Food Safety Facts on Bottled Water*, Canadian Food Inspection Agency, 2003. Retrieved June 18, 2003 from www.inspection.gc.ca/english/corpaffr/foodfacts/bottwate.shtml; **627** Cassava/Manioc Scones — Wells, Troth. (1990). *The New Internationalist Food Book*. Toronto: Second Story Press, p. 119. Copyright © Troth Wells/New Internationalist 1990; **628** How Do Starches Thicken Food? — Larson Duyff. (2000). *Nutrition and Wellness*. New York: Glencoe/McGraw-Hill; **630** How is Yogurt Made? — Larson Duyff. (2000). *Nutrition and Wellness*. New York: Glencoe/McGraw-Hill; **631** Painter et al. (2002). "Comparison of International Food Guide Pictorial Representations." *Journal of the American Dietetic Association* (102) 483-89) 2002; **636** What Makes Baked Goods Rise? – Larson Duyff. (2000). *Nutrition and Wellness*. New York: Glencoe/McGraw-Hill; **638-639** Larson Duyff. (2000). *Nutrition and Wellness*. New York: Glencoe/McGraw-Hill; **642** Wells, Troth. (1990). *The New Internationalist Food Book*. Toronto: Second Story Press, p. 105. Copyright © Troth Wells/New Internationalist 1990; **648** Reprinted from *Update: the changing*

farm face (2003) with permission of Ontario Agri-Food Education Inc.; **650** *The Farmer's Share*, Canadian Federation of Agriculture. Retrieved June 10, 2003 from www.cfa-fca.ca; **652** Graph: "Expenses to Gross Farm Receipts Ratio", adapted from the Statistics Canada publication "Farming facts", 2002, Catalogue 21-522, April 2003; **657** Graph: Fertilizer Use — Canadian Federation of Agriculture, No.2, 2003; **660** Proposed Common Outcome Goals — Environment. *Second Wave of Consultations* (May 2002), Agriculture and Agri-Food Canada. Retrieved June 12, 2003 from http://www.agr.gc.ca/cb/apf/index_e.php?section=info&group=consult&page=consult2_06, Safety Check — Excerpted from "Traceback system increases consumer confidence," Agriculture and Agri-Food Canada. Retrieved June 12, 2003 from http://www.agr.gc.ca/cb/supplement/art17_e.phtml; **661** Proposed Common Outcome Goals — Food Safety. *Second Wave of Consultations* (May 2002), Agriculture and Agri-Food Canada. Retrieved June 12, 2003 from http://www.agr.gc.ca/cb/apf/index_e.php?section=info&group=consult&page=consult2_05, Quote — Todd, Edward. (1867). *The Young Farmer's Manual*, p. 7; **662** *The Cell Switch*, Down to Earth, AgVision TV. Retrieved July 8, 2003 from http://www.agvisiontv.com/down2earth/story.cfm?segment=298; **665-666** Elements of sustainable development — *DFO's Aquaculture Policy Framework — Policy Context — Contributing to DFO's Sustainable Development Agenda*, Fisheries and Oceans Canada. Reproduced with the permission of the Minister of Public Works and Government Services Canada, 2003. Retrieved June 12, 2003 from http://www.dfo-mpo.gc.ca/aquaculture/policy/pg009_e.htm; **666** Canadian Fisheries and Aquaculture Production 1984-2001 — *Sustainable Aquaculture — Statistics*, Fisheries and Oceans Canada. Reproduced with the permission of the Minister of Public Works and Government Services Canada, 2003. Retrieved June 12, 2003 from http://www.dfo-mpo.gc.ca/aquaculture/statistics_e.htm; **674** Vitamin A Deficiency — *Micronutrient deficiencies*, World Health Organization. © Copyright World Health Organization (WHO). Retrieved July 10, 2003 at http://www.who.int/nut/vad.htm; **675** Graph: Vitamin A Supplementation — *Vitamin A Deficiency*, UNICEF Statistics. Copyright © UNICEF. Retrieved July 12, 2003 from http://www.childinfo.org/eddb/vita_a/index.htm; **676** Iodine Deficiency Disease (IDD) — *Micronutrient Deficiencies*, World Health Organization. © Copyright World Health Organization (WHO). Retrieved July 12, 2003 from www.who.int/nut/idd.htm; **677** Graph: Iodine deficiency disorders (IDD), UNICEF Statistics. Copyright © UNICEF. Retrieved July 10, 2003 from http://www.childinfo.org/eddb/idd/index.htm; **678** The Downward Spiral of Malnutrition — *Determinants of Malnutrition*, World Health Organization. © Copyright 2003 World Health Organization (WHO). Retrieved July 12, 2003 from http://www.who.int/nut/nutrition3.htm; **679** Graph: Progress During the 1990s — *Malnutrition*, UNICEF Statistics. Copyright © UNICEF. Retrieved July 10, 2003 from http://www.childinfo.org/eddb/malnutrition/index.htm; **680** World Food Program in 2002: A Quick Glance – *Facts & Figures*, World Food Programme © 2003. Retrieved July 10, 2003 from http://www.wfp.org/index.asp?section=1; **682** FYI — *Into School, Out of Hunger*, World Food Programme © 2003. Retrieved July 10, 2003 from http://www.wfp.org/index.asp?section=1, **A4-5** *Canada's Physical Activity Guide to Healthy Active Living*, Health Canada, 1998. Reproduced with the permission of the Minister of Public Works and Government Services Canada, 2003.

Statistics Canada information is used with the permission of the Minister of Industry, as Minister responsible for Statistics Canada. Information on the availability of the wide range of data from Statistics Canada can be obtained from Statistics Canada's Regional Offices, its World Wide Web site at http://www.statcan.ca, and its toll-free access number 1-800-263-1136